ninth edition

Stage
Makeup

Richard Corson

James Glavan
University of Texas at Austin

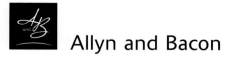

Allyn and Bacon

Boston   London   Toronto   Sydney   Tokyo   Singapore

Series Editor: Karon Bowers
Editor in Chief: Karen Hanson
Editorial Assistant: Jennifer Becker
Marketing Manager: Jacqueline Aaron
Editorial Production Service: Chestnut Hill Enterprises, Inc.
Manufacturing Buyer: Megan Cochran
Cover Administrator: Linda Knowles
Electronic Composition: Omegatype Typography, Inc.

Copyright © 2001, 1990, 1986, 1981, 1975, 1967, 1960, 1942 by Allyn & Bacon
A Pearson Education Company
160 Gould Street
Needham Heights, MA 02494

Every effort has been made to locate owners of the rights to photographs used in this
edition. The publisher welcomes information regarding their whereabouts.

Internet: www.ablongman.com

Between the time Website information is gathered and published, some sites may have
closed. Also, the transcription of URLs can result in typographical errors. The publisher
would appreciate notification where these occur so that they may be corrected in
subsequent editions.

Library of Congress Cataloging-in Publication Data

Corson, Richard.
    Stage makeup / Richard Corson, James Glavan.—9th ed.
      p. cm.
    Includes bibliographical references and index.
    ISBN 0-13-606153-2 (alk. paper)
     1. Theatrical makeup.   I. Glavan, James. II. Title.

PN2068 .C65 2000
792'.027—dc21
                           00-046879

Printed in the United States of America
10 9 8 7 6 5 4 3 2 1   VHP   05 04 03 02 01 00

Contents

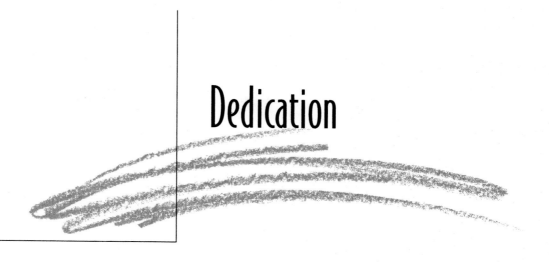

Dedication

The ninth edition of *Stage Makeup* is dedicated to the life and career of author, makeup artist, and teacher, Richard Corson.

It is not often that avocation and vocation come together. Richard Corson was one of those fortunates who achieved that happy state while still a student.

As a youngster he showed talent in sketching, drawing, and painting, and in school he developed a passionate interest in all things theatrical. He acted and directed and even had some of his one-act plays published. Dissatisfied with the state of stage makeup, which was often crude and amateurish, he put his artistic skills to use and developed a number of relatively simple techniques which noticeably improved the craft.

A Phi Beta Kappa student at DePauw and Louisiana State Universities, he chose his interest in makeup as the subject of his Master's thesis. This innovative work became the first edition of his first book, *Stage Makeup*.

Immediately in demand as a teacher, Corson used classwork to hone his techniques. He became fascinated with new products and experimented with them, and the new techniques he devised led to subsequent editions.

Because hairstyle and wigs, beards and mustaches were integral to a complete makeup, Corson created an appendix of sketches of hairstyles through the years to guide the actor. The sketches caught the eye of the distinguished British publishing house, Peter Owen Ltd., which commissioned an expanded version, a handbook to accompany *Stage Makeup*. There seemed to be no such sourcebook available, but no one, least of all Corson, anticipated the wealth of material to be explored.

Corson's insatiable curiosity led him to museums, galleries, theaters, and libraries throughout the Western hemisphere, where he found more and more material on the styles of the past, as well as the extraordinary and sometimes perilous means of achieving them. The handbook became a tome, *Fashions in Hair: The First Five Thousand Years,* the bible of hairdressers, stylists, and designers throughout the industry. Further explorations led to *Fashions in Eyeglasses,* which has been published in Japanese as well as English.

Corson's writing, however, never superseded teaching. Regular classwork gave way to seminars, workshops, and periodic engagements at major universities: Southern Methodist University, the University of Southern California at Long Beach, and the University of Minnesota, among others.

Later he embarked on a solo lecture demonstration, "An Actor Makes Up," which toured coast to coast for several years. This grew into a two-person program with more difficult and elaborate makeup demonstrations and complete scenes to accompany them. Always stressing his thesis that a makeup should not be simply a painted mask but rather an integral part of an actor's performance, each demonstration culminated in a real scene, such as the duel from *Cyrano de Bergerac,* a confrontation from *Merchant of Venice,* a comedic encounter from *The Importance of Being Earnest.*

Corson put touring on hold for three years in the 1950s to direct a program in New York City to train technicians for careers as makeup artists. Graduates went on to become prominent in television, ballet, and opera.

Although Corson rarely worked as a makeup artist per se, he occasionally designed a production and supervised its execution. His credits include *The Passion of Joseph D.* with Peter Falk as Stalin, Tony Richardson's production of *Arturo Ui,* starring Christopher Plummer, and Stella Adler's production of *Johnny Johnson.* Individual actors frequently consulted him about specific makeup problems.

Throughout his career, Corson remained steadfast in his belief in the individuality of the actor and his performance: that there be no one Hamlet, Shylock, or Cyrano "look," and that clichéd makeup is as abhorrent as a clichéd performance. He maintained that each actor should be as original in his appearance as in his characterization, thus making for an ever richer and more rewarding theater experience.

Richard Corson died on January 13, 1999. This ninth edition of *Stage Makeup*—compiled with the assistance of his colleagues and friends—will stand as a memorial to his career and his many accomplishments.

Mitchell Ericson

Foreword

I recall once needing a pair of ears for Abraham Lincoln. I didn't know if such a thing could be done, but I figured Dick Corson would, so I called.

"You want what?"

"Ears," I said. "For Lincoln. I'm doing Abe for the Phoenix Theatre—you know, Sherwood's play, and I'm working out the makeup."

"And you need ears."

"Yes, they were very big. Enormous, when you think about it," I said. "I figure without the ears it won't come out right."

"But with them . . . ?"

"Yeah."

"Why don't you come on over?"

Dick always had a sense of humor about me. We became friends after he helped carry a table to the theatre in Lakeside, Ohio, when I needed help and couldn't get it. That was many years ago.

"Now, let me explain, Hal, that I've never done ears like this before. It can be done, of course, but I'm not sure that it has been. There's not a lot of call for big ears, you know. There's a little casting problem, you see—undercuts and all that. How did you want to attach them?"

"I figured I'd just slip them over mine. Like mittens."

"Had you planned to glue them on?"

"Yeah. Once I slip them on, I'll glue them so they can't fall off. Actually, you shouldn't notice them much because his hair came out over them a lot. They shouldn't be grotesque."

"Just large."

"In case someone notices."

"I see."

Patiently he toiled over those ears. Then one night he called me. "Would you like to come down and slip them on?" I did, and they worked beautifully. It was the touch that made the makeup work, although I doubt very many people were aware of them. But Dick and I were enormously proud of them, and they made the makeup work so well in close-up that on the night we closed, the other actors in the cast waited in a local bar for me to take off the makeup so they could remember what I looked like.

Makeup requires patience. Corson was a patient man, a meticulous man, who went about his work with the care and thought of a scientist. He was multitalented and has used many of them in creating his books—*Stage Makeup, Fashions in Hair, Fashions in Eyeglasses,* and *Fashions in Makeup.* He took most of the photographs, did the intricate drawings, experimented on himself and his friends to get the many character effects, and he was a performer himself and understood the nature of the problems actors face on the stage. He was one of those totally dedicated people you sometimes meet or know in your life who make you feel that it's worthwhile to keep trying to do better.

It's been a great pleasure to see his book on makeup become established as the standard one in use wherever I go, knowing something of the toil that went to make it. In the early days when I was creating Mark Twain makeup he would come to see the show and we would discuss its effectiveness and how it could be improved. His eye I could depend on.

He's written the best book around on the subject. To all you actors who don't feel right unless you have the ears on, trust in Dick.

Hal Holbrook

Preface

Stage Makeup is intended to be used as a text and as a reference by actors and prospective actors who are or expect to be responsible for their own makeup—and by anyone who might in some way be involved with the makeup, whether as a designer, a director, a makeup artist, or a teacher.

As a textbook, it can be used by individuals learning either on their own or in a workshop. Both methods have their advantages. In learning by yourself, it's possible to work at your own convenience and at your own speed and to experiment with your own ideas and develop your own techniques. In a workshop that is not always possible. But a workshop does provide the advantage of not only having the guidance of a teacher but of seeing other students' work and learning from their successes and their failures. If you are or intend to be an actor, it is important that you work on your own face rather than on someone else's. Only if you are planning to be a makeup artist or a teacher is it really useful to work on faces other than your own. But a workshop is only the beginning. You should then continue to practice and experiment, applying what you have learned and developing your skill.

Whether you are working alone or in a group, taking photographs of your makeups will enable you to look at your work objectively. The photographs of student makeups in this book were taken as routine workshop procedure, using costumes and props from the costume shop and improvising when necessary. As most of the photographs were taken with an instant-picture camera, the students could make any improvements they wanted in the makeup before removing it and then have it photographed again for comparison.

Students seriously interested in makeup as a profession would do well to take courses in freehand drawing and to spend some time in art museums, studying paintings and observing how different artists have achieved their effects. They should also train themselves to observe people wherever they go—not just casually, but analytically, noting color and texture of the skin and hair, conformation of wrinkles, and size, shape, color, texture, and location of any blemishes. Students should also make note of any indications of possible profession or type of work and general lifestyle.

Students would also do well, if they have any talent for it at all, to take a course in acting to help them understand the actor's problems. And unless the student has the patience of a saint, the compassion of a doting mother, and the meticulous fingers of a jeweler, he or she might do well to consider choosing another profession.

R. C.

Acknowledgments

I am grateful to the publishers for trusting me with the revision of the ninth edition of Richard Corson's *Stage Makeup*. My charge was to simply incorporate new products and new techniques, and to expand the scope of the book to include makeup theory and technique for film, television, and for actors of color. It was my intention that the book retain Corson's makeup techniques, theoretical approach, his spirit, and his voice. With the passing of Richard Corson, my personal goal was to invite a number of individuals, including professional makeup artists, performers, teachers, and cosmetic company executives to participate in the revision process. The level of enthusiasm was overwhelming. To my surprise many were both thrilled and honored to share their expertise with the next generation of makeup students, teachers, and professionals. There was a unanimous expression of pride in the opportunity to give back to a book that had been their guide and inspiration for their own careers. I am grateful to all of them: James Black, Derrick Lee Weeden, Deidrie Henry, Thom Rivera, Vilma Silva, Olga Campos, and my dear friend Sally Wolf for their kindness in permitting numerous photographs to be taken as they worked on their makeup or had makeup applied to them for their current productions; Lyn Elam, Inga Loujerenko, Ben Schave, Kristen Chiles, Gil Adams, and Cole Noble for serving as models in demonstrating makeup products and techniques; costume designer, Esther Marquis for her lovely sketches; makeup artists Lenna Kaleva, Jeff Goodwin, Stephan Tessier, Olivier Xavier, and Adrien Morot for their generous contribution of photographs of character and prosthetic makeup from opera, television, and film productions; the various makeup companies for their cooperation; Dana Nye for his enthusiasm and support; Joe Blasco and Claudia Longo for their generosity; makeup artists Cinzia Zanetti, Michael R. Thomas, Joe Cola, Patricia Regan, and John Caglione for the many hours they spent answering so many questions; the lovely and resourceful Holly Byers who acted as my research assistant in Canada; Mitch Ericson, Hal Holbrook, and Uta Hagen for providing the Dedication, Foreword, and the Introduction; Kate Best for adding a touch of class to the book through her photographs and exquisite technique; contributing writers Amanda French, Joe Rossi, Marietta Carter-Narcisse, Toby Britton, and John McFall of Factor II; Dick Smith, one of the most imaginative and dedicated makeup artists in the country, for sharing with all of us the results of his own experimentation and the incredible photographs of his makeups; makeup artist Bill Myer for his friendship, good humor, and wealth of information; and, the wonderful faculty, staff, and students in the Department of Theater and Dance at the University of Texas at Austin for their support and patience. A special thank you to award-winning special makeup effects artist Matthew W. Mungle for his commitment to this book and generous contribution of photographs and step-by-step explanations of his prosthetic makeup techniques. Finally, I would like to acknowledge the generations of students who have been inspired by this wonderful book and who have gone on to advance the artform through their knowledge and ingenuity.

I also want to thank the following reviewers for their helpful comments: James Patterson, University of South Carolina; Rooth Varland, University of Mississippi; and Travis De Castro, Pennsylvania State University.

Thanks also to Gail Levee whose illustrations brought our hairstyles up to date.

Thank you Richard Corson for sharing with us your passion for *Stage Makeup*!

James Glavan

Introduction

The actor's dream is to play a wide range of characters, to explore many facets of life in roles that encompass all humanity. To fulfill this dream the actor requires not only talent and training but an unstinting devotion to the art.

In many areas of this endeavor actors are assisted by the artistry and technical skills of brilliant craftspeople. From the original script to the set, lighting, and costumes, every effort is made to achieve perfection. Curiously, in the field of makeup actors are left quite to their own devices. Except for the rare production so exotic or stylized that a specialist is necessary, actors must design and execute their own makeup.

It is therefore of considerable concern that many young professionals in the theater are unfamiliar with even so elementary a problem as projection of the actors' features, essential to the fullest communication of the characters' inner lives. Even on the rare occasions when a professional makeup artist is available, it is still the actors who are more aware than anyone else of the special problems posed by their own features and by the characters they are playing. Thus, it is the responsibility of each actor to learn the craft of makeup, that final dressing of the character which will enable him or her to perform the role as fully and as effectively as possible.

In addition to such fundamentals as the assimilation and projection of the character in terms of age, environment, and health, there is an area of psychological support that makeup can give actors comparable only to the assistance of a perfect costume. Just as robes or rags can give actors the "feel" of a character, so also can makeup. The visual image reflected in their dressing room mirrors can be as important to the actors as it will later become to the audience.

The authority of the arch of a brow or the sweep of a profile can be as compelling as Lear's crown and scepter. The psychological effect of shadows and pallor or glowing health can be as conducive to mood and manner on stage as in life, while an impudent tilt to a nose or the simple graying of the hair will inevitably make more specific the delineation of character. The most detailed and subtle characterization can be performed only with full freedom and authority when the actors know that the visual image supports and defines their work.

Actors untrained in makeup are deprived of an invaluable aid to their art—and little is done to remedy the situation. Large universities may give courses in makeup intermittently or not at all. Drama schools often merely glance at the problem or train in outmoded techniques. And actors must shift for themselves or hope for the casual assistance and hand-me-down techniques of fellow artists.

It is therefore most exciting and encouraging to all actors when a book such as this comes to our rescue. Richard Corson's approach to makeup is meticulous and eminently practical. Perhaps even more important is his stress on the creative aspects of makeup and the avoidance of stereotypes and formulae. The insistence on supporting technical skill with imagination and individuality reflects a positive and rewarding approach. With fullest exploitation of the mind and the senses, an unsuspected range of roles exists for each of us. It is through the assistance of the art and craft of makeup presented in this book that we can hope for a more complete realization of our goals in acting.

Uta Hagen

Illustrations

APPENDICES

Facial Anatomy

The first step in preparing to study makeup is to examine the structure of bone, muscle, and cartilage that lies beneath the skin. In remodeling a face to fit a particular character, you should know how the face is constructed. Even when you are merely trying to make your own face look its best, you need to be aware of which features you wish to emphasize and those you wish to minimize. Thus, actors or makeup artists, before they ever open their kit, should familiarize themselves not only with the basic structure of a human face but also with the particular structure of any face they make up, whether it be their own or someone else's.

Bones of the Face

A thorough and highly technical knowledge of anatomy is not really essential to the actor or to the makeup artist. It is not even necessary to remember the technical names of bones and muscles as long as you know where they are. There is, for example, no particular virtue in referring to the *zygomatic arch* when the term *cheekbone* is simpler and more generally understood. In a few instances, however, when the precise location of shadows and highlights is to be discussed, it is certainly advantageous to be able to refer to the exact area. The term *forehead* is useful only if we really mean the entire forehead. And in makeup we seldom do. There are two separate and distinct eminences, the *frontal* and the *superciliary,* which must ordinarily be considered separately in highlighting. In this case, then, the technical terms are useful.

Familiarity with the bones of the face becomes increasingly important with the advancing of the character's apparent age since muscles may lose their tone and begin to sag, flesh may no longer be firm, and the face,

in extreme old age, may sometimes take on the effect of a skull draped with skin. This is an effect impossible to achieve unless you know exactly where the bones of the skull are located.

Figure 1-1 illustrates a skull stripped of all cartilage, muscle, and skin. This is the basic structure of all faces, though there are, naturally, variations in exact shapes of bones.

Figure 1-2 is a diagrammatic representation of a skull indicating the names of the various bones and hollows (or fossae). The *maxilla* and the *mandible* are the

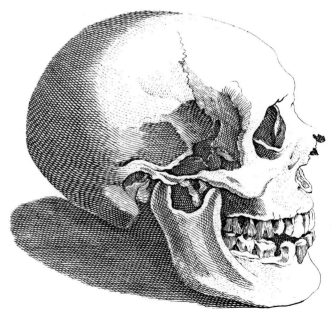

FIGURE 1-1 **A human skull.** *From Lavater's Essays on Physiognomy.*

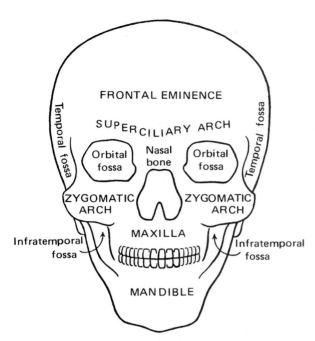

FIGURE 1-2 Diagram of prominences and depressions in the human skull.

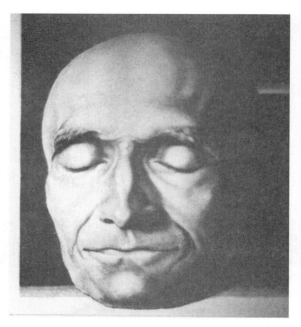

FIGURE 1-3 Head of a man in late middle age.

upper and lower jaws, and the *nasal bone* is simply the bony part of the nose. But observe that only the upper section of the nose is part of the bony structure of the skull. The lower, more movable part is constructed of cartilage attached to the nasal bone.

The importance of distinguishing between the two eminences of the forehead has already been mentioned. In some individuals these are very clearly defined, especially when the source of light is directly overhead, forming a slight shadow between the two. In other individuals the whole forehead may be smoothly rounded with no hint of a depression.

The *cheekbone* or *zygomatic arch* is one of the most important bones of the face for the makeup artist, and familiarity with its location and conformation is essential for accurate modeling. Some people have prominent cheekbones, easily observed, but others may need to prod the flesh with the fingers in order to find them. In studying the bones of your own face, you should locate them by feel as well as by sight. To feel the cheekbone, prod the flesh along the entire length, beginning in front of the ear, until you know its exact shape. Start with the top of the bone, then feel how it curves around underneath. Keep prodding along the bottom until you reach the enlargement of the bone under the eye. Familiarize yourself with the general shape and exact location of the bone. Observe, also, the angle of the cheekbone as it slopes gently down from the ear toward the center of the face.

Then there are the hollows in the skull. The *orbital hollows* (or eye sockets) are clear-cut (see Figure 1-3) and easy to feel with your finger. The *temporal* hollows are

what are normally referred to as the *temples*. These are not deep, but there is a slight depression that tends to show up increasingly with age. The *infra-temporal* hollows you will have already found in the process of prodding the cheekbone. The lack of bony support here allows the flesh to sink in underneath the cheekbone, resulting in the familiar hollow-cheeked effect. In extreme old age or starvation this sinking-in can be considerable.

Study the bone structure of your own face thoroughly. Then, if possible, study several different types both visually and tactually.

The skull is, as you know, covered with various muscles, which operate the mandible (the only movable part of the skull) and the mouth, eyelids, and eyebrows. In order that the study of these may be made more immediately applicable, they will be noted in Chapter 12 in connection with the individual features that they affect.

Construction of a Head

The best way to arrive at a practical understanding of the structure of the head is actually to construct one. This should be done with artists' modeling clay (such as Plastolene) on a thin but sturdy board. A piece of Masonite about 12 × 16 inches will do very well. Only the front half of the head (from the ears forward) need be done. Figure 1-4 shows such a head being modeled.

In addition to familiarizing yourself with the construction of a human head, there are two additional ad-

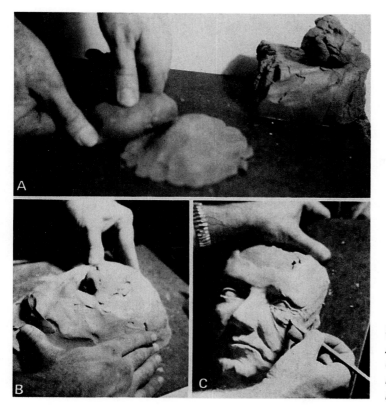

FIGURE 1-4 Modeling a head in clay.
A. Clay being pressed against the board to make certain that it sticks. B. Head shaped and nose begun. C. Completed head being aged with a modeling tool.

vantages in working with clay. One is the actual practice in modeling features—an essential step in making most three-dimensional additions to the face. The other is having available a head that can be remodeled indefinitely. This makes it possible to study the three-dimensional form of sagging flesh, such as wrinkles or pouches, that you are trying to reproduce with paint, as well as to experiment with various shapes of noses, eyebrows, or chins in planning a makeup for a specific character.

Modeling a Head in Clay

To model a face of approximately life size, you will need about nine pounds of an oil-base clay (see Appendix A), in a medium-soft to medium-hard consistency (#2 or #3 in Roma Plastelina). The area to be developed can be bounded by the hairline, the chin, and a point immediately in front of the ears. (See Figure 1-4.) The clay can be purchased at most art and pottery supply stores in two-pound blocks. Water-based modeling clays, which are considerably less expensive, are often packaged in twenty-five pound blocks and come in sealable plastic bags. For easy working, the clay can be cut into half- or quarter-pound cubes. These cubes should be kneaded and worked with the hands until the mass is soft and pliable. As each piece is softened, it should be pressed to the board with the thumbs, as shown in Fig-

ure 1-4A, and additional pieces mashed onto it in the same way. If this is done properly, the completed face can be carried about or hung on the wall with no danger that the clay will pull away from the board. (Figure 1-5A shows a whole head being modeled in clay.)

As each piece of clay is added, the general facial area to be developed should be kept in mind. A face about 7 to 9 inches long and about 5 or 6 inches wide works very well. The softened clay (except for about half a pound, which will be used later) should be molded into a mound resembling half an egg sliced lengthwise. It is by cutting away and building up the various areas in this mound that the face is developed.

Figure 1-6A shows a stylized head construction, emphasizing its three-dimensional quality. In 1-6B you can see how this is related to a real head. In many ways the head, especially the front half, is closer to a cube than to an egg. Although you will probably prefer to use the basic egg shape for your clay model, it is frequently helpful to visualize the cube in order to be sure that your head is really three-dimensional. It is important to be aware that the forehead, for example, has a front plane and two side planes (the temples). The depression for the eyes actually forms a sort of bottom to the forehead box, and the top of the head makes a rounded top.

The nose forms a smaller, elongated box with definite front, sides, and bottom. The front, sides, and bottom of the jaw should be clear-cut, with the lips following the rounded arch of the teeth.

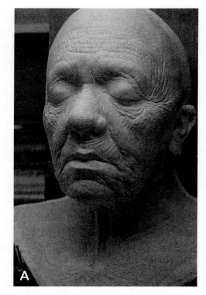

FIGURE 1-5 *A. Clay sculpture for prosthetic age makeup for the A&E mini-series, "Barnum." B. Detail. Sculpture by Stephan Tessier of TEXA FX Group, Montreal, Canada.*

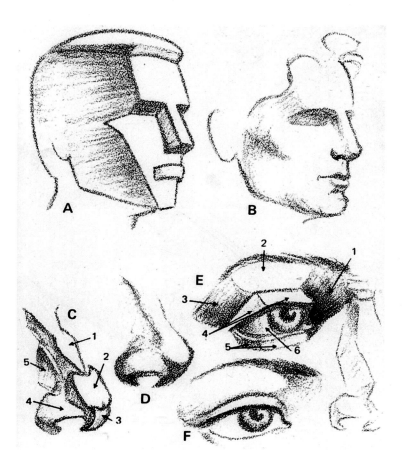

FIGURE 1-6 **Planes of the face.** *A, C, and E show planes of the head, nose, and eye flattened to clarify the construction.*

The classic face is divided into three equal parts horizontally, and that division should be your first step. The forehead occupies the top third, the eyes and nose the middle third, and the upper and lower jaws (including the mouth, of course) the lower third. It is a good idea to model the larger areas and develop the general shape of the head, defining the forehead, the jaw, and the eye sockets before starting on any detailed modeling.

Nose This is usually the simplest single feature to model because its size and location can easily be changed without seriously disturbing the rest of the modeling. This is where you will use the extra bit of clay that was left over. In adding the clay here or elsewhere, it is best to add more than seems necessary, for it tends to be easier to cut away excess clay than to add on to a feature that has been carefully modeled and then found to be too small.

Figure 1-6C shows a breakdown of the nose into its component parts. Plane 1 represents the slender nasal bone, and 2 and 3 show the two planes of the cartilage that forms the tip. In 4 we see the roughly cylindrical flesh of the nostrils, with 5 representing the side planes. D shows the nose as it actually looks to the observer. But notice in both C and D the subtleties of shape.

The front plane of the nose (1 and 2) is not of even width all the way down. It is narrow at the bridge, then widens and narrows again slightly as it fits into the still wider cartilage of the tip (2). Examine a number of noses carefully to observe this construction. In some noses (Figure 1-3, for example) it will be quite obvious. In others the change will be so subtle that it will be difficult to distinguish it. On your clay head, model these planes carefully to give the feeling of bone and cartilage beneath the skin. Since you will use this particular bit of modeling frequently in your makeup work, it is especially important to become proficient at it now.

Mouth
Modeling the mouth is a process of shaping and carving, working for the rounded fleshiness of the lips as opposed to a straight, thin gash in the clay. Start with a cylindrical shape, and model the mouth on that. (Refer to Figure 1-6A.) It is usually helpful in laying out the mouth to establish its exact center by means of the small indentation or cleft that extends from the nose down to the cupid's bow of the upper lip.

Eyes
Before beginning on the eyes, be sure the superciliary arch and the cheekbones are carefully modeled since these, along with the nose, will form the eye socket. It is usually wise to model an eye socket before building up an eye. This can be done quite simply by pressing firmly with both thumbs where the eyes are to be. Bear in mind that the space between the eyes is approximately the width of one eye. In other words, the eyes are normally the same width as the space between them.

As with the nose, the eyes are modeled with extra clay. A piece about the size of a walnut, set into each socket, should prove more than sufficient. This should give you a good start in laying out the correct planes.

Figure 1-6E shows schematically the planes of the eye, and 1-6F shows the normal eye for comparison. Planes 1, 2, and 3 represent the slope from the upper edge of the orbital fossa downward and inward to the eyeball—a slope that lies in three planes blending gently and imperceptibly into each other. Plane 1 is the deepest part of the eye socket, formed by the meeting of the nasal bone and the superciliary arch. Plane 2 is the most prominent part of the upper socket, pushed forward by the bone of the superciliary arch. This is in

essentially the same horizontal plane as the forehead. Plane 3 curves backward into the plane of the temple.

Plane 4 represents the upper lid, which comes forward over the eyeball and follows it around so that it is actually in three planes, only two of which are visible in this three-quarter view. Plane 5 represents the lower lid, which, though much less extensive than the upper, follows the same general pattern. Plane 6 represents the eyeball itself.

On your clay head it would probably be well to model the eye as if it were closed, as it is in Figure 1-3. If, however, you prefer the eyes to be open, you can carefully cut away a section of the lid in order to reveal the eyeball itself and give the lid thickness, or you can lay on thin pieces of clay to create the lids. The important thing is to have a three-dimensional eye, correctly placed in the face, well shaped, and set properly into the eye sockets. As with all other features, avoid flatness.

Next, smooth out rough edges and carefully check all planes of the face and of each feature. If the result lacks conviction, analyze it to find your missteps, and redo any problem areas.

But the best way to avoid major problems is first to lay out the proportions with great care, following the measurements of your own features, if you like. Then make sure that the basic head is three-dimensional. Avoid the tendency of some beginners to make heads that are either excessively egg-shaped or very flat. Develop a feeling for both roundness and squareness in the head. Be sure that your individual features are carefully constructed with all of their component parts. Relate the size and placement of features to the head and to each other. A careful modeling of each feature will then result in a three-dimensional head.

The important thing is to follow through each step logically and carefully, progressing from large areas to small ones, taking whatever time is necessary to do the work correctly.

PROBLEMS

1. Locate on your own face the various prominences and depressions shown in the diagram in Figure 1-2.

2. Collect photographs and works of art that can be used to illustrate the structure of the face.

3. Model a head in clay. (In most makeup classes there will probably not be sufficient time to do this. It should be done, however, by any student who is considering makeup as a profession.)

chapter 2

Light and Shade

Although some three-dimensional changes can be made in creating makeup for the stage, more often than not we create the illusion of three-dimensional changes, using the principles of light and shade.

When we look at an object—any object—what our eye observes depends on the light that is reflected from specific areas of that object to the eye. Thus, because of its structure, your own face will reflect light in a certain pattern, and this pattern of light reflection is what reveals the structure and causes you to look like you instead of like someone else.

But suppose you *want* to look like someone else. You can, if you wish, actually change the shape of your face with three-dimensional makeup. If you do that, the new face will reflect different patterns of light from your normal one, and you will no longer look like you. Instead of actually reshaping your face or parts of it, however, you could simply paint on patterns of light to match those your face would reflect if you were actually to change its shape, thus creating the illusion of the face you want the audience to see.

This is essentially what the painter does. (See Figure 2-1.) But instead of a painter's flat, white canvas, the makeup artist—or the actor—begins with a three-dimensional face—a face that will reflect, as the actor moves his head onstage, a continually changing relationship between the face and the source of light.

In spite of these differences between the painter and the makeup artist, the principles of their art remain the same. Both observe in life what happens when light falls on an object. Both see the patterns of light and shade that reveal to the eye the real shape of an object. Then, with colored paints of varying degrees of lightness and darkness, of brightness and grayness, both re-create those patterns. And if they are sufficiently skillful, observers will be led by those painted patterns of light and shade into believing that they are seeing the real thing. In the case of painted portraits, of course, that is not strictly true, for one is always aware that one is seeing a picture. In fact, only in *trompe l'oeil* paintings is it the aim of the painter to imitate reality so closely that view-

FIGURE 2-1 Light and shade used to create the illusion of a 3-dimensional head. *Oil painting.*

6

ers are fooled into believing they are actually seeing the real thing rather than a painted representation of it. But in creating a realistic makeup, the makeup artist *must* aim to convince the audience that they are seeing the real thing.

Since the basis of actual makeup technique lies, then, in understanding and applying the principles of *chiaroscuro* (or *light and shade*) that have been used by artists for centuries, our next step is to study these principles in theory, to observe them in life, and then to apply them in monochromatic drawing.

Flat and Curved Surfaces

How are we able to tell by sight alone whether a surface is flat or curved? The general outline of the object may provide a fairly reliable clue. But suppose we are trying to distinguish between a cylinder and a box of approximately the same size. If we cover up the ends, the outline will be exactly the same. But we shall still have no difficulty in determining which is which simply because the patterns of light and shade will be completely different, as illustrated in Figure 2-2. What, then, is chiaroscuro?

Perhaps the simplest way to approach it is to imagine the two forms in Figure 2-2 in total darkness. This would result, of course, in their appearing completely black. In other words, there is a total absence of light; and light, after all, provides the only means of our seeing these or any other objects. But if we turn on a light in the position of the arrow E, on the right, the light hits the objects and is reflected from them to our eyes, en-

abling us to see them. Observe, however, that the light does not illuminate the entire object in either case. Only those surfaces upon which the rays of light fall directly are fully visible because only they receive light rays to reflect to the eye. Surfaces that are situated away from the light source remain in darkness. That enables us to determine the direction in which the surface planes of an object lie and whether they are flat, curved, or irregular. In other words, it tells us the shape of the object.

Hard and Soft Edges

In both of the forms in Figure 2-2 part of the form is lighted, and part remains in darkness. But the shift from the lighted plane to the nonlighted or shadowed plane is entirely different in the two. In one there is a gradual shift from light through semilight (or gray) to dark. In the other the shift is sudden and sharp. Thus, we know that one object has a rounded surface and that the other has flat, angular ones. The sharp division between the two flat surfaces is known as a *hard edge,* and the gradual change between planes on the curved surface, though technically not an edge at all, is known as a *soft edge.* That is a principle basic to all character makeup.

Look, for example, at the two largest wrinkles in the face—the nasolabial folds, which extend from the nose to the lips. In a nasolabial fold, especially if it is well developed, as is the one in Figure 2-3, there is a definite crease in the flesh—and in drawing or painting, the effect of a crease is created by means of a hard edge, with the darkest dark next to the lightest light. The puffy part of the fold is somewhat like a half cylinder, with a gradual transition from the dark at the crease to a soft-edged highlight along the most prominent part of the fold and fading away into a soft-edged shadow.

This effect occurs—and can be reproduced with makeup—in various areas of the face, neck, and hands. Forehead wrinkles, eye pouches, sagging jowls, prominent veins in the hands—the illusion of all of these can be created with highlights and shadows—provided one

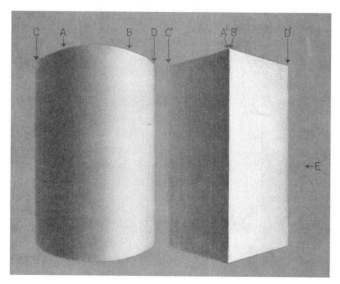

FIGURE 2-2 Modeling curved and angular surfaces.

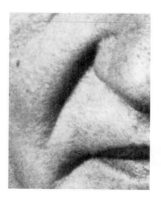

FIGURE 2-3 **Nasolabial fold.** *Note the combination of hard and soft edges.*

understands the principles of hard and soft edges and learns to apply those principles meticulously in doing character makeups.

Drawing with Highlights and Shadows

In order to make sure that you understand the principle and can apply it, draw some simple, three-dimensional objects, such as a cylinder and a box, with charcoal and chalk on gray charcoal paper. These will serve to demonstrate the principles of light and shade you will use in makeup.

Perhaps the simplest way to begin is to do a drawing similar to the one in Figure 2-2. Before beginning your drawing, pay particular attention to the areas indicated by the arrows. Arrow A designates the darkest area on the cylinder and B, the lightest. You will observe that neither of these areas is precisely at the edge of the cylinder. The edge of the dark side (C) is slightly less dark than the darkest part, whereas the light edge (D) is not quite so light as the highlight (B). The reason for this is simply that on the dark side a small amount of reflected light is always seen at the extreme edge, and on the light side the surface of the edge is curving away from us so abruptly that it seems to be less brightly lighted. If you were to draw a cylinder with maximum light and dark areas at the extreme edges, the cylinder would seem to stop abruptly at the edges instead of continuing around to complete itself.

The source of light in the drawing in Figure 2-2 has been arbitrarily placed in the position of the arrow E. Thus, the right side of the cylinder is in direct light, resulting in a strong highlight and a gradual diminution of light from this highlight to the darkest part of the lowlight, or shadow, on the opposite side of the cylinder. No matter from which direction the light is coming, it will create a highlight on the part of the object on which it falls and leave a lowlight on the opposite side—a natural phenomenon that must be carefully observed in doing makeup.

This phenomenon occurs no matter what the shape of an object may be. In the rectangular object in Figure 2-2, for example, there is a sudden change in the plane of the surface rather than a gradual one, and therefore, a correspondingly sharp contrast in areas of light and shade. This results, of course, in a hard edge and an apparent strengthening of both the highlight and the shadow at the edge. This optical illusion always occurs when strong lights and darks are placed next to each other. It can also be observed at the crease of the nasolabial fold in Figure 2-3. In the drawing (Figure 2-2) the hard edge is intensified by deliberately placing the lightest light next to the darkest dark. In other words,

both the strongest highlight and the deepest shadow are at the edge of the object nearest the eye.

In drawing such an object, there is an additional principle—that of aerial perspective—to be taken into consideration. According to that principle, first observed—or at least first applied—by the painter Ucello in the fourteenth century, the centralization of value (the relative brightness or darkness of a color) and of intensity (the relative brightness or dullness of a color) is inversely proportional to the nearness of the color to the eye. In relation to chiaroscuro, this means simply that, with distance, both black and white become more gray—in other words, less strongly differentiated. You have undoubtedly observed this effect in distant mountains or tall buildings or even in cars or houses at a considerable distance. Thus, the near edge of the rectangle is made to appear closer by increasing the intensity, no matter what the value may be. The far edges are made to recede by means of a decrease in intensity and a centralization of value. In makeup, this principle can be applied in highlighting the chin, for example, or the superciliary bone of the forehead in order to make them seem more prominent—in other words, closer to the viewer. Conversely, either one could be made to seem less prominent—farther from the viewer—by decreasing the strength of the highlight or perhaps even using a lowlight instead.

The term *lowlight* is sometimes used to refer to shadows used in makeup and to differentiate them from *cast* shadows. When undirectional light falls upon an object, it not only leaves part of the object itself in shadow, but it also casts a shadow of the object on any area around it from which the light is cut off. In other words, when an object intercepts the light, it casts a shadow. This shadow is known as a *cast* shadow. A cast shadow always has a hard edge, it follows the shape of an object upon which it falls, and it is darkest at the outer edge. Cast shadows are not normally used in makeup because of the continual movement of the actor and the resultant directional changes in light. Probably the only makeup for which they might be used would be one in which both actor and light source were immobile, as in a tableau or for a photograph. In Figure 13-7, for example, the makeup is copied from a painting, using the artist's lighting, which is primarily from one side, instead of imagining the light to be coming from above and center and adjusting the patterns of light and shade accordingly, as would normally be done in makeup.

In doing your own drawings, you might do well to begin with the flat-sided box. Start with your lightest light at what is to be the hard edge, and blend it gradually out toward the outer edge, allowing it to become slightly less light as you go. This can be done by applying the chalk directly, as carefully as you can, then blending with the fingers or with a paper stump to achieve smooth transitions. The precise technique you use is of little importance as long as you achieve the results you want. When the light side is completed, do the dark side in the same way, starting with a heavy application of charcoal at the hard edge next to the white.

In the cylinder there is a gradual transition from light to dark. Both the light and the dark can be applied in either horizontal or vertical strokes, then blended, leaving the gray paper to serve as the middle tone between the light and the dark.

Figure 12-76 illustrates the principle of modeling a third basic shape—the sphere—and the application of that principle to makeup. Notice how the same princi-ple is used in painting the apple cheeks in Figures 12-51 and 12-75B. In the sphere all shadows and highlights fall in a circular pattern.

Remember that whenever a single light falls on a three-dimensional object, those parts of the object not in the direct line of light will remain in shadow. Conversely, whenever there is a lowlight, or shadow, there is a corresponding highlight. When the surface changes direction abruptly, the shadow and the highlight are immediately adjacent. But when the surface changes direction gradually, shadow and highlight are separated by a gradation of intermediate shades.

PROBLEMS

1. With charcoal and chalk on gray paper (obtainable from your local art dealer or stationery store), draw a cylinder, doing the highlights first and completing them before beginning the shadows. Keep the chalk on one side and the charcoal on the other, letting the gray paper serve as a middle tone between them. (See Figure 2-2.) The gray paper can also be allowed to show through at the outer edges. This will decrease the apparent intensity of illumination on the light side and will represent reflected light on the dark side. Then draw a tall, narrow box like the one in Figure 2-2, carefully modeling it with charcoal and chalk, making the hard edge very clean and sharp.

2. Model a sphere in charcoal and chalk, keeping all edges soft. (See Figure 12-76.)

Color in Pigment

chapter 3

In addition to understanding the principles of light and shade, you should also be thoroughly familiar with the principles of color, which can then be applied specifically to makeup paints.

All color comes originally from the source of light. White light is a mixture of light rays of all colors. Technically, pigment has no color of its own but has, rather, the ability to absorb certain rays and reflect others. The rays it reflects are the ones that are responsible for the pigment's characteristic color. "Red" lips, for example, absorb all light rays except the red ones, which they reflect, making the lips appear red. A clown's white face reflects all of the component rays of "white" light and therefore appears white. Black eyelashes, on the other hand, absorb all the component rays in white light and therefore appear black.

But since we are concerned here primarily with the artist's point of view, suppose we merely accept for the moment the existence of color in pigment and begin by examining the relationships characteristic of the various colors we see.

Characteristics of Color

In order to be able to talk intelligently about color and to approach the problem in an organized way, it is convenient to know three terms usually used to designate the essential characteristics of color—*hue, intensity,* and *value.*

Hue   The hue of a color is simply the name by which we know it—red or green or blue or yellow. Pink and maroon are both variations of the basic red hue; brown is a deep, grayed orange; orchid is a tint of violet.

If we take samples of all of the major hues with which we are familiar and drop them at random on a table, the result, of course, is chaos. But as we place next to each other hues that are somewhat similar, we begin to see a progression that by its very nature becomes circular—in other words, a color wheel. That is the traditional form of hue arrangement and for our purposes the most practical one.

Since, however, the progression from one hue to another is a steady one, the circle could contain an unlimited number of hues, depending only on one's threshold of perception—the point at which two hues become so nearly alike as to be indistinguishable to the naked eye and, for all practical purposes, identical. But since a wheel containing hundreds of colors would be impractical, certain hues are selected at regular intervals around the circumference. The simplified color wheel illustrated in Figure 3-1A has been chosen because it is the one that is most familiar.

Intensity   Thus far we have been speaking only of bright colors. But more often than not we shall be using colors of less than maximum brightness. A gray-blue is still blue, but it is far different from the blue on the color wheel. Although of the same hue, it is lower in intensity. This color would be shown as being nearer the center of the wheel—more gray, in other words. Colors on the periphery are of maximum brilliance. Colors nearer the center are less brilliant (of lower intensity) and are commonly referred to as *tones.*

Value   In addition to being blue and low in intensity, a specific color may also be light or dark—light gray-blue, medium gray-blue, dark gray-blue. This darkness or lightness of a color is called its *value.* A light color has

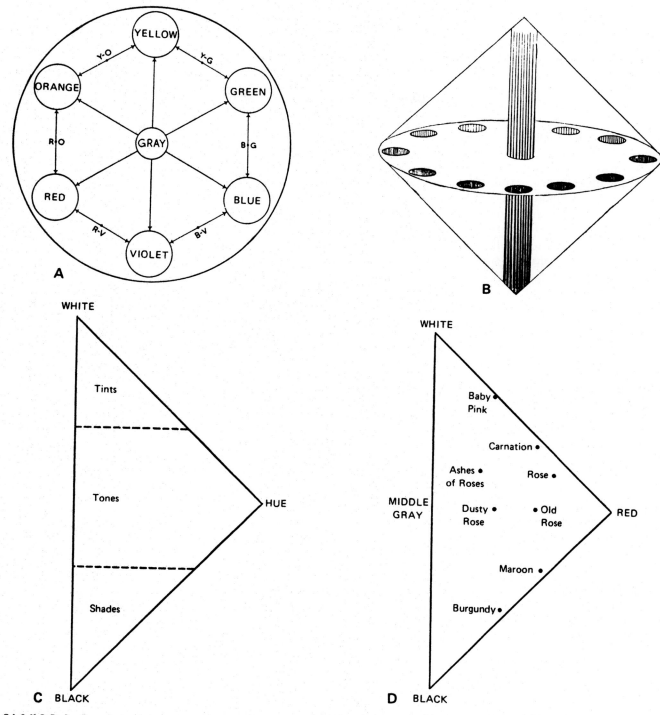

FIGURE 3-1 **Color diagrams.** *A. Color wheel. B. Double color cone. C. Color triangle. D. Location of values of red on the color triangle.*

a high value, a dark color has a low value. Pink is a high value of red; orchid is a high value of violet; midnight blue is a low value of blue. Since the color wheel is only two-dimensional, it obviously cannot be used to demonstrate values, the third color dimension. But this third dimension can be added simply by placing two solid cones base to base with the flat round color wheel between them, as in Figure 3-1 B.

From the color wheel we can go up or down within the cone. As we go up, we approach white, and as we go down, we approach black. Colors in the upper part of the cone are called *tints;* those in the lower part are called *shades.* (See Figure 3-1C.) Straight up the center from tip to tip there is an even progression from black to white; around the periphery, an even progression from one brilliant hue to another; and from any point on the outside to the center, a similar progression from a brilliant hue to gray.

Since any given point within the color cone represents a specific color, a vast number of colors is obviously possible. But every one can be located with reasonable accuracy in terms of *hue, intensity,* and *value.*

Color Mixing

If you don't have the exact color you need, you can, provided you have three primary colors to work with, mix virtually any color you want. These three primary hues are *red, yellow,* and *blue,* which can be mixed to achieve three secondary hues—*orange, green,* and *violet,* as well as an infinite number of intermediate hues. These hues will not, however, be so brilliant when obtained by mixing as when compounded directly from their sources in nature. Mixed colors always lose some intensity.

A glance at the color wheel (Figure 3-1A) will show why. Blue-green, for example, lies midway on a straight line between blue and green since it is obtained by mixing those two colors. Obviously, that brings it nearer to the gray in the center of the wheel than if it were placed on the periphery, where the primary and secondary colors are located. If the orange on the color wheel were obtained by mixing red and yellow, it too would fall nearer the center.

Colors falling opposite each other on the color wheel are called complements and when mixed will produce a neutral gray, as indicated on the color wheel. Blue and orange, for example, can be mixed to produce gray. However, if only a little blue is added to the orange, the result is a burnt orange. Still more blue will give varying intensities of brown.

The same result can be obtained by mixing black and white with the brilliant hue. Any color can be obtained by mixing three pigments—a brilliant hue, black, and white. The color triangle in Figure 3-1C illustrates the principle. This triangle should be imagined as a paper-thin slice cut vertically from the outside of the cone to the center. Since the triangle bounds the complete range of any one hue, a mixture of hue, black, and white at the three points can provide a color at any point within the triangle.

Pink, for example, can be obtained by mixing white with red. Mixing black with red will produce maroon. In order to achieve a dusty rose, both black and white must be added. Figure 3-1D shows where various tints, tones, and shades of red fall on the color triangle.

PROBLEMS

1. Translate the following color descriptions as well as you can into terms of hue, value, and intensity: vivid pink, bright orange, pale blue, deep violet, dusty rose, peacock blue, lavender, lemon yellow, brick red, salmon, orchid, turquoise, midnight blue, magenta, coral.

2. Following the principle of complements, what hue would you use to gray each of the following: red-orange, blue-violet, bluish green, greenish yellow, green? Assume that all colors are of maximum intensity.

3. Using red, yellow, blue, white, and black creme makeup or greasepaint, mix the following colors: orchid, turquoise, peach, coral, rust, olive green, cerise, dark brown, ivory.

A System for Designating Makeup Colors

Every actor or makeup artist, before beginning a makeup, is faced with choosing from hundreds of available colors those that can best help create his or her character. Unfortunately, one's choice is complicated by the fact that not only does each company have its own method of numbering its colors, but the numbers it assigns to its various colors do not always convey useful information about the colors they designate. The system described in this chapter was designed to alleviate this problem by coordinating the colors of the various makeup companies in a single system which, in essence, describes the color being designated in terms of its hue, value, and intensity.

Organizing the Colors

In this system every makeup color is identified by a number that indicates the hue, value, and intensity of the color. In the number S-9-d, for example, S indicates the hue (scarlet); 9, the value (medium); and d, the intensity (medium).

Hue Because of the large number of hues needed to cover the entire range of makeup colors, a few color names, such as *flame* and *chrome*, have been added to the more conventional designations, such as *red, yellow,* and *blue,* resulting in the following list of 39 hues (see below):

For those who may not be familiar with all of the added colors, perhaps it should be pointed out that scarlet is a bright, orangy red; *flame,* a hot orange; *chrome,* a warm yellow; *lime,* a yellowish green; *turquoise,* a blue-green, and *indigo,* a deep violet-blue. Note that in composite color names, such as turquoise-blue and blue-turquoise, the second word represents the stronger hue and is modified by the first word. That means that

turquoise-blue is a blue that is slightly turquoise, whereas blue-turquoise is a turquoise that is slightly blue.

In any particular makeup-color designation in this system of color classification, the hue is indicated by the first letter of the name of the hue or the first two letters for the composite names—for example, R (red), S (scarlet), F (flame), or RS (red-scarlet), SR (scarlet-red), FS (flame-scarlet).

Value The color values range from 1 to 20, 1 being very pale, and 20, very deep. Numbers 8 to 11 indicate a color of medium value. Thus, SF-1 is a pale Scarlet-Flame (or, in more familiar terms, a pale coral pink); SF-20, a deep Scarlet-Flame (a rusty brown); and SF-9, a warm flesh tone of medium value.

Intensity The intensity of the color is indicated by lowercase letters from a to j, a representing a high in-

39 Hues

Purple-Red	Chrome	Blue-Turquoise
Red	Yellow-Chrome	Turquoise-Blue
Scarlet-Red	Chrome-Yellow	Blue
Red-Scarlet	Yellow	Indigo-Blue
Scarlet	Lime-Yellow	Blue-Indigo
Flame-Scarlet	Yellow-Lime	Indigo
Scarlet-Flame	Lime	Violet-Indigo
Flame	Green-Lime	Indigo-Violet
Orange-Flame	Lime-Green	Violet
Flame-Orange	Green	Purple-Violet
Orange	Turquoise-Green	Violet-Purple
Chrome-Orange	Green-Turquoise	Purple
Orange-Chrome	Turquoise	Red-Purple

tensity and j, a low intensity approaching gray. SF-9-a, for example, would be a Scarlet-Flame of medium value and high intensity. SF-9-g would be a Scarlet-Flame of the same value but of low intensity.

Gray is technically a neutral (N), having no hue and no intensity. But it does have value, which is indicated as for the hue—N1, N2, etc.

The Makeup-Color Tables

The specific number/letter designation for each of the various makeup colors described above can be found in Tables 1 and 2 in Appendix J. In Table 1 available makeup colors are listed according to the names or numbers assigned to them by the various makeup companies. The most efficient way to make use of these tables of colors is to label all of your own makeup colors in accordance with the lists in Table 2. If you need a color you don't have, you can find out, by consulting Table 1, which company makes it. That will save time and will enable you to make a more accurate color selection than would be possible from the descriptive labels of the makeup companies.

But suppose you have been using one brand of makeup and have recently changed to another, and you now want to know what number in the new brand corresponds to a certain number in the old. First consult Table 2, where the various brands of makeup are listed according to their own numbers, along with the corresponding standardized numbers. Then turn to Table 1 for available colors listed under the standardized numbers. If the color you want is not available in the brand you are using, look for the nearest number with a listing for that brand.

Color Mixing

Sometimes you will need to mix colors in order to produce the exact color of makeup you want. Suppose, for example, that you decide you want an F-9-c foundation color. You have no F-9-c, but you do have lighter and darker F colors of the desired intensity. A mixture of the two should produce the correct color. (If your other F colors are not of the right intensity, additional mixing may be required.) If you have nothing at all in the F group, you might use an SF-9-c and an OF-9-c since both are of the same value, the same intensity, and of adjacent hues. They can therefore be mixed to produce the desired color. You can also mix two intensities of the same hue and the same value in order to produce an intensity somewhere between the two—as, for example, mixing F-8-a and F-8-c to get F-8-b.

To simplify your makeup kit, you can rely on mixing a few flesh colors with the more intense shading colors in order to create whatever flesh tones you want. For example, if you have an F-8-c foundation paint but find it isn't quite red enough, you can add a little red. If it is too dark, add some white. If the red makes it too brilliant, add some gray (black and white, if you have no gray). For a fairly grayed color, such as F-11-d, you might begin with F-11-c and simply add a little medium gray. Or if you had an F-11-e, you could mix it with F-11-c to obtain F-11-d.

If, on the other hand, you have F-11-c and want F-8-c, you can add white to lighten it. Or you can get what you want by adding an F color that is lighter and of the same intensity. Different hues can be mixed in the same way. An OF-9-c mixed with SF-9-c will give F-9-c since F falls midway between SF and OF.

Although at first reading this system of color designation may appear complex, once the method of classification is thoroughly understood, the grouping will seem simple and logical, and the advantages of having the makeup colors of the various companies organized into a single system of designation are considerable. The best colors and materials from the different companies can be used together without confusion, you can change from one brand of makeup to another without having to memorize a completely new set of numbers, and you can see at a glance what colors are available in various brands of makeup without having to rely on vague descriptive terms.

PROBLEMS

1. Indicate an approximate hue and value (such as light red, dark brown, medium yellow) for each of the following numbers in the color classification: R-2-a, V-1-b, SR-4-c, B-2-a, TB-6-a, SF-9-c, SF-8-g, T-12-b, P-8-b, N-8, B-13-a, C-7-a, 0–9-b, R-13-a, F-13-g, V1–7-a, GL-5-a.

2. Select five or six foundation paints from your kit. Then, using only red, yellow, blue, white, and black*, duplicate—as closely as possible—each of the colors.

3. If you are working in a class, mix several samples of paint; then trade samples with another student, and match his samples without knowing what colors he used to mix them. If you are working alone rather than with a group, mix several colors at random without paying any particular attention to the ones selected. Then go back and try to duplicate them.

*If your black paint is not a true black (not completely neutral, that is), it will throw off the color of the mixture. Most black paints in makeup tend slightly toward the blue. To find out whether or not you have a true black, mix a little with some white to make a medium gray. If the gray appears to be neutral, you have a true black, but if it seems to have a cast of any specific color (such as blue), it needs to be adjusted. That can be done by adding a tiny bit of the complementary color to the black. For example, if the gray appears bluish, add a very small amount of the darkest orange you have to the black and test again by mixing with white. If that is not done, and if the black is not true, you will not get the results you want in any mixing in which black is involved.

Lighting and Makeup

5

Since a makeup seen on a stage under colored lights never looks the same as it did in the dressing room mirror, it is to the actor's advantage to know what effect various colors of stage light are likely to have on his or her makeup so that he or she can make appropriate adjustments. The purpose of this chapter, therefore, is to consider what happens when colored light falls on colored pigment.

Color in Light

It was mentioned briefly in Chapter 3 that pigment depends for its color on the light that illuminates it. In other words, trees do not appear green at night—unless, of course, they are artificially illuminated. Nothing has color until light is reflected from it. If all the light is absorbed, the object looks black; if all the light is reflected, it looks white. If certain rays are absorbed and certain others are reflected, the reflected rays determine the color.

The various colors of rays that make up what we call white light can be observed when they are refracted by globules of moisture in the air, forming a rainbow. The same effect can be obtained with a prism. The colored rays are refracted at different angles because of their different wavelengths, red being the longest and violet the shortest. All matter has the ability to reflect certain wavelengths of light waves but not others, resulting in color sensations in the eye.

Just as white light can be broken up into its component hues, those hues can be synthesized to produce white light, as well as various other colors. As with pigments, three of the colors can be used as primaries and combined to produce any other color of light, as well as

the neutral white. However, the three primaries are not the same in light as in pigment. In light they are *red, green,* and *ultramarine (a deep violet-blue)*. In mixing lights, *red* and *green* produce *yellow* or *orange; green* and *ultramarine* produce *turquoise* or *blue-green,* and *ultramarine* and *red* produce *purple.* A mixture of all three primaries produces white light. On the stage these various colored rays are produced by placing a color medium in front of some source of nearly white light, such as a spot or a flood.

Light on Pigment

If the colored rays fall on pigment that is able to reflect them, then we see the color of the light. But if they fall on a pigment that absorbs some of them, the color is distorted. Suppose, for example, that red rays fall on a "red" hat. The rays are reflected, and the hat looks red. But suppose green rays are thrown on the "red" hat. Since the hat is able to reflect only red rays, the green rays are absorbed, nothing is reflected, and the hat looks black.

Imagine a "green" background behind the "red" hat. Add green light and you have a black hat against a green background. Change the light to red, and you have a red hat against a black background. Only white light (or both red and green lights at the same time) will give you a red hat against a green background.

The principle of light absorption and reflection can be used to advantage in certain trick effects as mentioned in the previous paragraph. But ordinarily your problem will be to avoid such effects rather than to create them. Usually—unless the makeup is to be seen in simulated moonlight or spotlighted with strong blues or greens—major adjustments will not be necessary.

The problem of becoming familiar with the specific effects of the vast number of possible combinations of light and makeup is a far from simple one. It is impossible to offer a practical panacea for all of the problems you may encounter. A chart could be made, but it would be inaccurate, for not only do exact shades of makeup vary among manufacturers and from stick to stick or cake to cake, but with todays' new technologies, light sources can also vary and vary greatly. Thus, the only practical solution seems to be to generalize and to leave details to the artist himself. Here are a few practical suggestions:

In the first place, try to do your makeup under lighting similar to that under which it will be viewed by the audience. Ideally, dressing-room or makeup-room lights should be arranged to take color media that can be matched with those used on the stage. Since dressing rooms are almost never so equipped, some special arrangement should be made if possible. A pair of small spots in a large dressing room, for example, can be very helpful.

Secondly, whenever possible, look at the makeup from the house. This can usually be done during a full dress rehearsal. If you are doing your own makeup, have someone whose judgment you can trust look at you from the house and offer criticisms. Since final approval of the makeup lies with the director, he is the logical one to do this, but may not be the person best qualified to give the actor constructive suggestions. If a makeup artist is in charge of all the makeup, he will check the makeup under lights and get final approval from the director.

In the third place, you ought to have some familiarity with the general effects of certain colors of light upon certain colors of makeup. Generally speaking, the following principles will hold:

1. Colors of low value will have a maximum effect upon makeup; colors of high value, a minimum.
2. A given color of light will cause a similar color of pigment to become higher in intensity, whereas a complementary color of pigment will be lower in both value and intensity.
3. Any color of pigment will appear gray or black if it does not contain any of the colors composing a given ray of light that falls upon it.

If a spotlight and appropriate color media are not accessible, the following list of colors of light, with their effects upon various colors of makeup, can be used as a guide. You should remember, however, that the effects listed are only approximations, and that the actual effects may upon occasion vary from those indicated here. The relatively recent development of higher color temperature lamps used in lighting equipment (higher temperature lamps often used in automated fixtures provide more blue light than conventional lamps) may also add some variation to the effects listed below. The names of the colors, rather than their numbers, have been used in this listing since they are more generally understood.

Pink tends to gray the cool colors and intensify the warm ones. Yellow becomes more orange.

Flesh pink affects makeup less strongly than the deeper shades and has a flattering effect on most makeups.

Fire red will ruin nearly any makeup. All but the darker flesh tones will virtually disappear. Light and medium rouge become a pale orange and fade imperceptibly into the foundation, whereas the dark reds turn a reddish brown. Yellow becomes orange, and the cool shading colors become shades of gray and black.

Bastard amber is one of the most flattering colors to makeup. It may gray the cool shading colors somewhat but adds life to a warm makeup color palette used on any skin tone.

Amber and *orange* have an effect similar to that of red, though less severe. Most flesh colors, except the dark browns, become more intense and more yellow. Rouges tend to turn more orange. Cool colors are grayed. Dark amber has, of course, a stronger effect than light amber.

Light straw has very little effect upon makeup, except to make the colors somewhat warmer. Cool colors may be grayed a little.

Lemon and *yellow* make warm colors more yellow, blues more green, and violets somewhat gray. The darker the color medium, of course, the stronger the effect upon the makeup.

Green grays dark and light skin tones and most cheek colors in proportion to its intensity. Violet is also grayed. Yellow and blue will become more green, and green will be intensified.

Light blue-green tends to lower the intensity of the foundation colors. Light red becomes darker, and dark red becomes brown. Use very little rouge under blue-green light.

Green-blue will gray medium and deep flesh tones, as well as all reds, and will wash out pale flesh tones.

Blues will gray most flesh tones and cause them to appear more red or purple. Dark skin tones may appear even darker. Blues and greens become higher in value, violets become more blue, and purples become more violet. The darker the blue, the stronger the effect.

Violet (light and surprise) will cause orange, flame, and scarlet to become more red. Rouge may seem more intense. Greens are likely to be a little lower in value and intensity. Be careful not to use too intense a red in either foundation or rouge. May be used as a substitute for blues when lighting darker skin tones.

Purple will have an effect similar to that of violet, except that the reds and oranges will be intensified to a much greater degree, and most blues will tend to look violet.

Color correction filters tend to raise the color temperature of transmitted light towards that of daylight. While they appear to be blue in color, they are in fact transmitting pink/red wavelengths of light and have proven to be very useful for all types of makeup.

Direction of Light and Its Effect on Facial Features

The *key light* is one predominant source of light that supplies the greatest amount of illumination on a performer. Performers who wish to appear smoother and younger should always be lit with a key light positioned high and in front of them. The key light position should illuminate the full face (especially the eyes) from a high enough position to create good cheekbone shadows, but not so high as to cast a large nose shadow over the upper lip, or shadows beneath the puffy under-eye pouches. When lighting older performers, the position of the key light is extremely critical. A person who has well developed nasolabial folds (smile lines extending from the nostrils to the outer corners of the mouth) should never be lit by a key light from a side angle (cross-light). A cross-light or side-light, even three-quarters front, will create unflattering shadows under the eyes, along nasolabial folds and around and under other undesirable facial sags and skin texture. A high, front key light will also help hide a double chin by camouflaging it with a well placed shadow.

Some lighting people, inexperienced in corrective lighting for the mature face, sometimes argue that illumination from a key light positioned straight on the face will be too flattering. Remember, lighting can be arranged to be either flat or create dimension by causing cast shadows on the face from the nose, cheekbones and other fleshy areas. Lighting that creates dimension through the use of cast shadows (from crosslight or sidelight) may be wonderful to create mood and dramatic impact, but is almost always devastating to corrective makeup. On the other hand, the lower jaw and cheekbone shadows created by a high, front key light can be complimentary to corrective makeup when properly controlled. (Cheekbone shadows are technically considered a blend of both natural and cast shadows, depending on the amount of protrusion.)

A skillful lighting person or Director of Photography (DP) will know how to increase or decrease the amount of shadow under cheekbones and under the jaw by raising or lowering the key light. This lighting procedure is the only one that should be used to give dimension to the mature face. And, even so, the light must not be positioned so high above the subject that it creates hard cast shadows under the nose, under the lower lip and/or under puffy eye pouches.

The lower the key light (still directed straight onto the subject's face) the flatter the face will become. This flattening effect is usually necessary to decrease the effects of aging. If this is the case the makeup artist must be sure to shade under the cheekbones, the sides of the nose and sometimes the side planes of the face to restore enough dimension to keep the face from appearing too flat or too round.

The makeup artist's application of highlighting and shading plays a very important role in the success or failure of this high, front key-light technique. Good lighting will fill in unwanted shadows only so far. The rest depends on the makeup artist's skill in applying corrective makeup highlights to reflect the light and makeup shadows to absorb the light. The highlights will lift the recessed areas while the shading will define and diminish areas to create flattering dimensions.

Fill light is produced by one or more instruments strategically placed to lighten shadows on the face, to lessen harshness and reduce contrast (light to dark ratio). In the theatre, every light that is not the key light is considered fill light. In the film or television studio it is frequently a diffused light placed on the opposite side of the camera from the key light. If the key light is placed high, in front of the subject and slightly to the left of the camera to directly illuminate the face, the fill light should be placed to the right side of the camera illuminating the side of the face less structurally prominent. A fill light may not be necessary when the key light is broad enough to illuminate the subject's entire face.

Backlight is supplied by one or more instruments illuminating from behind, giving the subject dimensional separation from the background. While light from this direction assists in defining the edges and shape of the subject it does not directly influence the makeup. It can, however, depending on its position, cause an unflattering appearance to subjects with thinning hair. Backlight from a high position may illuminate the scalp and accentuate the problem. Lowering the backlight or removing it will solve this problem.

If, as may occasionally happen, the primary source of light is to be from below rather than from above, the makeup should be done—or, at least, looked at—with light coming from below so that any necessary adjustments can be made. Previously unnoticed areas of the face, such as, the neck, ear lobes, and the hairline behind the ear must now be considered.

One problem remains. Since stage lights are likely to change from time to time during a performance, be aware of any radical changes, especially in color, and have your makeup checked under the various lighting conditions. If such changes do affect your makeup adversely and there is no opportunity for you to adjust the makeup to the lights, try to modify your basic makeup to minimize the problem under all lighting conditions. If this is not successful, consult the director about the possibility of some adjustment to the lighting.

PROBLEMS

1. What color would each of the following appear to be under the colors of light indicated: A yellow hat under red and green lights? A green hat under red and yellow lights? A red hat under blue and green lights? A red and green hat under yellow lights? A red and yellow hat under green lights? A green and yellow hat under red lights? A red and blue hat under blue lights'? A red, yellow, and blue hat under red, green, and ultramarine lights? A purple and white hat under red, green, and ultramarine lights?

2. It has been stated in the chapter that a given color of light raises the intensity of a similar color of pigment. Yet on a stage flooded with red light, all of the clear, bright reds seem to be "washed out." Why is this so?

3. In a lighting laboratory (Light Lab), the makeup room or on stage, set up the three basic lighting instruments: a key light; a fill light and a back light. Experiment lighting your makeup application using a variety of positions and levels of illumination.

4. Continue the experimenting in Problem 4 with a mature subject. Apply makeup and light the subject to produce the most flattering effect.

5. Continue the work in Problems 4 and 5. Photograph the subject with one or more of the following image capturing devices: a 35mm camera using portrait quality film, a digital camera, a hi-8 or digital video camera and a 16 mm movie camera. Analyze and discuss the results. (This problem would be better approached after having studied the entire book. Choosing the appropriate makeup and application techniques for each performance medium will insure greater success.)

Relating the Makeup to the Character

One of the basic purposes of most makeup is to assist the actor in the development of a character by making suitable changes (when necessary) in the actor's physical appearance. It seems reasonable, therefore, that our study of makeup should begin with an examination of the principles of character analysis.

Character Analysis

The first step in arriving at a suitable image for the character is to study the play. Directly through the stage directions and indirectly through the dialogue you come to know the character. You become acquainted not only with the character's physical appearance but also with his or her background, environment, personality, age, and relationships with other characters in the play. Although this probing into the character is essential for the actor, it is also essential preparation for the makeup. It is important to be able to translate the information into visual terms.

Take, for example, the nose of Cyrano de Bergerac. This would appear at first glance to be the basis for Cyrano's makeup. But is it sufficient to simply attach a large nose to the actor's face? Without it there is no Cyrano, but to what extent is the nose comic and to what extent tragic? What elements of nobility and courage and kindness should appear in the visual impression aside from the one exaggerated feature? And from a purely practical point of view, what effect will any given shape of nose have on the particular actor's face.

Such questions as these should be asked about any character you are analyzing. And, in answering each question, there is a choice to be made. You may not always make the right choice, but you should make a def-

inite one. A fine makeup, like a fine painting or a fine performance, is a product of thorough preparation, intelligent selection, and meticulous execution.

You may wish, for example, to reflect specifically on a character's face, state of health, disposition, and occupation. When these are specified in the script, it is essential not to deny them in the makeup. If Marguerite Gautier plays her death scene with rosy cheeks and a bloom of health, the credulity of the audience is going to be severely strained. Or if a pale, sallow-complexioned character is supposed to be a deep sea fisherman, the more alert members of the audience may suspect a sinister twist of the plot. Therefore, it is essential, at the very least, to provide the minimum requirements of the physical appearance so as to correlate what the audience sees with what it hears. But beyond this you have an obligation to use the resources of makeup creatively to solve more subtle problems.

It is, for example, not only possible but commonplace to find members of the same family who have similar backgrounds and similar environments, as well as a family resemblance, but who are still very different. The differences between the sisters, Goneril and Cordelia in *King Lear* for example, are crucial to the play. It will surely help both the actors and the audience if these differences can be reflected in the makeup. This requires an analysis to determine what each character should, or might, look like.

Such an analysis can be simplified by classifying the determinants of physical appearance into six groups: heredity, race, environment, temperament, health, and age. These are not, of course, mutually exclusive. Race, for example, is merely a subdivision of heredity and may be a basic consideration in such a play as *Joe Turner's Come and Gone* and of no significance at all in a play like *Waiting for Godot*, which was, in fact performed on Broadway with both white and black casts. Temperament is obviously a more important consideration than environment in studying the character of Lady Macbeth, whereas with Blanche in *A Streetcar Named Desire,* both environment and temperament are basic to an understanding of the character and the play. In any character analysis, therefore, it is well to concentrate one's attention on those groups which are of most significance to the character. It is not important to know precisely in which group any specific feature or character trait belongs. The divisions are laid out merely as a practical aid in organizing one's research.

Heredity

Generally speaking this group includes those characteristics, physical and mental, with which a person is born. The red hair of all the boys in *Life With Father* is obviously hereditary. Since it is required by the play, there is no choice to be made. But in most instances you must decide such things as the color of the hair, the shape of the nose, and the line of the eyebrow, and you must base your decision on a knowledge of the relationship between physical features and character and personality. In the character analysis it is a problem to choose exactly the kind of feature that will tell the audience most about the character and that will best support the character portrait the actor is trying to present.

Race

In realistic plays written to chronicle specific human experience, race is always a factor to be considered, whether it is mentioned in the play or not. Contemporary history plays such as August Wilson's *Seven Guitars,* Octavio Solis' *El Paso Blue,* and Amy Tan's *Joy Luck Club* paint a picture of American history fashioned out of unique cultural experiences. Demands of each script require specific cultural images to advance the dramatic action. Members of the same family should appear to be of the same race—unless there are adopted children of other races, a fact that would surely be brought out in the dialogue. Historical characters should appear to be of whatever race or combination of races they actually were—unless the playwright or director has decided to disregard the historical facts.

Environment

In addition to race and other hereditary factors, environment is of considerable importance in determining the color and texture of the skin. A farmer and a computer programmer are likely to have different colors of skin, and a color which is right for one would probably look incongruous on the other.

One must take into consideration not only the general climatic conditions of the part of the world in which the character lives but also the character's physical work conditions and leisure-time activities. Offices, mines, fields, foundries, night clubs, and country estates all have different effects upon the people who work or live in them. But remember that a character may have had a variety of environments. Monsieur Madeleine in Hugo's *Les Miserables* may be a wealthy and highly respected mayor, but his physical appearance will still bear the marks of his years of imprisonment as the convict Jean Valjean. If environment is to be construed as referring to all external forces and situations affecting the individual, then custom or fashion may logically be considered a part of the environmental influences, and a very important one. Influences arising from social customs and attitudes have throughout the centuries brought about superficial and self-imposed changes in appearance.

During most of the first half of the twentieth century it was assumed that men's hair would be short and that women's hair would be longer. A man might be capable of growing long hair and might even prefer long hair, but social pressures were at work to discourage him. During other periods of history, however, customs were different, and men wore their hair long and in some periods wore wigs. The drawings in Appendix F indicate the great variety in hair styles through the centuries, and, of course, those styles must be taken into consideration in analyzing a character and planning the makeup.

Similarly, the wearing of makeup off stage has varied throughout the centuries. If an eighteenth-century fop appears to be wearing makeup, no harm is done because he might very well have done so, but if any of the men in a realistic mid-twentieth century play are obviously made up, they immediately become less believable. Furthermore, styles in street makeup vary. The plucked eyebrows, brilliant rouge, and bizarre lips of the late nineteen twenties would seem anachronistic in most other periods. Similar eccentricities such as the heavy, stylized eye makeup of the ancient Egyptians can be found in other periods in history. (For information on fashions in makeup, see Appendix E.)

Remember that, on the stage, makeup should look like makeup only when the character would normally be wearing it. That means that your character must be analyzed in the light of the social customs to determine not only possible hair styles but also the accepted usage in regard to makeup. For every character that you make up, always analyze the skin color, hair style, and street makeup in terms of environmental influences.

Temperament

An individual's temperament, which can be interpreted as including personality, disposition, and personal habits, affects physical appearance in many ways. (See Figure 6-1.) The adventurer and the scholar, the Bohemian artist and the shrewd business person, the prize-fighter and the philosopher all are widely differ-

ent in temperament, and these differences are to a greater or lesser degree apparent in the physical appearance. The convivial Sir Toby Belch and the melancholy Sir Andrew Aguecheek, for example are, aside from all other differences, widely contrasting in temperament and could not conceivably look alike.

The March sisters in *Little Women* are products of the same environment and the same heredity; yet temperamental differences make them strongly indi-

FIGURE 6-1 Character makeups on the same actor showing differences in age and temperament. *Actor Colm Fiore in the film* Storm of the Century. *Makeup effects by Maestro Studio F/X, Inc., Quebec, Canada.*

vidual, and their individuality should be reflected in the makeup.

A shy, librarian in, say, 1953 would certainly not be ostracized if she wore false eyelashes, but it is most unlikely that she would do so. And the idea of her wearing green eyeshadow is preposterous. Yet green eyeshadow might be quite right for a dissolute, aging actress, such as Tennessee Williams' leading character in *Sweet Bird of Youth.*

The hair is an even more striking and obvious reflection of personality. One would expect the mature and socially correct Mrs. Higgins in *Pygmalion* to have her hair beautifully done, not a hair out of place, perhaps not in the latest fashion but in one considered proper for a woman of her years and of her elevated social station. The Cockney flower girl, Eliza Doolittle, on the other hand, might be expected to give her hair no attention at all, except, perhaps, to push it out of her eyes. When she is transformed into a "lady," her hair, as well as everything else about her, must reflect the change.

There are fewer opportunities for men to express their personality in this way, but the ones which exist must not be slighted. When a beard or a mustache is to be worn, it offers an opportunity to reflect personality. First of all comes the choice of whether to wear facial hair at all. And the choice is always related to fashion. In other words, it would take as much courage not to wear a moustache or beard in 1870 as it would to wear one in, say 1940. In 1960 it would take less courage than in 1940, but the mere fact of wearing a beard would still be significant and a clear reflection of personality.

Secondly, once the decision to wear the beard has been made, there is the equally important decision as to what kind of beard to wear. You must know first of all what kind of beards were being worn in the period. If fashions were very limiting, there is less freedom of choice; if the character departs from the fashion (and there are always those who do), it is doubly significant. But there are several periods in history, especially in the late nineteenth century, for example, when facial hair was the rule and the style was limited only by the imagination, taste, and hair growing capability of the individual. In such a period there is an extraordinary opportunity to express personality through conscious choice of style in facial hair.

The same principles apply, as well, to hair on the head. There are often limitations on styles for men, but even during periods when convention was very restrictive, as in the second quarter of the twentieth century, there was still some variation in length, in wave or absence of it, in the part, and in color.

An interesting case of temperamental differences resulting in both conscious and unconscious physical changes is found in the Madwoman of Chaillot. There are, in fact, four madwomen, each completely different from the others temperamentally, each showing that difference in her face. Countess Aurelia, the Madwoman of Chaillot, is calm, compassionate, clever, rather tragic, and completely charming. Mme. Constance, the Madwoman of Passy, is garrulous, argumentative, bad tempered, flighty, and quick to take offense. Mlle. Gabrielle, the Madwoman of St. Sulpice, is shy, retiring, and easily hurt. And Mme. Josephine, the Madwoman of La Concorde, is forthright, practical, and very businesslike. A makeup that would be appropriate for one of the madwomen would be completely wrong for any of the others.

These are not problems to be faced only with certain striking characters, like the madwomen or Sir Toby Belch, or on special occasions when circumstances demand it. They should be considered and solved for every character.

An actress of twenty-five who is playing a contemporary character of twenty-five must not assume that her hair style or her way of making up her eyebrows or her lips will automatically be suitable for the character. The problem becomes particularly acute in repertory theater or summer stock when an actor is playing a different role every week, sometimes with very little variations in age. It is then more important than ever that ways of distinguishing among the characters be found. This means finding the most revealing ways in which character might be expressed and use these to help develop individuality in the makeup.

Health

In most cases a character's state of health has nothing to do with the play. But sometimes, as with Mimi or Camille, there are noticeable changes that are important to the characterization or the plot. At other times, as with Elizabeth Barrett or with Laura in *The Glass Menagerie,* there is no specific illness, just a state of delicate health. A character may also be undernourished and must give physical evidence of this. By contrast, there are those who are overnourished and suffer from gout. And are others who are bursting with health and should show it in their faces.

Even when the health is not normal, a specific illness is rarely indicated. It is seldom necessary, therefore, to try to reproduce medically accurate physical symptoms. Any physical suggestions of the illness can usually be confined to changes in the skin color, the eyes, and perhaps the hair. As always, it is better to do too little than too much. Above all, avoid attributing to certain illnesses specific physical symptoms that are inaccurate and that will immediately be spotted by doctors and nurses in the audience. In certain areas of makeup it is best to curb the imagination and rely strictly on factual information.

Age

Since age invariably affects all people in physical terms, it is an essential consideration in every makeup, but not necessarily the most important one. How old is Falstaff, for example, or Lady Macbeth? Is it important to know this information precisely? Are there not more important facts to know about those particular characters. Before beginning the makeup, there must be some definite decision made about the age, and that decision will rest with the actor and the director. But in makeup we are interested in the apparent, not the actual, age, and this depends on the kind of life the character has led and how the character feels about it. Thus, the environment may have affected the character's apparent age, but so has his or her mental attitude. Is it positive or negative? Is he or she cheerful or morose? Does the character feel sorry for himself or herself, or is he or she glad to be alive? Do they look forward or backward? And how old do they think they are? Are they conscious of getting older each year, does time seem to have stopped? Do they really want to remain young?

Remember also that apparent age is related to nutrition and thus involves health, which depends on both nutrition and mental attitudes. As you can see, the various factors affecting the appearance are in many cases interrelated and cannot always be considered separately.

Discussing specific effects of age, can be only general and indicate the kind of changes that may take place. The conventional divisions of youth, middle age, and old age are serviceable for this discussion.

Youth (See Figure 6-2A.) There is an unfortunate custom in the theater of referring to any youthful makeup as a straight makeup. This means simply that you do nothing but heighten the color and project the features. Designating a makeup as "straight" can lead to neglect of essential work. Conceivably, the term has a certain validity in the event that a specific role is so cast that the actor's features are precisely right, with not a hair to be changed. If makeup is required that will change the actor to fit the character being playing, this is called a character makeup (Figure 6-3.)

Now, there are instances when there is no clearly defined character, or perhaps no character at all. In photographic protraiture, in some platform appearances, sometimes in choruses, it is expected that the actors appear as themselves, but it is rare to find an actor who cannot profit by some facial improvement. And a straight makeup does not improve, it merely projects. When we wish to improve an actor's face without relating it to a specific character, we use corrective makeup.

Makeup for youth, except when actors are appearing as themselves requires a character analysis. The physical attributes of youthfulness are usually a smooth skin, a good deal of color in the face, a delicately curved

FIGURE 6-2
Adolphe Appia.
A. Photographs at age 20 (Note the smooth skin, full lips and eyebrows, and gentle curves, characteristic of youth.) B. In later years.

FIGURE 6-3 Actor in character makeup playing a character of the same age showing the influence of environment on his physical appearance. *Actor John Ales in the film* Ride With the Devil. *Makeup by Jeff Goodwin of Transformations Makeup FX Lab.*

mouth, smooth brows following the shape of the eye, an abundance of hair, and so on. Those are, of course, average characteristics. Heredity, environment, temperament, and health may counteract the normal effects of youth, as in the case of Richard III. Despite the fact that Richard is a young man at the time of the play, he is hardly an average, normal one. Although there may be little in the face to suggest age, it will probably not seem particularly youthful. Temperament and environ-

ment will have had strong influences on his physical appearance.

Ophelia is a young girl, but her profound unhappiness and confusion, which finally result in a complete mental breakdown and suicide, must certainly, along with other elements in her personality, be reflected in some way, however subtly, in the makeup.

Middle Age (See Figure 6-4.) This is an indefinite period somewhere in the middle of life. It reaches its climax

Before

After

FIGURE 6-4 Age makeup on Kenneth Branagh. Adding 25 years and 25 pounds. *Makeup by Jeff Goodwin of Transformations Makeup FX Lab.*

perhaps in the fifties or even the sixties, depending on the individual. For purposes of this discussion it can be considered as including all ages between forty and sixty-five. But remember that in earlier times middle age came much sooner. In any case, it is the apparent rather than the actual age that is important in makeup.

Age can, and too often does, bring with it changes in the color of the skin and the hair, sagging muscles, hair loss, an increasing angularity in the lips, eyebrows, and cheeks, but the exact nature of these changes will depend on factors other than age. So it is important in every case to determine how seriously and in what ways age has affected appearance. And remember that the effects of age are modified radically by health, environment, temperament, and mental habits.

Old Age (See Figure 6-2B.) As a person advances beyond middle life, the skull structure usually becomes more prominent (Figure 12-36G), especially if the person is thin. A large person will have a greater tendency toward flabbiness, with pouches and puffs and double chins. (Figure 12-36F) Along with a general sagging of the flesh, the tip of the nose may droop (Figure 12-35A), hair may fall out (Figure 12-35L), eyebrows may become bushy or scraggly (Figure 12-16E), lips almost invariably become thinner (Figure 12-41B), teeth may fall out, skin and hair color will probably change, the skin on the neck may droop (Figure 12-41L) and the hands may become bony (Figure 12-54C), and the face may be a mass of wrinkles (Figure 13-15A). It is up to you to decide which of these effects apply to your character. Again, changes will be affected by health, environment, temperament, and mental attitudes.

The creative aspect of makeup lies in the mind of the artist and stems directly from the artist's understanding of the character. Following such a plan of character analysis means, of course, that all consideration of makeup cannot be left until the night of dress rehearsal. It is something that should be planned as carefully as the sets and the costumes. If, before you sit down at your dressing table, you have intelligently planned in specific terms the physical changes you wish to make, you will have mastered the creative part of your problem and will have left only the technical one of executing your ideas.

Physiognomy

Since the beginning of the human race people must have observed other people and drawn conclusions from their appearances as to their probable behavior. Through trial and error, certain correlations have been found that seem to hold up with reasonable consistency. Just as people draw these conclusions consciously or unconsciously in daily life, so they continue to do so when they see characters on the stage in the theater. The actor may choose to turn this to an advantage by becoming consciously aware of the correlations of physical appearance with character and personality traits. If not, the actor is taking the risk of assuming physical characteristics that could mislead the audience and detract from the believability of the character.

The practice of relating physical appearance to character and personality traits is defined by the dictionary as physiognomy. A familiarity with some of the principles of physiognomy can be enormously helpful in designing a face for the actor's character.

Much of this you already do unconsciously. Look, for example, at the faces in Figure 7-1. Study each character sketch and ask yourself why it suits the character. Is it a strong face or a weak one? Does it look optimistic or pessimistic? Sensitive or crude? Aggressive or timid? Determined or vacillating? Intelligent or not? Can you determine what there is about the face that causes you to react as you do?

Whether your response to the face is intuitive or analytical, it comes under the heading of physiognomy, and it is essentially what the audience does in relation to every character on the stage. Actors would thus do well to be aware of the ways in which an audience may relate physical appearance to personality and character traits.

In making changes in the face, remember that you are dealing with a whole face, not just a single feature, and those changes you do make will inevitably be affected by other areas of the face.

Eyes   Perhaps no other feature betrays the inner person so clearly as the eyes (See Figure 6-5.) In general, prominent eyes are found on dreamers and aesthetes (Figures 6-5A and B) who live largely through their senses, whereas deep-set eyes (Figures 6-5C and D) are more likely to be an indication of an observant, analytical mind. We might say that one is the eye of a Romeo, the other of a Cassius. Many eyes will be neither strongly one nor the other, and thus the individuality might be expected to include characteristics of both types.

The eyes and the mouth often change markedly during one's lifetime. These changes are usually associated with the aging process, but the kind of changes that take place will depend upon the sort of mental, emotional, and physical life one leads. The kind of wrinkles which develop through frequent laughter, for example, quite logically suggest a happy, kindly disposition.

Eyebrows   Eyebrows are one of the most expressive and easily changed features of all. Even a slight change in the eyebrow can effect the entire face. Eyebrows vary in placement, line, thickness, color, length and direction of the hairs. They can reveal mental or

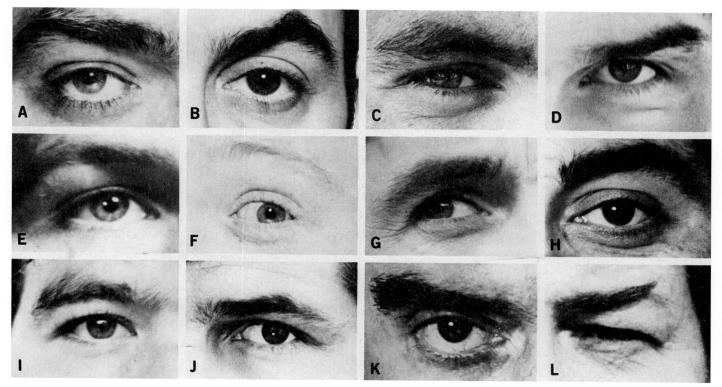

FIGURE 6-5 Character in eyes and eyebrows.

physical energy (Figures 6-5H and J, 7-1C and L), suggest weakness or lack of concentration (Figures 6-5F and 7-1A and J) and define a practical, intelligent personality from a simple, erratic one (Figures 7-1H and B.) If you want to suggest treachery or cunning, put a curve in the brow and angle it upwards (Figure 6-5K and 7-1D) This would also be an appropriate brow for Iago and Richard III and is, in fact, the brow of Henry VIII.

Nose

Noses can be classified as to size and shape (in profile). They can also be described in definitive terms such as Roman, Grecian, Aquiline, and retrousse; and with descriptive words such as strong, refined, aristocratic, cute, and inquisitive.

The nose is the boney feature that is relatively easy to remodel in three-dimensions. A very little added to or subtracted from the nose can, like a change in the eyebrows, alter the entire face. And since the change is so dramatic, it is important that the right kind of change be made. Once the decision to change the shape of the nose is made, questions such as what qualities would be appropriate for the character must be asked. Should it be straight or crooked, long or short, convex or concave, narrow or wide? Imagine, if you can a Lady Macbeth with a small, delicate, turned-up nose or a Snow White with a large Roman one. Utilizing research to study a variety of profiles and choosing one that seems appropriate is an invaluable next step. How it will look on the actor's face is a simple matter of experimentation.

Mouth

The size and shape of the mouth and the thickness and color of the lips affects the overall impression of character. The mouth can be large and expansive or small and contracted. It can curve upward or downward, be held loosely or tightly closed. Lips can be thin and straight or full and shapely. They can reveal a social personality or an introverted one. They can indicate warmth or reserve, a serious nature or one full of humor. The mouth is a good indicator of age, becoming thinner, more angular, and loosing color as one becomes older. (See Figure 6-6.)

The suggestions in this chapter are to be used only as guides. Use these brief suggestions with discretion and try always to correlate the features and not rely on only one to suggest the character. You will rarely be able to make all of the changes you consider ideal, but the purpose of character analysis is to discover the determining factors in the character's behavior and then to visualize as nearly as possible the final look.

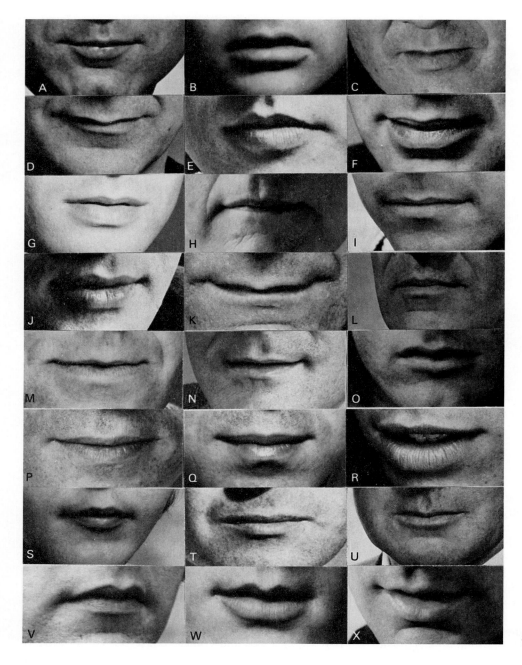

FIGURE 6-6 Mouths.

PROBLEMS

1. Choosing one or more of the character sketches in Figure 7-1, write a short essay explaining whether or not you agree with how the designer has interpreted the character through the sketch.

2. Choose three characters from well-known plays and write brief descriptions of how you think they should look, being specific about such features as mouths, noses, and eyes. Do not be misled by photographs of actors who may have played the parts, for in those you are seeing individual actor's interpretations, not the playwright's. Do not be concerned with practical problems of makeup design, application, or products.

chapter 7

Designing the Makeup

Once you have decided what you want the character to look like, the next step is to put your ideas into concrete form—either an experimental makeup or a sketch showing what you have in mind. Which you do will probably depend to some extent on whether you are an actor or a makeup designer. In either case, making a sketch or a drawing of the makeup can be extremely helpful. For a makeup designer, professional or nonprofessional, it is almost essential. (See Figures 7-6, 7-9, and 7-12.)

The Makeup Designer

If all of the makeups are being designed by one person, he or she will first study the play, then consult with the director, the costume designer, and, ideally, with the actors before designing the makeups and will also obtain photographs of the actors before making the sketches. Then, after the sketches have been approved by the director, the designer should make certain that the actors can do the makeup. If not, it is the responsibility of the makeup designer to teach the actors to do it, making sure they understand the instructions on the makeup charts. (See Figures 7-10 and 7-12.) And if the time for actually making up is going to be limited (as with quick changes or with the actors playing more than one part), it is the makeup designer's responsibility to make certain that the makeup, as designed, can be done by the actors (or the makeup artist) in the time available. Unless the makeups are unusually simple, all of this should ordinarily be taken care of before the first dress rehearsal. The makeup designer should be present at the first dress rehearsal with lighting in order to see the makeup in action on the stage. He or she can then consult with the director if necessary and suggest to the

actors any changes that need to be made. Only when the designer is completely satisfied that the makeups are being executed satisfactorily, should the actors be left on their own. In the case of a long run, the designer should check the makeups regularly.

In television and film, on Broadway, and in opera, the makeup designer is a professional makeup artist. In regional theater and dance companies the makeup design is often the responsibility of the actor or the costume designer and is executed by the actor. On occasion, a makeup artist will be contracted for special makeup effects. In academic theater the designer may be the makeup teacher, the costumer, or, ideally, one of the more advanced makeup students, who should, when competent to do so, be given the opportunity to design the makeups for public productions. Professional or nonprofessional, the designer should start work well in advance and have it essentially completed before dress rehearsals, which should be used for adjusting the makeup to the lighting and making any other changes that may be needed.

Although in most professional productions (and in some nonprofessional ones) the actors are expected to create their own makeups, there are productions that need the services of a makeup designer. And occasionally, in both professional and nonprofessional productions, a makeup artist may be called in to help actors who are not prepared, by training or experience, to do the makeup required. In that kind of situation the makeup artist does not usually submit designs to the director, but deals directly with the actors. Thus, instead of determining what the makeups are to be like, the makeup artist works with the actors in creating them.

When the makeup is finished, photographing it with an instant-picture or digital camera can be very helpful and may, in fact, lead to further work on the makeup. When the actors are satisfied with the makeup, they then learn—with the help of the makeup artist, if necessary—to do the makeup themselves, using drawings and photographs as a guide. The actors should also keep the photographs on a dressing table until they are secure in doing the makeup without them.

The makeup designer should always allow sufficient time—including additional sessions—for the actors to learn the makeup. If time for doing the makeup in a performance is going to be limited, the designer should make sure that the actors can do the makeup in the time available. And the designer should, of course, look at the makeup onstage and then make suggestions for any changes considered desirable.

The Actor as Designer

If there is no makeup designer for the production and no makeup artist is called in to help individual actors, the actors then become their own makeup designers. As such, they have the advantage of knowing, better than anyone else, the character as they want to portray it. They also have the opportunity to experiment with the makeup over a period of time until they achieve the results they want. An instant-picture camera can, if it is available, provide the means of actors looking at the makeup objectively. They can then make any changes or corrections that seem desirable.

In designing their own makeup, actors can begin either by sketching their ideas on paper, as a makeup designer does, or by experimenting directly with makeup on their own faces. They should, of course, choose whichever method works better for them.

If actors do sketches, they may wish to show them to the director for approval or suggestions. Or they may prefer to show the director photographs of makeup ideas they have been working on. Although neither of these will be expected, either can be useful in avoiding basic disagreements about the makeup the first time the director sees it at a dress rehearsal.

Costume Designer's Influence on the Makeup Design

The first images to appear when developing the look of any character will, more often than not, originate from the costume designer. After spending months in collaboration with the director, scene designer, and lighting designer, the costume designer will produce a sketch or rendering of each character in the production. These sketches are based on thorough research of the period in history in which the production is placed, on a thorough examination of each character, on the designer's intuition and aesthetic, and on a thorough understanding of the meaning and intentions of the story being told. The sketches are intended to represent the "look" of the production. They provide visual information about the character to the director, to the actor, to the costume shop, to the milliner (when appropriate), and to the hair and makeup departments. Some designers' sketches are to be interpreted literally and are such detailed and precise representations that fabric design, shoe styles, and even eye shadow and lipstick colors can be perfectly matched (see Figure G-17.) Other designers provide sketches that allow for greater interpretation.

Costume designers' renderings can often be used as character sketches revealing, not only the costume, but also the personality of the character through physical appearance. The sketches in Figure 7-1 have been selected from full costume renderings to illustrate the costume designer's insight into the character and how that might influence the makeup design for that character.

Sketches and Drawings

Two kinds of sketches or drawings can be used in designing makeups—*character* (those which present a visual conception of the character, as in Figure 7-1) and *makeup* (those which show the character conception adapted to the actor's face, as in Figures 7-5 and 7-6). Whether they are called *sketches* or *drawings* depends largely on the relative degree of spontaneity with which they are executed. A sketch (Figure 7-1, for example) is the more spontaneous and is usually done more quickly than a drawing (Figures 7-5 and 7-6). It is the makeup drawings, rather than the character sketches, that show what the actor can really be expected to look like when the makeup is finished.

Preliminary Sketches Preliminary sketches of the character can be done in any medium you choose—pencil (Figure 7-2), charcoal (or charcoal pencil) and chalk, pen and ink (Figure 7-3), pastel, or conté crayon. (Some of the materials used for the various mediums are illustrated in Figure 7-4.) They will usually be in black and white or sepia but can, of course, be in color if you wish. If you are inexperienced at sketching, it may be easier for you to use outlines of heads with features indicated, such as those shown on the worksheet in Figure 7-8. Student sketches, using similar worksheets can be seen in Figures 7-9 and 7-10. You may wish to do a number of sketches and then choose the one that seems best to express the character.

FIGURE 7-1 **Costume designer renderings used as character sketches.** *A. Marley by Shiela Hargett from A Christmas Carol. Southwest Texas State University. B. Francis Flute by Martin Pakledinaz from A Midsummer Nights Dream. Pacific Northwest Ballet. C. Scrooge by Esther Marquis from Charles Dickens' Christmas Carol, A Ghost Story of Christmas. The Alley Theatre. D. Antonio by Shiela Hargett from The Tempest. Southwest Texas State University. E. Amelia by Susan Tsu from Lost Electra. Asolo Theatre Company. F. Dr. Watson by Robert Morgan from Sherlock's Last Case. G. Kate Hardcastle by Susan Tsu from She Stoops to Conquer. Theatre Virginia. H. King Arthur by Desmond Heeley from Camelot. National Tour with Richard Burton. I. Dona Elvira by Robert Morgan from Don Juan. The Huntington Theatre. J. Trinculo by Shiela Hargett from The Tempest. Southwest Texas State University. K. Salome by Martin Pakledinaz from Salome. Santa Fe Opera. L. Dracula by Susan Tsu from Dracula, A Musical Nightmare. The Alley Theatre.*

FIGURE 7-3 **Portrait of Albert Einstein.** *Pen and ink drawing.*

FIGURE 7-2 **Pencil drawing.** *One of the wicked stepsisters in Cinderella. In ballet and opera, the stepsisters are usually danced or sung by men. The 1833 hairstyle is based on a drawing in* Fashions in Hair, *Plate 116.*

Adapting the Makeup to the Actor

If you have chosen to do preliminary sketches and have conceived them strictly in terms of the ideal—that is, if you have created an image intended to fulfill both the playwright's conception and the actor's interpretation—but you have not yet taken into consideration the practical necessity of adapting this ideal conception to the face of the individual actor, the adaptation should be done before the final drawings are made. There is no use presenting to the director or the actor a visual concept of the character that simply cannot be realized.

One of the simplest—and certainly most reliable—methods of adapting the ideal concept of the character to the face of the actor who is to play the part is to work from photographs—front and profile—of the actor, making sure, of course, that the photographs are recent enough so that the face will not have significantly aged. Place a sheet of tracing paper over the photograph (Figure 7-5A) and sketch the character in pencil (Figure 7-5B-H), being very careful not to change the actor's face in any way in which it cannot actually be changed with makeup. The drawings in Figure 7-6 were sketched from the photographs in Figure 7-7A and B. Figures 7-7C and D show the final makeup. Note the close resemblance between the drawing and the makeup—a result of working directly from a photograph of the actor. The drawing in Figure 17-7 was done in the same way.

If you have not previously worked from photographs in this way, you may prefer to begin by making a drawing of the actor's own face. This drawing can then be used with the character drawing (as in Figure 17-7) for a before-and-after comparison. This is the procedure:

1. Place a large glossy photograph of the actor under a sheet of tracing paper. You can tape both the photograph and the tracing paper to a drawing board, or if you prefer to use a pad of tracing paper, you can simply insert the photograph under the top sheet.
2. Using a sharp pencil with a medium (B) lead, trace the outline of the face and the features and fill in

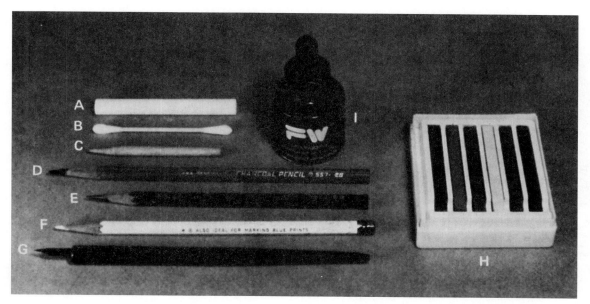

FIGURE 7-4 **Drawing and sketching materials.** *A. White chalk. B. Cotton swab. C. Paper stump. D. Charcoal pencil. E. Drawing pencil. F. White pencil. G. Drawing pen. H. Conte crayons. I. India ink.*

lips, eyebrows, eyes, and shadows. Paper stumps can be used for blending small areas, and the fingers for larger ones.

3. The hair should be sketched in but need not be done in great detail.

4. Remove the photograph and add finishing details to the drawing.

In making a drawing of the character from the photograph, follow the same procedure, but instead of copying the actor's features exactly, change those you wish to alter for the character, as illustrated in Figure 7-6.

Quick Changes

If there are quick changes to be made or if your facilities or your time for making complicated prosthetic pieces are limited, then you should make sure that the requirements for the makeup are reasonable. If they are not, you will need to modify your design to meet practical considerations. In Peter Falk's makeup for Stalin, for example, there was a fairly fast change to be made during intermission—from the first character drawing in Figure 17-7 to the second. Fortunately, the change could be made with cake makeup and the addition of a wig. Therefore, the requirements of the makeup were reasonable. (For suggestions on facilitating quick-change makeups, see Chapter 19).

Working Drawings

Working drawings should be provided for the actor or the makeup artist to follow in doing the makeup. They can be in the form either of drawings (such as the *makeup drawings* previously described or the ones used on the worksheets in Figures 7-9 and 7-10) or of diagrams of the face, with indications of changes to be made. The outlines of a face, front and profile, shown on the worksheet in Figure 7-8, could be used for the diagrams. Instructions for the makeup could then be connected to various parts of the diagram with arrows. However, since the drawings show approximately what the makeup will actually look like, whereas the diagrams do not, the drawings are much to be preferred. If you particularly want to relate your written instructions for the makeup to very specific areas of the face by means of arrows, that can be done as well with drawings as with diagrams.

The drawings, which can be in either black and white or color and which should include both a front view and a profile, must be carefully rendered to give an accurate impression of what the makeup will look like when it is finished. They can be done on an artist's drawing board, if you have one, or on a clipboard. The drawings (or photocopies of them) should be made available to the actor to mount on or near a makeup mirror (see Figure 17-8C).

FIGURE 7-5 **Making a character drawing from a photograph.** *A. Placing photograph of the actor under a sheet of tracing paper. B. Outlining the face with a drawing pencil. C. Shadows in the eye area being laid in with a pencil. D. Shadows being blended with a paper stump. E. Nose being reshaped. F. Jawline being aged. G. The character's hair being sketched in after the photograph has been removed. H. Finished drawing.*

FIGURE 7-6 Pencil drawings by Esther Marquis for Ebenezer Scrooge in "Charles Dickens' Christmas Carol, A Ghost Story of Christmas" at the Alley Theatre.

For black-and-white drawings, pencil is relatively easy to work with, especially when making revisions. The tracing-paper-over-photograph technique described under "Adapting the Makeup to the Actor" is likely to be the most accurate. If photographs of the actor are not available, pen or pencil drawings can be made directly on the makeup worksheets, as in Figures 7-9 and 7-10, or on separate sheets of paper.

For renderings in color (and color may be advisable for some makeups, especially nonrealistic ones), there are several possibilities. *Water colors* require the most experience for skillful handling and are not easily revised—an important consideration in doing makeup drawings. *Colored pencils*—including water-color pencils—are easier for the inexperienced to work with but not much easier to revise. *Pastels* and *colored chalk* are relatively easy to work with and have some similarity to makeup paints in color and technique of blending—also in their susceptibility to smudging. The smudging, fortunately, can be virtually eliminated, when the drawing is finished, by spraying it with fixative. It's a good idea to protect all such drawings with acetate or transparent plastic sheets.

In general, the advantages of black-and-white pencil drawings outweigh the advantages of drawings in color. If color is important, it can be indicated by referring to specific makeup numbers—either on the work-sheet or in the margins of the drawing, possibly with arrows leading to parts of the makeup for which various colors are to be used.

Work Sheets

When the final sketch for a makeup has been approved (if approval is required), you should then prepare a makeup worksheet to be followed in doing the makeup. The one in Figure 7-9 is both simple and practical. If you have not already done a finished drawing of the makeup, it can be drawn front view and profile on the worksheet, following the dotted lines or departing from them, using drawing pens or pencils (black or colored), water colors, water-color pencils, or conté crayon (black or sepia) or the makeup itself. When using pencils or conté crayon, the wrinkles and shadows can be blended with a paper stump or, for larger areas, with the fingers. When using a black lead pencil, it's possible to run your fingers lightly over the entire drawing to gray all the white areas, then to pick out the highlights carefully with an eraser. Since the edges of the erased area will be hard, those edges that should be soft in the makeup should be blended with a stump or with

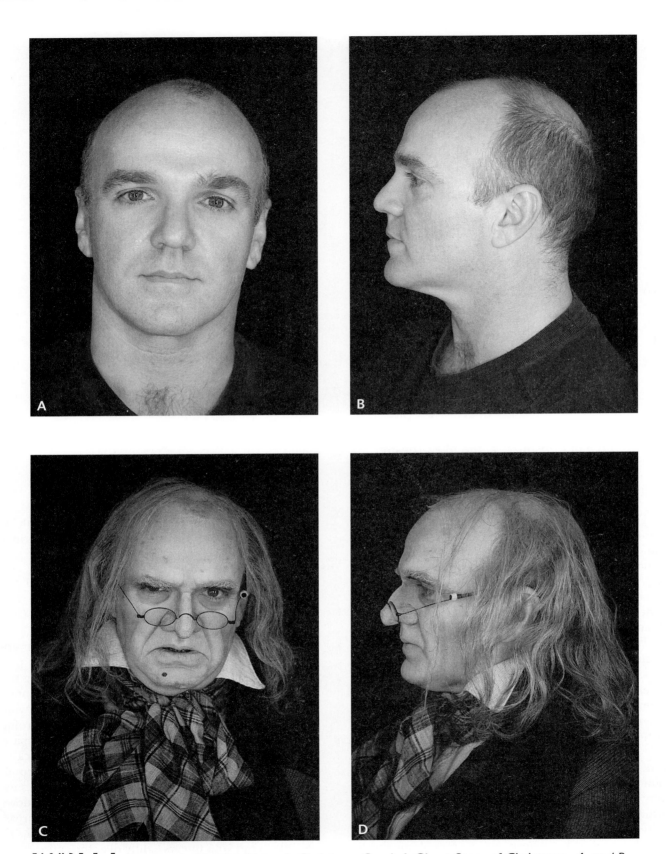

FIGURE 7-7 **Scrooge in Charles Dicken's Christmas Carol, A Ghost Story of Christmas.** *A. and B. Actor James Black. C. and D. Final makeup based on sketches in Figure 7-6.*

MAKEUP WORKSHEET

PRODUCTION: _____ **ACTOR:** _____
CHARACTER: _____

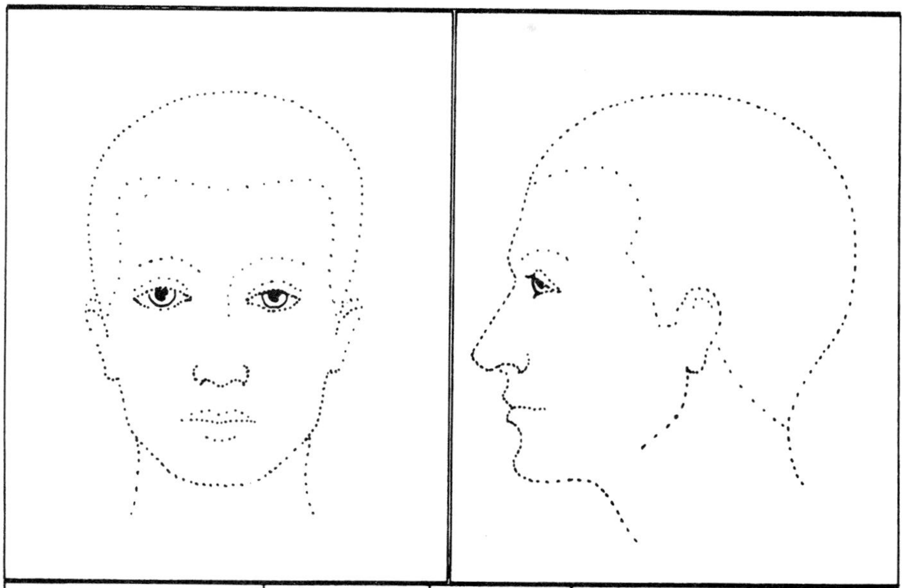

3-DIMENSIONAL MAKEUP	FOUNDATION	HIGHLIGHTS	EYE MAKEUP	STIPPLING
	ROUGE	SHADOWS		
NOTE:		HANDS		
		HAIR		

FIGURE 7-8 Makeup worksheet.

your finger into the adjoining gray area. When using makeup, simply place the makeup on the page and blend.

Precise information on makeup colors to be used, special techniques of application, hair styles, and any three-dimensional additions to the face, including beards and mustaches, can be entered in the appropriate spaces on the chart. Additional detailed sketches or diagrams can be included when necessary.

Figures 7-9, 7-10, and 7-11 show two styles of completed makeup charts/worksheets used to assist and train actors to complete their own makeup. After the final makeup has been approved, you should revise the worksheets, if necessary, to provide all the information required to reproduce the makeup. If possible, a photograph of the final makeup (Figure 7-12) should be attached to the chart. Having an instant-picture or digital camera and high-speed film available will make this a relatively simple matter.

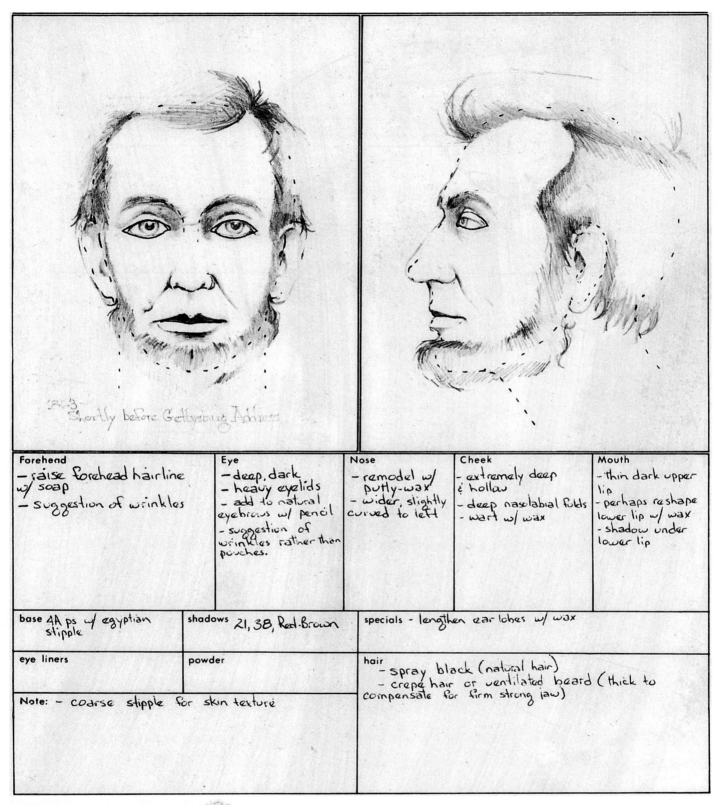

Forehend	Eye	Nose	Cheek	Mouth
– raise forehead hairline w/ soap – suggestion of wrinkles	– deep, dark – heavy eyelids – add to natural eyebrows w/ pencil – suggestion of wrinkles rather than pouches.	– remodel w/ putty-wax – wider, slightly curved to left	– extremely deep & hollow – deep nasolabial folds – wart w/ wax	– thin dark upper lip – perhaps reshape lower lip w/ wax – shadow under lower lip

1863
Shortly before Gettysburg Address

base 4A ps w/ egyptian stipple	shadows 21, 38, Red-Brown	specials – lengthen ear lobes w/ wax
eye liners	powder	hair – spray black (natural hair) – crepe hair or ventilated beard (thick to compensate for firm strong jaw)

Note: – coarse stipple for skin texture

FIGURE 7-9 **Makeup worksheet for Abraham Lincoln.** *By student Richard Brunner. For finished makeup, see Figure 7-11.*

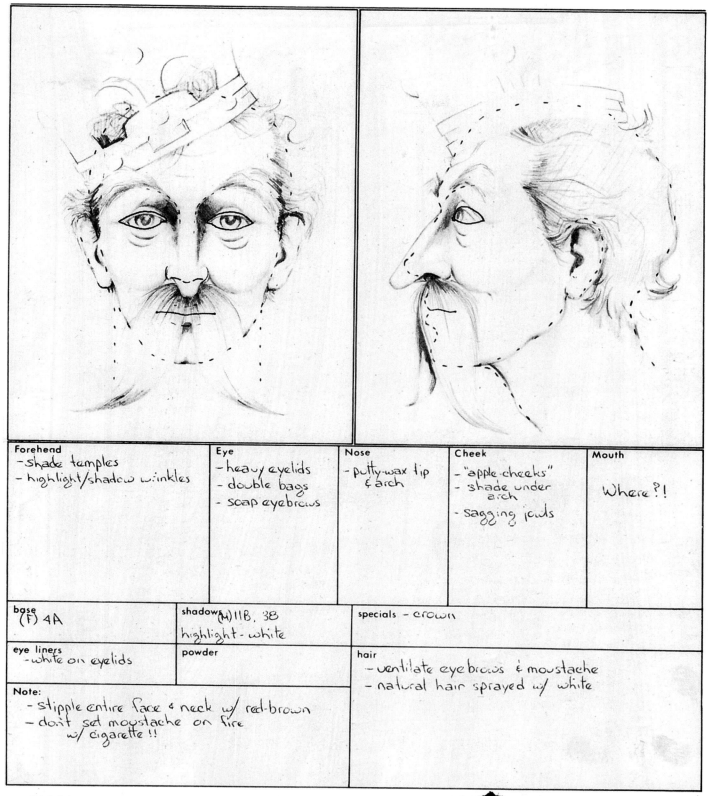

Forehead	Eye	Nose	Cheek	Mouth
- shade temples	- heavy eyelids	- putty-wax tip & arch	- "apple-cheeks"	Where?!
- highlight/shadow wrinkles	- double bags		- shade under arch	
	- soap eyebrows		- sagging jowls	

base	shadows	specials - crown
(F) 4A	(M) 11B, 3B	
	highlight - white	

eye liners	powder	hair
- white on eyelids		- ventilate eyebrows & moustache
		- natural hair sprayed w/ white

Note:
- stipple entire face & neck w/ red-brown
- don't set moustache on fire w/ cigarette !!

FIGURE 7-10 **Makeup worksheet for King Pellinore.** *By student Richard B⬛hner. For finished makeup, see Figure 7-11.*

FIGURE 7-11 Make-up Chart for Norma Desmond in the Broadway Tour of Sunset Boulevard starring Petula Clark. *By Broadway makeup artist Kate Best.*

FIGURE 7-12 **Makeups for Abraham Lincoln and King Pellinore.** *By student Richard Brunner. Pencil sketches for the makeups shown on the worksheets in Figures 7-9 and 7-10.*

PROBLEMS

1. Design realistic makeups for two or more fictional (as opposed to historical) characters. Use any medium you choose for the sketches.

2. Using tracing paper over an 8 × 10 photograph, make a character drawing for a makeup that an actor might reasonably be expected to be able to do alone. (The makeup may be for a specific character if you wish, but it need not be.)

3. Using the tracing-paper-and-pencil technique and an 8 × 10 photograph, adapt one of the character sketches you did for Problem 1 to the face of a specific actor.

Makeup Equipment

chapter **8**

Before beginning even to experiment with the application of makeup, it is necessary to have suitable equipment with which to work. And until you have learned the tricks of doing good work with whatever equipment happens to be available, you would do well to obtain the best you can afford. That does not mean that you need a *lot* of makeup. In the beginning, a small kit will serve quite well as long as it contains what you really need. From time to time, additional supplies can be added. Materials used in makeup are described in Appendix A.

The Makeup Kit

The term "makeup kit" refers to either a portable container of makeup or just the makeup itself.

Individual Kits

These are nearly always portable. (Group kits may or may not be, depending on where and how they are to be used.) They should be large enough to accommodate all of the makeup you usually carry, with room for additional items you may want to add later. You may choose to individualize your kit to fit your needs or select one of the convenient pre-packaged makeup kits available from a variety of manufacturers.

The kits should have compartments or divided trays to keep your materials organized and easily available. Whether they are made of metal, plastic, or wood is a matter of personal preference. What kind of makeup container you have—whether a case with trays or drawers designed specifically for makeup (Figure 8-1B, C, D, E) or a simple box with a few compartments—doesn't really matter as long as it holds the amount of makeup you need, keeps the makeup in order, is convenient to use, and is generally practical for you.

Group Kits

For a small group kit (or a well-stocked individual one) a large fishing-tackle box with cantilever trays (Figure 8-1A) can be used and is likely to be reasonable in price. These boxes come in various sizes. Similar boxes designed to be used as sample cases (Figure 8-1D, for example) may also be suitable for makeup.

If there is no reason to carry the makeup materials from place to place, then wood, metal, or plastic cabinets with small drawers or with shelves and pigeonholes are more easily accessible. The drawers or shelves can be labeled and the paints and powders arranged according to color. Dentists' cases with their many shallow trays and drawers (see Figure 8-2) are ideal for storing makeup.

Meticulous cleanup and attention to individual health issues must be taken, especially when utilizing group makeup kits. Disease and bacterial infections can easily be passed from one actor to another unless makeup and applicators are properly cleaned and disinfected between each usage. Here are some procedures for good makeup hygiene: never remove makeup from its container with your fingers; use instead, a palette knife or a small metal or plastic spatula transferring a small amount to a metal or ceramic mixing palette (see Figure 8-3E); when applying makeup to another person use a new, foam applicator sponge or a clean, disinfected brush; clean and disinfect brushes between usage, but discard used applicator sponges; clean brushes with a good commercially available brush cleaner (i.e., brush cleaners from Cinema Secrets, Brush-Off, Ben Nye, Kryolan, Mehron) or make your own by mixing 99% alcohol with acetone in a 1:1 ratio; sharpen eyeliner and eyebrow pencils between each use; never share liquid eyeliner or mascara (each actor should purchase his or her own product); apply powder eye color with a clean brush or sponge-tipped/cotton-tipped

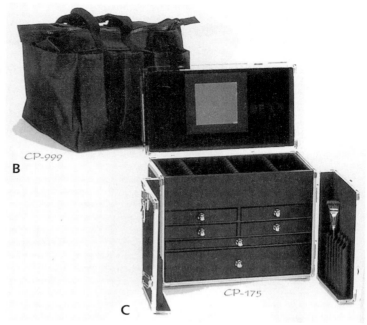

CP-999

B

CP-175

C

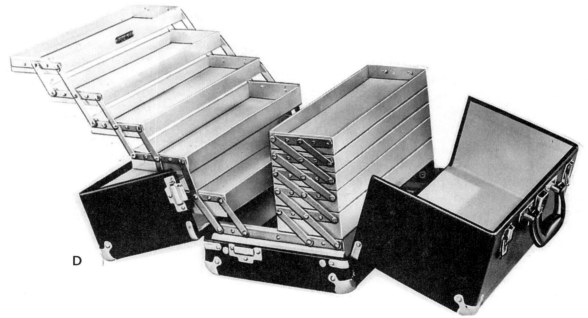

D

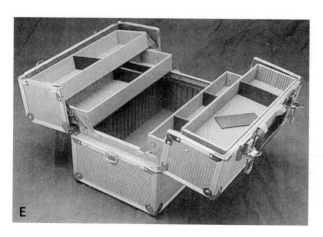

E

FIGURE 8-1 **Makeup cases.** *A. Cantilever fishing-tackle box, which can be filled with suitable items of makeup. B. Soft-sided, on-set make-up bag and C. Six-drawer, double door case by Japonesque Professional Make-up Supplies. D. Ten-tray case suitable for the professional makeup artist or for use as a group kit. (Fibre Products Mfg. Co.) E. Small aluminum makeup case by Kryolan.*

FIGURE 8-2 **Antique dental cabinet.** *Ideal for makeup storage for the professional makeup artist. Made of wood with marble base. There are shelves for bottles and jars behind the glass doors. This type of cabinet is occasionally available in antique shops. Modern dental cabinets can be obtained new from dental supply houses.*

applicators (discard between uses); and before you put creme formula makeup away, spray the surface lightly with a cosmetic-grade disinfectant (i.e., Sea Breeze) to prevent the growth of bacteria.

Makeup Palettes

A makeup palette box or clear plastic stackable, though they are not actually makeup kits, do to some extent function as one since they contain a number of colors. Palette boxes are available from a variety of manufacturers and provide the makeup artist with a convenient, space-saving selection of colors and products. There are palettes for foundations (regular and appliance), concealers, blushes, eye shadow, and lip colors (see Figures 8-3A, B). The clear variety are the most useful, since all of your choices are visible at a glance.

Or you can create your own palette by filling them with your own choice of makeup paints (Figure 8-3C, D). The paints can be removed from their original containers with a spatula, melted in a metal spoon, and poured into the various compartments of the palette or stackable (Figure 8-3E).

You can also buy inexpensive disposable mixing palettes at art supply stores. For use with makeup, the palette can be fitted into a suitable box. If the box you want to use is too small for the palette, take a pair of scissors and simply cut off as many rows of the palette as is necessary to make it fit the box.

Makeup Materials for the Kit

After you have determined what kind of makeup container will best fill your requirements, you will need to decide what you want in it—unless, of course, you prefer to buy a complete kit put out by one of the makeup companies—often at a considerable saving over the cost of the makeup materials purchased individually. There are several of these available—some with cake and some with creme makeup. (See Figure 8-4 and Makeup Kits, Appendix A.)

The main advantage in making up your own kit is that you can combine items you particularly like from various companies and can select only those items you think you will find useful. If you decide to do this, you may wish to refer to Appendix D (A Professional Makeup Kit) and select those materials best suited to your needs. The kit has been designed for the professional makeup artist. It can and should be used only as a guide in selecting products and tools.

The Makeup Room

Given the necessary materials, a makeup can be done in any surroundings, but the work can usually be accomplished more efficiently in a room specially designed to fill the requirements for makeup.

The focus of such a room, whether it is an individual dressing room or a large room for group makeup, is the makeup table and the mirror. The average dressing room has mirrors surrounded by rows of naked bulbs (see Figure 8-5). A more satisfactory arrangement would be to have the light source recessed and a slot provided for slipping in color mediums to approximate the stage lighting. This will never give the same effect as the stage lights, but it will come closer to it than the usual dressing room lights. If such an arrangement is not possible, at least be sure that the amount of illumination is adequate. If fluorescent lights are used, install color corrected tubes. Even when the lighting around the mirrors is adequate, individual lighted mirrors (Figure 8-6, A and B) are very helpful for close-up work. These self-contained, lighted makeup stations equipped with color

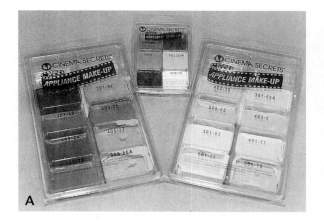

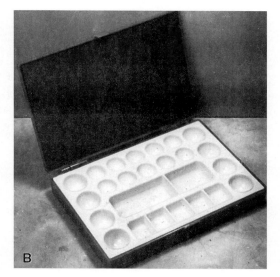

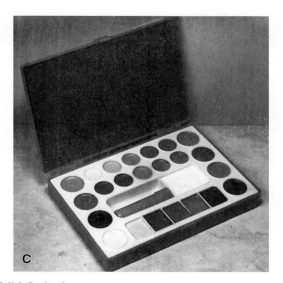

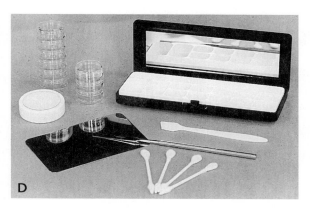

FIGURE 8-3 Palette box. *A. Clear plastic make-up palettes filled with Appliance Make-up in a variety of foundation and primary colors by Cinema Secrets. B and C. Grumbacher water-color palette box filled with creme or rubber mask grease paint (available from artists' supply stores). The makeup paints are melted in a spoon over a gas or electric burner or a candle flame and poured into the various compartments. The compartment might also be used to hold black stipple sponges, filled with an additional color, or left empty and used for mixing colors. box from Japonesque (see Appendix B). D. Palette box, clear plastic stackables and individual container by Japonesque. Stainless steel make-up spatula and mixing palette from Ben Nye.*

FIGURE 8-4 Student and professional pre-selected make-up kits are offered by Ben Nye, Kryolan, Stein, Graftobian, Kelly and Mehron (pictured is the Mehron Celebre Professional Creme Make-up Kit).

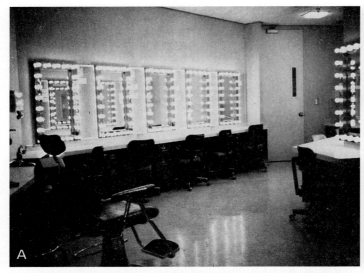

FIGURE 8-5 Makeup laboratory at the California State University at Long Beach. *Lab is furnished with padded chairs with casters, individual drawers between the chairs, mirrors with non-heating light bulbs, spotlighting in ceiling, 2 adjustable reclining makeup chairs, cork bulletin boards, colored chalkboard, 4 steel sinks, Corning-top electric range for prosthetic work, and built-in storage cabinets. A. Laboratory in new theatre, just after completion. B. and C. Room after the makeup department moved in. D. Ante-laboratory storage area with oven and sink. E. Advanced student, working under the supervision of instructor Bill Smith, applying prosthetic makeup for The Chairs.*

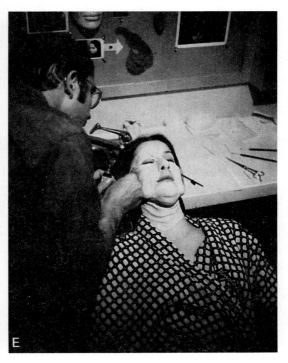

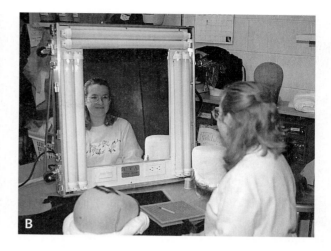

FIGURE 8-6 *A. Portable makeup mirror with adjustable lighting available from Kryolan. B. Portable make-up mirror with color corrected fluorescent lighting by CVA (Cases for Visual Arts).*

corrected fluorescent bulbs are useful as mobile makeup stations for touring and for transporting to various photographic and film locations.

No matter what type of illumination is used at the dressing tables, it is always desirable to have two spotlights in the general makeup room with colored mediums to approximate the lighting used for the play. The actor can then check the makeup as often as wanted, at a distance, under appropriately colored lights. The spots should be mounted one on each side of a full-length mirror at a sufficient height for providing a reasonable angle of illumination.

The dressing table should be about 29 inches high and should contain a drawer with a lock for storing the makeup between performances and for keeping the actor's valuables during performances. A dispenser for cleansing tissues either above or to one side of the mirror is a great convenience. Either a wastebasket or a special section built into the table should be provided for disposing of used tissues. If there is an additional space above or at the sides of the mirror, a row of small shelves or pigeonholes for makeup will help to avoid some of the usual clutter on the table. A row of cabinets above the mirrors can be very useful for getting personal belongings out of the way during performances or for storing wigs on blocks. It's a good idea to equip such cabinets with locks.

A stool is more practical than a chair for use at the makeup table—unless, of course, the chair is padded and has casters, as do those in Figure 8-5—since it enables the actor to get up and back away from the mirror quickly and easily without having to move the chair out and then maneuver it back into position when sitting down. A piano stool is especially practical since the height is adjustable. Padding and upholstering the stool, though not necessary, adds considerably to one's comfort when sitting for several hours at the makeup table.

In many regional theaters, including dance companies, performers customarily do their own makeup, but in opera, television, and film there will be a makeup person or even a makeup crew. This places an additional burden on dressing rooms, which are often overcrowded anyway. When that situation exists, there should be a special makeup room large enough to accommodate several actors in addition to the makeup people.

There should be running water in every dressing room. A makeup room should contain not only running water but also convenient facilities for storing makeup and wigs. Cases with small drawers are particularly useful. A reclining barber's or dentist's chair (see Figure 8-5B) is enormously helpful to the makeup artist and should be standard equipment in any makeup room.

A general makeup room, when there is one, should be as near to the dressing rooms and to the stage as possible. Since makeup may need to be hurriedly touched up between acts or during an act, having the makeup room near the stage is particularly important. Good ventilation is essential, and air conditioning is usually desirable.

The Makeup Workshop

The makeup workshop differs from the makeup room in that it is used primarily for laboratory work by the makeup artist. It may or may not be used for actual makeup. It should contain equipment and material for modeling and casting (including an oven for foam latex), for the construction and dressing of wigs, and for any

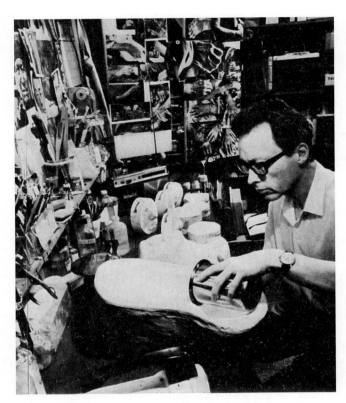

FIGURE 8-7 Makeup artist Dick Smith in his workshop. *Shown pouring foamed latex into one of the molds for Dustin Hoffman's makeup in* Little Big Man, *Figure 14-34. (Photo by Dick Smith.)*

experimental or preparatory work done by the makeup artist before actually applying the makeup. It should also contain ample storage facilities, allowing frequently-used items to be within easy reach. The workshop may or may not be equipped with a dentist's or barber's chair for casting or with a mirror and a makeup table. In other words, it should contain whatever is useful to the makeup artist for the work.

The university makeup laboratory shown in Figure 8-5 was designed to function as a makeup room, a workshop, and a classroom. Figure 8-7 shows a corner of a professional makeup artist's workshop.

The Makeup Morgue

One of the first requisites of a good makeup artist is a keen sense of observation and the ability to apply what you observe to the creation of your makeups. To help you remember what you observe, a makeup morgue (a term used to designate a file of clippings) is indispensable (See Figure 8-8). The morgue should contain, first of all, unretouched photographs of people. Illustrated magazines are a good source for these.

Reproductions of works of art are useful for historical characters. Much of this can be found in second-hand bookstores. In addition, your morgue should contain makeup catalogs, price lists, and any information you collect on makeup techniques. Anything, in fact, that relates to makeup should be included. Clear acetate sheets are very helpful in keeping smudges off your pictures.

Below are suggested classifications for your morgue. As your collection grows, you may want to make certain changes or add subdivisions.

AGE, Male	LATEX
AGE, Female	LIGHTING
ANATOMY	MAKEUP MATERIALS*
BALD HEADS	MAKEUP SKETCHES and
BEARDS and MUS-	DRAWINGS
TACHES	MAKEUP TECHNIQUES*
CHEEKS	MOUTHS and CHINS
CHINS	NASOLABIAL FOLDS
COLOR	NECKS and JAWLINES
CORRECTIVE MAKEUP	NONREALISTIC
DISFIGUREMENTS	NOSES
EARS	PAINTINGS, DRAWINGS
EQUIPMENT	PROSTHESIS*
EYES and EYEBROWS	RACES and NATIONALI-
FASHIONS	TIES*
FICTIONAL, Male	SCULPTURE
FICTIONAL, Female	SKIN TEXTURE
FOREHEADS	SUPPLIES
HAIR, Male	TEETH
HAIR, Female	WIGS, Male
HANDS	WIGS, Female
HISTORICAL, Male	WORKSHEETS
HISTORICAL, Female	

A very practical type of morgue is a set of loose-leaf binders with 8½ × 11-inch pages for pasting up your pictures. (See Figure 8-8A.) These pages can be rearranged or temporarily removed at any time. You will probably want to start with a single binder, then expand as your morgue increases in size.

If you want a convenient way to store your pictures until you have time to paste them onto the binder pages, an expanding file (Figure 8-8B) can be very useful. If you have a large collection of pictures, you may find a metal filing cabinet with removable manila folders (Figure 8-8C) more practical. If you also have or expect to have a number of books related to makeup, you should, of course, have bookshelves in your studio or workshop. You may or may not want to combine these with your drawing table and drawing materials, as in Figure 8-9. In any case, keep your pictures organized and ready for instant reference. Keep adding to your morgue continually. It is your private library and an important part of your makeup equipment.

*Can be subdivided.

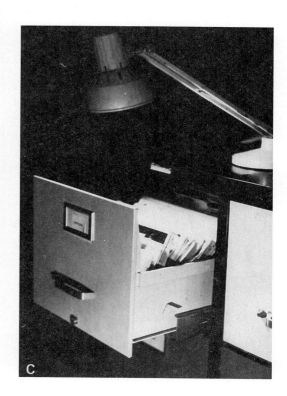

FIGURE 8-8 Makeup morgues.
A. Loose-leaf notebook with acetate
protective sheets. B. Expanding file.
C. Filing cabinet.

FIGURE 8-9 Corner of a makeup artist's studio with reference
books and drawing table.

1. Start your own makeup morgue with any photographs you may have already collected. Work out whatever filing system you find most convenient, but be sure there is adequate room for expansion. Label all material you find according to the category in which you file it. This will simplify putting it back each time you have used it.

Applying Makeup

Choosing the appropriate makeup, applicators, and application techniques for the various types of makeups can be a challenging process. Which type of makeup you choose will likely depend on one or more of the following:

1. Performance medium: television, film, theater, opera, dance
2. Skin type: dry, normal, oily
3. Surface to be painted: skin, latex, foam latex, silicone, gelatin
4. Personal preference

Once the makeup has been acquired, choosing the appropriate applicator for each type of makeup or makeup product will assist you in applying that product successfully. A full range of sponge applicators and makeup brushes are available for applying specific products to specific parts of the face and body. It is not necessary to acquire every product on the market, but professional makeup artists will argue that an assortment of quality brushes is a necessity. Good quality brushes are made with natural fibers (sable, squirrel, and camel) as well as from synthetic fibers (usually nylon) and come in a variety of shapes and sizes (see Figure 9-1). Sponge applicators are available in foam rubber and polyurethane in a variety of densities and textures (see Figure 11-2). Techniques for using sponges are discussed in Chapters 11 and 14.

Liquid Makeup

Foundations This type of makeup is available in opaque, transparent, powder, and airbrush formulas and can be used in all performance venues. The amount of coverage, surface texture, and sheen will determine how it is used and which formulation is chosen.

This greaseless foundation in regular and matte formulas can be used on both the face and the body and applied with a sponge, a brush, an airbrush, and with your fingers. It can be used on its own (does not need setting powder) or in combination with creme foundations for greater coverage (creme applied over liquid).

Liquid body makeup foundations move well over the skin and are formulated to cover a greater surface area of the body evenly and with relative speed. The foundations dry quickly, are often water resistant, and quality brands do not rub off on clothing. Creme and dry contour and accent colors can be used over liquid foundations.

Body Paints Liquid body paints used to decorate the face and body are available in a full rainbow of colors. Decorative and fantastical designs can be seen in theater and dance performances (see Figure 9-2), makeup competitions (see Figure 9-3), public festivals, and in commercial advertisements (see Figure 9-4). They can be mixed with water or setting liquids to produce a smudge-proof, water-proof surface that is easily removed with soap and water. They can also be applied with a sponge, brush, and airbrush.

Creme Makeup

Foundations When this type of makeup is applied to the face, it is usually transferred from the stick or the flat container with the fingers, with a brush, or with a foam-rubber sponge (see Figure 9-5A, B), any of which can also be used for blending. When used as the

1. Crease

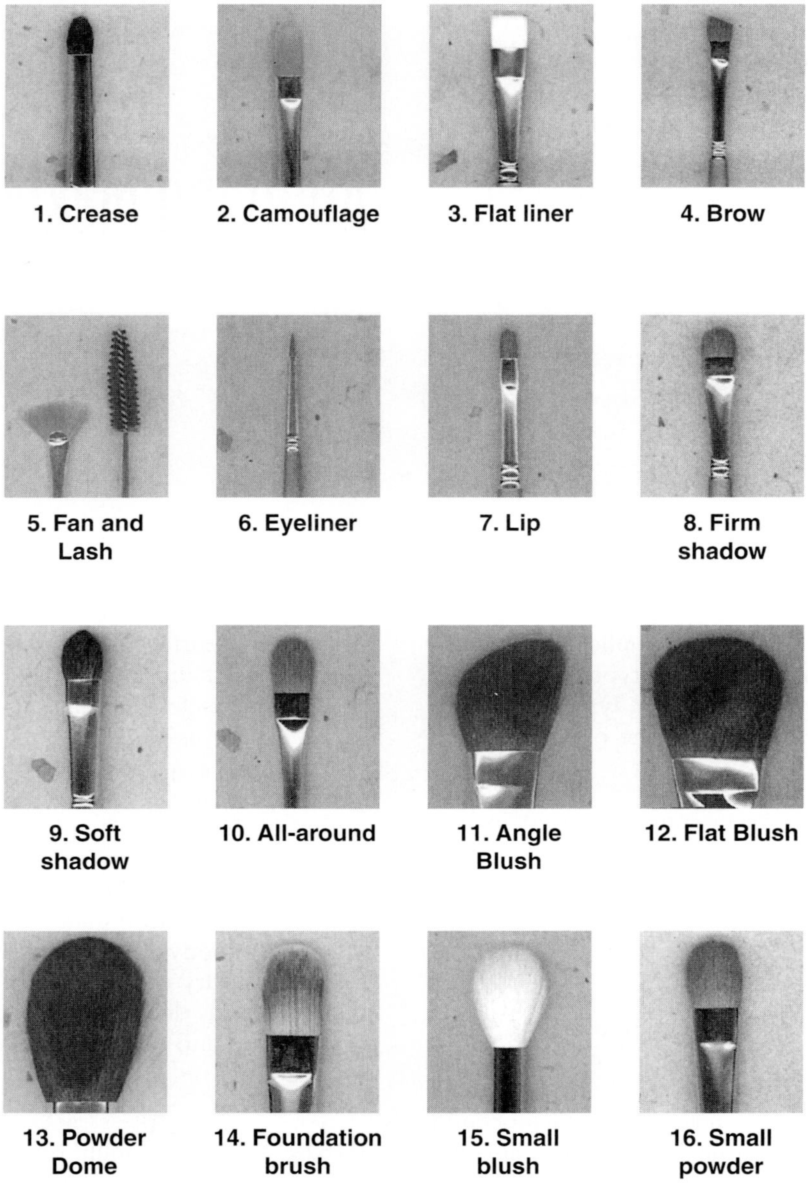

2. Camouflage

3. Flat liner

4. Brow

5. Fan and Lash

6. Eyeliner

7. Lip

8. Firm shadow

9. Soft shadow

10. All-around

11. Angle Blush

12. Flat Blush

13. Powder Dome

14. Foundation brush

15. Small blush

16. Small powder

FIGURE 9-1A Professional Makeup Brushes. *Brushes by Ve's Favorite Brushes.*

1. Crease—For creating soft lines around the eye.
2. Camouflage/concealer—For applying dense foundations and coverups.
3. Flat liner—For creating sharp lines.
4. Brow—Angled brush for shaping the eyebrows.
5. Fan—For blending; Lash—Spiral lash brush for applying mascara.
6. Eyeliner—Small, round, tapered brush for creating fine lines.
7. Lip—Beveled sides allow for accurate application of lip color.
8. Firm shadow—For applying eyeshadow.

9. Soft shadow—Soft and fluffy eyeshadow or used as a small powder brush.
10. Very favorite—All-around brush for foundation application, dry eyeshadow, soft eyeliner, contouring, dry shadows, also used wet for applying Aquacolor.
11. Angle blush—For applying contour and cheek colors.
12. Flat blush—Powder and dry colors.
13. Powder dome—Large powder brush.
14. Foundation brush—For brushing on foundations.
15. Small blush.
16. Small powder.

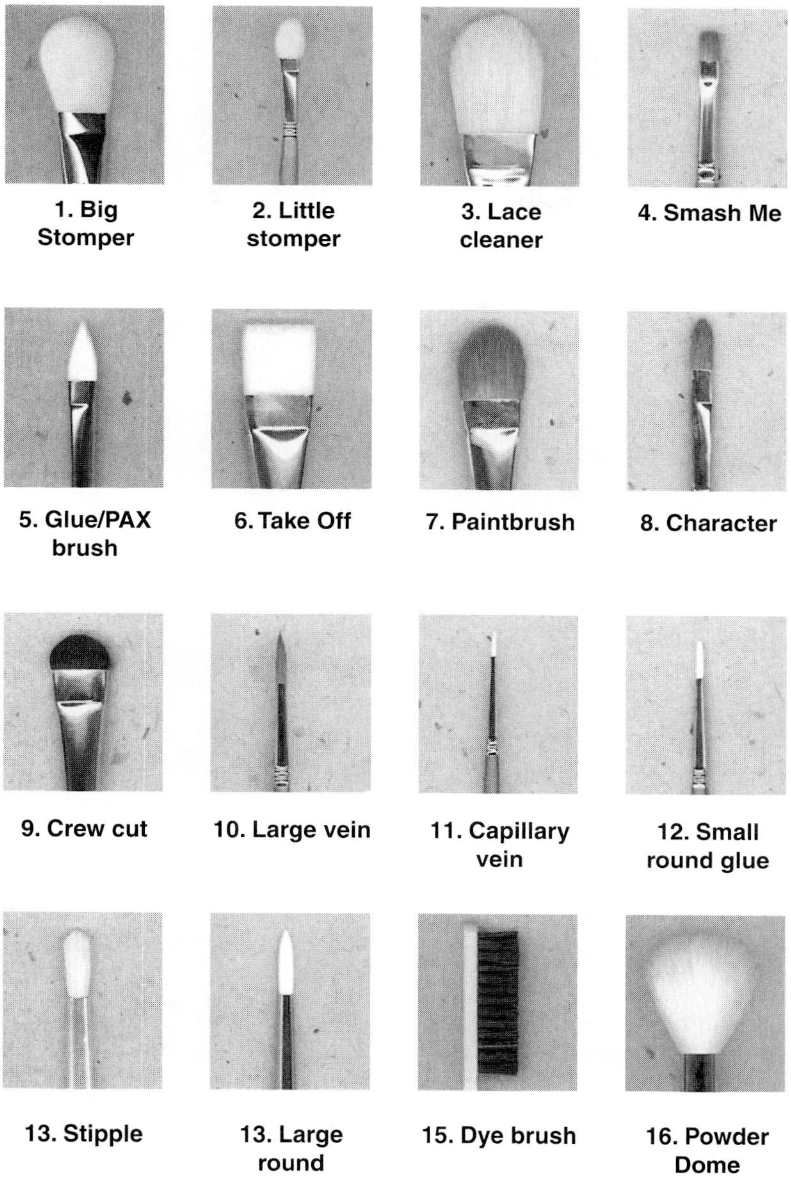

1. Big Stomper **2. Little stomper** **3. Lace cleaner** **4. Smash Me**

5. Glue/PAX brush **6. Take Off** **7. Paintbrush** **8. Character**

9. Crew cut **10. Large vein** **11. Capillary vein** **12. Small round glue**

13. Stipple **13. Large round** **15. Dye brush** **16. Powder Dome**

FIGURE 9-1B **Professional Makeup Brushes.** *Brushes by Ve's Favorite Brushes.*

1. *Big Stomper—Foam dome for pressing powder into appliance edges.*
2. *Little Stomper—Small foam dome for delicate spaces.*
3. *Lace Cleaner—For removing adhesive from wig lace and facial hair.*
4. *Smash Me—Used as a speckling tool by tapping against the counter.*
5. *Glue/PAX brush—For applying adhesives, PAX colors, and Aquacolors.*
6. *Take Off—For use with adhesive removers, adhesive, and makeup.*
7. *Paintbrush—For painting large areas with all foundations, from RMGP to Aquacolor.*
8. *Character—All-purpose brush.*
9. *Crew Cut—Used for blending powders and creme colors.*

10. *Large Vein—Used for painting in veins and other discolorations.*
11. *Capillary Vein—Used for tiny veins, eyeliner, and gluing edges.*
12. *Small Round Glue—Used for applying medical adhesive and Pros-Aide.*
13. *Stipple—Slightly stiff bristled brush used for texturing rubber appliances.*
14. *Large Round—Used for applying medical adhesive and Pros-Aide.*
15. *Dye Brush—Used for applying hair graying products and for adding scratches in bruise makeups.*
16. *Powder Dome—Made from fine white goat hair. For setting character and creature makeups.*

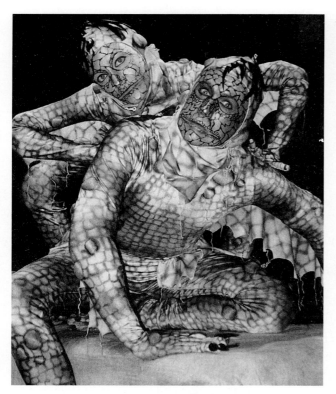

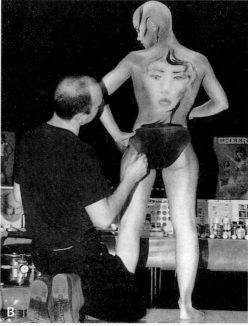

FIGURE 9-2 **Face painting for theatrical performance.** *Makeup design using Ben Nye's Lumiere Grande Colours by Amy Solomon. Actors Twyla Hafermann and V. Craig Heidenreich in* Seascape *at Actor's Theater of Louisville. (See page 404 for a color representation.)*

foundation color, the stick form of creme makeup can also be applied directly with the stick, then blended out with the fingers. If you need to mix colors in order to obtain the desired, shade, that can be done on the back of the hand, in a palette box, or on a mixing palette or tile. When applying creme foundations, use only enough to color the skin and conceal minor blemishes. Then powder the makeup and go over it lightly with a damp sponge. This removes excess powder and sets the makeup.

Highlights and shadows can be applied either before or after the makeup has been powdered. They can be applied *under* the base for subtle modeling effects or for covering heavy beards. Or you may wish to apply shadows under the base and highlights over. That helps to emphasize the highlights and minimize the shadows. When creme rouge, eye color, and/or highlights are applied *over* the base, they must, of course, be powdered. Creme rouge is usually applied with a foam-rubber sponge or with the fingers; contour colors, with a wide, flat brush, a foam-rubber sponge, or the fingers. (In general, makeup artists tend to use foam-rubber sponges for applying creme makeup, whereas actors are more likely to use their fingers.)

FIGURE 9-3 **Body painting for competition.** *A. Front view. B. Back view. Airbrush body paint using Kryolan's Aquacolor. Photograph courtesy of Kryolan Corporation.*

Face Powder

Although appropriate shades of face powder may, on occasion, serve as a foundation color for "natural" makeup applications, powder is most often used to set makeup (to keep it from moving) and to remove any undesirable shine. Face powder comes in two forms: pressed and loose. Pressed powder, which looks similar to cake makeup, is applied with a puff and pressed into,

FIGURE 9-4 **Body painting for commercial advertising.** *Hand painted with Ben Nye's MagiCake Aqua Paint. Photograph courtesy of Ben Nye Company, Inc.*

is applied with a sponge (see Figure 9-6) for large areas and with a brush for small ones. A natural silk sponge is best for the foundation color. The sponge should be damp but not wet. If the makeup does not come off on the sponge easily, you are not using enough water; if it seems thin and runs on the face, you are using too much water. If the paint seems to be thick and heavy, too much water may have soaked into the cake, or the sponge may have been rubbed too hard on the cake. In some brands of *dry* cake makeup the color comes off the cake much more readily than in others. If you use more than one brand of makeup, this difference may require some adjustment. If you have difficulty in getting color off the cake, simply use another brand of makeup.

After the makeup has been taken up on the sponge, stroke the sponge lightly across the face until the whole area is covered smoothly with a thin film of color. Cake makeup requires no powder. Performers with dry skin should, however, choose a creme formula foundation to help the skin retain moisture.

The wet formulas are glycerin-based and can also be used as eyeliner and for defining the eyebrow (see Figure 9-5). A pointed, round brush dipped in water and stroked across the surface is very useful in accomplishing this technique. As a face and body paint, Kryolan Aquacolor resists smudging and holds up well to perspiration.

Highlights and Shadows

These are normally applied over the foundation. It is possible, however, to apply them under the foundation for subtle modeling effects or for lightening a heavy beard. A combination of both methods can also be used. When the base is applied *over* shadows and highlights, it should be pressed on lightly with the sponge to avoid smearing the paint underneath and to allow the highlights and shadows to show through.

Cake foundations are also useful as highlights and shadows. When using appropriate light and dark cake colors, highlights and shadows can be applied with flat, sable brushes or with an angled brush or medium shadow brushes (see Figure 9-5D, E, F). Although a sponge can be used for larger areas, it is easier to control the paint with brushes. For smaller areas, including most wrinkles, $3/16$-inch, $1/4$-inch, and $1/8$-inch brushes can be used. Pointed Chinese brushes, $1/8$-inch round, and eyeliner brushes are useful for small details such as applying eyeliner, punctuating the eye crease, and shaping eyebrows (see Figure 9-5H, I, J). In general, it is best to use the largest size brush suitable for the particular job you're doing. Small brushes used for large areas are inefficient and may produce ineffective results.

If you are using a sponge to apply highlights and shadows, hold it so that only a small section of it touches the face. Apply the color directly to the face only in the area that is to be most strongly highlighted or shadowed.

not wiped onto the makeup. Loose powder can be applied with either a puff or a large powder brush (many professionals prefer using a puff). When applying loose powder, first distribute a small amount onto the surface of the puff, fold the puff in half and rub the powder into the fibers, open the puff and tap off any excess powder. Powder applied with a puff should first be folded in half around the forefinger (powder side out) and pressed firmly into the makeup (see Figure 9-5C). Powder applied with a brush should be lightly tapped onto the surface of the face. Excess powder is removed with a very soft powder brush or sometimes—especially for small areas—with a clean rouge brush. Face powder comes in no-color, translucent, and pigmented formulas. Experience and personal preference will help determine when to use which type.

Cake Makeup

Foundation

Cake makeup—dry such as Mehron's Star Blend or moist type such as Kryolan's Aquacolor—

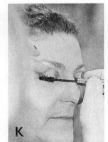

FIGURE 9-5 Opera makeup application techniques. *A. Soprano Sally Wolf before makeup application. B. Applying William Tuttle foundation with foam sponge applicator. C. Translucent setting powder applied with a powder puff. D and E. Shadows applied with a beveled all-around contour brush using Mehron's StarBlend Cake Makeup, Contour I and II. F. Applying highlights and cheek color with an Angle Blush brush using Mehron's StarBlend Cake Makeup, White and R/B Red. G. Eye shadow applied with a Shadow brush using Mehron's StarBlend Cake Makeup, Contour I and II. H, I, J. A black/brown mixture of Kryolan's Aquacolor used as an eyeliner to enhance the crease and to give definition and shape to the brow. It is being applied with a wet 1/8-inch tapered round brush. K. Applying the mascara with a spiral lash brush. L. Applying lip color with a lip brush. M. Attaching the wig after the makeup is finished. N. Soprano Sally Wolf as Dona Anna in Austin Lyric Opera's 1999 production of Mozart's* Don Giovanni. *Makeup by Leslee Newcomb.*

FIGURE 9-6 Applying cake makeup with a natural silk sponge (Actor Eugene Bicknell).

Dry Makeup

This includes all makeup that is applied dry to the skin—cake rouge, brush-on rouge, brush on eye-shadow, and face powder. All are, of course, used only as adjuncts to the various types of non-dry makeup.

Brush-on Eyeshadow/Eye Color These comes in smaller cakes and palettes in a variety of colors and are applied with a small shadow brush (see Figure 9-5G) or a tiny sponge on a stick. They can also be applied with a cotton tipped applicator. Natural bristled brushes tend to hold more pigment than synthetic brushes, therefore, delivering more product to the face. The choice to use a natural or synthetic brush will be determined by the desired effect and by personal preference. There are excellent quality brushes in both categories from which to choose. Any eyeshadow colors suitable for general shadowing can, of course, be used for that purpose. White and light flesh tints for highlighting are also available—more often in street makeup, however, than in theatrical.

Dry Rouge/Cheek Color/Bronzers Dry (or pressed powder) rouge is best applied with a brush (a rouge brush for larger areas and an eyeshadow brush for small ones), though a rouge puff, a powder puff, or, for small areas, a cotton tipped applicator can be used if a suitable brush is not available. Dry rouge can be applied over cake makeup, liquid makeup, or any creme or grease makeup that has been powdered (see Figure 9-5F).

It is possible to do a certain amount of shadowing with dry rouges and brushes, especially with dry rouges available in brown and gray as well as various shades of red.

Mascara

Mascara comes in two basic formats: the cake variety applied with a dampened brush; and the tube style with a wand applicator (see Figure 9-5K). While the tube and wand variety are convenient and readily available at any cosmetic counter it must be noted that they are not easily cleaned and sterilized and their use should be limited to personal, rather than group, makeup kits. Mascara also comes in regular and waterproof, and in thickening and lengthening formulas. Waterproof mascara is recommended for performance, but not for daily wear since it tends to dry out the lashes. The lengthening formula applies more evenly and goes on more smoothly than the thickening formula. Try applying several thin coats rather than one thick one.

Then with a clean section of the dampened sponge, using a very light touch, blend the color out over the entire area to be covered, letting it fade out as you go until it blends into the foundation color. It may be helpful to run a clean section of the sponge very lightly over the edge of the shadow or the highlight where it meets the foundation in order to help merge the two.

In working with brushes, the general technique is to lay on color in the darkest area of the shadow or the lightest area of the highlight, then clean the brush and blend the edges of the shadow or the highlight with the damp brush until they blend imperceptibly into the foundation. To save time, use separate brushes for highlights and shadows.

Whether you are using a sponge or a brush, it is always best to build up a highlight or a shadow with several applications rather than trying to get just the right amount the first time. It is much easier to add color than it is to subtract it. If a shadow does become too dark, it should be lightened by lifting the color with a clean damp sponge. Never try to lighten a shadow by brushing a highlight over it! Shadows and highlights can, however, be toned down or softened by stippling with a sponge, using lighter colors for shadows, darker colors for highlights, or foundation for toning down both at the same time. (For more detailed instructions in stippling, see Chapter 11.)

Lip Color

This product comes in a variety of formats: traditional lipsticks, color palettes, individual flat containers, lip color pencils, lip liners, and professional tube concentrates (see Figure 9-7). Other products including lip gloss, lip stains, lip balm, long lasting, matte finish, and those containing sunblock are also available. Lip colors can be applied directly to the mouth by using a traditional lipstick, by drawing them on with a lip pencil, and by painting them on with a brush (see Figure 9-5). When using long-lasting or matte formulas or for actors with dry, cracked lips, hydrate the lips first with a thin layer of moisturizer, lip balm, or petroleum jelly.

For a longer lasting lip color try one of the following techniques: (1) apply lip color, powder, then apply a second layer; (2) apply lip color, blot using a single-ply tissue (kiss the tissue rather than pressing it between your lips), then apply a second layer; (3) outline and then fill in entire lip with a lip pencil, then apply lip color with a brush to the edge of the lip line; (4) or use a combination of these three methods.

Concealers, Neutralizers, and Tattoo Covers

Also called cover-up or camouflage, concealers are used to hide or minimize unwanted facial discoloration, blemishes, birthmarks, beard shadow, and tattoos (see Figures G-19 and G-20). They range in consistency from highly pigmented opaque cremes to relatively transparent liquids. Nearly every makeup manufacturer produces some form of concealer (see Figure 9-8). The transparent formulas are generally used as a *neutralizer*. The neutralizing effect is accomplished when an unwanted discoloration is covered with a concealer containing the complimentary color to the discoloration. Heavy beardlines on men, for example, tend to appear in the blue color range. Applying a "beard cover" containing orange pigment (the compliment of blue) will, theoretically, neutralize the beardline, bringing it closer to the natural skin tone. This is how it works: when light hits the skin, it reveals the bluish cast of the beardline. When the blue reflects back through the orange-toned concealer it is neutralized and appears skin-toned. Dark circles under the eyes, often appearing purple in color, are neutralized with a yellow or golden-toned formula. Creme formulations must be powdered with translucent, no-color, or lightly pigmented powders. Carefully brush away excess powder and wipe lightly using a damp sponge.

The highly pigmented opaque creme formula concealers and the new airbrush concealers were developed to color correct by means of camouflaging skin imperfections such as acne blemishes and scars, scars caused by injury, birthmarks, tattoos, and extremely dark circles under the eyes. After choosing or mixing a color one or two shades lighter than the skin tone, apply to the skin with a brush or finger until the discoloration is no longer visible. Careful blending into the surrounding skin is essential. If the covered area appears slightly greyer than the surrounding skin, warm it up a little with a blush, foundation, or cheek color that matches the skin's undertone (red, orange, or yellow).

Moist or creme colors can be blended into the concealer, then powdered in order to set the makeup and remove the shine. Dry colors cannot be applied until the makeup has been powdered.

FIGURE 9-7 **Lip Colors.** *Lip palette by Kryolan; lipsticks by Ben Nye and Joe Blasco; lip pencils by Joe Blasco, William Tuttle, Namies, and Ben Nye; lip color brush; professional lip color concentrates by MAC.*

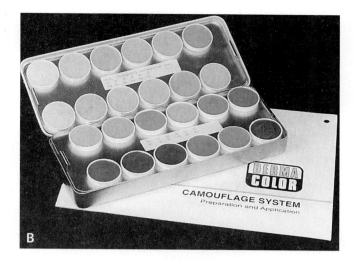

FIGURE 9-8 Concealer and Neutralizers. *A. Concealer wheels and neutralizer pencils by Ben Nye. B. Dermacolor Camouflage System by Kryolan.*

Tattoos   Should the script call for the addition rather than the elimination of a tattoo for a given character, one of the following techniques can be used:

1. Using a fine-pointed, 1/8-inch round sable brush, paint the tattoo design directly onto the skin surface using Reel Creation's Body Art Inks or Temptu's Body Art paints. The products, available in liquid and solid formulas, use 70% isopropyl rubbing alcohol as the solvent.

2. Place temporary tattoo paper transfers available from the same manufactures against the skin, then paint with alcohol to reveal a smudge-proof, water-resistant tattoo. After adding the appropriate colors, simply set the design with talcum powder. (Both manufacturers will reproduce your original design on a paper transfer.)

3. Have the design sculpted into a rubber stamp. Using a brayer, transfer fabric paint evenly onto the surface of the stamp. Press the stamp onto the skin. Using fabric paint or makeup, paint in additional colors, then stipple with skin-toned foundation for a more natural appearance and powder. (See Figure 9-9 and G-16).

4. Design the tattoo on a sheet of clear acetate. Cut out the design with a utility knife. Tape the stencil onto the skin and stipple with fabric paint or spray with airbrush cosmetics. Remove the stencil. (See Figure 9-10).

Appliance Makeup

Rubber-mask Greasepaint (RMGP)   This is a castor-oil-base greasepaint used primarily over la-

tex (regular and foamed), though it can be used over other three-dimensional makeup, such as derma wax, nose putty, and gelatin. The castor oil in the formula allows the makeup to lie on the surface of the appliance rather than absorbing into the surface like regular foundations. RMGP, also sold as Appliance Foundations by RCMA (Research Council of Makeup Artists), Appliance Make-up by Cinema Secrets, and RMG from Kryolan, apply easily and smoothly to the surface, blend well, and retain their color (see Figure 9-11). Unlike regular make-up, it is usually stippled on with a red-rubber sponge (see Figure 9-12). It is never powdered by rubbing or brushing the puff across the surface of the paint but always by pressing a heavily powdered puff firmly into it. Excess powder is removed by brushing lightly with a soft powder brush. If the makeup is to be stippled with various colors, that should be done after the rubber-mask greasepaint has been powdered.

PAX Paint   This combination of Pros-Aide medical adhesive and Liquitex acrylic paint was created to color foam latex appliances. It is applied with either a brush or a texture sponge (a sturdy polyurethane foam sponge textured on one side by removing bits of foam with your fingers). (See Chapters 13 and 14).

Airbrush Cosmetics

Airbrush-grade cosmetics provide an extremely light coverage with a seamless application that balances the natural skin tones. The speed of application is surprising, leaving a natural, sheer, smudge-proof, matte finish. Sprayed on in light layers they can cover imperfections, broken blood vessels, dark circles, blemishes,

FIGURE 9-9 Custom designed and crafted rubber stamp tattoo. *A. Using a brayer roll fabric paint on the stamp surface evenly. B. Press stamp onto the skin surface. C. Add coloration with fabric paint. D. Using a black stipple sponge apply foundation to the tattoo, then powder. Actor Thom Rivera as Alejandro in the Oregon Shakespeare Festival's 1999 production of* El Paso Blue *by Octavio Solis. (This actor can also be seen in Figure G-16).*

and age spots. When used for glamour makeup it takes no more than 5 to 15 drops of base, blush, and eye shadow to complete the entire makeup (see Figure 9-13). They can also be used as body makeup (see Figure 9-3); as a concealer; to diminish the effects of thinning hair; with stencils for face painting; for making temporary tattoos (see Figure 9-10); and for covering foam latex and gelatin prosthetic appliances.

Airbrushing tools include the airbrush, an air compressor, and an air pressure gauge. As the airbrush and cosmetics need only three to six pounds per square inch (psi) of air pressure to distribute the cosmetic evenly across the skin, the smallest air compressors are quite sufficient. Pressurized canisters allow for mobility on a set and for location work and can be stored in a canvas set bag.

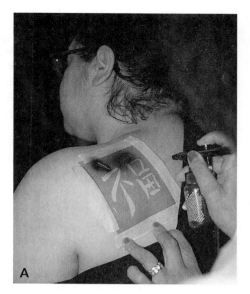

FIGURE 9-10 Temporary airbrush tattoo. *A. Airbrushing over an acetate stencil. B. Temporary tattoo using the Dinair Airbrush Makeup System.*

FIGURE 9-11 Rubber-Mask Grease Palette by Graftobian.

Mixed Techniques

If you wish to use cake makeup and creme makeup together, here are a few suggestions for ways in which that can be done.

Method 1 Use creme highlights and shadows over a cake makeup foundation. Then powder and add dry

FIGURE 9-12 Applying rubber-mask-grease paint with a red-rubber sponge, (Tom Lindberg).

rouge. (If moist rouge is used, it can be applied after highlighting and shadowing but before powdering.) The use of dry rouge, applied last, is especially advantageous because all of the rouging—cheeks, nose, wrinkles, etc.— can be done at once. Then add whatever stippling you wish. If you are stippling with creme makeup (see

FIGURE 9-13 Airbrush beauty makeup by Dina Ousley using the Dinair Airbrush Makeup System.

Chapter 11), powder after each color of stipple, and keep checking from time to time during the performance to see if additional powder is needed.

Method 2

With this method, creme highlights, shadows, and rouge are applied first—much stronger than usual but still well blended. Then cake makeup is patted on with a sponge until the makeup underneath shows through only as much as you want it to, after which rouge for cheeks and shadows can be brushed on. If highlights or shadows require touching up, that can be done over the base, preferably with cake makeup. This method can be used for very subtle aging. It would not be a good choice, however, if you want a strong three-dimensional effect. Nor is it suitable if the makeup is to be stippled (see Chapter 11)—unless, of course, you wish to use a light stipple in highlight areas and a dark stipple in shadow areas.

Method 3

Use creme highlights and cake shadows over a powdered creme foundation. This combines the advantage of highlights, which are easily blended, and shadows, which are not likely to develop a shine as the powder wears off. (With highlights, shine doesn't destroy the desired illusion; with shadows, it does.)

Method 4

For greater coverage apply creme foundation over liquid makeup and powder.

Corrective Makeup

chapter **10**

Corrective makeup (see Figure 10-1) is one that is designed to help actors to look their best. This may involve only minor adjustments, such as changing the curve of the eyebrows, or it may involve making the actor look younger. And, for the stage, it may involve changing the color of the skin.

The Foundation

In corrective makeup the purpose of the foundation is to provide a skin color that will enhance the actor's appearance under the stage lighting that is used for a particular performance. Since a skin coloring that looks normal and healthy off stage may look pale and washed out under stage lights, some additional color may be needed. If the skin does not need to be changed in color—this happens more often with dark-skinned actors than with light—the actor may not need to use a foundation. In this chapter, however, we shall assume that a foundation is needed.

Perhaps the easiest way to choose a suitable foundation (or base) color is to decide, first of all, what hue you want (R, SR, S, FS, etc.), then how light or dark the skin should be, choosing a number between 0 and 21 to indicate the value. A number 8, 9, or 10 is average for light-skinned men and a 5, 6, or 7 is average for light-skinned women. This average value is the one most frequently employed in corrective makeup, though it will vary with the actor's own coloring. For darker-skinned races the averages will be lower in intensity and usually in value and will match the undertones in the individuals skin color (see How to Determine Undertones in Chapter 19.) The fashionable makeup colors of the day may also affect one's choice. If pale skin is in fashion, women may wish to lighten

their foundation color. If summer tans are being worn, both men and women may wish to darken it. The actor's natural skin coloring will also have some effect on the color selected. Furthermore, a given color of makeup, unless it is rather heavily applied, will not look the same on a light skin as on a dark one.

As for the hue, you will normally choose, for corrective makeup, one that will help the actor look as attractive as possible under the lights being used on stage. Which color that is will depend, of course, on the performer's own skin color. A light-skinned performer may

F I G U R E 1 0 - 1 Female corrective makeup. *Actress Deidrie Henry in makeup (without wig) for the role of Vera Dotson in the Oregon Shakespeare Festival's 1999 production of* Seven Guitars *by August Wilson.*

look for a color in the S group, whereas an Asian will presumably avoid the redder hues and look for something with more yellow in it. Darker-skinned performers will usually require hues in a wider range of warm and cool tones; from warm and cool reds to golden yellows to olive tones. The F, SF, and OF groups contain a number of suitable shades. There are no hard-and-fast rules about what color an actor of any race may or may not use. The actor should choose one that looks attractive in the lighting in which he or she will be seen. A good rule of thumb is to first match the skin tone of the performer, check the color under the lighting in the performance space, then, if needed, raise or lower the color value to meet your needs.

Facial Analysis

Before corrective makeup is applied, the actor's face should be analyzed to determine how it can be made more attractive. If the two sides of the face are sufficiently different to appear obviously asymmetrical, the less pleasing side can be made up to match, as nearly as possible, the more pleasing one. Which side is to be corrected can usually be judged by covering first one half of the face with a sheet of paper, then the other. An even more effective technique is to take a full-face photograph, then to make a reverse print. Both the normal print and the reverse one can be cut vertically in half and the halves switched and pasted together. You will then have two photographs of the face with both sides matching, but one will be based on the right side, the other on the left. The less appealing face will indicate the side that is to be corrected. It is essential, of course, that the photograph be taken straight on if the technique is to work properly.

Decisions as to what is to be corrected will be based on personal taste, which may, in turn, be affected by current fashions. More often than not, however, fashions have to do with individual features—such as eyebrows and lips—rather than with overall proportions. But there are certain classic features and classic proportions that seem to transcend fashion and personal taste.

As noted in the chapter on facial anatomy, the classically proportioned face can be divided horizontally into three equal parts: (1) from the hairline to the eyebrows, (2) from the eyebrows to the bottom of the nose, and (3) from the bottom of the nose to the tip of the chin. If these three sections are not equal, they can be made to appear equal—or more nearly so—in various ways. But since a face not having classical proportions may sometimes be more interesting on stage than a classically proportioned one, making such a change is not necessarily advantageous.

If you decide that you do want to change the proportions of the face, the following suggestions can be used as a guide.

Forehead

If you want to create the illusion of a lower forehead, darken the area next to the hairline with a foundation color about two to three shades darker than the rest of the face. This color can be blended downward very gradually so that it disappears imperceptibly into the foundation. That makes the forehead appear lower because light colors reflect light and attract the eye, whereas dark colors absorb light and attract less attention. Following the same principle, a low forehead can be made to look higher by using a color about two to three shades lighter than the base and applying it at the hairline as before. That will attract the eye upward, emphasizing the height of the forehead.

The forehead can be made to seem narrower by shadowing the temples and blending the shadow onto the front plane of the forehead, thus apparently decreasing the actual width of the front plane by making it appear to turn sooner. Or it can seemingly be widened by highlighting the temples, carrying the highlight to the hairline. This will counteract the natural shadow that results from the receding of the temple areas and will appear to bring them forward. It will also seem to extend the front plane of the forehead horizontally. As always, there should be a difference of only two or three shades between the shadows and the base since deeper shadows at the temples tend to age the face. If the front lobes are too prominent, tone them down with a darker foundation color, and bring forward the depression between the frontal lobes and the superciliary arch with a highlight. If the temples are normally sunken, they can be brought out with a highlight.

Nose

If you want the nose shorter, apply a deeper color under the tip and blend it up over the tip. That will tone down the natural highlight and take the attention away from the tip. If a short highlight is placed on the upper part of the nose, that will attract the eye to that area and help still further to give the illusion of a shorter nose. If you want the nose longer, you can carry a highlight down over and under the tip, pulling the viewer's eye downward and apparently lengthening the nose.

If you want to widen the nose, run a broad highlight down the center and blend carefully. That will appear to widen the front plane of the nose—not the entire nose. You might also highlight the nares to attract the eye outward in both directions, thus giving an illusion of still greater width.

If you want to narrow the nose, reverse the procedure by shadowing the nares and the sides of the nose and running a very narrow highlight down the center.

Then blend the edges. That will give the illusion of a sharp and narrow bone and cartilage.

To flatten the nose, reverse the usual modeling by shadowing the front and highlighting the sides. Blend all edges carefully.

If the tip of the nose is fuller than you want it to be, shadow it slightly on either side of the painted highlight to tone down part of the natural highlight.

If the nose is crooked, run a fairly narrow highlight down the nose, then shadow it on either side wherever there is a natural highlight that reveals the crookedness. Blend the highlight and the shadows. The highlight may be straight, or it may bend slightly in the opposite direction from the real bend. Use whichever method proves the more effective.

In general, then, decide where you want to attract the eye of the viewer, and place the highlights in that area, shadowing areas that you want to recede or to seem smaller or less conspicuous.

Normally, in corrective makeup, highlights and shadows are about three shades darker than the base. But in making up the nose it is often possible and sometimes necessary to use stronger contrasts to achieve the desired effect. This applies particularly when you are using shadows to counteract strong natural highlights.

The corrective techniques just described, though effective from the front, have practically no effect on the nose in profile. That requires a three-dimensional addition. (See Chapter 13.) Obviously, the nose can't be cut down by that method, but it can be built up, as illustrated in Figure 13-5.

Jawline and Chin

If the jaw line is too square or too prominent, shadow the part that needs to be rounded off or toned down, carrying the shadow both under and over the jawbone, and blend carefully into the foundation. Wearing a fuller hairdo can also be helpful. If you want to make the jaw line more firm and youthful, run a stripe of highlight all along the jawbone, softening the lower edge and blending the top edge imperceptibly into the foundation. A stripe of shadow can be run along under the bone and both edges blended.

If the chin is too prominent—that is, if it juts forward too much—darken the whole chin with a light shadow. If it is too long in proportion to the rest of the face, it can be shortened by shadowing the lower part. Make sure that the edge of the shadow is thoroughly blended. If you want the chin longer, highlight the lower part, and if you want it more prominent, highlight the whole chin. If it's too square, round off the corners with shadows. If it's too pointed, flatten the point with a square shadow. A double chin can be minimized by shadowing it to make it less noticeable.

Wrinkles

Wrinkles can seldom be blotted out completely, but they can be minimized by carefully brushing in highlights where you find the natural shadows and subtly shadowing the prominent part of each wrinkle where you find a natural highlight. This applies also to circles or bags under the eyes.

Eyes

In making up the eyes, keep in mind that ideally eyes are the width of an eye apart. If they are less than that, you can make them appear to be farther apart than they actually are. For corrective makeup it is seldom that eyes need to be brought closer together, though that may be done for certain character makeups. Either of these changes can easily be brought about by making use of an optical illusion.

If the eyes and the eyebrows are made up as in Figure 10-2A, they will seem closer together. If they are made up as in 10-2B, they will seem farther apart. For women, false eyelashes can be used instead of—or along with—eye lining and eyeshadow to make the eyes look farther apart.

The lashes should be trimmed so that they are fuller at the outer corners, and they can be shortened and placed away from the inner corners of the eye so that they actually extend over only the outer two thirds of the upper lids.

Eyeshadow

Eyeshadows come in a variety of styles with the most popular being the creme and pressed-cake types. For a dramatic or fantasy effect try the metallic and pearlized liquid varieties. The creme formulas are sold in flat containers (cake style), as pencils, and in a creme stick. They come in a wide range of colors, go on smoothly, and blend easily, but have a tendency to gather into the folds of the skin, requiring constant maintenance to keep the color even and smooth. The pressed-cake eyecolor which can easily be applied either wet or dry, blends extremely well and is long lasting.

Eyeshadow for a corrective makeup application for women should consist of three color values: a highlighter and a medium and dark shadow. Choose natural colors that are harmonious with the actor's skin tone and that blend well into one another (i.e., bone, taupe, and charcoal/brown). Avoid using brighter colors unless they are slightly grayed and truly compliment the eyes. Whenever possible choose an eye shadow that is not the same color as the eyes. The color should compliment

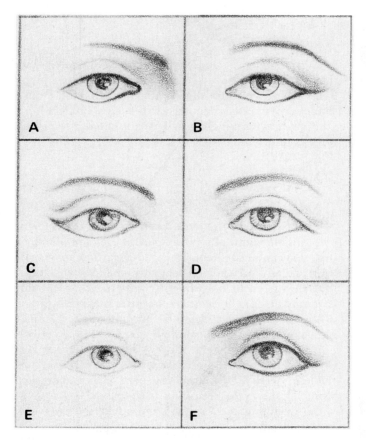

FIGURE 10-2 Eye illusions. *A. Shading the eye area and penciling the eyebrow to make the eye appear closer to the nose. Used on both eyes, it will give the illusion of the eyes being closer together. (See Figure 6-6C.) B. Shading the eye area and penciling the eyebrow to make the eye appear farther from the nose. Used on both eyes, it will give the illusion of the eyes being farther apart. (See Figure 6-6B.) C. Shading to turn the eye up at the corner. D. Shading to droop the eye at the outer corner. E. Highlighting (or absence of shading) around the eye to make it smaller. F. Shading the eye and darkening it and extending the brow to make the eye appear larger.*

the actor's eyes, not compete with them. Begin by powdering the eye area with a translucent or no-color powder before applying the pressed-cake eyecolor. This will create a smooth, oil-free surface.

Step 1. Using an eyeshadow brush or sponge-tipped applicator, apply the highlight sparingly over the entire upper lid from lashline to the crease and just under the outer half of the brow. You may also try a little in the inner eye area framed by the tear duct, nose and the eyebrow (Figure 10-3A and B).

Step 2. Apply the medium shadow over the upper lid to the crease starting at the outer edge of the eye and ending approximately two-thirds of the way toward the inner part of the eye and carefully blend up into the highlight with a clean brush or sponge-tipped applicator (Figure 10-3C). The fashionable practice of contouring the eye by carrying the shadow up from the outer corner of the eye towards the end of the eyebrow is not appropriate for corrective makeup. In Figure 10-5A the shadow has *not* been blended. Shadow on the lower lid is also fashionable from time to time but would not normally be used for corrective makeup.

Step 3. The darkest shadow will be used as a liner and applied with a small narrow brush along the lashline the entire length of the eye, or to separate the eyes slightly, begin two-thirds of the way toward the nose (the liner will last longer if applied with a damp brush). Leaving a space between the liner and the lashes can be avoided by placing the brush on the lashline and working the shadow into the lashes as you go (Figure 10-3C). Using a small clean brush, blend the shadow liner slightly up towards the lid. This line should be extremely fine at the inner corner of the eye, slightly wider at the center and gently taper to approximately one-eighth to one-quarter of an inch past the outside corner.

For some performance venues and on some faces it may be necessary to line the lower lid. Again, avoid creating a space between the lash line and the liner by applying liner on the base of the lash working from the top, not under the lower lash, then through the lashes and onto the lower lid (Figure 10-3D).

Many creme eye shadows tend to migrate and gather in the creases of the eye. This type needs constant attention to keep it looking smooth and natural.

Occasionally the eyelid is highlighted instead of shadowed (see Figure 10-5S) in order to make the eyes more prominent. The method usually used is described in detail in Chapter 12.

A touch of rouge on the bone just below the outer end of the eyebrow will add a youthful sparkle to the eye. This can be done with either creme or dry rouge. The red dot that is sometimes placed at the tear duct for the same purpose is much less effective and rather old fashioned.

Accents

The eyes can be accented by lining them, using a brush or an eyebrow pencil (Figure 10-4A). The brush can be used with cake or liquid eyeliner. If you find that the eyebrow pencil tends to smear, use cake liner instead. With either the brush or the pencil, draw a line along the upper lid close to the lashes. This line should usually start about two-thirds of the way in toward the nose or may even begin close to the tear duct. The line follows the lashes and extends about a quarter

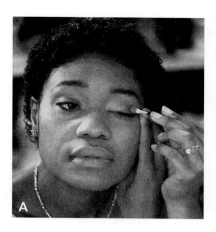
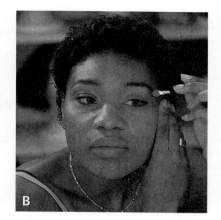

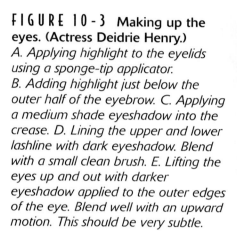

FIGURE 10-3 Making up the eyes. (Actress Deidrie Henry.)
A. Applying highlight to the eyelids using a sponge-tip applicator. B. Adding highlight just below the outer half of the eyebrow. C. Applying a medium shade eyeshadow into the crease. D. Lining the upper and lower lashline with dark eyeshadow. Blend with a small clean brush. E. Lifting the eyes up and out with darker eyeshadow applied to the outer edges of the eye. Blend well with an upward motion. This should be very subtle.

inch beyond the outer corner of the eye. It should end in a slight curve (Figure 10-2F), not a straight line, and when a natural effect is desired, it should fade out, not end abruptly.

Then draw a similar line on the lower lid, starting about a third of the way in from the outer corner or a third of the way out from the tear duct, as in Figure 10-3D, and moving outward along the eye, toward the top line. (A line starting in the middle of the eye, as in Figure 10-5B, should be avoided since it tends to divide the eye in half.) This lower line should usually fade out just before it meets the top line. Then both lines may be softened (for men they *should* be) by going over them with a narrow flat shading brush (Figure 10-4B) so that they really become narrow shadows instead of lines. Their purpose is to enlarge the eye slightly as well as to emphasize it. For a natural corrective makeup, they should not completely surround the eye, though for high-fashion makeup in certain periods they occasionally do. Sometimes a small amount of white is brushed or penciled in below the outer quarter inch of the top line in order to help enlarge the eye. Avoid lining the inside rim of the eyelid. The technique of adding white to the lower rim does tend to make the eyes appear larger, but may cause serious injury to the eye.

If the eyes are to be made to appear farther apart, the accents should be strongest at the outer ends and carried farther beyond the corner of the eye than usual (Figure 10-3E). If the eyes are to be closer together, the accents are shifted to the inner corners and should not extend to the outer corners at all.

Men should avoid lining the eyes when a natural effect is required. A bit of brown or clear mascara may be all that is needed. In large performance venues such as opera, ballet, outdoor theater, and houses with over eight hundred seats, eye liner is quite appropriate. Performers with extremely dark circles, bagging or puffiness, or excessive wrinkles should avoid blending the liner below the lash line or shadowing below the lash line since it tends to draw attention to that area of the face.

Eyelashes Women's lashes are nearly always darkened with mascara. Black is the preferred color although brown may be used on blonde lashes and for a more gentle, soft, natural look. Avoid fashion colors such as red, purple, or navy unless they are appropriate for a special character makeup.

Before applying the mascara, gently curl the lashes (Figure 10-6A), then hold the wand parallel to the eye

FIGURE 10-4 **Making up the eyes. (Actor Kristoffer Tabori.)** *A. Accenting the eyes with a makeup pencil. B. Softening the pencil with a brush. C. Penciling the eyebrows. Note that both the pencil and the brush are held at some distance from the tip in order to maintain a light touch.*

and stroke from the roots to the tips of the lashes (Figure 10-6B)—upward on the lower side of the upper lashes and downward on the upper side of the lower lashes (Figure 10-6C). Avoid clumps and keep the lashes separated for a natural effect. C and P in Figure 10-5 illustrate a failure to avoid clumps, though the effect in P is obviously intentional. If men's eyelashes are very light or very sparse, brown or black mascara will be helpful in defining the eye; otherwise clear mascara is suggested. Be extremely careful to avoid getting mascara into the eyes, as it can be painful. If you get smudges of mascara on the skin around the eye, they

should be carefully removed with a cotton swab dampened with water or, for waterproof mascara, with mascara remover.

Caution: Never share your mascara or your mascara brush with anyone else!

In removing mascara, apply the remover to a sheet of cleansing tissue folded into a small square, close one eye, and wipe off the mascara from the lashes on that eye. (Cotton balls should not be used, for they may leave a residue of fibers.)

Women often wear false eyelashes on the upper lid, less often on the lower. Normally, one false eyelash is

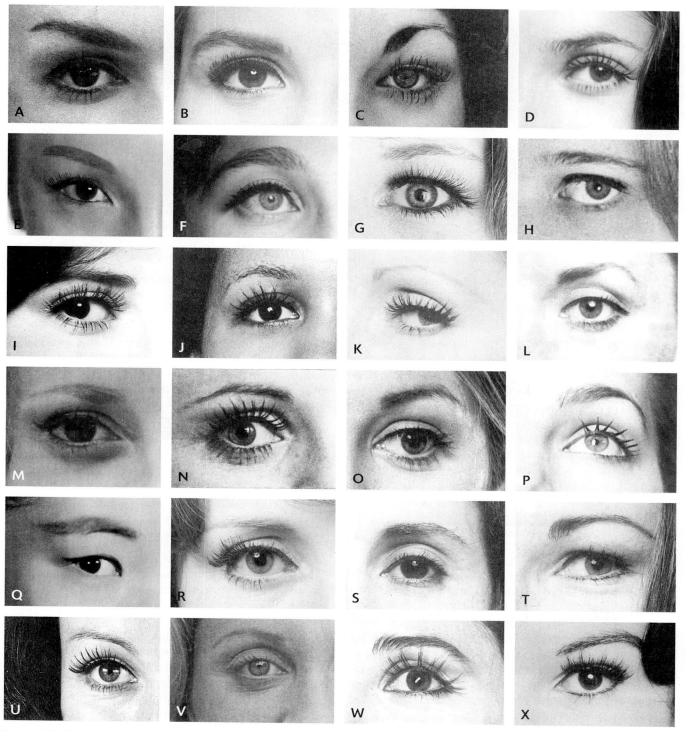

FIGURE 10-5 **Women's eyes.** *Illustrates both becoming and unbecoming treatment of eyebrows and the use and misuse of false eyelashes.*

cut in two and the hairs cut on an angle so that when the eyelashes are applied, they are long at the outer end and relatively short at the inner end. Be sure to cut the two halves of the lash in reverse so that you will have one left and one right lash. If the lashes are too full, snip out some of the hairs with small pointed scissors—*before* applying the lashes to the eyelid. You can also snip off the ends of some of the lashes to make them less even and more natural looking. Figure 10-5R shows lashes trimmed on an angle, and Figure 10-5K shows lashes

FIGURE 10-6 A. Curling the lashes with an eyelash curler. B and C. Applying mascara to the upper and lower lashes.

that have evidently not been trimmed at all. Using excessively long or heavy lashes may at times be fashionable but does not necessarily make the eyes more attractive.

False eyelashes, in both full top and bottom or as individual and cluster, are with practice, relatively easy to apply. Full false lashes add immediate length and fullness to the entire lash line. Single and cluster lashes add a more natural look by filling in sparse areas and adding a sense of sparkle to the eye. When using single or cluster lashes try mixing short, medium, and long together with short lashes towards the inner end, medium on the outer end and long in the middle. To achieve a "doe-eyed" effect attach the longer lashes to the outer end.

A better integration of the false eyelash with the natural lash line can be achieved by first applying a soft, narrow, dark line of color to the base of the lashes. This allows the lash band to disappear *into* the liner rather than just sit *on* the skin. Use a wet/dry pigment liner or shadow rather than a creme formula for better adhesion. Before attaching the lashes allow the adhesive to become slightly tacky for easy application. Gently curl and add mascara to your own lashes before attaching false ones will help hide the glueline and will aid in holding the lashes in place until the glue dries thoroughly. Finish by curling both sets of lashes and applying mascara.

Try this technique before applying mascara: add extra powder to the area below the eye and onto the front part of the cheek. If any mascara should fall onto the face simply brush it and the powder off with a powder brush.

The eyelashes are attached with a special eyelash adhesive or with surgical adhesive (see Appendix A). The adhesive is applied to the eyelash strip (Figure 10-7A), which is set in place along the bottom edge of the eyelid at the lash line, then secured by pressing care-

fully and gently with your fingers (Figure 10-&B) or a blunt ended orangewood stick, a paper stump or the end of a make-up brush. Avoid any space between the false lashes and your own. *Never use any sharp-pointed instrument near the eye!* If the eyes are to be made to seem farther apart, the lashes can be extended beyond the corner of the eye (Figure 10-5G). Apply false eyelashes and mascara only after the makeup has been powdered.

Eyebrows

For corrective makeup, men's eyebrows should always look natural, whereas women's may or may not. That does not mean that changes should never be made in an actor's eyebrows, but it does mean that they should not look made up. Unkempt, scraggly, or excessively heavy brows can be improved or controlled in a number or ways: by judicious plucking or waxing to remove hairs between the brows; by plucking or waxing to create an attractive arch; by carefully clipping unruly hair with a pair of small, sharp scissors; or by combing or brushing in a small amount of hair spray. If you're planning to pluck more than a few hairs, it would be wise to experiment with blocking out the portions of the brow to be plucked (see Chapter 12) in order to make sure you're improving the brows, not mutilating them.

In filling out or reshaping men's eyebrows with pencil, be sure to use short, light strokes following the direction of the hairs. Holding the pencil as shown in Figure 10-4C, rather than near the tip, will help to give you a lighter touch in applying the color. If you want to soften the penciling, stroke it lightly with a finger. Plac-

FIGURE 10-7 Applying false eyelashes. *A. Eyelash adhesive being applied to the lashes. C. Attaching the lashes to the skin. Remember to keep pointed objects away from the eye. Inga Loujerenko, ballerina.*

ing your eyebrow pencils in the freezer for five to ten minutes before sharpening will allow you to achieve a sharper point.

Pressed eyeshadow can also be used for both men and women to fill out (though not to reshape) the eyebrows. It is applied with a small, short bristled, angle-cut brush, which not only fills in the natural eyebrow if it needs filling in, but also produces the effect of a shadow under the brow, making it seem both wider and thicker than it actually is. Whether it can be used alone or should be used in combination with eyebrow pencil will usually depend on how much filling out is required.

If the brow is well formed and well placed or is lighter than the hair color, it can simply be darkened using pencil or mascara. With pencils, use short, quick, light strokes following the direction of the hair. For a more natural looking eyebrow simply transfer some pigment from the tip of the pencil to a stiff bristled eyebrow brush (it is often combined with an eyelash comb (see Appendix A) and brush onto the eyebrows. Remember that the intention is to darken the hairs, not the skin underneath—except when the natural brow needs filling out. Using a slightly lighter shade of pencil than the brow color will also aid in achieving a more natural look.

Changes in the men's eyebrows illustrated in Figure 10-8 would depend on the hair and on the entire face and even to some extent on the actor's personality or the aspects of his personality he wished to emphasize. For purposes of projection, however, B and D and possibly A (in Figure 10-8) should usually be darkened. If there is not much space between the eyebrow and the eye (as in Figure 10-8A and D), it may be advantageous to open up the eye area by lifting the outer end of the eyebrow to more nearly approximate the eyebrow in G. That could be done in D, for example, by brushing the hair upward and reshaping the outer end of the brow slightly with a pencil, giving more of a lift to the brow and thus

to the entire face. If it proved practicable, a few hairs might be plucked from the bottom of the brow in E. If one wanted a more masculine look, the brow in J might be filled out slightly with a pencil. You can judge for yourself the effect of the various brows illustrated—to what extent they enhance the eye, what quality of personality they suggest, and how they might be improved.

For women's corrective makeup, as for men's, it is not necessary to make the eyebrows fit one single pattern—rather, they should be as flattering as possible to the individual eye and to the face in general. Eyebrows that are too straight, too arched (Figure 10-5C), too slanted (Figure 10-5A), too thick (Figure 10-5F), too thin (Figure 10-5K), too close together, or too far apart might well be corrected. Raising the eyebrow over the outer corner of the eye, as in Figure 10-5B and as suggested for men in the preceding paragraph, can be very helpful in opening up the eye area. Compare, for example, eyebrows B and H in Figure 10-5. Exaggerating the upward curve too much, however, can become grotesque.

A very simple method of determining what shape of brow will look best on a particular face is to manipulate the natural brow with your fingers, as illustrated in Figure 12-22. That can save you a great deal of time in trial and error.

Cheeks

If the cheeks are too round, the part of the cheek to be made less prominent should be shaded with a base two or three shades darker than that used on the rest of the face. It is important, as always, to blend this lowlight imperceptibly into the lighter base. If the cheeks are too sunken, the procedure can be reversed by using a base a few shades lighter than the rest of the face to counteract the natural shadows that reveal the sunken cheeks.

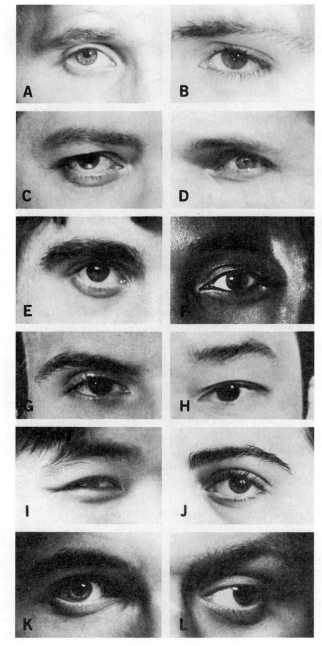

FIGURE 10-8 **Young men's eyes.** *Natural eyebrows without makeup. Some of them could be improved by darkening or reshaping for corrective makeup.*

Color of Rouge

Rouge or blush comes in both creme, powder, and gel formulas. Creme rouge should be blended into the creme foundation before it is set with powder. This rich formula is particularly useful for actors with dry skin. Powder or dry rouge is applied over the foundation (after it has been set) with a large powder brush or angled blush brush. It can be used on its own or combined with the creme formula. Gel blush

is extremely sheer and can be used without foundation for a more natural look.

Rouge or blush is usually applied after the modeling is done, though it is sometimes used as a shadow in modeling the cheeks. For men, a soft, natural color (such as SR-9½-d, RS-10-b, RS-10-d, or RS-11-b) should usually be used. In selecting a suitable brush-on rouge (as opposed to dry rouge, which can be used in the same way but does not come with its own brush), look for a shade that is not too pink.

For women, the shade of rouge chosen will depend on skin color, fashion, costume, and personal preference. With so many possible variations there can be no hard-and-fast rules. It is usually best to experiment with shades that you think *ought* to be suitable in order to find out which ones actually are the most effective. As a rule, the lighter the skin, the lighter the blush color, the darker the skin, the deeper the blush. For a natural look match the blush color to the actors' coloring when they blush or are flushed from physical exertion. While you should never match eye shadow to eye color, it is an appropriate technique to match blush color to lip color.

Fashions in rouge colors change, but for corrective makeup a flattering conservative shade should always be chosen in preference to an unflattering fashionable one. Costume colors—especially reds, oranges, and purples—may determine to some extent which color should be used. A magenta rouge, for example, is not likely to be the best choice for a woman wearing an orange dress, though magenta accessories might make such a combination possible. Personal preference may also be a factor, provided it does not lead one to choose an unbecoming or unsuitable color.

Placement of Rouge

Rouge should usually be placed on or slightly below the cheekbone rather than low on the cheek, though in glamorizing the face, a soft, medium shade of brush-on rouge can be effectively used as a shadow slightly below the cheekbone in order to sink in the cheeks. Rouge is usually applied after any modeling with highlights and shadows has been completed. Rouge should not be placed too near the eye or the nose. If the face is narrow, rouge should be kept even farther from the nose and placed nearer the ears in order to increase the apparent width of the face. If the face is wide, keep the rouge away from the ears and apply it in a pattern more nearly vertical than horizontal. For corrective makeup it should never be applied in a round spot, and it should always be carefully blended.

Fingers can be used to apply and blend the creme and gel formulas but the blush brush is recommended for all powders. Begin by dipping the brush into the powder, blow or tap off the excess, and apply blush first to a spot just below the cheekbone (Figure 10-9A), then blend up and back towards the hairline (Figure 10-9B). Avoid drawing a horizontal line across the face. A bit

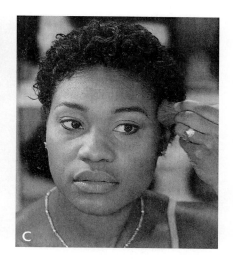

FIGURE 10-9 Applying cheek color with a large rouge brush. *A and B. Begin just under the cheek bone and apply rouge in long quick strokes on an angle up toward the ear and hair line. C. Add color to the temple and D. Chin.*

of color at the temple and along the chin (Figures 10-9C and D) will balance the entire look.

Rouge is not always used for men, but if color will help to make an actor look healthier or more attractive, a natural shade of bronzer could be used. It should be applied sparingly to areas where the sun naturally colors the face: the bridge of the nose, the brow bone, the cheekbones, and the chin. Whenever foundation is being used, the face should be powdered before using bronzer powder. This will insure a smooth even application and will avoid discoloration of the bronzer on oily skin, which tends to turn it a bit orange. It should usually extend over a wider area than it normally does for women–including the temples, if the face is not too wide. Above all, it ought to look as natural as possible. In case of doubt, use none.

Lips

Figures 10-10 and 10-11 illustrate lips of young men and women. In Figure 10-10, E represents the classical ideal–a graceful bow in the upper lip with a dip in the center and a full lower lip not quite so wide as the upper. But the lips need not match this model of classical perfection. Among the other lips in the group, some (A, for example) are well shaped and would not require correction. Although the upper lip in F is thin and out of proportion to the lower lip, the mouth is still attractive, and if it fits the face, it might better be left as it is. The lips in Figure 10-10I do not follow classical proportions, but they are interesting and attractive and should probably not be tampered with. The lower lip should certainly not be darkened. Its fullness works only because it remains light and does not contrast strongly with the skin. Note what happens in C when the lower lip is darkened.

In Figure 10-11, F is closest to the classical ideal. Most of the others might be improved with corrective makeup. In B, for example, the slightly crooked upper lip could easily be reshaped, perhaps giving it a more graceful curve and also widening it a bit in order to make it extend beyond the lower lip. Much the same is true of G. In E the upper lip could also be given a more graceful curve. It might be helpful in I if the upper lip

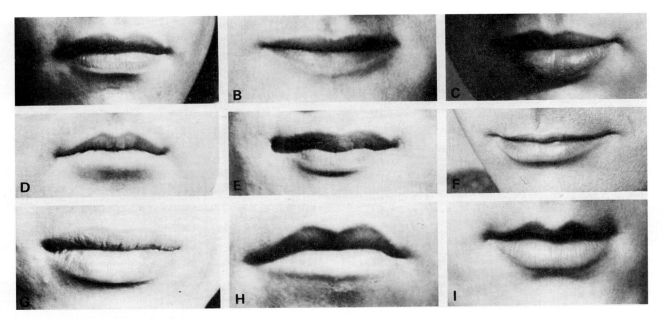

FIGURE 10-10 **Youthful lips, male.** *E is closest to the classical lip formation.*

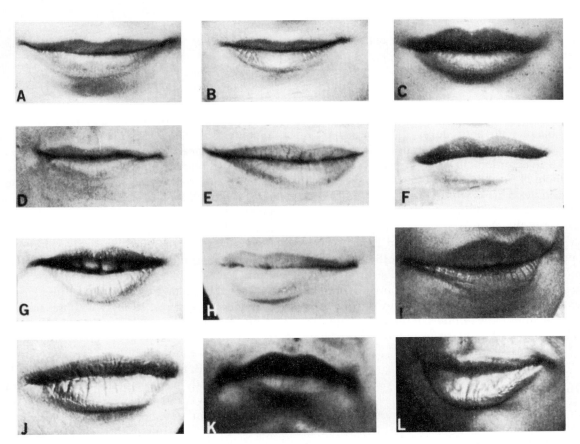

FIGURE 10-11 **Youthful lips, female.** *F is the most nearly classical lip formation.*

were to be thinned; filling out the lower lip would also help the proportion.

Reshaping

There are various ways of reshaping lips. Thin lips can usually be corrected for women by over-painting—that is, by first drawing on with a lip pencil new lips of the shape and size wanted. Then fill in with lip color. This overpainting should be done for men only if the results will seem completely natural. It's usually best to make the lower lip lighter than the upper. A thin highlight over the upper lip may help to define it. Note the natural highlights over most of the upper lips in Figure 10-10. A similar highlight can be painted in over the corrected lip.

If a man's lips are too full, it is usually best to leave them the natural color (Figure 10-10G). If they are already too red, the lower one can be lightened. If the upper one is very full, it too should be lightened. For women the fullness can be minimized by covering the lips with the foundation, then using the lip color only toward the inside of the lips and fading it outward into the foundation color. Deep colors should be avoided.

For too-wide lips, keep the lip color toward the center of the lips and cover the outer corners with the foundation color. The upper lip may be left slightly wider than the lower. If the mouth is too narrow, carry the lip color out to the extreme corners, particularly on the upper lip. It is seldom possible to carry the color beyond the natural corners of the mouth with any degree of success. The artifice becomes apparent as soon as the mouth is opened.

In the case of a turned-down mouth with a heavy upper lip and a thin lower one, the solution is to overpaint the lower lip to match the upper one and, if possible, to turn up the corners with paint. Or, if the outline of the upper lip is not too definite, it can be partially blocked out with foundation color and the lower one filled in to match. That much correction may not be possible for men.

For a mouth with a thin upper lip, the upper lip can—for women, at least, and sometimes for men—be overpainted to match the lower.

Lip coloring can best be applied with a narrow flat brush and blotted with tissue. The color should usually not be carried to the extreme corners of the mouth unless you wish to widen it. It is frequently helpful to define the lips by outlining them with a lip pencil, using the same or slightly darker shade than the lip color (Figure 10-12A). The outline should then be blended inward with your brush. Now apply the lip color with a brush or directly with the lipstick (Figure 10-12B).

For men, especially when no lip rouge is used at all, the outline of the lips can be defined very subtly with a brown makeup pencil, then blended. Further definition may be possible by deepening the natural shadow immediately below the center of the lower lip. If there is a natural shadow there, this will, of course, not be necessary; but if the natural shadow is slight, it may be helpful. It should, however, be done with great care so as to look completely natural. Observe the shadows under the lips in Figure 10-10.

Color

Lip coloring should be compatible with the rouge. And like rouge, it will depend—for women—on color of the skin, hair, costume, and perhaps on colors fashionable at the time. Lips and eyes should be kept in balance with each other. If accentuating the eye area keep the lip soft and vise versa. Bizarre fashions (such as white lipstick) should obviously be avoided in corrective makeup. For men a natural color (such as PR-9-d, SR-10-d, or RS-10-b) is safest. Often it is best not to color the lower lip at all.

FIGURE 10-12 Applying Lip Color. *A. Outline the lips with a lip pencil of the same shade as or slightly darker than the lip color. B. Filling in lips with lipstick. Actress Deidrie Henry.*

Neck

If the neck shows signs of age, it can be camouflaged somewhat by shadowing the prominent muscles and highlighting the depressions. Even a sagging neckline can be minimized, at least for the front view, by shadowing. The shadow should be strongest just under the jaw line and should blend gradually into the foundation, which can be darker on the neck than on the face. The neck shadow must never be allowed to come up over the jaw line. The jaw line itself can be defined with a shadow. That will tend to strengthen it and take the attention away from the neck.

Teeth

Dark or discolored teeth can be lightened with a white tooth color available from most theatrical makeup manufacturers. Professional whitening and/or bleaching techniques used by dentists are highly effective and relatively inexpensive. Irregularities (such as very long front teeth) can be corrected by shortening the teeth with black tooth enamel or black wax. More serious deficiencies, such as broken, missing, or extremely irregular teeth, require the services of a dentist. This can be expensive, but for professional actors—unless they are doing only certain types of character roles—it is important to have attractive teeth.

Hair

The actor's usual hair style should be considered carefully in relation to the shape of the face. If it can be made more becoming, it should be restyled. That can often be done merely by recombing in various ways and checking in the mirror, though it is sometimes better to consult a hairdresser whose work you know and can depend on. Medium long hair usually offers greater potential for change than does short.

If you want to make the face seem shorter and broader, avoid placing the bulk of the hairdo high on the head. Try, instead, to keep it flat on top and wider at the sides. If you want the face longer and narrower, the reverse will apply. If the face is too round, avoid a round hairdo that follows the shape of the face, since that would only emphasize the roundness. But a round hairdo could be helpful for a face that is too square or too angular. If the features are sharp, the hairdo should be soft around the face, not sleek—unless, of course, you have chosen deliberately to emphasize the sharpness.

If a man's hairline is receding slightly, it may be possible to restyle hair to conceal the fact. Or the hairline can sometimes be corrected by using eyebrow pencil of the appropriate color on the scalp. In doing this, never draw a hard, horizontal line; instead, use short strokes of the pencil following the direction of the hair. These strokes should be softened and blurred with the finger so that there is no definite line, and they should also be powdered to avoid shine. Darkening the base color at the hairline will also help. Makeup to match the hair color can be applied to small bald spots and can also be used with some success on the hairline. If the hair has receded beyond the point at which it can be corrected with paint, the actor should procure a toupee or a wig. The best ones are handmade and are expensive, but good inexpensive ones made with synthetic hair are also available. No matter what you pay for a wig or a hairpiece, be sure to have it skillfully styled.

PROBLEMS

1. Make your forehead (a) wider, (b) narrower, (c) higher, (d) lower.

2. Using only paint, change the shape of your nose, making it (a) longer and narrower, (b) shorter, (c) broader, (d) flatter.

3. Make your forehead more prominent and your chin less prominent, then your chin more prominent and your forehead less prominent.

4. Make your eyes (a) farther apart, (b) closer together.

5. Make one eye smaller and one eye larger.

6. Change the shape of your eyebrows without blocking them out.

7. Make your mouth (a) wider, (b) narrower.

8. Study your own face, noting prominent bones; size of eyes, nose, mouth, and chin; height of forehead; shape and thickness of eyebrows; shape, width, and fullness of lips, etc. Decide which features you'd like to change for your corrective makeup.

9. Do a complete corrective makeup on yourself.

Stippling

chapter 11

Stippling—a method of applying makeup by pressing the color onto the skin rather than stroking it on—is used for giving the effect of skin texture with paint, for toning down shadows or highlights that are too strong, for adding color to or changing the basic color of a makeup, for giving the effect of such skin blemishes as freckles and brown spots, and for helping to conceal the edges of three dimensional additions to the face. It is usually done with a sponge, occasionally with a brush.

Stippling with Sponges

Black plastic stipple sponges (Figure 11-1), red-rubber sponges (Figure 11-2), natural sponges (Figure 9-1), some household sponges, and pieces of polyurethane foam can be used for stippling. (See Sponges in Appendix A.) Red-rubber sponges are used primarily with rubber-mask grease and edge-cover adhesives, though they can also be used with creme makeup. Natural sponges are most always used with cake makeup. All sponges, including black stipple sponges can be used with creme makeup, greasepaint, cake makeup, or soft makeup in a tube.

The first step in stippling with a sponge is, of course, to apply the stipple color to the sponge. (To avoid creating hard edges or inadvertently transferring the shape of the square end of the black stipple sponge onto a face, sculpt it with scissors into an egg-shape. The rounded surface will assist you in reaching the many facial contours.) That can be done in four ways:

1. If you are stippling with regular creme, with creme contour or accent color, or with rubber-mask grease, press a flat surface of the sponge into the paint with just enough pressure to transfer paint to

FIGURE 11-1 **Stippling with a black stipple sponge.**

the surface of the sponge without clogging the holes. The sponge is then ready to use. In using creme sticks, you may prefer to stroke the stick across the surface of the sponge, especially if you are using a fairly large sponge.

2. If you are using creme-makeup crayons or creme stick makeup, stroke the crayon or the stick across a flat surface of the sponge. If you are using a small stipple sponge, you can simply press it into the top of the stick.

3. With makeup in a tube or heavily pigmented creme formulas such as concealers, tattoo covers, and clown foundations, apply some paint to the back of the hand, smooth it out, then press the sponge onto the paint on the hand. Or you can, if you prefer, spread the paint onto any convenient flat surface,

FIGURE 11-2 **Stipple sponges.** *(left to right) Triangular foam sponge, black stipple sponge (square and egg-shaped), red rubber sponge with small piece torn off for stippling.*

such as a piece of glass or tile, the top of a container of cake makeup, or the cover of your palette box if you happen to be using one.

4. In using cake makeup (moist or dry type), stroke the dampened (but not wet) sponge across the cake.

When the surface of the sponge is covered with paint, press the sponge gently onto the skin. If the stipple is too faint, keep pressing more firmly until you get the effect you want. *Always experiment first on your hand or on your arm before applying the stipple over makeup on the face.*

It is usually best to powder the makeup before stippling over it and also to powder over the stipple. If you are stippling with more than one color, powder after each color. When stippling with cake or other water-soluble makeup, it is, of course, not necessary to powder the stipple.

Stippling with Brushes

For stippling with brushes, small round sables, including eyeliner brushes, can be used. For freckles (Figure 11-3) or other spots of brownish pigmentation in the skin or for spots used for texture (see close-up of Hal Holbrook's Mark Twain makeup in Figure 11-4), narrow, flat brushes are preferable.

In stippling with brushes, the stipple paint is mixed on the back of the hand, in the cover of a makeup palette box, or on any appropriate flat surface, then taken from there with the brush and applied over the makeup. If you are using more than one color of stipple, it is not necessary to powder after applying each color, but only when all of the stippling has been completed.

Stippling for Texture

In stippling primarily for texture, one or more colors of stipple may be applied over the makeup, using grease paint, rubber-mask grease, creme makeup, or moist cake makeup such as Kryolan's AquaColor. Dry cake makeup is somewhat less effective for stippling but can be used.

If only one color of stipple is used, as in Figure 11-5C, choose a shade between the highlight and the shadow but not, of course, the same as the foundation

FIGURE 11-4 **Stippling with a brush.** *Detail from Hal Holbrook's makeup for Mark Twain. Three colors were used for the stippling and were applied with a small, flat brush. (For additional illustrations of Mr. Holbrook's makeup, see Chapter 17.)*

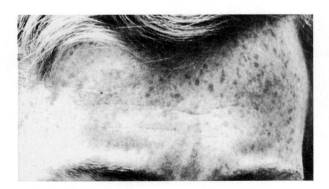

FIGURE 11-3 **Freckles.**

color—either a bit lighter or darker, a bit higher or lower in intensity, or of a different hue.

If you are not satisfied with the results from using just the one color of stipple, you can add additional colors. Three colors are usually more effective than one. Which ones you choose will depend on the effect you want—such as healthy, sickly, tanned, sunburned, or sallow. Keep in mind that colors used for men are usually darker than those used for women. And, of course, dark-skinned actors will require darker stipple colors than those with lighter complexions. The same holds true for light-skinned actors playing dark-complexioned characters.

The first stipple might be about four shades darker than the base. For characters who would normally have red or pink in the complexion, the second might be a shade of red—rose or coral, perhaps, or a bronze rouge. For characters without red tones in the complexion, the second stipple might be used to make adjustments in the color. If the color needs no adjusting, you can simply proceed to the third stipple, which should be lighter than the base but not so light as the highlight. If, after the stippling, the color of the makeup appears to need adjusting—more red, for example, or more pink or more yellow—stipple of the appropriate color can be added.

When you have chosen your stipple colors, apply the first one over the powdered makeup, being careful not to use too much. Avoid smearing the stipple or leaving dark blotches of paint. You should set this first stipple by patting translucent powder over it very carefully so as not to smear it. Slight smears can be retouched by stippling with a small brush.

Follow the same procedure with your second stipple color. If this is a red stipple, you can make it heavier on areas that you wish to appear more red in the final makeup. Powder again.

Then apply your third stipple. Its lightness or darkness will control to some extent the overall lightness or darkness of the final effect. Set this stipple with translucent powder.

Now stipple on the rouge. Even if you included it in the original makeup, you will probably need to add more. Then powder.

Finally, check the makeup and make any adjustments you wish to by additional stippling with a sponge or a brush.

It is also possible to do practically the entire makeup with stippling, including foundation, highlights, shadows, and rouge. This is one possible procedure:

1. Stipple the foundation directly on the skin, using three colors (or more, if you like) that, when juxtaposed in the stippling, will give you the color you want. This will, of course, be somewhat experimental. However, if the three you have chosen do not give you what you want, it's very simple to adjust the color by further stippling with whatever color seems needed. Powder after each application of stipple.

2. When the foundation color is satisfactory, carefully stipple on highlights, then shadows. As in working with a brush, always begin at the point of greatest intensity and work away from it toward the edge, stippling more and more lightly to create a soft edge. The density of the stipple can be increased in any particular spot or area by increasing the number of applications of the sponge. This is much safer than increasing pressure on the sponge, which can result in unsightly blotches. In shadowing, it is also possible to stipple the darkest part of the shadow with a deeper color. Hard edges or areas too small to stipple successfully with a sponge can be stippled

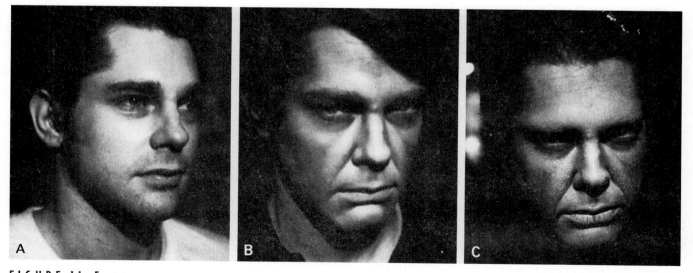

FIGURE 11-5 **Stippling for texture.** *(Actor Graham Beckel.) A. Without makeup. B. Sallow foundation with ivory highlights and rose shadows. Dry rouge (Bob Kelly Bronze) brushed on after powdering. C. Light stipple added for texture, then powdered. Hair combed back and slightly grayed.*

with an eyeliner brush. Errors in stippling, if they are not too serious, can usually be corrected by stippling over them with the foundation color. Powder after each stippling.

3. Stipple on the rouge wherever you normally would use it for the particular makeup you're doing—cheeks, nose, jowls, etc. Then powder.

An alternative method—and one which you might prefer for a more subtle effect—is partially to reverse the procedure and stipple on the highlights and the shadows first, making them fairly strong, then stipple on the foundation colors, and, finally, the rouge. Naturally, in stippling with the foundation colors you should proceed cautiously in order not to tone down the highlights and shadows more than you had intended to. However, if you find, when you have finished, that they have been toned down too much, it's a very simple matter to make corrections by additional stippling with your original highlight and shadow colors.

Stippling to Reduce Contrasts

Stippling can also be used to reduce contrasts in parts of the makeup that are too dark, too light, or too intense in color. Shadows that are too strong can be toned down with a lighter stipple, and highlights that are too strong, with a darker one. If both the shadows and the highlights are too strong, stippling with the base color will tone down both of them and reduce the overall contrast. If more texture is desirable, stipple the shadows with a color lighter than the base, and the highlights with a color darker than the base. For small areas, use small sponges or brushes, and be careful to confine the stippling to the area for which it is intended. If you inadvertently tone down an area too much, it can be corrected by further stippling with the original color.

Highlights and shadows in youthful makeups should not normally be stippled to reduce contrasts since stippling creates an illusion of texture. That, of course, would work against the smoothness of skin appropriate for most youthful makeups.

If the rouge in age makeups is too strong, it can be stippled with the base color to get the right intensity. Rouge in youthful makeups would not normally be stippled.

Stippling to Add Color

If you are not satisfied with the overall color of a makeup (too red, too yellow, etc.), it is possible to modify the color by stippling over the makeup with another color. This, of course, will also add a certain amount of texture. The cell size of your sponge will naturally determine the quality of the texture you are trying to create. Or you can use stippling instead of a foundation color by applying highlights and shadows directly onto the skin, then stippling to add an overall color.

If, when you have finished the stippling, you find that the color is still not quite right, you can add additional colors of stipple to correct it. Remember, however, that the more stipple you put over the makeup, the more you are toning down the highlights and shadows underneath. If you inadvertently tone them down too much, you can, of course, restore them by further stippling with the highlight and shadow colors. You may also want to use stippling for adding red to the cheeks, nose, jowls, and other areas of the face. Be assured that when and if you have exceeded maximum coverage you can simply remove the makeup and continue experimenting until you are satisfied with the results.

Unless you are using dry cake or wet makeup such as Ben Nye's, MagicCake Aqua Paint, you should usually powder the makeup before and after each stipple color is applied.

Natural skin texture and discoloration (blotchiness, age spots, bruises) can be simulated for intimate theatre settings, for television and for film. The accuracy of the application should please the eye. That is, it should, in close proximity, look "real" to you. Techniques for achieving a natural looking skin should include some modification of the makeup. Products such as castor oil, GP-20, PAX medium, alcohol, and makeup sealers can all be mixed with makeups to create various translucent effects. Some tips for using these products are:

1. Castor oil can be mixed with creme or cake makeup or with Rubber Mask Grease Paint (also called Appliance makeup).
2. GP-20, a base for many commercial liquid makeups, is used to make a variety of products and color more translucent It can be mixed with dry cake makeups, and pigmented powders,
3. PAX Medium made from Pros-Aide, an acrylic matte medium, was developed to be added to PAX paint (see Appendix A and Chapter 14) when coloring foamed latex and other three-dimensional appliances.
4. Makeup sealers, fixatives, and mixing liquids can be added to dry and moist cake and body makeup for sheer, waterproof coverage.
5. Alcohol mixed with any makeup can create sheer washes of color. It is the required solvent for the variety of waterproof temporary tattoo and body art ink pigments manufactured by Reel Creations and Temptu. Using alcohol on the tip of your brush, pick up a small amount of color and apply immediately. Since it will dry very quickly, you will need to work in small areas at a time.

All of these products when mixed with makeup can be applied with any number of commercially manufactured sponges. A custom-made sponge applicator used to effect skin discoloration and age spots can be made in the following way:

Cut a piece of 1-inch polyurethane foam into a 1- × 2-inch rectangle. Choose a firm rather than soft quality foam. On one long side draw several (up to ten) irregular shapes in a variety of sizes. These shapes will simulate age spots or discolorations. Tear or pinch away the negative space leaving the shapes on the surface. This stipple sponge, or more precisely a sponge stamp, will produce larger and more defined shapes than commercial stipple sponges. It can be used for regular makeup applications, replacing standard sponge applicators, but is particularly effective when using translucent formulas or glazes.

Stippling to Conceal Edges

In using latex pieces, eyebrow covers, bald caps, and various constructions with cotton and tissue, there are sometimes visible edges to be concealed. For the stage, film, and television this can be done by first stippling over the edge with appliance adhesive, Duo Surgical Adhesive or Pros-Aide with a red rubber sponge Allow them to dry thoroughly and then powder.

The rubber-mask grease or other coloring products (see, Chapter 14) are applied with a red-rubber sponge, which is pressed firmly onto the skin repeatedly, resulting in a thicker-than-usual foundation. Powder is then pressed firmly onto the rubber-mask grease, and the excess is dusted off with a powder brush, as usual. (Since the rubber-mask grease is pressed on without being smoothed out afterward, the technique is referred to as "stippling," even though the skin is completely covered with the paint.) Various colors of stipple can be applied over this with a black stipple sponge (Figure 11-1) or with brushes. The purpose in this case is not primarily to give texture to the skin, but to use the stippled patterns of light and dark colors to break up the tiny line of shadow (if present) created by the thickness of the edge being concealed.

Modeling with Highlights and Shadows

chapter 12

You have already studied the general structure of the face. The next step is to learn to modify the appearance of this structure through the use of highlights and shadows. Although the illusion created may involve making cheeks rounder, chins more pointed, or noses crooked, more often than not, it will include some aging.

In youth, firm muscles and elastic skin fill out the hollows and smooth over the bumps in the bony structure of the skull. But with age and the accompanying sagging of muscles, this bony structure becomes increasingly evident. Therefore, the first thing to do in learning to age the face is to visualize the bones of the skull and to locate them by prodding with the fingers.

Unquestionably, the single most important factor in learning to create the illusion of three-dimensional changes in bones and flesh through the use of two-dimensional painting techniques is a thorough understanding of what happens when directional light falls on a three-dimensional object (see Chapter 2). Once this is understood, the solution to most problems concerning realistic modeling in makeup can be found simply by asking three questions:

1. What is the exact shape of the structure (a cheekbone, for example, or a wrinkle) that is to be represented?
2. Where is the light coming from? (On the stage it will normally be from above rather than from below.)
3. What happens, in terms of light and shadow, when a light from that direction falls on a structure of that shape?

The answers to these questions will make it clear where the structure (wrinkle or cheekbone) would be light and where an absence of light would make it appear dark. These light and dark areas can then be painted onto the face, creating for the observer the illusion of prominent bones and wrinkles where they do not actually exist.

Before beginning to do this, it's a good idea to take time to practice the technique of modeling hard and soft edges.

Modeling Hard and Soft Edges

It would be best to do the following practice on the back of your hand or the inside of your wrist or your arm if any of those areas is sufficiently free of hair. Choose a medium flesh tone for the foundation, a medium dark color (such as S-13f, FS-13-g, or PR-12-g) for the shadows, and a very light color (such as OF-1-b, OF-1-c, F-1-a, FS-1-a, FS1-c, or FS-3-a) for the highlights. Use a wide or an extra-wide flat brush. With your brush, take up a small amount of paint and transfer it to the back of your hand—*not* in a spot you plan to use for your practice. Then work from the paint on your hand, using your hand as a palette. This enables you to control the amount of paint on your brush much more effectively than when you work directly from the stick or the container of makeup. (This applies, of course, only to creme makeup or to greasepaint, not to cake makeup. Makeup can be taken directly from cakes without using a palette.) If you are using paint from a palette box (see Appendix A), you can use the inside cover of the box as your palette. Both the hand and the palette box cover can also be used for mixing colors.

The following procedures for modeling hard and soft edges, though they are quite specific as to how to do what and in what order, are not intended to deter you from experimenting with other techniques for achieving the same results.

Soft Edges

In making a soft-edged highlight (or a soft-edged shadow), begin with the area of greatest intensity.

1. Using a stainless steel spatula, remove make-up from the container onto a mixing tray, stainless steel palette or ceramic tile.
2. With a brush or sponge cover a section of skin with a medium foundation.
3. Using your brush, take up some highlight color from your hand or your palette.
4. With a single, firm stroke of your brush, make a stripe of highlight color. (If you have used a brush of the correct width, taken up the right amount of paint, and used the right amount of pressure in applying it, you will need to make only the one stroke before blending the edges.)
5. Either wipe your brush clean or use a clean brush, then draw the brush lightly along one edge of the highlight, overlapping the edge. Repeat this until the edge blends imperceptibly into the foundation. If you are using cake makeup, the brush should be slightly damp, and you should wipe the makeup off the brush after each stroke, redampening it when necessary.
6. Repeat step 3 with the opposite edge. This should give you a strong highlight with two soft edges. If it is not strong enough, repeat the entire procedure on top of what you have already done.
7. Repeat step 2 with a medium shadow color, applying the stripe of paint a short distance away from the highlight.
8. Repeat step 3 on the side of the shadow away from the highlight.
9. Do the same on the other side of the shadow. In the blending of the shadow color toward the highlight, avoid any overlapping of the highlight color with the shadow. When you have finished, there should be a gradual transition in value between the lightest area of the highlight and the darkest area of the shadow. In other words, you should now have modeled, in essence, a cylinder. (see Figure 2-2.)

Hard Edges

Hard edges are used in realistic makeup only to create the effect of a crease in the flesh. For a hard edge to be fully effective, the lightest light must meet the darkest dark without any overlapping, smearing, or fuzziness. Hard edges should be clean and sharp. The following steps can be used to practice making a hard edge:

1. Cover a section of skin with a medium foundation color.
2. With your brush, take up some highlight color from your hand or your palette.
3. Holding the brush so that the bristles are perpendicular to the edge you intend to paint, draw it care-

fully along the skin where you want the hard edge to be. If the hard edge is to fade out at one end (as it usually should), gradually lift the brush so that it touches the skin more and more lightly as you move along. If there are irregularities in the edge, go over the entire edge again in the same in order to make corrections.

4. Wipe your brush clean. If you are using cake makeup, the brush should be damp.
5. If you want the highlight to be considerably wider than it now is (as on the upper lip when highlighting the nasolabial fold), place your brush in the same position as in step 3 and, barely touching the skin, draw the brush away from the hard edge, pulling some of the paint outward. How far you pull the paint out depends, of course, on the width you want the highlight to be. Moving down along the highlight, keep repeating this stroke for the entire length of the highlight. If you do *not* want to widen the highlight but only to blend the edge, skip this step entirely.
6. In order to soften the outer edge of the highlight, wipe your brush clean, then holding it parallel to the hard edge, stroke it very lightly over the outer edge of the highlight, overlapping the edge with the brush. Keep doing this until you have a soft edge that blends into the foundation color.
7. Examine the highlight. If it needs strengthening, repeat the entire procedure on top of what you have just done. Keep doing this until it is as strong as you want it to be. It would be well at this point to powder what you have already done.
8. Using your shadow color and working in the opposite direction, follow the same procedure as for the highlight, being extremely careful to maintain the clear, sharp edge, and never to let the shadow overlap the highlight. (See Figure 2-2.)

When you have learned to model hard and soft edges convincingly, you can then apply the technique in creating the illusion of three-dimensional changes on the face.

Modeling the Face and the Neck

In order to make sure that the final makeup will fit the actor's face, you should always be aware of how every highlight and every shadow relates to the structure of the face, including bone, cartilage, muscle, fatty tissue, and skin. To demonstrate this, model your entire face and neck by using highlights and shadows to bring out the bone structure and to create the effect of sagging muscles and flesh.

Begin by covering your entire face with a medium deep (8, 9, or 10) cake, creme, or greasepaint foundation color in a shade suitable for aging. This should be a grayed color (d, e, or f) in a warm hue (R, S, FS, or SF). Then, using a pale cream or ivory color, highlight areas of the face as they might look in middle or old age, with bones becoming more prominent and flesh sagging. (See Figure 12-1, which can be used as a guide but should be adapted to your own face rather than copied exactly.) For this exercise make the highlights *very strong,* but soften the edges except when creating the effect of creases. Subtle modeling effects can be introduced after you have a thorough understanding of the

basic concepts and have practiced the techniques. The following information provides a series of steps for laying in a foundation of highlights and shadows. Detailed instructions for contouring specific areas of the face are then presented later in the chapter.

1. Using a wide (Figure 12-2H) or extra-wide (Figure 12-2I) flat shading brush, highlight the frontal area marked H1 in Figure 12-1.
2. Still using your wide brush, apply similar highlights to the superciliary arch, emphasizing the area just above the eyebrows, marked H2 in Figure 12-1. If you look at your forehead in profile, you may find

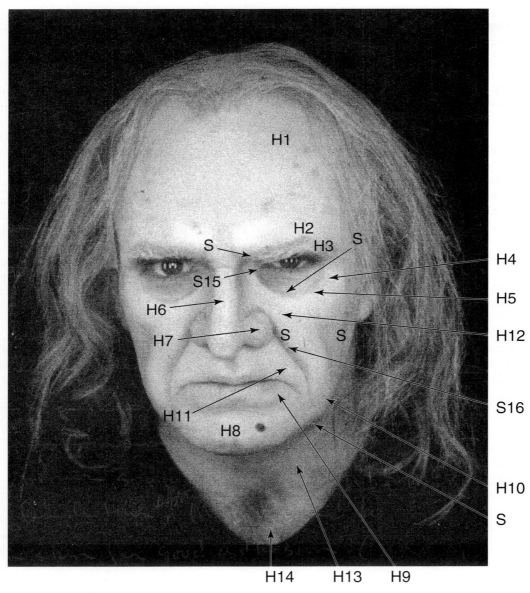

FIGURE 12-1 **Highlighting and shadow for age.** *Actor James Black as Scrooge at the Alley Theatre. (This exercise is designed to begin the modeling process by highlighting the prominent areas of the face. It is equally as valid an exercise to begin with the shadows.)*

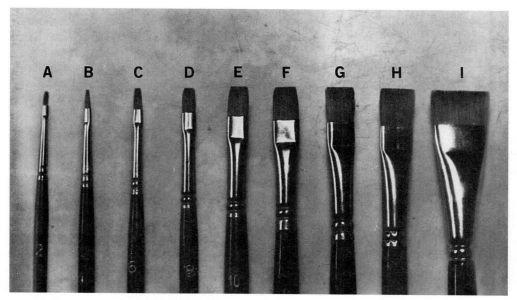

FIGURE 12-2 **Flat sable brushes.** *A, B, and C, Narrow. D, E, and F, Medium. G and H, Wide. I, Extra wide. All brushes by Kryolan, illustrated in actual size. (Kryolan numbers are 2, 4, and 6 for narrow; 8, 10, and 12 for medium; 14 and 16 for wide; and 5/8-inch for extra wide.)*

a horizontal break or a change in direction of the planes about halfway up. If you do, this break will represent the top limit of the highlight area.

3. Since the top of the orbital bone above the outer corner of the eye (H3) nearly always catches the light, highlight it, softening the edges. A medium brush (Figure 12-2E or F) can be used for this. You may also wish to highlight the lid itself, though if you were creating a very deep-set eye, it would be shadowed instead.

4. Using a medium-wide (Figure 12-2G) brush, highlight along the *top* of the cheekbone (H4), softening both edges of the highlight. (See Figure 12-32.) To locate the top, lay one finger horizontally across your temple, press firmly, and move it down until you find it being pulled outward by the cheekbone. Then press *downward* against the bone. Where your finger rests will be the top of the bone. It is the top plane of the bone, not the outside or the underside, that normally receives the most light.

5. If you want a pouch under the eye, continue the cheekbone highlight to the pouch, letting it stop with a hard edge along the lower boundary of the pouch and making it strongest at the very edge of the pouch (H5).

6. Using a medium brush (Figure 12-2E or F), highlight the bone and the cartilage that form the top or front of the nose (H6) since these invariably catch the light strongly (See Figure 12-26A, B.) Keep the highlight off the sides.

7. With the same brush, add a small highlight (H7) to the tops of the nares. (See Figure 12-26C, D.)

8. Highlight the chin (not too strongly since it picks up a significant amount of light by virtue of its position on the face) with a wide or a medium-wide brush. Be sure to keep the highlight below the break between the lip and the chin, making it strongest right at the break (H8), where there will be a fairly hard edge in the very center. (See Figure 12-48A, B.) This edge softens as it moves away to the right and to the left.

9. Now you can begin to use sagging muscles and flesh along with the bone structure in placing your highlights. The flesh at the corners of the mouth may puff out or sag with age, catching the light. Highlight this area (H9) with a medium or a wide brush. (See Figure 12-48C, D.)

10. The jaw line (H10) normally catches a highlight; but since, in age, it is the sagging flesh rather than the bone that is most strongly lighted, highlight this area with a wide or an extra-wide brush, keeping your edges soft and emphasizing the irregularity caused by the sagging flesh. (See Figure 12-41A, B, C.) If your own jawbone is firm and youthful, you can use photographs, paintings, or drawings to determine what might happen to it and how it might catch the light if there actually were sagging flesh.

11. The upper lip, all the way from the nose to the mouth, catches light, especially at the crease of the nasolabial fold (H11 in Figure 12-1). With a wide or an extra-wide brush, held as shown in Figure 12-36C, D, start your highlight at the nose, making a very sharp, clean edge along the crease, then fade it out (Figure 12-36E) as it moves toward the center of the lip.

12. Now observe the area marked H12 in Figure 12-1. This is the top of the nasolabial fold. It may not always be this pronounced, but the area is nearly always prominent in age. It catches a strong highlight with soft edges. Be sure not to carry the highlight all the way to the crease. A medium brush can be used. To the outside of the crease is an area (S16) that folds under and away from the light and therefore should not be highlighted.

13. Since, with age, the sterno-cleido-mastoid muscles of the neck (H13) usually become more prominent and catch the light, highlight them as you would a cylinder. If your own are not obvious, you can usually find them by turning your head as far as possible to the side and feeling the opposite side of your neck with your fingers.

14. There is likely to be a little light picked up by the larynx and the tracheal column (H14). Make the edges of the highlight soft.

Now, if you have done your highlighting skillfully, your skull structure should be more apparent, and your flesh, in some areas, should have begun to seem more puffy and perhaps to sag. Observe yourself in a spotlight at some distance from the mirror to determine to what extent this has happened. Although the highlights ought to be stronger than you want them to be in the finished makeup (see Figure 12-3A), they should, nonetheless, have begun to give an effect of age.

You will notice, provided you have used a sufficiently dark foundation color, that, as a result of the contrast between it and the very light highlights, the foundation color appears darker than it actually is. As a result of this optical illusion, you will need to add less shadow color than would be required if you had used a lighter foundation color. You may, in fact, need only to deepen the shadow slightly in certain areas—the eye sockets, for example, the deepest part of the wrinkles, or the underside of the jowls. Use your shadow color sparingly. Avoid adding any more than is necessary in order to create the three-dimensional effect that you want.

15. Brush a little deep shadow into the part of the eye socket next to the nose (S15 in Figure 12-1), keeping the edges soft. A medium-wide brush is a good choice for this area. This shadow continues up underneath the inside edge of the browbone and fades into the crease of the eye. It may also continue down onto either side of the nose blending and fading as it nears the tip. The soft edges of this shadow should not be blended onto the front plane of the face (H12) or onto the ridge of the nose (H6). Unless the eyes are to appear sunken in, avoid the eyelid and the area marked by H3. You may choose to

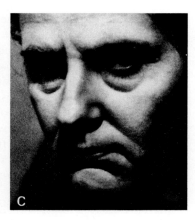

FIGURE 12-3 **Modeling the face with highlights and shadows.** *A. Highlighting completed. Makeup by student Milton Blankenship. B. Applying shadows. Makeup by student Joe Allen Brown. C. Highlights and shadows completed. Makeup by student Gigi Coker.*

contour the eye by shading the inside (continuing the shading from S15) and outside (use a slightly higher value than at S15 or simply apply less color) areas of the lids.

16. Using the same color and a medium-narrow flat brush (1/4 inch to 1/2 inch), merely suggest a shadow beginning at the root of the nasolabial fold just above S16. The edge of the shadow along the crease should be hard; the edge toward the cheek should be soft.

17. Deepen any other areas (such as those marked S in Figure 12-1) that obviously need deepening.

18. If you have been using creme or grease makeup, it should now be powdered. Press translucent powder into the makeup, and remove the excess with a powder brush. (Be sure to choose a translucent powder that does not darken the highlights too much.)

You may find that, although you have achieved a three-dimensional effect, the results are quite stark and unnatural. The next step, therefore, is to add a touch of rouge–not only on the cheeks, but also on the nose, on the jowls, and in some of the shadow areas. Use a natural shade of dry rouge and apply it with a rouge brush. You may even wish to add rouge around the eyes to make them look weaker. *Always be very careful not to get the rouge into the eye.* Look again in the mirror to see how the rouge creates the effect of blood under the skin and begins to bring your makeup to life. With every realistic makeup you do, always consider the possibility of touching shadow areas with rouge for a more lifelike effect.

If the makeup is still too white or too contrasting, the solution–not only here but in most makeups that need toning down or pulling together–is to use stippling.

Stippling

Colors darker than the highlight and lighter than the deep shadow are usually best for stippling. Use your base color, if you like, or for a pinker effect, either use a pinker color or add a stipple of rouge. If you want the foundation color more yellow, stipple with something yellowish. This is a good opportunity to experiment with different colors of stipple. In any case, stipple gently, barely touching the sponge to the face, so as to give added texture to the skin. Keep examining the results in the mirror as you go, and observe that, as you tone down the highlights, the makeup begins to lose its three-dimensional quality. It is important, therefore, to avoid over-stippling. (For more detailed instructions in stippling, see Chapter 11.)

The preceding instructions are for an exercise in modeling technique not necessarily related to a particular character. To check the effectiveness of your modeling before you stipple, it's a good idea to take a close-up black-and-white photograph of your makeup with an instant-picture camera, making sure that the light is coming from the direction you imagined it to be coming from when you did the makeup.

After you have studied the photograph carefully to see if the makeup looks the way you meant it to, turn it upside down and look at it again. That will help you determine how convincingly three-dimensional the modeling really looks. Then, after making any improvements you would like to, it would be a good idea, for purposes of comparison, to photograph the makeup again, both before and after it has been stippled.

The next step is to refine the approach to a makeup by making choices related to a particular character, beginning with colors for foundation, highlights, and shadows.

Foundation Colors

In selecting the foundation color (unless you already know approximately what color you want), you would do well to analyze the character as suggested in Chapter 6. On the basis of your analysis, decide first on the appropriate hue (such as red or orange), then on the value (the relative lightness or darkness of the skin color you want), and finally on the intensity (the brightness or grayness of the color). That should automatically lead you to the correct section of the color tables, and from the listings there you can select one that seems appropriate. If you do not have the color you select, choose the nearest one you do have, and mix the color you want, using the colors you have available. You may, of course, wish to choose a darker foundation color than the character would normally require in order to decrease the amount of shadow needed, as was done for the preceding exercise.

If your own skin–whether it is dark or light–is the right color for the character, then you may not need a foundation. If you choose to use one for other reasons (to cover skin blemishes, for example), it can be the color of your own skin.

Highlight Colors

Since highlights, in a realistic makeup, represent the character's skin color seen in strong light, they will usually be of a higher value of the foundation hue. For corrective makeup they will normally be about three shades lighter and for a very subtle aging effect, a bit more. For a greater aging effect, increase the contrast between the foundation color and the highlight.

Some useful highlight colors for light-skinned performers are Mehron's Shado-Liner #17, Ben Nye's Ultralite and Natural Lite, Joe Blasco's TV White, Bob Kelly's Ivory, Kryolan's Hilite and TV White, and in cake makeup, Mehron's 1B and Kryolan's TV White. Kryolan's and Bob Kelly's sticks for covering blemishes can be used when you prefer makeup in stick form for highlighting.

Dark-skinned actors can choose a color six to eight shades lighter than their own skin. Mehron's Lt. Buff and Warm Honey, Ben Nye's Soft Caramel and Ivory, Joe Blasco's Darkskin Highlight (DH1), Kryolan's O34 and F16, and Bob Kelly's Medium Fair and Tantone foundation colors are good possibilities.

Highlights used in age makeups will nearly always be toned down somewhat by being stippled and should, therefore, usually be lighter—sometimes considerably lighter—than you want them to appear in the final makeup. How much they are toned down can be controlled by stippling.

Shadow Colors

Whereas shadow colors for modeling in corrective makeup are usually about three shades darker than the base, they can be many shades darker for stronger contrasts in age. They may be of the same intensity as the foundation or grayer, but they should rarely be brighter. For character makeups it is advisable to use two shadow colors—a medium one (which is applied first) and a deep one, which adds depth to the shadows. The medium shadow can be either a grayed version of the foundation color or, more often than not for light-skinned performers, a shade with more red in it than the base. In realistic makeup, shadows that are too cool for the base color tend to look dirty. If the actor is going to be wearing a red costume, more red than usual can be used in the shadows. The deep shadow should be several shades deeper in value than the medium one. Low values and intensities of Red, Scarlet-Red, Red-Scarlet, and Scarlet are the ones most commonly used for light-skinned makeup and for some Native Americans. For Asian performers, the shadow colors might have a slight olive or yellow undertone. For many darker skinned performers the need for shadow colors is minimal and in some cases simply not necessary. With heavy character makeup being the exception, the deep skin tones provide their own natural shadow effect.

There is no universal shadow color suitable for all base colors, but there are currently available ones that can be used with a number of different foundation colors. For medium shadows, Bob Kelly's Medium Rose Shadow, Ben Nye's Character Shadow, Joe Blasco's Lightskin Shading #2 and Darkskin Shading #2, Kryolan's Shadow #1, #2, and #3, and Mehron's Mocha Rose (RC11) are especially effective. For deep shadows, Joe Blasco's Gray-Violet, Mehron's Smokey Taupe (RC 12), Bob Kelly's Grey Violet (S1-17), Ben Nye's Dark Brown, Extra Dark, and Misty Violet Shadows, and Kryolan's Shadow #4 and #5 are all useful.

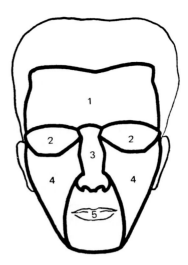

FIGURE 12-4 Division of the face into areas.

Both medium and deep gray shadow colors are also available. Any of these can, of course, be mixed with other colors to lighten them, darken them, gray them, or change the basic hue. Or you can mix your own shadow color for each makeup to go with the foundation color you're using. If there is a shadow color of your own mixing that you find useful with various foundation colors, you might mix up a batch in a small flame-proof container and heat it over a gas flame, a candle, or an electric burner, then pour it into small containers or a palette (see Chapter 8) for future use.

If you are using cake makeup (dry or moist type) and have a shadow color that is not red enough, instead of mixing colors, as you would with creme or grease makeup, you can apply the shadow, then add red to it afterward by brushing on dry rouge as you are completing the makeup.

Now that you have experimented with highlights and shadows in restructuring the face as a whole and considered the problem of choosing colors for specific characters, the face will be divided into areas so that you can examine in detail the modeling of these areas. The five area divisions—forehead, eyes, nose, cheeks, and jaws—are diagrammed in Figure 12-4. Each area will then be subdivided into planes for more detailed analysis. The discussion of each area will indicate the various possible treatments of that area.

Area 1: Forehead

Planes The forehead is divided into five planes, as shown in Figure 12-5. Planes A and C are the frontal and

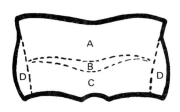

FIGURE 12-5
Area 1: Forehead.

the superciliary bones; D, the temporal hollows; and B, the slight depression between the two prominences.

A simple method of aging the forehead is to highlight and shadow these planes. The two prominences, A and C, catch the light (Figure 12-6A and C) and should, therefore, be highlighted. The depression, B, falling between them, may be slightly shadowed. Be careful, however, in doing a realistic makeup, not to emphasize the transverse shadow too strongly. If you are using a fairly dark foundation color, you will probably not need to add any shadow at all since the foundation color, if dark enough, will itself serve as a shadow.

The highlighting can be done with a brush, a sponge, or the fingers. Figure 12-7 illustrates the technique that can be used with a brush. A wide or an extra-wide brush should be used. If you have only narrow

brushes, then use your fingers for creme or grease makeup or a sponge for cake.

For a prominent overhanging brow, carry a strong highlight all across the front plane of the superciliary arch, rather than just over the eyebrows, and shadow deeply across the bridge of the nose to sink it in.

The temples (Figure 12-6D) are nearly always shadowed for age. These shadows may be barely perceptible in middle age but are usually quite pronounced in later years. The shadows tend to be more intense at the inner edge and to lighten as they approach the hair.

In placing the highlights, keep in mind the light source on the stage. With light coming from above, a strong light will fall on the upper part of the frontal bone. If there is a horizontal division approximately in the middle of your forehead (most clearly observable in profile), the area coming forward below this division will catch another strong highlight, and the area immediately above the division will be less strongly lighted. This is the area where you may or may not wish to use a very slight shadow. When there are no wrinkles to crease the skin, all edges of highlights and shadows will be soft. If you want to make the forehead more rounded or bulging, apply the highlights and shadows in a curved pattern.

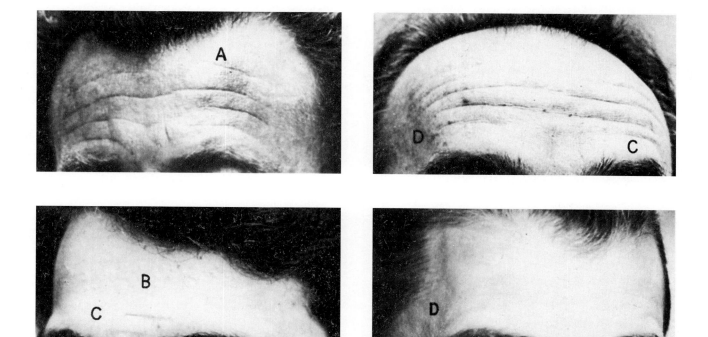

FIGURE 12-6 Foreheads. *A and C indicate prominences that are normally highlighted for age; B, a slight depression that may or may not be lightly shadowed; and D, a depression that is usually shadowed for age.*

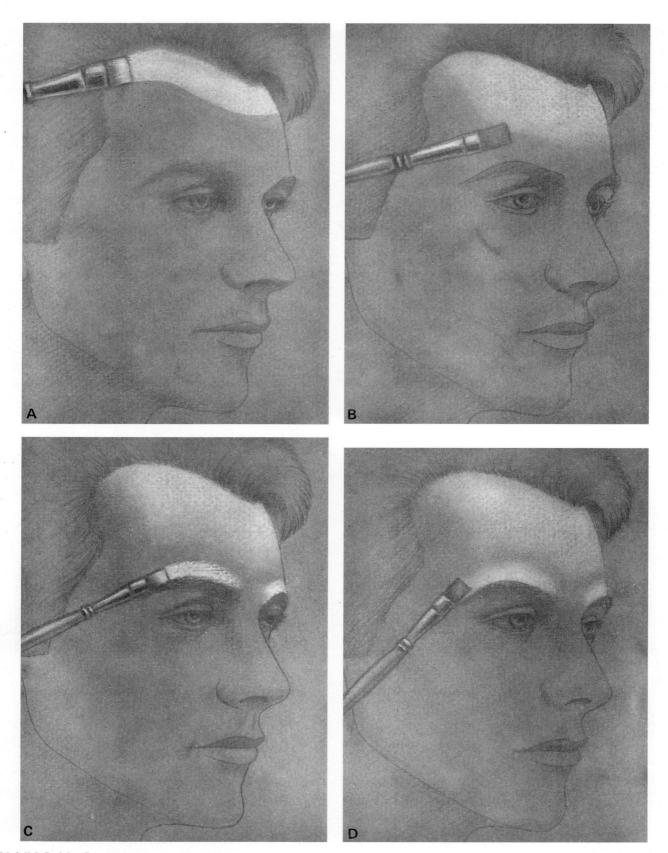

FIGURE 12-7 **Highlighting the forehead.** *A. Highlighting the frontal bone with an extra-wide brush. B. Blending the lower edge of the highlight. C. Highlighting the superciliary bone with a medium-wide brush. D. Blending the superciliary bone highlight with a clean brush. E. Highlighting the vertical edge of the frontal bone with a wide brush. F. Blending the edge of the highlight with a clean brush.*

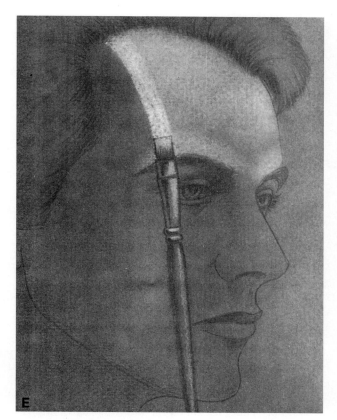

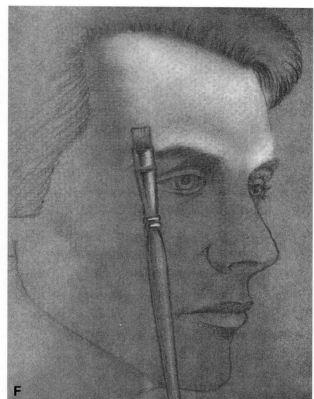

FIGURE 12-7 Continued.

Wrinkles

Wrinkles If you want to give the effect of a wrinkled forehead, make sure that you model the wrinkles meticulously and that you follow the natural wrinkles—otherwise, you will have a double set of wrinkles when the forehead is raised. Young people who have not yet developed any natural creases and cannot form any by raising the forehead may wish to use photographs of wrinkled foreheads as a guide.

Before beginning to model forehead wrinkles, observe your own or someone else's natural wrinkles, and with your light source from above, note where the wrinkles catch the light. Is it above or below the crease? Carefully examine photographs in your morgue and those in this chapter (especially Figure 12-8) to see exactly how the light pattern falls, giving the effect of a series of half cylinders. (The lower photograph shows what happens when the light source is from below.) Once you understand the principle involved, you will never make the mistake of painting wrinkles upside down, and you will always keep your hard edges crisp and clean in order to form sharp creases. Following the steps given below may be of help:

1. Using a medium flat brush with your highlight color and holding it so that the flat end of the brush lies

parallel to, and barely touches, one of the natural creases in the forehead (Figure 12-9A), draw the brush along the crease, fading the color out at each end. Make sure the paint touches the natural crease at all times but never crosses it. It is best not to try to model wrinkles with the forehead raised, since the paint is very likely to smudge in the creases, resulting in messy edges.

2. Holding the brush in the same position (Figure 12-9B) and starting near but not *at* one end of the highlight you have just applied, move the brush along the length of the wrinkle again, almost to the end, this time pulling it downward in a series of short, vertical strokes in order to increase the width of the highlight. Be sure, however, not to make these strokes the full width you want the finished highlight to be since space must be left for blending.

3. Using a clean brush, soften the lower edge of the highlight until it blends imperceptibly into the foundation. This should be done by drawing the flat of the brush along the highlight, overlapping the edge. (See Figure 12-9C.) Repeat this until you have a good blend. If you blend downward, the highlight will tend to become too wide. However, highlights for forehead wrinkles are usually wider than the

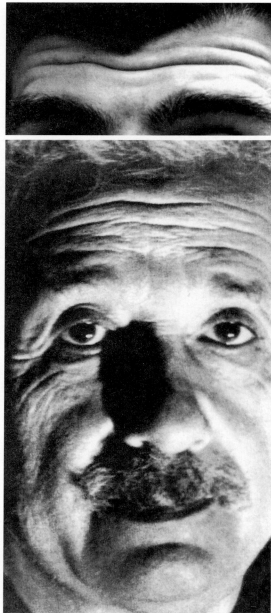

FIGURE 12-8 Forehead wrinkles—light coming from above and from below. *Note the reversal of highlights and shadows as a result of the reversal of normal lighting.*

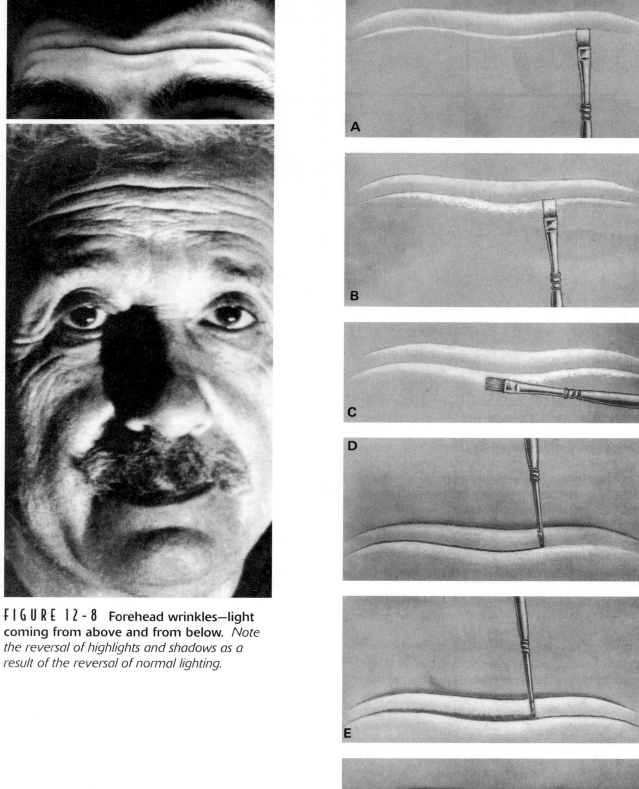

FIGURE 12-9 Modeling forehead wrinkles with paint. *A, B. Highlighting the wrinkle. C. Blending the highlight. D, E. Shadowing wrinkle. F. Blending shadow.*

shadows because of the angle of the light source. If the light were coming from directly above, highlights and shadows would be the same width. But as the light source moves forward, the light area is naturally increased and the dark diminished. Observe the relative widths of highlights and shadows in Figure 12-8. Make sure that the ends of wrinkles, instead of being thick and blunt, are fine and delicate, disappearing imperceptibly into the foundation.

4. Since you must treat not only the wrinkles in a wrinkled forehead, but the entire forehead area, highlight the superciliary arch and the frontal bone, making all edges soft.

5. Using a very narrow brush, paint a line of shadow immediately adjacent to the hard edge of the highlight. (Figure 12-9D.)

6. Following the technique described for blending the highlight in step 2, pull the shadow upward, away from the crease, keeping it narrower than the highlight. (See Figure 12-9E.)

7. With a clean brush, and using the technique described for softening the edge of the highlight in step 3, blend the upper edge of the shadow into the foundation color. (See Figure 12-9F.)

8. Check your wrinkles for roundness and depth, making sure that hard edges are strong and crisp and that soft ones fade away subtly. Check also for pro-jection—in a spotlight, if possible—and make any necessary adjustments. Then powder—unless you are using cake makeup, in which case powdering will not be necessary.

9. Unless there are reasons for its not being done (wanting a pale and bloodless look, for example), a touch of rouge should be added to the shadows and should extend into the highlights. A small, soft brush can be used to apply the rouge. If you prefer to use moist rouge, it should be applied with a narrow shading brush before the makeup is powdered.

10. If the wrinkles look too strong and obvious, stipple the entire forehead, as illustrated in Figure 12-10B, with the base color or any other color or colors you consider appropriate. Using more than one color tends to give a more natural effect. Stipple carefully, watching the effect as you go so that you don't wipe out everything you've done. If the stippling grays the shadows too much, you can add more rouge. If you use a red stipple, extra rouge will probably not be necessary.

In making wrinkles, you may prefer to use flat-cut pencils (see Figure 12-11) for *applying* the color. For *blending* the color, however, brushes should be used, though cotton swabs (Figure 12-12) can be substituted if a proper brush is not available.

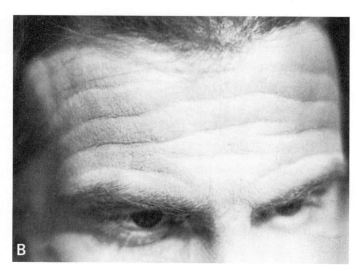

FIGURE 12-10 **Modeling wrinkles.** *Makeup by student Douglas Parker. A. Applying creme-makeup highlights and shadows for forehead wrinkles. B. Forehead wrinkles powdered and stippled.*

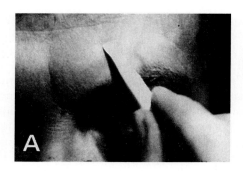

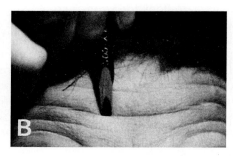

FIGURE 12-11 A. Highlighting and B. shadowing forehead wrinkles with flat-cut makeup pencils.

FIGURE 12-12 Blending forehead-wrinkle highlights with a cotton swab. (Student J. C. Stahl).

Area 2: Eyes

No feature is more important in suggesting character than the eyes, and none can be changed in a greater variety of ways. Figure 12-13 illustrates a few of the changes that can be made in a single eye. For photographs of youthful eyes and eyebrows, see Figures 10-5 and 10-7; and for aged ones, Figures 12-16, 12-17, 12-18, and 12-19. In studying these photographs, always

determine the light source in the photograph and make the necessary adjustments for stage lighting.

PLANE A (Figure 12-14) extends forward from the eye to the bridge of the nose and is nearly always shadowed for age. It is seldom highlighted except for Oriental makeups or for counteracting heavy shadows in deepset eyes. The center of this plane is usually one of the darkest parts of the whole orbital area. (See Figure 12-13F.) The lower edge fades into the shadow on the side of the nose. The outer edge is soft and turns into a highlight on the bridge of the nose. The inner edge is always soft, fading into plane B. In general, the greater the age, the deeper this shadow. A medium or a wide brush can be used for this area.

PLANE B is the transition area between Plane A and Plane C. The shadow colors applied to Plane A are usually lightened as they cross B and approach C.

PLANE C is often rouged for youthful makeups and is usually highlighted for age makeups (Figure 12-15A). In old age, the skin in plane C may sag and actually cover a part of the open eye. (See Figures 12-16A and K.) Although we cannot do that with paint, we can approach the effect by strongly highlighting C_1 and shadowing the lower edge of C_2 (Figure 12-19A). A medium or a wide brush can be used for C_1 and a narrow one for C_2. If the light is coming from above, the lightest part of the highlight will be nearest the eyebrow—in other words, on the superciliary bone where it forms the outer edge of the eye socket. It will gradually recede into a soft shadow as it approaches the B-C division, whether or not a fold is to be made. (See Figure 12-13F.)

The deepest part of the shadow is at the bottom of the area, and it turns very gradually into a highlight as it approaches C_1. The dotted line indicates only a general division of the whole plane, not a specific one. The inner edge of plane C is a definite division, however, and should be heavily shadowed if sagging flesh is to be represented. If not, then the transition to B is a gradual one.

It is usually best to use two colors for the narrow shadow that creates the impression of a fold of flesh. With the basic shading color, a medium shadow can be applied along the division between B and C and blended carefully to form two soft edges. Then the simulated crease can be deepened with a darker shadow. This deep shadow should also be lightly blended. If the whole orbital area is to appear sunken, then plane C may be shadowed rather than highlighted.

Frequently, wrinkles (commonly known as crow's feet) cut across the outer edge of plane C_2, as in Figure 12-16A. If you use these wrinkles, be sure to make them true wrinkles, not lines (see discussion of forehead wrinkles). Model the wrinkles first with highlights, using a 1/8-inch brush or an eyeliner brush, then add the shadows with an eyeliner or a pointed Chinese brush, keeping the creases very sharp and clear.

PLANE D is the eyelid itself and may be either highlighted or shadowed. If the whole eye is to appear

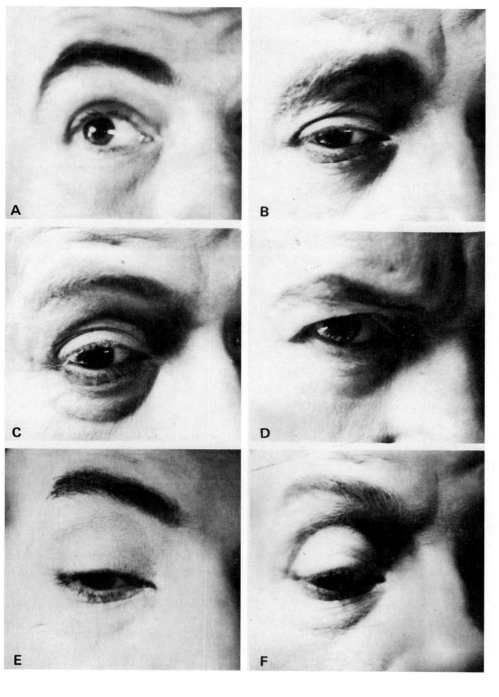

FIGURE 12-13
Changing the eye with makeup. *All makeups are on the same eye. Cake makeup used throughout, except for darkening the brows and lining the eye in E. Outer end of the brow in E was blocked out with spirit gum. (Makeup by Richard Corson.)*

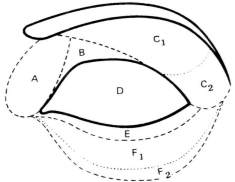

FIGURE 12-14 Division of the orbital area into planes for highlighting and shadowing.

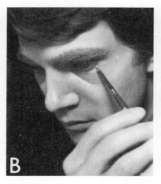

FIGURE 12-15 **Modeling for the Orbital Area.** *(Actor Eugene Bicknell.) A. Highlighting plane C with a medium brush. B. Highlighting plane F with a narrow brush. The top edge should be hard. (The highlight under plane F$_2$ is actually part of the nasolabial fold and will be illustrated in that section.) C. Shadowing plane A of the eye with a medium-wide brush. D. Shadowing plane F of the eye with a medium brush.*

sunken, plane D may be shadowed; but if the eyeball itself protrudes, catching the light, D should be highlighted and the upper division between it and the other areas deeply shadowed. (See Figure 12-13F.) When D catches a highlight, C$_1$ normally does too (Figure 12-16B), though there may be a deep shadow between the areas.

PLANE D is sometimes highlighted in the same way for glamor makeups, with the eyeshadow used only on the lower part, close to the eye. For either age or glamor, the actor may, at times, want to create the effect of a more prominent lid than he or she has naturally. This can often be faked quite successfully with paint. (See Figure 17-11.) With a medium brush and your highlight color, draw the enlarged lid on the natural eyelid in approximately the pattern shown in Figure 12-13F. Then, with a deep shadow, outline the new lid and, with a medium brush, shadow upward toward the eyebrow, just as you would if there were a natural crease. The secret of modeling this false eyelid convincingly is to make the shadow edge very dark so that it gives the effect of a deep crease. (See Figure 17-11H.) The effect is more convincing if the eye is not opened too wide.

If the character would be wearing eyeshadow, it will usually be concentrated largely on plane D, though fashion has sometimes decreed that the color be extended over the whole orbital area. In any case, for realistic plays, if the eyeshadow is supposed to be apparent, the placement and the color should be determined on the basis of what choice the character would make. Would she follow the latest fashion or would she not? (If she would, what *was* the latest fashion at the time?) Would she choose a conspicuous color or a conservative one? (A color that might seem conservative in one period might be conspicuous in another.) Would she take care to avoid colors that clashed with her cos-

tume or wouldn't she? (Eyeshadow colors that do clash with the costume can be somewhat jarring and should be used only when that effect is intended.) Would she wear false eyelashes or wouldn't she? (If she wouldn't, don't let the eyelashes be obviously false.)

To give the effect of weak eyes, which may accompany extreme old age, the lower part of D and all of Plane E can be rouged with a narrow brush. Using red around the eye opening tends to give an effect of age or weakness of the eyes or may indicate that the character has been crying. In using red around the eyes, apply and remove it with great care so as not to get any into the eyes. And never under any circumstances use *any* makeup inside the lashes, next to the eye itself. If there is a warning on any particular red makeup not to use it around the eye, use another shade of red or another form of red makeup that is not considered unsuitable for use in that area.

PLANE E is usually shadowed for age (see Figure 12-18F), the division between E and F usually having a fairly hard edge. Since a strong shadow under the eye (plane E) tends to add strength, it should usually not be very pronounced for extreme old age. Rouging helps give an appearance of weakness and age. As noted earlier, any red makeup this close to the eye should be applied and removed very carefully.

PLANE F is seldom shadowed in its entirety. Usually the shadow starts at the inner corner of the eye (Figure 12-17I), then fades out along the lower edge, never reaching the outer corner. This can be done with a single shadow color (Figure 12-13B, D, and F) or with two. A deep shadow color (dark brown, gray violet, or dark gray) can be added–also beginning under the inner corner of the eye but fading out sooner than the medium shadow. A medium or a medium-narrow brush can be used. (See Figure 12-15D.) Be careful not to shadow

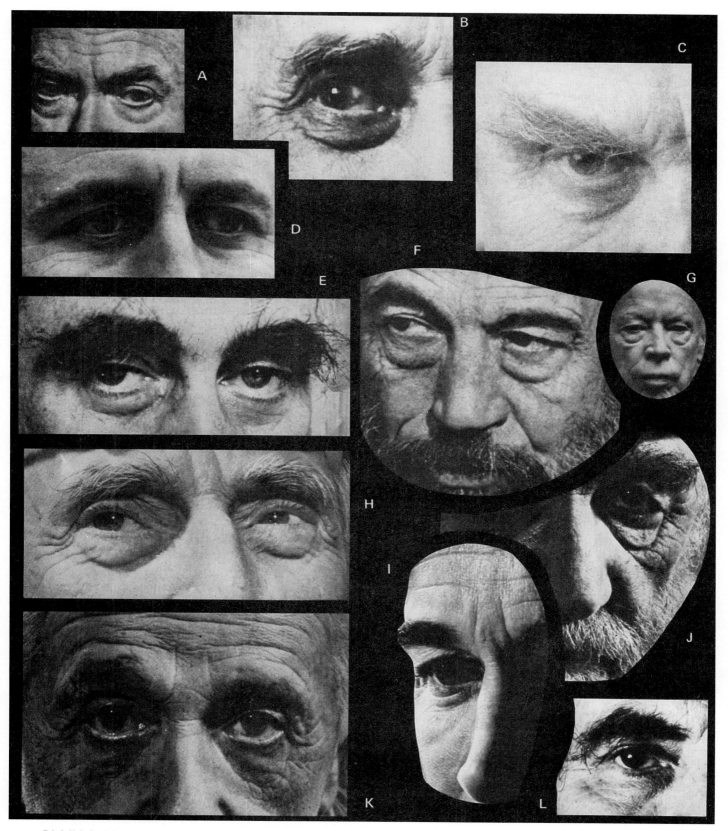

FIGURE 12-16 Eyes and eyebrows.

plane F too heavily unless you mean to suggest dissipation, illness, or lack of sleep.

The whole F plane sometimes becomes rather wrinkled (Figure 12-16K), and diagonal wrinkles may cut across the lower edge of F_2 on the side away from the nose (Figure 12-16H). These should be carefully modeled like tiny cylinders, An eyeliner brush or the narrowest available flat brush can be used. If you want plane F slightly puffy, it can be highlighted as shown in Figure 12-15B, using a narrow brush. This same kind of highlight is used when making a full pouch (see the following section).

The secret of shading the various planes of the eye effectively lies in a constant variation of intensity of shadow and highlight and in some variation in color. Not one of these areas should ever be flatly shadowed or flatly highlighted. You should start your shading at the point of maximum intensity, then decrease it gradually in other parts of the area. The use of two colors in the shadow and the addition of rouge can be very helpful in achieving a convincing effect.

Eye Pouches
In order to make a pouch (Figure 12-16), highlight F, and shadow F_2 as if you were modeling a half cylinder that ended abruptly along the bottom edge of F_2. The entire lower edge of F_2 should be hard, with a deep shadow that blends up across F_2 and turns into a highlight on F_1. The division between F_1 and F_2 should always be a soft edge. The cheek area below the pouch will catch light coming from above and will therefore be strongly highlighted.

One of the secrets of making a convincing pouch is to keep the shadow heaviest at the bottom, where the fold of skin naturally falls, creating a deep shadow, and to let it become thinner and thinner, usually fading out almost completely before it reaches the corner of the eye (Figure 12-18K). The fact that these subtle variations must be made in a very small area means that pouches, in order to be convincing, should be modeled with care and precision, keeping the hard edge clean and sharp. Always use both a medium and a deep shadow, and make sure the pouches look rounded at the bottom, where the sagging skin turns under. A flatly painted shadow will look exactly like paint, not like a pouch.

If you have the beginning of a natural pouch of your own, it will be easy to determine the correct size and shape. If you do not, then you should decide on the basis of what seems to fit in best with your eye.

Following is a step-by-step procedure for modeling a relatively simple eye pouch with paint, as illustrated in Figure 12-18. Other pouches will require a similar technique, with some variations, depending on the particular effect desired.

1. Very carefully highlight the area around the pouch (Figure 12-18A), keeping the edge of the highlight next to the pouch very strong and sharp and clean. Pull the highlight away from the edge, as illustrated in Figure 12-18B. Then, with a clean brush, soften the lower edge of the highlight so that it disappears into the foundation color. (See Figure 12-18C.) This highlight should be modeled with a medium or a medium-wide flat brush. Holding the brush as shown in Figure 12-18A will give you a clean, sharp edge.

2. Highlight the inside of the pouch with a narrow brush, as shown in Figure 12-18D. If the lower lid (plane E) is going to be shadowed, the highlight can begin at the division between E and F, with a definite edge. If the lower lid is puffy and becomes part of the pouch (Figure 12-16F), the upper edge will be immediately below the eyelashes. In either case, soften the lower edge of the highlight in order to make a gradual transition—as if you were modeling a tiny half cylinder. This can be done either by stroking it gently with a clean narrow brush or by patting it lightly with a cotton swab.

3. With a medium shadow, model the fullness at the bottom of the pouch, keeping the lower edge very clean and sharp and letting the upper edge fade out toward the highlight (Figure 12-18E). This fading out can be done, as with the highlight, by using either a clean narrow brush or a cotton swab. (For an alternative procedure for steps, 3 and 4, see the paragraphs following step 10.)

4. With your deepest shadow color and your smallest brush, deepen just the bottom edge (not the side edges) of the pouch (Figure 12-18G), then pull the paint upward slightly to soften the upper edge of the shadow. Have the courage to make this shadow extremely dark. (Note the darkness of this lower edge in Figure 12-16F and H.)

5. At this point you may wish to add a touch of rouge to the area between the shadow and the upper highlight, using a small brush. Or you can add the rouge later. (See step 10.)

6. If the lower lid (Figure 12-18E) is not actually part of the pouch itself, as in Figure 12-16A, it is usually shadowed. This can be done with a flat brush approximately the same width as the lower lid. It's usually best to begin at the outer corner of the eye and brush across the lid, allowing the shadow to fade out a bit as it approaches the inner corner of the eye. (See Figure 12-18F.)

7. Powder the pouch with a puff, and remove excess powder with a powder brush. (If you are using cake makeup, this step will, of course, not be necessary.)

8. If the pouch looks too smooth for wrinkled skin in the rest of the face, or if the contrasts are too strong for the rest of the makeup, stipple it very carefully with your sponge.

9. The stippling should now be powdered.

10. If you have not added creme rouge in step 5, or if you have and it is not strong enough, brush the lower part of the pouch with dry rouge, using a small eyeshadow brush.

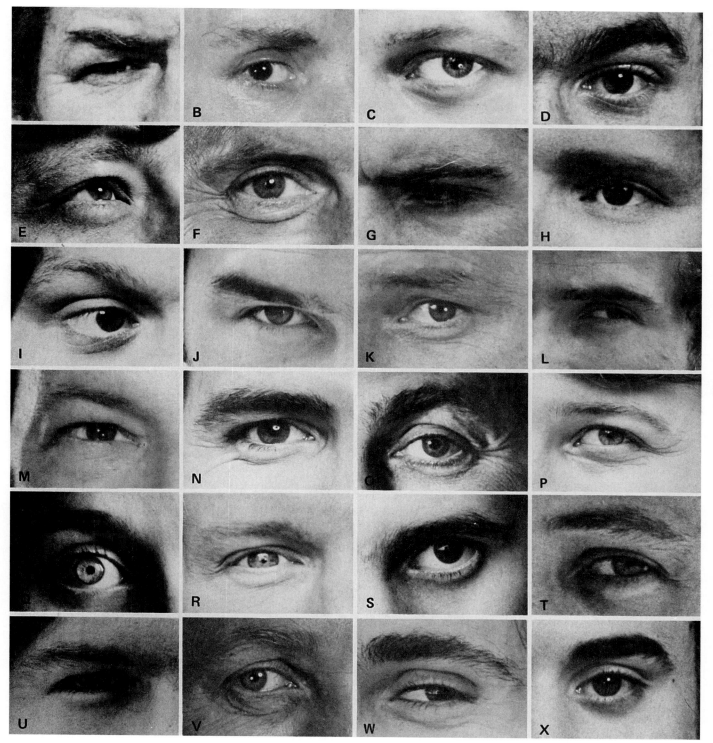

FIGURE 12-17 Male eyes and eyebrows.

It is possible to vary this technique for modeling pouches by substituting red for the medium shadow. Highlights are applied as usual (steps 1 and 2). The variation comes in step 3. Instead of applying a medium shadow, model the area with red, bringing the color up a bit higher than you normally would for the shadow. This color can then serve as the red between the shadow and the highlight, thus eliminating step 5.

For step 4, instead of using a brush, you can, if you prefer, use a dark pencil that will be compatible in color with your deep shadow. In working with a conventionally sharpened pencil, draw your hard edge with the point, then shade with the side of the lead. With a flat-cut pencil (Figure 12-11B), run the sharp edge along the crease to form a hard edge, then pull the pencil upward, away from the crease, to complete the shadow in the same manner that you would use a flat brush. In shading with your pencil, decrease the pressure of the pencil as you move away from the hard edge, then blend the edge with a clean brush to soften it.

Check your morgue and the various illustrations in this book for other types of eye pouches and for ideas on aging the eyes without the use of pouches.

Asian Eyes

Because Asian eyes require very special treatment, it will be more practical to consider them separately. An examination of photographs of Oriental eyes will show that they are occasionally quite slanted (Figure 10-5Q) and sometimes not slanted at all (Figures 12-17U and 12-35D).

The lid itself ordinarily disappears completely under a fold of flesh that is really an extension of planes A, B, and C in Figure 12-14. (See Figure 12-19A.) This fold overlaps the lower lid slightly at the tear duct (Figure 12-19B). It is this *epicanthic fold* that is particularly characteristic of people of Asian descent. Sometimes there is also an overlap at the outer corner of the eye (Figure 12-19C).

One of the most striking characteristics of Asian eyes is the flatness of the orbital area. Because the eye itself is prominent and the bridge of the nose is not built up, the dip between the two (plane A) is likely to be relatively slight (Figure 12-19D).

If the Asian eye is to be achieved with paint alone, it is usually necessary to highlight the entire orbital area, and especially plane A, in order to bring the eye forward and counteract the natural shadows. Sometimes there is a slightly puffy effect in plane E (Figure 12-19E). If you wish to create this effect you can model it as a pouch or as a transverse wrinkle with the usual shadow and highlight.

In addition to the highlighting, two small shadows are necessary. One is a crescent-shaped shadow at the tear duct, which gives the illusion of the epicanthic fold. This shadow must be precisely placed, as shown in Figure 12-13E. The second shadow is placed on the outer third of the upper lid and may extend very little beyond

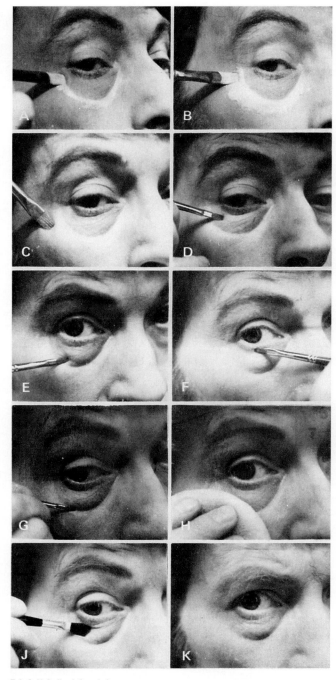

FIGURE 12-18 Modeling a deep eye pouch.
A. Outlining pouch with highlighting, using medium brush. B. Widening highlight by pulling paint away from hard edge. C. Softening outer edge of highlight with clean brush. D. Highlighting top of pouch with small brush. E. Shadowing bottom of pouch with medium shadow. F. Shadowing lower lid with medium shadow. G. Deepening bottom edge of pouch with very dark shadow. H. Powdering pouch. J. Adding dry rouge with soft eyeshadow brush. K. Finished pouch, after stippling. Stippling is used here primarily to add texture.

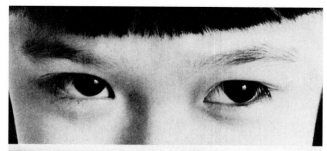

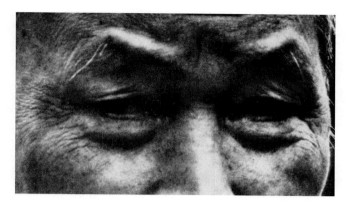

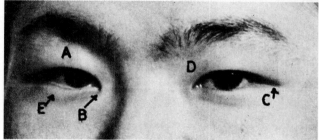

FIGURE 12-19 Asian eyes. *B is the epicanthic fold.*

FIGURE 12-20 Eyes of an elderly Chinese.

the eye. For women who would be using makeup, a slight upward curve to this shadow is often effective.

The eyebrows normally are slanted slightly upward or are rather short and relatively straight. Instead of following the eye downward in a curve, as is usual for youthful brows in Caucasians (Figure 12-13A), Asian brows may taper off quite abruptly at the ends (Figure 12-13E). There are, however, variations. (See Figures 10-5Q, and 12-19.) For aged Asian eyes, see Figure 12-20.

For Caucasian eyes that do not adapt easily to this painting technique, three-dimensional makeup (Chapter 13) may be required.

Asians who wish to play Caucasians can shadow plane A, simulate a tear duct with makeup, using a touch of red for the mucous membrane, and extend their eyebrows downward (Figure 12-74B). They may or may not find it necessary to highlight planes B and C and shadow the division between them. Slanting eyes, unless they are very pronounced, are not always a problem, for Caucasian eyes are sometimes slanted. But if they are a problem, the slant can be counteracted to some extent by bringing the shadow at the outer corner of the eye downward instead of upward.

Eyebrows

Changing the eyebrows for corrective makeup has been dealt with in Chapter 10. But besides having the potential for making the face more attractive, eyebrows provide a particularly useful means of characterization. Figure 12-13 illustrates a few such changes that can be

made with an eyebrow pencil, paint, and an eyebrow brush in order to age the eye as well as to suggest character. (See also Figure 12-21.)

But using the eyebrows to suggest character can be just as important in makeups for youth as for age. Figure 6-6A, for example, shows a straight (not a corrective) makeup with no changes for character. In B and C the eyebrows and the eyeshadowing have been changed—not to improve the face or to age it but to create a look more appropriate for a specific character. In this case, the principles of optical illusions for making eyes appear farther apart and closer together (see Figure 10-3) have been used. Note how the general look of the face has been altered as a result of this relatively simple change. And note also what character impressions each change creates.

In determining what you want to do with the eyebrows for characters of any age, it's a good idea to manipulate the natural eyebrows with your fingers, as previously suggested in Chapter 10 and illustrated in Figure 12-22, in order to help determine the effect on the face of different eyebrow shapes and positions. Unless your eyebrows (or those of your subject) are unusually adaptable, you might do well to add hair to them, cover them completely with additional hair, or block them out (Figure 12-23) by one of the methods suggested below or others you may devise. If part of the natural brow can be used, you may prefer to block out only the part that needs to be eliminated, as was done in Figure 12-13E, for example.

In blocking out the brows, the problem is twofold—to flatten the hairs against the skin so that they will stay down for the duration of the performance and to cover the flattened hairs by some method that will conceal their color, using a flesh tone to match the rest of the skin.

Blocking Out with Soap
In soaping, rub a moistened bar of soap repeatedly over the brows, which must be free of grease, until they are flattened down (Figure 12-24A.) In flattening the brows, spread the

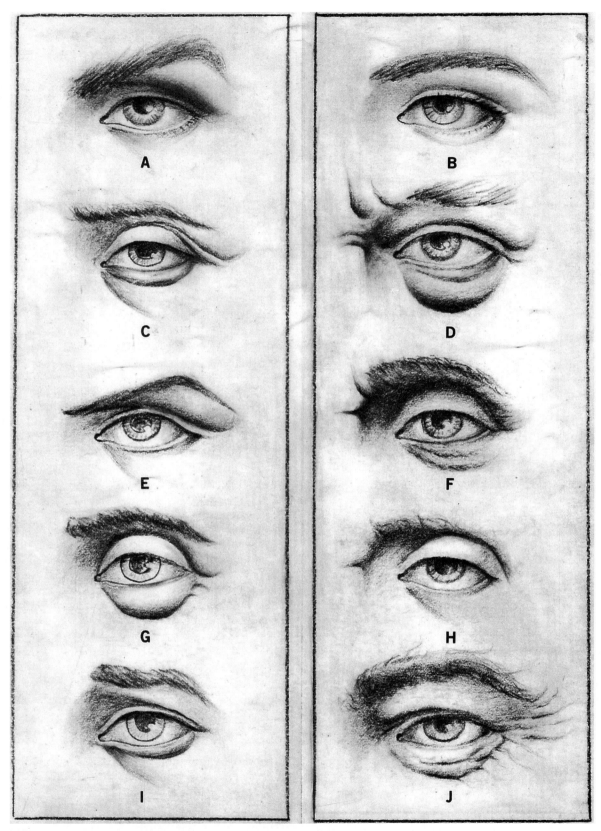

FIGURE 12-21 **Changing the eye.** *Ten sketches of possible makeups for the same eye. All of the changes can be made by blocking out all or part of the eyebrow in A and creating a new brow and by remodeling the eye area with highlights and shadows.*

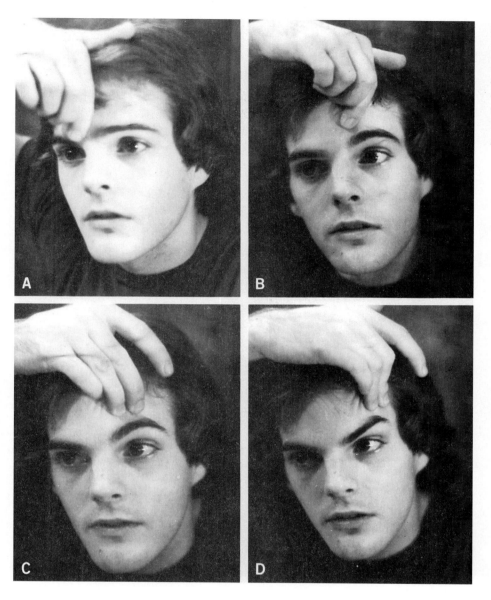

FIGURE 12-22 Manipulating the natural eyebrow before beginning the makeup. *A simple method of selecting the most appropriate shape and position of the eyebrows for the character. (Demonstrated by actor Jeffrey Hillock.)*

FIGURE 12-23 Sixteenth-century lady. *Eyebrows blocked out. Putty-wax nose. Makeup by student Carolyn Bain.*

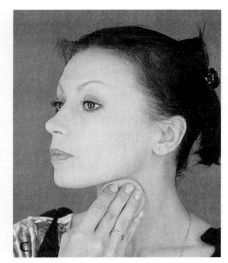

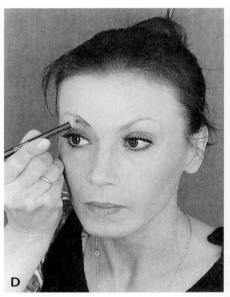

FIGURE 12-24 **Partially blocking out eyebrows** *Makeup by Inga Loujerenko, principle ballerina, Ballet Austin. A. Both ends of the brows have been flattened with soap, then covered with sealer. B. Creme makeup is applied. C. Then powdered. D. New eyebrows are sketched on with a brown eyebrow pencil. E. Finished makeup. For a complete step-by-step application of ballet makeup see color section.*

hairs with a fine-tooth comb, as shown in Figure 12-26B. When they are dry, cover them with creme foundation or with rubber-mask grease. Make very sure that you blend the paint carefully into the skin at the edge to prevent the outline of the brows from becoming obvious when the makeup is finished. Then press powder into the paint and remove the excess with a powder brush. If the brows still show through, add alternate layers of paint and powder until they are effectively blocked out. If the brows are heavy, one or more coats of plastic sealer can be applied over the dried soap. For firm adhesion, be sure to spread the sealer beyond the soaped area. Apply the makeup over the dried sealer. Unless the brows are very light, soaping is probably the least satisfactory method of covering them, since with this method the hairs are more likely to loosen during a performance, allowing the brows to become visible. The brows in Figure 20-3 have been soaped out.

Blocking Out with Spirit Gum

A more effective method than soaping is to flatten the hairs with spirit gum. Brush the gum well into the brows, comb the hairs upward at an angle onto the forehead, then when the gum is very tacky, press the brows down with a damp cloth so that they will lie flat and give as smooth a surface as possible. When the spirit gum is dry, it should be covered with sealer in order to keep the paint from loosening the gum. Rubber mask grease, greasepaint, or creme stick can then be stippled over the brow, using more than one coat if necessary. Cake makeup should not be used; it will not adhere properly to sealer.

The spirit gum can be removed with alcohol or spirit-gum remover or, if necessary, with acetone. Be very careful, however, not to let the liquid run down into the eyes. The safest procedure is to dampen cotton or a cloth with the remover, then bend over so that the eyebrow is lower than the eye *before* removing the spirit gum. Or you can use a makeup remover that will remove both makeup and spirit gum. (See *Makeup removers* in Appendix A.)

Blocking Out with Wax

You can also mat the brows down with derma wax or, preferably, with Kryolan's stick of Eyebrow Plastic (Figure 12-26A), blending the wax carefully into the skin at the edges, then covering it with one or two coats of sealer. If the brows are very heavy, it may help if you flatten them with spirit gum and let it dry before applying the wax, in order to help keep the wax from loosening. In flattening them, spread the hairs with a comb (Figure 12-26B). After the sealer over the wax is dry, makeup can be applied. Rubber-mask greasepaint gives the best coverage.

Blocking Out with Plastic Film

Eyebrows can also be blocked out by covering them with plastic film (see Appendix A). These are the steps involved:

1. Prepare the plastic film by painting liquid plastic (see Appendix A) on glass (Figure 12-25A) or any smooth surface, such as formica, that will not be affected by the plastic, or on the outside of a grapefruit (Figure 12-25C), an orange, or even a large lemon. For eyebrow covers, the fruit is preferable since it gives a simulated skin texture. The plastic can be applied with a brush (Figure 12-25A), an orangewood stick (Figure 12-25C), or a glass rod. Using a rod or an orangewood stick saves cleaning the brush. Three coats of the plastic should be sufficient. Each coat should be thoroughly dry before another coat is applied. In order to avoid trimming, paint the plastic on the glass or the fruit in the shape and size required to cover the eyebrow, overlapping it all around.

2. When the plastic is dry, powder it, then lift one end with tweezers or a fingernail. Powder the underside as you pull it up (Figure 12-25B and D).

3. Cover the eyebrow with eyebrow paste, derma wax, or spirit gum (Figure 12-26A). Then comb the brow upward (Figure 12-26B), spread the hairs, and press them flat against the skin.

4. Press powder into the flattened brows (Figure 12-26C). If the brows are dark, it may be helpful to stipple the brows with a little makeup. Confine the makeup to the brows, and keep it off the surrounding skin. If grease or creme makeup has been used for this stippling, powder again.

5. Apply spirit gum to the skin around the brow (Figure 12-26D) or to the plastic piece, then very carefully lay the plastic piece over the brow (Figure 12-26E), making sure there are no wrinkles or rippling of the edges. Press the plastic down firmly with a damp sponge.

6. Using a small brush dipped in acetone, go over the edges of the plastic (Figure 12-26F) in order to dissolve them and blend the plastic into the skin. (If you are going to apply three-dimensional eyebrows—

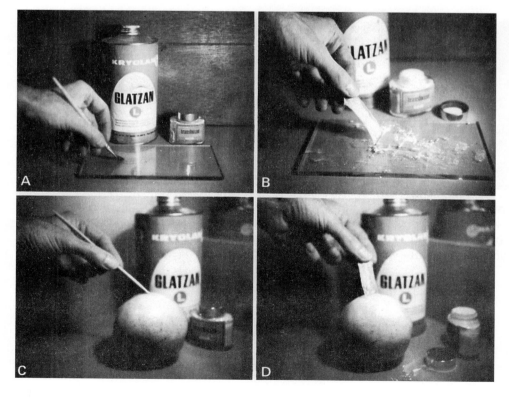

FIGURE 12-25 Making plastic film for covering eyebrows. *A. Painting liquid plastic on glass. B. Removing dry and powdered film. C. Spreading liquid plastic on grapefruit. D. Removing dry and powdered film.*

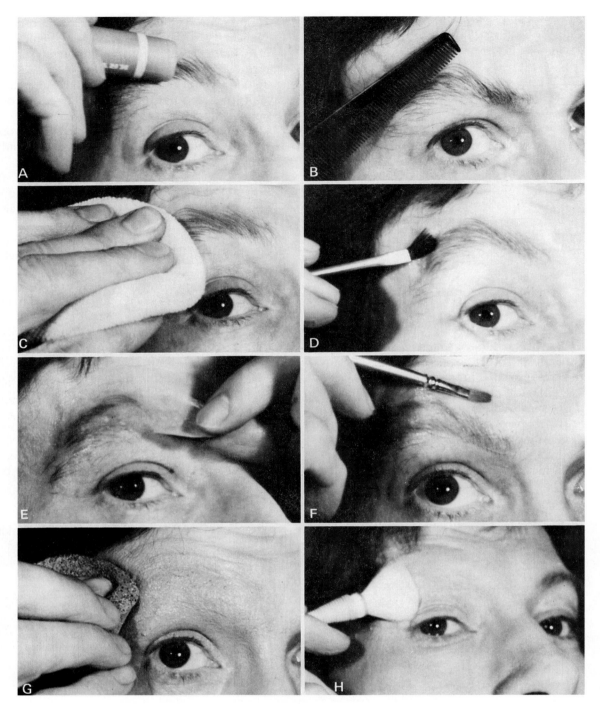

FIGURE 12-26 **Blocking out eyebrow with plastic film.** *A. Covering brow with Kryolan's Eyebrow Plastic. B. Combing hair upward to flatten it. C. Pressing powder into the flattened brow. D. Painting spirit gum around eyebrow. E. Covering eyebrow with plastic film. F. Dissolving edges of plastic film with acetone for blending. G. Stippling rubber-mask grease over brow area. H. Dusting powder off blocked-out brow.*

crepe hair or real hair ventilated on lace–it should be done at this point.)

7. Stipple your makeup (rubber-mask greasepaint gives the best coverage) over the plastic and onto the skin area around it (Figure 12-26G), then powder, pressing the powder into the makeup with a puff. Remove the excess powder with a powder brush (Figure 12-26H). If the makeup is not covering adequately, stipple on more makeup, then powder again.

Painted Eyebrows
In addition to coloring the natural brows and filling out and reshaping them with pencil, it is possible to pencil or paint certain types of eyebrows over natural brows that have been blocked out (See Figures 12-23, 12-24). If the penciling is to give the illusion of natural hairs, it should be carefully done with short, light, sketchy strokes in order to avoid a flat, painted look.

Crepe-Hair Eyebrows
Crepe hair can be added to the natural brows or applied over brows that have already been blocked out. When using hair to fill out the natural brows, add a few hairs at a time, touching the ends with spirit gum and putting them in place with a pair of tweezers. The added hairs can be trimmed after the spirit gum has dried.

When the brows are to be blocked out with spirit gum, crepe hair can be attached to the whole spirit-gummed brow or to any part of it while the gum is still tacky. In fact, if any part of the natural brow is to be covered by a false brow of at least equal thickness, it is usually best to attach the crepe hair, a few hairs at a time, directly to the gummed area rather than to apply the whole false brow over a blocked-out one. The makeup to cover any exposed part of the natural brow can be applied after the false brow is securely in place.

For natural-looking crepe-hair eyebrows, it is usually best to mix at least two colors. If you want the hair to have a natural sheen, you can apply a small amount of brilliantine, hair dressing, petroleum jelly, or even cold cream to the surface of the brows. If you want smooth, neat-looking brows, comb very carefully, pull out loose hairs, and trim away scraggly ones. Further instructions for using crepe hair can be found in Chapter 15.

Ventilated Eyebrows
When false eyebrows are to be used for a number of performances, real or synthetic hair ventilated on lace is more satisfactory than crepe hair. Instructions for ventilating are given in Chapter 16.

Aging the Eyebrows
In aging the eyebrows, first decide exactly what effect you want, then determine how that can best be achieved. The brows may take a variety of forms. They may be sparse (Figure 12-17E and K), irregular (Figure 12-16K), bushy (Figure 12-16E), or overhanging (Figure 12-16L). They may be wide (Figure 12-17D), narrow (Figure 12-17M), thick (Figure 12-17D), or thin (Figure 12-17K). But in suggesting age they should never look plucked unless that is really appropriate for the character.

Eyebrows can be aged quickly, when that is necessary, by running a white stick liner, white creme stick, or stick hair whitener through them against the direction of hair growth (Figure 12-13B). This can also be done with clown white, cake makeup, white mascara, or shoe polish (not recommended)

Area 3: Nose

If the nose tends to flatten out under lights or if it is to be altered in appearance for either corrective or character requirements, it will need a certain amount of remodeling. The nose area has seven planes (Figure 12-25).

PLANE A is the very small depression usually found, except in the classic nose, between the superciliary arch and the nose. It is shadowed for age and usually contains one to three vertical wrinkles (Figures 12-16A and D, and 12-42H). The two appearing at the inner ends of the eyebrows have their inception in plane A of the eye socket (area 2) and usually become narrower as they continue upward (Figure 12-37). The center wrinkle may be narrow at both ends and wider in the middle. These are the frowning wrinkles and if made rather deep, they will lend severity to the facial expression. Like all facial wrinkles, they should follow the actor's natural ones if there are any. Painted wrinkles must never conflict with an actor's natural wrinkles–including those that appear when the actor smiles or frowns.

PLANE B is the prominent part of the nose and is highlighted both in indicating age and in sharpening and narrowing the nose. If the nose is too long, the lower end of the plane can be left the base color or lightly shadowed (Figure 12-29B) as indicated for corrective makeup. The width of the highlight will largely determine the apparent width of the nose. (See Figure 12-29.) If the nose is too sharp and needs to be broadened or flattened, plane B can be left the base color or

FIGURE 12-27 **Planes of the nose.**

lightly shadowed. If the tip is to be broadened or rounded slightly without the use of prosthesis, it can be done by rounding and broadening the highlight (Figure 12-29A). Applying and blending the highlight on plane B is illustrated in Figure 12-28A and B.

The effect of a broken nose can be achieved by giving the illusion of a crook or a curve in plane B. (See Figures 12-29D, 12-30.) This is done by using not only a crooked or a curved highlight to reshape plane B but also shadows to counteract the natural highlights on those parts of plane B which should not be prominent on the crooked or broken nose. In Figure 12-30, for example, A represents a normal nose, and B, C, and D show three possible shapes which could be created by the application of highlights and shadows to the nose in A.

Once you have decided on the shape you want, this is the procedure:

1. Using a flat shading brush of the width the highlighted area is to be, paint a strong highlight on plane B to create the shape you want for the new nose. Drawings B, C, and D in Figure 12-30 are diagrammatic representations of two possible broken or crooked noses which could be created with highlights and shadows on the nose in drawing A. Note that in neither case does the highlight extend beyond plane B into plane C. Any extension of the highlight onto the sides of the nose (plane C) would result in part of the highlight's disappearing whenever the head was turned at more than a very slight

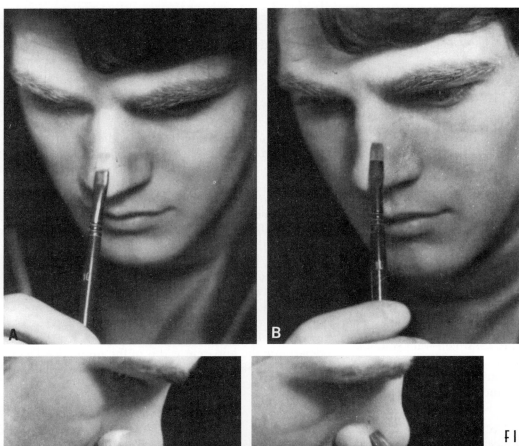

FIGURE 12-28
Highlighting the nose.
(Actor Eugene Bicknell.)
A. Highlighting plane B with a medium brush. B. Blending the edges of the highlight with a clean brush. C. Highlighting the nostrils with a medium brush. D. Blending the highlight with a clean brush.

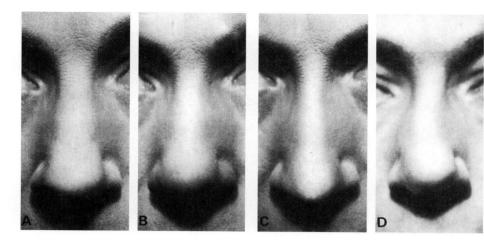

FIGURE 12-29 **Remodeling the nose with paint.** *A. Wide. B. Shortened. C. Long and thin. D. Crooked.*

angle. The edges of the highlight should, of course, be slightly softened.

2. The three shaded areas in Figure 12-30B and D and the two in C show the correct placement of the shadows for the noses illustrated. The purpose of the shadows is to counteract those natural highlights which would destroy the illusion of the crooked nose. In other words, the shadowed areas are supposed to look as though they are part of the side of the nose. To work effectively they must be fairly dark and be confined to plane B. They must not extend into plane C. Since any part that did extend into plane C would not be receiving as much light as the part on plane B, the part that extended would seem darker than the rest of the shadow and would tend to destroy the illusion. All edges of the shadow should be softened and blended into the highlight on one side and into the foundation on the other. To check the effectiveness of the illusion, look at the nose in a mirror with a spotlight on the face from at least several feet away. This particular illusion should always be checked at a distance–in a spotlight, if possible–to determine how effective it really is.

3. Unless you are using a water-base makeup, powder the nose, making certain that the shadows do not shine. If they do, the illusion will be destroyed. And keep checking from time to time throughout the performance. A real broken nose can be straightened by reversing this procedure, as explained in Chapter 10.

PLANE C is nearly always shadowed for age. For realistic makeups, the edges between planes B and C, as well as the outer edges of plane C, must always be soft. If the nose tends to flatten out under light, as it sometimes does in youthful makeups, plane C can be subtly shadowed to give the nose greater depth.

PLANE D may be shadowed with plane C, especially if the nares are too wide, but usually a highlight on the upper part of the nare, as in Figure 12-28D, will give the nose more form. To widen the nares, highlight plane D (see Figure 12-28C and D). To make the nostrils appear larger, outline them with a black eyebrow pencil. (See Figure 12-31.)

PLANE E is usually shadowed for age, but the fact that it receives only reflected light from the floor and sometimes a little from the footlights, if there are any, means that it is automatically in natural shadow. Carrying the highlight from plane B down into E will give the nose a droopy effect.

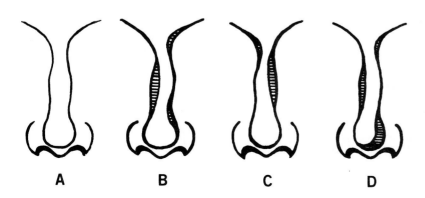

FIGURE 12-30 **Placement of highlights and shadows for crooked noses.** *A. Normal nose. B., C., and D. Crooked noses. The shaded areas show the placement of shadows: the unshaded areas would be highlighted.*

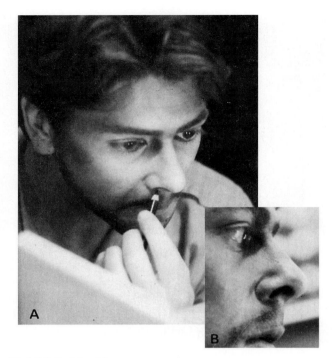

FIGURE 12-31 **Enlarging the nostrils.** *A. Enlarging nostrils with a black eyebrow pencil. B. Closeup of enlarged nostril. (Actor Kristoffer Tabori.)*

Area 4: Cheeks

The use of rouge for cheeks and lips will depend on the natural skin pigmentation and on whether natural or artificial coloring is being represented. For creating natural coloring in the cheeks for youth, avoid rouges that are either too purple or too orange. The lighter values are easier to control than the deeper ones. The SR, RS, S, and FS shades from 6 to 12 (*a, b,* and sometimes *c* or *d* intensity) are useful for light-skinned women, and RS10-d, RS-11-b, FS-9-b, or similar shades are effective for light-skinned men. Dark-skinned female performers will often choose a rouge color of high intensity that is not too blue or too orange (this often depends upon the color of the costume). While subtle shades may be appropriate for print work and on film, they will simply dissappear on stage. The R, SR, RS, and S shades from 12 to 16 and all in *b* intensity should be appropriate. Study people to determine the natural placement. There is a great deal of variation. Rouge may be high or low, near the ear or near the nose, confined to a small area, or spread over most of the cheek. Note also other areas of the face—such as nose, forehead, and chin—that may show some color. For all performers, a touch of rouge in these areas can increase the realism of the makeup.

In representing street makeup, ask yourself what color the character might choose, how much she would use, and where she would place it. Would she follow the fashions or be ultraconservative? Might she use too much or none at all? Would she apply it carefully or carelessly? Might she notice whether it clashed with her dress, or wouldn't she care?

In other words, the problem of the addition of artificial coloring should be considered from the point of view of the character, since it is, after all, a choice over which she (or sometimes he) presumably has control. But remember one thing above all—if a character would not be wearing makeup, it is your responsibility to not let her look as if she is.

Modeling As you have already discovered in the study of facial anatomy, the cheekbone (Figure 12-33) is rounded, so that when light is coming from above (the usual assumption in makeup for the stage), the upper part of the bone receives strong light, whereas the lower part, which curves downward and inward, does not receive direct light and therefore appears considerably darker. This means that in modeling the cheeks for age or to achieve the effect of prominent cheekbones in youth, the cheekbone should be highlighted and the hollow below it shadowed. (See Figure 12-35E.) The following is a step-by-step procedure for modeling the cheekbone:

1. First, prod the bone (as you have done before in the study of anatomy) in order to find the underside of the bone that curves back in and does not receive direct light. Then, with a medium or a medium-wide brush, lay on a strip of highlight along the top of the bone (Figure 12-34A), making sure that it is actually on top of the bone, where light from above would hit most strongly, and not on the side of the bone, which would be strongly highlighted only if light were coming from the side. With a clean brush, blend the upper edge out so that it disappears into the foundation, and very carefully soften the lower edge as if you were modeling a cylinder.
2. With a medium or a medium-wide brush, lay on the shadow color along the lower half of the cheek-

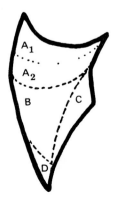

FIGURE 12-32 **Planes of the cheek.**

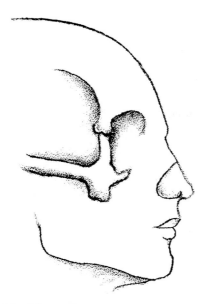

FIGURE 12-33 Cheekbone.

FIGURE 12-34 **Highlighting the cheekbone.**
(Actor Eugene Bicknell.) A. Applying the highlight to the top of the cheekbone with a wide brush. B. Blending the edges of the highlight with a clean brush.

bone, (Figure 12-34), taking care to leave a space between the shadow and the highlight above.

3. With a clean brush, soften the lower edge of the shadow, which should now blend into plane B of the diagram in Figure 12-32. Then very carefully soften the upper edge of the shadow so that there is a gradual transition from the light (A_1) to the dark (A_2). Avoid a definite line between the two.

4. Natural modeling of the cheeks for a woman can be accomplished by the careful placement of a dry or creme rouge in a lower value or of a higher intensity than the foundation just under the cheekbone. This will serve to add color to the cheek and contour to the face. Adding a brown contour, if not carefully blended, can often make the face appear dirty.

How much the cheek sinks in and how prominent the bone is will depend on the intensity of the highlight and the shadow. For youthful makeups the contrast may be fairly subtle. For age makeups it may be relatively strong.

The treatment of plane B varies considerably with individuals. The area just below the cheekbone usually catches a little light (Figure 12-35E), and the bottom of that area will, of course, be in shadow as it curves around the jawbone. But in between, various things may happen. Study some of the faces in Figure 12-35 and in your own morgue. Then analyze your own face, or the one you're working on, in order to determine what treatment is likely to work best, making sure it is suitable for the character. If it isn't, you may have to compromise between the ideal cheek you have in mind and the specific potential of the face you're making up.

Placed just under the cheekbone, cheek color can also perform as contour shading when the color is lower in value or of a higher intensity than the foundation.

Nasolabial Folds

Plane C includes the nasolabial folds–the wrinkles running from either side of the nose downward to the mouth. These folds vary considerably in form and development. (See Figures 12-35, 12-36.) Each one has one hard edge and one soft edge. Wherever there is a crease in the flesh, as there is in the nasolabial fold, a hard edge is automatically formed (Figure 12-37E). Outward from this crease, the shadow lightens (Figure 12-37B) and turns gradually into a highlight as the crest of the fold is reached (Figure 12-37A, A'). Here is one possible technique of application:

1. With a medium or a medium-wide flat brush, starting near the inner corner of the eye, bring a stripe of highlight down along the fleshy area between the nose and the cheekbone (see Figure 12-38A). The upper edge of the highlight, falling along part of plane F_2 (Figure 12-14) of the orbital area, should be kept fairly hard. The width and the conformation of this highlight will depend, of course, on the type of nasolabial fold you have in mind, which must, in turn, be related to the face of which it is a part. If the fold is to be full at the nostril and taper off into nothing near the mouth, the highlight will follow a similar pattern. It will become not only narrower and closer to the crease as it moves downward but also less strong so that at its lower end it may simply disappear into the foundation. This can be done in a single stroke by twisting your brush as you go down in order to narrow the stripe and also by using less and less pressure. Other types of nasolabial folds will, of course, require different conformations of the highlight. These you can work out through observation and experimentation.

FIGURE 12-35 Cheeks and nasolabial folds.

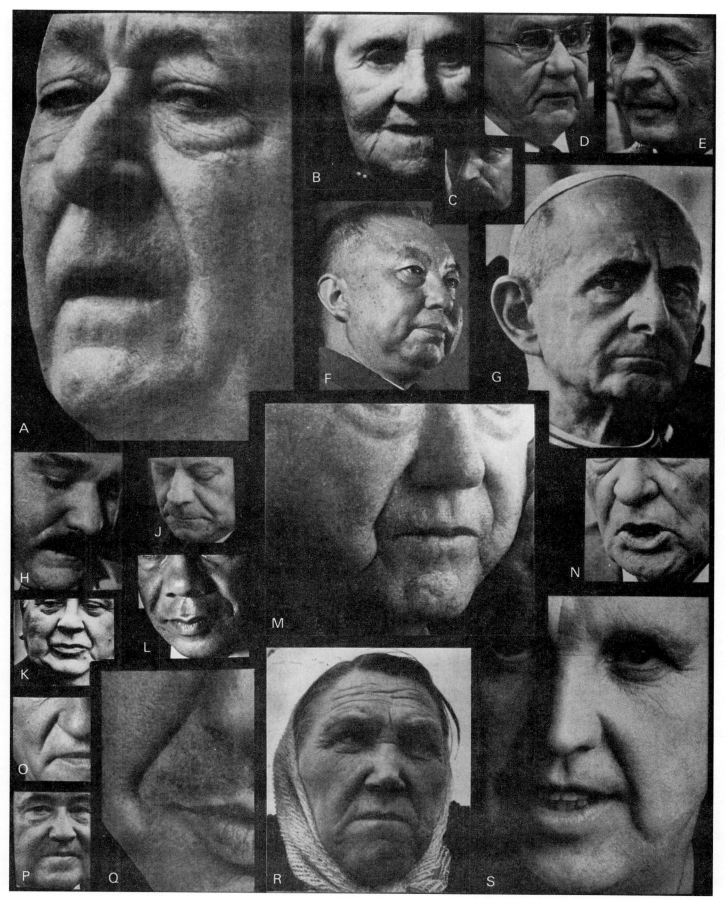

FIGURE 12-36 Cheeks and nasolabial folds.

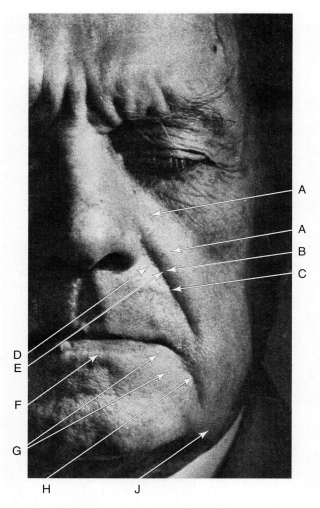

FIGURE 12-37 Placement of highlights and shadows for age. *(See text.)*

the nare and end near the mouth. Make sure that the outer edge of the stripe coincides exactly with the crease and does not overlap it. This is your hard edge, and it must be kept sharp and crisp.

4. Starting with a clean brush at the top of the crease, pull the brush away from the crease, this time letting the highlight fade out as it leaves the crease (Figure 12-38D). Repeat this movement until you have gone the entire length of the crease.

5. Repeat the same horizontal strokes once more (Figure 12-38E), this time fading the highlight imperceptibly before it reaches the center of the lip. Additional strokes can be made for proper blending.

NOTE: If you chose to begin your fold with step 3 instead of step 1, steps 1 and 2 should be done now.

6. Using a medium flat brush held at right angles to the crease, with the ends of the bristles butting against it (the same way as in step 1, but from the opposite direction), paint in a narrow arching stripe of medium shadow color (Figure 12-38F), tapering it as you go down. The lower end should fade away into nothing. The inside edge of this stripe must follow exactly the hard edge of the highlight, barely touching it but never overlapping it. (Instead of a shadow color here, you may wish to substitute red, carrying it out farther beyond the crease than you would the shadow, as was suggested in the instructions for modeling eye pouches. If you do this, the deep shadow—step 7—will be somewhat wider than indicated in the instructions.)

7. With a clean, narrow brush, soften the outside edge of the stripe by pulling it away from the crease (Figure 12-38G) so that it blends imperceptibly into the foundation. There should be just a little of the foundation color showing as a middle tone between the highlight and the shadow. Wipe your brush and soften the outside edge of the shadow by overlapping it with the brush, held parallel to the crease (see Figure 12-38H), and moving the brush downward the entire length of the shadow.

8. With your narrowest flat brush and a deep shadow color, go over the hard inside edge of the medium shadow, fading it out at the bottom. (This is a repetition of step 6, using a deeper shadow color and a narrower brush.)

9. Wipe your brush and, barely touching the outer edge of the deep shadow, soften it along its entire length. (This is a repetition of the technique in step 7 but without carrying the shadow so far from the crease.) (If you have used red instead of a medium shadow for step 4, you will need to make this deep shadow wider.) You should now have a sharp, clean edge with a strong contrast between light and dark.

10. In order to give the fold an even more three-dimensional effect, extend a touch of light or medium shadow downward from the eye pouch along the

2. With a clean brush, blend the lower inside edge of the highlight (see Figure 12-38B) and the part of the upper outside edge which does not fall alongside plane F_2 of the orbital area.

NOTE: You may prefer to begin your nasolabial fold with step 3 instead of step 1, in which case steps 1 and 2 should be done following step 5.

3. Begin by smiling into the mirror to locate the crease of the fold on your own face. Relax the smile. With the edge of the flat medium brush, pick up a small amount of highlight. Remember to regularly sharpen or flatten the tip of your brush by lightly drawing the edge across the makeup, mixing palette, or the back of your hand, first on one side then the other. Now, while holding the brush at right angles to the natural crease in the skin and the ends of the bristles butting up against the crease, as in Figure 12-38C, paint a fine arching line downward along the crease, leaving a narrow stripe of strong highlight. It should begin along the side of

FIGURE 12-38 Modeling a nasolabial fold. *(Actor Eugene Bicknell.) A. Highlighting the top of the fold with a medium brush. B. Blending the lower edge of the highlight. C. Making a hard edge along the crease with an extra-wide brush. D. Pulling the highlight away from the crease. E. Blending the highlight into the foundation. F. Applying a medium shadow along the crease. G. Pulling the shadow away from the crease. H. Blending the outer edge of the shadow. Steps F, G, and H have been repeated with a deep shadow, which has been kept narrower than the medium shadow.*

highlight. Observe this shadow in Figure 12-35A, for example.

11. If the fold seems well modeled but too strong, stipple it with your foundation color or with any other color or colors you think would be helpful. (See Chapter 11.) Be very careful to avoid overstippling and, as a result, losing the three-dimensional quality of your fold.

12. Unless the character the actor is playing is to be very sickly—some red should be added to the fold. There may be only a little, or there may be a great deal. Observe people for amount and placement. The red can be applied after powdering by brushing on dry rouge or by stippling on creme rouge with a black stipple sponge. If you are also stippling with other colors, you can add the red at the same time. However, after the stipple is powdered, you can still add additional red, if you want to, by brushing with dry rouge.

The preceding instructions are intended for one specific form of nasolabial fold but can easily be adapted to other forms—narrow at the top and wider at the bottom (Figure 12-35F), narrow at the top and bottom and wider in the middle (Figure 12-36L), short (Figure 12-35K), full and puffy (Figures 12-35A and 12-36F), or long and sharply defined and sometimes joined to other wrinkles (Figure 12-35G). For folds which curve outward at the bottom and form what are usually called apple cheeks, see the discussion following.

Apple Cheeks

The term as used here refers not to enormous fat cheeks, no matter how apple-like they may be, but to a nasolabial fold that spreads out and turns into a ball of flesh centered around the knob of the cheekbone. (See Figure 12-35I.) The nasolabial fold begins as usual, sharp and clear, but very narrow at the top and widening as it goes down. As the fold turns outward, the crease disappears and the shadow becomes quite wide, so that in essence you are painting a small sphere. In fact, one of the best ways of beginning the apple cheek is to smile as broadly as possible, then place a spot of highlight on the most prominent part of the round fleshy area that is formed. This highlight will usually be centered on the ball of the cheekbone under the eye. Then, using a wide brush and a medium shadow, paint in the shadow area as if you were modeling a sphere. Starting with the brush in the crease of the nasolabial fold, sweep down from the nostril, following the natural crease until it turns toward the chin. Then move away from the nose, around the ball of the cheek, and into the shadow under the cheekbone. This will give you a very narrow shadow at the beginning and a wide one on the lower part of the "apple." The top edge of this shadow should be very soft and fade imperceptibly into the foundation. The bottom edge gradually softens as it moves away from the nose. (See Figures 12-39 and 12-58B.)

Apple cheeks will look more apple-like with a generous touch of rouge. They are not invariably red, but more often than not there is some color. The red can ei-

FIGURE 12-39 Apple cheeks.
A. Student Joe Allen Brown. (For other makeups by the same student, see Figures 12-3B, 12-71, and 20-2.) B. Student Clista Towne-Strother. (Compare with Figure 12-75.)

ther be substituted for the medium shadow or be brushed on with dry rouge after the modeling has been completed and powdered. Stippling can also be used to redden the cheeks, provided you also want to add texture. In applying dry rouge, start at the nostril and brush downward and outward, following the form of the sphere but usually keeping the stronger color near the nose. You may want a little rouge on the nose as well.

Jawline

Plane D of area 4 is the mandible, or jawbone. One of the most effective ways of adding age to the youthful face is to create the illusion of sagging jowls. The correct placement of the jowls can usually be determined by gently squeezing the flesh of the jaw between the fingers to see where it creases naturally or by pulling back the chin and turning the head in various ways until creases or bulges appear. (See Figure 17-5B.) It is also possible to estimate the usual position from photographs in Figures 12-36G, 12-35E and K, and 12-42.

The point at which the front and back areas of sagging flesh meet can nearly always be located by pressing the thumb or a finger upward somewhat beyond the

FIGURE 12-40 **Highlighting crease in cheek.** *The highlight is being applied along a natural crease created when the actor smiles. (Actor Eugene Bicknell.)*

middle of the jaw until you locate an indentation in the bone. This will be the correct point for ending the front sag and beginning the back one.

There are too many possible variations in jaws and sagging muscles at the jawline to make it possible to give precise instructions for modeling that will fit every case, but general principles can be adapted and applied to individual faces. In any case, this is the procedure for modeling one particular kind of jowl:

1. Using a wide brush, sweep the highlight color down from the ear, around the curve in the jawbone, then up (see Figure 12-43A). This upward curve will take place at the indentation in the jawbone described above. Then sweep the brush in another wide arc along the lower part of the jawbone, leaving a small triangle of the foundation color showing at the point where the second arc begins. (See Figure 12-43B.) The second arc should end at the point you have already determined. A third and smaller arc starts at this point and then becomes part of the chin highlight. (See Figure 12-43B.)
2. Using a wide brush, fade the top edge of the highlight upward into the cheek area (Figure 12-43C).
3. Using a clean brush, soften the lower edge of the highlight. (See Figure 12-43D.)
4. Using a medium highlight, make two small triangles just below the two points at which the arcs of the jawline highlights meet. These triangles should have fairly hard edges along the two diagonal sides and a very soft edge along the bottom. Figure 12-43E and F shows the first triangle. Be sure to leave enough space to add a shadow between the main jawline highlights and the little triangles.
5. Using a medium-narrow brush (Figure 12-43G), paint a medium shadow beneath the large highlight and above the small triangular ones, touching the lower highlight but not the upper one. Because this represents the underside of the sagging flesh, which would normally be in shadow, it should be modeled like a cylinder with the upper edge fading into the highlight. The lower edge can be softened slightly with a clean narrow brush, or it can be left hard (see Figure 12-43H).
6. In order to increase the three-dimensional quality of the fold of flesh above the two triangles, darken the lower edge of the fold with a deep shadow color (Figure 12-43I), then soften the upper edges of this shadow with a clean brush. The lower edge can also be softened slightly but need not be. The jowls should now appear to be three-dimensional.
7. A more realistic effect can usually be achieved by adding a touch of rouge. (See Figure 12-43K.) This can be done after powdering by stippling with creme rouge or brushing on dry rouge.
8. Stipple with one or more colors, then powder. (See Figure 12-43L and M.)

FIGURE 12-41 Neck and jaw lines.

CHAPTER 12 : Modeling with Highlights and Shadows

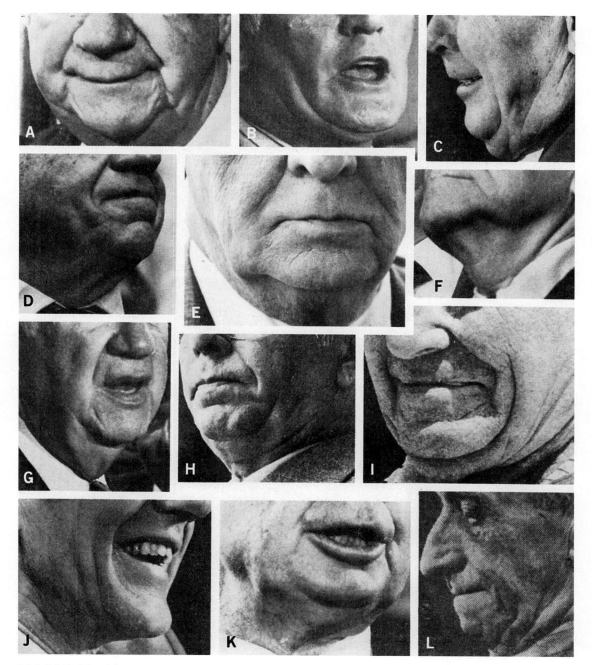

FIGURE 12-42 Jaw lines.

With some faces, there may be a deep vertical crease cutting up from the jawline across the cheek. This varies with the individual, but this is the basic technique:

1. With a medium-wide brush, sweep a highlight down from the upper plane of the chin to the bottom of the jawline, then back up in a small curve. (Figure 12-44A.) Blend both edges.
2. Locate any natural or potential crease in the flesh. This can usually be done either by squeezing the flesh together or by twisting the head around until

a crease forms. Note that with light coming from the front, the roll of flesh behind the crease will catch the light; highlight this area, as shown in Figure 12-44B. The lower part of the highlight should be rounded to give a sagging effect. The crease edge will, of course, be hard and the other edges soft.
3. With your highlight, make another sag (C) at the turn of the jawbone. Soften all edges.
4. Using a medium shadow, make an arc (D) under the first highlight, carrying it up along the crease (E). This crease edge will be hard, the others soft.

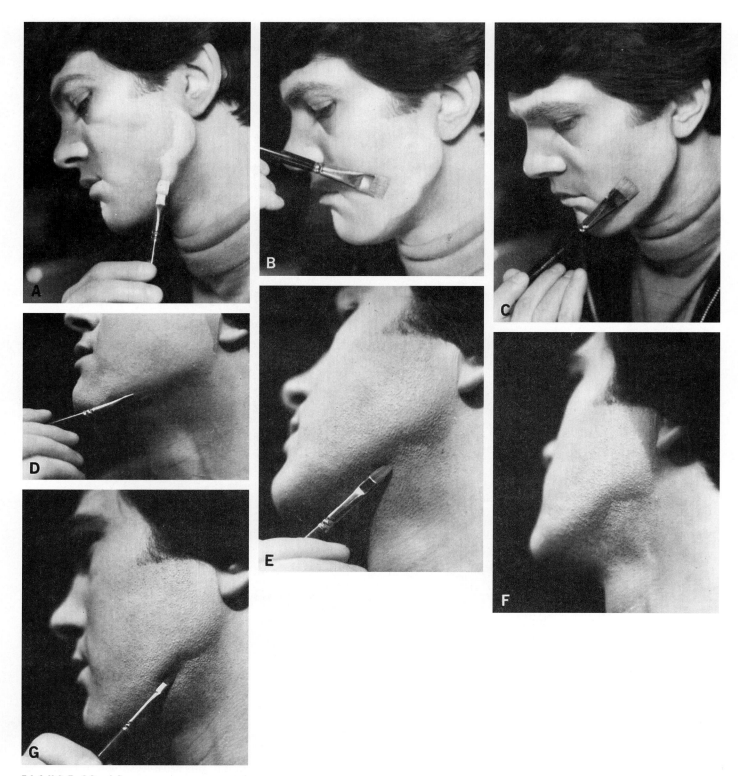

FIGURE 12-43 Modeling sagging jowls. *(Actor Eugene Bicknell.) A. Highlighting the jawbone with a wide brush. B. Blending the upper edge of the highlight. C. Using a clean, extra-wide brush for additional blending of the edges. D. Softening the lower edge of the highlight with a clean brush. E. Adding triangles of highlight with a medium brush. F. First of two triangles of highlight completed, with the bottom edge blended into the foundation. G. Adding a medium shadow, with a hard edge on the bottom where it meets the triangle of highlight, and a soft edge on the top, blending into the soft edge of the upper highlight. H. Medium shadow completed. I. Deepening the bottom edge of the shadow next to the lower highlights. J. Modeling completed. K. Adding dry rouge with a soft eyeshadow brush. L. Stippling the highlights and shadows. M. Completed jaw line.*

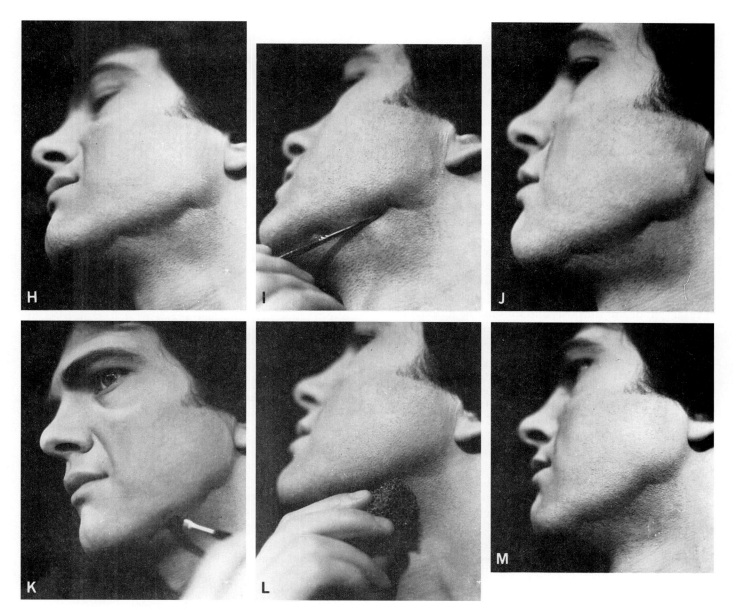

FIGURE 12-43 Continued.

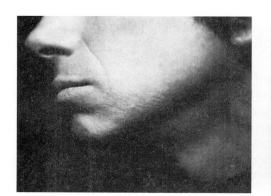

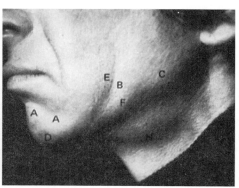

FIGURE 12-44 Aging the jawline.

Both shadow and highlight should fade out before reaching the cheekbone.

5. Add two more areas of shadow (F and G) under the two remaining highlight areas, softening the top edge. The bottom edge may be semi-hard or slightly softened. In the illustration (Figure 12-44) the area toward the chin is semi-hard, whereas farther back it is slightly softer. Note the very dark triangle of shadow just below the crease in area F. Sagging muscles in the neck (Figure 12-43H) can contribute to the effectiveness of the sagging jawline.

In aging the jawline, it is often helpful, especially with youthful actors, to work from within as well as without. A small bit of sponge (either foam rubber or natural silk) can be placed between the lower jaw and the cheek to make the cheek protrude. Absorbent cotton or cleansing tissues can also be used. Naturally, the sponge must be sanitary. A new sponge or a sponge that is reserved for this purpose, and for the one individual, should be used, and whether new or not, it should be sterilized before use. The exact size and shape can be determined by experimentation, starting with a slightly oversize piece and cutting it down. Once the pieces are cut to the right size, they can be preserved for future use. They should be thoroughly washed and dried after each wearing and kept in a tightly covered box or jar.

The actor may object at first to sponges in the mouth, but it is not difficult to adjust to them. They do not interfere with articulation or projection, though they may change the quality of the voice slightly.

For a greater effect of puffiness in the cheeks, as well as in the jowls (as for the aged Victoria, for example), a large piece of sponge or cotton can be used. It would be well to start with an entire small or medium-size sponge and then cut it down as much as necessary. The larger the sponge, of course, the more uncomfortable it is likely to be and the more difficulty it is likely to cause for the actor. If sponges are to be used at all, they must be used for a number of rehearsals to enable the actor to become accustomed to them. No actor can be expected to go through a dress rehearsal, let alone a performance, with a mouth unexpectedly full of sponges. Studying people and photographs of people and modeling sagging jaw lines in clay before modeling them in paint can be very helpful.

Area 5: Mouth and Chin

This area includes seven planes (Figure 12-45). When there are well-developed nasolabial folds, the outer edge of plane A is always hard (Figure 12-37E). The highlight (Figure 12-37D) decreases in intensity as it approaches plane B, which may or may not be shadowed.

Depending on the natural formation of the actor's upper lip, it is sometimes possible to model the areas A,

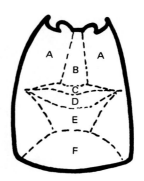

FIGURE 12-45 Planes of the upper and lower jaws.

B, and C in such a way that areas A and B appear to curve outward, with area C sinking in, as if the character had no upper teeth. This can be done by modeling the areas like a horizontal cylinder—strongly highlighting the upper part of areas A and B, then letting the highlight fade into a medium shadow on the lower part of A and B and into a deep shadow on area C.

Conversely, the upper lip can be made to seem to protrude by highlighting the lower part of plane A and fading the highlight upward into the foundation color as it approaches the nose.

The treatment given the lips for a specific character can be analyzed on the basis of color, size, shape, and texture.

Lip Color

In deciding on the color for the lips, determine first whether you are representing natural lips or painted ones. If natural, then choose a color that will look natural on stage. What that color is to be will probably depend on the character's age, race, sex, and state of health. In any case, it should relate to the color you have already chosen for the rouge, if any.

If the character's lips would be painted, the decision will be made in terms of what lip coloring she would choose to wear and how heavily she would apply it. Fashion may or may not be a factor; personal taste or lack of it certainly would be. Normally the lip coloring will match the rouge unless the character would be likely to mismatch them or unless the lips would be painted and the cheeks natural (in which case, the color might or might not match.) Lip makeup is usually applied with a flat sable brush.

Size of Lips

The size of the lips (both width and thickness) will depend to some extent on the actor's own lips and how much they can be changed. For a realistic makeup, a very narrow mouth, for example, cannot successfully be made into a very wide one, but a wide one can sometimes be narrowed. The techniques for changing the apparent size of the lips have already been discussed as part of corrective makeup in Chapter 10.

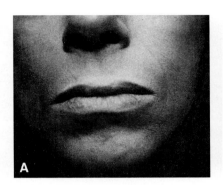
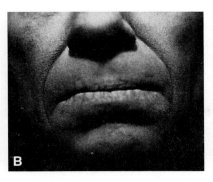

FIGURE 12-46 **Changing the mouth.** *All makeups on the same actor. A. Youthful mouth—upper lip reshaped. B. Aged mouth. Upper lip slightly convex; lips wrinkled with highlights and shadows.*

Reshaping the Lips

Reshaping the lips may or may not involve a change of size. It will involve either changing the apparent natural shape to fit the character (Figure 12-47) or painting on a new shape as the character might. The reshaping by the character would presumably be intended either to produce what she considered a more becoming shape or to follow a particular fashion, such as the bee-stung lips of the twenties or the Joan Crawford mouth of the thirties.

Lip Texture

Observe in Figure 12-48 the variations in lip texture, which have to do largely with age, environment, and health. In youth the texture is usually smooth, but later in life, depending on the condition of the skin generally, the lips may be rough, cracked, or wrinkled. It is, therefore, important in aging youthful faces that the lips be aged as well. (See Figure 12-46B.) This caution is based on observation of too many makeups in which youthful lips in a wrinkled face have destroyed the believability of an otherwise effective makeup. Suggestions for aging the lips are given below.

Aging the Lips

In addition to causing changes in texture, aging and changes inside the mouth (loss of teeth or wearing of false ones) can bring about changes in shape, size, and general conformation of the mouth.

Lips are likely to become thinner (Figure 12-41B, G, M and J), and they may be cut by numerous vertical wrinkles, as in Figure 12-41H and I.

If the mouth is to be wrinkled, it is helpful to make it smaller and, if possible, thinner—unless, of course, it is already small and thin. Thinner lips can be accomplished by first applying foundation to both lips along with the rest of the face, then powder. Shape the lips by lining them with a natural lip tone on the bottom and a slightly darker shade on the top. After filling in the lips, blot with a tissue to remove any excess oil (if creme foundation is used). The lips should now be pursed tightly and gently stippled with a natural highlight. When the lips are relaxed the wrinkle effect will appear.

Painted on wrinkles can be accomplished with a narrow brush, modeling the wrinkles carefully and using strong highlights with very narrow, deep shadows to form deep creases. Be sure that each highlight has one hard edge and that the hard edge is very sharp and clean. (See Figure 12-49.) If the wrinkles are too strong, they can be toned down by stippling. The important thing is to make them convincingly three-dimensional.

The most effective changes in texture can best be accomplished with three-dimensional makeup (see Chapter 13). But in using paint, you can stipple the lips or break the smoothness of the outline with wrinkles. The stippling is done along with that of the rest of the

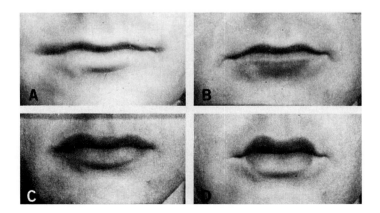

FIGURE 12-47 **Reshaping the lips.** *A. Natural lips. B. Lips thinned. C. Lips made fuller. D. Lips made very full and mouth narrowed. Makeup by student David Moffat.*

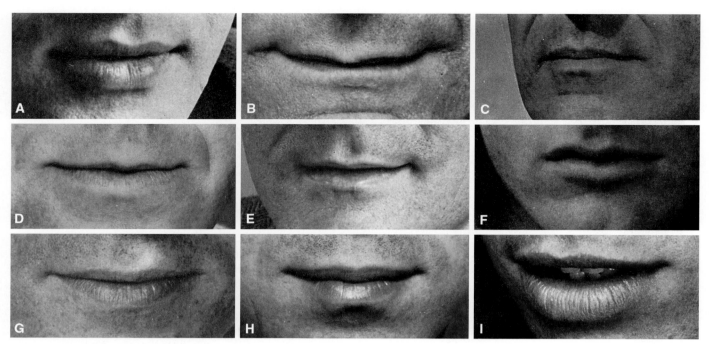

FIGURE 12-48 Mouths, male.

face, using the same colors. The lips should already have been reshaped, and if there are wrinkles cutting into the lip area, they should also have been done before the stippling.

In addition to the lips, the area around the mouth should also be aged. In old age, and sometimes in middle age, there is often considerable sagging of the muscles, particularly at the corners of the mouth. This frequently results in a crease angling downward from the corners of the mouth, with a roll of flesh above it (Figure 12-48B). Light falling on this roll of flesh from above will create a soft-edged highlight on top and a shadow with one hard and one soft edge below, just as it does with a nasolabial fold or a forehead wrinkle. The area immediately below the fold will be highlighted with one hard and one soft edge (Figure 12-50C and D).

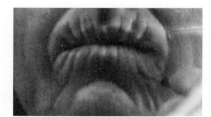

FIGURE 12-49 Aging the mouth. *Painting on wrinkles with highlights and shadows, which will later be stippled. Makeup by student Barbara Murray.*

This highlight may very well become part of a larger sagging area that does not usually have a sharp crease below it but often ends—in part, at least—where the chin begins. The exact conformation of this area and of the fold above varies considerably—not only with age, but with the individual. It's best to study faces and photographs, then adapt the information you have accumulated in your mind to the requirements of the specific character, relating it, as always, to the individual actor's face.

Study also the variations in plane A immediately below the lips, noticing particularly that this area can be either concave (Figure 12-36Q) or convex (Figure 12-41G). Concave is normal in youth, but it may sometimes become convex in old age.

Chin Suggestions for changing the chin to make it more attractive have already been given in the chapter on corrective makeup. These same techniques can be used for character makeup.

The chin itself changes relatively little with age, except for the changes in the texture of the skin, which can be achieved with stippling. What is usually called a double chin (Figure 12-51) is actually a sagging neckline, resulting from a relaxing of the muscles of the jaw and neck area. It begins just behind the chin and cannot be effectively simulated with paint unless the actor already has the beginnings of one that can be highlighted. Lowering the head slightly and pulling it back will help to emphasize whatever fullness is already there. (See Figure 12-51.)

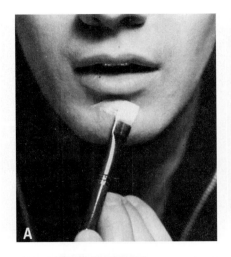
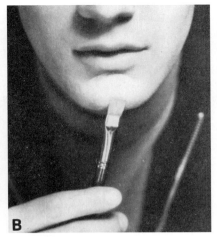

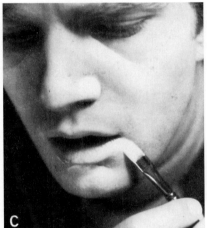
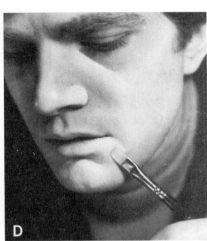

FIGURE 12-50 **Highlighting the chin and the mouth area.** *(Actor Eugene Bicknell.) A. Highlighting plane F of the chin with a wide brush. B. Blending the highlight with a clean brush. C. Using a medium brush to highlight part of the lower lip and the area below the corner. D. Blending the soft edges of the highlight with a clean brush.*

A crease may develop, with age, between areas E and F (see Figure 12-42D). Or there may be a rather abrupt change of plane without an actual crease. In either case, the top of the chin should be more strongly highlighted than it would be in youth in order to emphasize the increased angularity. (See Figure 12-50A and B.)

Neck

The neck, of course, ages (see Figures 12-41 and 12-42) along with the face and sometimes even more rapidly. A youthful neck, like youthful lips, can destroy the believability of an otherwise effective age makeup. It has already been mentioned that both the front and the back of the neck should be made up. For juveniles, nothing else is likely to be necessary. But for age, the neck requires modeling.

There are four prominences in the neck that are important in makeup. They are labeled A, B, C, and D in Figure 12-52. Because the muscles, along with the top of the larynx and parts of the tracheal column, catch the

FIGURE 12-51 **Sixteenth-century lady.** *Makeup by student Carol Doscher.*

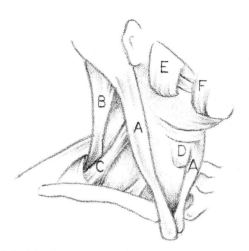

FIGURE 12-52 Muscles of the neck and jaw.

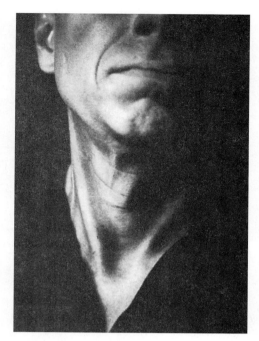

FIGURE 12-53 Neck aged with cake makeup.
(Makeup by Richard Corson.)

light, they should be highlighted. All of these, being roughly cylindrical in shape, should be modeled like cylinders, with the highlight fading around to a shadow. The hollow at the breastbone, where the sterno-cleido-mastoid muscles almost meet, is usually in shadow. In old age there may be two folds of flesh starting above the larynx and hanging down like wattles (Figure 12-41C, H, and M). Small ones can be effectively painted on for a front view (Figure 12-53) but are, of course, ineffective in profile.

It is also possible to model the wrinkles that form around the neck and diagonally upward toward the ears. To determine the correct placement of the wrinkles, it is usually necessary to twist and turn the head until natural wrinkles are formed. These can be carefully modeled with highlights and shadows. For aging plumper characters, these transverse wrinkles should nearly always be used, but they should be wider and fewer in number.

Hands

In representing youth, the hands should always be made up to go with the color of the face. The extent of modeling needed for bone, knuckles, and veins of the hands will depend on both age and the care that the hands have been given. Usually, unless the character tends to be quite pudgy, the bones of the hands, in age, tend to become more prominent and the veins begin to stand out (Figures 12-54). The bones, both in the back of the hand and in the fingers (Figure 12-54) should be modeled like cylinders, with highlights along the top and shadows along the sides. The joints may sometimes swell and often, with light skins, redden. A little rouge will give the color. The swelling can be suggested by rounded highlights on top of the joint and narrow, crescent-shaped shadows around them.

A dark-skinned actor who wants to create the effect with makeup can make his hand into a fist and cover the joints with very dark brown makeup. The hand can then be straightened out and the dark brown makeup wiped off the surface of the joint, which can be shadowed, slightly highlighted, and powdered. This technique will leave natural-looking dark ridges in the deepest part of the wrinkles on the joints.

The veins, if at all prominent, should appear three-dimensional, not flat, which means that there should be a highlight along one side of every vein and a shadow along the other. (See Figure 12-55.) Decide arbitrarily which way the light is coming from. Veins should be treated as elongated cylinders. Their roundness will be particularly pronounced as they cross over bones. They are nearly always irregular, often forking out and meandering across the hand. If the actor's natural veins are visible, they can be followed; and if the actor's veins are prominent, they should be followed. Otherwise, it is possible to place the veins wherever they appear to be most effective. Be careful, however, not to use too many. A few veins carefully placed and convincingly painted will be far more effective than a complicated network.

The color of veins will depend on the type and color of the hand. A pale, delicate, fine-skinned hand will naturally reveal much more blue in the veins than a deeply tanned or a black or a brown one, on which the veins may not appear blue at all and can be modeled with the normal highlight and shadow colors. Often veins that are not extremely prominent are a light

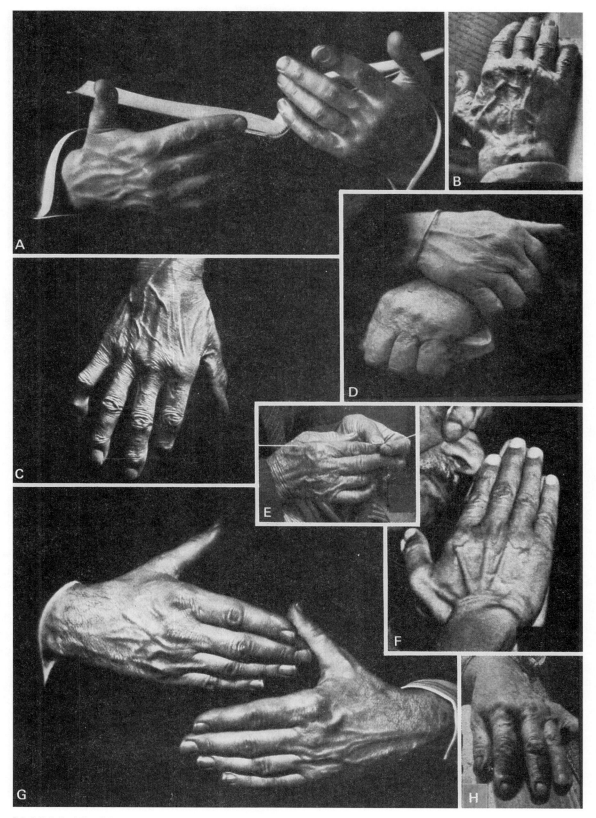

FIGURE 12-54 Hands.

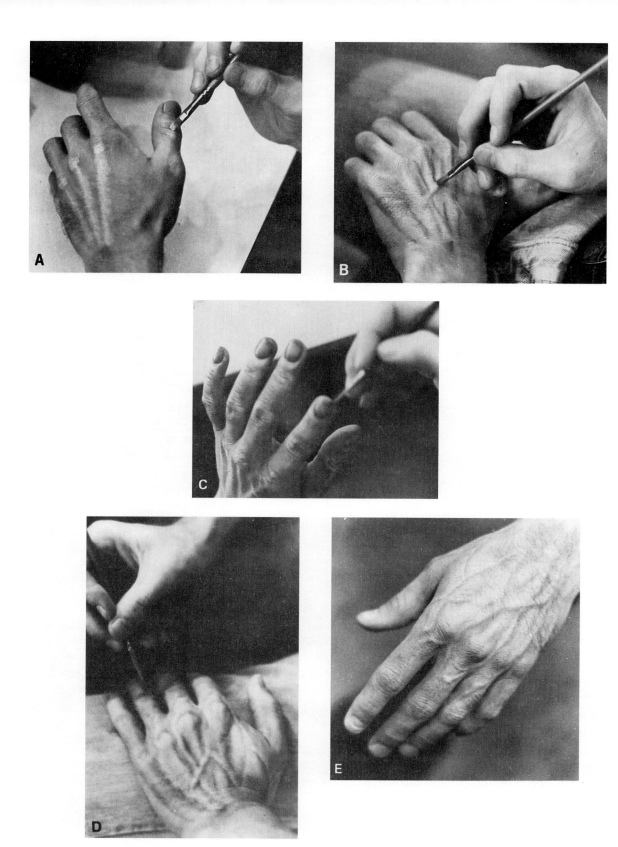

FIGURE 12-55 **Aging a male hand.** *Makeup by student Milton Blankenship. A. Highlighting the bones of the hand. B. Shadowing between the bones. C. Adding details. D. Finished makeup after powdering. E. Adding an aging effect to the fingernails.*

greenish blue, in which case a very pale tint of blue-green can be used for highlighting. Very prominent veins under a delicate white skin are likely to be a much deeper blue, with no green cast, and would be expected to have blue-gray shadows. Observe the coloration in elderly hands—of the skin as well as the veins.

The brown spots so often found on older hands can be painted on with a yellowish brown—about the same color as freckles (FO-13-c/d). They should be of various sizes and unevenly distributed. If the hand is to be rough textured, it should be stippled or given a three-dimensional skin texture (see Chapter 13).

Fingernails

In aging the hands, always make sure that the nails are aged in harmony with the rest of the hand. The aging may involve filing or cutting the nails (either real or artificial) to a length and shape appropriate for the character, and it may also require changing the color and the apparent texture of the nails, both of which can be done with creme makeup and makeup pencils, used with latex, sealer, flexible collodion, or spirit gum.

The color can be brushed on (see Figure 12-55E) when using creme makeup or stroked on when using creme-makeup crayons or makeup pencils. In general, creme-makeup crayons are preferable to regular creme makeup. Makeup pencils, if you happen to have the right color or colors, are especially useful for creating the effect of ridges in the nails. Vertical strokes can be applied with a white pencil, leaving slight spaces between the strokes to allow the natural color of the nail to show through. Or, instead of leaving spaces between the strokes, you can make alternating strokes of two colors, such as white and ochre, to give a yellowish cast to the nails. You can also achieve the same effect by applying creme makeup or makeup crayon with a very narrow brush.

Pencils can also be used for coloring the nails without giving the effect of ridges. After the color has been penciled on, you can blend it with a fingertip so as to color the entire nail—evenly or unevenly, whichever is appropriate. You may wish to apply the color heavily to conceal the natural color of the nails or sparingly to allow some of the natural color to show through. Any color applied to the nails should be powdered before proceeding with the next step.

When the nails have been appropriately colored, they should be coated with clear latex, sealer, or non-flexible collodion. No matter which one you use, it should be powdered when it has dried in order to remove the shine and give a duller finish to the nail—unless the character would be wearing clear nail polish, in which case the powder should be omitted or clear nail polish used instead of the latex, sealer, or collodion.

An alternative method of aging the nails is to coat them with spirit gum, then, with one finger, to tap the gum until it becomes tacky, at which point you can press white or neutral face powder into the gum. That gives a dull whitish effect suitable for some aged characters.

If dirt under the nails is appropriate, gray or gray-brown creme makeup can be applied with a small brush.

To create the effect of colored nail polish on aged nails, you can use red makeup pencil or apply lipstick, creme makeup, or makeup crayons with a narrow brush to make vertical stripes of color, as previously suggested. The red should then be powdered and coated with latex. If you want the effect of frosted nail polish, powder the latex; otherwise, leave it unpowdered. Red pencils can be used on the nails without a protective coating of spirit gum; but since some reds stain the nails (or the skin), direct application of the pencils to the nails is not advisable—unless, of course, you have already experimented with the red you plan to use and have determined that it does not stain.

For removing makeup from the nails, latex can be peeled off, sealer and collodion removed with acetone, and spirit gum, with spirit-gum remover or acetone.

Teeth

Teeth, if too white and even for the character, can be darkened with an appropriate shade of tooth enamel. The effect of chipped or missing teeth can be created with black tooth enamel or black wax. Black eyebrow pencil can also be used, but it may require touching up during the performance. The teeth should always be dried with a tissue before being blocked out.

Black tooth enamel can also be used to make the edges of the teeth uneven. If they are already uneven and the character should have even teeth, the process can be reversed.

For stained or discolored teeth (Figure 12-56), you can rub brown mustache wax on the teeth with the fingers, then partially remove it with a cotton swab. If you want additional color along the sides of the teeth, you can add more wax with another cotton swab. The teeth must, of course, be dried before any wax is applied. The wax can be removed with a cleansing tissue.

If you do not have brown mustache wax, you can color clear mustache wax or derma wax with brown cake makeup by scraping the top of the cake with a knife to obtain a small amount of brown powder, then mixing the powder with the wax, using a palette knife or a modeling tool. When the powder is thoroughly embedded in the wax, it will, of course, be impervious to saliva in the mouth. For nicotine stains, you can use an appropriate shade of cake makeup or mix colors if you don't have the right shade. Non-toxic tooth enamels and colors are available in shades such as Black, White, Nicotine, and Decay.

FIGURE 12-56 **Discoloring the teeth.** *Actor, James Black, rubbing "Nicotine" tooth color by Ben Nye on his teeth in preparation for the role of Scrooge, in The Alley Theatre's production of Charles Dickens'* Christmas Carol, A Ghost Story of Christmas.

Reshaping the Face

There are times when, in addition to working with individual features, you may wish to think in terms of reshaping the face–making it more square, long, wide, round, or oval–in order to make it more appropriate for a particular character. (See Figure 12-57.) This can be done–at least to some degree–by means of highlights and shadows and beards, mustaches, hair, and eyebrows.

The Long Face A face can be made to look longer by increasing the apparent height of the forehead and the apparent length of the nose (Figure 12-58A) and the chin by highlighting. (See Chapter 10.) Narrowing the face by subtly shading the sides of the forehead and the cheeks will also make it seem longer, as will a high, narrow hair style or one which covers the sides of the face. A pointed goatee (Figure 12-60B) or a long, narrow beard will have the same effect. A long nose and long nasolabial folds (Figure 12-57B) will also contribute to the illusion.

To make a long face look less long, follow the suggestions below for the wide face.

The Wide Face To make a face look wider, you can do just the reverse of lengthening–lower the forehead (which can be done with the hairstyle, as well as with the makeup) and shorten the chin (if doing so would not be inappropriate for the character), highlight rather than shadow the sides of the forehead and the cheeks,

shorten the nose, flatten and widen the hairstyle, and dress any facial hair horizontally (Figure 12-57C) rather than vertically. Making the eyebrows farther apart will also help, as will avoiding long nasolabial folds and making apple cheeks instead. In order to decrease the apparent width of a wide face, follow any of the suggestions for the long face that seem appropriate.

The Square Face To make a face more square, the forehead should be vertical at the temples, giving a squared-off effect, and should usually be made to look as broad as possible. This can be done by highlighting the temples and even blocking out the hairline, if necessary, in order to take it farther back at the sides. The top hairline should be fairly straight across. If much hair needs to be blocked out, it would usually be better to wear a wig that will cover the natural hairline and provide a hairline more suitable for the character.

The jaw can be highlighted at the sides, if necessary, to make it look wider, and the chin can sometimes be squared off a bit. A square-cut beard can be very helpful. Straight eyebrows will also contribute to the illusion.

If the face is noticeably longer than it is wide, follow the instructions for the wide face in order to give a squarer look.

A square face can be made to look less square by rounding off the forehead, the jaw, and the chin, wearing a longer and more rounded beard, and giving the face an illusion of greater length (see *The Long Face*).

The Oval Face A face–unless it is already too round–can be made to look more oval by rounding off the upper corners of the forehead either by shadowing or by changing the hairline and doing the same to the jaw with shading or with a beard, creating a sweeping curve down to a rounded chin. A round face can be made to look less round by shadowing the sides of the cheeks, curving the shadow gently downward at an angle toward the chin.

The Round Face To round a youthful face and keep it youthful, follow the principles used in modeling a sphere, as illustrated in Figure 12-59, in which drawing A illustrates the shading and highlighting for a sphere, and drawing B, the outline of a youthful face. The effect of roundness is achieved with a highlight (B_5) made in a round pattern in about the center of the cheek, and a thin, crescent-shaped shadow drawn in an arc from close to the eye, past the nostrils and the mouth, and around to the back of the jaw, as shown in B_4. All edges should be soft, and the shadow very subtle. Although some faces cannot be made to look round without the use of three-dimensional makeup, an *effect* of roundness can usually be achieved by rounding various features or areas of the face, as illustrated in Figure

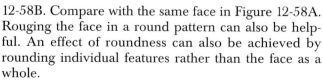

FIGURE 12-57 **Three-dimensional and painted character makeup.** *A. Actor Randall duc Kim in his own makeups for B. Titus Andronicus and C. Falstaff.*

three shades darker than the base. When "aging" a round face, this same technique can be used, as illustrated in Figure 12-51. You may also wish to age the face with sagging apple cheeks (see Figure 12-41F), which give the impression of a happier disposition than would long, drooping nasolabial folds.

In this chapter we have concentrated on makeup for the face, the neck, and the hands, but other exposed parts of the body may require makeup as well. Cake makeup can be used for relatively small areas; but to cover large areas, body makeup is usually more practical. For details, see *Body Makeup* in Appendix A.

Bringing the Makeup to Life

Bear in mind, as you work on any realistic character makeup, such as those in Figures 12-61 and 12-62, the actor you are making up (whether it be yourself or someone else) is the only one who can bring the makeup to life and until he or she gets into character, the makeup will be incomplete. Assuming the character before the makeup begins and as needed thereafter is an essential part of the creative process. Bear in mind also that whenever the makeup is being photographed or checked, either in the mirror or onstage, the actor should *always* be in character.

12-58B. Compare with the same face in Figure 12-58A. Rouging the face in a round pattern can also be helpful. An effect of roundness can also be achieved by rounding individual features rather than the face as a whole.

In addition, whatever effect of roundness you have achieved with makeup can often be enhanced with the hairstyle and facial hair (see Figure 12-60). A rounded collar in the costume may also help.

A naturally round face cannot be made thin, but it can be thinned somewhat by highlighting the cheekbones and shading the whole cheek with a color two or

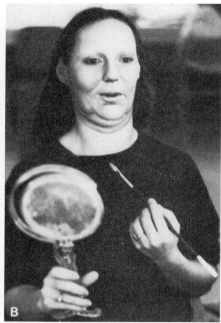

FIGURE 12-58 Length and roundness in the face. *A. Increasing the illusion of length in the nose. B. The same face with the illusion of roundness created in the cheeks, the jowls, and the neck. The horizontal effect in the modeling of the rounded areas also creates an illusion of greater width in the face as a whole. Makeup by student Clista Towne-Strother.*

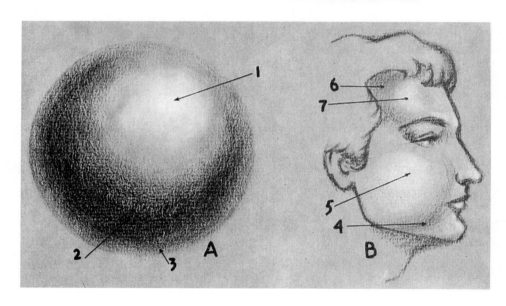

FIGURE 12-59 Modeling a round cheek.

FIGURE 12-60 Changing the shape of the face. *A. The illusion of width is achieved by carrying the light foundation color from ear to ear and pulling the hair and beard out horizontally. B. The face and the nose have been narrowed by shadowing. The nasolabial folds and the long narrow nose help to lengthen the face. (Makeup by Richard Corson).*

FIGURE 12-61 **Aging a young face.**
A. Opera student Tracey Staver. B. Tracey Staver as Judge Turpin in the musical, Sweeney Todd, *at the Cincinatti Conservatory of Music. Creme foundation with creme highlights and shadows. Maroon-colored pressed and creme blush applied over shadows to add life and color to the skin. Soaped eyebrows covered with plastic sealer and foundation then powdered before attaching ventilated eyebrows. Mustache and beard (mixture of human and yak) applied over clean skin for secure adhesion (makeup by Lenna Kaleva).*

FIGURE 12-62 **Five character makeups on the same actor.** *The makeups were created—except for facial hair and wigs—using the principles and techniques discussed in this chapter. (Makeup by Richard Corson).*

1. Design and execute makeups for a pair of characters, both youthful, but sufficiently different that the difference will be apparent in the makeup—as, for example: Katharina and Bianca (*Taming of the Shrew*); Barbara and Sarah (*Major Barbara*); Ophelia (*Hamlet*) and Audrey (*As You Like It*); Canina and Columba (*Volpone*); Joan of Arc (*St. Joan*) and Laura (*The Glass Menagerie*); Romeo and Hamlet; Stanley Kowalski and A Young Collector (*A Streetcar Named Desire*); Marchbanks (*Candida*) and Leo (*The Little Foxes*); Charles Lomax and Bill Walker (*Major Barbara*); Antonio and Launcelot Gobbo (*Merchant of Venice*); Mosca (*Volpone*) and Orlando (*As You Like It*).

2. Follow the step-by-step instructions under *Modeling Hard and Soft Edges* early in the chapter.

3. Following the instructions under *Modeling the Face and the Neck with Highlights and Shadows*, model your face—first with highlights only, then adding shadows, rouge, and stipple.

4. Model your cheekbones with highlights and shadows, taking care to follow your bone structure. You may want to stipple with one or more colors after you have finished.

5. Model a broken or a crooked nose.

6. Practice doing nasolabial folds until you can do them convincingly. If you think it will be helpful, you might model them on your clay head first before modeling them with paint.

7. Do at least three different aged eyes. Make sure that one of the eyes has a full pouch, and keep working on the pouch until it is convincingly three-dimensional. With at least one of the eyes, begin by blocking out the eyebrow.

8. Age your mouth.

9. Age your forehead, using only highlights and shadows.

10. Age your forehead, using wrinkles.

11. Age your neck and jaw line.

12. Age your hands.

13. Age your teeth.

14. Design and execute a makeup for a middle-aged character from a play.

15. Choose from your morgue or from photographs or works of art in this book, three elderly people. Determine what makes them look old rather than middle-aged.

16. Design and create a makeup for an elderly character from a play.

17. Do worksheets for the makeups you designed for problem 1, Chapter 7.

Three-Dimensional Makeup

chapter 13

In modeling with paint, there was no attempt to make actual changes in the natural shape of the actor's features but merely to give the impression that such changes had been made. Three-dimensional makeup involves actually building up parts of the body—usually the face, neck, or hand—with various materials, such as nose putty, derma wax, cotton, cleansing tissues, latex, gelatin, and liquid plastic. *Molded* latex processes will be discussed in the next chapter.

Nose Putty

Nose putty is used primarily for changing the shape of the nose (see Figures 13-1 and 13-2), though it does have other uses as well. An actor who settles for his or her own nose instead of the nose of the character is failing to take advantage of a particularly useful and relatively simple means of physical characterization.

The use of nose putty need not be restricted to fantastic noses or even to large ones. There are minor changes that can easily be made in order to give the actor a nose more suited to the character. But whether the changes are major or minor, the less putty you need to use, the easier the shaping and the blending will be.

Building up the Nose   The first step in building up the nose—the easiest feature to change three-dimensionally—should be to make a profile sketch of the shape you want, bearing in mind that no matter what the shape or size of the addition, it must appear to be an integral, living part of the face. This means that whatever additions you make to the nose must give the impression of being supported by bone and cartilage and

must be so carefully blended into the natural skin that it is impossible to tell where the real nose leaves off and the false one begins.

Once you have a clear plan firmly in mind and know exactly what you intend to do, applying and shaping the

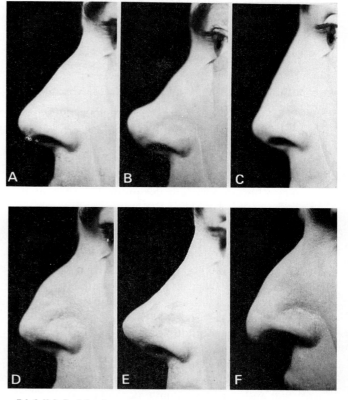

FIGURE 13-1 **Putty noses.** *B-F show reshaping of nose A with nose putty.*

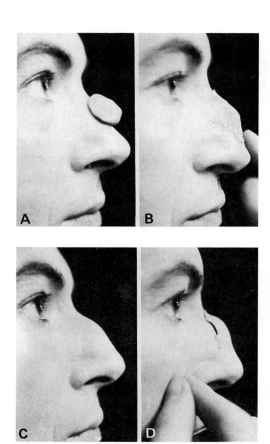

FIGURE 13-2 Modeling the nose with putty.
A. Ball of putty on nose. B. Putty being shaped and blended with fingers. C. Finished nose, made up and powdered. D. Removing the putty with a thread.

nose putty is not difficult, but it does require patience. This is the procedure:

1. Keep your sketch in front of you and use two mirrors to give you a profile view of the nose as you work.

2. Make sure the skin is free from all grease and makeup before applying the putty. Use 70% alcohol sparingly on an absorbent cotton swab to cleanse the skin.

3. Separate a small piece of putty from the mass and knead it with your fingers until it is very pliable. If the putty is too stiff and the heat of the hand does not soften it sufficiently, immerse it in hot water for a few minutes or place it near a radiator or in a microwave oven for a few seconds. Although it is possible to soften putty by the addition of a small amount of cleansing cream, the method is not recommended. There is a tendency to add too much cream, resulting in a putty that loses its ability to stick, becoming too soft and mushy and quite unmanageable.

4. Stick the softened ball of putty on the part of the nose that is to be built up the most (Figure 13-2A), pressing it into the skin for good adhesion. If it does

not seem to be securely attached, remove it, then paint the nose with spirit gum and let it dry before reapplying the putty. Or you can use both spirit gum and cotton under the putty, as described in the section on *Derma Wax*. To assist you in smoothing out the surface, coat your fingers lightly with K-Y Lubricating Jelly (not petroleum jelly) to keep the putty from sticking to them. If you have no lubricating jelly, you can substitute setting gel. (In case you have neither lubricating jelly nor wave set, a very light coating of cleansing cream can be used.)

5. Carefully blend the edges of the putty into the skin, shaping the nose as you work (Figure 13-2B). Use more lubricating jelly on your fingers if the putty sticks to them. Always confine the putty to as small an area as possible, being especially careful to keep it off areas *surrounding* the nose. If, in blending the edges, you tend to keep pulling the putty outward until it has spread well away from the area you want built up, blend in the opposite direction–toward the center of the nose.

6. When the blending is finished, you can make final adjustments in the shape. Using your sketch as a guide and two mirrors to check the nose from all angles, cover your fingers with more lubricating jelly and keep pressing, prodding, and massaging the putty until you have precisely the shape you want, always keeping in mind the image of flesh and skin over bone and cartilage. A final light massaging with lubricating jelly will help to eliminate unintentional cracks and bumps and give a completely smooth surface.

7. When the surface of the putty is smooth, the edges perfectly blended, and the lubricating jelly dried, stipple the putty with your black stipple sponge to give skin texture (see Figure 13-5K). Then, if the putty is lighter or less red than the skin, stipple it with rouge–dry rouge (applied with a damp sponge) or creme rouge (applied with either a stipple sponge or a flat red-rubber sponge). If creme rouge is used, powder it well, then brush off the excess powder. A method of giving three-dimensional texture to putty by using a small latex negative of a section of the surface of a grapefruit, orange, or lemon is explained in Chapter 14. The method uses the same principle followed in creating texture on plastic eyebrow covers, illustrated in Figure 12-25C and D.

8. Powder the nose, pressing gently with the puff. Remove excess powder with a powder brush.

9. Stipple the foundation color (preferably creme or grease) over the entire nose (see Figure 13-5I), using a natural sponge for cake makeup and a flat red-rubber sponge for creme or grease. If this does not adequately cover the putty area, powder, then stipple on more of the foundation color. If you are using dry cake makeup, it will probably dry lighter than the same makeup applied directly to the skin. For that

reason, it is not the best choice of makeup to use over nose putty. However, the problem can sometimes be corrected by coating the light area with more lubricating jelly. The water-soluble jelly will mix with the makeup and dry with a slight waxy sheen. Powdering will counteract this. If the color matching is still not satisfactory, coat the problem area with rubber-mask grease, making sure to blend the edges of the grease thoroughly into the skin, then powder. If the color of the rubber-mask grease you are using does not match the foundation color you plan to use for the makeup, you can either use the rubber-mask grease for the entire makeup or cover it, after it has been powdered, with the foundation color you are using on the rest of the face.

10. For most characters, you will want to add rouge to the nares and other parts of the nose to give it a more natural appearance. This can be done after the foundation coat has been applied or when the various colors of stipple or other finishing touches are being added. If it is done afterward, moist rouge can be stippled on, or dry rouge can be brushed on.

Figures 13-3 and 13-4 illustrate a variety of noses.

Removing the Putty
A thread can be used to remove the putty. Starting at either the base or the bridge of the nose, run the thread along the nose under the putty (Figure 13-2D), pulling the thread tight with both hands. This does *not* preserve the putty nose intact for future use—it is simply a more efficient way of removing the putty than pulling it off with the fingers. Any bits of putty remaining on the nose after the bulk of it has been detached with the thread can be removed by massaging with makeup remover until the putty is soft enough to be wiped off with tissues. Always do this gently in order to avoid irritation.

Building up the Chin
Nose putty can also be used on other bony or cartilaginous areas, such as the chin, but it is seldom practical to do so. On this part of the face where there is a great deal of movement of the muscles, bubbles will very likely appear in the surface of the putty and ruin the effect. However, if you try this technique on the chin, follow the same steps suggested for building up the nose.

Derma Wax

Derma wax (see Appendix A) is softer than nose putty. It can be shaped and blended more easily, but it is also more easily damaged when touched than is nose putty and can loosen and fall off unless it is very firmly attached to the skin. Experiment with a variety of waxes from the different manufacturers. (Naturo Plasto Morti-

cian's Wax, from Alcone and Namies, has been used quite successfully.) Like nose putty, it should be confined to bony parts of the face. (See Figure 13-5.) For close work you may wish to blend the edges of the wax into the skin with alcohol and a soft brush.

Before using derma wax, apply a coat of spirit gum to the area of the skin to be covered in order to keep the wax from loosening. Let the spirit gum dry, then follow the same procedure as for applying nose putty.

Cotton under Derma Wax
For still greater security, cotton fibers can be added to the undercoat of spirit gum before applying the derma wax, as follows:

1. Coat the nose with spirit gum. (Figure 13-5A.)
2. Tap the spirit gum repeatedly with your finger until it becomes very tacky. (Figure 13-5B.)
3. Place a layer of absorbent cotton over a slightly smaller area than that to be covered with derma wax (Figure 13-5C), then press the cotton firmly into the spirit gum.
4. When the spirit gum is dry, pull off all the loose cotton. (Figure 13-5D.)
5. Press a small amount of derma wax onto the cotton, and push it around firmly with one finger to make sure the cotton fibers are embedded in the wax. (Figure 13-5F.)
6. Press a ball of derma wax into the center of the wax which has just been applied (Figure 13-5G), and mold it with the fingers into the precise shape you want. (Figure 13-5H.) Be sure that the edges are well blended. Using lubricating jelly on the fingers makes the blending easier.

Makeup can be applied directly over the derma wax (Figure 13-5I), or the wax can be coated first with sealer (see Appendix A). If cake makeup is to be used, apply it directly to the wax with no coating of sealer. The makeup for the nose is completed in the usual way (Figure 13-5J through L).

Derma Wax over Nose Putty
Derma wax can also be used over nose putty to provide a smooth surface and an imperceptible blend into the skin—not that this cannot be done with putty, but doing it with wax may be easier and in some cases can save time.

Latex over Derma Wax
For greater protection than sealer will give to the surface of the derma-wax construction, latex can be used. This is the procedure:

1. Coat the wax construction with latex. This can be done with the fingers.
2. When the latex is dry, powder it.
3. Use a rubber-mask grease foundation over the latex.
4. If the wax needs texture or wrinkles, they can be added at this point by pressing the wax with the

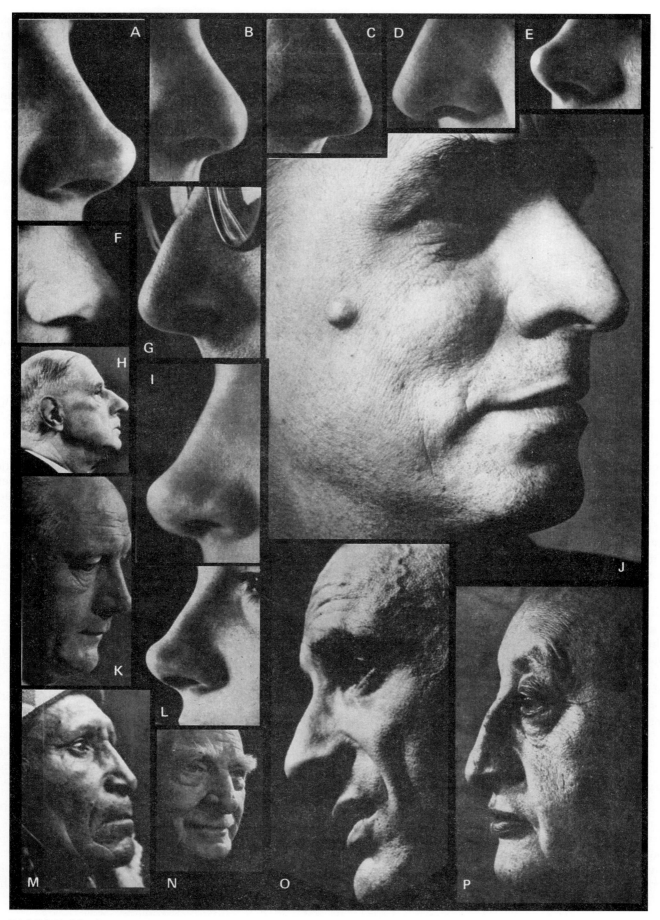

FIGURE 13-3 Noses.

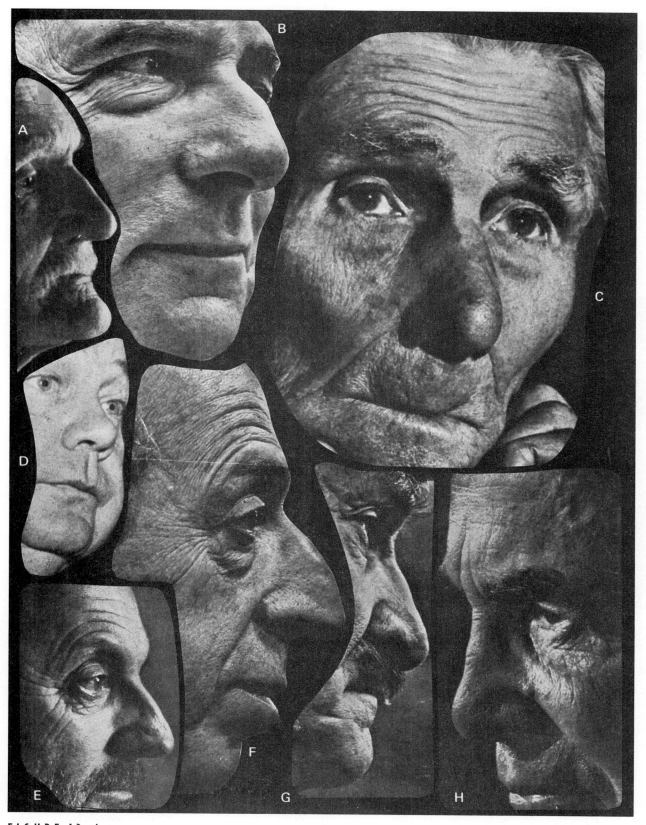

FIGURE 13-4 Noses.

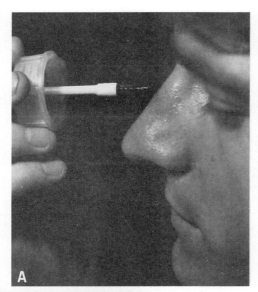

FIGURE 13-5 **Building up the nose with derma wax over cotton.** *(Tom Lindberg.) A. Applying spirit gum to the nose. B. Tapping the spirit gum to make it tacky. C. Applying the cotton. D. Pulling excess cotton off the nose after the spirit gum is dry. E. Cotton foundation for the derma wax. F. First application of derma wax. A small amount of wax is pressed into the cotton, then blended into the skin. G. Second application of derma wax. A ball of derma wax is pressed onto the nose at what is to be the most prominent part. H. Blending the derma wax with lubricating jelly. I. Applying creme makeup foundation with a red-rubber sponge. J. Powdering the nose. K. Pressing the wax with a stipple sponge to add skin texture. The entire nose was then stippled with creme rouge and a dark and light creme makeup for additional texture effect. L. Completed nose. M. Removing the derma wax with tissue.*

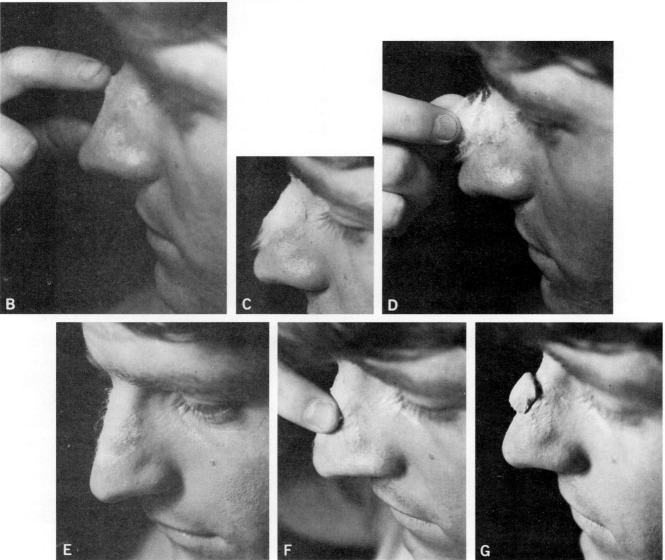

FIGURE 13-5 Continued.

latex negative of a grapefruit skin or with the tip of a brush handle to give a skin-texture effect or with an orangewood stick or a modeling tool to form wrinkles. In doing this, be careful not to puncture or tear the latex skin which protects the wax.

5. Complete the makeup.

Removing Derma Wax

If the derma wax has been applied directly to the skin without any sort of adhesive, most of it can simply be removed with the fingers and the remainder wiped off with makeup remover and tissues.

If spirit gum has been used under the wax, an all-purpose makeup remover (which removes spirit gum along with the rest of the makeup) may work better. If it doesn't, use some spirit-gum remover.

If you have used both spirit gum and cotton under the wax, you might do well, after peeling off as much of the construction as you can with your fingers, to remove the remainder with spirit-gum remover before using your regular makeup remover. If latex has been used over the derma wax, that can be peeled off first and the wax removed as usual.

Putty-Wax

A half-and-half mixture of nose putty and derma wax combines to some extent the advantages of each—the greater adhesives of the nose putty and the ease of blending of the derma wax. The mixture can be made

FIGURE 13-6 (l-r) Derma wax by Joe Blasco, Putty-Wax by Mehron, Silicone Putty by Art Anthony.

up an ounce or so at a time by melting the two together in a double boiler or in the microwave (do not allow this mixture to boil). The mixture can then be poured into a container, cooled, and used as needed. If you are mixing only a small amount, it's simpler to remove half the contents of a metal container of derma wax, add a piece of nose putty to the remaining half, and place the container in a shallow pan of simmering water. When the wax and the putty are both melted, they can be stirred thoroughly, then cooled.

Putty-wax (available from Mehron) is applied in the same way as nose putty. If it doesn't adhere properly, use spirit gum or spirit gum and cotton under it. (See sections on *Nose putty* and *Derma wax*.)

Putty-wax has been used for the makeups in Figure 12-23.

Removing Putty-Wax

Putty-wax can be removed in the same way as derma wax. If spirit gum or spirit gum and cotton have been used under it, see the instructions for removal in the sections on *Nose putty* and *Derma wax*.

Silicone Putty

Developed for the film industry, this translucent putty (see Figure 13-6 and Appendix A) has excellent adhesive properties and easily blends into the surrounding skin. It stays flexible, holding surface texture and shape and is not affected by heat or cold, thus avoiding the "melting" and rather sticky properties of putty and wax. It is used for buildups (noses, chins, etc.), cuts, gashes, and bullet holes. Silicone putty is manufactured in a variety of translucent colors that give a realistic skin-like appearance. Colors can be custom blended with the addition of cosmetic grade pigments (Bob Kelly), pressed powders, foundations, eye shadows and cheek colors, flocking, and intrinsic silicone colorants (colors that are mixed into the product) (Factor II, Inc., see Appendix A).

Like nose putty and derma wax, silicone putty should be confined to bony parts of the face, hands, and body. Try this procedure:

1. To match skin tone, simply add small amounts of loose powder (or scrape the surface of pressed powders), fibers, or colorant to the putty, kneading between your fingers until the color is blended thoroughly.
2. Clean the skin thoroughly of all grease and makeup with absorbent cotton and 99% alcohol or an astringent or toner. Apply an appropriate amount of putty firmly to the skin, smoothing the surface and blending edges into the surrounding skin with your fingers (if needed, try applying spirit gum first for greater adhesion). There is no need to lubricate your fingers when working with this product.
3. Using a small, flat natural bristled brush, apply a small amount of silicone solvent to the edges. Brush carefully until the putty blends into the skin completely.
4. Adjust the shine of the putty with a very light application of a matte powder.
5. Adjust the color by adding light washes of extrinsic silicone pigments (colors painted onto the surface such as Factor II), Temporary Tattoo colors (Reel Creations, Inc., Temptu Body Art), or Dermacolor (Kryolan) diluted with 70% alcohol.

Silicone putty can also simulate cuts and bruises. Simply slice into or texture the surface of the putty with a palette knife, tooth pick, or other appropriate object. Color as above and add blood as needed. To simulate bullet wounds, the putty can be sculpted or pressed into a plaster or vacuformed mold that has been lightly coated with a silicone mold release (see Appendix A) or petroleum jelly.

Gelatin

Powdered gelatin mixed with hot water provides an efficient means of creating such three-dimensional effects as moles, warts, wounds, scars, and welts (see Figure 13-20) that do not require great precision in modeling. The mixture makes a very thick liquid that solidifies as it cools. That means that you must work rapidly, for once the gelatin has congealed on the skin, it cannot be reshaped—unless, or course, you add more warm gelatin. If that does not give you the effect you want, you had better peel it off and begin again. Makeup can be applied to the congealed gelatin along with the rest of the face. The recipe, application procedure, and coloring techniques for prosthetic gelatin are discussed in Chapter 14.

Latex

Natural rubber latex is the sap harvested from the rubber tree. Ammonia, the smell with which it is commonly associated, is added as a preservative to help keep it from decomposing and coagulating. There are different types of latex developed for different purposes. Natural, prevulcanized latex without any fillers is often called pure gum latex or balloon rubber. This type makes thin translucent products such as balloons, rubber gloves, and condoms. It is not recommended for brushing or slushing into molds. Other prevulcanized latexes contain a variety of thickeners and fillers designed to either build up layers inside a mold or to be painted on in heavy layers to form thick rubber molds. When purchasing latex, be sure to describe exactly what kind of product and process you are planning in order to receive the appropriate one.

Adding color to latex, whether it be bright colors or fleshtones, will assist you in applying makeup or color to the finished piece. Latex, in a color that closely matches the final skin or surface tone will require less makeup and provide a more even coverage. Sold in tubes and purchased from your local paint or hardware store, universal colorants or tinting colors are generally used to color interior and exterior house paints. They can be thinned with distilled water (regular water may upset the pH balance and cause some gellation of the rubber) and used to color the latex. Poster paints mix well without harming the latex, but a generous amount is needed to produce even the lightest of colors. The best colorants are pigment dispersions, specifically manufactured to color latex. (See Appendix A, Latex.) Latex can also be tinted with a few drops of food coloring (use mostly yellow, some red and a tiny bit of blue). When coloring liquid latex, remember that it turns darker when it dries.

You could also choose to simply use pre-tinted latex from the manufacturer in order to provide a foundation color. When using tinted latex, remember that it turns much darker after it dries.

Liquid latex (see Appendix A) can be used for casting in plaster molds (see Chapter 14) and for painting on flat, smooth surfaces (glass, for example) in order to create pieces, such as welts and scars, that can be transferred to the skin after the latex has dried (see Figure 13-25); and for applying directly to the skin to create three-dimensional wrinkles and skin texture. When using latex on the skin, use only the type that is intended for that purpose. Because latex can be irritating to some skins, it is advisable to test the skin first for allergic reactions. If latex causes irritation or feels as if it is burning the skin, *don't use it,* or try another brand or another technique that does not involve applying latex directly to the skin. You may also try applying a skin barrier (Barrier Spray by Mehron, Aquacream by ADM Tronics, Top Guard by Premiere Products, Inc., see Appendix B.)

One method of using latex for aging is to apply clear latex (which is white when in liquid form but dries clear) over an age makeup. If you use creme makeup or greasepaint, use as little as possible, set it with translucent powder, and spray with a sealer (Sta-Spray and Sealer by Joe Blasco, Final Seal by Ben Nye). If you use cake makeup, which is water-soluble and tends to mix with latex, again, spray with a sealer to avoid smearing the makeup. Then, working on one area of the face at a time, pull the skin tight with the fingers and, using either a red-rubber or a foam latex sponge, stipple the latex over the completed makeup. When each area is dry, dust it with powder, then release the skin, which should form wrinkles. If you want deeper wrinkles, apply additional coats of latex in the same way. When the entire

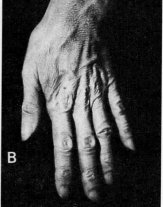

FIGURE 13-7 **Hand aged with latex over makeup.** *Makeup by student Catherine Smith. A. Hand aged with cake makeup. B. Clear latex applied over the makeup.*

face has been covered, the makeup can be touched up with rubber-mask grease, greasepaint, creme makeup, or makeup pencils (provided you have suitable colors). When using makeup other than RMGP, the latex must be stippled with a light coating of castor oil to protect it from the cosmetic oils.

If you prefer, you can simply apply the latex first, then add any makeup that seems appropriate.

Latex can also be used to age the hands. But if the hands are hairy, either shave the hair first or make absolutely certain that the hairs are protected from becoming embedded in the latex, for that would almost certainly result in a good many of them being removed with the latex after the performance. To protect the hairs, coat hairy parts of the hand with spirit gum first, making sure that all of the hairs are embedded in the spirit gum, which should then be allowed to dry before the latex is applied.

Before applying the latex, stretch the skin tightly by making a fist. Then the latex can be applied, allowed to dry, and powdered. When the hand is relaxed, wrinkles will form. In Figure 13-7 the hand was aged first with cake makeup, sprayed with sealer, then wrinkled with clear latex. For deeper wrinkles, use several coats of latex, making sure that each coat is dry before applying the next. Drying time can be shortened by using a hair dryer.

Before applying latex to the faces of women and girls or boys of pre-shaving age, it is important to consider the fact that facial fuzz will become embedded in the latex, which will cause considerable discomfort and irritation on removal. Unfortunately, applying a barrier such as petroleum jelly or a light coating of creme makeup will cause the latex to eventually separate from the skin, defeating the purpose. If shaving is out of the question, try coating the hair with spirit gum as mentioned above.

Plastic Film

Liquid plastic film can be used in the same way as clear latex. *But make sure you use the plastic film intended for application directly on the skin* (see *Plastic film* in Appendix A). The liquid dries very quickly—a considerable advantage.

Old Age Stipple

Dick Smith has created a remarkably effective latex stipple for aging the skin. This is the formula: (1) Place 90 grams of foam latex base in an 8-ounce paper cup. (2) In another paper cup mix together 10 grams of talc U.S.P., 6 grams of pulverized cake makeup of whatever shade you want for the makeup, and 1 teaspoon of plain Knox gelatine. (3) Stir 3 tablespoons of hot water into the powders, one at a time, until they are dissolved. (4) Stir the solution slowly into the latex, then pour the mixture into glass jars. (5) Place the open jars into hot water for 10 minutes, and stir occasionally. (6) Cap the jars and keep them refrigerated until needed. (7) To prepare the mixture for use, heat a jar of the mixture in hot water until the contents become liquified. (8) To use the latex mixture, stipple it over the stretched skin, and keep the skin stretched until it is dry and has been powdered.

Old Age Stipple (Kryolan, RCMA), Wrinkle Stipple (Ben Nye), Old Skin Plast (Kryolan) are available in a variety of skin tones. It can also be painted with sheer layers of rubber-mask grease paint (RMGP, also called appliance makeup) and creme and cake foundations (cake and creme foundations may be mixed with castor oil or GP-20 for a smooth, sheer application of color). Apply as usual: stretch the skin; stipple latex onto the skin; dry thoroughly; powder, then release, and apply makeup. (See Figures 13-8 and 13-9.)

Another recipe for old age stipple combines the water-based adhesive Pros-Aide with Liquitex Matte Medium. Stretch the skin and stipple as recommended in the previous paragraphs. Adding a high grade of cosmetic talc to help bulk up the recipe will assist you in building up layers. Thinner solutions will produce finer wrinkles; slightly thicker solutions will produce larger and deeper wrinkles. This formula is nearly transparent, will dry with a slight shine, and will remain tacky to the touch. It should be lightly powdered. Because of this natural transparency, it can be applied over a powdered foundation for a natural looking aging technique.

FIGURE 13-8 **Hands aged with old age stipple.** *Actor, John Sawyer, as Shadrack from the film* Shadrack. *(Makeup by Jeff Goodwin of Transformations Makeup FX Lab.)*

Before

After

FIGURE 13-9 Face aged with old age stipple. for TV movie of the week, *The Search for Grace.* *Actress, Ann Donnell as Sarah. (Makeup by Jeff Goodwin of Transformations Makeup FX Lab.)*

Latex and Tissue

This technique involves the use of liquid latex and cleansing tissue (Figure 13-10). It is usually best to cover the whole face with tissue in order to avoid unnatural contrasts in texture between the tissue-covered wrinkles and the relatively smooth skin. This is the procedure:

1. Be sure the skin is clean and dry. Then use a non-irritating liquid latex to paint the area to be wrinkled. *Avoid getting latex into the hair, eyebrows, eyelashes, or beard.* If the eyebrows are to be covered, block them out first by one of the methods suggested in Chapter 12 so that there are no free hairs. Then they can be safely covered with latex. If there is fuzz on the face, either shave first or else lightly cover the skin with creme foundation, powder it, then apply the latex, but remember that this can contribute to loosening of the latex during the performance. You may wish to use a skin barrier first.
2. Tear (do not cut) a single thickness of tissue to the approximate size and shape of the area to be covered, pull the skin tight with one hand, and with the other apply the tissue to the wet latex. For the area around the mouth, a broad smile will probably stretch the skin sufficiently. For best results, work on only a small area at a time.
3. Paint another layer of latex over the tissue and let it dry or force-dry it with a hair dryer.
4. Release the skin and powder the latex. Wrinkles will form.

5. When all of the latex work is finished, color the surface by using one of the following methods: (1) stipple (do not rub) the surface with rubber-mask grease paint; (2) paint a very thin layer of castor oil onto the surface, then stipple with regular creme foundation; (3) stipple with PAX paint (see Appendix A). If you have used a fairly dark latex, apply a lighter foundation color, catching only the tops of the wrinkles, leaving the darker latex showing through in the creases or tiny depressions. That will emphasize the texture as well as the wrinkles that have formed. Stippling with various colors of paint will produce a more natural effect.
6. Complete the makeup as usual with highlights, shadows, and powder. In order to take advantage of the texture, keep the shading subtle. Touch-ups can be done with makeup pencils if you wish.

The latex can be peeled off quite easily after the performance.

If you want to build up parts of the face when using this technique, it can be done with either derma wax, putty-wax, nose putty or silicone putty. It is best to keep the addition small, and care should be taken to blend it smoothly into the skin. The following method can be used:

1. Apply small amounts of putty or wax directly to the skin for jowls, nasolabial folds, etc. Avoid building up the mouth area if possible, and be sure to blend the wax or putty smoothly. Use spirit gum first if you prefer. If you use putty or wax on the nose and

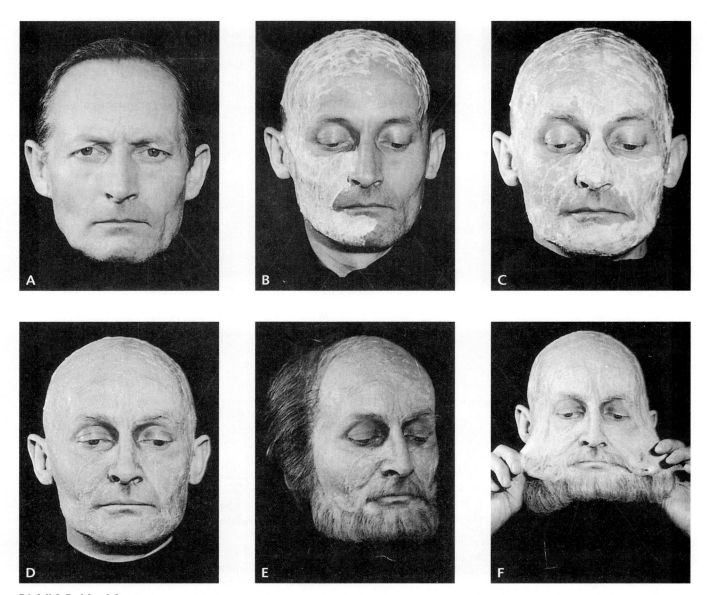

FIGURE 13-10 **Makeup with latex and tissue.** *A. Model without makeup. B-C. Latex and tissue being applied. Head has been covered with a plastic cap. D. Shadowing begun. E. Makeup complete with wig, beard, and additional shadowing. F. Removing the makeup. (Courtesy of Kryolan Corp.)*

tissue on the rest of the face, be sure to give the nose some texture by pressing the surface of the putty or the wax with a grapefruit rind or by stippling with a black plastic stipple sponge or a stiff-bristled brush to create tiny holes in the surface.

2. Follow the directions above for applying latex, tissue, and color

In removing the makeup, peel off the latex. Most of the wax or putty will probably come off with it. Then use any good makeup remover. If you have used spirit gum first and it does not come off with your makeup remover, use spirit-gum remover or alcohol.

Should the actor perspire excessively or if there is considerable muscle movement, the latex and tissue

technique may work itself loose from the skin. A solution to this problem is to use spirit gum as an adhesive

Spirit Gum, Tissue, and Latex

1. Avoiding the eye area, coat the stretched skin with a good spirit gum, first letting the gum become tacky (or inducing tackiness by tapping the gum rapidly with the finger as described earlier and illustrated in Figure 13-5B). Use old age stipple around the tender eye area.

2. Stretch the skin and apply single thicknesses of tissue that have been torn, not cut. Avoid straight

edges. If you want to push the tissue into deeper wrinkles than those that will form naturally, do so at this point. Let the spirit gum dry or force-dry it with a hair dryer.

3. Stretch the skin again and apply a coat of latex. Let the latex dry or force-dry it with a hair dryer before releasing the skin.
4. Powder the latex.
5. Complete your makeup as suggested above (step 5, *Latex and Tissue*).

The makeup can be removed by brushing spirit-gum remover along the edge, then pulling the layers of tissue and latex up gradually, brushing with remover as you go in order to loosen the spirit gum.

Latex, Cotton, and Spirit Gum

In Figure 13-11 latex, cotton, and spirit gum have been used for the abnormal, leathery skin of the young Elephant Man, whose eyes alone reveal his youthfulness. This is the technique:

1. Paint the skin with spirit gum, working on one section of the face at a time (remember to avoid painting the eye area with spirit gum, choosing instead the Age Stipple technique). The forehead is a good place to start. (See Figure 13-11A.) The eyes or the mouth can be done last. If you cover the eyebrows, flatten them out first with Kryolan's Eyebrow Plastic, Special Plastic, or derma wax so that they will not get stuck in the latex.
2. Tap the spirit gum with your finger until it is tacky, then lay on absorbent cotton (Figure 13-11A through E) and let the gum dry. Be sure the fibers follow in the direction you want the wrinkles to go—that is, vertically over the mouth, almost vertically down the cheeks, and horizontally on the forehead.
3. Pull off most of the cotton (Figure 13-11F). The less you leave on, the less pronounced the three-dimensional effect will be.
4. Cover the cotton with latex, using your finger rather than a brush. This step should be done with the skin tightly stretched. *Avoid getting latex into the hair, eyebrows, eyelashes, or beard!* Only one section of the face should be done at a time. The mouth can be stretched with a broad smile, which must be held until the latex is dry. The skin of the cheeks can be pulled taut with the fingers (Figure 13-11L). A hair dryer can be used to speed the drying. When the latex is dry, release the skin, and it will fall naturally into wrinkles (Figure 13-11M).
5. If the eyebrows are covered, crepe-hair or ventilated eyebrows (see Chapter 15) can be attached with latex or spirit gum.
6. When all of the latex work is finished, choose one of the following methods introduced in step 5 under *Latex and Tissue:* (1) stipple (do not rub) the surface with rubber-mask grease paint; or (2) paint a very thin layer of castor oil onto the surface, then stipple with regular creme foundation; or (3) stipple with PAX paint (see Appendix A). Stippling with various colors of paint will produce a more natural effect. Be sure to finish this dimensional makeup with subtle highlights and shadows. With a velour puff, press a generous amount of powder into the grease and creme makeup, then remove the excess with a powder brush.

Most of the makeup can be peeled off, but because of the undercoat of spirit gum, it will peel less easily than latex usually does. The remainder of the gum can be cleaned from the skin with spirit gum remover or 70% alcohol. In pulling the latex off and in dissolving the spirit gum, be extremely careful around the eyes and the eyebrows. To avoid pulling hairs out of the eyebrows, pull very slowly and brush a little alcohol or spirit gum remover into them as you go.

This technique can also be effective on the hands (see Figure 13-12).

Cornmeal, Wheat Germ, or Bran with Latex and Spirit Gum

In order to give the skin a rough texture, with or without wrinkling, cornmeal, wheat germ, or miller's bran (Figure 13-13C) can be used with the latex. This is the procedure:

1. Apply spirit gum to the skin and allow it to become tacky or induce tackiness by tapping the gum rapidly with one finger.
2. When the gum is sufficiently tacky, cover it with cornmeal, wheat germ, or bran. This can be done with the hands. Do not try to apply it with a tissue; the tissue will tend to stick to the spirit gum and tear, leaving small pieces that may be difficult to remove. If you want the skin to look wrinkled as well as rough, stretch it before applying the cornmeal, wheat germ, or bran.
3. Apply latex with the skin stretched or not stretched, as you prefer, and let it dry or force-dry it with a hair dryer. It is also possible, when using cornmeal, to mix it with the latex before applying it to the skin.
4. Complete the makeup as in step 5 under *Latex and Tissue* (Figure 13-13C).

Bran and latex, appropriately made up, can also be used to simulate wounds, growths, or diseased conditions of the skin.

When applying makeup to the hands be sure to carry the makeup far enough up the arm to be covered by the sleeve of the costume.

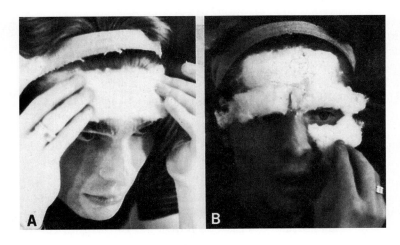

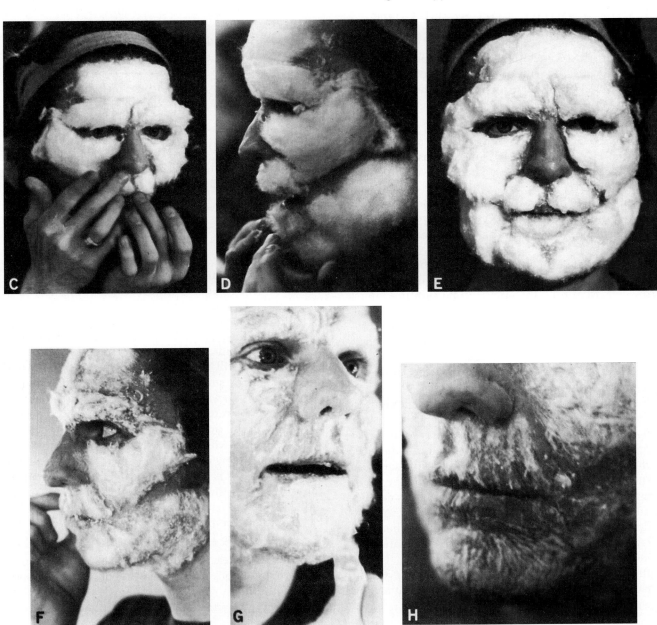

FIGURE 13-11 **Skin texture with latex, cotton, and spirit gum.** Makeup for The Elephant Man *by student Milton Blankenship. A. Applying thick layer of cotton over spirit gum after the gum has become tacky. B. Applying cotton to the cheekbones. C. Applying cotton to the upper lip. D. Applying cotton to the jawline, chin, and lower lip. E. Thick layer of cotton completed. F. Pulling off excess cotton. G. Applying latex to the chin area. H. Chin after latex has been dried. I. Stretching skin on cheek and jaw area as latex is being dried. J. Wrinkles on cheek and jaw after latex is dry. K. Drying latex on upper lip. L. Stretching skin over cheekbone as latex is being dried. M. Rubber-mask grease applied over the dried latex.*

FIGURE 13-11 Continued.

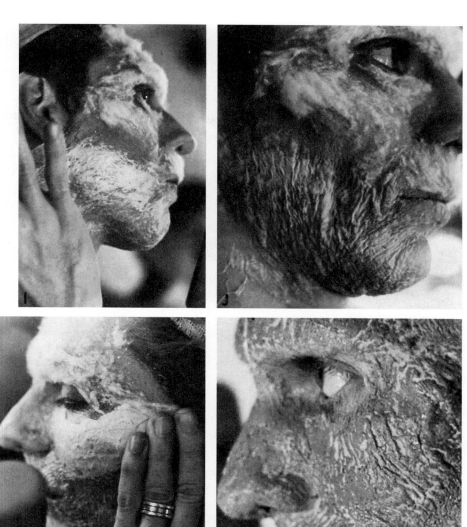

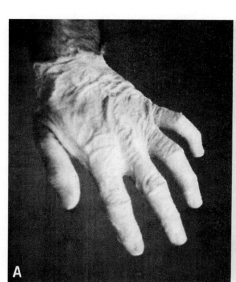
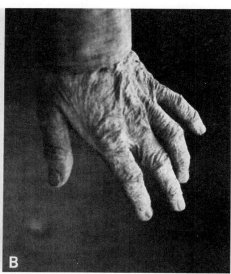

K

L

M

A

B

FIGURE 13-12 Hand aged with latex, cotton, and spirit gum. *Makeup by student Larry Lane. A. Cotton attached to the hand with spirit gum, then coated with latex. B. Foundation, three colors of stipple, and brown spots applied over the latex.*

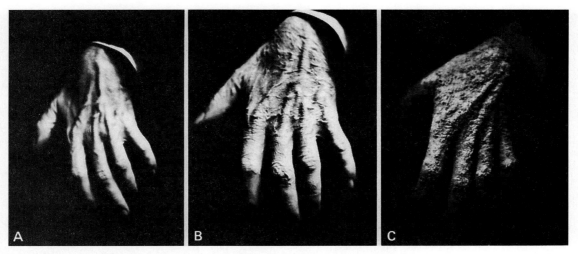

FIGURE 13-13 **Hand aged with different techniques.** *A. Cake makeup. B. Tissue and spirit gum over cake makeup. C. Latex and cornmeal.*

Special Constructions

The constructions that follow can all be made by direct methods. Some of them might also be done with the molded latex technique discussed in the next chapter.

Black Eye

A black eye involving only swelling and bruising can be simulated with paint. It may involve only the orbital area or the cheekbone as well. In either case, it changes color as it ages. There is more red at first, but then the inflammation subsides, leaving a deep purple color (giving the "black" effect), medium or dark gray, and the greenish yellow color typical of bruises which are no longer inflamed. See the photograph of a painted black eye in Figure G-21 in the color section.

The various stages of a black eye can be simulated by mixtures of red, purple, black, white, and greenish or lemon yellow (try Ben Nye bruise wheels and Kryolan 24-color Dermacolor palette). The purple can be deepened with black, and if the mixture is not red enough, red can be added. Or it can be stippled with black and red. Black and white can be mixed for the gray. For the yellowish tinge, lemon yellow can be mixed with just a little light gray (white with a touch of black) or stippled with light gray. All of the color can be applied with a brush or with a small black stipple sponge.

If the cheekbone is to be involved, you can highlight it just below the corner of the eye. The area immediately below the eye (including the lower lid) and the superciliary bone above the outer corner of the eye can also be highlighted. For light-skinned characters, white can be used for these highlights and stippled down later. For dark-skinned characters, it would be better to use a color a few shades lighter than the base.

Gray shadow can then be stippled below all of the highlights and in the eye socket. Purple and black stipple can be added when appropriate. The shape of the darkened area will usually be a somewhat irregular oval. All edges of both highlights and shadows should be kept soft.

To begin, choose a bony area of the face above or below the eye as the impact point. This point can easily be highlighted creating the illusion of swollen skin (remember, light colors protrude while dark colors recede). Then, take your stipple sponge and cut it into several different shapes, some pointed, some rounded off. Take the pointed stipple sponge and apply a small amount of red to the bruised area. Do not make it a solid color! Using another sponge, stipple purple in a smaller area around the point of impact, overlapping the red in some areas (a fresh bruise is more red and pink in color so use the purple judiciously). Now, take a clean latex sponge and lightly blend the colors out in feather-like strokes creating steaks and swirls giving the appearance of interesting patterns of broken blood vessels. Blend the two colors together in some areas, leaving them separate in others. You can, at this point, repeat the previous steps to intensify the colors. When you are finished, powder the bruise with translucent powder and brush away any excess. Then mist over the entire area with water (i.e., Evian aerosol spray) to reduce the powdery look and bring out the natural looking colors.

Fresh bruises are mostly pink and reddish in color, turning purple and red, then purple and blue as they get older. The next stage is slightly greenish, then it turns yellow and finally disappears as the blood pigments are absorbed gradually into the bloodstream. To make the older bruise, simply follow the same steps using more purple and blue, adding green and yellow around the edges.

FIGURE 13-14 Skin texture and wrinkles.

FIGURE 13-15 Skin texture and wrinkles.

Jeff Goodwin

Jeff Goodwin, film and television makeup artist of Transformations Makeup FX Lab states, "continuity wise, every person heals differently and at their own rate of speed, but it is usually safe to say that your average bruise will disappear in five to seven days. So, carefully consider your continuity and properly carry over your injuries. I hate to see films in which the actor gets a blackeye or bruise and in the next story day it is miraculously healed and gone away. Remember to break down your scripts carefully and plan for these things ahead of time. Also, there is no excuse for neglecting to collect good and accurate visual research, especially for physical conditions caused by aging, disease or accidents."

Blindness

The actor can usually suggest blindness by keeping the eyes nearly closed (see the photograph of Helen Keller, Figure 13-14K). For blindness involving disfigurement of the orbital area, you might cast a blind eye and make a molded latex, gelatin, or silicone piece from it (see Chapter 14 for casting methods); or if you have a plaster cast of the actor's head but don't have time to cast the blind eye, you could model a blind eye on the cast in clay, then paint latex over the clay. Although that would not have the texture or the detail of a cast piece, it would give you a molded piece that would fit the actor.

Whatever kind of piece you use, it should, of course, be appropriately painted or made up. For an open, staring eye, for example, or even a partially opened one, you might paint the eye on with either makeup or acrylic paint or for a more "real" look, order a glass eye from a special effects makeup supplier (Alcone, Burman's, Factor II) or from your local taxidermist. You might even glue on false eyelashes. To enable the actor to see through the eye, a hole could be cut into the piece and gauze glued to the back, then painted to conceal it.

Bruises

Even when accompanied by swelling, a bruise can usually be simulated with paint. (See Figures G-23 and G-24 in the color section.) For light-skinned characters, red, gray, purple, greenish yellow, and light cream or ivory can be used. The fresher the bruise, the more red; the older it is, the more yellow. For darker-skinned characters, the colors should be adjusted to the color of the skin. The color being used can be either dabbed on the bruised area and then blended together with a brush, or stippled on. In either case, make sure that all edges are soft. If the bruised area is to be very swollen, you may want to build it up first with derma wax, silicone putty, or gelatin (gelatin kits available from Kryolan, Ben Nye, Paramount; for gelatin recipe, see Chapter 14, *Welts*.)

Burns

Minor burns can be simulated by stippling the skin with red makeup applied with a red-rubber sponge. For deeper burns, coat the skin with latex, which can be pulled loose and allowed to hang if you want it to. A single layer of cleansing tissue placed over the latex and then covered with another layer of latex will give more body to the hanging skin. Cotton can be used with the latex for burnt flesh. Makeup can then be applied over the latex. For close work try some of the following commercially available products: RCMA, Blister and Scar making material; Kryolan's, Tuplast; Art Anthony's, Flesh Putty; and any of the gelatin products mentioned under bruises.

Cuts

Superficial cuts can be painted on, with or without the use of artificial blood. Deeper cuts usually require building up the area with wax or putty, then cutting into it with a dull instrument, such as a palette knife (Figure G-23). Plastic sealer can be painted over the construction at this point if you wish.

The inside of the cut can be painted red with grease paint. For a cut that is still bleeding, a few drops or even a stream of artificial blood can be added to the cut with an eye dropper and allowed to run out onto the skin.

In some areas, such as the neck, where building up with putty or wax may not be practicable, latex can be painted directly onto the skin and allowed to dry thoroughly. The skin can then be pushed together into a crease in the middle of the strip of latex. The latex will stick to itself, forming a deep crease (Figure G-22) that can be made to look like a cut with the addition of red makeup. Blood may or may not be running from the cut.

For a horizontal cut in the throat, be sure to use a natural crease in the skin if there is one. Pinching of the skin is not recommended but is sometimes done.

Ears

If you are making up such characters as sprites, leprechauns, devils, or aliens it may be necessary to make pointed ears. Although molded latex pieces (see Chapter 14) should be used for close work, the following simple, direct construction can be used in an emergency:

1. Sculpt a pair of ear tips using Roma Plastilina. Check for correct scale, shape, and proper fit by periodically setting them on the actor's own ear.

FIGURE 13-16 **Phantom of the Opera.** *Ear modeled with putty-wax. Stylized silent-screen makeup by student Richard Brunner.*

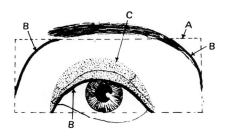

FIGURE 13-17 Diagram of Asian eyelid made with adhesive tape.

2. Paint four to six layers of liquid latex onto the surface (this depends upon the quality and type), allowing each layer to dry completely. The final two layers should be stippled on with a piece of red sponge to simulate skin texture. Edges should be feathered to allow for a smooth transition between the latex ear tip and the actor's ear. A thick, straight edge would be very difficult to disguise.

3. Attach the tip with appliance adhesive, or water-soluble spirit gum (this type of spirit gum is easily removed).

4. Paint with RMGP (rubber-mask grease paint) and powder.

Eyelid, Asian

(For real Asian eyelids see Figures 12-17U, 12-19, 12-20.) If the eye is so deepset as to make it difficult or impossible to create the effect of an Asian eye with paint, and if a latex eyelid (Chapter 14) is not practicable, a satisfactory effect can usually be achieved with adhesive tape. The choice to include as highly a slylized makeup as Asian eyelids in the overall production concept must be made with the consideration of the entire company. This is one method:

1. Tear or cut slightly over 2 inches of tape from a roll at least 1-inch wide. This tape is represented by the broken line (A) in Figure 13-17.

2. Mark and cut as shown by the heavy lines (13-17B). This forms the eye opening and rounds off the up-per edges so that the tape will be easier to conceal. (It is best to make a paper pattern first, then mark the tape.)

3. Cover the area indicated by C with makeup on the *back* of the tape. This gives a nonsticky area over the actor's own eyelid.

4. Attach the tape (usually slightly on the diagonal) so that the top falls just below the natural brow and covers the downward sweep of the outer end (Figure 13-18A). In order to prevent the eyebrow's appearing to be cut off too abruptly, lift a few hairs from under the tape and let them fall on the outside. Stipple the edges of the tape with latex cream adhesive to help conceal them.

5. When the latex is dry, cover the tape and the skin with foundation color (Figure 13-18B), and finish the makeup. If you are using cake makeup, cover the tape and a little of the skin around it with grease or creme makeup first; powder; then apply the cake makeup. In order to counteract the flatness of the tape, shadow the lower edge and highlight the center to give a puffy effect (Figure 13-18C).

The cutting of the tape can be greatly simplified by cutting 4 inches instead of 2, folding it double, sticky sides together, marking and cutting either side, then separating the two pieces. This will ensure that both eyes are exactly alike. If you place a piece of waxed paper between the two sticky sides, you will have no trouble getting them apart. Be sure the tape is not uncomfortable, that it does not interfere with the normal action of the eyelid, and that the actor can see without difficulty.

It is also possible to make Asian eyelids with liquid plastic, using the technique described in the following section for making sagging eyelids. The main point of difference, aside from the change in shape, is that when the tab at the bottom (corresponding to A' in Figure 13-19A) is folded up to create the almond-shaped opening for the lid, it will have to be clipped in several places in order to give a smooth curve.

A simpler tape construction can be used with equal effectiveness on certain eyes. This consists of a crescent-shaped piece of adhesive tape, the outer edge of which is attached to the side of the nose and under the inner

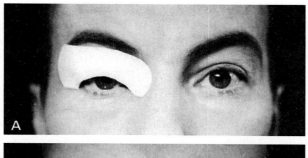

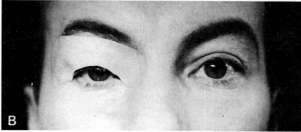

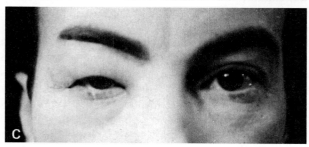

FIGURE 13-18 Asian eyelid made with adhesive tape. *Edges are stippled with latex and the tape darkened with rubber-mask grease. Makeup is completed with eyebrow pencil and creme makeup. Notice how the flat tape is slightly rounded with shadowing.*

end of the eyebrow. The inner edge of the crescent (which should be very nearly a half moon) hangs free. The purpose of the piece is to conceal the deep depressions (plane A, Figure 12-14) that are normal to the Caucasian eye.

Eyelid, Sagging

A sagging eyelid (Figure 13-19) can be constructed in much the same way as an Asian eyelid, except that the tape should slant down from the inner end of the eyebrow to the outer corner of the eye. The upper edge of the tape can correspond exactly to the bottom of the natural brow; or the tape can be used to block out part of the brow, and a new brow can be glued onto the tape or attached to the skin above the tape. The projection (A') is folded under, along the dotted line, before the tape is attached to the skin. This gives the appearance of a fold of flesh.

Plastic film (see Appendix A) can be used instead of the tape in constructing the eyelid and is much preferred since it has greater flexibility, is less bulky, and has thinner edges. The piece shown in Figure 13-19C

can be cut from a sheet of plastic film or formed by painting liquid plastic (see Appendix A) onto glass to conform to a pattern of the piece placed under the glass (Figure 13-19B).

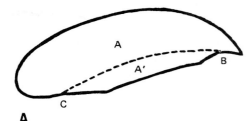

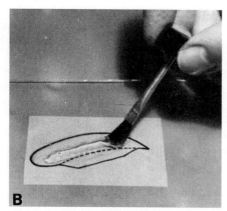

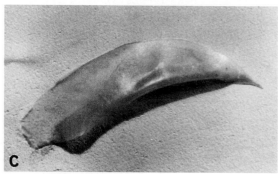

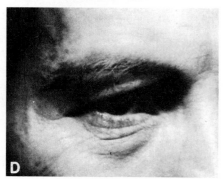

FIGURE 13-19 Sagging eyelid. *A. Pattern for the sagging eyelid shown in C. and used for the makeup in D. (Reproduced here in the exact size used.) B. Painting plastic eyelid on glass. Pattern is placed under the glass. C. Plastic eyelid folded and ready for use. D. Plastic eyelid attached but not made up.*

The advantage of this method is that edges can be kept very thin, whereas the center portion can be given more firmness with additional coats of plastic. Since many coats of plastic may be needed to give the desired thickness, dropping the liquid plastic onto the area to be built up instead of brushing it on will speed up the process.

When the plastic piece is dry, it should be powdered, then removed from the glass (see discussion under *Scars* and *Welts*.) The tab (A') should be folded under and glued down or secured with translucent plastic tape (see *Adhesive tape* in Appendix A). The piece can then be applied with spirit gum. Before pressing it down into place, make sure that it is exactly where you want it. If you want to experiment first with various placements, coat the edges of the plastic with stubble adhesive (see Appendix A). The piece will then adhere temporarily to the skin. This experimentation should be done before any makeup is applied to the area.

In experimenting with the placement, try it with various expressions, such as a frown or raised eyebrows.

If any reshaping of the piece is necessary as a result of this experimentation, it can be done before the spirit gum is applied. Should this trimming result in any thickened edges, they can be thinned by placing the piece on the glass and brushing the edges with acetone until they are thinned down.

Makeup can then be applied as usual. As with any prosthetic piece, never use this eyelid for a performance unless it has first been worn for at least one entire rehearsal—preferably more.

Clear latex can be used in essentially the same way and builds up more quickly, though it may take longer to dry. If you plan to use the eyelids for a number of performances, making molded latex eyelids (see Chapter 14) is much more efficient.

Fingernails Long fingernails can be cut out of used photographic film or sheets of acetate and glued onto the natural nails with spirit gum. They can be colored with nail polish or paint. Ready-made false fingernails, if they are long enough, provide a simpler solution to the problem.

Moles (Figures 13-20 and 13-21.) These raised and sometimes hairy spots on the skin can be created with such materials or combinations of materials as derma wax, gelatin, cotton and spirit gum, gelatin and alfalfa or chia seeds, latex, and wheat germ. They can be formed directly on the skin before any makeup is applied or they can be made on any convenient smooth surface and attached with spirit gum after they have solidified. They can be appropriately colored when the rest of the makeup is applied. If a mole is to be hairy, the hairs can be embedded in the material as the mole is being made. If the mole is to be small and smooth, a few drops of latex can be transferred to any flat glass or other smooth, nonabsorbent surface with an orangewood stick, a small glass rod, or a brush handle and then allowed to dry. The latex must be thick enough so

FIGURE 13-20 **Making a mole with gelatine and alfalfa seeds.** *A. Ingredients for the mole: gelatine, alfalfa seeds, and hot water. B. Mixing the ingredients. C. Forming the mole on the skin, using an orangewood stick. D. The finished mole. (Enlarged.) E, F. Gelatine moles, natural size.*

that it will not spread out when it touches the surface. And it must dry completely before it can be used.

Since gelatin has a natural, flesh-like appearance, it is likely to require less makeup than other materials and may sometimes require none at all. When color is needed, powdered rouge or scrapings from cake rouge, cake eyeshadow, or cake makeup foundation can be added to the powdered gelatin before the hot water is added, or the gelatin mole can be touched up with cake eyeshadow, creme shading colors, or light, medium, or dark brown eyebrow pencils.

Moles can also be made by mixing liquid latex with alfalfa or chia seeds (and with scrapings from the top of an appropriate shade of brownish cake makeup if you want the mole to be colored), then pouring or spooning enough for one mole onto glass (or other smooth surface) and letting it dry. When it is dry, the top of the mole should be powdered, but the bottom must not be. If you want to attach the mole directly to the skin before applying any makeup, brush a spot of clear latex onto the skin and let it dry. Then carefully lift the mole off the glass with tweezers and press it onto the spot of dried latex on the skin.

Perspiration and Tears

The effect of perspiration can be created by applying glycerin, Bob Kelly's Perspiration, Kryolan's Sweat, or Paramount's Glycerian over the finished makeup. These products can be applied with the fingers, with a stipple sponge, or with a manual spray bottle.

Tears, if unable to be produced by the actor, can be induced by either rubbing menthol under the eyes or by blowing the vapors into the eyes through a tube using menthol crystals (available at Namies or your local pharmacy).

Pimples

Although pimples can be created three-dimensionally with latex, derma wax, sesame seeds, etc., they can also be painted on with tiny highlights, shadows, and creme rouge.

If there are to be a lot of them, and the whole area that they cover is to be reddened, the reddening can be done first by stippling, to whatever degree is appropriate, with a somewhat muted creme rouge. In order to determine the appropriate shade, observe the color of real pimples. The pimples, varying in size and irregularly placed, can then be modeled with highlights and shadows, using a very small brush. If, after the makeup is powdered, the pimples need toning down, that can be done with additional stippling, either with the creme rouge or with the foundation color, whichever is more appropriate.

For a single pimple or a few fairly large pimples, begin with a round, reddish spot a bit larger than the raised portion of the pimple in order to create the effect of an inflamed area around the pimple. To create the raised portion of the pimple, place a small, round highlight in the center of the reddish spot. Then, with a tiny brush, shadow around the bottom of the highlight as if you were modeling a sphere. The edges of all three colors in the pimple must be soft. Unless you are using cake makeup, the pimple or the pimpled area should, of course, be powdered.

Scabs

Scabs can be made directly on the skin with derma wax, spirit gum and cotton, or gelatin. When gelatin or spirit gum and cotton are used, the scab can be made on any smooth surface (glass, marble, formica) and, when it has dried, attached to the skin with spirit gum. Or it can be made directly on the skin. It can be appropriately colored either before or after it has been applied. Scabs can also be cast in latex and attached with spirit gum. (See Chapter 14.)

When gelatin is used to make the scab, the gelatin can be colored by adding various shades of dry rouge and cake makeup (especially browns and deep reds) before it is applied to the skin. Additional coloring can be added, if necessary, after the gelatin has solidified. When derma wax is used, spirit gum and cotton should be applied to the skin first—unless the skin is hairy, in which case the cotton may not be necessary. Or spirit gum and cotton can be used without the derma wax. In either case, coloring is added after construction of the scab has been completed.

Scabs can also be made by first painting the area of the scab with latex, then immediately placing a pinch or two of Red Zinger tea on the wet latex and letting the latex dry. Use a soft brush to remove any of the tea which is not anchored in the latex. For a thick scab, use more latex so that more of the tea will adhere to it. Or if you find, when the latex has dried, that the scab is too flat, simply paint on another coat of latex and add more tea. If the scab isn't exactly the color you want, touch it up with creme makeup colors and powder it.

With all of these direct methods, any hairs on the skin will become embedded in the artificial scab, as they do with real scabs, and will help to hold it in place.

Fresh scabs will often begin as areas of coagulated dried blood. They are nearly black in color at the center and appear more red at the edges. Choose a dark red blood product that dries with a slight sheen (try Fabulous sun burn gel at Cinema Secrets, K.D. 151 Blood, see Appendix B). Build up several layers at the center, blend the edges slightly to reveal the red coloration and let dry completely. Finish with a spray sealer or spray bandage.

Scars

The traditional method of creating scars of the type illustrated in Figures 13-21D, F, and I is to paint the area to be scarred with nonflexible collodion before any makeup is applied. As the collodion dries, it will wrinkle and draw the skin. If the scar is not deep

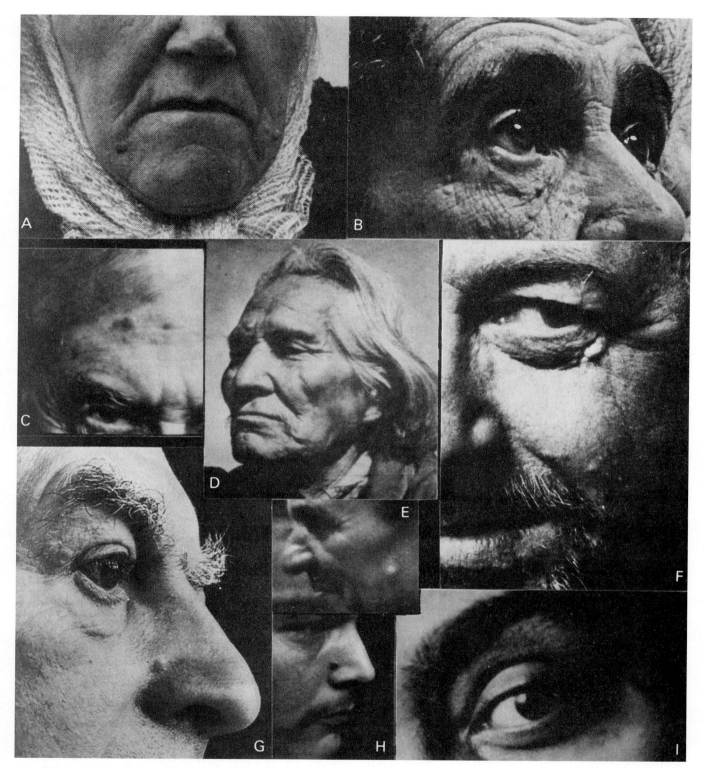

FIGURE 13-21 Scars, cuts, moles, and warts

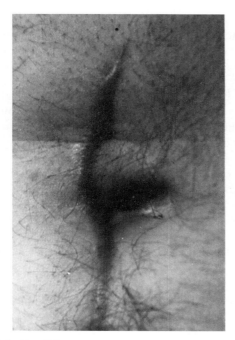

FIGURE 13-22 Surgical scar resulting from repairing a knife wound.

may not be needed over the collodion, depending on the effect you want. For additional protection to the skin, apply cleansing cream, moisture cream, or any good skin cream to the skin first, then wipe off the excess before applying the cake makeup. *Avoid using collodion close to the eye.*

For recent scars that still retain a bit of red or pinkish color use pigmented collodion (Collodacolor by Michael Davy, see Appendix B).

Collodion scars can be peeled off or removed with acetone. Because dermatologists consider this prolonged creasing of the skin undesirable, this method of making scars cannot be recommended. In addition, collodion may irritate the skin, though applying the collodion over the makeup rather than directly to the skin should cause less irritation. However, if there is any irritation at all, this method should not be used. Latex scars, which can be painted directly on the skin or attached with medical adhesive (Figure 23 B and C), can be used instead.

One simple but effective method is to use cleansing tissue or absorbent cotton with latex and spirit gum. The spirit gum is applied first, then a very thin piece of cotton or tissue, then latex. The scarred area can be roughened as much as you like by pulling up bits of cotton or by wrinkling the tissue. Derma wax and other materials can also be used. (See Figure 13-23A.) Special coloring for the scar may or may not be necessary.

If latex has not been used in making the scar (or sometimes even if it has), it's a good idea to coat the scar with sealer after the makeup has been completed. That will not only protect the scar but also give it a slight natural sheen.

enough, successive coats can be applied. Each coat should be allowed to dry completely before another is added. The makeup is then applied as usual.

A better method is to use cake makeup as a foundation and apply the collodion over it. Makeup may or

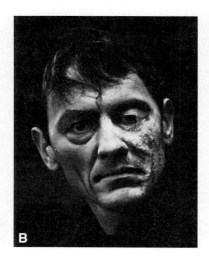
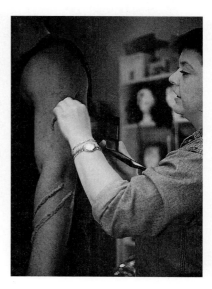

FIGURE 13-23 **Scars and welts.** *A. Welt with cut. Derma wax with blood-red creme rouge in cut. Makeup by student Paul Lynch. B. Scar tissue. Left eye partially covered with adhesive tape and left side of face covered with layers of latex. Makeup by Bill Smith. C. Intrinsically colored three-dimensional latex scars applied with Telesis V surgical adhesive on actor Derrick Weeden, as Othello at the Oregon Shakespeare Festival. (Makeup by Ranny Beyer.)*

Another method is to pour or brush latex onto glass and, with a palette knife or an orangewood stick, swirl it and shape it into the size and kind of scar you want. Then allow it to dry, or force-dry it with a hair dryer, peel it off the glass, and apply it to the skin with spirit gum. When you complete the makeup, color the scar appropriately. This is a variation of the molded latex scars or welts described in Chapter 14. It is a particularly good technique for arena staging. For greater projection, combine the latex with cotton or tissue.

Three-dimensional latex scars as seen in Figure 13-23C can be colored intrinsically using cosmetic grade pigments. Form the raised scars by pouring pigmented latex into a plaster negative mold (#1 industrial molding plaster), allow to dry, powder, remove from the mold, and trim the edges. First, apply a skin barrier (Top Guard by Premiere Products, Inc.) to the actor's body where the scars are intended to be attached, then coat the scars and the skin with a pressure sensitive, silicone-based adhesive (Telesis V by Premiere Products, Inc.) and allow both to dry for five minutes. Firmly press the scar onto the actor's skin. Apply makeup to the scar and blend to match the actor's skin color, then powder. Use a strong, gentle solvent to remove the appliance (Super Solv by Premiere Products, Inc., see Appendix A).

Similar techniques can be used to make scars with plastic scar material (Tuplast by Kryolan), plastic sealer, or liquid plastic film. The plastic, as in the latex process can be poured or painted into a negative plaster mold.

The mold must first be sealed with two light coats of white shellac, allowed to dry thoroughly between coats, and then coated with a thin layer of petroleum jelly. Once it is cured, the plastic can be removed and attached to the skin with one of the pressure-sensitive adhesives. Another technique is to pour or smear the plastic onto glass, then swirl with an orangewood stick to make bumps or ridges (Figure 13-24). This will give a semitransparent scar that can be applied to the skin with spirit gum (if flexibility and strength of the bond are a concern, spirit gum may not be the best choice; use one of the adhesives mentioned above). The scar can be colored and given more body by adding tinted face powder as the plastic is being swirled with the orangewood stick. For stronger coloring, powdered rouge can be used. If you don't have powdered rouge, simply scrape the top of a cake of dry rouge to produce a powder. Figure 13-24B shows scars with and without powder and rouge.

When the plastic scars are pulled off the glass, both sides should be powdered, as with latex pieces. When the scars are applied to the skin with spirit gum, the edges of the plastic can be dissolved and blended into the skin by brushing them with acetone. The makeup can then be applied. The plastic scar can be left without makeup or can be partially or completely made up with appropriate colors. As with latex, materials such as cotton or string can be used in the plastic scar. Figure 13-24C shows a plastic piece on the face before the edges have been blended.

FIGURE 13-24 Plastic scars, welts, and growths. *A. Making the pieces with liquid plastic. B. Finished pieces, some with color added. C. One of the pieces attached to the skin with spirit gum. Makeup has not yet been applied.*

Gelatin can also be used for making scars. A surgical scar, for example, could be easily and quickly duplicated directly on the skin with gelatin. Or it could be made on glass or formica first, then attached with Pros-Aide.

Another method of making a raised scar is illustrated in Figure 13-25. Although it involves a number of steps, it is really quite simple and requires only following the illustrations and the captions. Having done that, you may wish to experiment with your own variations. The technique was devised for the 1986 Broadway revival of Eugene O'Neill's *The Iceman Cometh*. For ready-made Vacu-form positives or scars and wounds, see Scars and Wounds in Appendix A.

Warts
Warts can be made with nose putty, derma wax, gelatin, molded latex, silicone, polyurethane, or latex foam. Nose putty, derma wax, and gelatin warts can be built up directly on the skin, whereas molded latex or foam warts must, of course, be molded first, then attached with spirit gum. Makeup can be applied to the wart with a small, flat shading brush. It can then be powdered along with the rest of the makeup.

Nonmolded latex warts, however, can be constructed directly on the skin by the following method:

1. Dip an orangewood stick, a glass rod, or the handle of a plastic rat-tail comb into a bottle of latex, then remove it and let it dry.
2. Starting at the top of the latex coating, which should not be powdered, remove the latex from the stick, rod, or comb handle by rolling it down from top to bottom, using the thumb and the forefinger.
3. When the latex is all off, squeeze it together into a lump. If you want to reshape it further—to make it flatter on the bottom, for example—you can cut it with scissors.
4. Dab a spot of spirit gum (no smaller than the bottom of the wart) onto the skin (which must be free of makeup or grease) at the spot where the wart is to be placed, then tap the gum lightly with one finger until it becomes very tacky.
5. Press the bottom of the wart firmly into the spirit gum.
6. When the spirit gum is dry and the wart is securely attached to the skin, you can smooth out the surface of the wart with derma wax, blending it carefully into the skin, using a small, flat shading brush.
7. Powder the wart carefully and brush off excess powder with a powder brush. The wart is now ready to be made up.

The advantage of making a wart by this method is that if properly attached, it is unlikely to fall off or to be knocked out of shape if accidentally touched.

For stronger bonds use a pressure-sensitive adhesive such as Appliance Adhesive by Ben Nye, Pros-Aide by ADM Tronics Inc., or one of the Telesis adhesives by Premiere Products, Inc.

Welts
Welts, like warts, can be made with nose putty, derma wax (Figure 13-23A), gelatin, molded latex, silicone, polyurethane, or latex foam. As with warts, welts of nose putty and gelatin can be built up directly on the skin, whereas molded latex or foam welts must be molded first, then attached with spirit gum. The method chosen may depend on the length of the welt and where it is to be used. A welt across the cheek, for example, could probably be made by whichever method was more convenient. But a long welt or a welt that is to be used under clothing and then revealed during the course of the play might better be made up in advance and attached with spirit gum.

Wens
Similar to a wart in appearance but larger and more rounded, wens are usually flesh-colored and are most often found on the top of the head, the forehead, or the back of the neck. They can be made in the same way as warts; but because of their size, they should usually be made of foam latex or by the direct latex-and-wax method described for warts. They can also be made with gelatin (preferably molded), in which case they have to be made immediately before the performance and cannot be reused.

Wounds, Open
Various materials, such as derma wax, putty wax, silicone puttys, gelatins, scar plastics, and tissue and latex, can be used to create open wounds. And various non-makeup items can be combined with those materials to produce interesting effects.

The first step was to apply spirit gum to the area. The spirit gum was then tapped with one finger to make it tacky. The tea leaves were pressed into the spirit gum, and the entire area of the wound was painted with latex. When the latex was dry, it was made up to match the rest of the skin, and the central area was colored with two shades of creme rouge. The latex at the center of the wound was then cut open with scissors. (This was done with extreme care in order to avoid creating a *real* wound!) The opening was filled with stage blood, which was allowed to flow out, then smeared over the wound and onto the skin surrounding it.

There are many qualities and colors of stage blood manufactured for a variety of effects: Arterial, veinal, wet, dried, pooling, squirting, running, shiny, sticky, thick, thin, dark, red, blue, brown, transparent, opaque, staining, non-staining, and edible. It must perform in a manner that is visually appropriate for the intended effect. Should you choose to develop your own recipe, here are a few suggestions:

1. Avoid liquid detergents and soaps with the hopes of creating a washable blood. Mixing colorants into

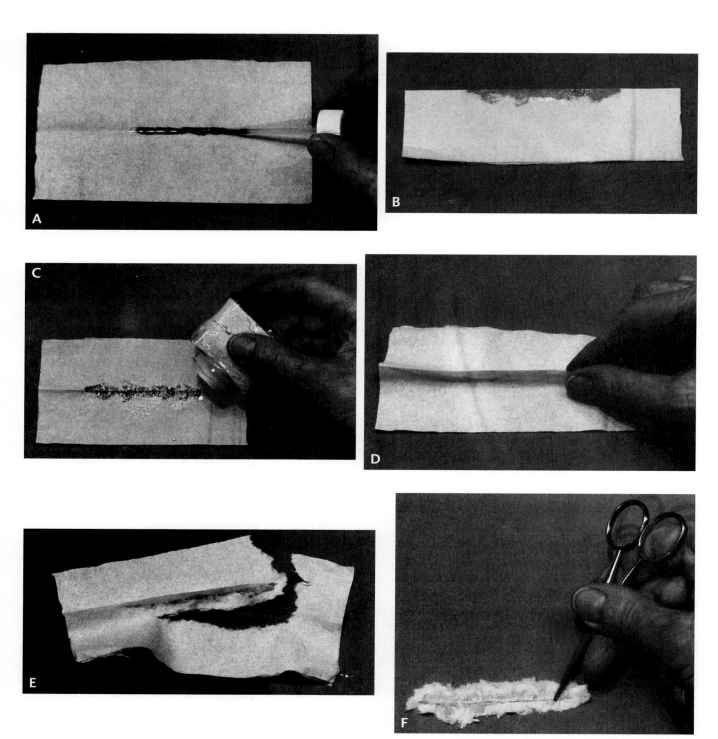

FIGURE 13-25 **Making a scar.** *A. Sheet of cleansing tissue. B. Spirit gum being applied along crease in tissue. C. Spirit gum powdered and tissue folded along crease. D. Tissue opened out. E. Tissue turned upside-down and spirit gum on tissue powdered. F. Crease in tissue pressed together. G. Tissue being torn around spirit-gummed area. H. All excess tissue removed. I. Ridge in tissue being flattened with scissors. J. Latex being applied to tissue. K. Tissue being folded, with latex inside. L. Excess tissue torn away. M. Sealer being applied to scar. N. Finished scar, powdered. O. Scar creased with orangewood stick, then attached to skin with spirit gum or latex.*

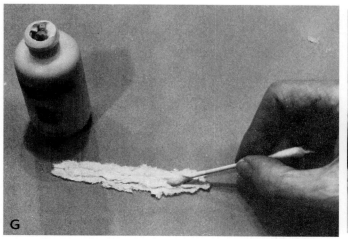

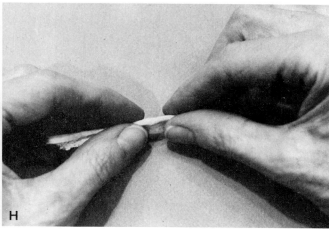

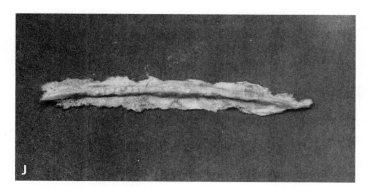

FIGURE 13-25 Continued.

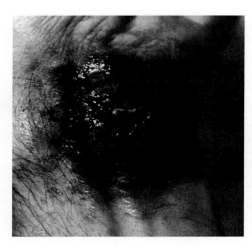

FIGURE 13-26 **Puncture wound in wrist.** *Created with Red Zinger tea leaves and latex.*

soaps has the reverse effect. Acting as a surfactant the soap breaks down the surface tension of the fibers allowing the colorant to penetrate deeper into the garment. It may also cause the blood product to foam.

2. Create a blood product that remains flexible and shiny and peels off the skin or other smooth surfaces by mixing your colorant into Phlex-glu.

3. Karo syrup and food coloring are a simple and effective product. The syrup will suspend the dye and keep it from staining fabrics (it is important to test blood products on fabric samples before using them on finished costumes.) This is also safe as mouth blood.

4. Produce a no-drip blood by mixing one tablespoon peanut butter with one quarter teaspoon of vegetable oil, add two drops of water and red and blue food coloring as needed. Safe as mouth blood.

5. Use Hershey chocolate under blue gels or dark stage lighting. Safe as mouth blood.

6. If blood comes into contact with the costume, be sure to choose fabrics that are washable. Dry cleaning will often lock in the stain. Always test the fabrics before using any blood product. To remove blood products from costumes, immerse them in warm soapy water as soon as they come off stage. It is always a good idea to have a costume double or back-up costume when they are repeatedly exposed to blood products.

PROBLEMS

1. Model a nose with derma wax, then add skin texture, foundation, rouge, and stipple.

2. Model a nose meticulously, using derma wax (preferably flesh-colored). Then, instead of making up the nose with a foundation color, as you normally would, stipple it with what you consider to be the best possible colors to match your own nose in order to make the new nose look completely convincing to anyone standing and talking to you. (Yes, it can be done.) It would be advisable, of course, to avoid exaggerated shapes and to make only a small addition to your own nose. For this experiment, do not use sealer over the derma wax, but do powder it. If the powder is obvious, even after being dusted off with a powder brush, pat it lightly with a damp sponge. The best test of the makeup is, of course, to deliberately talk to someone who is unaware that the nose is not entirely your own in order to find out if it is noticed.

3. Model a nose with derma wax and cotton. Then add skin texture, foundation, rouge, and stipple.

4. Model a nose with nose putty, then add skin texture, foundation, rouge, and stipple.

5. Experiment with the various methods for creating the effect of wrinkled skin, and do a complete makeup using one of the methods.

6. Do a few special constructions, such as welts, warts, moles, scars, or burns.

7. Using whatever materials you wish to, create your own technique for making scars, wounds, or unsightly growths.

8. Design and execute a makeup using one or more three-dimensional makeup techniques.

9. Apply several kinds of blood products to a variety of white fabric samples: silk, cotton, wool, and a synthetic. Then clean each sample to remove the blood. This experiment will assist in determining the kinds of fabrics best suited for costumes in productions using stage blood.

chapter 14

Prosthetic Makeup

The most effective method of creating most three-dimensional additions to the face, neck, and hands is to use molded prosthetic pieces. For the stage, however, this type of makeup is not always practical since actors normally do their own makeup, and the creation of molded prosthetics may require the services of a professional makeup artist.

However, the actors and young makeup artists who want to experiment with casting prosthetic pieces can certainly do so and will no doubt find it both interesting and useful. But whether the actors learn to make their own prosthetic pieces or have them made for them, the advantages of using this type of makeup are obvious—it can provide three-dimensional additions to the face impossible to achieve with nose putty and derma wax or other direct constructions (see Figure 14-1); the pieces can be modeled and remodeled on a plaster head until they are perfect and can then be reproduced indefinitely; and, unlike direct additions to the face, they can (for the stage, at least) be used several times.

Casting For Prosthetics

The first step in creating a three-dimensional appliance is to reproduce the actor's face, or some part of it, in plaster. To do this, a negative mold is made with a flexible alginate (see Appendix A), as illustrated in Figure 14-2A-G.

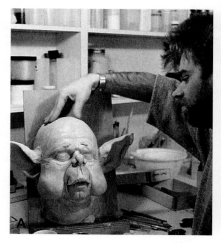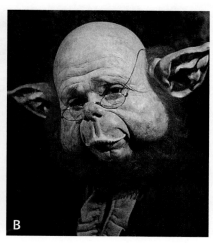

FIGURE 14-1 **Foam latex gnome.** *A. Clay sculpture. B. Foam latex character makeup for French Canadian children's television show using GM Foam System, Glatzan bald cap, and crepe hair shaped with Krylon Crystal Clear. Makeup and photography by Stephan Tessier of Texa FX Group, Montreal, Canada.*

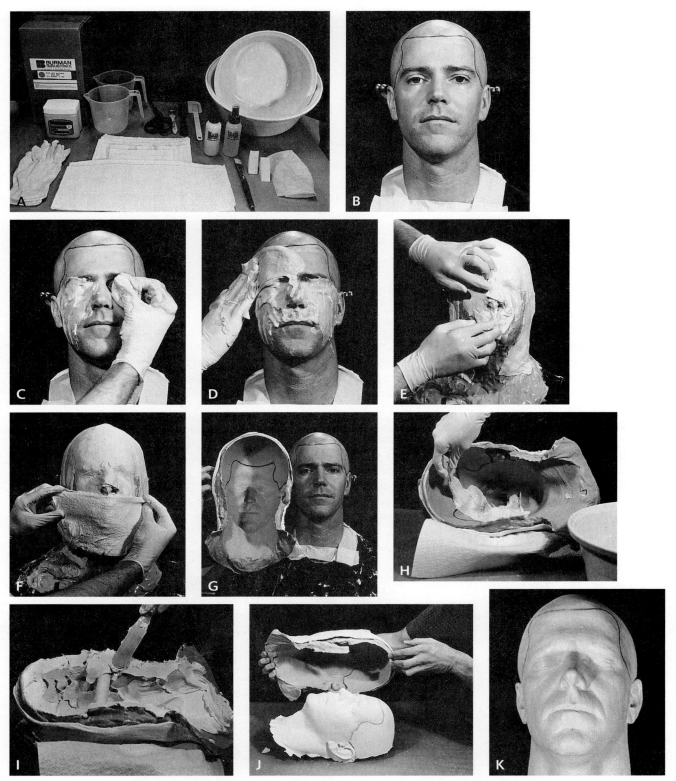

FIGURE 14-2 **Face casting.** *A. Alginate (40 oz. for a full ¾ face cast); water (60 oz. for above mix); warm water for plaster bandages; flexible plastic bowls for mixing alginate, plaster bandages and plaster; pre-cut plaster bandages (3–6 inch rolls); kitchen or metal spatula; disposable rubber gloves; bald cap (rubber or plastic); glue, brush, sponge and remover for cap; 1-inch disposable brush; scissors (small and large); petroleum jelly; measuring cup (at least 4 cup capacity); indelible ink pencil. B. Applied bald cap and face prepared for alginate cast. C & D. Alginate application. E & F. Strips of plaster bandage being laid over solidified alginate. G. Face cast removed. H. Brushing first layer of plaster or dental stone into negative mold. I. Adding the handle. J. Removing alginate from plaster cast. K. Finished and cleaned face cast. Casting by Matthew W. Mungle. Model, Michael Cristillo.*

Preparing The Subject

If the entire face is being cast, it is best to have the subject sitting in an upright position, not lying down, to avoid distorting the face. A barber or dentist chair is ideal. A plastic makeup cape (Figure 14-2B) or a painter's lightweight plastic drop cloth can be used to protect the clothing. It may or may not be taped to the skin at the neckline. The solidified alginate can be easily removed from the plastic later.

If the top of the head or the entire head is to be cast, a plastic or a latex cap (Figure 14-2B) can be used to protect the hair. In any case, it's a good idea to mark the hairline on the cap with an indelible ink pencil (available in art stores), which will later be visible on the cast.

While the face requires no special preparation (except for a light coat of petroleum jelly on the eyebrows, eyelashes, and cap), it is essential that it be made clear to the subjects that they are in no danger. It must be explained to them that if for any reason the alginate interferes with their breathing, they need only expel their breath forcefully, open their mouths and break the mold, or remove the alginate from their noses or mouths with their hands. Most subjects, once they have confidence in the operator, find the process pleasant and relaxing.

It is important that the facial muscles be relaxed during the mold making process. A smile or the raise of an eyebrow can ruin the mold. It is to everyone's advantage, especially with nervous subjects, to let them watch a mold being made on someone else first, clearly explaining the entire process as it unfolds. Having the actor view a commercially produced video of the entire casting process may also help alleviate any fears. It is usually best to work in a private room that is relatively quiet with no extraneous noise or conversation and where the subject does not feel that he or she is being watched by a number of people. Classical music playing in the background sometimes helps to break the silence and may calm your subject. If others are watching (and this should be permitted only if the subject is willing), it is essential that they understand from the start that they must be quiet! Any remarks or noises that disturb the subject or tend to make the person smile must not be permitted since they may very well result in a ruined cast and the work having to be done all over again.

It is also desirable for the person or persons doing the casting to avoid casual conversation with others unrelated to the work being done. Knowing that he or she has the operator's undivided attention helps to give the subject confidence. Although it is not absolutely necessary, giving the subject a pencil and paper as a means of communication can add to a sense of security. If this is done, it would be best for someone other than the operator to be responsible for reading what the subject has written. The subject can also be given appropriate hand signals to enable the operator to ask questions and get "yes" or "no" responses without the subject's having to answer by writing.

If, in spite of the reassurance the subject still seems apprehensive, it may be suggested, after making it clear that there is nothing unusual about it, that the person allow someone to hold his or her hand. This can be very comforting to some subjects and therefore helpful to the operator as well. In any case, never leave the subject alone until the mask has been removed. The subject will feel more secure knowing someone is there.

Negative Alginate Mold

It is very important to have all the materials needed to cast the face laid out before starting the face casting procedure (Figure 14-2A).

The primary type of facial casting material used is an alginate impression material, a seaweed derived powder, which when mixed with water becomes a flexible material easily removed from the skin. The setting time of different types of alginates may vary depending on the temperature of the room and water. A colder room and water retard the setting time whereas a warmer room and water hasten the setting time.

It is recommended that you mix a small batch of alginate to test the setting time before casting your subject's face. Various alginates require different mixing proportions and set up times. For this casting process Accu-cast alginate (see Appendix A under alginate) was used. When applying alginate to the face, two people should work together, one on the left side and one on the right. Alginate impression materials set up quickly, some within minutes, so it is to your advantage to apply it as rapidly as possible. Should you decide to patch a hole or add to a thin area, remember that wet alginate will only stick to wet alginate. Once it cures it will not stick to itself. This is another reason to work quickly. To avoid surface bubbles in the plaster, gently press the alginate onto the face taking special care around the eyes (keep them closed), nose, and mouth (Figure 14-2C and D). The final thickness should be approximately ¼ to 1/3 inch. A thick layer will add too much weight causing soft areas of the face to sag. A very thin layer may cause the alginate to tear. Both will leave distortions in the final cast. Wearing rubber gloves throughout the entire process is recommended.

When the nose is being cast, you should work very carefully around the nostrils with the fingers or a small spatula, making sure that both nostrils are clear at all times. It will give a nervous subject a greater feeling of security if you cover the nose and leave proper holes for breathing before covering the mouth. Otherwise, leave the nose until last, when the subject is likely to feel more relaxed about the whole procedure. Then you can work around the nostrils very carefully and fill in the holes after the mold has been removed. You should explain to the subject that if alginate should cover the holes accidentally, the subject need only expel his or her breath forcefully to remove it. Avoid using straws in the nose since it may distort the nostril area.

When casting the ears, push the alginate into all of the folds to avoid air pockets. An overly thick application might benefit the overall stability around the ear but may interfere with the proper removal of the mold.

When the alginate has solidified (from 4 to 8 minutes), it must be supported by a "Mother" mold. This mold is made by laying wet strips of pre-cut plaster bandages (see Appendix A) over the alginate (Figures 14-2E). The following sizes will facilitate the rapid application of this reinforcement step: six-inch wide, three layers thick plaster bandages; two 16-inch strips for the back sides of the face; two 8-inch strips for the forehead and the bridge of the nose area; one 1-inch strip for the center area of the nose; two 2-inch strips for each side of the nose; five 10-inch strips for the mouth area, each frontal side of the face, the chin area, and the neck area.

When the plaster hardens, it will provide a rigid form to hold the shape of the alginate (Figure 14-2F) after it is removed. Working carefully around the nostrils, press the bandages together under the nose to avoid covering the breathing holes. This will add greater strength. Covering only the front part of the ears with plaster bandages will make removing the mask easier.

Remove the alginate by first asking the subject to lean forward slightly, bring the hands to the face to support the mask and move all of the facial muscles (smile, frown, etc.) to aid in loosening the mold. It can then be removed easily (Figure 14-2G). It is best to loosen it first near the ear to let in the air. Remove it carefully and slowly, running your fingers around the edges between the skin and the alginate. The alginate does not stick to skin but may stick slightly to hair if it has not been lightly coated with petroleum jelly.

When the negative mold is finished, the positive plaster cast should be made immediately to prevent the possibility of shrinkage of the alginate as it loses its moisture.

Positive Plaster Cast
Before pouring the plaster positive cast, place a small piece of wet plaster ban-dage on the outside of the nose area and carefully fill in the nostrils from the inside of the mold with a small batch of thick alginate (use warm water to hasten the setting time) or by using two small oval pieces of wet clay. In preparing the plaster, first measure three cups of cold water into a bowl (preferably a plastic one), then slowly sift in white hydrocal (see Appendix A) until it reaches the top of the water level. Another method is to follow the manufacturers recommended water-to-plaster ratio of 100 parts of Industrial White Hydrocal to 40–43 parts of water by weight (see Figure 14-3). One hundred ounces of plaster equaling six pounds four ounces and forty to forty-three ounces of water equaling approximately two pounds ten ounces will usually fill a medium-sized mold. Remember to add the weight of the container to the overall weight of each ingredient. Let the mixture stand without stirring until the top of the plaster level looks like a dried river bed. The white hydrocal mix may be stirred at this time with your hand (wear a rubber glove) or a kitchen spatula. After the plaster has been stirred, the bowl should be hit a few times on the bottom with the palm of the hand to force air bubbles to the surface.

Although plaster can be poured when it is thin and watery or as thick as mayonnaise, an in-between consistency (like that of heavy cream) usually works best. If it is too thin, it will be hard to manage and will take longer to harden; if it is too thick, it may not conform to the shape of the mold. It should be pointed out, however, that thin plaster results in a harder, more durable cast than does thick plaster.

The wet plaster should first be painted carefully over the inside surface of the negative alginate mold with a 1-inch disposable brush, coating the mold completely (Figure 14-2H). Then the rest of the plaster can be either spooned or slowly and gently poured into the mold. To avoid having too heavy and cumbersome a cast, brush the plaster away from the center and up along the sides of the mold, leaving a shell of plaster rather than a solid block. If the plaster is too thin to do

FIGURE 14-3 Plaster comparison chart.

*Mfr	Parts water per 100 parts plaster needed by weight	Mfr's name for product	Setting range, in minutes	Dry compressive strength, lb. Per sq. in.
USG	64–66	Industrial Molding Plaster	25–30	2,000
USG	54–56	Pattern Shop Hydrocal	20–25	3,200
USG	40–43	Industrial White Hydrocal	20–30	5,500
USG	35–38	Ulracal 30	25–35	7,300
USG	28–32	Hydro-Stone	20–25	11,000
USG	21–23	Super X Hydro-Stone	17–20	14,000

*USG = U.S. Gypsum Co., 125 S. Franklin, Chicago, IL 60606. (Call 1.800.621.9523 for the nearest distributer.)

this, let it sit until it begins to thicken. When filling the mold, be sure it is adequately supported so that the shape will not be distorted. Be very careful to protect the nose, which is especially vulnerable to damage. Setting the face cast in a bowl filled with old rags or towels will give enough support.

Implant a wooden or plastic (PVC) dowel in the back of the cast while the plaster is still wet as a handle for easy removal and handling (Figure 14-2I). If you plan to hang the cast on a wall for storage, form a loop from a length of wire (part of a coat hanger will do) and embed the ends in the plaster before it hardens, leaving the loop outside and near the top of the cast. This can prove to be a great convenience.

When the plaster is thoroughly hardened in the mold, the alginate can usually be removed from the plaster cast in one piece (Figure 14-2J) and sometimes be used to make a second cast of the same head. But this second casting should be done immediately, before the mold begins to shrink. If the mold is set aside and allowed to shrink, it can be used to cast a shrunken head, a miniature of the original. If for any reason you should want to do that, make sure the edges are not allowed to curl up, since that will give a deformed head. Keeping the cast moist with a wet towel will help. After the castings are done, the alginate may be discarded. The surface of the plaster cast should now be scraped cleaned, ridding it of imperfections such as air bubbles, eyebrows, and eyelashes.

Before using the plaster cast, allow it to dry thoroughly. This may take several days. Then spray the cast with two light coatings of Krylon Crystal Clear Acrylic (see Appendix A). You now have a reproduction of the actor's face (Figure 14-2K) on which you can model in clay the features you want to reproduce in latex.

Clay Models

The modeling of individual features (Figures 14-4, 14-5, 14-17, 14-18, and 14-19) is done with artists' modeling clay (Chavant NSP Medium, see Appendix A), which requires no special technique. You will do it largely with your fingers, though clay modeling tools (Figures 1-4C and 14-5) may be helpful for creating the details. Be sure the clay is perfectly smooth, completely blended at the edges, and modeled in exactly the form you want the latex piece to take. You can simulate skin texture by dotting the clay with tiny depressions to represent pores. Remember that the slightest mark on the clay will be reproduced on the finished piece.

A useful trick for making skin texture pads quickly is to make a latex negative of a grapefruit, orange, or lemon skin, as mentioned in Chapter 13. This is done by painting liquid latex onto a section of the outside of the fruit, preferably one with skin that is not too smooth. Five to ten thin coats will probably be necessary. When the latex is thoroughly dry, powder it, remove it from the fruit, and you will have a textured piece that can be

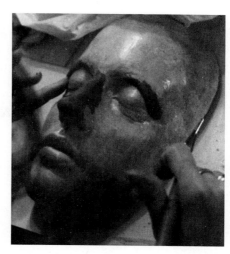

FIGURE 14-4 Modeling nose and sagging eyelids in clay on a plaster cast. By student Catherine Smith.

pressed into the clay, transferring the pore textures. All clay models should be textured. Eyelids should only have a slight texture to them to blend with natural skin texture.

Negative Plaster Mold

The next step is to make a negative mold of the clay feature just as you made a negative mold of the actor's face. This casting from the clay, however, must be done with plaster or a harder stone such as dental stone or Ultracal 30 (see Appendix A) rather than alginate. First, with some extra

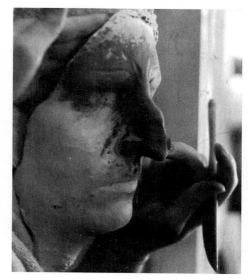

FIGURE 14-5 Modeling one-eyed witch's nose on a plaster cast of the student's face. *The right superciliary arch has been built up to distort the face. The left eye will be obliterated with clay. Makeup being created by student Barbara Murray.*

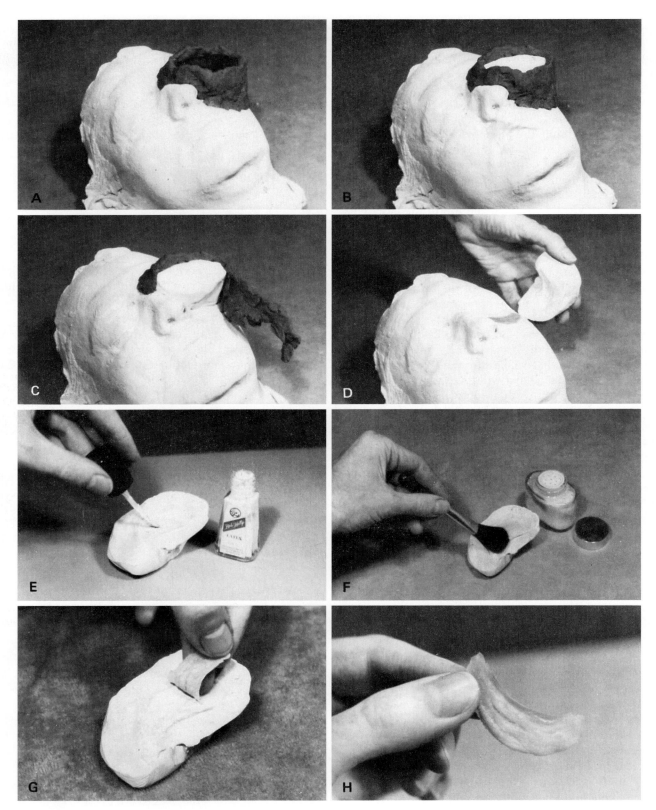

FIGURE 14-6 **Casting an eye pouch.** *A. Clay wall around eye area. B. Plaster poured in and allowed to harden. C. Clay wall partially removed. D. Negative plaster mold of pouch removed. E. Negative mold painted with latex. F. Dried latex being brushed with powder. G. Latex pouch being removed from mold. H. Latex pouch trimmed and ready for use.*

FIGURE 14-7 **Casting a latex nose.** *A. Plaster cast with nose modeled in clay, surrounded by a clay foundation for the cylinder to be used as a dike. B. Cardboard cylinder (a moist cat-food container with both ends removed) pressed into the clay. C. Pouring plaster into the cylinder. D. Removing the plastic mold. E. Latex nose being removed from the negative mold. F. Attached latex nose being made up for Kristoffer Tabori for his Dauphin in* St. Joan. *For the completed makeup, see Figure 14-8.*

clay, build up a wall around the modeled feature to prevent the plaster from spilling over the cast. You can make the wall entirely of clay (Figure 14-6A), or you can make a low foundation of clay (Figure 14-7A) and set a cardboard tube (Figure 14-7B), a can, or a plastic container with both ends open, into the clay. The cardboard cylinder shown in Figure 14-7B was made from a container of cat food. The metal top of the container was, of course, removed when the contents were used. The bottom was then cut off in order to get rid of the metal rim, after which the edge was appropriately shaped to fit into the clay foundation.

When the cylinder is anchored securely in the clay and the clay pressed against it to prevent leakage, as has been done in Figure 14-7B, grease all exposed parts of

the plaster cast and the clay sculpture that will be touched by the plaster when it is poured. This can be done with petroleum jelly. In using a clay foundation with a cylinder pressed into it, it is easier to grease the cast and the sculptured clay *before* pressing the cylinder into the clay foundation.

When the cast and the sculptured clay have been greased and the wall is firmly in place, make up your plaster or dental stone just as before and pour it over the new feature, giving plenty of thickness so that the mold will not break when you remove it.

When the plaster is hard, pull off the clay wall (Figure 14-6C). If you are using a cylinder in a clay foundation rather than a wall entirely of clay, you may wish to remove accessible portions of the clay foundation first, though this is not always necessary. Then maneuver the mold around until it can be easily slipped off. Now you have a negative mold (Figure 14-6D) from which you can make any number of prosthetic pieces. If, by chance, air bubbles have left little holes anywhere in the mold, fill them up with plaster.

Positive Latex Cast

There are two techniques for making latex prosthetic pieces from the plaster molds. One is a *painting* method; the other is a *slush* method.

For either method liquid latex is used (see Appendix A). The latex can usually be purchased in either flesh or natural white, which is almost transparent when it dries. It can also be tinted with food coloring or with special dyes. It is not necessary for the latex piece to match the base color, but if it is too different from the skin coloring, it may be more difficult to cover. The solidified latex will always be darker than the liquid latex.

The main requirement for a positive latex piece is to make the central parts of the piece thick enough to hold their shape and the edges thin enough to blend into the skin without an obvious line. In the brush technique (Figure 14-6E) a layer of latex is painted into the negative plaster mold, which requires no surface preparation. The type of brush used is a matter of choice. A soft bristle lets the latex flow on more easily, but it is also very difficult to clean; and unless extreme care is taken, it will probably not last very long. A stiff bristle is easier to clean but doesn't give as smooth a coat of latex. A flat, medium-stiff bristle is perhaps the most generally practical. Inexpensive brushes should be used. Brushes in use should be kept in soapy water and washed out thoroughly with soap the moment you have finished with them. Once the latex has solidified, it can seldom be removed from the brush.

Before painting in the first coat, it would be well to estimate about where you want the edge of the piece to be and to mark that with a pencil on the plaster. Then you can be sure to keep the latex thin along that line. Subsequent coats are painted in after the preceding coat is completely dry. Each subsequent coat can begin a little farther from the edge in order to provide a gradual thinning. The number of coats needed depends on the thickness of the coats. You will probably need a minimum of five, depending on the thickness of the latex and the requirements of the particular piece.

With the slush method, some of the latex is poured into the mold and gently sloshed around to build up layers of the latex. This is done by holding the plaster mold in the hand and moving or rocking it so that the latex runs first up to and just beyond the proposed edge, as marked with a pencil. Subsequent movements should keep the latex nearer and nearer to the center and farther and farther from the edge. If you have a problem in making the latex go exactly where you want it to, you can maneuver it with a clean modeling tool or an or-angewood stick. When you think you have built up enough thickness, drain off the excess latex or take it up with cleansing tissues or absorbent cotton. Absorbing it instead of pouring it avoids a build-up of latex at the point at which it is poured. You can avoid the whole problem by pouring in a little at a time. It is better to have too little than too much since more can always be added.

Before removing the latex piece, be sure it is completely dry. In deep molds, such as noses, this may sometimes take several hours. Forcing hot air into the mold with a hair dryer can speed up the drying considerably. Then dust the surface of the latex with face powder to prevent its sticking to itself. (See Figure 14-6F.) Once it has been dusted, it will never stick to itself or the mold again, even if you wash the powder off immediately. Then loosen the latex at a spot along the edge and carefully slide a small brush filled with powder between the latex and plaster, working towards the edges, gently lifting it away from the plaster (Figure 14-6G.) As you do so, dust more powder inside to keep that surface of the latex from sticking. Keeping your hands from rolling the delicate edges of the piece is of utmost importance at this stage. Sometimes the piece comes away easily, sometimes it has to be pulled, but it will come. If you do have to pull hard, however, be sure not to pull it by the tissue-thin edge, which is likely to tear. Also, avoid pulling so hard that you stretch the piece permanently out of shape. As soon as you are able to loosen a little more of the piece, grasp it farther down to pull out the remainder. Tweezers can be helpful.

After you have removed the piece, try it on the actor who is to wear it or on the cast of the actor's face. Check all blending edges to make sure they are very thin and lie flat against the skin. If the first piece you make from the mold is imperfect, make note of the problems. If they can be corrected by adjustments in the application of the liquid latex, make another piece, correcting the errors. If the problem is with the mold, see if there are any minor corrections that can be made. If not, make another mold—or as many more as necessary. When you have one you're satisfied with, label it with the date and the name of the actor, the character, and the play. If you then make duplicate molds, as you might want to do in order to make several pieces at once, number each one in the order in which it was made. There may be slight differences in the molds, and the identifying number could be useful. The plaster mold can be used indefinitely as long as the actual casting surface remains in good condition.

Prosthetic Pieces

Noses

There are three basic criteria for a useful, workable latex nose—it must be rigid enough to hold its shape without wrinkling or sagging, the blending edges should be tissue thin, and the blend should, if possible, take place on a solid, rather than a flexible, foundation (on the actor's nose, that is, rather than on the cheeks or the nasolabial folds).

The first two of these criteria depend on the distribution of latex in the plaster cast and have already been discussed. The third requires careful placement of the clay used in building up the nose of the plaster cast. The actual modeling of the clay corresponds closely to the modeling of a putty nose—the accurate following of natural nose structure, the careful blending of edges, the limiting of the clay addition to as small an area as possible, and the final addition of skin texture.

The principal difference between modeling a clay nose and a putty one is that putty may, if necessary, cover the sides of the nose completely, but clay should not do so. It should, if possible, stop far enough short of the outer boundaries of the sides of the nose to allow for a blending edge of latex beyond the section that is being built up. (See Figure 14-7A. For the makeup using this nose in the final scene of *St. Joan,* see Figure 14-8.)

The latex piece need not cover the entire nose. On the contrary, the smaller the area it covers, the easier it will probably be to work with. A tilted tip or a small hump, for example, does not require modeling a complete nose. If the piece you make involves the nostrils (Figure 14-7E), they can be cut out of the piece after it has been cast in order to permit normal breathing.

Because the final latex piece can be no better than the clay nose from which it was cast, considerable care should be taken in the modeling. Once the model is perfected and cast, achieving an effective latex nose is largely a matter of careful manipulation of the liquid latex in the cast.

Eyelids

Sagging eyelids are very helpful in aging youthful eyes. Figure 14-4 shows a pair being modeled in clay on a plaster head. In modeling the lids, work from photographs of older people, using more than one, if you like, and combining the most useful and adaptable features of each. The latex eyelids can stop just below the natural brow, which must then be aged; or they can cover the brow, making it possible to attach aged brows to the latex piece with crepe hair and latex or to ventilate eyebrows into the latex piece (see Chapter 15). Remember that only the edges that are to be attached to the skin should be thin. The edge that falls diagonally across the eye area hangs free and should be appropriately thick.

Latex eyelids are particularly useful in Asian makeups. In modeling them, be sure to give the clay sufficient thickness over the center of the eyeball so that the movement of the real eyelid will not be impeded. Before modeling Asian lids, study the Asian eyes in your morgue, as well as those in Figures 12-19, 12-20, 12-35D, and 12-36F.

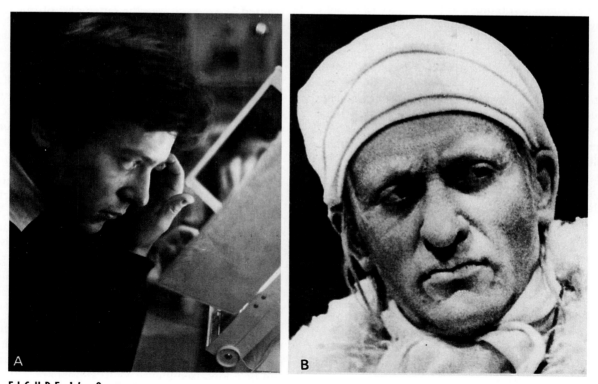

FIGURE 14-8 A. Actor Kristoffer Tabori in B. The final scene of Shaw's *St. Joan. The nose is shown being cast in Figure 14-7.*

Eye Pouches   These are invaluable aids to aging and are one of the simplest pieces you can make (Figure 14-6). Again, you should work from photographs of real people (see Figure 12-16). Some pouches will be fairly smooth and definitely pouch-like. Others will be somewhat flat and a mass of fine wrinkles. There are countless variations. If there is a definite line of demarcation to the pouch you wish to make, then it will not be necessary to leave a thin edge on the bottom of the piece, though there should be one at the top. As usual, remember to give it skin texture.

If molded eye pouches are needed in a hurry, they can be made in a few minutes by using gelatin instead of latex–provided, of course, you have the molds. As mentioned in Chapter 13, however, there are disadvantages to gelatin pouches–they are heavier (and therefore less comfortable) than latex pouches, they can be used only once, and there is a possibility that they might be loosened by excessive perspiration.

In making gelatin additions in plaster molds, there is usually no need to apply a separator, such as vegetable oil or petroleum jelly to the mold, though you may prefer to do so. The gelatin should, of course, be poured into the mold before it congeals. Be sure to keep the gelatin at the level of the smooth area surrounding the negative mold so that the gelatin positive will lie flat against the skin. If, when the gelatin has congealed in the mold but has not yet been removed, the surface of the gelatin is rough, smooth it out by stroking it with cotton dipped in hot tap water. This will melt the surface of the gelatin and remove any excessive roughness that might prevent its fitting tightly against the skin.

Ears   Rubber cauliflower ears can be slipped over the actor's real ears very simply. Rubber tips can be used for such characters as Puck or the leprechaun in *Finian's Rainbow*. Also, small ears can be enlarged–as they must be, for example, in a makeup for Abraham Lincoln.

The technique in making ears, partial or complete, is to make a shell that will fit over the natural ear. This requires a *split mold*. After you have modeled the clay ear on the plaster cast of the actor's natural ear and built your clay fence, place the cast so that the ear is horizontal. Then pour plaster up to the middle of the rim of the ear. It's a good idea to let the surface of the plaster be somewhat uneven. If the plaster is fairly thick, this will happen automatically, giving a bumpy or undulating surface. When the plaster is dry, grease the surface and pour in more plaster, covering the ear. When this plaster is dry, remove the clay fence, as usual, then very carefully pry the two sections of plaster apart and remove both from the clay ear.

You can then fit the sections back together. If the surface is uneven, this will be no problem, for there will be only one way they will fit. This will give you a deep mold with a crevice into which you can pour the latex

and slosh it around to cover all the surfaces of the negative mold. Any excess can be poured back out. It is better to build the ear up with several coats rather than trying to do the whole thing at once, letting the layers dry completely between layers. Be sure to keep the latex thin at the edges, which will be glued to the natural ear, and thick around the rim so that the ears will hold their shape.

When you are sure the latex is dry (it's a good idea to force-dry it with a hair dryer), powder the inside, then carefully pry the mold apart, powdering as you do so. The ear should then be trimmed around the edges. After the latex ear has been slipped over the natural ear and glued down, it should be made up to match the face.

In painting the mold with latex, you may not be quite sure how far out to bring the latex. After you have made and trimmed your first ear, however, you will be able to see where the boundaries should be. Then you can mark these boundaries on the plaster cast with a pencil to serve as guidelines for all future ears made from that mold. This will make it possible to keep the latex thin at all edges that are to be glued down.

Chin   Receding chins can be built up or straight ones made to protrude; round chins can be made more square or square chins rounded. Goatees can be pasted on latex chins as well as on real ones and will not need to be remade for each performance. Frequently a chin can be combined in the same piece with a scrawny or a fat neck. If the chin addition is to be very large, a foamed latex piece (see the latter part of this chapter) would be preferable.

Wrinkled Forehead   A wrinkled forehead can be modeled in clay on a plaster cast of the actor's head and a negative plaster mold made from the clay positive. Latex positives can then be made from the negative plaster mold. Ready-made latex forehead pieces are available. (See Figure 14-9.)

Neck   It is possible to age the neck effectively from the front with paint, but the profile is difficult to change. A latex piece will, however, produce an old neck from any angle. You can have prominent muscles and sagging flesh or transverse rolls of fat, or sagging jowls. For this type of construction, however, *foamed* latex, gelatin, or silicone should be used. (See the latter part of this chapter and Figure 14-31.)

Bald Caps   One of the best methods of creating the effect of a bald head is to cover the hair with a latex or a plastic cap. The cap can be worn plain, or hair can be added (see Figure 14-10 and Chapter 16).

In making a latex or plastic cap, balloon latex or plastic cap material should be painted or stippled (a

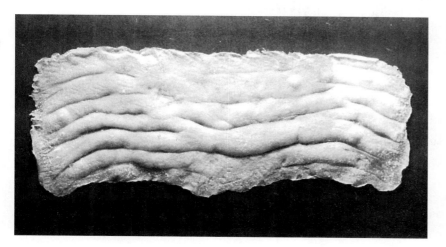

FIGURE 14-9 Molded latex forehead piece.

combination of the two is usually preferable) onto a positive plaster, ceramic, or plastic head (the plaster can be made, the other two can be purchased from Kryolan, see Figure 14-11) suitably shaped to an average head size. The surface of the form should be very smooth and if made of plaster should be coated with two layers of Krylon Crystal Clear Acrylic Spray and then buffed with Carnuba wax. Gradually build up the thickness of the latex or plastic cap material by applying six to seven layers of material to the form. Using a latex sponge applicator paint the first layer over the entire head shape to approximately two inches past the hairline in front and three to four inches past the hairline in back. The second layer should end at the hairline, with each successive layer being applied at one-inch increments away from the hairline toward the crown (layer three is one inch from the hairline, layer four is two inches from the hairline, and so on). The final layer should be stippled onto the entire head shape, starting at the crown and working toward the hairline. This layer should be feathered to one-half inch past the hairline. Allow each layer to dry completely between applications. The back of the cap should be left long so that it will cover all of the neck hair and can be tucked into the collar. If this back tab is not needed, it can be cut off later.

To remove the cap from the form, begin by rolling the cap material from the edges to within a quarter inch of the hairline. Powder the entire surface with translucent face powder. Using the rolled edge to grip the cap, begin pulling it slowly away from the form, powdering the underside regularly. See Figure 14-12 for general instructions for applying the bald cap.

FIGURE 14-10 **Wig attached over bald cap.** *Gelatin nasolabial fold and jowl appliances. Stretch and stipple aging (Old Age Stipple) around eyes. Makeup by special makeup effects artist Matthew W. Mungle. Actor Christopher Walken in* Blast From the Past. *Photograph courtesy of Matthew W. Mungle.*

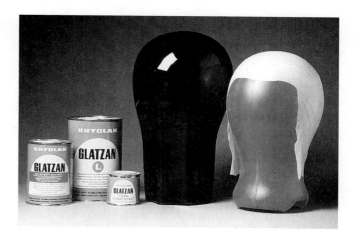

FIGURE 14-11 **Glatzan plastic bald cap material, ceramic cap head, plastic cap head.** *Photograph provided by Kryolan Corporation.*

Purchasing ready-made bald caps (either latex or plastic) will, of course, save a great deal of time. The ready-made cap illustrated in Figure 14-12 is made of extra-thin latex, with an unusually long nape, which can be shortened if you wish. Complete instructions for applying the cap come with it. (See also *Plastic caps* in Appendix A.)

Hands   Wrinkled and veined hands can be made up in the form of gloves, invaluable for quick changes.

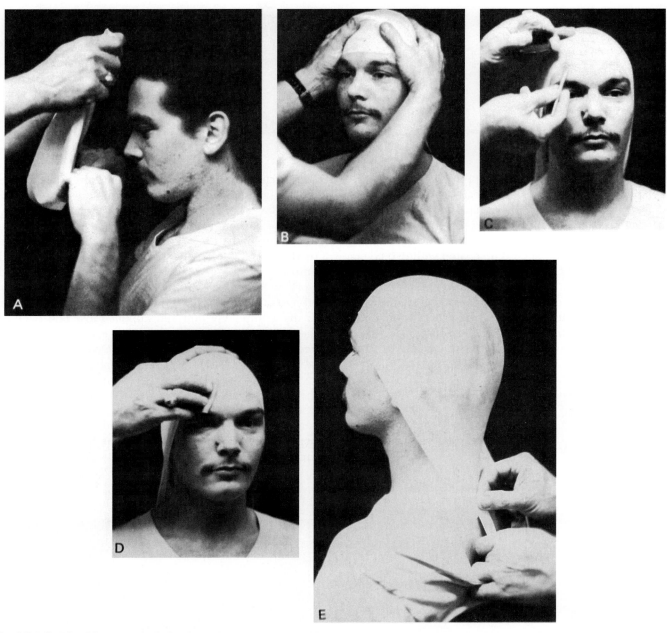

F I G U R E 1 4 - 1 2 **Applying a latex cap. (Caps available from Cinema Secrets, Namies, Michael Davy, Alcone.)** *A. Subject assisting in putting on the cap. (Subject's hair can be plastered down with water, hair-setting gel or hairspray. For a completely smooth transition between forehead and hairline use Gaf Quat.) B. Front of cap being smoothed out and distance from eyebrows adjusted. C. Applying Pros-Aide or Telesis adhesive under front edge of cap. D. Pressing down front edge of cap firmly with dampened chamois or cloth. E. Attaching lower end of cap to skin with adhesive tape. F. Making marks to indicate front edge of ear and point at which ear joins head. G. Cutting cap to second mark. This should be done with great care! H. Applying adhesive to underside of edge of cap, then bend head back slightly before pressing firmly into place. I. Front edge of cap being stippled with Duo surgical adhesive or Pros-Aide for better blending. After stipple has dried and been powdered, cap is made up with rubber-mask greasepaint or PAX paint. J. In this illustration, rubber-mask greasepaint is being applied with a sponge.*

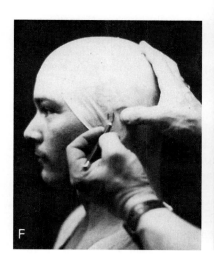

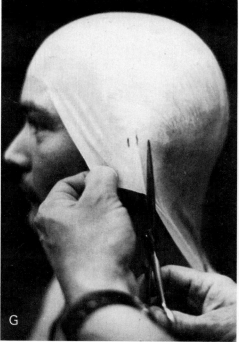

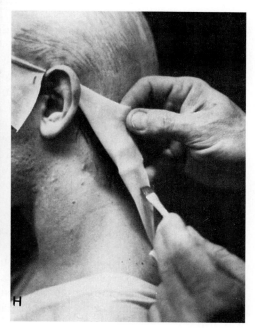

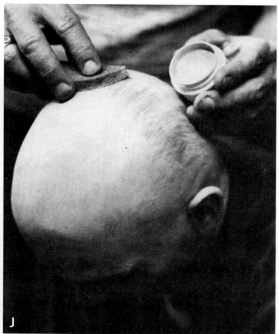

FIGURE 14-12 Continued.

The gloves can be made by making up the hands with wax to build up knuckles, bones, and veins, then casting them, one at a time, by laying the hand, well oiled, palm down in wet plaster and pushing down until the plaster covers the lower half of the hand, including the fingers. Let the plaster set until it has solidified. Before casting the back of the hand, make sure there are no free hairs that might become embedded in the plaster. If you can't flatten the hairs sufficiently with wax and petroleum jelly or cold cream, cut them off. If the subject objects to this, make plaster casts of the hands with alginate, then make a negative plaster mold from the positive plaster cast.

Whether you are casting directly from the hand or from a positive plaster cast of it, when the bottom half of the negative mold has solidified, remove the hand from the mold and grease the exposed area of the hardened plaster, return the hand to its original position, then pour fresh plaster over the hand. When the plaster has hardened, gently separate the two halves of the mold by moving the hand. When the two halves of the mold are thoroughly dry, they can be put back together and secured with masking tape. The mold is then ready for the latex, which can be poured in, sloshed around, then poured out. This can be repeated four or five times, each coat being allowed to dry thoroughly or force-dried with a hair dryer before the next one is added. For each drying period, place the mold with the fingers up so that latex will not accumulate in the finger tips. Extra coats may be added just to the back of the hand in order to stiffen knuckles, bones, and veins. These coats should dry with the mold flat and the palm up. Be patient and make sure that the latex is completely dry before separating the cast. Otherwise, the glove can be ruined.

Latex pieces to be pasted on the back of the hands are, of course, much simpler to make since only the back of the hand needs to be cast. (For hands aged this way using foamed latex, see Figure 17-6I.)

It is also possible to buy thin, snug, rubber surgical gloves and to attach the pieces to the gloves instead of to the hands.

Application of Prosthetic Pieces

Attaching the Piece
Latex pieces should be attached to the skin, which must be free of grease, before any makeup has been applied. Cleaning the skin with either rubbing or 99% alcohol will make for a better adherence of the appliance. The appliance may be glued with Pros-Aide, Beta Bond, Telesis Adhesives (See Appendix A under adhesives) or spirit gum (this should be avoided if possible as the appliance may tend to loosen during a performance with spirit gum). Latex should also be avoided as a glue as it has a tendency to build up on the appliance and will loosen if the actor perspires freely.

These are the steps to be followed in attaching a latex piece (a nose for example) with spirit gum or other adhesive.

1. Place the piece exactly in position on the face, and check for a good fit (Figure 14-12A).
2. If the piece needs trimming, do it very carefully by tearing the latex, keeping the blending edges thin and irregular (Figure 14-12B). Thin, irregular edges are easier to conceal than straight ones. If you are applying a nose and the nostrils have not yet been cut out, that should also be done. Then try the piece on again and do any further trimming. Now place the piece on the face and powder over all edges

with face powder a few shades lighter or darker than the natural skin.
3. Remove the piece from the face and brush adhesive along the powder line on the skin on all inside edges of the prosthetic (Figure 14-12C). Allow the adhesive to become tacky before applying the piece to the skin.
4. Place the piece very carefully into position (Figure 14-12D). Adjusting the position of the piece after the edges are in contact with the skin can result in unsightly corrugations. These are very difficult to conceal.
5. Press the edges down firmly with the fingers, with a lint free cloth or a chamois. Press straight down (not at an angle) will help avoid creating wrinkles. An orangewood stick or the end of a make-up brush can be used to supplement the fingers in the areas that are less easily accessible (Figure 14-12E).

Concealing the Edges
Using a small piece torn from a make-up sponge stipple the edges of the piece with latex cream adhesive (see Appendix A) to help conceal them. The adhesive should, of course, be allowed to dry before the makeup is applied. If the edges are thicker than they should be or if they have a tendency to corrugate, the following procedure (or variations of it) may solve the problem:

1. Apply the piece as usual, using spirit gum or other adhesives (Figure 14-13A through E).
2. Paint all edges of the piece with matte spirit gum or other adhesive, slightly overlapping onto the skin (Figure 14-13F), then tap the spirit gum with the finger until it is almost dry. Press it firmly with a wet cloth or a damp sponge (Figure 14-13G) to set it.
3. Press face powder firmly onto the spirit gum with a puff (Figure 14-13H), then remove excess powder with a powder brush.
4. (Optional) Apply a coat of plastic sealer over the powdered spirit gum (Figure 14-13I) and allow to dry. Powder the sealer.
5. Apply Duo surgical adhesive along the edge of the piece (Figure 14-13J), allowing it to overlap onto the skin. Allow to dry or force-dry with a hair dryer, then powder.
6. Apply rubber-mask grease as usual.

It is important to note that sealing the spirit gum protects it from the rubber-mask grease paint. The RMGP will affect the spirit gum by turning it gummy and will lessen its adhesive strength.

Applying the Makeup
Rubber-mask grease, rather than the usual foundation paints, should be used over latex pieces and should be stippled on with a red-rubber sponge (Figure 14-13K). When you use rubber-

mask grease paint only for the latex piece and not for the rest of the makeup, be sure to stipple it over the edges of the piece and onto the skin immediately surrounding the piece. Then blend the edges of the rubber-mask grease into the skin with the fingers (Figure 14-13L) or with a brush in order to keep the edges from showing through the makeup used for the rest of the face. It can then be powdered by pressing in as much powder as it will absorb and brushing the excess off lightly with a powder brush. The rubber-mask grease needs more frequent powdering than regular creme foundations to keep it from developing a shine. This application, including powdering, can be repeated one or more times if it seems necessary to do so in order to conceal the edges.

If a fairly large area of the face is covered by a latex piece or if there are a number of pieces used, you would probably do better to apply the rubber-mask grease over the entire face rather than just on the pieces.

Stippling

To help conceal the edges of latex pieces, the rubber-mask grease foundation should be stippled with other colors. (See Chapter 11 for suggestions on stippling.) The stippling can be done with creme makeup or grease paint instead of rubber-mask grease if you prefer. The following procedure or variations of it can be used:

1. Using a black stipple sponge or latex sponge applicator (Figure 14-13O), stipple the piece with a color three or four shades darker than the base, concentrating on the edges of the piece and the adjacent areas of skin. Then powder.
2. Repeat step 1 using a color three or four shades lighter than the base. Powder.
3. Using a black stipple sponge or latex sponge applicator, add some red creme rouge if it is appropriate in that particular area of the face. (On the nose it usually is.) Powder again. If you wish to add additional red, that can be done very easily by brushing on a dry rouge of the appropriate shade.
4. Check to make sure that the edges of the latex piece are not apparent. If they are, do some detailed stippling along the edges, using a small pointed brush. Where the edge is revealed by shadows, use a light stipple to counteract the shadows; and where it is revealed by highlights, use a dark stipple. Check the effect in your mirror as you go along, continuing to stipple until the results are satisfactory. The careful application of the correct adhesive and proper placement of the appliance at the start will reduce the need to overly camouflage the appliance edge with makeup.

Removing a Latex Piece

If the piece has been attached with spirit gum or other adhesive and if you expect to use the piece again, avoid pulling it off. Remove it instead by carefully loosening the edges with spirit-gum remover. This can be done by dipping a fairly firm-bristled flat brush into the remover, inserting the bristles between the edges of the latex piece and the skin, then running the bristles along under all of the edges. (Figure 14-13P.) The remover will dissolve the spirit gum as you go. The piece can then be lifted off easily. Pulling the piece off before the spirit gum is dissolved can stretch the edges, resulting in corrugations. After the piece has been removed, any spirit-gum residue should be cleaned off with more remover. This can be done with a wad of cotton. Makeup can be removed from the piece with alcohol or spirit-gum remover.

Foam Latex

Although the hollow, shell-like latex pieces work well on bony parts of the face, their hollowness may become apparent on softer areas where there is the possibility of considerable movement. This problem can be overcome through the use of foamed latex, with which it is possible to make three-dimensional, spongy jowls and sagging necks that look and move like natural flesh.

Working with foam latex involves the combining of three to five compounds (based on the particular manufacturer's formulation) in various amounts in a specific order over a given amount of time. The procedure is considerably more complicated than the slush-mold process previously described. The ingredients include the following: a relatively thick, creamed natural latex base with a high concentration of solids and ammonia; a curing agent containing sulfur to vulcanize and preserve the foam and other agents which keep the foam cell structure from breaking down; a surfactant or foaming agent to aid in lowering the surface tension of the latex enabling it to froth more easily; and a gelling agent that converts the foam from a liquid to a solid.

The shelf life for the latex base is approximately one year, although with regular attention (weekly vigorous shaking) it will last nearly twice that long. The components, however, will last quite a long time with little attention.

Closed Molds

For foamed pieces it is necessary to use two molds: a positive and a negative instead of the one open mold used with liquid latex. The positive mold duplicates the actor's own features, the negative mold duplicates the clay sculpture and corresponds to the single mold used for painted-in latex pieces. When the two molds are fitted together, the space or spaces between them will correspond precisely to the clay addition that has been built up on the plaster cast. This space is then filled with foamed latex by first pouring it into the negative mold, then fitting the positive mold

FIGURE 14-13 **Applying a latex nose.** *Actor Tom Tammi applying a ready-made latex nose, using special precautions to deal with problem edges. A. Fitting the nose. Edges and nostrils have not yet been trimmed. B. Trimming the nostrils. C. Applying the spirit gum to the inside edges of the nose. D. Applying the spirit-gummed nose. Edges are being pressed down firmly with the fingers. This could also be done with a cloth or with a chamois. E. Pressing down edges around the nostrils with an orangewood stick. (Note: The next few steps—photographs F, G, and H—are intended to be followed only when there is a potential problem in concealing the edges due either to their excessive thickness or to their tendency to corrugate.) F. Applying spirit gum over the blending edge. The spirit gum is then tapped with the finger until it becomes almost dry, after which it is set by pressing it with a damp sponge. G., H. Powder is then pressed into the spirit gum. I. Applying sealer over the spirit gum. The sealer is allowed to dry, then powdered. J. Applying Duo adhesive over the sealer. This is allowed to dry, then powdered. K. Applying rubber-mask grease to the nose with a red-rubber sponge. L. Blending the rubber-mask grease into the area surrounding the nose. Then powder. M. Applying creme stick makeup. This is then blended into the rubber-mask grease. (Or the rubber-mask grease could be used over the entire face.) N. Powdering the creme stick. O. Stippling the nose. After the nose has been powdered, three colors are applied with a black or red stipple sponge. Each color is powdered after it has been applied. P. Loosening the nose with spirit-gum remover.*

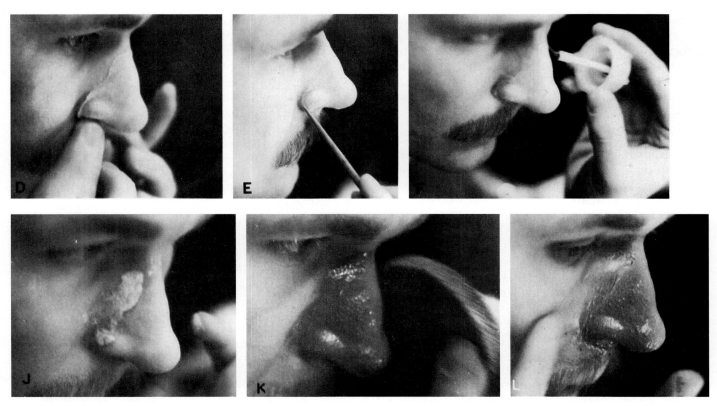

into the negative mold. This will automatically squeeze out the excess, leaving the space between the two molds filled with latex foam. The foam in the closed mold is then cured (baked in an oven), after which the mold is separated and the foam, a spongy three-dimensional piece, is removed. The casting is done with Ultracal 30 or dental stone (see Appendix A), which is harder, less porous, and more durable than plaster. Instructions for making a closed mold can be seen in Figures 14-41, 14-42, 14-43.

Foaming the Latex
The companies that make latex for foaming have their own formulas for combining the various ingredients (either three, four, or five depending on the brand) in order to produce the foam. Whenever you use any foam latex for the first time,

carefully follow the directions that come with it. Any experimentation should wait until after you have observed the results produced by following the maker's instructions. When you do begin experimenting with variations in the procedure, be sure to keep a precise record of all such variations, including all materials used and exact amounts of each, temperatures (both room and oven), beating times, and volume of foam. Date each entry and comment on the results. If the results are not entirely satisfactory, you might include any suggestions which occur to you for changes to be made in the next experiment. With each new experiment, only one variation should be made.

When "running" a foam batch, it is the amount of ammonia in the foam that most affects the gelling process. Excessive amounts of ammonia will keep the foam from gelling, too little will cause it to "set up" in the bowl. When difficulties arise in the foamed latex process they are often caused by the amount and speed with which the ammonia evaporates from the foam and may be traced to such diverse sources as room temperature and humidity, the speed of the mixer, the type of beater used (improper foaming), and even the depth and rotation speed of the mixing bowl. Other sources can include too short a curing time, too low or too high an oven temperature (foam too soft or too hard with an unpleasant odor), baking time, and excess moisture in the mold (latex skin becoming detached from the foam on or after removal from the mold).

Since formulas vary from brand to brand and since you will be following the instructions for your particular brand, the information given here is intended primarily for those who are not acquainted with the process but would like to have some idea of what is involved. Specific amounts of the various ingredients will not be included.

To mix the compounds:

1. Before beginning the mixing, paint the mold release onto the positive and negative molds (foam latex kits usually include a mold releasing agent). Curing the mold by painting the surface with a 1:1 mixture of castor oil and alcohol and baking at two hundred degrees for three hours before coating it with a releasing agent will help the foam latex cure properly.
2. Weigh exact amounts of the curing agent and foaming agent into the mixing bowl.
3. Weigh and add the exact amount of latex base specified. (Use a triple beam gram scale.)
4. Add the appropriate amount of colorant (can be obtained from the manufacturer). Pigment dispersions, made specifically for coloring latex, are recommended. Universal color tints are not recommended for foam latex appliances. Polypropylene glycol contained in the colorants causes the foam cell structure to break down.
5. In an electric mixer, whip the compound at a low speed for 1 minute then increase the speed to a high and whip up to approximately 3½ or 4 (occasionally even to 5) volumes. This should take approximately 2 minutes. The bowl in which you whip should be marked in advance for the desired numbers of volumes. The 3½ volumes should give a firm foam. For a softer foam, increase the volumes.
6. Reduce the speed at least half for a few minutes then to speed 1 or 2 for a few more minutes to refine the foam.
7. With the beater still running, add the pre-weighed gelling agent and beat for 30 seconds.
8. Reduce the speed, if possible, and mix for 1 to 2 minutes more.

To transfer the foam to the mold:

1. There are two ways to transfer the foam latex into your negative mold: by pouring and by injecting. The pouring method works well on small appliances (noses, eye pouches) and for those no larger than the size of a face cast. You can also use a spoon to scoop foam into the mold, being careful to avoid adding large bubbles. Filling deep cavities and wrinkles by spooning or spreading the foam with a spatula before pouring the remaining foam will help alleviate the possibility of trapped bubbles. Foam injection guns can be used to transfer foam into larger molds. The design of the mold must include at least one injection hole (large enough to accommodate the gun nozzle) and vent holes for displaced air and excess foam (see Figure 14-14). When using the injection method, the positive and negative molds must first be assembled and clamped together before the foam is injected. This exercise, however, utilizes the pouring method.
2. Once the foam has been added, place the positive mold into the negative allowing the weight of the positive to settle the foam (this should take only a few moments). Then press the two parts together, closing the mold. This will automatically squeeze out the excess, leaving the space between the molds filled with the foam latex. The mold can now be held together with clamps, mold banding straps, or rubber mold bands (see Burman Industries, Appendix B).
3. After giving the foam time to set (usually 8–15 minutes) place the mold into a preheated oven not to exceed 200 degrees F. The curing time will depend on the size of mold and the thickness. It will usually be a minimum of 3 hours. Another method is to set the mold in a cool oven, set the oven at 200 degrees for 1½ hours, then let cool in the oven for 3 hours.

FIGURE 14-14 Injecting foam latex. *The three-part Ultracal-30 mold is secured with clamps and mold banding straps. Kryolan A-150 Foam Latex is then injected into the mold using the injection gun. Makeup artist Dennis Penkov from Berlin, Germany. Photograph courtesy of Kryolan Corporation.*

Dick Smith

By the year 2001, Dick Smith will have been a professional makeup artist for 56 years. In 1940 he entered Yale University to pursue a career in dentistry, but after seeing *Dr. Jekyll and Mr. Hyde* with Spencer Tracy, his interest began to change. He found a book on stage makeup and transformed himself into Mr. Hyde, scaring his classmates. From then on, when time permitted, he made himself up as the Frankenstein monster, the phantom, the werewolf, the mummy, Quasimodo, etc.–each time testing his work on hapless Yale men. Makeup became his passion.

After being discharged from the Army in 1945, Smith moved to New York and tried to find work in film as a makeup artist. After 6 months of rejections, he was finally hired by NBC-TV in New York. He was the first staff makeup man in the television industry. During his 14 years at NBC, Smith taught himself about all types of makeup, invented quick-change techniques for "live" television and makeup colors for color television, ran a department with as many as twenty artists whom Smith trained, and created countless beauty, character, and appliance makeups. In 1956 Smith moved from New York City to Larchmont, New York, with his wife and two sons where he spent the next 37 years preparing his creations in the basement of his home.

In 1959, after leaving NBC, Smith became director of makeup for David Susskind's television productions for two years. Two dramas, *Moon and Sixpence* and *The Power and the Glory* starring Sir Laurence Olivier were the most memorable. After Susskind lost his drama series to the new television game shows, he produced his first film which became Smith's first work with film as well. The film was *Requiem for a Heavyweight* starring Anthony Quinn who played a battered old prizefighter.

In the 1960s Smith created the makeup for a number of films including *Mark Twain Tonight* for television (which won the Emmy for makeup), *Midnight Cowboy* and *Little Big Man* starring Dustin Hoffman (who was aged to 121 years), and others.

With the 1970s came the era of "special makeup effects," which refers to a physical change in the performer's face while the camera is rolling, caused by a special makeup device or technique. Smith started it all using bleeding bullets in *The Godfather* and many macabre effects in *The Exorcist*.

In this new era, Smith and other artists like him no longer worked on a film from beginning to end. After *Godfather II* and the *Sunshine Boys* in 1975, he would only create special makeup or effects and was on the set for their filming. Additional makeup artists would handle all other makeup. The following films required such special work from Smith: *Taxi Driver, Marathon Man, The Sentinel, The Deer Hunter, Altered States, Night Hawks, Ghost Story, The Hunger, Amadeus* (won U.S. and British Academy Awards for makeup), *Starman, Poltergeist III, Everybody's All American,* and *Dad.* Smith was makeup consultant for *Death Becomes Her* in 1991 and *Forever Young* in 1992.

Dick's life work, *The Advanced Professional Makeup Course,* is a 700-page illustrated home study course sold to students and professional makeup artists around the world. Since 1992, he has lectured twice yearly at a school in Tokyo which has developed a course in special effects based on his written work.

---

4. Once the mold is cured, turn off the oven, open the door slightly, and allow it to cool down gradually. When removing the mold from the oven, use gloves, oven mitts, or an old towel. The mold may still be quite hot. Set the mold on a table with the vent hole up and pull gently on the piece of rubber sticking out of the hole. This will begin to loosen the appliance from the plaster. Do not tear it (this may cause damage to the piece), simply cut it off. Then set the mold on end and slowly separate the two halves. Pulling the mold apart too quickly may cause damage to the foam. The foam piece will usually stick to one side or the other, but should it stick to both sides, gently pry it loose with a flat, round-ended tool until both pieces are separated. To preserve the delicate edges, powder the foam generously and start working the foam loose from the center rather than from the edges of the piece. Avoid excessive handling of the edges before they are powdered.

Pull off any ragged edges of the piece (never cut edges), but not too closely or too evenly. They should be very thin and somewhat irregular. When the foam is completely separated from the mold and the flashing, set the appliance in a safe place. Now wrap the mold in old towels or place it back in the oven to avoid damage caused by rapid cooling.

Check the foam appliance for holes, tears, or surface imperfections. These are the biggest problems for anyone running foam latex. For serious or continuous problems seek professional assistance (see Foam Latex, Appendix A). The best material with which to make repairs is more foam latex. Mix a small batch and spatula it onto tears, seams, holes, or other imperfections, allowing it to gel and set it back in the oven to cure. Check the piece every thirty minutes until the foam bounces back when touched. To protect your foam appliance, include an extra mound of foam to check for doneness.

Another product that can be successfully used for patching small imperfections is Pros-Aide (see Adhesives, Appendix A). Allowed to thicken naturally (simply leave the lid off a small bottle) or thickened with Cab-O-Sil (fumed silicone dioxide used as a thixotropic agent), Pros-Aide can be applied with a small metal spatula, dried with a hair dryer, and then powdered.

It is possible but not necessary to clean foam appliances by washing them in soap and water to remove the separating agent and any chemicals remaining in the foam. These chemicals may cause irritation on highly sensitive skin. The process may damage the delicate edges, so care must be taken. Add two to three drops of Ivory Liquid detergent per gallon of water and squeeze the foam with your fingers for a few minutes. Rinse well under fresh water until the water runs clear. To remove excess water press the foam between paper towels and return it to the plaster positive until completely dry. Should the edges begin to curl and fold over onto themselves, generously add powder and carefully unfold the edges. (Note: If for any reason you should want to change the color of your foam latex appliance, simply dip it in fabric dye intended for natural fibers).

Making and applying a foamed latex appliance. *The photographs on the following pages illustrate the creation of the makeup for Dustin Hoffman as the 120-year-old man in the film* Little Big Man. *Makeup created by Dick Smith, S.M.A.*

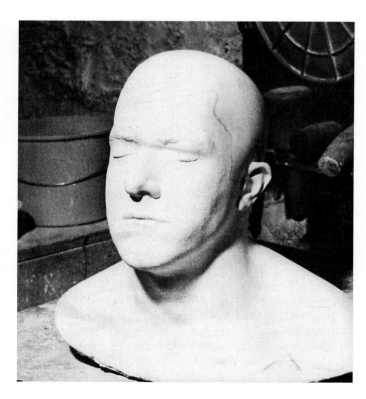

FIGURE 14-15 **Making a plaster cast of Dustin Hoffman's head and shoulders.**

FIGURE 14-16 **Plaster model of Dustin Hoffman's head.** *Clay models of every part of the latex mask were later sculpted over copies of this head or sections of it.*

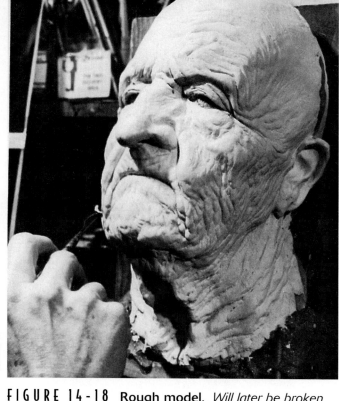

FIGURE 14-17 Makeup artist Dick Smith making clay model for front half of the latex prosthetic.

FIGURE 14-18 Rough model. *Will later be broken down into 8 parts—brow, nose, upper lip, eyelids, bags, lower lip and chin, and sides of face and neck.*

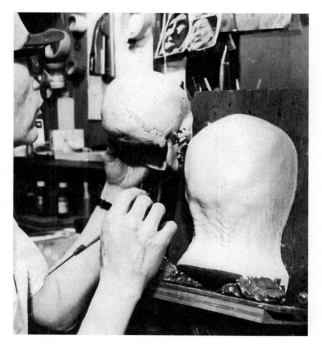

FIGURE 14-19 Modeling back of head on a plaster section of Dustin's head.

FIGURE 14-20 Making molds of clay models of bags, chin, and nose.

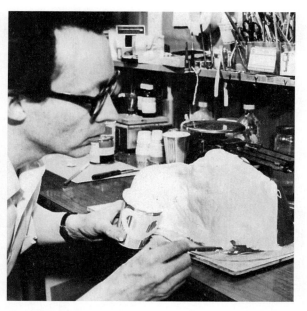

FIGURE 14-21 Making special epoxy mold of clay model of the largest part of the mask—sides of face and neck.

FIGURE 14-22 Finishing outer surface of the mold of the sides of the face and neck section. *This exterior part of the mold is made of hard plaster.*

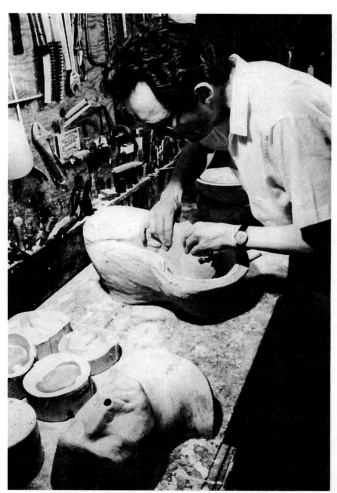

FIGURE 14-23 **Removing latex.** *After mold has been baked to cure latex and positive cast of Dustin's face has been lifted out, the latex mask section is then carefully removed. (Pouring latex into the mold is illustrated in Figure 8-7.)*

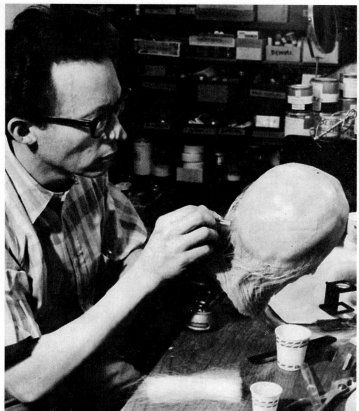

FIGURE 14-24 White hair being implanted bit by bit in back section of latex mask.

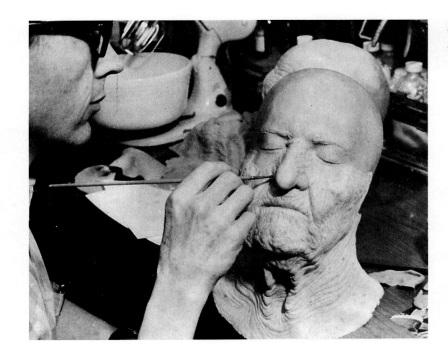

FIGURE 14-25 Painting "liver spots" on part of the latex mask.

FIGURE 14-26 Finished mask sections.

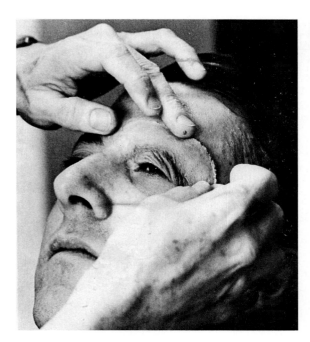

FIGURE 14-27 Attaching foam latex eyelid. *Piece is made thin enough and with enough folds sculpted into it so that it blinks naturally.*

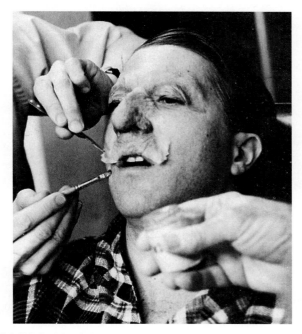

FIGURE 14-28 Nose and lip piece. *Slomon's Medico Adhesive (makeup artists now use medical adhesives such as Appliance Adhesive B, Pros-Aide, or Telesis adhesive) used near mouth for better adhesion.*

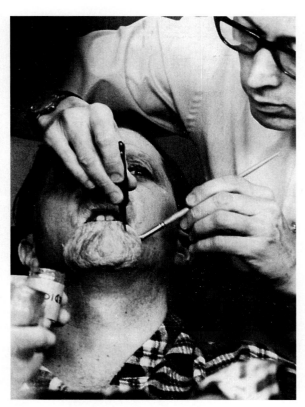

FIGURE 14-29 Chin and lower lip being attached. *All of the pieces were pre-colored to save time, leaving only minor coloring to do after they were glued on.*

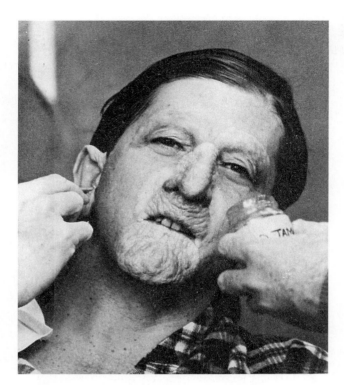

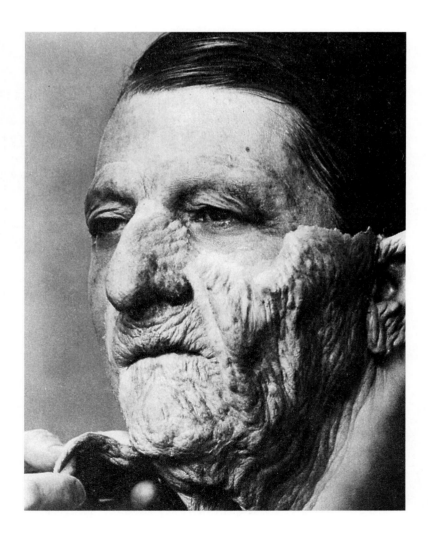

FIGURE 14-31 Attaching large latex piece for cheeks and neck.

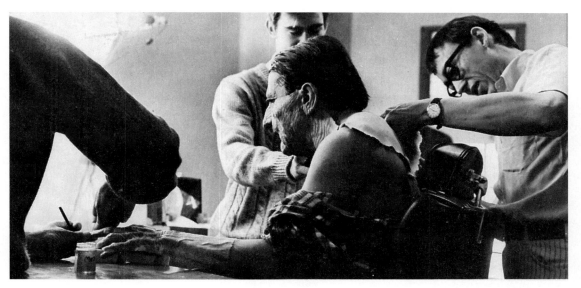

FIGURE 14-32 Applying shoulder hump and hands.

FIGURE 14-33 Hands with latex gloves and fingernails.

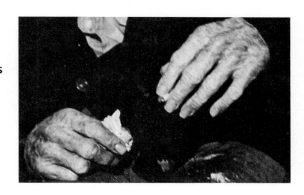

FIGURE 14-34 Headpiece being put on. *Piece was constructed of two overlapping sections of foam latex, which were glued together before being put on.*

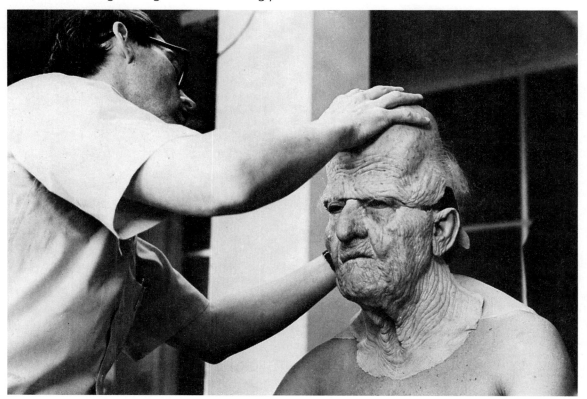

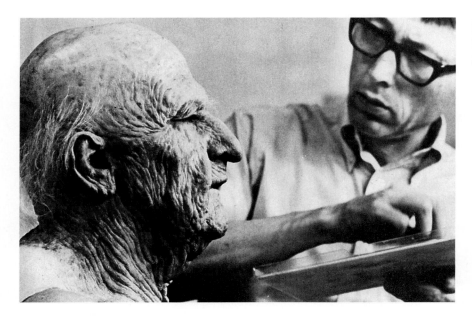

FIGURE 14-35 Final touch-up of foam latex makeup. *Makeup by Dick Smith, S.M.A.*

FIGURE 14-36 Dustin Hoffman as the 120-year-old man in *Little Big Man*. *(Photographs of Figures 14-23, 14-24, 14-25, 14-26, 14-27, 14-29, 14-30, and 14-31 by Mel Traxel, Cinema Center Films. All others by Dick Smith.)*

Application

Foamed latex pieces can be attached with Pros-Aide, Pros-Aide II, silicone adhesives, prosthetic adhesive, or Prosthetic Adhesive B (Dow Corning 355, also called Prosthetic Adhesive A by RCMA, is no longer available). Spirit gum is not recommended because of its tendency to react to salt in perspiration compromising the adhesive bond.

Unlike a "shell" latex appliance, foam latex pieces must be attached to the entire surface area of skin covered by the piece. Because most of the pressure sensitive adhesives have similar working properties, Pros-Aide will be used for this application method:

1. Clean the face of all makeup, dirt, and skin oils with 99% alcohol on a cotton swab.
2. Hold the foam latex appliance against the face to check for proper placement. Starting at the center of the face and working towards the edges, brush on Pros-Aide to just outside the edges of the appliance. Let the Pros-Aide dry slightly, then press the piece into the adhesive (having two people working will expedite the process). The various drying times of the different adhesives will determine how large an area can be covered at one time. For an even stronger bond paint adhesive to both the face and the inside of the appliance and allow it to dry before application. It is important to attach the appliance symmetrically.
3. Attach the delicate edges last by wetting them lightly with a little 70% alcohol. The alcohol reactivates the glue which in turn is absorbed into the foam. (To more easily apply adhesive behind your appliance, bend the ferrule of your brush at about three quarters of an inch above the bristles to an angle of approximately forty-five degrees).
4. Once the appliances are glued, seal the edges by stippling them with Pros-Aide using a piece torn from your red stipple sponge. Allow it to dry, then powder with a translucent setting powder.

Painting Foam Latex

Two products commonly used for coloration on foam latex are rubber-mask grease paint, a castor oil based appliance makeup and PAX paint, a mixture of Pros-Aide and Liquitex artist acrylic paint. These two products can be used separately or in combination.

Rubber-Mask Grease Paint

Rubber-mask grease can be applied to the pieces with a sponge or with brushes. The degree of coverage that can be achieved ranges from highly opaque to extremely transparent. It can be used straight from the container or thinned with castor oil or the cosmetic fluid GP-20 (diluted with water) for transparent glazes. This glazing technique provides the makeup artist with the ability to create layers of natural looking skin coloration for intimate theater settings and for television and film (see Figures 14-36, G-30, and G-31). After the foundation colors are applied you may then want to adjust the color generally or locally (as with rouge, for example) by stippling on additional color with a coarse sponge (make a custom-shaped sponge from a 1-inch by 2-inch block of polyurethane foam. Along one long side draw eight to ten irregular shapes in a variety of sizes and cut or tear away the background or negative space leaving the shapes on the surface). This helps to add texture and skin discoloration while relieving the flatness of the rubber-mask grease foundation. To finish, press powder into the makeup to set it and remove the shine. If variations in surface sheen are required this can be accomplished by adding more or less powder in certain areas. Glazes can now be added to the powdered makeup for further texturing. To suggest broken blood vessels, lightly cover the area with a mixture of red silk or rayon flocking and K-Y Jelly. Further texturing can be accomplished by using a coarse sponge or a brush to stipple additional colors over the powdered makeup—red-brown, grayed purple, dull brick red, rose, gray, lavender, creamy yellow, or whatever colors seem appropriate. RMGP glazes can also be used over PAX to create similar effects as mentioned above.

PAX Paint

PAX, developed by the Academy Award winning makeup artist, Dick Smith, is made by mixing one part Pros-Aide to one part Liquitex. This creates an opaque flexible paint that moves equally well on the skin as it does on appliances, better in many ways than RMGP. Mixed with non-toxic Liquitex earth-tone colors (burnt sienna, raw umber, burnt umber, raw sienna, red oxide, yellow ochre, titanium white, and black) it is relatively safe to use on healthy skin. (It is the responsibility of the artist to collect all scientific data relating to any product with which the artist or the subject might come in contact and to use good judgment in determining how and/or whether to use the product.) It is extremely durable, an excellent cover for appliance edges, it photographs well, and does *not rub off on costumes*! As with RMGP, apply and blend PAX with a patting motion using a firm polyurethane foam applicator. Any makeup or adhesive can be used on PAX.

What makes this product appealing is also its biggest disadvantage. The strength of its adhesive properties causes some difficulty in removing it from the skin. It is, therefore, not recommended for application near the eye area. Gentle, yet strong prosthetic adhesive removers specifically formulated to remove PAX are available and work quite well (see Adhesives & Solvents, Appendix A).

PAX can be modified in a variety of ways. The following are some suggestions for using PAX:

1. Mix Pros-Aide with Liquitex Matte Medium to form PAX Medium, a colorless material that when added to PAX can produce a paint with varying levels of transparency. Adding various levels of transparent coloration to the appliance will help you create a more realistic looking skin. It will also assist you in blending the paint off into the skin around the eyes, the edges of the face, and off the edges of the appliance should you choose to use makeup on the skin.
2. Add water (or PAX Extender, see PAX, Appendix A) to PAX paint to produce a thinner, even more transparent product. It can be thinned as much as 24 parts of water to 1 part PAX and used as a wash to tint areas of the face (i.e., sunburns). Thinned PAX Medium can be used as a sealer over makeup on pre-painted bald caps to protect them during the application process.
3. Add more Pros-Aide to your original recipe to create a stronger adhesive bond. Adding less will make a paint that is easier to remove.
4. Any product, except acetone, can be applied over PAX.
5. Since PAX products dry with a slight shine and the surface remains a bit sticky, it is important to powder with a slightly translucent setting powder (choose a slightly warm tone).
6. Avoid applying layers of thick PAX over soft foam. This will cause unnatural folds and wrinkles and the surface will appear thick skinned and heavily made up.

Before working with foamed latex, study the series of photographs of the television makeup for Hal Holbrook's *Mark Twain* in Figure 17-6 and of the movie makeup for Dustin Hoffman in *Little Big Man*, Figures 14-15 to 14-36.

Cold-Foam Process

Polyurethane Foam A quick and relatively simple method for making foamed pieces in a closed mold, this process involves the use of a polyurethane foam with a latex skin. Carefully follow the instructions which come with the foam you're using. In general, however, this is the procedure:

1. Cover surfaces of both the positive and the negative mold with a release agent, such as castor oil or petroleum jelly (Figure 14-37A). Wipe off any excess before proceeding. (Using rubber-mask grease adds color to the latex skin.)

2. Coat the inside of the negative mold with latex (Figure 14-37B), keeping it thin at the edges, then let it dry.
3. Add the catalyst to the foaming compound (Figure 14-37C) and stir well (Figure 14-37D), making sure the two are thoroughly mixed. Continue to stir until the moment the mixture begins to foam. Do not lean over the mixture at this point to observe the foaming since the foaming process releases toxic fumes.
4. Pour the mixture immediately into the negative mold (Figure 14-37E).
5. Press the positive mold tightly into the negative mold (Figure 14-37F), and let stand for the time specified in the instructions.
6. Carefully separate the two molds and remove the piece. If the latex skin separates from the foam, reattach it with spirit gum.

Silicone Foam

This is a soft foam that does not require a latex skin. The brand you are using may already be flesh colored. If you want to deepen the color, add colorants before adding the catalyst. The foam is simple to mix and can be removed from the mold in from 7 to 10 minutes. It is fully cured in 24 hours. Follow the manufacturer's directions.

Foam Gelatin

This two-component, self-foaming gelatin behaves in a similar manner to polyurethane foam (known as a/b or cold foam). When the foaming agent is added to the melted gelatin it produces a lightweight, flexible appliance. It is safe, non-toxic, produces no hazardous fumes or chemicals, and is reusable. Foaming gelatin can produce appliances in minutes, even using your current latex molds. Mix the foaming agent with the melted gelatin and pour or spoon into a chilled mold. Use a light coating of petroleum jelly as a mold release. Seal all surfaces with Silicolor, apply to the skin with spirit gum, and blend edges with witch hazel on a cotton-tipped applicator. Foam gelatin appliances can be colored with rubber-mask greasepaint or airbrush cosmetics. (See Appendix A).

Teeth

For enlarged, crooked (Figure 14-38), or fanged veneer teeth, acrylic caps can be made to fit over the natural teeth. The following materials, most of which are

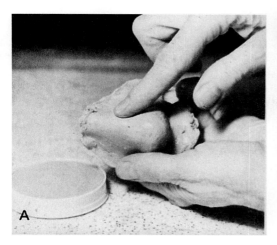

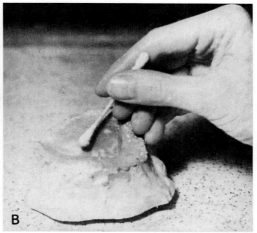

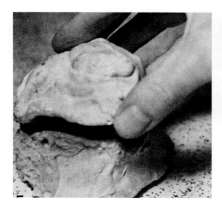

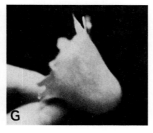

FIGURE 14-37 **Making a nose with polyurethane foam.** *A. Coating the surface of the positive mold with rubber-mask grease. B. Coating the surface of the negative mold with latex. C. Adding the catalyst to the foaming compound. D. Stirring the catalyst and the foaming compound. E. Pouring the foam into the negative mold. F. Pressing the positive mold into the negative mold. G. The finished nose after it has been removed from the negative mold.*

available from dental supply or special makeup supply houses, will be required (Figures 14-39 and 14-40A).

To make teeth, follow this procedure:

1. Mix the alginate (instructions included with dental alginate). Dental alginate is different from face casting alginate and has a faster setting time. Fill a disposable mouth tray (upper or lower) with alginate, which gels in 1 to 3 minutes, and immediately place

it in the actor's mouth (Figure 14-40B). Either upper, lower, or both may be used. Be sure to get the right size for the actor's mouth, or get several sizes and keep the extras for possible future use. The mouth trays, though called "disposable," can be cleaned, disinfected, and reused. Make sure to get the alginate up into the gum area. If necessary ask the actor to pull his or her lip out to facilitate the alginate getting into the gum area. After 2 to 3 minutes, to

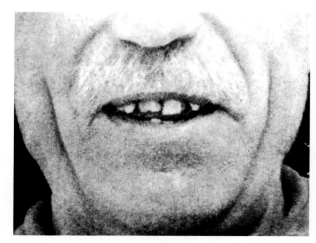

FIGURE 14-38 Teeth of an elderly man.

FIGURE 14-39 Acrylic powder and liquid for making false teeth.

test for dryness, feel the overflow that has been forced through the holes in the tray. If it feels dry, wait another 30 seconds to make sure that all the alginate has gelled before removing the tray.

2. Have the subject close his or her mouth around the tray and blow several times, puffing the cheeks out. This will loosen the *vacuum* between the teeth, gums, and alginate. Remove the tray from the mouth, mix the dental stone (see Mixing Chart, Figure 14-3) in a small bowl, and immediately brush it into the negative mold of the teeth and gum before the alginate starts to shrink. The purpose of brushing rather than pouring the stone is to make sure that all the crevices are filled and that there are no air holes. You may also tap the cast on the table while the stone is still liquid to release any trapped bubbles.

3. When the dental stone has hardened, separate it from the negative impression, which can then be discarded. The disposable tray can be either discarded or washed, sterilized, and kept for future castings.

4. Fill the rubber form (Figure 14-40C) with dental stone, and immediately set the positive cast of the teeth into it. Take care not to immerse too much of the gum area into the stone as you will need this to register your teeth veneers). Let the stone dry until it has hardened completely.

5. Remove the rubber form from the stone cast and clean any excess stone off the cast. Be careful not to damage the teeth cast as registration is very important (Figure 14-40D).

6. When the teeth are thoroughly dry, spray them with a light coat of Krylon Crystal Clear Spray. It may be advisable at this time to make a duplicate mold of the original teeth cast with silicone impression material. This assures that you will have a negative mold of the teeth in case anything happens to the original cast. Check step 10 for instructions on making this mold.

7. Using a non-sulfur based, light-colored modeling clay, carefully sculpt the false teeth desired on the cast of the actor's own teeth (Figure 14-40E). The sculpture of the teeth should slightly wrap around the back of the teeth for better hold with the finished product.

8. Sculpt a clay casing around the teeth, staying at least 1/8 inch away from the sculpted teeth in front and back (Figure 14-40F and Negative Mold Making, step 2).

9. Spray the whole teeth cast with 3 very light coats of Krylon Crystal Clear Spray.

10. Mix the silicone impression material. As with any two-part silicone product, first mix part A with part B together in one container, then transfer this mixture into a second container. Continue mixing. This step insures that all materials are mixed completely. Quickly and carefully build up a generous coat on the whole teeth cast (Figure 14-40G). Let it cure. If a second coat is needed it may be added at any time and will stick to the first.

11. Apply a plaster bandage mother mold to the outside of the silicone cast. Let harden (Figure 14-40H).

12. Remove plaster bandage mother mold and silicone mold from teeth cast placing the silicone back into the mother mold. Clean all the clay off the teeth cast with 99% alcohol or acetone (Figure 14-40I).

13. Coat teeth cast with 2 light coats of Alcote PVA separating agent. Let each coat dry. Then, coat the teeth cast with a light coat of petroleum jelly.

14. Pour ¼ oz. acrylic powder into a mixing cup and add ¼ oz. acrylic liquid. Stir the mixture until it makes a soupy liquid. Pour the mixture into the negative cast of the sculpted teeth (Figure 14-40J).

15. Quickly push the positive stone cast of the teeth into the negative silicone mold containing the acrylic mixture. Let the acrylic cure (it cures fairly fast).

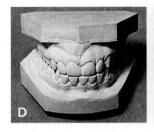

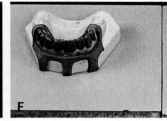
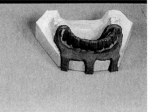

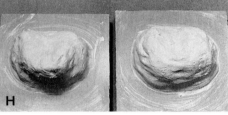

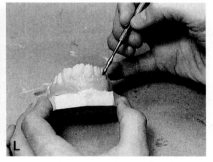
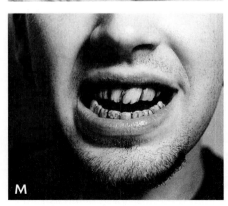

FIGURE 14-40 **Making false teeth.** *By Matthew Mungle. A. Materials for making teeth veneers: (l-r) petroleum jelly; dental stone; small plastic mixing cups; two-part flexible silicone material, Cutter Sil Light or any other brand; mixing bowls; ½ roll plaster bandages; Krylon Crystal Clear Spray; dental impression cream; Alcote. PVA separating agent; disposable mouth trays; modeling clay; palette knife; (not shown) dental teeth coloring kit or non-toxic acrylic paints, stirring rod, modeling tool, spoon, small scissors, nail file, utility brush, powdered acrylic, and acrylic mixing liquid. (Figure 14-38). B. Dental tray with alginate. C. Rubber base form. D. Cleaned casts (upper and lower). E. Sculpted teeth. F. Clay casing around sculpted teeth. G. Silicone impression material applied to sculpture. H. Plaster bandage mother mold. I. Removed silicone negative and cleaned positive. J. Pouring acrylic into silicone negative. K. Removal of silicone negative and acrylic teeth still on positive. L. Applying gums to teeth. M. Painted and finished teeth in actors mouth.*

16. Remove the plaster bandage mother mold and the silicone negative from the teeth cast. This will leave the acrylic teeth attached to the teeth cast (Figure 14-40K). Carefully remove the acrylic teeth from the cast and trim the excess acrylic from the teeth with scissors and a finger nail file.

17. Gums may be added at this time if desired. Remove the teeth from the cast and apply petroleum jelly to the stone cast. Mix a gum colored acrylic and spatula it onto the gum area of the stone teeth cast. Quickly press the acrylic teeth onto the cast making sure the teeth contact the gum acrylic (Figure 14-40L). The gum acrylic area can be modeled before it sets. Before trying the teeth on the actor, make sure all edges are smooth.

18. Color the acrylic teeth appropriately, using a dental coloring kit or tooth color (liquid or wax) from the manufacturer or cosmetic company. For a high gloss shine, paint the teeth with a clear gloss paint from a dental coloring kit (available at dental stores).

The false teeth can be kept on the stone cast of the teeth, kept in a plastic box or in container of mouthwash when not in use.

Figure 14-40M shows a finished set of teeth being worn by an actor.

Advanced Mold Making

Occasionally it will be necessary to make molds for aging or changing the features of an actor's face. In this case a mold must be made without any undercuts to make what is called a *wrap-around* prosthetic appliance. The following materials are needed for mold making and sculpting: alginate (40 oz.); water (60 oz.); water for plaster bandages; plaster bandages; Ultracal 30 (UC) Krylon Crystal Clear Acrylic Spray; burlap (see Appendix A, pre-cut into 4-inch squares); metal or kitchen spatulas; disposable rubber gloves; wood rasp; Chavant NSP Medium clay sculpting tools; brushes; 99% alcohol; drill; router *key* bit; $1/4$- and $3/8$-inch drill bits.

1. Starting with a full face cast mounted on a formica board or on the top of a counter (Figure 14-41A), sculpt out all the *undercuts* around the jaw line and neck area with water clay (see Appendix A). An undercut (Figure 14-41B) is an area of hard plaster that curves under the cast and therefore would make a negative mold impossible to remove from a positive mold without breaking a delicate edge. With water-based clay, sculpt all of the undercuts out of the face cast. Undercuts may appear in back of the jaw line, around the neck area, and between the cheekbones and the ear area. The next step is to take an impression of this form with alginate and reproduce it in a harder plaster, Ultracal 30 (UC) (see Appendix A). In order to mold the flared-out face cast you will need to spray the whole form with two or three light coats of an acrylic spray such as Krylon Crystal Clear Acrylic Spray (see Appendix A) and paint the plaster with a light coat of petroleum jelly to keep the alginate from sticking to it.

2. Mix 40 ounces of Alginate into 60 ounces of water and coat the cast with an even coat ($1/4$- to $1/3$-inch thickness (Figure 14-41C).

3. After the alginate has set, gently remove it from the face cast and place it back. This will assure that the alginate and plaster bandage mother mold will come off in one piece (Figure 14-41E).

4. Cover the set alginate in plaster bandage as you would with a face cast (refer back to face casting) to create a mother mold, supporting the shape of the alginate (Figure 14-41D).

5. Once the plaster bandage has set, carefully remove the alginate/plaster bandage mold together (Figure 14-41E).

6. Measure 1 cup tepid water into a plastic mixing bowl and sift in 2 cups UC. Let set for 1 minute. Mix thoroughly by hand, using rubber gloves. Tap the bottom of the bowl with your hand to release any excess bubbles that may have accumulated in the UC. Paint the UC mix into the alginate negative with a 1-inch disposable brush and follow by building up the thickness as the material starts to thicken (Figure 14-41F). This layer should be at least $1/4$-inch thick. Let set, usually about 5 to 10 minutes.

7. Mix 2 cups tepid water with 4 cups UC and let set 1 minute. Mix and paint one light coat onto the set UC. Dip two layers of burlap squares into the UC mix and gently press into the negative alginate mold. Continue this procedure, overlapping burlap squares, until the whole mold is covered. Roll two layers of burlap saturated with UC and reinforce the edges of the mold (Figure 14-41G). Place a metal pipe into the back of mold and reinforce with burlap. An additional small batch of UC may be mixed and painted onto the surface as a finishing coat.

8. After the mold has set for at least three hours it can be pulled and cleaned (Figure 14-41H). Let this mold set overnight. The mold is now ready to sculpt on.

Sculpting

To sculpt an old age or character face, begin by building up high and low areas, cheekbones, nasolabial folds, jowls, and neck waddles (Figure 14-42A) in Chavant NSP medium-density clay (see Appendix A). The thickest area of your sculpture could be up to 1 inch, the thinnest area should be no thinner than $1/32$ inch. It is important to look at the sculpture in different lighting situations (i.e., full frontal, side lighting, etc.) to estimate the curves of folds and wrinkles. It is very important that the edges of the sculpture be blended out creating a smooth transition between clay and plaster.

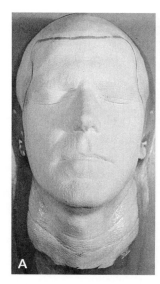
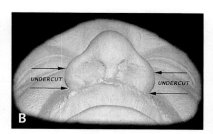

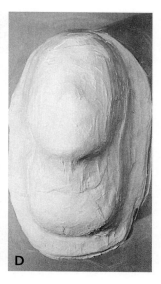
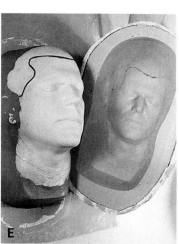
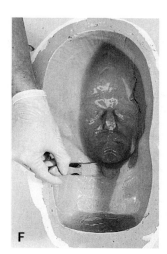

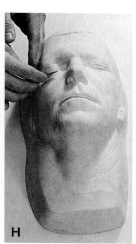

FIGURE 14-41 **Making a new cast without undercuts (called a flared positive).** *A. Clay used to eliminate undercuts from original cast. B. Close-up illustrating undercuts on nose area. C. Alginate applied to cast. D. Plaster bandage applied over alginate. E. Alginate negative removed from plaster positive. F. Brushing in first coat of Ultracal-30 into alginate negative. G. Attached handle and reinforce with burlap to the edge. H. Cleaning flared positive.*

Edges can be cleaned with a brush or cotton-tipped applicator and acetone. A brush and 99% alcohol may be used to smooth out any rough areas of clay.

Various sculpting tools may be utilized to achieve different wrinkles and folds (Figure 14-42B). Textures may be added with rubber stipple sponges, sculpting tools, or from rubber latex skin texture pads (Figure 14-42C) described in the *Clay Models* section of this chapter. Slight over-texturing of pores into the clay will assist the plaster or stone in duplicating details in the negative.

Negative Mold Making
After you are satisfied with your sculpture you will need to make a negative mold of it to capture all the details of the clay.

1. Drill indented *keys* into the mold with a rounded router bit and drill. These indented keys will stabi-

lize the negative mold, make the positive a tighter fit, and keep it from shifting around when placed in the negative mold (Figure 14-43A). Surface keys, where stone meets stone, can also be utilized to stabilize the positive into the negative mold. It may be necessary to shave off any undercut areas around the nose and eyes in order for the negative to be removed without chipping (Figure 14-43A).

2. Using Chavant NSP medium clay, roll 12-inch long, ¼-inch wide snakes. These will be used to make the casing around the sculpture (Figure 14-43B). Clay should also encircle the indented or surface keys. Water clay can be used for larger areas. Stay at least one eighth of an inch away from the edge of the sculpture with the clay casing.

3. Once the casing is completed, clean the stone area between the clay sculpture and the clay casing area

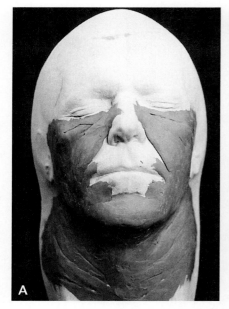
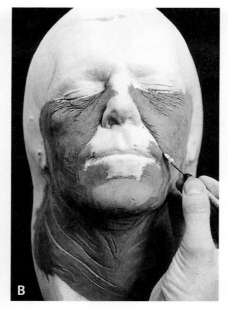
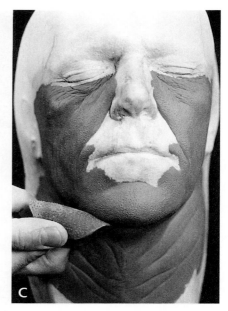

FIGURE 14-42 **Sculpting the wraparound appliance.** *A. "Blocking out" the appliance in clay. B. Sculpting wrinkles and folds. C. Texturing with texture pads.*

with acetone on a cotton-tipped applicator. This will insure that your edges of the final prosthetic appliance will be as thin as tissue. Then spray the sculpture with three light coats of Krylon Crystal Clear Spray. A light coat of petroleum jelly should be painted into all indented and surface keys only after they have been cleaned off with acetone.

4. Mix 1½ cups water to 3 cups UC. Tap the bottom of the bowl to release any bubbles from the mixture. Gently paint the surface of the sculpture with the UC and a disposable brush (Figure 14-43C) being careful not to trap any air pockets between the clay and the UC mix. You may want to blow a little air on the surface to relieve any bubbles. Continue patting the UC mixture on until it starts to thicken. This coat should be approximately ¼- to ⅓-inch thick.

5. After this first *splash* coat has set, mix 2 cups water with 4 cups UC and paint a thin layer onto the previous coat. Dip two layers of 4-inch burlap squares into the UC mix and gently apply this to the mold. Continue this process until the whole mold has been covered. Make small rolls of burlap dipped into UC and apply these to the outer edges of the mold for reinforcement. (Figure 14-43D). With two rolls of burlap dipped into UC, make a bird's nest on top of the mold. Fill it with UC to create a flat surface. This will act as a pedestal when the mold is turned over.

6. Let this mold set overnight, then clean off the sharp edges with a wood rasp.

7. Open the mold by pulling or using a furniture clamp or C clamp and three blocks of wood (Figure 14-43E).

8. Remove all clay from both molds. Clean the clay residue off with 99% alcohol or acetone. *Be sure to use a respirator when using chemical solvents.* Use only wooden tools on the surface of the sculpted area to avoid damaging the stone.

9. Drill vent holes through the positive mold into areas where the casings were placed next to the sculpture (¼-inch and ⅜-inch drill bits are recommended). This will allow for the excess gelatin to run out of the mold creating a thinner edge on the prosthetic appliance (Figure 14-43F).

10. This same process is used to make a nose appliance mold (Figure 14-43G).

Making a Gelatin Wrap-around Appliance

Mixing Gelatin
Supplies Needed

Sorbitol
Glycerin
Distilled water
Gelatin (300 Bloom)
Zinc oxide
Joe Blasco Ruddy Light Skin Powder or any colored powder
Red flocking
Large tongue depressor or stirring utensil
Small strainer
Large microwavable bowl

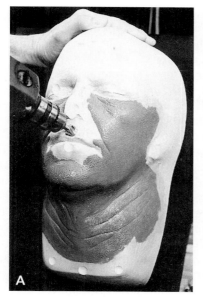
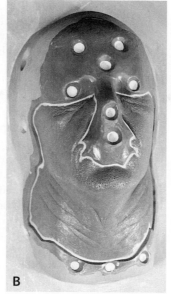
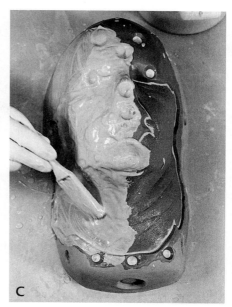
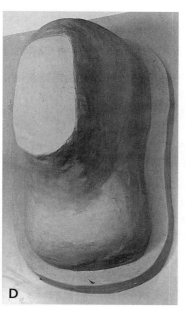

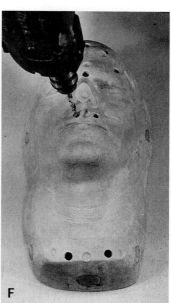

FIGURE 14-43 **Developing a mold for the prosthetic appliance.** *A. Drill keys into the positive. B. Add a clay casing around the entire sculpt and cast (both light and dark grey indicate the casing). C. Brushing on the first coat of Ultracal-30 over the entire sculpt. D. Burlap reinforcement is applied over entire sculpt. Use burlap to build the birds nest on top and to reinforce edges. E. Opening mold with furniture clamp and wood. F. Vent holes being drilled. G. Positive cast of original nose with negative cast of new nose. (Photos courtesy of Matthew W. Mungle.)*

Cups
Measuring spoons
Measuring cup

Basic Gelatin Formula

2 oz. sorbitol
3 oz. glycerin
1 tbsp. distilled water
3 tbsp. gelatin
1/8 tsp. zinc oxide
1/2 tsp. Joe Blasco Ruddy Light Skin Powder
1/4 tsp. Red Flocking

Note: This formula may be multiplied to create larger batches of gelatin. The amount of gelatin used may be raised or lowered to create a firmer or softer gelatin formula.

Procedure

1. Measure the sorbitol, glycerin, and distilled water into a large microwavable bowl and mix.
2. Measure the gelatin, zinc oxide, loose face powder, and red flocking into a separate container and mix.
3. Sift the powders through a small strainer into liquids and mix thoroughly.
4. Let this mixture set for twelve hours or overnight allowing the gelatin granules to absorb the moisture of the liquid.
5. Microwave the gelatin mixture in the bowl for 30-second increments until the gelatin granules are thoroughly melted. Do not let the mixture boil. This procedure may have to be repeated several times. After the granules have been melted, the mixture may be left in the bowl and stored or it may be poured into a plastic zip lock bag and stored flat.

Remember, this mixture will be extremely hot. DO NOT let it touch the skin.

Pouring Gelatin Appliances
Once the positive and negative molds are made, either a foam latex appliance or a gelatin appliance may be produced. The advantage of a gelatin appliance is that it requires a lighter makeup application, provided the gelatin color is a close match to the actor's skin color. It moves more like real skin, the materials are less expensive, and the appliance is less time consuming to produce. The only disadvantage is that the gelatin can *melt* on the face if the actor tends to perspire freely. There are steps, however, that can be taken to prevent this from happening (see the *Gelatin Prosthetic Application* section).

1. To pour and remove a gelatin appliance from a stone mold, you will have to coat the mold with a releasing agent. Spray vegetable oil, which is available in grocery stores, is the most economical choice. However, a more effective releasing agent is Epoxy Parfilm (see Appendix A) or the combination of the two. Spray the positive and negative molds with a heavy coating of the release agent and let it set for at least 30 minutes. The release agent will soak into the plaster and *pickle* the mold (Figure 14-44A). After 30 minutes, spray a lighter coat onto both molds making them ready to accept the hot gelatin mixture.
2. Heat the pre-mixed gelatin formula and carefully pour it into the negative mold (Figure 14-44B). Pick up the mold and roll the gelatin around onto all the sculpted areas.
3. Quickly press the positive into the negative (Figure 14-44C) and place barbell weights or any heavy object onto the positive mold only (Figure 14-44D). Let set for at least 45 minutes. Time will vary depending on the thickness of your mold.
4. Remove the weights and open the mold as shown in Figure 14-43E. Carefully pull the gelatin away from the molds and powder with baby powder (Figure 14-44E). To keep the gelatin appliances from wrinkling or the edges from being folded under, place the appliances on a vacu-form face cast or on a face cast covered with plastic. The appliances must be kept in a sealed plastic bag away from heat and humidity until ready for use (Figure 14-44F).

Applying Gelatin Appliances
(See Figure 14-45 for a list of supplies.)

1. Clean the skin with a tissue dampened with 99% alcohol. Be careful not to get alcohol near the eyes (Figure 14-46A—model before makeup application). Clean the front and back of the gelatin appliances with a tissue dampened with acetone.
2. Apply a pre-made rubber bald cap or bald pate with Beta Bond adhesive (see Appendix A). Add stretch and stipple old age (Old Age Stipple) on the forehead and around the eyes (Figure 14-46B).
3. Start the application of the wrap around gelatin appliance by applying adhesive to the skin and back of the appliance. Pros-Aide and Beta Bond are two types of adhesives that work well with gelatin appliances (see Appendix A). The adhesives are contact glues (pressure sensitive) and work best when both sides are allowed to dry, then are pressed together. If re-gluing or re-setting the piece is necessary, 99% alcohol may be used as a solvent to lift the appliance off the face. No extra glue will be necessary to tack that area back down. Begin at the chin and work up to the cheeks and eyes of both sides of the face (Figure 14-46B). Finish the application by gluing the neck down. Gluing is best achieved in small sections to insure the whole appliance has been glued down. Press any bubbles out between

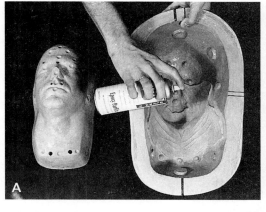

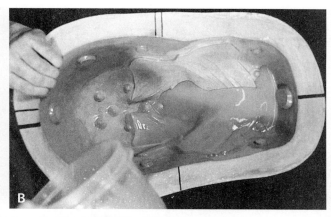

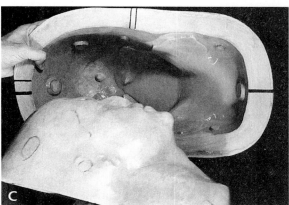

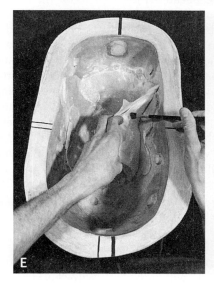

FIGURE 14-44 **Making the gelatin appliance.** *A. Negative mold being sprayed with mold release. B. Gelatin mixture being poured into mold. C. Positive mold being pressed into negative mold. D. Weights applied to positive. E. Powdering the gelatin appliance as it is being removed. F. Store the gelatin appliance on the form in a plastic bag. (Photos courtesy of Matthew W. Mungle.)*

the appliance and the skin. If the actor perspires freely, it is advisable to coat his or her skin with five coats of plastic sealer such as Sealer A from W.M. Creations, Inc. (see Appendix A) to prevent the perspiration from attacking the gelatin and melting it. The back of the appliance may also be coated with plastic sealer.

4. Make sure all the appliance edges are glued with adhesive.

5. With a cotton-tipped applicator and witch hazel, blend or *melt* the edges of the appliance into the surrounding skin (Figure 14-46C).

6. Apply any additional pieces. For this makeup example, a nose tip and ear lobes were also applied (Figure 14-46D).

7. After application and blending of all appliances are complete, apply a light coat of Pros-Aide or Beta Bond adhesive to all the edges with a cotton-tipped

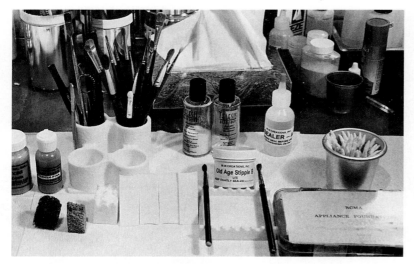

FIGURE 14-45 **Materials used for applying the gelatin appliance.** *Brushes; sponges (white foam and stipple sponges); tissues; brush and adhesive holders; adhesives (Beta Bond, Pros-Aide and Spirit Gum, see Appendix A under Adhesives); adhesive removers; 99% alcohol; acetone; old age stipple (see Appendix A); witch hazel astringent (available at drug stores); cotton-tipped applicators; plastic sealer (W. M. Creations Sealer A); Stacolor (see Appendix A); rubber-mask greasepaint kit; scissors.*

applicator. Let the adhesive dry, and stipple a light application of Sealer A with a small torn white foam sponge or red stipple sponge over the edges only. To protect the gelatin appliance, the whole appliance may be coated with sealer.

8. Apply a light, translucent application of Stacolor Pink-6205 (see Appendix A), thinned with a very small amount of 99% alcohol with a torn red or orange stipple sponge (Figure 14-46E). Because the skin contains enough red pigmentation, Stacolor is applied only to the gelatin. Stacolor is used for this step because it does not rub off when you begin to apply the skin-tone foundations. When skin-toned Stacolors are used instead of makeup the appliance becomes smudge-proof, waterproof, and grease (oil) free. Reel Creations and Temptu tattoo colors may be substituted for this step.

9. Apply rubber-mask grease paints with a torn white foam sponge to create skin depth. It will be necessary to apply at least three to four different shades of makeup bases to accomplish the look of skin discoloration and old age spots. Reduce or thin the bases with either castor oil or GP-20, using very light applications to achieve a more realistic skin tone effect. Heavier application of makeup as needed on foam latex appliances is not necessary. Applying the skin tone bases very thinly will allow the translucency of the gelatin show through (Figures 14-46F).

10. Finish the makeup with additional shading and wrinkle lines. Extra reds may be added to give more *life* to the prosthetic appliances (Figure 14-46G). Eyebrows and eyelashes are also grayed with hair white or a light makeup base.

11. Apply a properly styled and cut lace wig and glue it down with spirit gum to finish the prosthetic makeup (Figure 14-46H). Other designs using gelatin appliances can be seen in Figures G-28 and G-30.

12. Remove the gelatin appliances by first using the proper remover suggested for Beta Bond or Pros-Aide. Pros-Aide may also be removed with 70% alcohol and a flat brush. Once the appliance is removed, the remaining residue can be removed by soaking a puff in Isopropyl Myristate and gently rubbing the area until it disappears. The Isopropyl Myristate leaves an oily film and is milder for the skin than products such as Detachol which tends to leave the skin red and dry. Aging latex "stretch and stipples" are best removed by first coating the area with liquid hand soap, letting it set for a few minutes, then applying a warm wet towel to the area and repeating the process one or two more times. Adhesive residue may be removed in the same manner with adhesive removers. The skin can then be cleaned with a mild medicated cleanser (Noxema, for example), and treated with a 100% pure aloe vera gel and Vitamin E cream.

Silicones

The translucent appearance of the human skin has been a challenge for makeup artists for many years. With the introduction of silicones, it is now possible to create the color of skin in a more lifelike appearance without the use of lights and makeup. Designing a prosthetic piece in silicone can be a very simple procedure. A basic understanding of the material, however, is foremost in completing any silicone project.

There are four different grades of silicone elastomers defined by their usage: industrial, food, medical, and implant grade. *Industrial grade* includes the varieties of one-part RTV (room temperature vulcanizing) silicones found at local building supply or hardware stores. Squeezed from a tube or sprayed from a can, these sil-

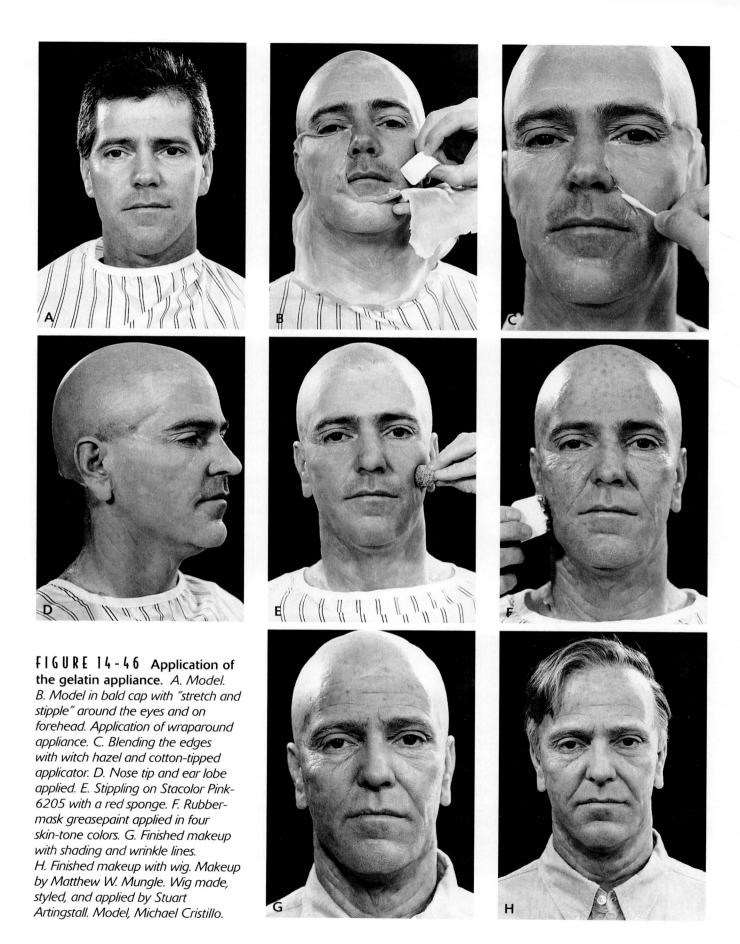

FIGURE 14-46 Application of the gelatin appliance. *A. Model. B. Model in bald cap with "stretch and stipple" around the eyes and on forehead. Application of wraparound appliance. C. Blending the edges with witch hazel and cotton-tipped applicator. D. Nose tip and ear lobe applied. E. Stippling on Stacolor Pink-6205 with a red sponge. F. Rubber-mask greasepaint applied in four skin-tone colors. G. Finished makeup with shading and wrinkle lines. H. Finished makeup with wig. Makeup by Matthew W. Mungle. Wig made, styled, and applied by Stuart Artingstall. Model, Michael Cristillo.*

Matthew Mungle

Academy Award winner, Matthew W. Mungle, was born in Durant, Oklahoma, in 1956. Matthew was one of four children of Atoka dairy farmers Jene and Becky Mungle. As a boy he can recall seeing *Frankenstein, Dracula,* and *Creature From the Black Lagoon.* He was fascinated with the makeup, experimenting with face casts and prosthetics on willing family members and friends. In 1964 with the release of *The Seven Faces of Dr. Lao,* Matthew credits the film as having been his greatest influence and deciding factor in becoming a makeup effects artist.

After his tenure at Oklahoma State University as a theater arts major, he was eager to get to Hollywood and begin learning his craft. Matthew arrived in Hollywood, California, in the fall of 1977, and soon applied and was accepted into Joe Blasco's Makeup Center. Matthew credits Joe Blasco with his professional start in the industry. Today, Matthew is a veteran voice to other up-and-coming artists hoping to find a working niche within the industry. "If you want to be a makeup artist, then you need to learn and perfect all areas of the craft."

Matthew's professional career began on low-budget projects that taught him to think fast on his feet, but it would not be long until he achieved his first major success with *Edward Scissorhands* in 1990. With over 100 film and television projects to date, Matthew has worked on a genre of box office successes, including *Bram Stoker's Dracula,* which earned him his first Oscar in 1992; *Schindler's' List,* giving him another nomination in 1993; Oliver Stone's *Natural Born Killers;* creating Arnold's pregnancy stomach in *Junior;* special makeup effects on *Outbreak; Congo;* and *Primal Fear;* and aging James Woods to 72 in *Ghosts of Mississippi,* which earned him his third Oscar nomination in 1996.

Aging has become one of Matthew's strongest calling cards within the industry and an area of makeup effects that's definitely the most challenging. His fascination with artificially making someone young look old prompted him to research more viable methods, such as with *gelatin*–first used in the 1930s, but later abandoned when the hot lights caused it to melt. However, with today's less intense lighting and faster film, Matthew has resurrected the nearly transparent substance, which when applied looks and moves like real skin. "I'm intrigued with how women and men age differently. Both get jowls and tend to get that fold of skin over the top lid of the eyes and bags under the eyes. But men's ear lobes get longer. Women's skin, on the other hand, tends to get crepey and translucent."

Matthew's recent film credits include psycho-thriller *I Know What You Did Last Summer* (1997) and it's 1998 sequel, *I Still Know . . .* (1998); the hilarious off-beat Mike Myers film, *Austin Powers* (1996); *Dr. Doolittle* with Eddie Murphy (1998); *54* starring Mike Myers as Steve Rubel (1998); Universal's *One True Thing* with Meryl Streep (1998); and Universal's *Psycho* (1998). Recently released projects include *Bowfinger* starring Steve Martin and Fine Line's *Blast from the Past* starring Sissy Spacek and Christopher Walken. Currently, Matthew has just completed the new *Flintstones: Viva Rock Vegas* for Universal and began filming *The Perfect Storm* for Warner Brothers and *Soul Survivors* for Artisan.

Although his work schedule dictates much of his time, Matthew and business partner, John E. Jackson, also run Nu-Products, which manufactures and distributes their own specialty line of makeup effects products.

In addition, Matthew continues to supervise the teaching of a *special advanced prosthetics technique course* at the world-famous Joe Blasco Makeup Center in Los Angeles, and in September of 1999 was invited to conduct a special 3-day seminar on *advanced prosthetics* for Screen Training Ireland in Dublin.

icones are used as caulking compounds and aerosol lubricants and coatings.

Tested for their ability to remain in contact with the skin surface or pierced through the skin's surface, products made from *medical grade* silicones range from prosthetic reconstructions to catheter implants and blood carrying systems to silicone-coated syringe needles. Silicone products tested for their ability to safely remain inside the body are considered *implant grade* silicones. Other products, such as baby bottle nipples and three-dimensional prosthetic devices used to enhance age and character makeups are made with *food grade* silicone. It is this latter group that is of interest for this discussion.

Two basic types of RTV silicone elastomer systems fall under the heading of food grade silicone: tin condensation cure and platinum addition cure silicones. They are differentiated from one another by the type of chemical reactions used for their curing process. Tin cure systems employ a silanol polymer and use tin as a catalyst, while the platinum system utilizes vinyl polymers and platinum catalysts. Both polymers react with their curing reagent and are accelerated by the catalyst producing a silicone elastomer. The chemical reaction inherent within the tin system produces ethyl alcohol as a by-product which quickly evaporates. Inevitably, this small loss of material results in some slight shrinkage as curing occurs and the alcohol evaporates. This is why tin silicones exhibit more shrinkage than platinum cure systems. This chemical reaction in which the molecules combine with the evolution of a by-product is usually called a condensation process, hence the name for the product line.

All of the platinum silicones rely on the addition reaction between the vinyl polymers and hydride curing reagent to create a silicone elastomer. This entire process is aided and accelerated by the platinum catalyst. Heat may also be utilized to greatly accelerate the platinum curing process without compromising the physical properties of the material. One advantage to this reaction is there is no by-product formed in this chemical reaction making it virtually odorless. The final result is a translucent, flexible, skin-like product that when filled with the appropriate pigments and then applied becomes indistinguishable from the actor's own skin.

Tin condensation cure silicones generally cure at lower temperature than platinum; therefore, they cannot be accelerated by the addition of heat! The benefit to a tin system is it will cure practically anywhere, against virtually any mold surface, using any mold release. It is by far the simplest silicone elastomer to use. Tin silicones will actually cure in a mold that has been contaminated by latex, if a little care is taken to clean the mold. One negative side to tin silicones is they are generally not recommended for extended contact with skin tissue. This problem is easily solved by the addition of a layer of medical-grade brushable silicone to the inside of the prosthetic (between the appliance and the skin).

Platinum silicones in general exhibit superior physical properties such as tear strength and elasticity. This is the reason they are generally the material of choice for any prosthetic appliance that is to come into contact with skin. The negative side to platinum silicones is that they are very susceptible to contamination. They will not cure with any exposure to various organic products, especially foam latex, latex gloves, and Roma Plastilina. This type of silicone is highly sensitive to the sulfur contained in these products. If you choose a platinum silicone, you must create a new sculpt using the proper sculpting medium (sulfur-free Chavant clay), fabricate a new mold using all of the proper casting compounds (white hydrocal over the gray Ultracal-30), pigments, and mold releases (from the manufacturer) and mixing equipment (glass, stainless steel, clear polypropylene–avoid polystyrene). When every detail has been properly monitored, place the closed mold into a conventional dry heat oven to accelerate the cure. Do not use an oven that has had foam latex molds placed into it on a previous occasion as this can contaminate the entire piece.

The following exercise will demonstrate the technique for utilizing silicone in developing age prosthetics using a tin condensation cure silicone, Rhodia (VI-SIL) V-1082. The properties of the tin cure system allow it to be used in any pre-existing mold, even those that contain residue from previous foam latex appliances. This is especially useful for artists who wish to experiment with silicone without having to repeat the lengthy process of making new molds. This is the procedure:

Cleaning the Pre-existing Mold

1. The first step in casting these appliances is to clean the mold thoroughly. Scrub the molds with acetone and a soft bristle brush. This will eliminate any physical debris and remove some residual latex contamination. (The molds pictured here are epoxy surface faced, hydrocal positives, and epoxy negatives.)
2. After the acetone has had a few minutes to evaporate, rinse the molds thoroughly with IPA (isopropyl alcohol) and allow to dry.

Mold Release

3. Apply mold release. Silicone, in general, should not need a mold release. However, it has been found that the minimal use of a proper mold release does make release a bit easier. (See Figure 14-47 for choosing the proper mold release for a variety of mold making compounds). Test your products before casting a complete appliance. Ivory liquid or petroleum jelly are more effective release agents when painted into a warm mold.

FIGURE 14-47 Mold release chart for Tin Condensation Cure Silicones.

Mold	Silicone	Mold Releases
Gypsum	Condensation Cure	Petroleum Jelly Liquid Soap F-901 Tin Foil Substitute A-801 PVA A-301 Petroleum Spray
Epoxy Surface Coat	Condensation Cure	1 coat A-301 and 1 coat A-801 PVA
Epoxy	Condensation Cure	Epoxy Parfilm A-505 Ease release

4. Before introducing the tin cure silicone into the mold, paint medical grade silicone onto the plaster positive (this step is not necessary when using platinum systems). Two coats of 891 Med A Silicone should be applied directly to the surface of the positive mold with an artist's brush to an overall even thickness (see Figure 14-48A and B). The first coat can be thinned by first dipping the brush into E.T.F. (Extrinsic Tri Fluid) or 1:1:1 Trichloroethane, then completely covering the mold with Med A just beyond the margins of the appliance to create a smooth even surface. Wait twenty to thirty minutes for this first coat to dry, or accelerate this process with the use of a heat gun. A second coat can then be applied but should not extend to the outer margins of the appliance. This will enable you to produce clear thin margins at the edge of the prosthetic device.

Adding Color to Silicone

5. The silicone should be intrinsically pigmented with a silicone liquid pigment coloring system. To replicate the coloration and the mass of the prosthetic appliance in Figure 14-53, combine 30 grams of FX-1082 base with 3 grams of catalyst, 3 drops of red I204, 3 drops of white I-200, and 4 drops of suntan I-227 (see Appendix B, Factor II).

   The pigments are added to the silicone drop by drop and recorded. To determine the opacity of the silicone it is necessary to add the white pigment first. Usually 4 drops of white pigment per 10 grams of silicone will produce an initial opacity. It is important not to forget that the other pigments will also produce a certain degree of opacity. Using white and the primary colors (red, yellow, and blue) it is possible to achieve a good basic skin color. The numbers of drops are recorded on a color sheet for future reference. When the base color is finished so that it matches an overall color on the actor, the silicone is vacuumed to remove all air in the material.

Vacuum De-aeration

6. The act of mixing silicone incorporates air into the mixture. There are a number of ways to remove the air before you place the material into a mold. One way is to pour the mixture into a glass baking dish and set it in the refrigerator or freezer allowing the bubbles to rise while slowing down the reaction. The standard way is to place the material into a vacuum chamber (see Figure 14-49) in a container at least four times the volume of the mixed material. This allows room for the material to expand during the process (see manufacturer's specifications). During the process, the material needs to rise to the top of the container in a violent form and fall back to the bottom of the container without going over the top. This is absolute proof you have successfully pulled vacuum on the material. Continue to hold the vacuum for a couple of additional minutes.

Painting the Silicone

7. After breaking the vacuum and removing the material from the container and before filling the mold, try laying in small amounts of more intensely pigmented silicone into the surface of the negative mold (called intrinsic painting). This will produce an appliance that will appear more life-like. This may take some time and experience. For the inexperienced, it is advisable to fill the mold with the base color and then extrinsically paint the appliance after it has cured. Now transfer the silicone into the mold by painting in small amounts at a time or carefully pouring from an edge. Once the pigmented silicone is placed into the mold, be careful not to entrap any air bubbles, and close and clamp the molds (see Figure 14-50). FX-1082 will cure overnight at room temperature. When the appliance is removed from the mold, it must be trimmed and cleaned with soap and water, then wiped with alcohol (Figure 14-51).

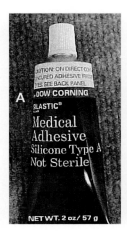
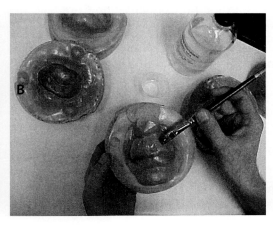

FIGURE 14-48 A. 891 Silicone Medical Adhesive Type A. B. Applying the 891 Med A to the plaster positive.

FIGURE 14-49 A. Vacuum chamber. *B. Silicone placed in the vacuum chamber. C. Vacuum pump.*

8. Before adding painted details to the surface of the appliance, clean it with acetone. Avoid touching the surface of the appliance; handling the appliance at this point will prevent a good integral bond of the extrinsic pigments. So if you touch it, you must completely re-prepare the surface of the appliance with acetone.

9. The next step is to add coloration to the surface of the appliance (called extrinsic painting) to create the desired overall effect (see Figure 14-52). Thin the colors with Extrinsic Tri-Fluid, 1:1:1 Trichloro-ethane, to a thin wash and paint them onto the appliance using a very fine artist's sable brush. The vehicle E.T.F. (Extrinsic Tri-Fluid) causes the surface of the silicone appliance to swell, opening the pores of the silicone, and allows the pigment to enter the spaces and internally become part of the appliance. When the E.T.F fluid evaporates, the pores will close, and the surface of the appliance will return to its original form. It is not possible to change the base color of the appliance by using extrinsic coloration techniques. The reason for getting the in-

trinsic color to match as close as possible is to minimize the amount of extrinsic pigmenting required. This is a fine and delicate art form. Considerable time and attention to detail is essential. When the coloring is to everyone's satisfaction (Figure 14-53 and G-31), seal the appliance. Apply three layers of the same, but uncolored, silicone. Each application must be cured individually and returned to room temperature before putting a new layer down.

Applying the Silicone Appliance

10. Apply a silicone appliance in a similar manner as foam latex and gelatin appliances. The exception here is to avoid adding adhesive to the edge of the silicone. Using a silicone adhesive (Secure or Telesis) or a water-based adhesive (Pros-Aide), paint the entire inside of the appliance stopping at an eighth to a quarter inch from the edge. Allow the adhesive to dry and become tacky (the silicone adhesives dry quickly so working in small areas is suggested). Press the appliance onto the skin, then wet the

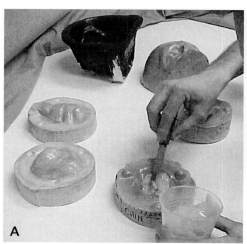

FIGURE 14-50 **Adding silicone to the mold.** *A. Apply silicone to the negative mold. B. Pressing smaller molds together and hold with mold bands. C. Clamping larger molds together.*

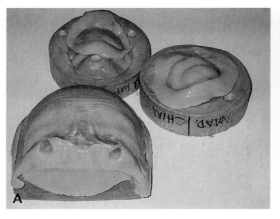

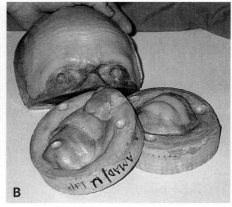

FIGURE 14-51
Opening molds.
A. Silicone appliance with flanges. B. Appliances with flanges removed.

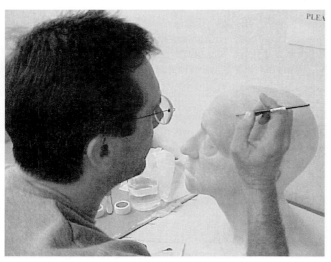

FIGURE 14-52 Extrinsic painting of the gelatin appliance. *Makeup artist David Trainer.*

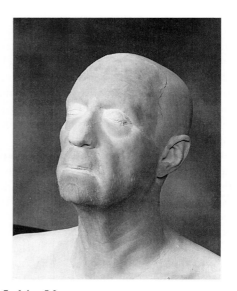

FIGURE 14-53 Finished silicone appliance mounted on the head cast of F. Murray Abraham. *Appliance made and painted by David Trainer from molds donated by Dick Smith. Molds made by Dick Smith for F. Murray Abraham in the role of Salieri for the 1984 movie,* Amadeus *(see Figure G-32 for a color image of the original makeup in foam latex). Products and technical advice by Factor II.*

edges with water and they will disappear. No edge stippling is required.

Removing the Silicone Appliance

11. Remove the appliance with an alcohol-based remover such as Detachol or Bond Off (Ben Nye). Clean the adhesive residue from the appliance with 70% alcohol.

PROBLEMS

1. Cast a life mask.

2. Model a simple prosthesis (such as a nose or a pair of eye pouches) in clay on the plaster cast. Then make an open mold from the clay model and a latex prosthesis in the open mold.

3. Design and execute a makeup using the latex prosthesis you have made.

4. If you are interested in working in foam latex and have the necessary equipment available, design and execute a makeup using this method. Keep a careful record of procedures and results, specifying precise amounts used, volumes, temperatures, and timing.

5. If you wish to do so, experiment with more complicated open-mold and/or closed-mold prostheses.

6. Make a simple prosthesis from the cold foam process using a closed mold.

7. Design a makeup requiring dental prosthesis, then make the teeth, and execute the makeup.

8. After you have developed your sculpting and mold-making skills, try making an old age wrap-around appliance using the procedure for gelatin appliances.

9. Make a nose, chin, or forehead appliance from silicone. This process requires skill in developing your ability to accurately match skin tones. Begin with small projects while you practice color mixing.

Beards and Mustaches

The first step in constructing a beard or a mustache is to make a rough sketch of what you have in mind. Presumably you will have done this when designing the makeup. Illustrations in this book and in your morgue should be helpful. The style you choose will, of course, depend on the period of the play and on the personality of the character.

You can make or buy beards or mustaches of real or synthetic hair ventilated on a lace foundation. This type of beard is the quickest to apply, the most comfortable to wear, and the most convincing. It is also the most expensive, but it will last for many performances, if not for many years. If you will be using a beard or a mustache for only a few performances and if your budget is limited, you will probably want to use crepe hair. In any case, you should become proficient in the technique of applying it. This applies primarily to men, of course, and to women who plan to make up men. And women do sometimes use crepe hair for eyebrows in character makeups.

Crepe Hair

Crepe hair is hair that has been permanently kinked by means of weaving on strings and boiling. Wool crepe is relatively inexpensive and, if skillfully manipulated, very effective. It can be used for beards, goatees, mustaches, sideburns, eyebrows, and occasionally to add to the natural hair. It is not usually satisfactory, however, for movie or television close-ups.

Various shades of hair are available, and for realistic beards or mustaches, several shades should be mixed. This can be done by straightening braids of both shades, then combing them together. This will give a far more realistic effect than would a flat color. It is especially important for realistic makeups that pure black or pure white crepe hair never be used without being mixed with at least one other color. Black usually needs some gray or brown or red; and white, some blond or light gray.

Preparation of Crepe Hair

Crepe hair comes in braids of very kinky, woolly strands, which for straight- or wavy-haired actors should normally be straightened before the hair is applied. This is done by cutting the string that holds the braids together and wetting the amount of hair to be used. The portion of the hair that has been dampened can then be straightened by stretching it between the legs or arms of a chair, two clothes hooks, or any other solid objects not too far apart. Both ends of the stretched hair are tied with string to whatever moorings are being used and left to dry.

The damp hair can be straightened much more quickly, however, with an electric iron, but be careful to avoid scorching the hair. Pressing under a damp cloth or using a steam iron (Figure 15-1) is preferable.

After the hair is dry, it should be carefully combed with a wide-toothed comb, then cut into lengths as needed. A great deal of the hair will probably be combed out of the braid. This extra hair should be removed from the comb, gathered in bunches, and recombed as often as is necessary to make it useable for eyebrows, small mustaches, and the shorter lengths of hair needed in making beards. In combing, always begin near the end of the braid and work back, combing gently. Otherwise, you may tear the braid apart.

In case slightly wavy hair is desired, the crepe hair should be stretched less tightly while drying. Sometimes

FIGURE 15-1   Straightening crepe hair with a steam iron.

it need only be moistened and allowed to dry without stretching. It is also possible to use straightened hair and curl it with an electric curling iron after it has been properly trimmed. Crepe hair can also be curled by wrapping the straightened hair diagonally around a curling stick (a broom handle will do), securing with string, and allowing it to dry or force-drying it with an electric dryer. Spraying the hair on the stick with hair spray or coating it with wave set will give it more body.

Occasionally it is possible to use unstraightened hair if a very thin, fluffy kind of beard is needed. To prepare the hair, pull out the braid as far as it will go without cutting the string, grasp the braid with one hand, the loose end of the hair with the other, and pull in sharp jerks until a section of the hair is detached from the braid. The hair can then be spread out and fluffed up with the fingers. One method of fluffing is to pull the hair at both ends. Half of the hair will go with the left hand, half with the right. The two strands can then be put back together and the process repeated until there are no dark spots where the hair is thick and heavy. The curl is thus shuffled around so that it is no longer recognizable as a definite wave. If the hair is then too fluffy, it can be rolled briskly between the palms of the hands. This is nearly always done for mustaches when straightened hair is not used. The pulling and fluffing technique is particularly useful when skin should show through the beard in spots, as it sometimes does on the chin. It can also be used in an emergency if there is no straightened hair and no iron available to straighten it.

Mixing Colors

Because combing wool crepe, even with a wide-toothed comb, tends to waste a good deal of hair, mixing can be accomplished more economically by first cutting the various shades of hair into whatever lengths you are going to need, always allowing extra length for the trimming. You can then proceed in one of two ways—either take strands of hair of each color and gradually put them together until the portions of the various colors you want mixed are assembled into one pile, or put together all of the hair you want mixed and keep pulling the strands apart and putting them back together until they are sufficiently mixed. The principle, though not the technique, is the same as for shuffling cards.

The first method will probably give you a more even mixture. For some beards you will want to choose colors that are not too strongly contrasting in hue or value; for others you will want stronger contrasts. You might even, for example, use such strongly contrasting colors as black, white, and red.

If you wanted to give more subtlety to the color variation in a beard, you might work with three colors (which can be referred to as *a, b,* and *c*), mixing *a* and *b* to produce one mixture, *a* and *c* to produce another, and *b* and *c* to produce a third. Added to your original three colors, that would give you six different shades, which might vary only in value-variations of gray, for example—or in both value and hue—perhaps some red or brown mixed with the gray.

Application of Crepe Hair

The hair is commonly applied with spirit gum over the completed makeup. If creme makeup or greasepaint is applied in a very thin coat and well powdered, the gum should stick. How well it sticks will depend largely on how much the actor perspires and on the quality of the spirit gum used.

You will already have determined the shape of beard you want. In applying the hair, always be aware of the natural line of hair growth, as shown in the diagram in Figure 15-2. The numbers indicate the most practical order of application. The procedure is as follows:

1. Paint the area to be covered by hair with spirit gum one section at a time, and allow the gum to become quite tacky. Lightly tapping the gum repeatedly with the tip of a finger will speed up the process. It's a good idea to have some powder handy to dust on the fingers or on the scissors whenever they get sticky. During the application, the scissors and the fingers can occasionally be cleaned with alcohol or spirit-gum remover.

2. Separate a dozen or so hairs from one of your darkest piles, and, holding them firmly between the thumb and the forefinger of one hand, cut the ends on the bias (Figure 15-3). The hairs should be longer than required for the finished beard or mustache—they can be trimmed later. The darker hair should usually be used underneath; the lighter, on top. In observing bearded men, however, notice that in

FIGURE 15-3 Cutting crepe hair. *Hair being cut on the bias before being applied to the face.*

gray or partially gray beards, certain sections of the top layer are often lighter than others. Those areas normally match on both sides of the face.

3. When you have made sure that the gum is sufficiently tacky, apply the hair first to the underside of the chin (Figure 15-4A), Usually the application should be in three layers. Push the ends of the first layer into the gum under the chin, about ½ or ¾ of an inch back from the tip (#1 in Figure 15-2). Press with the scissors, a towel, or a damp chamois for a few seconds (Figure 15-4B), then add a second and a third layer (#2 and #3 in Figure 15-2), the latter starting from the lowest point on the neck where the hair grows naturally. The hair along the edge of this line should be very thinly spread. If you are making a full beard, the hair should be carried up to the highest point at which the beard grows on the underside of the jaw.

4. Next, apply hair to the front of the chin. The hair can first be attached in a roughly semicircular pattern, following the line of the tip of the chin (#4 in Figure 15-2). Then add thinner layers of hair (#5 and #6), following the line of the beard as outlined by the spirit gum. For full beards the hair should be built up gradually, starting at the chin and proceeding to the sideburns (Figure 15-2, #7-12; and Figure 15-4C). As the hair is usually not so heavy on the sides of the face, a few applications will be sufficient. Each application of hair should be pressed and allowed to dry slightly before another is made. Remember that ordinarily the thin layer of hair at the edge of the beard will be somewhat lighter in color than the hair underneath.

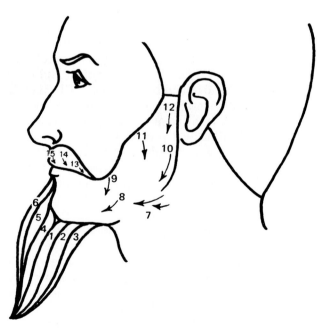

FIGURE 15-2 Diagram for applying crepe hair beard. *Layers of hair are applied in the order indicated by the numbers.*

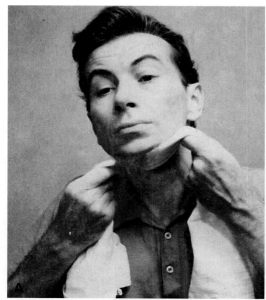

FIGURE 15-4
Constructing a beard with crepe hair and spirit gum. *Straightened hair is built up gradually in layers, using two or more shades of hair. All loose hairs are pulled out before the final trimming. Notice how the thinner hair on the cheek blends into the skin. (Makeup artist Richard Corson.)*

5. When you have completed the application and have allowed the spirit gum time to dry, gently pull all of the hair in the beard in order to remove any stray hairs that are not firmly anchored. A beard that will not resist this gentle pulling is not secure enough to wear on stage.

6. Holding your barber's shears vertically or nearly vertically, trim and shape the beard according to the style required, using a hand mirror when you need a profile view. If the beard is to be straggly, little or no trimming may be required; but a neat beard requires careful shaping.

7. Usually you will want to spray the beard with hair spray so that it will hold its shape. An unkempt beard may not need spraying; but, on the other hand, you may wish to use the spray to maintain the disorder.

Mustaches should not be stuck on in two pieces (except for distance work in which accurate detail is not necessary) but built up in the same manner as beards, starting at either end and working toward the center, letting the hair fall in the natural direction of growth (Figure 15-2, #13-15). One end of each hair should always be free. The ends of the mustache may be waxed to make them hold their shape. Better yet, the whole mustache can be sprayed with diluted spirit gum (see *Atomizer*. Appendix A) or hairspray.

In extending the sideburns, either separately or as part of a beard, it is sometimes possible, if the actor's hair is long and his sideburns are fairly full, to undercut the natural sideburns so that at least a quarter inch of real hair can be made to overlap the false hair, thus avoiding an obvious join. If, however, the natural sideburns are closely cropped, it will probably be more practical to continue the front edge of the false sideburns upward slightly in front of the real ones as far as necessary in order to make a smooth blend into the natural hair.

Removal

In removing the crepe hair, brush on spirit-gum remover along the top edge of the beard or the mustache, then pull the hair off gently, continuing to brush on the remover as you go. When all of the hair has been removed, clean the area where it was attached—first with the spirit-gum remover, then with your usual makeup remover.

Latex Base

If you need the hair construction for more than one performance, you can make it up on a latex base rather than attaching it directly to the skin with spirit gum (Figure 15-5). It is recommended that you have a clean face with no natural facial hair of any sort before you begin as removal of the latex can often be difficult. This includes the soft, fine hair often found on a woman's face. Before painting latex on the face, it's a good idea to protect the skin with a light coating of cleansing cream or oil. Then powder the oiled skin and

FIGURE 15-5 Crepe hair beard and mustache. *Beard constructed on latex, using four colors of crepe hair—light gray, medium gray, light gray-brown, and blond. Mustache made of real hair ventilated on lace (see Figure 15-9B). Makeup by Bill Smith. (For another makeup by Mr. Smith, see Figure 13-33C.)*

brush off the excess powder. If you should feel a burning sensation on your skin when you apply the latex, try another brand. If no other brand is immediately available or if you find all brands irritating, use spirit gum.

If you prefer to make the beard on a plastic face rather than on a real one, see Figure 15-6.

Following is the procedure for making a mustache. Essentially the same procedure would be used for beards and sideburns.

1. Paint the entire mustache area with liquid latex. If the character is to be aged, carry the latex application partially over the upper lip until the lip is as thin as you want it to be. When the first application is dry, add successive applications—usually two or three—until the latex seems thick enough to form a firm base.

2. When your crepe hair is ready to attach, paint on a final coat of latex and immediately push the ends of the hair into it. The ends will be firmly anchored when the latex dries. Because latex dries quickly, you should do only one small area at a time.

3. Pull out all loose hairs, and trim the mustache.

The mustache may now seem to be anchored solidly enough to leave it on for the first performance,

FIGURE 15-6 **Mustache on a plastic head.** *(The head is available from Bob Kelly.)*

but if there is much movement around the mouth or excessive perspiration, the latex may loosen and pull away from the skin. It is safer, therefore, to remove it as soon as the latex is dry and reattach it with spirit gum. This can be done simply by lifting one edge of the latex with a fingernail, tweezers, or an orangewood stick and pulling the mustache off. The back of the latex should be powdered immediately to prevent it sticking to itself. Rough edges should be trimmed before putting the mustache back on. In trimming the latex, be sure to leave as thin a blending edge as possible.

In reattaching the mustache, apply the spirit gum to the back of the latex, but only around the edges—unless there is to be so much movement that you would feel more secure with a greater area of adhesion. Let the gum become slightly tacky before attaching the piece to the skin. After the piece is in place, press with a towel for a few moments, just as in applying the hair directly with spirit gum. To conceal the edge of the piece, add a row of hair to the skin along the top edge of the mustache. This added row of hair will usually be the lightest hair you have prepared for use in making the mustache. On light-skinned actors, light hairs blend into the skin more readily than do dark ones.

Removal   In removing the beard and mustache that has been re-applied with spirit gum, apply alcohol or spirit-gum remover around the edges of the latex to loosen it. Do not try to pull it off without first loosening

the gum, as this may stretch or tear the latex. When the mustache has been removed, clean all the gum from the back of the latex with remover. It is possible to reattach the mustache with latex, but since the problem of security still remains, this is not advised. In making both a beard and a mustache with a latex base, make them separately or cut them apart after they are made in order not to restrict movement of the jaw.

If you mistakenly applied the latex over natural facial hair, try using baby oil or mineral oil to aid in the removal. Gently peel back a corner of the latex, near an edge, and carefully work a Q-tip dipped in the oil underneath the latex, moving in the same direction as the hair grows. This should cause the latex to release the hair. If you would like to try to reuse the beard and mustache, you will need to clean the latex with alcohol and lightly powder it so that the latex will not stick to itself. Remove the excess powder before reusing.

Beard Stubble

For an unshaven effect (see Figure 15-7), yak hair, human hair, or crepe hair is cut into tiny pieces and attached to the beard area with beard-stubble adhesive. There are several variations in the method. This is the simplest:

1. Wash the face with soap and water or clean it with alcohol or astringent to remove all grease. If the skin under the stubble is to be made up, use transparent liquid makeup.
2. Choose the color of hair you want, then cut up tiny bits of it onto a piece of paper, your makeup table top, or any smooth surface.
3. Cover a small section of the beard area with a beard-stubble adhesive (see Adhesives, Appendix A). Uncolored mustache wax can also be used for the same purpose.
4. Push a dry rouge brush into the pile of hair bits (quite a few will stick to the brush), and, with the brush, transfer the bits to the face. Spread the hair

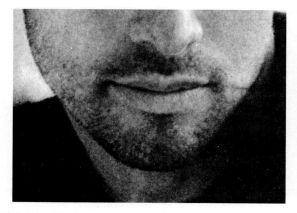

FIGURE 15-7 **Beard stubble.**

bits out fairly evenly and try not to pile them up in clumps. It would be best to have an extra rouge brush for this purpose.

5. Another method is to form a small loose ball from the bits of hair, then carefully pat it against the adhesive.
6. Repeat steps 3 and 4 until the entire beard stubble is complete.

It is also possible to use matte spirit gum instead of the stubble adhesive, and it may be advisable to do so if there is likely to be any sort of activity that might dislodge the stubble from the wax adhesive. The spirit gum can be applied over whatever makeup you are using for the character. Regular spirit gum is not advisable because of the shine. When the gum is almost dry, the stubble can be attached by touching a fairly large clump of it to the gummed area repeatedly until the entire area is covered. Loose hairs can be brushed off and final touching up can be done with the fingers or with tweezers. The spirit gum can be used over any makeup, though grease or creme makeup must, of course, be thoroughly powdered. The stubble adhesive works better on clean skin and is used for natural effects for the stage and in film and television (see Figure 15-8).

When attaching stubble to foamed latex prosthetics colored with PAX paint (see Chapter 14) try mixing the adhesive Secure BT-404 (Factor II) with the solvent Hexamethyldisiloxane (HD solution) in a 1:1 ratio. This solution will dry shiny and clear, but will remain slightly tacky. To eliminate the shine, stir in the matting agent TS-100 or Cab-O-Sil a little at a time to create a smooth, paintable solution. The method for applying the stubble onto this surface will follow the same procedure as mentioned in the above exercise.

Removal
Beard stubble applied with a wax adhesive can be removed with any oil-based makeup remover. When applied with spirit gum, it can be removed with spirit-gum remover or alcohol.

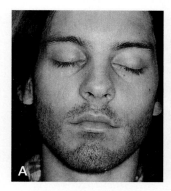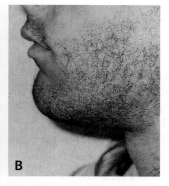

FIGURE 15-8 Beard stubble. *Applied with Naturo Plasto, Mortician's wax on actor, Toby Maguire, in the film, "Ride With the Devil." (Makeup by Jeff Goodwin at Transformations Make-up FX)*

Beard Shadow
If, instead of a beard, only a beard shadow is required, simply stipple the beard area (over the finished makeup) with an appropriate color. With medium or dark brown hair, charcoal brown is usually effective, but a lighter color would, of course, be used for lighter hair. For black hair, a dark gray makeup or gray mixed with black might be used; and for gray hair, a lighter gray. Experiment with colors to determine the right one. Unless you are stippling with cake makeup, the stipple should always be powdered.

In stippling with creme makeup, spread the color onto the back of the hand, then press the stipple sponge into the color on the hand rather than pressing it directly onto the cake. That gives you better control over the amount of color on the sponge. Then, touching the sponge very lightly to the face, do all of the stippling with great care in order to avoid mistakes, which can be very time-consuming to correct. If you do make a mistake, try correcting it, if only a very small area is involved, by first blotting the mistake carefully with a tissue, then powdering it with a cotton ball or a cotton swab and, using a small brush, covering the spot with the foundation color. Powder again, then re-stipple. Depending on the size of the spot, it may be best to do the re-stippling with a small pointed brush rather than with your stipple sponge. Colors labeled "Beard Stipple" (usually a charcoal brown) are available.

Eyebrows

Yak hair, coarse human hair, or crepe hair can be used to supplement the natural brows, or they can be used to make completely new ones, as suggested in Chapter 12. In adding to the natural brows, it is possible to attach the crepe hair to the skin over the brow and comb it down into the brow or to stick tufts of crepe hair into the brow. The method used will depend on the form and the thickness of the natural brow and of the brow to be constructed.

Sometimes it is necessary to block out the eyebrows completely (see Chapter 12 for details) and build new ones. Ideally, this should be done by ventilating real hair onto net (see following section), but it can be done using the beard stipple method. When using latex as an adhesive, be very careful not to get it into the real eyebrows, for it may be impossible to remove the latex without removing the hairs as well. Once the hairs have been completely matted down with spirit gum, wax, or sealer, however, it is usually safe to apply latex over them.

Removal
When using spirit-gum remover on the eyebrows, always protect the eyes by bending over so as to cause the liquid to flow away from the eyes instead of toward them. When applied with latex over blocked-out eyebrows, the hair can simply be peeled off.

Ventilated Pieces

The most convincing and convenient beards and mustaches are made of real or synthetic hairs individually knotted onto a net foundation. This knotting process is usually known as ventilating, though it is sometimes referred to as working, hand tying, or knotting the hair. The process is required in the making of full wigs, parts of wigs, toupees and, as mentioned above, facial hair. Although it is time consuming and takes a great deal of patience, it is quite rewarding work for the hair, even in close-ups, appears to be actually growing out of the skin. The piece, when finished, is easily attached and removed and, with proper care, will last for some time. Since learning to ventilate from reading a book can be difficult, it is recommended to those who wish to improve their technique and speed to enroll in a class, or apply for an internship or an apprenticeship program.

Materials

Foundations may be of silk net, nylon net, wig lace, cotton net, silk gauze, or a combination of gauze and net. The gauze is a somewhat stiff, thin, tough, closely woven fabric. The better nets are also thin, fairly stiff, and somewhat transparent, so that when they are glued to the skin they become invisible from a short distance. (Figure 15-9A and B). The mustache in Figure 15-9D and E was ventilated onto silk gauze.

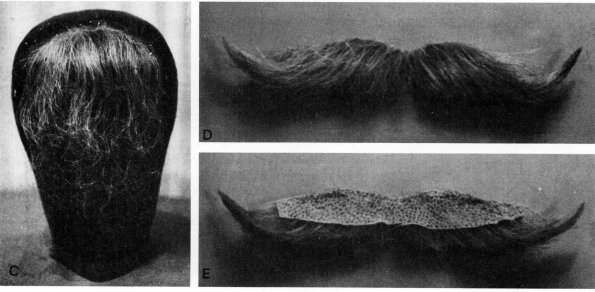

FIGURE 15-9 Ventilated mustaches. *A, B. Front and back of mustache ventilated on lace. C. Mustache (on wig block) ventilated on lace, shown before trimming. D, E. Front and back of mustache ventilated on gauze.*

Both human and synthetic hair are used, but when greater stiffness is desired, yak hair may be substituted. It is less expensive, it can be dyed any color, and it does not mat or snarl as readily as human hair does.

The finest human hair is available in a full range of natural colors. Human hair that has been dyed is less desirable since the color may fade in time. Coarser human hair can be obtained at more reasonable prices. Hair comes in various lengths, tightly bound with string at the cut end, and may be either straight or curled. Hair is purchased by weight, the price depending on quality and color. Grays are usually the most expensive.

Various types of synthetic hair are available in a number of colors and at prices considerably lower than for human hair. Some types have a high sheen, giving a rather artificial look; others have less sheen, some of them being virtually indistinguishable in appearance from real hair. Real and synthetic hair are sometimes mixed but it is not recommended as the two are styled differently. For sources of all types of hair and wig lace, see Appendix A.

Construction of Ventilated Pieces

The first step in constructing a beard or a mustache is to collect the appropriate tools (see Figure 15-10). This will include: human or yak hair in the colors required; a set of drawing cards; a ventilating needle; a ventilating needle holder; a piece of nylon netting or wig lace; a canvas head block; a pattern; and silk or dressmaker pins with large, flat heads. Then draw the outline of the proposed piece on the face with an eyebrow pencil. This, of course, will indicate only the area of the skin from which the hair would normally grow—not the

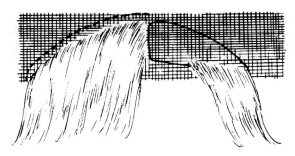

FIGURE 15-11 **Ventilating a mustache onto net or gauze.** *The solid line represents the outline of the mustache, which should be drawn on paper underneath the net or, if gauze is used, on the gauze itself. The dotted line represents where the gauze or net will be trimmed.*

shape or styling of the beard or the mustache. In other words, a long handlebar mustache may grow from the same basic area as a short-clipped mustache. The only difference is that the hair itself is longer. The diagram in Figure 15-11 will serve as a general guide for outlining the area of growth. For individual variations in beard growth, see Figures 15-12, 15-13, Appendix G, and illustrations in your own morgue.

After the area is marked on the skin, lay a small piece of plastic wrap over the marked area making sure that you do not cover the mouth or nose and cover with a piece of transparent tape. Trace the outline onto the tape with a permanent marker then cut out along the traced lines. This will give you an accurate pattern. For mustaches this is a very simple process, but for beards there is an obvious complication since the hair grows both over and under the jawbone. The solution is to place a larger piece of plastic wrap on the face, without covering the mouth, that goes from one sideburn to another and under the chin. Completely cover the plastic wrap with transparent tape following the shape of the face, covering all areas that will have hair on them, and making sure to support the area under the jaw with tape as well. Again, draw the shape of the beard onto the taped surface with a permanent marker.

The third step is to pin or tape the pattern to a wig block, a beard block (Figure 15-14A,B,C), or a plaster cast of the actor's face, and lay a piece of lace over it. The lace should be at least an inch longer and wider than the pattern. It will be trimmed later. In Figure 15-11 the solid line represents the pattern of a mustache showing through the lace. The pattern should be pinned down with silk or dressmaker pins if you are using a canvas block or with transparent tape if you are using a wooden block or plaster cast. Next, position your lace on the block over the pattern so that the holes run in a vertical direction. The holes in most nylon netting or wig lace will actually run in a direction: horizontal or vertical. Hold the lace over dark fabric and you should

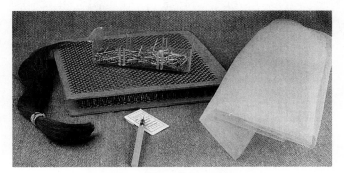

FIGURE 15-10 **Ventilating tools.** *(clockwise from left) Human hair hank, a set of drawing cards, silk or dressmaker pins, fine netting, ventilating needle holder, ventilating needle packet. (drawing cards, ventilating needle and holder from Kryolan, netting from De Meo Brothers)*

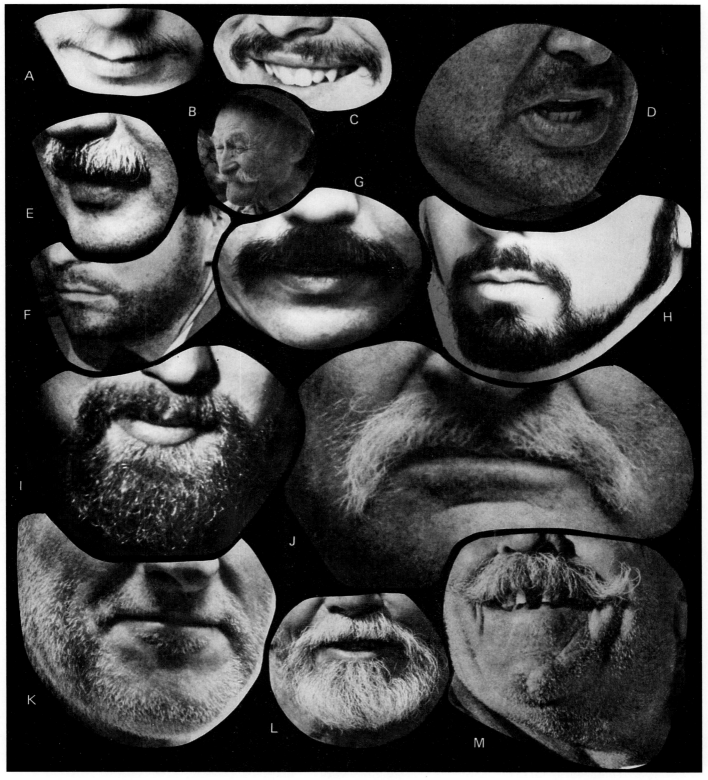

FIGURE 15-12 Mustaches and beards.

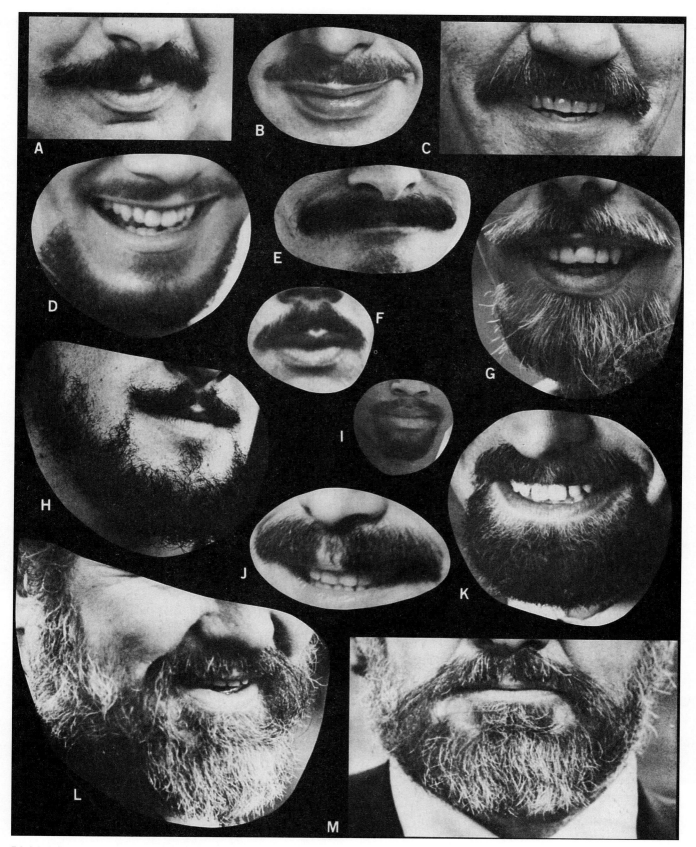

FIGURE 15-13 Mustaches and beards.

FIGURE 15-14 Attach patterns to a beard or canvas wig block. *A. Beard block. (Seen here with a ventilated beard by Kryolan.) B. Mustache pattern from tape and plastic wrap attached to a canvas wig block. C. Mustache pattern in paper pinned over black tape attached to a canvas wig block.*

be able to tell the difference. The lace should be pinned down with silk or dressmaker pins if you are using a canvas block, with tape on a plaster cast, with staples or wig points if you are using a wooden block. When pins or staples are used, be sure the lace is secured firmly, with the head of the pin or staple resting tightly against it so that it is not pulled out of shape in the knotting process. Begin by placing a pin in the top center of the netting approximately ¼ inch away from the edge of the pattern. Place another pin in the bottom center of the netting, opposite of the top pin, pulling slightly. Now do the same on the left and right sides of the netting. Fill in the perimeter of the edge of the lace with pins placed no more than ¼ inch to ½ inch apart (Figure 15.15)

The ventilating needle is shown in Figure 15-16. It consists of a handle about 3 inches long into which the needle is inserted. The needle is about 1½ inches long and curved with a sharp fishhook at the end. The size of this hook regulates the number of hairs that will automatically be drawn from the hank when the needle is inserted. Needle sizes are designated by number, starting with 00–the larger the number, the larger the needle. For the body of a beard, a #1 or a #2 needle can be used, but for the edges a #00 is needed so that the knots will not be obvious. Larger needles should be used only where the knots are to be covered by subsequent layers of hair. For mustaches it is best not to use a needle drawing more than two or three hairs. For the top few rows a needle drawing only one hair should be used.

Preparing the Hair It is important to know which part of the hair is the root and which is the end. This is more important, however, for wigs than for facial hair. Place one side of the drawing cards on the table in front of you so that the teeth are bent away from

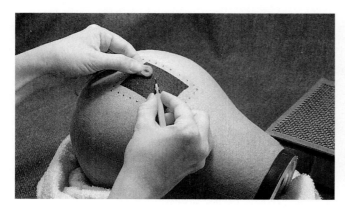

FIGURE 15-15 Ventilating a mustache on a canvas wig block.

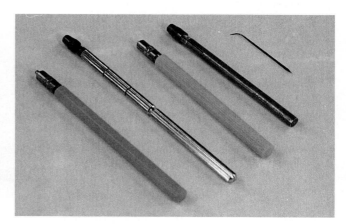

FIGURE 15-16 Closeup of various holders and a ventilating needle.

you. Place a small amount of the hair in the drawing card so that there are 2 to 2½ inches of the *root* end of the hair (facing towards you) hanging over the edge. Place the other half of the drawing card on top of the first side with the hair in it, again, making sure that the teeth are pointing away from you. Press down on the drawing cards over the hair so that the teeth mesh together. This will allow you to "draw" the desired amount of hair from the card to ventilate into your sample (Figure 15-17A, B and C.)

Place the ventilating needle in the holder. Practice holding your needle as you would a pencil. Roll the needle between your fingers so that the hook on the needle goes toward you and away from you. Put the needle down in a safe place to prevent it from rolling off the table.

Figure 15-18 illustrates the ventilating technique. Always keep in mind, in ventilating, that your hands must be pulling against each other from the moment the needle catches the hairs until the hairs are knotted. Releasing the tension of the hairs before the knot is tied will probably result in their slipping off the needle. Releasing it before the ends of the hair are completely free of the knot may result in a loose knot, which will then have to be tightened by pulling it with the fingers.

Hold the canvas block with the prepared netting in your lap or supported on a table with towels around it to prevent it from rolling. This is the procedure for ventilating:

1. Pull a small amount of hair out of the drawing cards (Figure 15-17C.) Go down the bundle of hair approximately 2 inches and bend it over. This is known as the *turn over*. (1) Pinch the hair between the thumb (2) and index finger (3) of your left hand approximately ¼ inch to ½ inch down the turn over. (See Figure 15-19A and B.) Allow the ends of the hair to be loosely supported in the rest of your fingers. At first the tension of your pinch will be very tiring, but once you get used to the process, you can tighten and ease up as needed. Now you are ready to ventilate.

2. Take your ventilating needle (6) in your right hand and hold it as you practiced. Slide the needle through a hole on the netting, passing under or *catching* a bar and come out through the next hole (7). Bring the bundle of hair to the needle and catch a few hairs on the ventilating hook (the number depends upon the size of the needle). Pull the hair out of the bundle a short distance. With both hands in tandem, slide the hair back through the holes, under the bar, taking care to keep the hook from catching the lace or netting. That can be done by rolling the needle slightly with the thumb and the forefinger in a counterclockwise direction and, at the same time, pushing the needle gently upward against the strand of the lace under which the hook must pass, enabling the smooth side of the needle to pass freely under the strand of the lace without the hook becoming caught in the net. This may take a little practice, but will soon become automatic.

Then withdraw the hook far enough to clear the lace comfortably (Figure 15-18B); but be careful not to draw it too far, or you may pull out the short end of the hair from between the thumb and index finger.

3. Now that you have a loop of hair attached to the needle, move the needle forward and catch the hair in the neck of the needle as illustrated in Figure 15-18C. Roll the hook of the needle away from you so that the hair is wrapped around the neck. With both hands in tandem, pull the hair and needle toward you and swing the needle to the right. You should see or feel the hair on the neck slide up the neck and be caught by the hook of the needle (Figure 15-18D and E). Drop the hook behind the hair and twist the needle one half turn clockwise. Leave your left hand stationary and pull the hair that is held by the hook through the loop of hair still on the needle (Figure 15-18G). Pull the hair all the way through to the right and out of your left hand. If you tighten the tension of the hair in your left hand as you pull the hair out with your needle, the knot will

FIGURE 15-17 **Using the drawing card for ventilating.** *A. Hair is placed on the drawing card with root end toward you. Notice that the angle of the metal teeth on the card are curling away from you. B. The two halves of the drawing card are firmly pressed together. C. Pinch a small amount of hair at the root end and draw it from the card.*

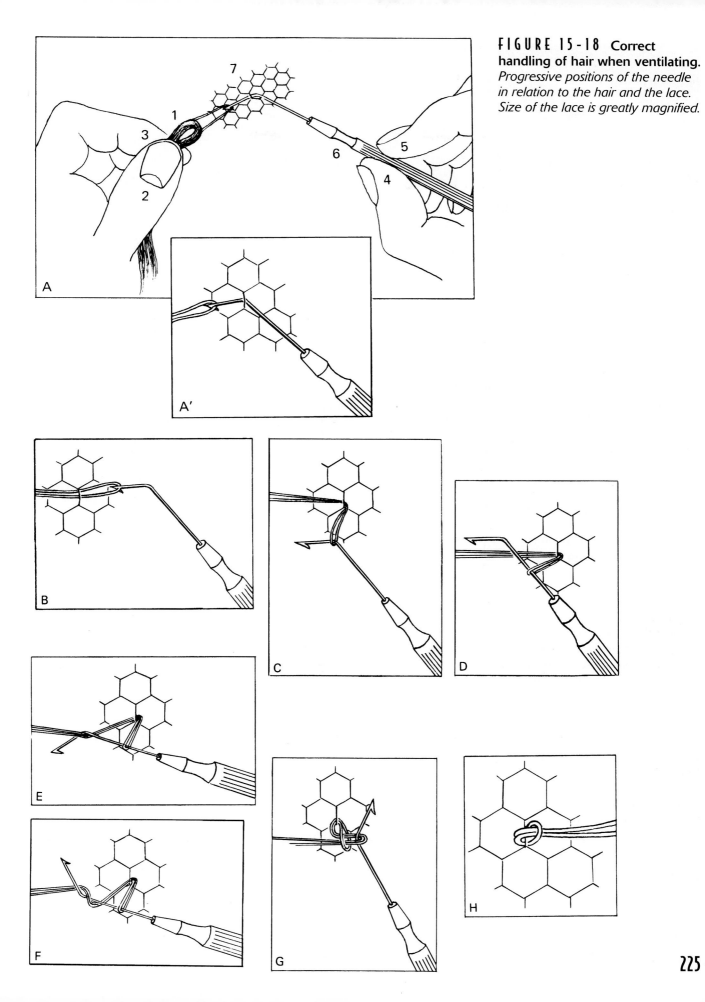

FIGURE 15-18 Correct handling of hair when ventilating. *Progressive positions of the needle in relation to the hair and the lace. Size of the lace is greatly magnified.*

225

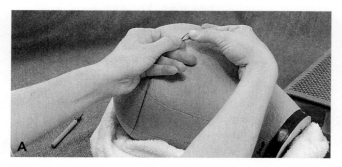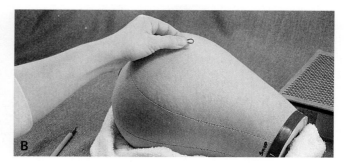

FIGURE 15-19 **Ventilating hair onto lace.** *A. "Bending" the root end of the hair (turn over) into a small loop. B. Hold the loop firmly (pinching the loop) and keep it smooth and organized during the ventilating process.*

tighten to the bar of the net. You should have a nice, clean knot (Figure 15-18H). The hairs will then lie in one direction, moving away from the left hand. Always move the right hand in the direction you want the hairs to lie.

As you become more comfortable and familiar with the process of ventilating, you will loosen your grip by relaxing your hands, resulting in the elimination of much of the motion in your left hand, letting the right hand and needle do the lion's share of the work. If you are left handed, reverse the hands as described above and pull the hair out towards the left.

The most important part of ventilating is to stay calm and focused and to take regular breaks. Novice as well as experienced ventilators should develop stretching exercises to reduce muscular tension and to avoid more serious physical conditions such as tendinitis and carpal tunnel syndrome.

In making a mustache, always begin at the outer corners and work along the bottom and upward. The top hair should always be the last to be knotted in. When the hair is in, trim the net about a quarter inch beyond the hair, as shown by the dotted line in Figure 15-11. The lace immediately under the nose may have to be trimmed closer than that, but avoid trimming it too close since the edges will eventually ravel and will have to be cut down still further.

You may want to do some preliminary trimming of the mustache before trying it on, for when you finish the ventilating, the hair will probably be as long as that in Figure 15-9C. When you are learning to trim and style beards and mustaches, carefully study photographs before you do any trimming at all. If you can find a photograph of exactly the style you want, so much the better. Cut the hair carefully with a good pair of barber's shears, a little at a time. Be sure to try on the mustache before doing the final trimming.

In constructing a beard, place the pattern on a form (such as a beard block or a plaster cast of the head) so that the original tucks can be taken. Then attach the edges of the pattern to the block with transparent tape. Identical tucks can be taken in the net. These can be folded down as you attach the edges of the net to the block with pins. You can secure the tucks by sewing them flat with fine thread of the same color as the netting, or with *invisible* thread which is a monofilament thread, ventilating through the thicknesses of net. When you ventilate in the folded area, be sure to catch all of the layers of the netting for added strength to the piece.

If you want to make the body of the beard foundation with gauze, simply lay the gauze over the beard pattern as you would the net, but trim it down 3/8 to 1/2 inch below the upper outline of the beard. The gauze should not show when the beard is finished. Then lay on a strip of net along the edge, overlapping the gauze about 1/2 inch and, of course, overlapping the edge of the pattern also. Along this edge, the hair can be ventilated through both net and gauze, tying them together.

For both beards and mustaches you should nearly always use more than one shade of hair. Facial hair is often darker underneath, lighter on top and along the edges. (See Figure 15-13M.) The lighter hair along the edge, being nearer the color of the skin, is extremely helpful in making a subtle, realistic blend. With gray hair, the differences in color are especially marked. There may sometimes be dark brown or even black hairs underneath and white ones above. This can be reproduced very subtly in ventilating, since the hairs are put in individually. A few red or auburn hairs will give a gray beard added life. Observe real beards—gray ones are rarely, if ever, the same color throughout. There may be a salt-and-pepper effect, with dark and light hair mixed, or the gray may be in streaks or areas, more or less matching on both sides of the face.

Application of Ventilated Pieces

A full beard can be applied in one piece or, if desired, cut into sections—usually three for actors or five for singers—each section being applied separately. In dividing the beard into sections, cut the lace very carefully, avoiding, if possible, cutting any of the hair. (Figure 15-21 shows a beard cut into three sections, plus a mustache.) Following are the three basic steps for applying a beard, whether in one, three, or five sections:

1. Place the piece on your face to determine the correct position. If you have a beard or a mustache with a partial gauze foundation, you can secure it to the skin with double-faced toupee tape. If you are using a mustache with no gauze, set it on the face, then observe very carefully where it goes so that you can estimate where to place the spirit gum.

2. Brush a thin coat of matte spirit gum onto the clean skin, covering the entire area beneath the lace. For beards, you will normally place the gum only under the edges of the lace, though it is possible and sometimes desirable to cover the entire area if there is to be strong muscular activity, as in singing, or if for any reason you feel the need of the additional security. *Never use latex on wig lace!*

3. Let the spirit gum become slightly tacky. Then press the lace into the gum with a damp or dry chamois or dry powder puff, being careful to press the lace straight down without letting it slide on the skin. This sliding could stretch it, causing unsightly corrugations or ripples, which might become permanent. Use a clean section of the cloth or chamois each time you press. Keep pressing until the lace is dry. Then, with a toothbrush, or an eyebrow brush, lift any hairs that may have inadvertently been stuck down by the gum.

Dressing Ventilated Pieces

When the beard or the mustache is securely attached, it can be combed with a wide-toothed comb. But remember, in combing any hairpiece, always to hold the comb at an angle so that there is no possibility that the teeth will dig into the net foundation and tear it. This means holding it at the reverse angle from the one usually used in combing your own hair. Also, when the hair is fairly long, always begin combing at the ends and work toward the roots. Human hair in hairpieces of any kind become matted and tangled much more easily than the same hair would while growing on the head. This is because half of the hair is going against the natural direction of growth. In other words, the hair is knotted somewhere between the roots and the end, both of which are extended outward. A human hair is not quite the simple, smooth filament it appears to be—there are little scale-like projections, all going in the same direction. You can usually feel the difference by running a hair quickly between your thumb and fore-

finger in the direction of growth and then against the direction of growth. When hairs are not all going in the same direction, these tiny scales catch onto each other and cause matting. Therefore, special care is needed in combing any kind of hairpiece made from human hair.

If the hair does not naturally fall just as you would like it to, comb it with water, set it (pushing it into waves or making pin curls—on the ends of beards or mustaches—for example), and let it dry before recombing it. When the hair is dry, spray it with hair oil or hair spray, or apply a gel or cream dressing, then comb the hair and do whatever trimming and shaping may be needed. If you want the hair to look dry or unhealthy or dirty, you can use colored powder or cake makeup to dull it.

Human hair can also be curled with a curling iron if you prefer. Heat should never be used on synthetic hair. Steaming is preferred. In order to maintain the wave in synthetic hair, it may be necessary to spray it with hair spray.

The ends of a mustache can be shaped with mustache wax, derma wax, or hair spray. The mustache and the goatee in Figure 15-20 were dressed with Kryolan Eyebrow Plastic and hair spray.

FIGURE 15-20 **Cavalier** *Mustache and goatee. Ventilated with synthetic hair on nylon net and dressed with Kryolan Eyebrow Plastic and hair spray. (Makeup, including mustache and goatee, by student Douglas Parker.)*

Removing and Cleaning Ventilated Pieces

To remove the beard or the mustache, dip a stiff brush into spirit-gum remover or alcohol, and press the bristles into the lace edge. *Do not scrub and do not pull up the lace by force.* Any good lace or net is very delicate and requires considerable care in handling to avoid stretching or tearing it. Keep flooding it with the remover until the gum is softened and the lace comes up by itself. Then dip the lace edge (or the entire piece if there is spirit gum on all of it) into a dish of acetone to remove all traces of spirit gum and makeup. The lace must be kept absolutely clean if it is to remain invisible on the skin. It may be desirable, even when the gum has been used only on the edge, to soak the whole piece in acetone from time to time. Always use proper ventilation, gloves, and a respirator when using acetone.

Beards and mustaches should be carefully stored so that they will be kept clean and the lace will not be damaged. It is best to stuff beards with cotton or tissue paper and to keep each one in a box large enough so that it will not press the beard or the mustache out of shape.

Adapting Beards

One great advantage of ventilated pieces is that they can be restyled, often merely by combing, for a variety of characters. It is possible, for greater flexibility, to make a full beard in three pieces-one center and two side sections—with, of course, a separate mustache (Figure 15-21).

Then the pieces can be used singly or in any combination, as shown in Figure 15-22, in which all six makeups are done with a single wig and the four pieces shown in Figure 15-21. This is only a sampling of the variety of styles that could be obtained by redressing various facial hair pieces and applying them in different combinations.

It is most useful for any wig department, small theater group, or for the actor to build up a stock of ventilated beards and mustaches. The time invested initially will surely pay off in the end, giving you a stock of realistic beards and mustaches that can be saved and used to enhance productions for years to come.

FIGURE 15-21 Full beard in sections.
Sideburns, mustache, and beard made of real hair ventilated on nylon net. These pieces can be recombed, straightened, or curled and used in various combinations, as illustrated in Figure 15-22.

FIGURE 15-22 **A Versatile Beard.** *Late nineteenth-century beard styles made by combining the four ventilated hair pieces shown in Figure 15-18. The same hairlace wig was recombed and used throughout.*

PROBLEMS

1. With crepe hair, duplicate one or two beards and mustaches from photographs.

2. Design and execute, using suitable crepe-hair applications, makeups for two different characters.

3. Using real or synthetic hair, ventilate a mustache or a beard based on a drawing, a print, or a photograph.

4. Do another complete makeup for a specific character from a play using your ventilated beard or mustache. Do a makeup worksheet first.

Hair and Wigs

chapter 16

The hair is always an important element in any makeup and is invaluable as a means of suggesting period, personality, and age (see Figure 16-1). There is so much effort required for collecting research, developing a character analysis, and creating makeup sketches that failure to make the hair suit the character can compromise an otherwise skillful makeup. If you are creating a likeness of a famous individual, then the appropriate research should guide you in the right direction. If you are creating a new character, then your research should include several style possibilities for that character. Thorough research and planning are vital to the design process and will serve you well in your collaborations with the costume designer, director, and actor, as you select a style that is both flattering to the actor's features and appropriate for the character.

You have many options with which to achieve the hairstyles. You can use the actor's natural hair, you can use wigs, or you can use a combination of the two (see Figure 16-2).

Natural Hair

Restyling   More often than not the actor's own hair can be appropriately styled for the character being played. The hair can be parted on the side, in the middle, or not at all. It can be combed or messy, straight or wavy, close to the head or fluffed out.

For both men and women it is possible to wave the hair, if it is naturally straight, by setting it with pin curls,

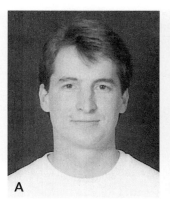

FIGURE 16-1 Opera student Matthew Smith as Mangus in the opera *The Knott Garden*. *Before and after. Makeup, wax nose, wig, and facial hair by Lenna Kaleva.*

FIGURE 16-2 Student actor as The Pirate King in the operetta *The Pirates of Penzance*. *Highlighting the actor's own hair with makeup to match the fall. Makeup, fall, and facial hair by Lenna Kaleva.*

rollers, hot rollers, or by curling it with a curling iron. If the hair is to look well groomed, it can be sprayed with a commercial hair spray, or hair dressing can be applied with the fingers and combed through the hair.

For characters whose hair would be expected to look dull and lifeless, face powder the color of the hair can be dusted on, or a little cake makeup or liquid body makeup of the desired shade can be applied with a sponge. If the hair is to look stiff and matted, it can be heavily sprayed with a liquid setting lotion or hair gel, shaped with the fingers, and dried with a hairdryer and diffuser.

Cutting
There are times when cutting the hair is the simplest method of achieving the correct hairstyle for a character. If actors are willing to have their hair cut, they can be sent to a barber or a hair stylist with sketches and visual research of the desired style.

Occasionally the style required might be so unflattering to modern eyes (though appropriate for the period) that actors may well object to having their hair cut. This can also occur if actors are involved in a play and doing commercial or film work at the same time where they are expected to maintain a certain style for continuity purposes. If actors are not willing to change their own hair, wigs may be used instead. (See the section on *Wigs and Hairpieces* in this chapter.)

Coloring
Another design option for creating the hair for a character is the addition of color. There are three methods for accomplishing this: permanent, semi-permanent, and temporary color (see Figure 16-3).

Permanent color is as the name implies. To minimize the chances of irreparable damage to the actor's

hair, it is *strongly* recommended that a professional cosmetologist who has experience coloring hair make such a change. Please note, hair that has never seen harsh chemicals, as those involved in coloring, permanent waves, or relaxers, will take the color much better than hair that has been processed. Be aware that over-processing can cause damage to the hair.

Semi-permanent color is often used to temporarily color graying hair to help it blend in with the natural hair color. Semi-permanent color can be used to change an actor's hair color if the run of performances is limited to one or two weekends or if the actor is unwilling to make a permanent change. If you intend to use a semi-permanent color for an extended run, expect to refresh or re-color the hair every week and a half to two weeks. This will largely depend on how often the actor washes his or her hair.

Temporary hair color comes in a variety of forms including liquid, mousse, spray, and gel. It is readily available at most beauty supply stores and is the easiest coloring option. It simply washes out with regular shampoo. You can successfully change the hair color from light to dark with this product but lightening dark-colored hair would best be achieved with a spray-on color. Temporary color should not be used if actors have a tendency to perspire profusely. The color will lift from the hair as they sweat and will stain the skin and the clothing.

You should always follow all directions. Preparation and careful application is a must with hair coloring products. Some of them will stain the skin and all will stain fabrics. In the case of most permanent colors, it is important that you also use proper ventilation as the chemicals involved often have a very harsh scent. As always, if you do not feel comfortable doing the coloring yourself, contact a local professional.

Graying
There are many products on the market for adding gray color to natural hair. There are sprays, sticks, creams, and liquids (see Figure 16-4). They come in many shades, including silver and white, but do not always look natural on everyone. One of the major concerns with hair whiteners is that flat white and gray can often appear to have a bluish cast or can turn chalky on dark hair colors. Hair whitener applied over dark hair may require a warmer yellow or orange tone mixed into a base. It is to your advantage to test your colors under performance lighting when possible.

When choosing a graying product, consider the hair styling process prior to and after it is grayed. Most problems occur when petroleum or oil-based hair styling products are used. With the exception of aerosol colorants, most graying formulas will simply not adhere to these styling products. Even when using spray-ons it is difficult to retain the intensity of the color after the hair has been combed or brushed through. If gray hair color

FIGURE 16-3 Coloring products and tools.

FIGURE 16-4 **Graying products and tools.**

needs to be applied over styling products, a water-soluble brand will provide a more suitable surface on which to paint.

Aerosol colorants are not recommended for actors if head coverings and touching of the hair are part of the action within the performance. These spray-ons, when dry can produce a rather comical powder-puff effect sending dust-like particles floating through the air. Color sticks can be substituted for adding streaks or coloring specific areas. Liquids can also be used for overall graying effects, but will, on occasion, come off on hats.

No matter what kind of graying product you use, it is important that you avoid blending color into the skin around the hairline. A medium or soft bristled toothbrush is an excellent tool to assist you in accurately applying fine streaks of color in the hair. Toothbrushes are particularly useful for applying small amounts of color to the hairline at the temples and sideburns and to eyebrows and facial hair. A disposable mascara wand is another handy tool that will allow you the same control. For covering larger areas a very soft bristled brush, such as a baby brush, can be used. Be sure to protect the costume by covering it with a smock or cape. Many of the graying products have an oil base and will not easily wash out of the clothes.

Here are some tips for applying color to the hair:

1. Spray-on products can be used as directed or sprayed into a small container and applied with a toothbrush. If the spray-on color is to look natural, it is important that you carefully comb through the style after the color has dried.
2. Liquid colors should also be applied with a brush or toothbrush by pouring the color into a bowl or dipping the brush into the color, blotting the excess on a towel or tile, and brushing the color into the hair. Liquid color can be combed after it has dried.

Note: liquid graying products must be mixed well or shaken vigorously before application.
3. Stick colors should be applied by carefully drawing the color through the hair. Comb or brush as necessary.
4. Cream or pancake makeup of the appropriate color can also be used and applied with a makeup brush (see Figure 16-2) or with a toothbrush. The pancake makeup will require water to make it work. Dip the brush into the water, tap off the excess liquid, and scrub the brush over the pancake. Apply as with liquid color.

Shoe polish is not recommended as it can damage actors' hair (some actors, however, find shoe polish a useful tool.) Using white powder or cornstarch is also discouraged, as it will have the same dusty effect as spray-on hair color.

Wigs and Hairpieces

If it is not possible or is impractical to use the actors' own hair, then a wig or hairpiece must be used. Wigs are often worn in period productions to create the illusion of historical accuracy. They can also be worn when actors will not or cannot cut or color their hair, or when an actor has no hair at all. By definition, wigs cover the entire head and hairpieces are used to supplement a wig or the natural hair. If you are considering the use of a wig, do not wait until the last minute. Wigs are not as cooperative as you might think and the desired style may take a few tries before you get it right. Wigs can be purchased at specialty retail supply shops and at most costume stores. Look in your Yellow Pages and go explore! There are also many companies that will provide catalogues from which you can order by mail or by phone.

Wigs are usually made of human or synthetic hair. Human hair wigs can be colored, set, curled, and styled just like the hair on your head, but easier to reach. Synthetic wigs can also be set and styled, but are extremely difficult to color. It is best to purchase a synthetic wig in the appropriate color.

The Parts of a Wig
A store bought wig will look different on the inside than a handmade wig. The foundation will often include a base made of lace elastic and a rubber latex skin crown (see Figure 16-5). The hair on the body of the wig is made up of rows of wefting sewn to the lace elastic and the remainder is machine punched into the skin crown (see Figure 16-6A, B). There is usually extra elastic in the center back that is used for fitting the wig to different head sizes.

A handmade wig will often have several types of wig-making netting or lace in the foundation (see

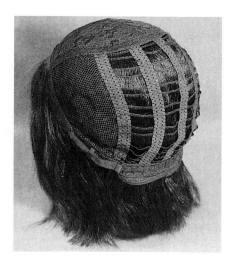

FIGURE 16-5 A store-bought wig foundation.

Figure 16-7A, B). A heavier vegetable net is often used in the perimeter, lighter weight caul netting is used in the crown, and a medium and lightweight wig netting is used in the front of the wig. The hair on the wig can be rows of wefting sewn onto the foundation or the wig can be completely hand tied or ventilated. If the wig has not been made for a specific individual, then there will be elastic or another device in the center back to allow it to be tightened.

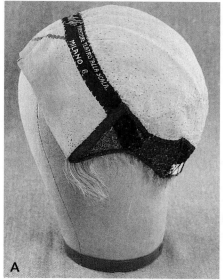

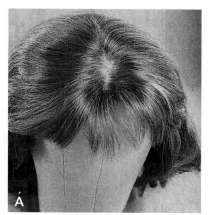

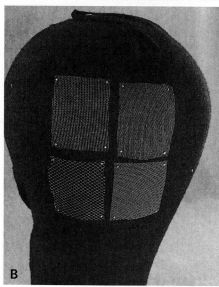

FIGURE 16-6 Store-bought wigs. *A. Rubber crown of a store-bought wig. The hair has been punched into the rubber. B. Wefting. (clockwise from the left) A store-bought wig, a short piece of wefting, wefting as it can be purchased in a bundle. The elastic at center back of wig is used to tighten the wig to fit the actor.*

FIGURE 16-7 Examples of wig-making laces. *A. An example of one type of hand-made wig foundation. Silk and caul netting with silk transformation instead of a ventilated hairline. B. Examples of wig making laces. (clockwise from the left) Fine netting used for the front hairline and facial hair, medium netting used for transition from fine net to original foundation, caul net, vegetable net. (All from De Meo Brothers in New York.)*

Measuring for Wigs

Taking measurements for a wig has several purposes: measurements will tell you what size head block to use; they will give you points for drawing a hairline; and they can be used to send to various companies that rent wigs.

Measurements *a* through *e* are used most often. Measurements *f* through *h* are most helpful when the wig is custom made for the actor (see Figure 16-8).

a. *Around the head* (behind the ears) from the front center of the hairline to the nape of the neck and back. (Average measurement: men, 23–24 inches; women, 22–23 inches.)

b. *Over the top* from the front center of the hairline to the nape of the neck. (Average measurement, 12–14 inches.)

c. *Ear to ear* over the top of the head at ¼ inch above the join. (Average measurement, 11–12½ inches.)

d. *Temple to temple front* across the forehead above the eyebrows. (Average measurement, 6–7 inches.)

e. *Temple to temple back* across the widest part of the head. (Average measurement, 16 inches.)

f. *Sideburn to sideburn* over the top of the head. (Average measurement, women, 12 inches, men will vary on length of sideburn.)

g. *Bottom of ear to bottom of ear* back of the head over the nape. (Average measurement, 6 inches.)

h. *Nape* bottom hairline on the neck. (Average measurement, 4 inches.)

Most measurements should be taken with the actor's hair loose and down. However, if the wig is to be styled with an upswept or a short look, it is recommended that long hair be pinned up in pincurls and

---

Wig Measurements and Information

Note: Remember to add an extra 1/2" to 1" to your measurements if the performer has hair that reaches center back or longer OR is at least shoulder length and thick!

a. **Around the head** (hairline) _____

b. **Over the top** (hairline to nape) _____

c. **Ear to ear** (over the top) _____

d. **Temple to temple** (front) _____

e. **Temple to temple** (back) _____

f. **Sideburn to sideburn** (over the top) _____

g. **Bottom of ear to bottom of ear** (back, over nape) _____

h. **Nape** (back, bottom hairline on neck) _____

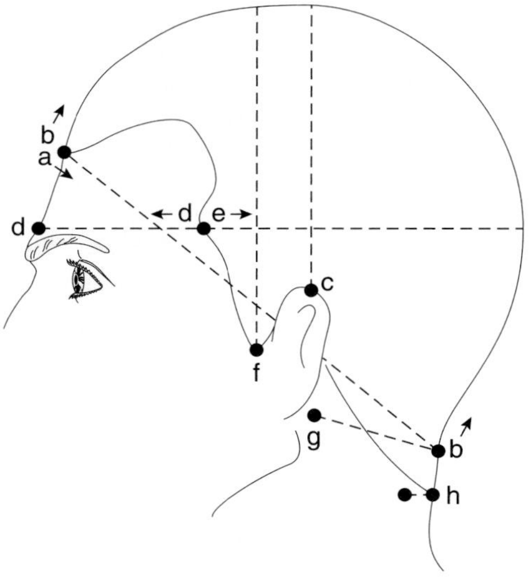

Hair information:
Color number:　　human _____　　synthetic _____
Highlights　　　　human _____　　synthetic _____

Texture: _____
(thick, fine, naturally curly . . . .)

Length: _____
(top of shoulders, center back, short man's cut . . . .)

Other Notes:

FIGURE 16-8　Wig measurement information sheet.

new measurements taken. This will add approximately ½ to 1 inch to all the measurements.

It is also wise to observe the length and texture of the actor's hair. Keeping a visual reference library of company members or of student actors by taking photographs with a Polaroid camera can be of great assistance. Taking notes will also help you remember certain details which can and should include observations related to color. This is particularly important when you need an exact hair color match when buying a fall or chignon. Hair color rings that include dozens of numbered color samples are available from most wig companies, like CMC in California (see Appendix B). These color rings can be purchased and used to match the actor's hair color to a swatch number. Then simply order the correct hair goods.

Selecting Wigs

By the time you are ready to select a wig, you should have finished your research, taken accurate measurements, and decided upon the hair color and style to best complete the look of your makeup. Budget considerations may affect the decision to invest in synthetic or human hair wigs. The price of both human hair and synthetic wigs will depend upon color and length. If you need a wig that is graying, you can always get one that is the proper base color and gray it yourself using one of the coloring methods listed in earlier in this chapter.

Styling Wigs

Human hair wigs can be set and styled just like your own hair. You can even curl a human hair wig with a curling iron. Synthetic wigs can also be set and styled. You can even change the style from curly to straight and back again. The secret to styling synthetic hair is steam. Set the wig in rollers and then steam the hair with a clothes steamer, then set it under a bonnet hair dryer or in a wig dryer for approximately thirty minutes on medium heat, after which it can be removed and allowed to cool. To finish styling the synthetic wig, first remove the rollers and then using clips or pins to hold the style in place, lightly steam the wig again. Allow to dry, remove the clips and touch up as necessary. To remove excess curl, simply pull the hair straight with a comb, following the comb with the steamer.

Falls and Chignons

Falls are hairpieces used to lengthen the back of the hair. A full wig can be used as a fall if it is set back on

FIGURE 16-9 Wig used as a fall. Natural hair used in front and blended into the wig. Wig by Amanda French. Makeup by student actor, Kristen Chiles, as Zee in the University of Texas at Austin production of *Blind Horses*.

the head and the natural hair in the front is blended into the style (see Figure 16-9).

A chignon is a hairpiece that is used as an addition to the natural hair (see Figure 16-10). It can add height, volume, and depth to a style. It can be used as extra curls, braids, or buns.

A switch is a type of chignon that is also used as an addition to the natural hair. It comes in the shape of a ponytail and is made of wefting. It can be shaped into a bun, but it is most often used as a braid or a length of curls. It is also quite useful when you need to lengthen an existing ponytail.

Attaching falls and chignons to existing wigs can improve the versatility of any company's wig stock.

FIGURE 16-10 (from the top) A hand-made fall, a chignon, and a switch.

Cleaning Wigs

The process for cleaning and conditioning human hair wigs can be identical to caring for your own hair. After taking down the style and carefully brushing through the wig, wash it in warm water using a mild shampoo and a light conditioner, then rinse well. Towel dry and carefully comb through the wig using a wide toothed comb. Allow the wig to dry thoroughly or place it in a wig dryer before putting it away. The process of washing a human hair wig will remove all of the curl, so be sure to leave plenty of time if you need to restyle it for the next performance.

Synthetic wigs can also be cleaned and conditioned. After taking down the style and carefully brushing through the wig, wash it in cold water using a mild shampoo. Use a light conditioner on the wig and rinse well in cold water. Towel dry and carefully comb through the wig with a wide tooth comb. Allow it to dry thoroughly. Washing a synthetic wig in cold water will retain its curl. Washing a synthetic wig in warm or hot water will make the curl fall or come out completely. Using a conditioner on a synthetic wig will help to control frizz and static electricity.

The following are two suggestions that may dispel any myths about caring for a synthetic wig:

1. Please do not wash a synthetic wig in the washing machine. You will do severe damage to the wig, and it will take you days to comb out all of the tangles.
2. Please do not use a fabric detergent or fabric softener on a synthetic wig. They are too harsh, they do not completely rinse out, and your actor may be sensitive to the chemicals.

Adding a Natural Hairline

It is possible to add a natural hairline to the front of a purchased wig. This can be accomplished by stitching fine netting or wig lace onto the front edge of the wig and ventilating into it a natural hairline. The measurements recorded on the measurement sheet will assist you in determining the shape and size of the new hairline (see Figure 16-11A, B.) This is the procedure for *fronting* the wig shown in Figure 16-12:

1. Using a seam ripper, remove the binding from the front edge of the wig. This ¼-inch tape contains a row of hair which should be saved and later used for ventilating into the new lace front.
2. The remaining ¼-inch seam allowance on the wig should be carefully pressed flat. When using a synthetic wig, simply dampen the seam allowance and dry it with a hair dryer. Avoid touching the iron to synthetic hair.
3. Place the wig loosely on a canvas head block of the appropriate size. Loose placement will later accommodate pincurled hair. For actors with short hair or for wigs styled in shorter lengths, a close fit against the head block will be necessary.
4. Place the wig on the head block and arrange it so that the center, back hairline is at approximately the same place as that of the actor's. Using a 1¼-inch long, round headed pin, secure the back hairline to the block. Now secure the front hairline just behind the seam allowance with five pins, one at each of the following locations: at the center front; at the sideburns; and centered between the center front and sideburns. Control the hair with a piece of twill tape (see Figure 16-13).

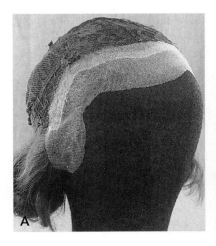 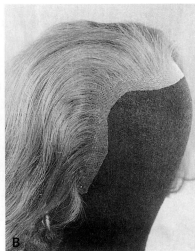

FIGURE 16-11 A. Medium and fine netting added to the front of a store-bought wig to make a natural hairline. (Inside view.) B. Ventilated hairline. (Outside view.)

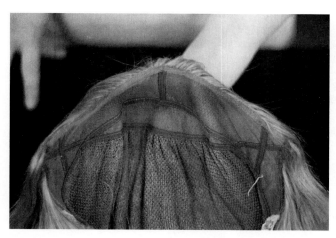

FIGURE 16-12 Inside of locally purchased wig showing the front hairline finished with ¼-inch tape binding.

5. To determine the new hairline:

a. Transfer measurement *b* (see Figure 16-8) from the measurement chart to the head block starting at the center, back hairline (see Figure 16-14 A). Bring the tape measure over the head and place a pin at the center front. For example, if the measurement is 12 inches, place the number twelve on the tape measure at the CB hairline, bring the tape measure over the head, and place a pin on zero at the CF (see Figure 16-14 B).

b. Transfer measuremnt *c,* from the measurement sheet to the head block to determine how the wig will fit over the ears (see Figure 16-14C).

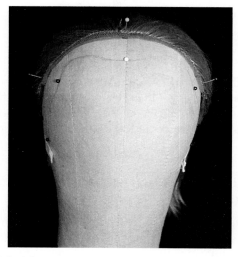

FIGURE 16-13 After removing the commercial front of this wig, it is placed on a canvas head block and secured with round headed pins.

b. Transfer measurement *f* to the head block to determine the length of the wig at the sideburns. Place two pins, one at each sideburn (see Figure 16-14D).

c. Transfer measurements *d* and *e* from the measurement sheet to the head block to determine temple placement (see Figure 16-14E, F).

d. Draw in the new hairline with a pencil or permanent marker directly on the canvas block using the pins as a guide (see Figure 16-15A). An optional method is to wrap the front of the block in plastic wrap covered with Magic tape before the wig is attached. This will protect the surface of the canvas from unwanted markings. Another method, often used in making full wigs, is to take an impression or make a skull cap of the actor's head by wrapping it completely in plastic wrap and Magic tape. The actor's entire hairline can then be transferred directly to the cap with a permanent marker.

6. Position the wig lace over the front of the block with the holes of the lace running vertically to the center front of the wig. Carefully drape the lace onto the new front area until it fits smoothly between the edge of the wig and the hairline. Secure the lace with the round headed pins as demonstrated in Figure 16-15B. Trim the lace to approximately 1 inch from the pins.

7. Using silk or cotton/polyester thread in a color that matches the wig, sew the lace to the edge of the wig. Starting above the ear, sew through all layers securing the first stitch with a double knot. Using a small whip stitch, continue to attach the lace to the wig along the wig edge (Figure 16-15C). An optional sewing technique is to connect the lace to the wig using a ventilating needle and transparent nylon thread. The stitch utilizes the same technique as ventilating hair (Figure 16-15D). For narrow allowances, as seen in this example, the ventilating stitch should be executed in a zigzag pattern for strength and for minimizing its visibility. On wider allowances, two rows of stitching are recommended. Once the stitching has been completed, trim the lace close to the stitching line with a good pair of scissors (Figure 16-15E). Hair can now be ventilated into the new lace front. See Figure 16-16 for proper ventillating posture. The procedures to ventilate follows.

If the hair is to be combed back, simply work from the wig edge toward the front hairline, pulling the hair toward the back of the wig after each knot. Brushing or combing it occasionally as you work will keep stray hairs from getting in your way. The amount of hair you use will depend on how thick you want the hair to be. Ordinarily, it is desirable to keep the wig as light in

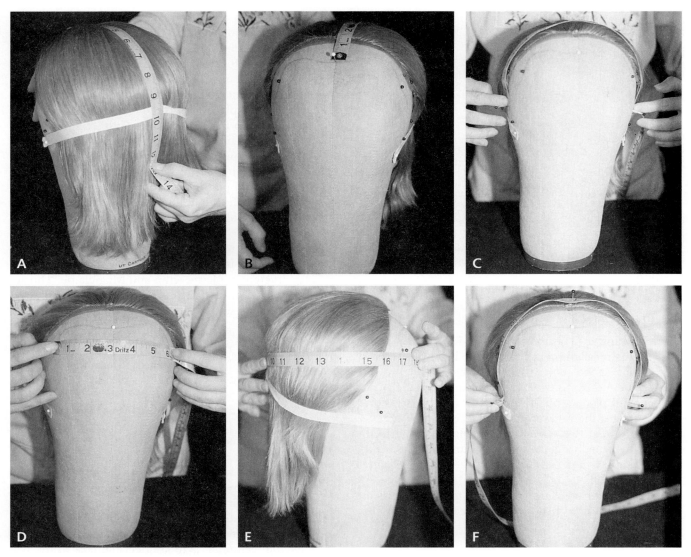

FIGURE 16-14 Steps for determining the shape of the new hairline when "fronting" a wig. *A. and B. Marking the distance from the center back to the center front hairline. C. Measuring the distance from ear to ear D. and E. Finding the temple placement. F. Measuring for sideburn placement.*

weight as possible within the limits set by the effect you are trying to achieve. The hair can be knotted into the binding tapes as well as through the net.

As you approach the front hairline, use a smaller needle and space your hairs evenly and closer together. It is, in fact, usually a good idea to stop ½ to 1 inch from the front edge, turn the wig block around, and work the hair from the opposite direction, beginning at the edge of the hairline, allowing the hair to hang down as if over the face. When you reach the previous stopping place and the ventilating is finished, comb the front section back. It will stand slightly up and away from the forehead making the hairline somewhat less obvious. (See *Constructing Ventilated Pieces,* Chapter 15).

Trimming the excess lace from the new hairline largely depends upon the technique of the wig maker and size of the performance venue. Wigs for the opera stage often have lace edges in excess of 1 inch, while those for film can be less than ¼ inch. In general, the more intimate the viewing, the narrower the lace edge becomes.

Putting On and Securing a Wig

There is nothing more humiliating than losing your hair on stage, especially if you had not intended to do so. Actors must enter the stage feeling confident that their wigs are securely fastened to their heads. Putting on a wig is a simple process, but one that takes much practice. An actor should always seek assistance from a professional before putting on a wig. The correct procedure follows.

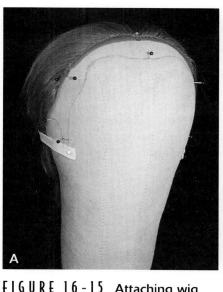

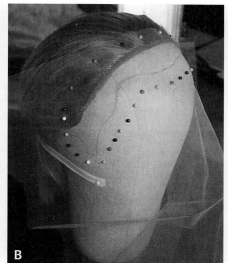

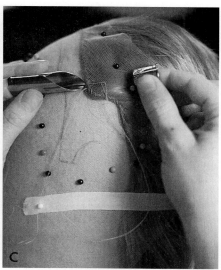

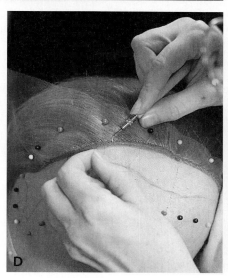

FIGURE 16-15 Attaching wig lace to the front of the wig.

A. Draw in the new hairline B. Drape the wig lace over the wig and secure with pins C. Stitching the wig lace to the wig using needle and thread D. Attaching wig lace to the wig using a ventilating needle and transparent nylon thread. E. Trimming the wig lace.

To begin with, have the proper tools (see Figure 16-17):

The wig
Bobby pins
A wig cap the same tone as the wig (or as close as possible)
A rat-tail comb
Medium hair pins
Large hair pins (if possible)
Spirit gum (if the wig has a lace front to be glued to the face
A small piece of chamois cloth or a powder puff

Pincurls

First, roll the actor's hair into pincurls. Not only do the pincurls secure the actor's hair underneath the wig, they are also the anchors for the hair pins used to pin the wig to the actor's head. Take a small section of hair (approximately 1" × 1") in the front center of the

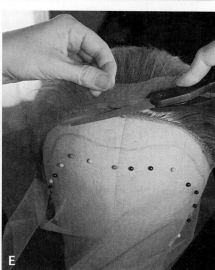

FIGURE 16-16 Proper ventilating position.
Amanda French, wig and make-up designer.

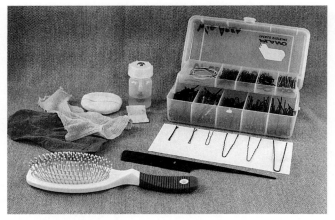

FIGURE 16-17 **Tools for putting on a wig.** *(clockwise from the left.) 2 examples of wig caps, powder puff, spirit gum, small piece of chamois cloth, small tackle box with pins, large hair pin, medium hair pins, small hair pin, bobby pins, rat-tail comb, brush.*

head and wrap it around two fingers of your hand as in Figures 16-18A, B. Carefully slide your fingers out holding the curl flat against the head as in Figure 16-18C. Secure the curl with two bobby pins crossing each other at a right angle. Make sure to catch the curl along with the hair underneath. The pins should make a cross or an x over the curl. Continue making pincurls around the hairline, systematically filling in the top as you go (see Figures 16-18D, E). You should have at least ten pincurls by the time you are finished. Make sure they are all tight and flat to the head.

Wig Cap Next, put on the wig cap. The wig cap serves three purposes: (1) to hold the pincurls tight against the head; (2) as an extra anchor in which to pin the wig; and (3) to help absorb some of the perspiration from the actor's head. Start by stretching out the wig cap with your hands. It will be easier to put on and is more comfortable for the actor if it has been

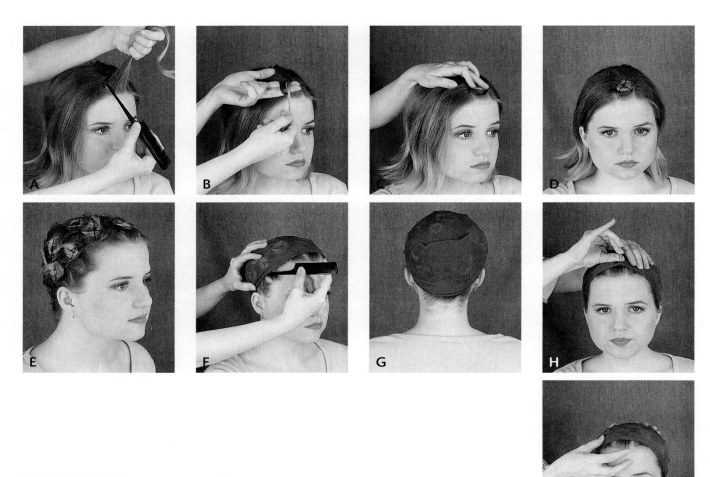

FIGURE 16-18 **Preparing the actor's hair before putting on a wig.** *A. Sectioning the hair for a pincurl. B. Wrapping the hair around two fingers. C. Hold the curl flat to the head. D. Finished pincurl. E. Complete head of pincurls. F. Tucking in the stray hairs. G. Tuck in the excess wig cap. H. Pinning through the cap I. Pushing the pin under a pincurl (Wig design and execution by Amanda French. Model, Mern Davis.)*

stretched to a larger size. Place one edge of the wig cap on the actor's forehead at approximately ½ inch below the hairline. Have the actor hold the wig cap in place, this will free your hands to stretch the cap over the head. Pull the cap out and down over all of the pincurls to just below the hairline at the nape of the neck. Be sure to cover the tops of the ears as you gently release the cap. The actor can now release the wig cap as well. Carefully slide the wig cap back revealing the fine hairs at the front hairline. Stop at the edge of the center front pincurls. After sliding the wig cap up off of the ears, take the "tail" end of the rat-tail comb and carefully tuck any stray hairs up into the cap (see Figure 16-18F). Then tuck the excess wig cap at the top of the head under itself making a tidy horizontal fold. (see Figure 16-18G). Using a small hair pin (these are different from bobby pins), pin the wig cap to the pincurls at the center front, at the temples, and on either side of the nape following the pinning technique shown in Figures 16-18H, I.

Attaching the Wig

Now put the wig on over the wig cap. You should be standing behind the seated actor and both of you should be facing the mirror. Take the wig and hold it over the head, placing the center front of the wig on the forehead just below the hairline. Set the wig down onto the head and slide it back into place. Using the sides of the wig at the ears as a handhold, make sure that the wig is evenly placed and centered (see Figure 16-19A).

You can easily hurt an actor while pinning the wig to his or her head. You can avoid this by placing one hand under the wig at the spot where you intend to insert the pin. Push the pin through the wig until it touches your hand. Remove your hand and gently push the pin under and into the pincurl. Use medium pins along the front hairline and large pins toward the back. Repeat the process as necessary. Once you get used to the feeling of the pin going through the wig netting, using your hand will most likely not be necessary. It is recommended that you pin the wig to the head in places similar to that of the pinning of the wig cap. Then pin as the weight of the wig requires and the actor feels is necessary. Once you have finished pinning the wig to the head, the wig should be secure and should not come off until it is removed! (See Figures 16-19 B, C, D, E.)

Gluing the Lace

It is preferable that the makeup be complete and powdered before the wig is glued to the face.

The first step is to observe where the lace sits on the face. The object is to keep the spirit gum in the area of the netting, not in the hairline of the wig or of the actor. Starting at the center of the forehead, gently lift the netting and apply a quarter-inch wide brush stroke of glue to the skin below. Release the netting making sure that it still sits flat to the head. Do not press the netting into the glue at this time. Move on to one of the sides. Lift the netting, apply the glue to the skin, then release the netting. Repeat this procession the other side.

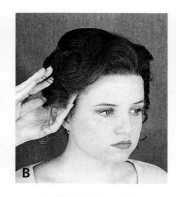

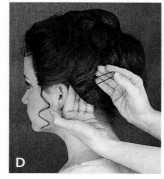
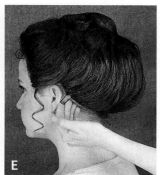

FIGURE 16-19
Securing the wig. *A. After placing the wig on the head, slide it into its proper position. B. Pushing the medium size hair pin into the wig against the hand C. Slide the pin under a pincurl D&E. Pinning the same way in the back using the large hair pins.*

Take a small piece of chamois cloth or fresh powder puff and start in the center front of the lace, gently pressing the lace into the spirit gum. (See Figure 16-20.) Repeat this process on both sides of the wig. Using the cloth or puff allows the netting to adhere to the spirit gum, cuts the shine of the spirit gum, and keeps the gum off of your fingers! Throw the cloth or puff away once it is full of dried spirit gum.

Removing the Wig

Removing the wig is the exact reverse process of putting on the wig. You will need the following tools:

Spirit gum remover or 99% isopropyl alcohol;
Tissues;
Cotton balls;
Q-tips;
A medium size hair pin;
A brush.

If you have a lace front wig that has been glued to the face, you must start by loosening or removing the spirit gum. First, dampen a cotton ball with spirit gum remover or alcohol. Make sure it is wet, but not dripping. It is recommended that you keep tissues close by, as you do not want any remover to fall into the eyes of the actor. Gently press the cotton ball with remover onto the lace at the glue line.

Once the spirit gum begins to dissolve, take a medium size hairpin or Q-tip soaked in remover and carefully slide it under the lace. When sliding a hairpin under the lace, move it in the direction that the hair naturally grows, then gently separate the lace from the skin.

FIGURE 16-20 Gently press the netting into the spirit gum with a small piece of chamois cloth.

Now remove the anchor pins from the wig to release it from the head. Lift the wig up and away from the head and carefully place it on the wig block. Remove the pins from the wig cap. Put the wig cap where it will be washed or keep it with the wig to be used again. Take out the pin curls and brush out the hair.

Learning how to design hairstyles and dress and care for wigs is an important part of the makeup process. If you also know how to construct wigs, you are in an advantageous position. In the professional theater, actors are not usually expected to design or to dress their own wigs. In the non-professional theater, however, both actors and makeup artists may sometimes be expected to do both. A thorough knowledge of the techniques involved with hair design and construction for both natural and synthetic wigs will not only contribute greatly to the effectiveness of the makeup but will positively affect the quality of the entire production.

PROBLEMS

1. Design a makeup for a middle-aged or elderly character from a play using a wig, facial hair, or both.

2. Add a natural hairline to a store-bought wig.

3. Practice applying a wig using the techniques in this chapter.

Creating a Likeness

For most makeups there is considerable latitude in choice of details—the height of the forehead, the line of the eyebrows, the shape of the nose. But in recreating real people whose faces are well known, the objective should be, of course, to achieve as accurate a likeness as possible.

The first step is to compare the face of the character with that of the actor who is to portray the character, noting points of difference and of similarity. The comparison should include shape of the face; shape, length, and color of the hair and the beard; color of the skin; and precise conformation of individual features, including height and width of the forehead; length, breadth, and shape of the nose; distance from nose to mouth and from mouth to tip of the chin; width of the mouth; thickness and shape of the lips; line of the jaw; prominence of the cheekbones; line and thickness of the eyebrows; size, shape, prominence, and slant (if any) of the eyes; distance between the eyes; and the line, in profile, of the forehead, nose, mouth, chin, and neck. The points of similarity can be emphasized and the differences minimized. If the actor's nose is too small, it can be enlarged and reshaped with putty. If it is too large, it can be shadowed to make it seem less large, and attention can be drawn to other features. Wigs, beards, and spectacles can be enormously helpful.

An excellent way of training yourself to observe details and to reproduce them is to copy portraits. Photographs, with their myriad of details, may prove less useful to the beginner than works of art (paintings, drawings, engravings) with their simplifications. In using these artists' representations, however, you should keep in mind that your objective, except when you are deliberately working with stylization, is to achieve a re-

FIGURE 17-1 Creating a likeness in a makeup workshop. *Note the careful arrangement of the portrait and the close-up mirror for easy comparison between the portrait and the likeness. (Makeup by student Clista Towne-Strother.)*

alistic, believable makeup. It should be your purpose to recreate in three dimensions the artist's subject, not to reproduce his technique.

Whereas the artist is permitted to show brush marks and to use a cross-hatching of lines to represent shadows, the makeup artist, in doing a realistic makeup, is permitted no such license. You may also have to make certain compromises in minor features that cannot reasonably be duplicated on the actor's face. But a good likeness can usually be achieved in spite of inevitable minor variations from the original.

Woodrow Wilson

In creating the makeup for Woodrow Wilson shown in Figure 17-2, it was immediately obvious that the actor (Mr. Wilson Brooks, Figure 17-2A) had a bone structure lending itself easily to the makeup. Since President Wilson's face was wider, Mr. Brooks' hair was puffed out a little at the sides to increase the apparent width of the head, and a small ventilated hairpiece on nylon net was used to match Wilson's hairstyle. Observe carefully the following relatively minor but extremely important changes in individual features:

1. Wilson's eyes have a heavy-lidded effect caused by sagging flesh that actually conceals the upper lid completely when the eye is open. For this makeup a latex piece was used over the eye. The piece was made by the method described in Chapter 14. Since Wilson's eyebrows were straighter than Mr. Brooks', the latex was allowed to cover part of the inner end of each brow. The shape of the eyebrows is always

important and should be copied as accurately as possible. In this case the inner ends were raised slightly, the brows darkened, and the point just beyond the center of each brow was exaggerated. Shadows under the eye were deepened with cake makeup.

2. The nostrils were highlighted, though it does not show in the photograph, and the nose was narrowed slightly by shadowing.
3. The shape of both upper and lower lips was altered slightly, and the lower lip was highlighted. Shadows at the corners of the mouth were deepened. Observe also the highlights and shadows just below the mouth.
4. A slight cleft in the chin was painted in with highlights and shadows.
5. Forehead wrinkles were accentuated with highlights and shadows. The superciliary arch was highlighted.
6. The cheekbones were brought out with highlights and shadows, and the nasolabial folds were deepened. Although the line of Mr. Brooks' folds is not quite the same as Wilson's, the difference has little effect on the likeness. An actor's own wrinkles, particularly the nasolabial folds, can be deepened or flattened out, shortened or lengthened; but if they are at all pronounced, the natural line should be followed. Otherwise, a smile will reveal that the real fold does not coincide with the painted one, and the credibility of the makeup will be destroyed.
7. The ears were made to stick out slightly with nose putty.
8. The final touch was added with a pair of pince-nez.

It was observed frequently during the making up that very slight changes—reshaping the lips or the eyebrows, a shadow here, a highlight there—made consid-

FIGURE 17-2   Actor Wilson Brooks as Woodrow Wilson.

erable difference in the likeness. Because it is impossible to have every detail perfect, it is important to make the most of what the actor's face will permit.

Mark Twain

Actor Hal Holbrook (Figure 17-3), in his brilliant recreation of Mark Twain, is as meticulous in his makeup as in his acting. No detail is too small or too unimportant to be given careful attention each time the makeup is applied. And for every performance he devotes more than three hours to perfecting these details. That his makeup takes so long is perhaps less significant than that he is willing to spend that amount of time doing it. In discussing his problems of recreating Mark Twain physically, Mr. Holbrook says: "The jaw formation is similar, and so is the cheekbone. My eyes have the possibility. His eyes had an eagle sort of look, but you can create that with makeup. And, of course, his nose was very distinctive-long and somewhat like a banana. Mine's too sharp. The nose alone takes an hour. I have a smooth face, and if I don't break it up, the texture is wrong. Also, I have to shrink three and one-half inches. Part of this is done by actual body shrinkage—relaxation all the way down as though I were suspended on a string from the top of the head. Part of it is illu-

sion—the way the suit is made and the height of the furniture on stage. The coat is a little bit longer than it should be. There's a downward slope to the padded shoulders. There's a belly, too—not much of one, but it pulls me down. The lectern, the table, and the chair are built up a little higher."

Materials   The makeup is done with a combination of creme stick, grease-stick liners, pencils, and powder. Three shades of creme stick are used—FS-5-c/d for the base, OF-2-b for highlights, and S/FS-10-e for shadows. Three grease sticks are also used—a deep brown, a maroon, and a rose. All three are used for shadows and accents and the red for additional pink color in the cheeks, on the forehead, eyelids, and ears, for example. There are also brown and maroon pencils for deep shadows.

Application   Except for the base and the first general application of creme-stick shadows to the cheeks and eye sockets and sides of the nose, all of the makeup is done with brushes, most of them flat sables in various widths. The smaller wrinkles are done with 1/8-inch and 3/16-inch brushes and some of the larger areas with a 3/8-inch brush. The makeup is taken directly from the stick. The color is sometimes taken up from the two sticks and mixed on the brush; but more frequently, the

FIGURE 17-3 Actor Hal Holbrook as himself.
Chicago Tribune, photo by John Austad.

FIGURE 17-4 Hal Holbrook as Mark Twain.
Chicago Tribune, photo by John Austad.

FIGURE 17-5 **Making up as Mark Twain for the stage.** *Chicago Tribune,* photos by John Austad.

arious shades are applied separately, one after the other. Mr. Holbrook uses three shadow colors–the S/FS-10-e, the maroon, and the dark brown–and he sometimes adds a bit of rose to give the shadow more life.

All shadows and highlights, as can be observed in Figure 17-5A, are exaggerated since they are to be powdered down. If cake were being used instead of grease, this initial heightening would not be necessary. However, once one has determined what effect the powder will have, one way is as effective as the other. For the detailed brushwork used on this makeup (the whole makeup is approached almost as if it were a painting), the creme-stick and grease method is probably easier. As always, choice of materials is a personal matter.

One of the greatest problems in making up youth for age is to eliminate expanses of smooth skin. It is at this point that otherwise technically competent makeups often fail. The problem has been solved in this case by covering the smooth expanses with wrinkles, puffiness, hollows, and sagging flesh. You will notice in the accompanying photographs, especially Figure 17-5D, that the entire face and the neck (except for the forehead, which is concealed by the wig blender, and the upper lip, which will be concealed by a mustache) are almost completely covered with shadows and highlights. Very little of the original base color shows through.

After the makeup has reached approximately the stage shown in Figure 17-5B, the cheek area in front of the ears is stippled (using a small brush) with dots of maroon, rose, and the creme-stick base. This is then softened somewhat with a clean 3/8-inch brush. When further toned down with powder, the effect, even in the dressing room, is remarkably convincing. (See Figure 17-4.)

After the stage shown in Figure 17-5B has been reached and that much of the makeup powdered, the lower part of the forehead, across the bottom of the side-burns to the ears, is covered with spirit gum, and the wig is put on in the usual way (Figure 17-5C). Ordinarily it is safer to put the wig on first, then apply the spirit gum underneath the blender, though with a very tight wig this may be difficult. Practice makes it possible, however, to apply the spirit gum in the right place and to put the wig on exactly right the first time so as to avoid the difficulties with the gum. The blender in this case extends down to the eyebrows.

The next problem, and a crucial one, is to adjust the blender perfectly so that there are no wrinkles, no air bubbles, nothing to destroy the illusion. This must be done quickly, before the spirit gum becomes too tacky. Again, it takes practice to know exactly how to adjust the blender and what sort of minor imperfections are likely to cause trouble later. Once the blender is perfectly adjusted, it is pressed hard with a towel all along the edge in order to stick it tight to the skin and to make it as smooth as possible. The blender is always cleaned with acetone after the performance in order to make sure the edge will be as thin as possible.

In concealing the edge of the blender, the creme-stick base is applied to the blender somewhat irregularly with a 3/8-inch brush. Then the shadow is applied with a brush to the temples, crossing the edge of the blender. A little light red is worked spottily into either side of the frontal area, keeping away from the hairline. Wrinkles are then drawn on the blender with maroon and the shadow color and highlighted with OF-2-b. Then the temples are stippled with maroon and rose and the shadow color. This is a very important step, since it further helps to hide the blender line by breaking up the color in the area. (See Figure 17-5D.)

The eyebrows are made shaggy by sticking several tufts of gray hair with spirit gum into the natural brows. The mustache (ventilated on gauze) is attached with spirit gum, the hair is combed, and the makeup is completed. (See Figure 17-4).

The preceding paragraphs about Mr. Holbrook's makeup were written for the third edition of *Stage Makeup*. It is interesting to note that by the time *Mark Twain Tonight* appeared on Broadway in 1966, Mr. Holbrook had made several changes in his makeup—notably, from a blender wig to one with a lace front (putting on the wig was far easier and the effect from the audience was essentially the same) and in the use of sponges for stippling (as described in Chapter 11) instead of brushes. The effect was equally good though

not quite the same. Whereas the sponge method took away the youthful smoothness of the skin, which then looked convincingly aged, the brush technique, giving equal age, suggested discolorations of the skin typical of old age. For Mr. Holbrook's television special in 1967 a three-dimensional makeup had to be created for Mark Twain using foamed latex (see Figure 17-6). Since then, Mr. Holbrook has made further changes in his makeup for the stage—a latex nose, false eyebrows, and a plastic cap underneath the wig to conceal his own hairline.

There are several lessons to be learned from Mr. Holbrook's makeup:

1. An effective makeup should be carefully planned and rehearsed. Any but the simplest sort of makeup may well require a certain amount of experimentation, sometimes a great deal. Even experienced makeup artists do careful research and planning on any makeup involving historical characters.

2. The makeup should be an integral part of the characterization. Mr. Holbrook over a period of years studied photographs and even an old film of Mark Twain, read everything he could find by or about him, and talked with people who had known or seen him. His makeup developed along with his performance and was the result of considerable planning and experimentation.

3. It is essential, in making up, to adapt the makeup to the actor's face. Mr. Holbrook does not duplicate a portrait of Mark Twain on his own face. As he makes up, he continually twists and turns and grimaces in order to make sure that every shadow or wrinkle he applies follows the natural conformations of his own face so that there is not the slightest chance that a passing movement or expression will reveal a painted wrinkle different from a real one.

4. One of the secrets of aging the youthful face is to concentrate on eradicating *all* signs of youth, including a smooth, youthful skin. This Mr. Holbrook has done. The numerous wrinkles in the Mark Twain makeup are less important individually than for their effect in breaking up smooth areas of skin with light and shade and color. Unwrinkled areas are textured with stippling. Mr. Holbrook has taken a positive approach to every area of the face and has made sure that nothing remains to betray the actor beneath the makeup.

Because the remarkable recreation of Twain's likeness is essential to the effectiveness of the performance, Mr. Holbrook feels that he must cut no corners and that even if the audience were unaware of any imperfections, he would know, and in his own mind the performance would suffer. This is an example of the dedicated artist to whom no amount of effort is too great if it will in any way contribute to his performance.

FIGURE 17-6 **Television makeup for Hal Holbrook's Mark Twain.** *The series of photographs on the following pages show the step-by-step creation of Dick Smith's makeup for the CBS-TV special of* Mark Twain Tonight. *Although Mr. Holbrook does his own makeup for the stage (see Figures 17-3, 17-4, and 17-5), three-dimensional constructions were required for television. Mr. Smith spent eight to ten weeks preparing for the makeup. This involved making more than 50 casts (A) and a number of experimental tests. Three complete makeups were created before the final one was chosen. With the help of an assistant, Mr. Smith was able to cut the 5-hour application time to 4½ hours and removal time to 1 hour. The method of making casts and foam-latex pieces like those on the following pages is described in Chapter 14.*

The makeup involved both expected and unexpected problems. In order to prevent the smearing of makeup when Mr. Holbrook put his hands into the pockets of his white suits, Mr. Smith painted the backs of the hands (after the foam-latex pieces had been attached) with a mixture of latex and acrylic paint. Then at the dress rehearsal it was discovered that the edges of the large latex appliances were working loose around the mouth because of muscular activity—a common problem with any prosthetic application in that area. The use of Slomon's Medico Adhesive in troublesome spots successfully prevented any loosening of edges during the performance.

Although the three-dimensional television makeup shown here would obviously not be practical for regular use in the theater, some of the techniques might very profitably be incorporated into makeups for the stage. The first step was to flatten Mr. Holbrook's front hair with spirit gum. B. After the gum was brushed on, it was pressed down with a wet towel. Stipple latex was then applied to the eyelids, dried with a hair dryer, and powdered to prevent sticking. C. Foam-latex eye pouches were attached with stipple latex and adjusted with tweezers. D. Eyebrows were flattened with spirit gum and covered with foam-latex pieces. E. The foam-latex nose was attached with spirit gum and stipple latex. F. The large foam-latex appliance (neck, jowls, nasolabial folds) was set in place and attached with spirit gum on the lower parts and stipple latex on the top edges. The edges were blended with Scar Plastic Blending Liquid. G. Piece completely attached. H. Duo adhesive was then applied as a sealer. I. Meanwhile, foam-latex pieces were being attached to the backs of the hands by an assistant.

J. A plastic forehead piece was needed to give the effect of seeing the scalp through the thin and fluffy front hair of the wig. K. After it was attached with gum, the edge of the plastic piece was dissolved with acetone to blend it imperceptibly into the natural skin. L. A light rubber-mask greasepaint base was applied over the entire face, then stippled with other colors, using a coarse sponge (M) and in some cases a brush. N. Eyebrows were attached over the latex covers. O. The wig was then put on, the front lace glued down with matte plastic, and the hair brushed. P. After the mustache (ventilated on a net foundation) was attached, the entire makeup was touched up wherever necessary. Q. shows the final result.

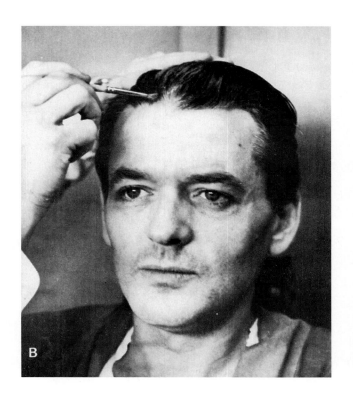

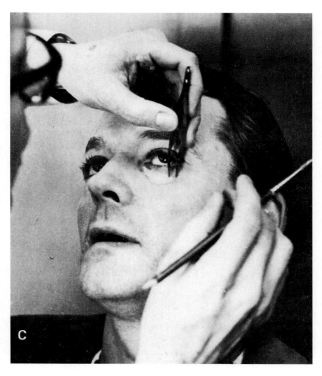

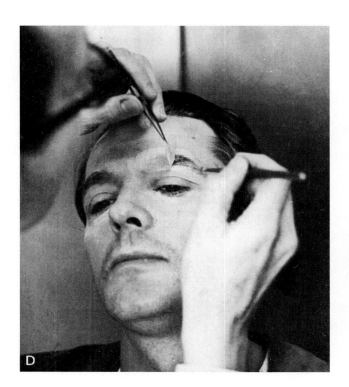

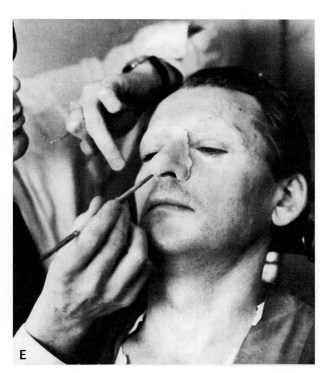

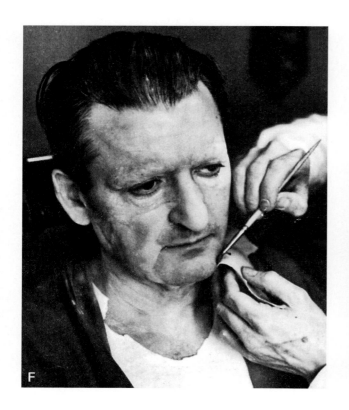

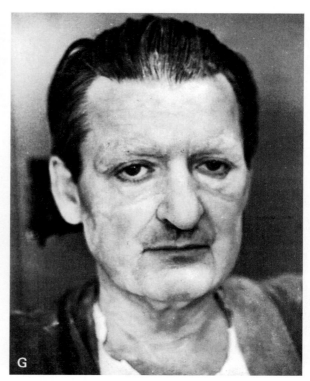

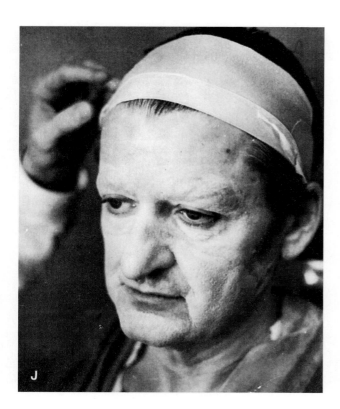

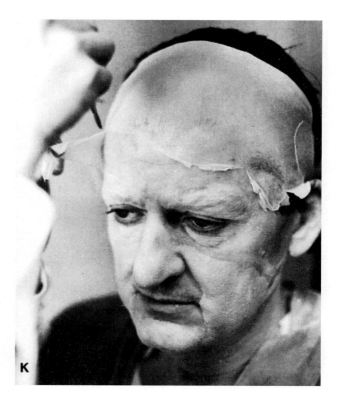

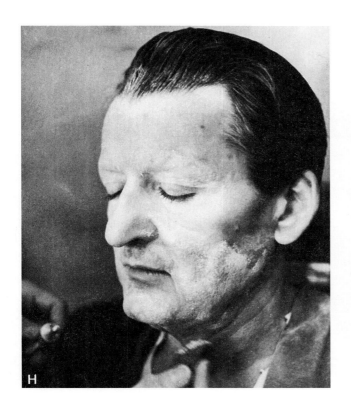

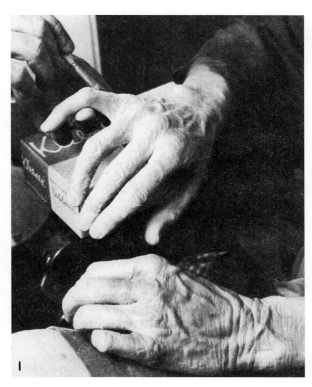

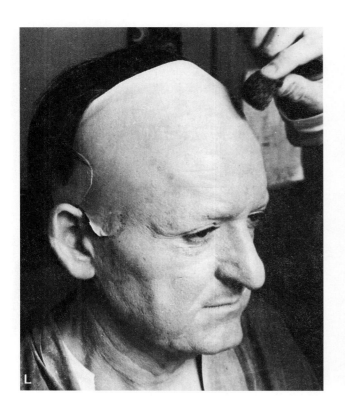

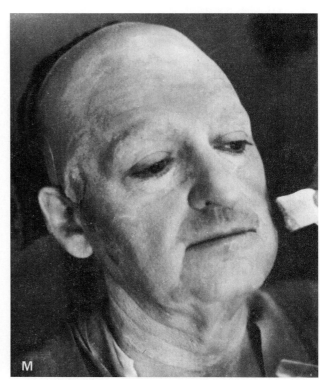

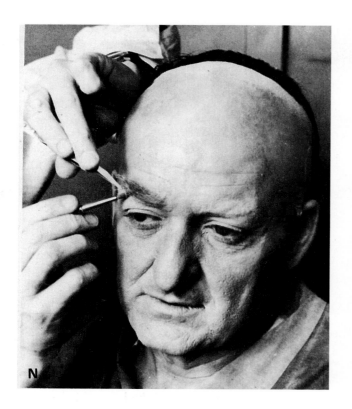

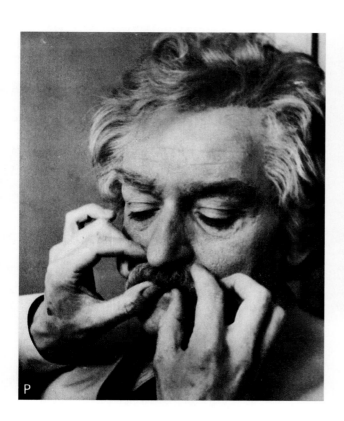

FIGURE 17-7 Pencil sketches of Peter Falk as himself and as Josef Stalin.

Stalin and Trotsky

In designing the makeups for historical characters, such as Stalin and Trotsky in Paddy Chayefsky's *The Passion of Josef D.*, it is helpful, as suggested in Chapter 7, to work from photographs of the actor. In doing character drawings from these photographs, one should be careful to do only what can actually be done with makeup in the given situation. If, for example, the makeup has to be done quickly (as in the change from the young Stalin to the older one, shown in Figure 17-7), changes should be kept simple. Although it is not necessary, there is some advantage in doing a sketch of the actor as well as of the character. Having both sketches for comparison, as in Figures 17-7 and 17-9, adds considerably to the effectiveness of the presentation in discussing the makeup with the director and the actor and in reassuring them that the transformation is feasible.

In using this method, be sure, as suggested in Chapter 7, that the photograph is a reasonably recent one, and use both front view and profile. If all your preliminary work is based on a firm jaw and a smooth skin, an unexpectedly wrinkled face with sagging muscles can be disastrous. Furthermore, a face that appears, from the front, reasonably easy to make into the likeness of a historical personage can present problems in profile.

Peter Falk as Stalin

The major elements in the change to the young Stalin were the mustache and the eyebrows. Adding the mustache (real hair ventilated on lace) was a simple matter; changing the eyebrows was not quite so simple. Whereas Mr. Falk's eyebrows were heavy and slanting down, Stalin's had to be thin and slanting up. Thus, the actor's natural eyebrows had to be completely blocked out. This was done with spirit gum and fabric. (See Chapter 12.) After the foundation, highlights, and shadows had been applied, the beard area was darkened somewhat with gray, then stippled with dark brown for an unshaven effect. Finally, the mustache was attached with spirit gum, and Mr. Falk's own hair was arranged to suit the character. For the more mature Stalin, the wig was put on (Figure 17-8C) and the lace front attached with spirit gum. Then the youthful makeup was covered with a cake foundation and appropriate highlights and shadows added.

Alvin Epstein as Trotsky

Alvin Epstein presented an additional problem in that he was expected not only to look like Trotsky but to achieve the likeness in a quick change. He was playing three characters, each one totally unlike any of the others; but only Trotsky needed to be a recognizable historical personage.

In addition to adding a wig, a goatee, and a mustache (Figure 17-9), Mr. Epstein reshaped and darkened his own blond eyebrows. The pale, translucent skin that Mr. Epstein wanted for Trotsky was achieved with white cake makeup lightly applied, then partially removed with liquid cleanser, letting the natural skin color show through and leaving a very slight shine. The bone structure was then accentuated with highlights and shadows and the eyes with black and light red. A touch of red was added immediately under the eyebrows.

The Mad Hatter

Likenesses can also be based on illustrations of fictional characters (Figure 17-10). Once it is determined, by examining the face in the mirror at the same angle and with the same expression as that in the illustration, that a likeness is possible, the procedure is essentially the same as when working with a drawing of a real person. For the Mad Hatter, the eyebrows, eyelids, and nose were the features requiring the most obvious changes. Figure 17-11 shows the step-by-step procedure.

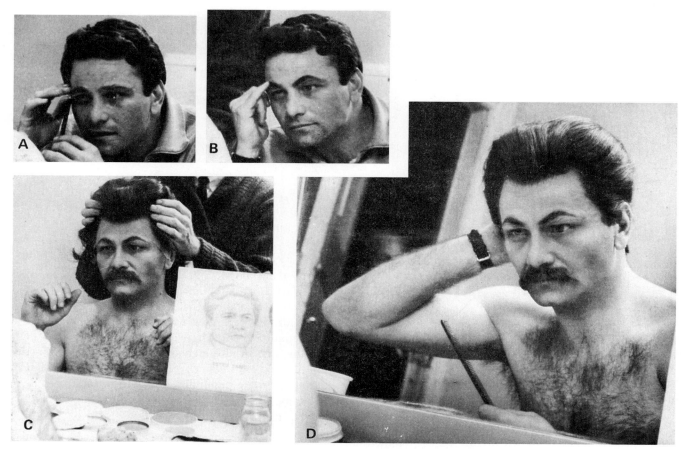

FIGURE 17-8 Peter Falk to Stalin. *A. Blocking out natural eyebrows. B. Human-hair eyebrows, ventilated on net, being attached with spirit gum. C. Wig being adjusted, front lace not yet trimmed. D. Makeup completed, wig being combed. Photos by Werner J. Kuhn.*

Alvin Epstein

Epstein as Trotsky

FIGURE 17-9 Pencil sketches of Alvin Epstein as himself and as Trotsky.

FIGURE 17-10 The Mad Hatter from Alice in Wonderland. *Based on the Tenniel illustration.*

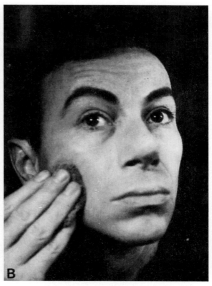

FIGURE 17-11 **Makeup for the Mad Hatter.** *A. Nose being built up with putty-wax. B. Cake makeup foundation being applied. C, D, E. Face being modeled with highlights and shadows. F. Eyebrows being made up. G. Hairlace being pressed into spirit gum. H. Finished makeup. Model and makeup artist, Richard Corson.*

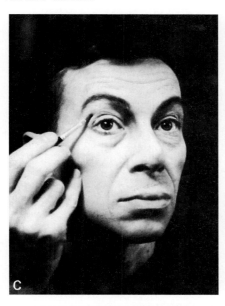

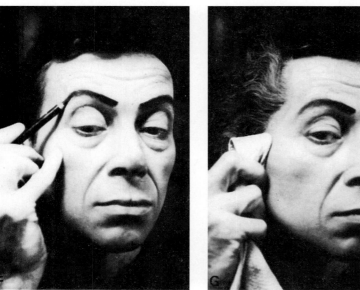

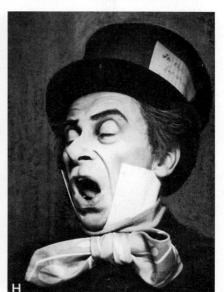

1. Make yourself up as a historical character from a play.

2. Create a likeness from a portrait—not necessarily of a historical figure and preferably a painting rather than a photograph. Make sure before you begin that a recognizable likeness is possible.

chapter 18

Natural Makeup for Film and Television

Film and video makeup allows for as many variations in character as in the stage makeup process. The full range of techniques used for straight makeup, corrective makeup, modeling with highlights and shadows, and three-dimensional makeup often apply for film and television. The major difference between theater and film and video makeup is the materials and the overall intensity of the effect.

Film

Faces recorded on film for a motion picture must, in most cases, be made up to please the eye. Any effect or technique that appears unnatural or over done will most likely be "seen" on film. Film industry makeup artists generally use highly refined products that are similar to creme-type foundations but have a lighter consistency and produce a more natural look than standard creme foundations. Foundations such as Visiora's MV series (Figure 18-1), Max Factor's Pan-Stik, MAC Matte foundations, Bobbi Brown Creme Stick, Chanel creme foundations, Rino Carboni of Rome, RCMA creme foundations, Ben Nye's Creme foundations, Kryolan's TV Cream Makeup Stick, and Mehron's Celebre (Figure 18-2) are examples of product lines with color choices and consistencies suitable for this medium. An extremely light coverage is applied with a triangular-shaped sponge and blended into the skin until it virtually disappears. Depending on the quality of the actors' skin, the foundation should be applied only to those areas of the face where it is most needed. It is of utmost importance for performers, especially film actors, to have healthy, clear, smooth skin and develop a good skin care program.

FIGURE 18-1 **Visiora line of cosmetics.** *These include: Powder Compact (PC); Liquid Face and Body Makeup (CN); Liquid Face Makeup (VN); and Creme Face Makeup (MV).*

FIGURE 18-2 Mehron's Celebré Professional Creme Makeup.

Television/Video

Electronic reproduction or the process of recording an image on video tape at the current television standards is unlike the way today's film stock captures an image. While film, color photography, and the human eye see light in fine points (similar to a pointillist's painting) the video image reproduces the picture in horizontal lines. There are approximately 500 of these lines on a standard color television and the equivalent of 1000 lines represented on 35 mm film. The higher horizontal resolution measurement of 35 mm film stock indicates the viewed image to be twice as clear as the television image. Because the video image does not capture as much information as film stock or the human eye, the electronic process must enhance details by exaggerating the difference between colors, shapes, and lines. In addition, the cameras are adjusted to precisely define the edges of objects, adding clarity to each shape. This process, known as *edge enhancement,* is designed to separate objects or shapes from one another. For example, if a character is wearing lip color, the electronic process will exaggerate the edge of the mouth and carefully separate it from the skin tone. This, however, could be a problem if the performer has pigment changes in skin tone or natural wrinkles, since they too would be exaggerated. These problems will soon be reduced with the introduction of advanced technologies such as high definition television and computer chip driven video cameras. They promise to all but eliminate the need for edge enhancement and with it the medium's idiosyncratic makeup techniques.

Makeup for video should have a higher degree of coverage than for film and must eliminate surface shine to counter the harsher lighting. Natural reflective highlights and minor changes in skin tone may be perfectly acceptable to the eye and to the film camera, but on video, because of the increased contrast and edge enhancement, minor shine may appear as a hot spot and the soft glow of natural redness in some skin types becomes exaggerated and blotchy. Harsher lighting also has a tendency to lighten natural skin tones. With this in mind, choose or custom blend a foundation one half shade darker than the skin tone. The foundation must be applied evenly and blended carefully to produce a smooth, streak-free surface. Powdering the foundation first with a clear, translucent, colorless powder will prevent the foundation from darkening. After the makeup is complete, a pigmented face powder one half shade darker than the foundation may be added to those areas of the face naturally colored by the sun. Professional foundations such as William Tuttle (Figure 18-3), RCMA, Cinema Secrets' Ultimate Foundations, Joe Blasco's creme foundations, and Ben Nye's Matte foundations, and commercial products such as Gerda Spillman, Senna, MAC Matte Foundations, Shu Uemura cake foundations, work well in this medium. An-

FIGURE 18-3 William Tuttle Color Foundation and Neutralizer.

other important consideration when selecting foundations for video recording is to choose one that will reduce the redness or *ruddiness* in the skin's undertones. Redness in the skin may, in some studio systems, be enhanced in video processing.

A major advantage for the makeup artist working in video is the ability to view the recording immediately after shooting. Video playback, in contrast to film developing, allows for instant judgment of the makeup effect. Color-corrected monitors, available in the studio control room, allow the makeup artist the opportunity to carefully inspect the makeup before and during recording. "Set monitors", however, are not color-corrected and are seldom used for this purpose.

Choosing a Foundation

Foundations serve a variety of purposes in makeup application: to color the skin; to naturally even out the color variations found in all skin tones; and to provide a surface on which to contour and accent.

Choosing the appropriate foundation generally depends upon the distance between the performer and the viewer and the medium through which the make-up is being viewed. As a general rule, with the exception of non-realistic makeup styles, the closer a viewer comes to the performer, the more natural the make-up should appear. While stage make-up techniques are often intended to project facial features, make-up for film and television require more subtlety, often to the point of showing no make-up at all. And while stage make-up foundations often deepen the skin color to compensate for variations in brightness and color of stage lighting, the new sensitive film stock and improved video cameras capture color as it naturally appears.

An important consideration when choosing a foundation to match the skin tone is whether a natural or

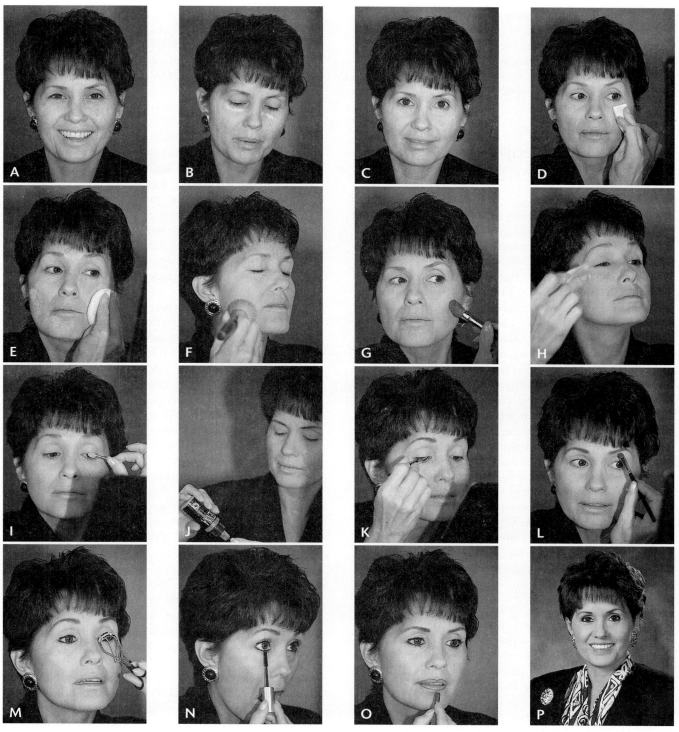

FIGURE 18-4 Makeup for video and television. *A. News broadcaster Olga Campos without makeup. KVUE Channel 24, Austin, Texas. B. Mary Kay Full Coverage-Ivory Concealer applied on under-eye discoloration. C. Edges of concealer blended into surrounding area. D. Mary Kay Liquid Foundation Fawn Beige, SPF-13 or Joe Blasco TV Makeup Creme Foundation Natural Beige #3 Foundation applied with a triangular-shaped foam sponge. E. A generous amount of Mary Kay Translucent loose setting powder is pressed into the foundation using a clean powder puff. F. Excess powder is removed with a large powder brush. G. Studio Gear Henna cheek color is applied on the cheekbone with a blush brush. H. Excess blush is toned down using the foundation sponge. I. Studio Gear Barely There eyeshadow used to highlight the eyelid is applied with a sponge-tipped applicator. J. Senna Black eyeliner is transferred from its tube to a small container and mixed with eyeliner sealer. K. The eyeliner is then applied at the lash line with an eyeliner brush. L. The brow is being filled in with Studio Gear dark brown eyeshadow on a flat, firm dome-shaped brush. M. Lashes are curled before applying Maybelline Lash by Lash Black mascara. N. The wrong way to apply mascara. Never point the end toward the eye. O. Define the edges of the lips and then fill in with MAC Mahogany lip pencil. For longer lasting lip color, use a brush to paint over the pencil with MAC Retro Matte Lipstick. P. Completed Makeup. (See Figure G-8 for a color image of the finished makeup.)*

artificial light source is being used. The variation in color temperature of the light can effect the overall color quality of the make-up requiring an adjustment to the foundation. A close working relationship with the director and the director of photography will assist you in organizing makeup test shots before principle photography begins.

Natural Makeup for the Female Performer

Creme-style foundations should be applied with a fine polyurethane foam sponge. Pick up a small amount of color from the container and apply it as thinly as possible, giving the skin as little coverage as needed (Figure 18-4A, B, C and D.) After covering a small area of the face, check the color for a correct match. Color must always be matched on the face, not from the container or on the back of the hand. The base should be blended carefully at the hairline, leaving no traces of makeup color on the hair, eyebrows, or lashes. Color should be blended to the lash line on both the upper and lower lids and to just under the jawline where it meets the neck. The area under the jawline is a good blending off point for two reasons: (1) it is high enough to avoid rubbing off on the wardrobe; and (2) it is usually in the shadows from overhead lighting or daylight. Continue the foundation on the neck back toward the hairline and onto the top surfaces of the ears. Remember that a subtle shift in color to the naked eye may become far more noticeable to the video camera.

Cake foundations, when used, must be applied with care to avoid the characteristic dry powdery look. Since cake foundations have a tendency to "sit" on the surface of the skin, the film and video cameras, in most cases, see the makeup as an unnatural addition.

Powder Most creme foundations, including the newer, lighter formulas require setting powder. Most makeup artists prefer the finely ground translucent powders, while others use the tinted varieties which can add the warmth back into the foundation often lost under bright or harsh lighting. Powder is applied generously with a powder puff and then removed with a soft powder brush (Figure 18-4E and F.) The face should appear to have a natural sheen for film work and a matte finish for video. The matte finish may look unnatural and flat to the eye, but the video camera will electronically process the smooth consistent surface into a natural looking effect. Excess powder can be removed with a slightly damp sponge.

Concealer Concealers are most often used to cover dark circles under the eyes and to eliminate redness and other skin discoloration's on the face. They are available in a variety of formulas from sheer neutralizers such as Joe Blasco's Red and Blue neutralizers to more opaque camouflage systems such as Dermablend and Kryolan's Dermacolor. Other suggestions for concealers include Laura Mercier Camouflage Concealer, Yves Saint Laurant Touche Eclat, Lancome MaquiComplet, Tuttle WB Stipple, Stila Face E, Max Factor Erase, Shu Uemura Mark Cealer, Clinique, MAC NC Foundations, and RCMA concealers to name a few. Choose one that is slightly lighter than the foundation (one to two shades) and with a subtle yellow tint to counter the common purple undertones found around the eye, a subtle green tint to counter red discolorations, and a subtle orange tint to balance the blue areas caused by heavy beard shadow. Avoid using white and very light colored concealers. They can appear chalky on the skin and create a raccoon effect around the eyes.

For under-eye concealer to be effective, proper placement is of utmost importance. Apply the concealer with the fingers or a concealer brush under the eye up to the lower lashes and on the inner most corner of the eye (often the darkest area.) (See Figure 18-5B.) It should be used only on the discolored area and blended carefully toward the natural highlights. If the concealer is used outside the discolored area it may increase the effect of the "bags" and cause other areas to appear puffy. Smooth and blend with a light patting motion for an even application and greater coverage. Do not over blend. Powder with a translucent setting powder or with one that is slightly lighter than the concealer.

Should concealer be applied before or after the foundation? Many makeup artists believe that a practical method for determining the amount of concealer to be used is dependent on the amount of visible discoloration appearing through the foundation after it has been applied to the face. Too much concealer may indeed be just as unattractive or cause just as much focus as the original discoloration. After all, the purpose of the concealer/foundation combination is to leave the skin looking smooth and natural (Figure 18-4B and C).

Cheek Color or Blush Cheek color adds a natural healthy glow to the skin. Whether you choose a cream, gel, or dry formula, finding the proper color can be confusing. One method for developing an appropriate color is to mix together equal amounts of foundation and a primary red. This is an excellent reference point from which to choose cheek colors. Be sure to integrate creme and gel formulas into the foundation before the setting powder is applied. Choose colors that compliment the lips and provide a matte finish. They should not be too bright, too dark, or too shimmery or frosted.

Cheek color is applied on the cheekbone with the fingers (creme and gels) or a brush (cake and powders),

FIGURE 18-5 Natural Makeup for film and intimate theater settings. *A. Actress, Kristen Chiles without makeup. Skin care products include Rachel Perry Tangerine Dream Facial Cleanser and Neutrogena Combination Skin Moisturizer. B. Physicians Formula Light Under eye concealer is applied over Almay Moisture Renew Matte Finish Ivory Powder foundation. C. Covergirl Blush Iced Cappucino is applied with a blush brush and is being used as cheekcolor and for contouring. D. The same blush is used to provide a kissed-by-the-sun coloration to the forehead, bridge of nose, apple of cheeks, and chin. E. Brown pencil eyeliner is applied only to the top lash line. It is then smudged to soften the edge. F. Ulta Prestige Marble eyeshadow is applied to the lid and crease. The crease is then darkened with Ulta Prestige Coffee Bean shadow. G. Makeup application to this point. H. Correct method for applying mascara to the top and bottom lashes. (L'Oreal Lash Out Black). I. Lips are first lined with Mary Kay lip pencil in Raisin. J. Only the top lip is filled in with The Body Shoppe-Colorings in Bronze lipstick. Press lips together to transfer excess to the bottom lip. This technique produces an effective contour to the lower lip. K. Finished makeup. (see Figure G-7 for a color image of this makeup.)*

and should not be used to attempt contouring or shading under the cheekbone. It should appear and act as a soft glowing highlight. Place the cheek color near the hairline (avoid tinting the hair, especially blonde hair) and blend toward the center of the face (Figure 18-4G). Blend carefully to avoid creating a horizontal line across the cheek (Figure 18-5C and D). All traces of color should blend away before they reach the outside corner of the eye. Unless a fuller "apple cheek" effect is desired, keep cheek color off of the front plane of the face.

Eye Shadows

Dry eyeshadows in three harmonious shades (light for highlighting, medium for the upper lid, and dark along the lash line) should be used to naturally accent the eye. These shades should blend together invisibly. While creme formulas are easily applied and blend smoothly, they tend to migrate into the creases of the eye necessitating regular attention to maintain a consistent appearance throughout filming.

The area of the eyelid between the lashes and the crease should be highlighted with an ivory, bone, or vanilla dry shadow (Figure 18-4I). The highlight is strongest over the highest projection of the eyelid and should then be blended away from the center in all directions. The area of the brow bone directly under the arch of the brow should also be highlighted. Using the same color, apply a small amount to the outer half of the brow, blending out and down toward the crease.

For a natural makeup application use a brown, grey-brown, taupe, or cocoa shadow. Apply the shadow with a crease brush (Figure 9-1A.1). Starting at the outer edge of the upper lash line, follow the crease to approximately two-thirds of the way toward the inner eye. The shadow can be applied into or slightly above the crease (Figure 18-5E). Using a firm shadow brush (Figure 9-1A.8) blend upwards toward the brow. Blend the shadow from dark to light before reaching the highlighted area under the brow. The darkest shade is used as an eyeliner (see the following section).

Eye shadow in a natural makeup should always have a matte finish. Avoid opalescent or pearlized colors. Remember that subtlety in application and blending are key to a successful film or television makeup. Eyeshadows by Stila, MAC, Philosophy, Chanel, Senna, Bobbi Brown, and Max Factor are often used.

Eyeliner

The purpose of eyeliner in a natural makeup is to enhance and darken the lash root line and therefore must be similar to or darker than the hair color. Four types of eyeliner should be considered: pencil, powder, cake, and liquid. The *pencil* liner can be easily blended creating a soft, natural eyelash line (Figure 18-5F), but the waxy color is affected by body heat and can smudge during a long shooting schedule. Using a dark *eyeshadow* along the lash line creates an even softer line than the pencil and is quite easy to control.

Although *cake* and *liquid* liners require a bit more skill to apply, they have the advantage of drying and do not smudge as easily. Cake and liquid liners can be left with a hard edge or blended with a damp brush or cotton-tipped applicator (Figure 18-4J and K.)

For performers with blonde hair and light skin, a light brown, sable, or slate colored liner should be used. Performers with red hair can choose light brown or auburn liner colors based on skin and hair coloration. Light brown hair with light skin tones should use a medium brown, cocoa, or charcoal eyeliner. Those with medium to dark brown colors should use a dark brown, mahogany, or charcoal eyeliner.

The width of the eyeliner at the inner edge of the upper lash line (toward the nose) should be quite thin and then widen as it moves away from the center of the face ending at the last lash. If liner is needed on the lower lashes it is usually thinner at either end and slightly thicker at the center of the eye. Great care should be given to making these lines thin and blended. The goal is to frame and enhance the eye. (See Figure 18-4J and K.)

Eyebrows

The eyebrow should look well-groomed, defined, and be of a color slightly darker than the hair. A well-groomed eyebrow may actually allow you to use less makeup. The shape should follow the natural brow line and can be tweezed, waxed, or shaved (see Figure G-15B) to remove excess hairs. (Be aware that small bumps can appear after waxing caused by ingrown hairs which can be painful and unsightly. They can be avoided by first cleaning the brow with a toner before the waxing process and then exfoliating the area regularly with a gentle cleansing scrub. Applying a drop of Benzoin Peroxide to the area once a day for several days after waxing will also prevent this problem.) When tweezing, first pluck any hairs between the brows above the bridge of the nose, then carefully remove stray hairs from below the brow. The highest point of the arch should be created at approximately three-quarters of the distance along the brow from the inner edge.

The thickness of the brow is not as important as its shape. The brow should be thickest near the center of the face, gradually become thinner at the arch and then taper into a fine point. If the natural brow does not follow this direction, light strokes with an appropriately colored pencil can be used to alter the shape.

Adding color to the eyebrow can help to frame the face. It is important to add enough color to fill in the brow without creating a painted-on look. Brow color can be applied with a pencil or with a brush and brown eyeshadow (Figure 18-4L). Should the brows look too dark or artificial after using a pencil try applying brown eyeshadow instead with a small, hard, flat brush angled at the tip. For thin and short brows, fill in the sparse areas with a pencil using short hair-like strokes, then apply shadow with a brush over the entire brow. Finish the application by brushing the brow with a stiff eyebrow brush or toothbrush into the desired shape.

Mascara
Black or brown mascara should be used for nearly every makeup application when trying to achieve a natural look. Brown appears most natural, produces a gentle soft looking lash and can be used on those occasions when no makeup is required. Blonde lashes look best with a reddish-brown colored mascara for film work and black mascara for television (the intense video lighting will wash out lighter colors.) For those performers with extremely dark hair or for dark-skinned performers, black mascara is preferred.

While waterproof mascaras are not recommended for daily wear (they tend to dry out the lashes), their durability can be useful for video or television production. Holding the wand parallel to the floor, apply a lengthening formula mascara (thickening formulas tend to clump on the lashes) to the underside of the top lashes and to the upper side of the lower lashes (Figure 18-5H). Apply two to three thin layers, letting the mascara dry between coats. Here are a few mascara tips: (1) always curl eyelashes before applying mascara (Figure 18-4M); (2) avoid pointing the tip of the wand toward your eye (Figure 18-4N); (3) mascara on the lower lid may accentuate discoloration and puffiness, (4) for a fresher, cleaner look apply mascara only to the upper lash, (5) avoid bright colored mascara; (6) and always use less mascara on the lower lashes. Brands often used by professional makeup artists include Maybelline Great Lash, L'Oreal Lash Out, Lancome Defencil, and Max Factor 2000 Calorie.

Lip Color
The purpose of lip color in a natural makeup is to heighten the color of the lip, even out the skin tone, and add definition to the lip line. Without it, the camera, especially in video, may confuse the often soft or broken edges between the lip and the surrounding skin. The color should be similar to the performer's natural color which can then be toned and contoured with either brown or ivory. The upper lip, usually in a natural shadow, can be slightly darker in color while the lower lip is slightly lighter or brighter and often highlighted to create a fuller appearance. One method to accomplish a natural looking lip is to first create a defined edge using a brush or pencil and then blend the color softly out onto the lip. This method does not require coloring in the entire lip area (Figure 18-5I and J). Another method is to first cover the entire lip with a natural lip pencil (Figure 18-4O), then apply lip color with a brush. This method insures longer lasting coverage and assists the makeup artist when reshaping the lip is necessary. Some popular lip colors are by Cargo, Chanel, Philosophy, Bobbi Brown, Max Factor, Lorac, and MAC (Figure 18-6).

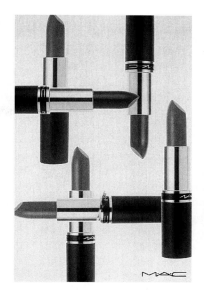

FIGURE 18-6 Lipsticks by MAC (Makeup Art Cosmetics).

Makeup for the Male Performer

The approach to makeup for men working in film and video has changed dramatically in recent years. Improvement in film stock and video technology require far less makeup than in the past. As mentioned previously, film will see the makeup more naturally than video and must be used sparingly or sometimes not at all. Most men on television—actors, reporters, news anchors, and politicians—use makeup to counter the effects of video processing.

Foundation
Foundation should be applied over a cleanly shaven face. If the beard shadow is quite dark, an orange-tinted beard cover may be applied under the foundation to balance or neutralize the blue-grey cast. For most men, however, the foundation on its own will provide enough coverage. Avoid eliminating the beard shadow completely, for the appearance of some shadow will help to maintain a masculine image.

As a general rule, light-skinned men are made up to appear slightly tanner, while those with dark skin should appear a slightly warmer shade than their natural skin tone. The foundation should be applied and blended in a similar manner to female makeup.

Powder
When capturing an image on film, the foundation, if applied sparingly, may not need to be powdered immediately. A slight sheen is natural and gives the skin a healthy appearance. When natural skin

oils begin to appear through the makeup, apply powder and provide touch-ups to remove the shine and refresh the application. For video, however, foundations must be powdered to remove any appearance of shine. Men should pay particular attention to maintaining a matte finish on bald spots and receding hairlines.

Eyeliner

Except in cases where the lashes are blond or extremely faint, eyeliner is rarely used on men. Should this be necessary, either apply a soft, faint line at the root of the eyelash with a sharp pencil and blend with a clean brush until the line disappears, or apply a light coating of brown mascara to the lashes. Any sign of eyeliner on a man's lash line will tend to look feminine.

Concealer

In video production, under-eye cover is generally used in the same manner as on women. Be mindful to blend the color evenly into the surrounding skin to create a natural look.

Cheek Color

The flattening out of facial colors and contours created by the application of foundation is usually not as problematic for men as it is for women. A stronger bone structure and the slight beard cast tend to minimize the effects of the foundation. If cheek color is to be used, a bronze tone can help to create a natural outdoor ruddiness. Avoid using shades of red on the cheeks and cheekbones unless a specific character makeup is being requested.

Lip Color

The upper lip can be darkened slightly by lining it with a brownish-bronze lip color. Mehron's RC-10 and Kelly's Medium Rose are examples of excellent upper lip colors. The lower lip can be lightly colored with a bronze lip color or can simply be left untouched.

Working with a Makeup Artist

Having a working knowledge of theatrical makeup is crucial for stage performers. Actors working in live theater are, with few exceptions, responsible for applying their own makeup. Film and video projects, however, will nearly always have a makeup artist on set who is solely responsible for how the actor's makeup appears on camera. For some actors, it may at first seem awkward, for others it will be a great relief. The professional actor about to make the transition from stage to screen should become familiar with the organization and responsibilities of the makeup department. The actor must also become familiar with what is expected of he or she by the makeup department to insure a professional, appropriate and expedient makeup application.

The Makeup Department

There are five classifications in the makeup category: Key Makeup Artist; Assistant Makeup Artists or "Second"; Body Makeup Artist; Key Hairdresser (Hairstylist); and Assistant Hairdresser. The Makeup Category is responsible for all makeup, hairdressing, wigs, beards, mustaches, body makeup, prosthetic appliances and special effects.

The duties of this department can be summarized as follows:

During the span of time allotted for pre-production activities, the department heads will study or *break down* the script to determine the makeup and hairdressing requirements. This will include the type and number of characters, and the number of performers and extras that will need attention. They will then work with the director to design believable characters and discuss specific makeup application techniques for each performer. Finally, a preliminary makeup schedule and makeup charts for each performer will be prepared. The makeup charts are distinguished by character and scene number, and contain a complete list of all items and products used for each character. Included is a detailed explanation of how each product will be used.

As production begins the key makeup artist will instruct the assistant makeup artist(s) and hairstylists on the design and requirements of the production. He or she will also schedule and assign category artists (additional makeup artists and/or hairstylists) to specific actors and/or extras. On a daily basis throughout the entire shooting schedule, they will apply all required makeup and hairstyles. Other responsibilities include makeup touchups between takes, and developing and maintaining complete and accurate continuity records during filming. Accurate continuity records will insure that an actor with a black eye, for example, will appear with the same black eye, on the same eye over the course of successive shooting days. Careful attention to makeup continuity during filming will be of great assistance during the editing process.

The professional makeup artist is trained to pay attention to every detail. They notice when the back light is picking up flyaway hairs or creating a hole in a hairstyle, they make sure that lipstick is not feathering, that the nose and forehead are not shiny, that there is no broccoli in the teeth and that hands are the same color as the face. In short, they make sure the performer is camera ready throughout the entire shooting schedule.

Responsibilities of the Performer

The following is a list of Makeup Do's and Don'ts, compiled from interviews with professional makeup artists, to assist the performer making his or her first appearance in the makeup trailer or on set:

Do . . .
   . . . arrive on time with enough time to eat before you get into makeup.
   . . . arrive COMPLETELY barefaced (no makeup, no liner, no mascara.)
   . . . arrive with your face clean and moisturized.
   . . . sit quietly in the makeup chair.
   . . . ask the makeup artist any questions or requests before the makeup application begins!!
   . . . try to stay away from overly salty or spicy foods (including onions and garlic) for a few days before shooting to avoid puffiness.

Don't . . .
   . . . bring food, coffee, breakfast, etc. to the makeup chair.
   . . . study your lines during makeup.
   . . . talk on your cell phone or to other people around you. We usually have a deadline and others to makeup as well.
   . . . touch makeup items unless you ask.
   . . . change your makeup. If you have concerns, ask politely if changes are possible.
   . . . DO NOT touch your face after makeup!!

It may be appropriate, for reasons of health and safety, for an actor or performer to bring a small personal makeup bag with a few essential items. Although it is not appropriate to insist that the makup artist use an actor's makeup (most makeup artists have professional products that work for the given performance medium), it is an option if the actor has contracted a skin contagion or if the actor notices a lack of hygiene in and around the artist's kit.

This makeup bag or kit should include the following: a few new professional sponge wedges; a new powder puff; one liquid foundation blended to your skin tone and slightly darker; one professional creme foundation; a set of professional brushes—liner, blush, brow, two shadow brushes, a lip brush, and a small bottle of 90% alcohol for sanitizing the brushes; black mascara; disposable mascara wands; blush, lip pencil and lipstick in shades to flatter your complexion (this is especially important for men and women of color to make sure that you always have an appropriate skin tone.)

As a final suggestion to any performer anticipating a long day of filming, here is a list of items to bring with you to make the you more comfortable: a good medicated lip balm; toothbrush, tooth paste, floss and mouthwash; a nailbrush and hand cream; body lotion (for men and women of color to prevent ashiness); eye drops, lens solutions, contact case, and glasses; feminine products; and breath mints or gum.

Conclusion

The magic of makeup in all mediums is aided by the visual principle of diffusion. Diffusion has the effect of softening irregular skin texture, eliminating fine wrinkles, and allowing wig lace to all but disappear. It is a phenomenon unaided by filters or lens adjustments. Each medium has its own method. Diffusion in the theater is caused by space or atmospheric distance. Diffusion in films is affected by the distance the projected image must travel, the enlargement process, and the quality of the projection surface. Video diffusion is primarily caused by the quality of the line resolution of the receiving unit (the television).

While techniques and materials may vary to accommodate their respective technologies, makeup for film, video, and the stage are fundamentally the same: foundations must be applied; facial features must be defined; and character must be revealed. It is very likely that the same well-executed natural makeup could appear and be appropriate for stage, film, and video. The principles for applying highlights and shadows, straight and character makeup, three dimensional and prosthetics are remarkably similar throughout all performance mediums. What does define the mediums from one another is how they are viewed by the audience: fixed seating and distance in the theater; or flexible vantage points and enlarged images on film and video. The proximity of the viewer to the performer is the primary factor in determining the intensity of the makeup application. It is not, however, the only consideration. Attention must be paid to variations in lighting, the sensitivity of film stock, and the requirements of today's electronic video equipment. The density, color and texture of any makeup effect will be influenced by one or more of these variables.

PROBLEMS

1. Apply makeup using makeup techniques for video and television. Capture the image before and after the makeup application on video tape, play the tape in class, and analyze the results.

2. Apply makeup using makeup techniques for film processing. Capture the image before and after makeup application on a 16 mm or 35 mm film stock. Process the film, project the film for the class, and analyze the results. (If this not possible, remember, if it looks good to the eye it will look good on film.)

Makeup for Darker Skin Tones

The representations of color found in darker skin tones are as diverse as the ivory color of almonds to the deep black of ebony wood. The color range is so varied that it often becomes difficult to identify individual skin tone and then match that tone with an appropriate cosmetic. Only recently have major cosmetic manufacturers, commercial and theatrical, made a conscientious effort to include a broader range of shade selections in their primary cosmetic lines for persons of color. Historically, actors of color and their makeup artists have had to be creative and rather ingenious in formulating their own foundations and accent colors. Even with the expanded range of available colors it is nearly impossible to find a shade that matches every skin tone. Developing the skills to properly analyze skin tone will assist in the successful selection and/or custom blending of the most flattering and appropriate foundations, powders, shadows, blushes, and lipcolors that will work for any medium including film, television, video, print, and stage.

The primary challenge associated with applying makeup to actors of color is to match the skin tone and choose appropriate accent colors. This is not, however, as simple as it may seem. Many products become muddy or ashy against the skin and will often leave a slightly grey cast after application. In many instances one or more of the following might contribute to this problem: (1) improper training; (2) limited choices of products; (3) lack of understanding of how to properly choose products; (4) fear of dark complexions; (5) inability to determine the undertones in the skin coloration in people of color. Understanding the concept of undertones is the key to mastering makeup for actors of color.

Dark skin, generally recognized in colors of cream, tan, olive, copper, earth brown, dark red-brown, and ebony, regardless of ethnic origin and genetic mixture, can be separated into warm and cool categories or

FIGURE 19-1 A. Actress Deidrie Henry. *B. Deidrie Henry as Vera Dodson and Andrea Frye as Louise in the Oregon Shakespeare Festival's* Seven Guitars. *(1999). (Photograph by Christopher Briscoe.)*

FIGURE 19-2 Vilma Silva as China and Thom Rivera as Alejandro in the Oregon Shakespeare. Festival's *El Paso Blue*. **(1999).** *(Photograph by David Cooper.)*

palettes. A warm palette is dominated by the color yellow and a cool palette by the color blue. The first step in determining a performer's color category is to simply drape them in a pure white and then a creme colored cape or shirt (this is best done outdoors or in color-corrected lighting.) An objective visual observation is all that is necessary. Which looks better? If the bright white looks better, they fall into a cool palette. If the cream color looks better, they fall into a warm palette. There are some who will look good in both and therefore take on both palettes.

Determining Undertones

Skin tone is not always the most important factor in determining undertones. Skin tone may fade with age or deepen with sun exposure but the basic undertone will never change. The skin contains a combination of three pigments: melanin which produces a brown tone; carotene which produces a yellow tone; and hemoglobin which produces a red tone. The various combinations of these pigments creates the undertones, not the lightness or darkness of the skin. Other factors to consider are the natural hair color, the color of the eyes, and the complexion. The following steps will assist you in analyzing skin tone and determining undertones:

1. Hold a piece of white paper next to the inside portion of the wrist (you might also try cutting a one inch diameter hole in the paper and setting it on the wrist). The white paper will allow you to see the true color. Ignore any prominent vein coloring (veins have a blue-green cast). Look for the color lying just beneath the surface of the skin. It is likely to be blue, blue-pink, green, red, yellow, gold, or gold-orange. Do not confuse yellow undertones with a sallow complexion which is usually due to age or sickness.

2. Like skin, the hair also has undertones. Examine the hair color nearest the root under proper lighting and notice the prominent highlights. Look for a blue-black, reddish-burgundy, blonde, gold, ash, drab, silver-grey, or yellow-gray cast. Choose the most conspicuous color. Is it warm or cool? If the hair color is no longer natural, the color palette can be modified to accommodate the change. For example, if the natural hair is golden-brown (warm) and is changed to jet black, the palette automatically becomes cool. Even though the skin tone, foundation, and powder remain warm, due to the cool hair color, the person takes on a cool palette of coloration for the eyes, cheeks, and lip color. Hair undertones, then, are the determining factor when choosing the palette for accent colors. In general, warm and cool palettes will be determined by the following hair colors:

Warm   Light to medium-dark brown with golden highlights
        Red or auburn
        Light- to medium-dark blonde with golden highlights
        Taupe, beige, grey (not silvery white)

Cool   Dark-brown to blue-black
        Salt and pepper or silver-white
        Dark brown to jet-black with mahogany or burgundy-red highlights
        Platinum blonde or ash blonde
        Light- to medium-brown hair with ash or drab highlights

3. Examine the eyecolor. Blue, blue-green, blue-grey, and blue with gold flecks may indicate a cool palette, while hazel, brown, and brown with gold flecks may indicate a warm palette.

4. A person's complexion is also another tool in determining the skin's undertones. For example, dry skin is usually associated with a cool palette, freckles with a warm palette, and one with exposed surface capillaries can be either cool or warm.

Once the undertones have been categorized as warm or cool, each category is then divided into two groups: Group I and Group II–Cool; and Group I and Group II–Warm (see Figure 19-3). Group I Cool is defined by a cool red or mahogany undertone; Group II Cool is defined by cool red that is often mixed with green or an ebony undertone; Group I Warm is defined by a warm golden undertone; Group II Warm is defined by a warm copper undertone.

Within each group in Figure 19-3 probable skin tones, hair color, and makeup colors are listed. The skin tone is directly related to the foundation color. For a light to medium olive-brown skin tone, a light to medium olive-brown foundation should be chosen. The foundation must, however, contain a small amount of

FIGURE 19-3   Undertones and color palettes for darker skin.

Group I Cool–Blue-based color palette

Undertone:	Cool–red *(mahogany)* *(this group has more red than Group II–Cool)*
Skin tone:	Light to medium olive-brown, light to medium brown, rose-brown
Hair color:	Medium brown, dark brown, blue-black, black with reddish-burgundy highlights, silver grey
Makeup/Accent colors:	Deep red, blue-red, true red, brown-red, purple, fuschia, violet, aubergine

Group II Cool–Blue-based color palette

Undertone:	Cool–red, sometimes green *(ebony)*
Skin tone:	Medium to darker from dark olive to blue black (sometimes the skin looks dry or slightly ashy)
Hair color:	Medium brown to black
Makeup/Accent colors:	Deep red, raspberry, cognac, berry, magenta, burgundy

Group I Warm–yellow to yellow-orange color palette

Undertone:	Warm–*golden*
Skin tone:	Fair, light yellow-brown to light golden-brown
Hair color:	Blonde, red-auburn, brown, grey-taupe, grey-brown
Makeup/Accent colors:	Peach, apricot, salmon

Group II Warm–yellow-orange to red-orange color palette

Undertone:	Warm–*copper (this group has more red than Group II Warm)*
Skin tone:	Medium to dark yellow brown, medium to dark golden-brown (the skin may have a slight oily appearance)
Hair color:	Medium to dark brown, blue-black with reddish-burgundy highlights
Makeup/Accent colors:	Clear red to orange red or true red, red-brown

undertone color to perfectly match the skin. The makeup color palettes including blush, lip color, and eyeshadow are determined by the undertones of the skin and the hair. They are either cool or warm, blue-based color palettes or yellow-based color palettes, and are defined by how much or how little red pigment they possess. A yellow to yellow-orange palette, for example, using peach, apricot, and salmon accent colors contains less red than the color palette using orange-red and true red for its accent colors.

Choosing a Foundation

When choosing a suitable foundation, look for formulas containing a mixture of yellow, red, and yellow-green tones with the brown pigment. Check the color for clarity by smearing a sample onto a white piece of paper. Are the added tones clearly visible in the foundation or does the foundation simply appear muddy? If any of the foundation samples appear to have a white cast to them, they will not be appropriate for dark skin shades. These foundations may contain talc or titanium dioxide and will leave an ashy or grey cast on the skin. The additives are used to create an opaque formula to enhance coverage. Manufacturers who produce a broad range of foundations and accent colors appropriate for actors of color include Interface, Bobbi Brown, Trish McEvoy, Black Opel, Fashion Faire, Iman, RCMA, MAC, William Tuttle, Gerda Spillman, Joe Blasco, Mehron, Ben Nye, and Kryolan (to name a few).

After you select the basic color palette in a light to medium or medium to dark range, it is advisable to include a few "mixing colors" in addition to the foundations. Good mixing colors are foundations that are highly pigmented with yellow, yellow-green, red, or orange-red. These mixing colors are indispensable in any makeup kit and are used to adjust the undertones in the basic brown foundations. Some examples of useful mixing colors are Visiora's 101 and 102, William Tuttle's Chocolate Cream and Toasted Almond, Fashion Faire's Copper Glo and Tawny Glo, RCMA's Shinto series, Joe Blasco's Ruddy Dark-skin series, and Interface's Fox.

As mentioned in previous chapters, foundations are used to give the skin an even texture, to enhance skin tone, and to provide a smooth canvas on which to add color and dimension. The following techniques provide you with the ability to begin building dimension into the face with the initial foundation application:

Technique A

1. Choose three foundation shades: a medium shade that matches the skin tone; a concealer/highlighter that is one shade lighter; and a third which is one shade darker than the skin tone.
2. Because many actors of color are darker across the brow area and on the chin and somewhat lighter on the cheeks, it is necessary to balance the tones by applying the lighter foundation to the darker areas and the darker foundation to the lighter areas. Blend the foundations colors with care.
3. Now apply the lighter shade as a concealer under the eye and lightly down the center of the face (forehead, nose, around the mouth and chin) and blend well.
4. Apply the medium foundation over the entire face.
5. Powder the front planes of the face with a setting powder one to two shades lighter than the concealer and the surrounding areas with a slightly darker shade. The powders must be blended with care.

Technique B

1. Apply matching foundation with a sponge applicator to the entire face to balance the skin tone.
2. Apply a light yellow-orange foundation/concealer under the eyes, across the forehead, down the center of the nose, and around the mouth and chin.
3. Apply a loose powder in a lighter shade over the entire face.

During the summer months, as the skin begins to darken, the medium may become the highlighter and the darker shade may become the foundation.

Concealers, Highlighters, Neutralizers

Concealers and neutralizers for dark skin are used much the same way as for other skin tones: to cover imperfections such as scars, blemishes, discolorations, and under-eye circles (see Chapter 9, Concealers). For medium to very dark complexions, it is important to use concealers and neutralizers in the orange to orange-red family of colors such as Interface's Fox, Ben Nye's Beard Cover, or Fashion Faire's Copper Glo and Tawny Glo. These products work well to neutralize or eliminate dark spots on the face, especially for those suffering from

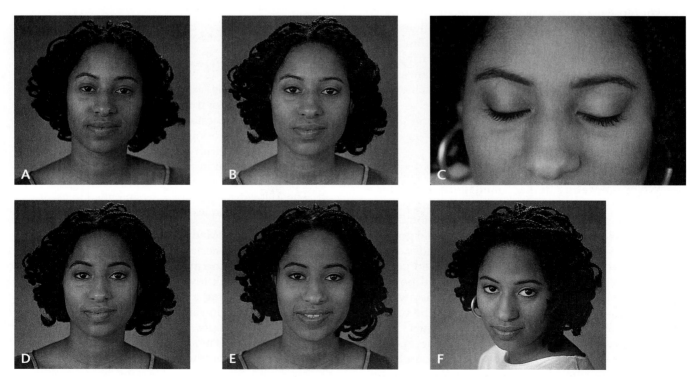

FIGURE 19-4 Natural makeup application on dark skin. *A. Model without makeup. B. Model with foundation, eyeliner, and eyeshadow. C. Close-up of eye makeup. D. Added highlights, concealer, and contouring. E. Added lip and cheek color. F. Finished makeup. (Makeup by Joe Rossi)*

hyper-pigmentation (see below). Concealers must not always be distinguished as a particular product, but are a function of any product that provides the appropriate coverage, enough to diminish the effects of unwanted discolorations.

Unlike concealers and neutralizers, highlighters are used to exaggerate and project bone structure and facial features. Use highlighters in the gold to orange to orange-red family of colors such as Trish McEvoy's Face Shine, Black Opal's Golden Glow, Senna's Face Bronzing Quad, Visiora's CC225, and MAC Cream Color base in Gold or Bronze. Foundation colors one to two shades lighter than the primary foundation are also recommended for under the eye and for other areas of discoloration or uneven skin tone. Highlighting under the eye may not even be necessary since natural discolorations do not contrast as much against darker skin.

Contouring

The same theoretical approach and techniques discussed in Chapter 12 can be used when contouring light to medium skin tones. Contouring or shadowing with darker colors on dark to very dark skin, however, can be impractical and often unflattering. When the skin is very dark it is best to simply highlight the features and allow the color of the skin to act as its own contour. This works for the eyes, cheeks, nose, jawline, forehead, and temples.

For those occasions when your director (film, video or theater) insists on more contouring, small amounts of black can be blended into the foundation color. While some makeup artists believe contouring very dark skin does not work under any circumstances, others will do what is necessary to successfully achieve the desired effect.

Powder

When powdering darker foundations use either a *true* no-color powder or a finely ground tinted powder two to three shades lighter than the foundation. When the natural oils in the foundation mix with the powder, the powder will darken by two to three shades. Use a loose powder for lighter coverage and pressed powder when a truly matte finish is expected. Avoid powders containing talc or other white substances. They will appear dusty and leave a powdery residue on the surface. Most manufacturers including Bobbi Brown, Black Opal, Ben Nye, Fashion Faire, MAC, Clinique, and Prescriptives provide pigmented powders to compliment the darker foundations. Add to your makeup kit a soft yellow-orange powder to mix with an orange-brown, yellow-brown, or red-brown tones.

Blush

The primary concern when choosing a blush or cheekcolor is to avoid those products that appear ashy (a dusty grey color) on the skin. This is a concern consistent with most cosmetic products for people of color. Suggestions for choosing colors for specific skin tones and color palettes are listed on the color chart in Figure 19-3. For application techniques, refer to Chapters 9, 12, and 18. For added dimension, lightly blend in a small amount of pink powder as a highlight to any warm cheekcolor.

Eyeshadow

Powdered eyeshadow provides a softer, more even consistency and will help absorb the natural oils from the skin. Apply eyeshadow with a cotton swab applicator for a soft look, a sponge-tipped applicator to create a smooth and even texture, and with your fingers for heavier coverage. Choose deep natural tones such as sable, coffee, and espresso or vibrant jewel tones such as blue-green, purple, and wine or shades of grey, navy blue, and muted green. Highlight the lid and below the brow with bone, matte yellow, pink, light coral, or beige in warm or cool tones as suggested by the undertone palette. With dark skin often providing its own shadow, contouring the crease may not be necessary.

Lip Color

Lip color can be custom blended by mixing equal amounts of primary or true red with the foundation color. While this is not necessarily a rule it will guide you towards a family of colors appropriate for a given skin tone. This method, along with the correct undertone palette of colors will assist you in making appropriate choices for any skin tone in a variety of performance venues.

The following suggestions are intended to assist you in developing techniques for proper lip color application:

1. *Uneven lip color:* Many dark-complexioned men and women have a certain amount of discoloration on the lips. It is found most often in the lower lip which tends to be pink towards the center. Even out the color by applying a base color with brown pencil over the entire lower lip. Set the pencil with a light dusting of translucent powder and blend off with a damp sponge. Then apply the lip color over both lips. This will produce a more accurate and long-lasting lip color. Using the same pencil technique for men, apply a lip conditioner over both lips, replacing the lipcolor and powder.

2. *Full lips:* Full lips cannot be made smaller, but you can create the illusion of smaller size. To downplay the size of full lips, simply use soft natural tones. Bright colors and colors of high value will only draw more attention. Remember, colors of high value and intensity project while low value, low intensity colors recede. Another method is to first line the lips just inside the natural lipline before filling in with a soft, natural color.

3. *Skin tone and lip color:* As a general rule, the darker the skin tone the darker the lip color. For performers working in large venues, however, choosing a color that assists in projecting the facial features far outweighs the need to follow the latest fashion trends. Contouring the lower lip with highlights of vanilla, gold, or bronze will help to add shape and dimension.

The following list of cosmetics is presented here as an example of one performer's skin care and makeup regimen for performance. A color illustration of the finished makeup application on dancer/choreographer, Mercedes Ellington, using these products can be seen in Figure G-10:

Skin Care:	Lancome Primordial Intense
	Lancome Hydra Zen
	Lancome Viabolic Yeux (eye area) with vitamin C
Concealer:	Lancome MaquiComplet Beige III
Foundation:	Lancome Maquivelours Beige Sable III
	Matte Finish (powder): MAC Studio Fix C-4
Brows:	Maybelline Blonde pencil
Eyeshadow:	MAC Gris and La Prairie Glacee with Benefit 911 over the eyelid. Chanel Fantasie D'Ete on the brow bone blended with Makeup Center Brick Blush above the crease.
Eyeliner:	Yves St. Lauren #1 Moire or L'Oreal Noir.
Mascara:	L'Oreal Voluminous Black
Lipstick:	MAC Foil as a base with Chanel Crimson/Scarlet as a top coat. (A *true* Red)

Adhesives

On very dark skin, some adhesives such as spirit gum, tend to crystallize in extreme weather conditions. To remedy this, apply a small amount of foundation over the lace and crystallization with a small stiff brush until it blends into the skin tone or simply remove the lace pieces during the earliest break, clean and re-apply.

Lighting

Working under intense, bright lighting is not usually a problem for dark-skinned performers. Bright lighting does not "wash out" the skin tone as it does for their lighter-skinned colleagues and therefore requires less adjustment to the makeup. Warm lighting colors are often advantageous to darker-skinned performers. They accentuate the yellow-red undertones already present in the skin. The challenge comes as the inescapable cool blue shades of evening light wash across the stage. Skin tones and facial features in the Group I and II Cool palette often become darker and bluer and can loose much of their definition. The problem is compounded when the wardrobe is also in the same cool palette. Remember that makeup is only flattering or enhanced by the quality of light it is seen under. A close working relationship with the costume designer, lighting designer, lighting director, or director of photography will assist you in having your work appear as you had intended. It is your responsibility as a professional makeup artist to gain the experience and develop the confidence to form effectual collaborative relationships with professional colleagues.

Skin Types and Conditions

Making informed choices about skin care and makeup needs is based on a better understanding of the unique skin types and skin conditions of darker-skinned performers.

Skin Types
There are three basic types of skin: dry, oily, and combination. Dry skin lacks a natural sheen, looks dull, is prone to develop lines and wrinkles, and tends to age prematurely. This type of skin has small pores, is lacking moisture, and has under-active sebaceous glands (produces sebum, the skin's natural oil). Recommendations for skin care include cleansing creams, cleansing lotions, and moisturizers (day and night) formulated for dry skin. Moisturizers should be applied under creme-style foundations, blushes, eye color, and lipsticks.

Oily skin appears shiny and is greasy to the touch. This type of skin has active sebaceous glands and is generally characterized by the appearance of large pores. This type of skin is slightly thicker than other types and is susceptible to pimples and impurities under the surface. To prepare for makeup application, clean the skin twice a day using a facial soap (not body soap) followed by a facial cleanser, both formulated for oily skin. Clean the skin gently; excessive scrubbing with a wash cloth may only cause the skin to produce more oil. On a weekly basis, apply a cleansing mask (specifically for oily skin) to remove impurities left behind from daily cleaning. The drying action will absorb excess oils and give the skin a smoother appearance. Apply an oil-free moisturizer for daily wear, but avoid nightly applications and products called night creams. They tend to aggravate oily skin. Many actors with oily skin recommend regular exfoliation with an alpha hydroxy acid. This product helps promote soft, smooth, younger looking skin by slowly removing dry skin cells without the damaging effects of other more abrasive cleansers.

In general, the darker the skin, the more shiny it will appear. Mattifying creams (that dry to a matte finish) and oil-control lotions can be applied under oil-free foundations to help stop excessive shine. Powdering the concealer generously before applying the foundation will also help to reduce the effects of oily skin. Should the powder appear ashy after application to very dark skin, simply remove it and apply only the foundation.

Anti-shine products such as Interface's Self Control, AntiShine, Smashbox, Mehron's Touchup, and Origin's Zero Oil can also be used but must be applied sparingly. They can be applied before or after the foundation. Test each product before the initial application as some of them may turn grey or ashy on dark skin.

The most common skin type is the combination skin. This type of skin usually has an oily T-zone (across the forehead and down the center of the face from forehead to chin) and normal to dry areas surrounding the zone. Each area has different needs and must be cared for separately.

Skin Conditions
Hyperpigmentation is recognized by small black spots appearing on the face usually from the incorrect extraction of impurities from enlarged pores. It is also seen as heavy darkness under the eyes, on the lids, on the cheek area, and around the mouth and neck. Hormonal changes in women during pregnancy can often cause this condition. It is impossible to cover the dark areas with a lighter foundation. It will simply become a lighter dark spot. This apparent dark brown discoloration will most often have a blue undertone and can be neutralized with a product in the orange to orange-red color range. First apply a very light wash of a foundation that best matches the skin tone. Next, apply the neutralizer with a brush to the discolored areas. Blend the foundation and the neutralizer together eliminating all edges. Powder and apply makeup colors as usual.

Pseudofolliculitis is the medical name for the inflammation of the follicle or ingrown hair. Many men with overly curly hair suffer from this condition. It can cause infection and lead to scarring. Products such as Tend Skin and Bump Stop can be used before and after shaving to help prevent this condition. Facial massage and regular exfoliation with a gritty facial scrub before shaving are also recommended. Some men who have prob-

lems shaving use depilatories such as Magic to remove facial hair. Depilatories are rather strong chemicals that dissolve the hair but must be monitored carefully to avoid burning the skin. Use minimum makeup to cover this condition as the makeup can be unsightly and focus attention on the problem.

Vitiligo is a condition characterized by the loss of pigment on areas of the skin. Opaque camouflage systems such as Kryolan's Dermacolor, Mehron's Tattoo Cover, and Dermablend products can successfully add color back into these areas.

Keloids are large dark scars caused by injury to the skin or by infection (see Figure 19-5). People predisposed to keloids should see a skin care specialist before considering cosmetic treatments such as ear piercing.

The Basic Makeup Kit

A well stocked makeup kit should contain a variety of products in a range of colors from alabaster to ebony. Given the fact that most of the difficulties in choosing appropriate color palettes occur with medium to very dark blue-black complexions, great care must be made in selecting products for these skin tones.

The following list of items is recommended for the professional makeup artist. Individual makeup kits for the performer need only include those products that compliment the performer's face and character range. This may include a proper foundation, a powder that does not change the value of the foundation or turn it muddy, and accent colors in both warm and cool palettes that compliment the skin and a variety and range of possible wardrobe colors.

I. Skin Care
   Makeup remover
   Oil-free cleanser
   Alcohol-free astringent/toner
   Oil-free/hydrating moisturizer
   Broad spectrum UVA/UVB sun screen
   Castor oil—for use under dry eyes. Mix a small amount with concealer, then apply. It is also used to condition brushes that are used for creme applications.
   Benadryl—cream/spray for allergic reactions
   Hydrocortisone cream 1%—for allergic reactions
   Styptic—liquid/pencil to stop bleeding
   Lip balm
   Makeup wipes
II. Foundations
   Creme
   Creme to powder
   Liquid
   (Colors should range from alabaster to ebony in warm and cool palettes with red and yellow mixing colors.)

FIGURE 19-5 A. Actor
Derrick Lee Weeden. *B.
Derrick Lee Weeden as Othello
in the Oregon Shakespeare
Festival's* Othello. *(1999). Three-
dimensional latex scarring
(keloids) on body and arms.
(Photograph by David Cooper.)*

III. Concealers/Highlighters
Light to medium to dark in creme and pencil
form
Orange to cover brown/blue discolorations
Beard cover
Orange-red foundation
Yellow to cover red discoloration
Mellow yellow
Erase
Gold to highlight medium to very dark skin
tones
Tattoo cover
IV. Powders
Loose
Pressed
An assortment including: translucent,
yellow, yellow-pink, light, medium,
dark (not very dark)
V. Cheek Color/Blusher
Powder
Creme
Gel
Liquid
An assortment including:
light to medium skin tones, neutrals such
as, apricot, beige, brown, and
aubergine
dark to very dark skin tones, red, orange,
violet, brown, gold, bronze
VI. Lip Colors
An assortment including:

metallic colors, gold, white, silver, pink
warm and cool colors
clear lip gloss
lip pencils in several shades
VII. Eye Colors
Powders—loose, fairy dust, pressed
Pencils—white, black, brown, taupe, auburn,
plum
Cremes—same
VIII. Eyelashes
Assortment of shapes and sizes in brown and
black:
individual
short
long
angled
full
demi
Duo adhesive in white and dark
IX. Mascara
Cake—black, brown, clear
Liquid—same
X. Eyebrow Kit
Powder
auburn, taupe, brown, black, charcoal
Mechanical pencils
blonde, taupe, brown, black, grey, ebony
XI. Other
Derma Shield/Liquid Bandage to protect open
wounds and cuts before applying makeup
Anti Shine to remove shine

PROBLEMS

1. Practice your ability to determine skin undertones.
   a. Catagorize the performer's skin tone into a warm or cool color palette.
   b. Determine the undertone.
   c. After analyzing the skin and hair undertones, the eye color, and complexion, determine the undertone group in which to place the performer: Group I or II Cool or Group I or II Warm.

2. Analyze a variety of dark foundations for clarity of undertone colors. First, develop a foundation test chart on a piece of white paper. Smear a sample from several foundations on the page using a small metal or plastic spatula (the larger the sampling the more information you will have). Label each foundation with the manufacturer's name and color. Look for yellow, yellow-gold, yellow-orange, orange-red, copper, reds, and blue colors mixed with the brown foundation. Are the colors clearly visible or muddy when mixed with the foundation? Also, analyze the makeup for signs of talc or titanium dioxide which will appear ashy, chalky, or muddy.

2. Using the information gathered from problem #1, develop a complete color palette for the individual including foundation, concealer, powders, cheek color, eyeshadow, lipcolor, eyebrow, and mascara for a natural makeup effect. Design a makeup chart using your choices. Apply the colors directly to the chart. (Do not be afraid to make mistakes. It will take time and practice to master this technique. But, you must start somewhere.)

3. Using the makeup color palette and chart from Problem #2, develop a detailed step-by-step makeup application procedure (including skin preparation) for the same model. Apply the makeup to the model following your procedure. Make adjustments to the procedure when needed. Photograph your makeup application under proper lighting.

4. Follow the same steps as in problem #3 with natural or straight makeup for a large procenium theater.

5. Follow the same steps as in problem #3 with natural or straight makeup for video/television.

6. Follow the same steps as in problem #3 with makeup designed for fashion photography. (Refer to your makeup morgue.)

7. To determine your skin type and develop a proper skin care regimen, see a professional skin care specialist (dermatologist or aesthetician).

Nonrealistic Makeup

chapter 20

Nonrealistic makeup comprises makeups not only for realistic and nonrealistic characters made up in one of various nonrealistic styles (Figures 20-1, 20-2B, 20-3, and 20-4), but also for nonrealistic, that is, fanciful or nonhuman characters—such as trolls, demons, and apes—made up in a realistic style (Figure 20-9).

FIGURE 20-1 Joe York as Frank N. Furter in *The Rocky Horror Show* at Zachary Scott Theater Center, Austin, Texas. *An example of* Theatricalism. *(Photograph by Kirk R. Tuck.)*

Nonrealistic Styles

The nonrealistic styles can range from theatrical realism or *theatricalism* (Figures 20-1, 20-2B, 20-3, 20-4, for example) to nonrealism (Figures 20-4B, 20-5, and 20-6). When this nonrealism results from imposing a particular style on the design of the makeup, it is referred to as *stylization*.

Stylization
In designing a stylized makeup, you might begin by thinking in terms of using line, color, and form to heighten, exaggerate, simplify, clarify, satirize, symbolize, or perhaps amuse. Instead of consulting photographs for inspiration, you might consult paintings (Figure 20-5), drawings (Figure 20-8), prints, caricatures, masks (Figures 20-6), mosaics (Figures 20-7), toys, sculpture, or stained glass. Then, from your various ideas, you could select for your designs those that seemed best suited to the character, the play, and the style of production.

For a stylized production of a French farce using black-and-white sets and costumes, for example, black-and-white makeups are an obvious, but potentially amusing, choice. For a Medieval morality play, you might design makeups to look like mosaics (Figure 20-7, for example) or stained glass. For the production of a play by Brecht, you could relate the makeups to the work of German artists of the period.

Relating the Makeup to the Audience
In addition to relating to the style of the production, to the play, and to the character, a nonrealistic makeup should also relate to the audience. Although audiences are usually quite willing to go along with innovations in

FIGURE 20-2 Alan Sues as Professor Moriarty in *The Adventures of Sherlock Holmes.* An example of theatricalism. *A. Alan Sues as himself. B. Alan Sues as Professor Moriarty. (Photograph by Martha Swope.)*

FIGURE 20-3 The Red Queen from *Through the Looking Glass.* Natural eyebrows soaped out. Putty wax nose. An example of theatricalism. *Student makeup by Rebecca Colodner.*

FIGURE 20-4 Mephistopheles. *Makeup in two different styles. A. Theatricalism. B. Stylization. Makeup by Richard Corson.*

FIGURE 20-5 Makeup in the style of painter Karl Schmidt-Rottluff.

FIGURE 20-7 Thirteenth-century mosaic head. *San Marco, Venice.*

FIGURE 20-6 Makeup copied from an Oriental mask. *By student Elaine Herman.*

FIGURE 20-8 The duchess from *Alice in Wonderland.* *With Alice, Cook, Baby, and Cheshire Cat. Illustration by Sir John Tenniel.*

style, there are certain areas of resistance the actor or the makeup artist should be aware of. Our ideas about some nonrealistic characters may be rather nonspecific and are thus open to fresh interpretation. But our ideas about other nonrealistic characters—such as those in *Alice in Wonderland* and *Through the Looking Glass,* for ex-

ample, are not so flexible. Sir John Tenniel created visual images of the characters in *Alice* (Figure 20-8, for example) that have become the definitive representations of those characters, and most audiences will tend to relate to them more readily on stage if they look rather like the ones with which they're familiar.

Nonrealistic and Nonhuman Characters

Makeups for nonrealistic and nonhuman characters may or may not be nonrealistic in style. Sometimes—as when an actor is playing a flower, for example—there is no choice since an actor simply cannot be made up realistically as a flower. Or as a cat. But the actor can be made up quite realistically as an ape (Figure 20-9).

The following suggestions may provide some ideas for dealing with a variety of nonrealistic characters. When referring to these suggestions, bear in mind that the descriptions are based largely on literature, art, and folklore; and though they may sometimes be stated dogmatically, they represent only a convenient point of departure. You may wish to vary them to suit your purpose.

Angels   First determine the style of the production and the sort of angel required. If an ethereal angel is

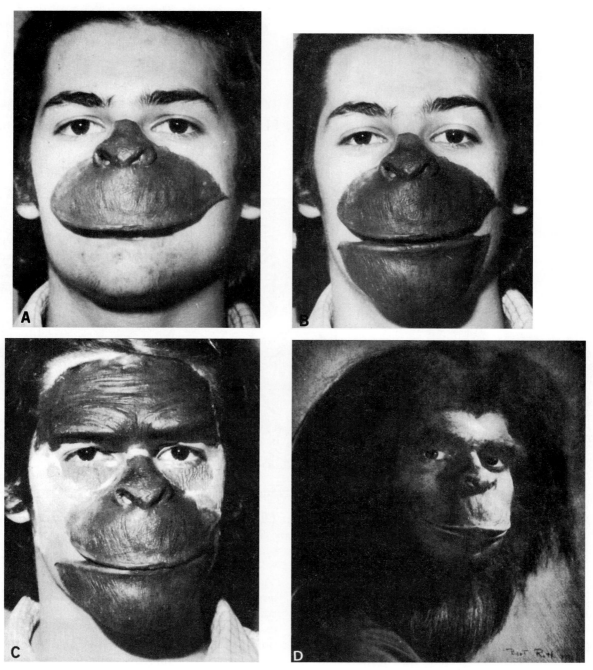

FIGURE 20-9 **Ape.** *Foamed latex mask, made in three pieces. Makeup by Bert Roth, S.M.A.*

called for, you may wish to work with pale lavenders, blues, or whatever color seems appropriate. The features will probably be idealized human ones. But if you were doing *The Green Pastures,* the angels could achieve the comic effect required only with a realistic makeup.

Animals

When animals are played by humans (Figure 20-10), the style of the makeup may be either realistic or nonrealistic. Papier maché heads or masks (Figure 20-11) or latex constructions (Figure 20-9) can be used and sometimes should be; but if the style of the production permits, you may prefer merely to suggest animal features on a human face. That can be done in a completely nonrealistic or a modified realistic style with paint (Figures 20-12 and 20-13), or the paint can be combined with three-dimensional makeup. Crepe hair can also be used. Split lips can be drawn on (Figure 20-12), foreheads can be lowered, real or painted whiskers can be added, and paws can be made from gloves.

Birds

Bird faces can be built up with three-dimensional additions or completely stylized with painted details. Sometimes the two may be combined. Birds with small beaks and large eyes (owls, for example) are, of course, easier to do with paint than are large-beaked birds. Brightly colored feathers can be attached with spirit gum. A complete mask would, of course, be more practical if the makeup had to be repeated. For smaller-beaked birds being done with makeup rather than masks, putty might be used instead of latex. Color can be as realistic or as fanciful as the birds themselves.

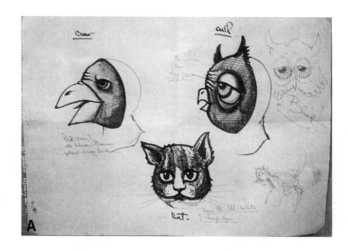

FIGURE 20-11 Bird and animal masks. *By Bill Smith. A. Sketches. B. Masks.*

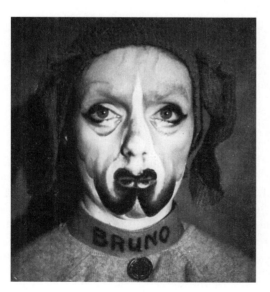

FIGURE 20-10 Bruno. *Stylized makeup for children's play. Improvised headdress. Makeup by student Barbara Murray.*

Clowns

Circus clowns wear stylized makeups of various types, each individually designed. Traditionally, they always design their own makeups and never copy the makeup of another clown. *Shakespearean* clowns are not really clowns at all in the contemporary meaning of the word and require a makeup—either *realistic* or *theatrical*—appropriate for the individual character.

The first step in designing a makeup for a circus clown is to decide what sort of clown you want—sad, happy, elegant, shy, brash, suspicious, ineffectual. Then design an exaggerated, stylized makeup to fit the conception. For a sad clown, for example, the eyebrows and the corners of the mouth will probably slant downward. A happy clown will, of course, have the corners of the mouth turned up. If your clown is to be an

FIGURE 20-12 **Stylized rabbit.** *Makeup by Barbara Murray. A. Blocking out eyebrows with Kryolan Eyebrow Plastic. B. Eyes being made up. C. Areas of color being painted on. D. Completed makeup with improvised headdress. Teeth are painted on over the lips.*

"Auguste" (see Figure 20-14), he will presumably have white paint accenting the eyes and mouth, pink cheeks, and a red nose. Sketching your design on paper first is likely to save time and result in a better makeup.

Clown white (see Appendix A) is usually used as a foundation. All exposed areas of flesh should be evenly colored. Then with pencils, brushes, and shading colors, you can duplicate your design. Bulbous clown noses can be molded with latex or purchased ready-made. Red-rubber balls are sometimes used. The hair should be treated in a style harmonious with the rest of the makeup. A skull cap or a wig is usually worn.

Death   Death is usually pictured as having a skull for a head (see Figure 20-15). The facial bones can be highlighted with white or ivory and shadowed with gray, charcoal-brown, or both. If the head is not going to be covered, a white skull cap or a plastic or a latex cap should be worn. The cap, which should cover the ears, can be painted the same color as the face and the edges blended carefully into the foundation. The eyebrows should always be blocked out (see Chapter 12).

If the makeup is to be luminous, the white paint can be dusted with fluorescent or phosphorescent powder (see Appendix A) before any shading is done. Or fluo-

FIGURE 20-13 **Tiger.** *Makeup by student Kathy Ross.*

FIGURE 20-14 **Auguste clown makeup.** *By "Ambrose."*

FIGURE 20-15 **Death.** *Cake makeup. Makeup by student Dennis Drew.*

rescent or phosphorescent paint can be brushed over the completed makeup in the appropriate places. With fluorescent makeup, an ultraviolet ray must be used on a dark stage to cause luminosity.

If Death is to appear part of the time disguised as a human, a normal though pale, makeup can be used instead of white and the fluorescent paint or pigment applied only to the bones of the skull. Under normal stage lights the makeup will look normal, but under the ultraviolet ray the skull will appear. If the hands are to be visible, they should, of course, be made up in harmony with the makeup on the face. It is also possible to present Death in other ways—as a coldly beautiful woman, perhaps, or as a black-hooded figure with no face at all. Or as a clown.

Devils and Demons

(Figures 20-16, 20-17, 20-18) The conventional devil (Figure 20-16) usually has a long face with sharp, pointed features, prominent cheekbones, long, hooked nose, well-defined lips, dark, upward-slanting eyebrows close together, and deep-set eyes. He may also have a mustache and a small, pointed beard. Conceptions of demons are usually less conventional and more imaginative.

Dolls

China or porcelain dolls can be made up with a creamy white, ivory, or pale pink foundation. The rouge, usually pink, should be applied in a round spot in the center of each cheek, and the spot should be blended somewhat at the edges. The lips should be small with a pronounced cupid's bow. The natural eyelashes can be darkened with mascara or false ones added. The eyes should be made to took as round as possible. An inexpensive wig with shiny, synthetic hair is usually preferable to an expensive one. Other types of dolls will, of course, require other kinds of makeup.

Elves

Elves are usually pictured as very small with pointed or butterfly-shaped ears, large mouths, small turned-up noses or long pointed ones, and round or slanted eyes. The hair may be short or long. Older elves

FIGURE 20-16 **Devil as jester.** *From an old print.*

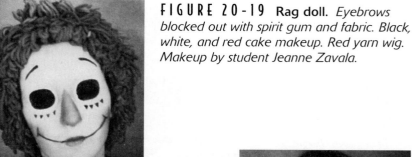

FIGURE 20-17 Sixteenth-century devil's head.

FIGURE 20-18 **Demon.** *English door knocker.*

FIGURE 20-19 **Rag doll.** *Eyebrows blocked out with spirit gum and fabric. Black, white, and red cake makeup. Red yarn wig. Makeup by student Jeanne Zavala.*

FIGURE 20-20 **Marionette.** *Eyebrows blocked out. Cake makeup with black eyebrow pencil. Makeup by student Sarah Barker.*

usually have beards. Red cheeks are appropriate for good-natured elves of any age.

Fairies

Fairies tend to be diminutive and graceful unless they have turned bad, in which case they will appear more evil and witch-like. Wicked fairies (Carabosse in *The Sleeping Beauty,* for example) are more like wicked witches and are sometimes played by men, giving them stronger, less feminine features. Emphasis in the makeup should, of course, be on wickedness—dark, slanting eyebrows, close together, evil, piercing eyes, etc. (See *Witches.*) Good witches may tend to look more like fairies.

The skin color for good fairies is usually light and delicate—shell pink, lavender, orchid, pale blue, or green, gold, or silver are possibilities. Red shades, being more human, should be avoided. Metallic flakes or sequins are sometimes used. The flakes usually adhere to greasepaint. If they don't, you might try rubber-mask grease, or you might use stubble paste (see Appendix A) as an adhesive. Sequins can be attached with a latex adhesive or spirit gum.

The features should be delicate and well formed. The ears may or may not be pointed. A delicate lip coloring should be used but no cheek rouge. The eyebrows and sometimes the eyes may be slanted. The hair of female fairies is usually long and golden.

Ghosts

Ghosts are usually thought of as being pale and rather indistinct. Highlighting is, of course, essential in achieving an appropriate ghostly effect. As for the makeup, pale, bloodless colors—such as white or lighter, grayed tints of blue, lavender, greenish yellow, or yellowish green—might be used. The bone structure can be highlighted with white or pale tints of the base color and shadowed with gray, especially in the eye sockets, which should be the most deeply shadowed areas of the face. Hair on the head and on the face can be white or gray.

The ghost of a specific character should usually resemble the character—except, of course, in color. The makeup in Figure 13-10E, though not intended as the makeup of a ghost, might, with less warmth in the coloring, be so used.

A gray nylon stocking worn over the face (with or without makeup underneath) will increase the effect of ghostliness.

Gnome

Gnomes are commonly thought of as living underground. They are always mischievous and nearly always unfriendly. They may be very ugly, even deformed. A long nose, prominent cheekbones, jutting brow and receding forehead, pointed chin, receding chin, fat cheeks, sunken cheeks, large ears, very bushy eyebrows, no eyebrows, pop eyes, small and beady eyes, and bulging forehead are possible characteristics. Older gnomes may have long and flowing beards. The skin may be very wrinkled and either very pale or very sallow. (Figure 20-21)

Goblins

Goblins are believed to be evil and mischievous. Rough and swarthy skin, slanted slits for eyes, enormous mouths, flat or long and carrot-shaped noses, extremely large ears, and pointed teeth are possibilities to be considered in the makeup.

Grotesques

Grotesques are creatures (human or nonhuman) that are in some way distorted or bizarre. The Weird Sisters in *Macbeth* are sometimes made up as Grotesques.

Monsters

This category covers a variety of creatures, from mechanical men to werewolves. If the monster is to be animalistic, the hair should grow low on the forehead and perhaps cover a good deal of the face. The nose usually needs to be widened and flattened. False teeth made to look like fangs will make the monster more terrifying. But if the creature is to appear in a children's play, it should be conceived with some discretion. Gory details, such as blood streaming from an open wound and eyes torn out of their sockets, might well be saved, if they are to be used at all, for adult horror plays. Foreheads can be raised and heads squared off, eyes rearranged, teeth made large and protruding, and so on. Skin-texture techniques—tissue with latex, tissue and spirit gum, latex and bran or cornmeal—can be used to good effect.

Ogres

An ogre is usually conceived to be a hideous monster who feeds on human beings. Prosthetic applications will undoubtedly be needed. You might consult the suggestions for making up a gnome and then exaggerate them.

Pan

Pan is the mythological Greek god of forests, flocks, and pastures. His head and body are those of an elderly man, and his lower parts are those of a goat. He is usually depicted with horns.

Pierrot

Pierrot and Pierrette are often made up with a white foundation covering all exposed flesh. Ivory or very pale pink can be used if preferred. The lips should be small and quite red with a pronounced cupid's bow. The natural brows should be blocked out and high arched ones painted on with black eyebrow pencil. The eyes should be well defined, and the rouge should be two round spots. For a more completely stylized makeup, rouge, lips, and eyebrows might all be in the shape of diamonds or other simple geometric figures. The design of the costume should harmonize.

Statuary

All exposed flesh should be made up, the color depending on the color of the material of which the statue is supposedly made. Grays, grayed blues, grayed greens, and grayed violets are useful for shadowing. Avoid warm tones unless the statue is of a color that would require warm shadows. Whether or not the makeup should be powdered will depend on the material of which the statue is supposedly made. If the finish would naturally be shiny, a creme or a grease foundation without powder can be used. A dull finish requires a water-soluble or a powdered creme or grease foundation.

Gold, silver, or bronze statues can be made with metallic body makeup. The effect is excellent, but the technique should be used with care (see discussion in Appendix A under *Metallic Makeup*).

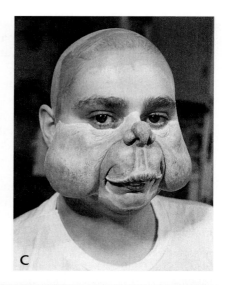
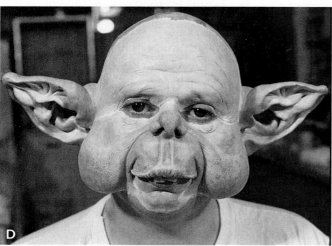

FIGURE 20-21 **Foam latex Gnome.** *By TEXA FX Group using GM Foam System for a French children's television show. A. Clay sculpt by Stephan Tessier. B. Subject, Olivier Xavier. C. Application of Glatzan bald cap, foam cheeks, and chin using Pros-Aide adhesive. For perfect edges, brush Pros-Aide on the skin and let dry; apply prosthetic; paint a little 70% isopropyl alcohol onto appliance edge (it will soak through and reactivate the glue); seal edges with Pros-Aide. D. Forehead and ears are attached and painted with PAX, PAX Wash, and a touch of rubber-mask greasepaint. E. Wig and beard are pre-shaped on a form and set with Krylon Crystal Clear then applied with matte spirit gum. (Makeup and photographs by Stephan Tessier of TEXA FX Group of Quebec, Canada.)*

Toys

Makeup for toys other than dolls—as, for example, tin or wooden soldiers or marionettes (see Figure 20-20)—can best be copied from the actual toys. Their unreality should be stressed in order to counteract the obvious lifelike qualities of the actor.

Trolls

Trolls live underground or in caves and are usually thought of as being stupid, ugly, and hateful. They have been described as having large, flabby noses, enormous ears, rotten teeth, and disgusting skin. For the skin, the face might be covered with latex over mounds of derma wax. For a rougher texture, miller's bran could be added. (For wonderful illustrations of trolls, goblins,

brownies, elves, and other fairy creatures, see *Faeries,* a book by Brian Froud and Alan Lee.)

Vampires

A vampire is a preternatural being that spends its days in a coffin and comes out only at night to drink blood. Since it never sees the light of day, it invariably has a pale, bloodless complexion—with the exception of the lips, which are sometimes abnormally red. Dark hair is conventional, with dark eyebrows slanting upward. The face should usually be thin and rather emaciated.

Witches

Traditional witches (see Figure 20-22), usually have sharp, hooked noses, prominent cheek-

FIGURE 20-22 Witch from *Snow White and the Seven Dwarfs*. *Derma wax on chin, nose, and knuckles. Makeup by student Nancie Underwood.*

FIGURE 20-23 Three witches, a devil, and a demon.

bones, sunken cheeks, thin lips, small sunken eyes, prominent pointed chins, numerous wrinkles, straggly hair, clawlike hands, warts and hair on the face, and seldom more than one or two good teeth. The complexion may be light or dark, sallow or swarthy, gray or puce. It might even be yellow, red, blue, green, or violet.

Witches can, however, be good or bad, young or old, ugly or beautiful. And the makeup can be realistic or stylized. Whereas a wicked old witch might have a face the texture and color of a dried apple, a good young witch might have a face of alabaster with hair of metallic gold. A bad (but sophisticated) young witch, on the other hand, could have a face with a glint of steel, slashed with jet black eyebrows over heavily lashed, slanted eyes. And then there are those witches who look exactly like everybody else and not like witches at all.

PROBLEMS

1. Make sketches for makeups based on visual images suggested to you by three of the following adjectives: Gross. Mean. Fantastic. Disoriented. Confused. Odd. Square. Melting. Broken. Discordant. Eroded. Slimy. Strange. Startled.

2. Design a realistic and a nonrealistic makeup for the same character.

3. Design two makeups for nonrealistic characters from plays, and execute one of the makeups. Following are some suggestions for possible characters: Oberon, Titania, Puck, Peaseblossom (*A Midsummer Night's Dream*); Mephistopheles; one of the Witches (*Macbeth*); Ko-ko, Pooh-Bah, Katisha, the Mikado (*The Mikado*); The Green Thing (*The Gods of the Mountain*); Red Queen, White Queen (*Through the Looking Glass*); King of Hearts, Queen of Hearts (*Alice in Wonderland*); He (*He Who Gets Slapped*); Ariel, Caliban (*The Tempest*); Elvira (*Blithe Spirit*); Pagliacci; Ghost (*Hamlet*); Trolls (*Peer Gynt*); Insects (*The Insect Comedy*); one of the Orcs (*Lord of the Rings*).

Makeup Materials

The following pages contain an alphabetical listing of materials from various makeup companies. The materials can be obtained directly from the companies, from makeup supply houses, or occasionally from your local drugstore. Addresses of the makeup companies and various distributors of their makeup are listed in Appendix B.

Absorbent Cotton Used for stuffing in the cheeks to enlarge them and for building up the face, neck, or hands in combination with spirit gum or latex.

Accent Colors Colors used to "accent" the face, such as rouge, lipstick, and eye makeup, or to decorate it—as in clown, Kabuki, or other stylized makeups. Bright reds, oranges, yellows, blues, greens, purples, and all metallic colors are in this category. These are available from the various makeup companies in creme makeup, cake makeup, and greasepaint and are listed, in their brochures, under various headings—Lining Colors, Cheek Color, Rouge, Lipstick, Eyeshadow, Pressed Shadow, and so forth.

Acetone A clear liquid, highly flammable solvent used to remove many adhesives and collodion from skin, brushes, and hairpieces. Also used to melt (trim) edges of plastic bald caps and dissolve dried Pros-Aide. It can be mixed with isopropyl myristate to increase its cutting power during cleanups. It can be added to green soap and baby oil to create an effective prosthetic adhesive remover (mix 1 part baby oil to 6 parts acetone to 13 parts green soap). Since it evaporates very rapidly, it should be kept tightly sealed. When reference to acetone is made, it means *pure* acetone and **not nail polish remover.** Obtainable at paint and hardware stores. Avoid breathing the fumes, and keep it away from the eyes.

Adhesives

Spirit gum the adhesive most frequently used for attaching wigs, beards, and mustaches. Made from tree sap or synthetic resin it can be thinned with acetone. It can also be made to dry extremely fast when thinned with a small amount of Hexane. "Matte" sprit gum can be made by adding TS-100. The water soluble variety is practical for practice work and "speed" lay-on jobs (laying or building a beard directly onto the face with crepe or natural hair).

Duo (eyelash or surgical adhesive) is a cream latex-based adhesive used for attaching false eyelashes and for stippling to help conceal edges of prosthetic pieces. Works well for "stretch and stipple" aging jobs as well. Available at local drugstores.

Medical adhesive (prosthetic adhesive, silicone adhesive, prosthetic "A") is a quick drying, silicone-based adhesive for applying prosthetics. This product is also good for rubber (not plastic) bald caps. Available from Ben Nye, Paramount, Graftobian, Mehron, RCMA, Bob Kelly. Joe Blasco's adhesive is called Sensitex.

Pros-Aide I and II (prosthetic "B," acrylic adhesive) from ADM-Tronics is a milky colored acrylic water-based emulsion adhesive that dries clear and becomes a flexible acrylic non-water-based material when dry. It is generally used for applying prosthetics and plastic bald caps. It is used to make PAX paint and Bondo. Can be diluted by as much as 24 parts water to 1 part Pros-Aide. Pros- Aide II is not quite as strong or as difficult to remove as Pros-Aide I. Prosthetic adhesive "B" called Special Adhesive II is available from Kryolan.

Beta Bond a strong adhesive used to attach gelatin and foam latex appliances. Available from Premiere Products.

FIGURE A-1 **Adhesives and removers.** *(From l-r) A. Pros-Aide I and II (the Original and the Sequel) by ADM Tronics, Inc.; B. Pros-Aide by Burman Industries, Inc.; C. Pros-Aide Remover by ADM Tronics, Inc.; D. Super Solv Adhesive Remover by Premiere Products, Inc.; E. Telesis Beta Solv and Beta Bond Adhesive and Remover by Premiere Products, Inc.; F. Duo Surgical Adhesive; G. Sensitex Appliance Adhesive by Joe Blasco; H. Spirit Gum by Mehron; I. Matte Spirit Gum by Joe Blasco.*

Telesis IV and V replacement adhesives for Dow 355. "V" is less expensive and behaves most like 355, except for a slightly slower drying time. Available from Premiere Products.

(Tips for using adhesives: spirit gum on lace goods; eyelash adhesive and latex around the eyes; spirit gum for quick changes of rubber noses and prosthetic adhesives for extended wear; Pros-Aide for plastic bald caps; and medical adhesive for rubber bald caps). See Figure A-1.

Adhesive Removers These solvents are used to remove a variety of adhesives from skin, wig lace, and prosthetic appliances. Adhesive removers are generally available from the companies providing the adhesives and should be ordered at the same time.

Bond Off A mild solvent used to quickly remove either medical adhesives or spirit-gum residue from the skin or prosthetic. Available from Ben Nye.

Detachol Strong, but gentle remover for adhesives, prosthetics, and heavy makeup applications. Available from Alcone, Namies, Factor II.

Super Solv Non-oily, hydrocarbon-based, pleasant scented, extra-strength adhesive and prosthetic remover. Allows rapid removal of adhesives and prosthetics without damage to appliances and latex pieces. Available from Premiere Products, Inc.

Isopropyl Myristate This is the gentlest adhesive remover and must be used with patience.

Orange Solvent An excellent remover for oily residues on just about anything.

244 Remover A Dow Corning class of cyclic silicones designed to dissolve oils and greases. Removes makeup without leaving the skin greasy. Also removes medical adhesives. Available from Alcone and Namies.

Prosthetic "A" Thinner Used as a thinner and solvent for medical adhesives. It also thins Telesis and other silicone materials such as Flesh Putty.

RCMA Adhesive Remover A highly efficient cleanser for removing all types of RCMA adhesives and sealers from the skin. Not designed for cleaning lace hair pieces.

RCMA Adklen A professional adhesive remover in a semi-solid formulation that does not run.

RJS Adhesive Remover This is a very gentle, thick cream-type remover for adhesives and adhesive residue. The thinner green-colored type is used for general cleanup.

M.E.K. (Methyl Ethyl Ketone) A strong, flammable solvent used in bald cap plastic and other effects plastic. Requires good ventilation. This product is a known carcinogen.

Hexane An extremely strong solvent used to "melt" edges of rubber bald caps. It can be used to dilute some adhesives to help them dry faster. Use sparingly and with proper ventilation. This product is a known carcinogen.

Adhesive Tape Occasionally used to draw the skin in order to change the shape of the eyes or the mouth or to construct false Oriental or sagging eyelids. A clear plastic tape called Dermacil is available in drugstores in ½-inch and 1-inch widths.

Kryolan has a clear plastic tape in ½-inch and 2-inch widths as well as an unusually effective double-faced adhesive tape, which comes in large and small rolls and is made with a very thin layer of strong adhesive on a brown paper tape. When the tape has been pressed into place, the brown paper is peeled off, leaving the adhesive. In using the tape, *tear* off the length you want–don't cut it. Tearing the tape makes it much easier to separate the tape from the brown paper. The same type of tape is also available from Bob Kelly and other wigmakers in precut, short strips packaged in small plastic boxes for the convenience of toupee wearers who want to carry a small supply of tape with them.

All Kryolan tapes are available from Alcone and from the various Kryolan distributors. Both cloth and plastic toupee tape can be obtained from wigmakers, and both can be used to attach mustaches and beards for quick changes, as well as to secure toupees. (See Toupee Tape).

AF (Appliance Foundation) Thinner A thinner and extender formulated for use with prosthetic makeup and rubber-mask greasepaint. Available from RCMA.

Alcohol 99% isopropyl is the usual type for makeup purposes. 70% is also effective, but leaves a slight residue. They can be used to thin temporary tattoo inks, to revive dried inks, and to thin prosthetic colors (although RMGP may lose some of its workability). The high percentage alcohols can also be used as a solvent to remove prosthetics in a manner that will allow them to be saved for additional use. Alcohol can cause dryness and skin irritation, but is handy in a pinch. Obtainable at local drugstores.

Alginate A non-reusable impression powder for taking face casts and duplicating molds. It comes in regular and prosthetic grade and in a variety of formulas based on working time (3 min., 6 min., 8 min.) Available from dental supply stores, Burman Industries, Cinemafx, Namies, Frends, Complexions, and Alcone. (See Chapter 14.)

Antishine Products designed to control shiny skin and maintain a matte finish under hot studio conditions. They are completely transparent allowing the natural skin tone to appear through. Can be applied under and over foundations. Available in light, medium and dark from Make-up International Ltd. as Supermatte Antishine and from Mehron as Touch Up.

Aquacolor Wet Makeup A Kryolan moist cake makeup. Available in three sizes and many shades.

There is also a water-soluble, nonmetallic makeup in gold, silver, copper, and bronze called Aquacolor-Interferenz. Both have excellent coverage. (See also *Cake Makeup*.)

Atomizers Useful for spraying diluted spirit gum on crepe hair to help it hold its shape, and alcohol on the face and on rubber pieces to remove spirit gum.

Bald Caps See *Plastic and Rubber Caps*.

Barrier Products In cream, spray, and paint on types, barrier products are water and perspiration resistant formulas applied to the skin to reduce irritation from cosmetics and adhesives and to increase the adhesion of prosthetic devices. Available as Kryolan's Fixer Spray, Mehron's Barrier Spray, Blasco's Sta-Spray, Factor II's Skin Prep, ADM Tronic's Aquacream, and Premiere Products' Top Guard.

Beard Block (See Figure 15-14.) A shaped wooden block used in ventilating beards. Available from wigmakers' supply houses. A plastic beard block mounted on an aluminum pipe is available from Bob Kelly. (See Figure 15-6.) Urethane beard and face blocks with plastic pipes in the back and at the neck are available from Mane-Sta and Makeup Designory. A plaster cast of the actor's head can be substituted if no beard block is available or if a more nearly perfect fit is required. The hair-lace can be taped to the plaster with masking tape. If you want to attach the plaster head to a wig-block holder, embed a 1-inch pipe into the plaster while it is still wet–the pipe will fit over a standard holder.

Beard Stubble Adhesive An adhesive wax in stick form used to attach beard stubble for an unshaven effect. It is made by Kryolan and is available from their distributors. Bob Kelly has a somewhat similar product called *Beard Stubble Adhesive Stick*.

Beards Instructions for making beards can be found in Chapter 15. Excellent ready-made ventilated beards and mustaches are available from Kryolan. (See Figure A-2, A-3.) Ready-made beards can also be purchased from Alcone, some wigmakers, and retail costume companies. Made-to-order beards and wigs are available from Bob Kelly.

Black Wax Used for blocking out teeth. It is softened in the hand, then applied to the teeth to be blocked out after they have been dried with a tissue. It can also be used to block out parts of teeth to make them appear broken or uneven. It can be removed with a dry tissue. Black tooth enamel (see *Tooth Enamel*) serves the same purpose. Using black eyebrow pencil as a substitute for black wax is discussed in Chapter 12. Black wax is

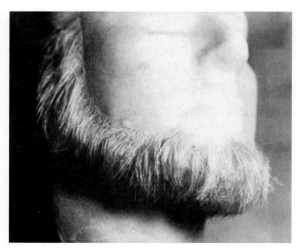

FIGURE A-2 Ready-made beard. *Available from Kryolan.*

FIGURE A-3 Ready-made goatee. *Available from Kryolan.*

available from Stein; black and brown from Graftobian and Bob Kelly. (See Tooth Enamel).

Blemish-Cover Sticks These are small makeup sticks in lipstick cases used to cover skin blemishes or minimize wrinkles. They usually come in a limited number of shades, ranging from light to medium flesh tones. The lighter shades can also be used for highlighting. They are particularly useful for quick changes (see Chapter 19). Available as Kryolan's Erase, Ben Nye's Creme Neutralizing Crayons, William Tuttle's Concealor Pencils.

Blood, Artificial Stage blood can be classified into two categories, according to the use to which it is to be put—external (used outside the body) or internal (flowing from the mouth). External blood should never be used internally. For internal blood, gelatin capsules, obtainable from your local pharmacist and makeup effects store in various sizes, can be filled with blood formulated specifically for internal use, held in the mouth,

then crushed at the appropriate time to release the blood. (For certain external uses, capsules of blood can be held in the hand and crushed.) In deciding which brand of blood to use, you should consider the ease with which the blood can be removed from costumes and from the skin. Some brands of blood can be wiped off the skin easily without leaving a stain, whereas others leave a temporary stain, which can be removed with soap and water. Consider also the thickness of the blood and how believable it looks as it runs on the skin. The color, of course, should also be believable.

Artificial blood is obtainable from makeup companies and their distributors. It often comes in fresh, old, dried, arterial, and veinal colors; and in regular, thick, squirting, and coagulated formulas. The following list includes the company and the type of blood product they carry: Ben Nye, Stage Blood, Thick Blood (arterial gel), and Fresh Scab; Mehron, Stage Blood, Dark Blood, Squirt Blood, and Coagulated Blood Gel; Joe Blasco, Artificial Blood, Artificial Blood (Dark), Old Dried Blood; Bob Kelly, Artificial Blood; Kryolan, Transparent Blood (non-staining, non-drying), Special Film Blood (washable), Fixblood (waterproof, quick-drying, peelable), Magic Blood Powder (appears in contact with component B), Fresh Scab, and Eye Blood; Graftobian, Stage Blood, Blood Gel, and Blood Paste; Cinema Secrets, FX Blood, Blood Gel, and Mouth Blood; Paramount, Stage Blood, bags and capsules; Reel Creations, Inc.–Reel Blood Original Formula, Lung Blood (for dark skin, dark clothes, dark surfaces), Aged Blood, and Thick Blood (fresh, aged, and dried); K.D. 151 Blood, Blood Jam and Jelly, Mouth Blood, Flowing Blood Syrup, Pumping Blood, Drying Blood Jelly, and RCMA Blood Type A, B, C, and D.

The above list includes blood for external use, blood for internal use, blood for bloodshot eyes, washable blood, thick blood, packets of blood (external and internal), capsules of powdered blood (internal), and plastic blood in tubes (called *Fixblood*) for a dried blood effect. The *Fixblood* dries quickly, does not rub off, and is removed with acetone. Kryolan also has what they call *Magic Blood,* consisting of two reacting chemicals, both liquid, one of which is applied to the skin and allowed to dry. Then, at whatever point the other liquid touches it, the two chemicals combine and turn dark red. This might be used, for example, by applying one liquid to the skin and the other to a dull knife blade, then drawing the blade lightly across the skin to create the effect of a cut. Magic Blood should, however, be used cautiously. *It is not a toy, it should not be played with, and it should not be used by children. It should never be used near the eyes or any mucous membranes. It should be applied only on normal, healthy skin, and it should be removed thoroughly after use.*

Fabulous, a product parenthetically known as *sunburn gel stain,* can also simulate coagulated blood from cuts and gashes. Available from Cinema Secrets.

FIGURE A-4 Blood products from REEL Creations, Inc.

FIGURE A-5 MagiColor Face and Body Paint. *Available from Ben Nye.*

For blood coming from the mouth, Cinema Secrets' *Mouth Blood* (mint flavored and formulated specifically for use in the mouth) is excellent in both color and consistency. Red toothpaste can also be used. Mixing it with adhesive powder for false teeth will produce an effect of dried blood.

Body Makeup Available as an opaque liquid, a transparent liquid, or a powder. Opaque liquid body makeup is a greaseless foundation comparable to cake makeup except that it is in liquid form. It can be obtained from Mehron (111 Liquid Makeup), Visiora (CN-Liquid Body Makeup), Kryolan (Aquacolor Liquid and Liquid Body Makeup), William Tuttle, Joe Blasco, Ben Nye (MagiColor), Dinair (Airbrush Cosmetics), in a variety of shades. It is applied with a sponge, brush, or airbrush and is removable with soap and water or makeup remover. REEL Creations, Inc. manufactures a waterproof body makeup that is easily sprayed on with an airbrush or pump-type sprayer. Another body makeup called Dansproof is specifically formulated for professional dancers. Dansproof is a water resistant, self-setting creme foundation that does not require powder. Available from Kryolan. (See also *Texas Dirt, Character Powders* and *Metallic Makeup*.)

Bondo (PAX putty, PAX butter) Thickened Pros-Aide that can be used to fill in holes, build up shapes, or to smooth out and blend edges of prosthetic appliances and bald caps. It is made by mixing just enough Cab-O-Sil with Pros Aide to prevent the mixture from running. Apply the mixture with a flat dental spatula or a small wedge of red stipple sponge. The name "PAX butter" refers to the same material when made with PAX paint (colored). Can be removed with PAX AT-TAX by Art Anthony and PAX On-PAX Off by Foam Paint Products or other Pros-Aide removers.

Brush Cleaner A liquid for cleaning and disinfecting brushes. It comes in bottles, canisters, and spray bottles. Available from Ben Nye, Mehron, Kryolan, Parian Spirit, Cinema Secrets, and Brush Off by Crosby & Co. Makeup removers and shampoo are also effective.

Brushes, Chinese or Japanese (See Figure A-7F.) Watercolor brushes with a fine, sharp point, useful in accenting wrinkles. Obtainable at art supply stores and in some Asian import shops.

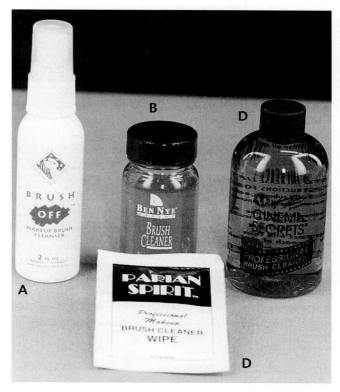

FIGURE A-6 Brush cleaners. A. Brush Off. B. Ben Nye. C. Cinema Secrets. D. Parian Spirit.

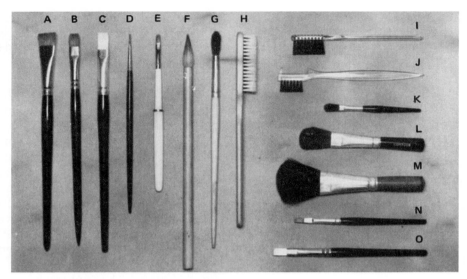

FIGURE A-7 **Brushes.** *A-B. Long-handled flat sable brushes (Kryolan). C. Long-handled flat synthetic brush (Ben Nye). D. Long-handled pointed sable brush (Kryolan). E. Sable lip brush in white plastic holder (Kryolan). F. Pointed Chinese water-color brush. G. Camel's hair utility brush (Bob Kelly). H. Brush for cleaning hairlace. I. Eyebrow brush. J. Eyebrow brush-and-comb (Kryolan). K. Soft brush for applying dry eyeshadow. L. Contour or rouge brush. M. Powder brush (Mehron). N. Short-handled flat sable brush. O. Short-handled flat synthetic brush (Bob Kelly).*

Brushes, Dye (See Figure A-7H.) Also called hair coloring brushes are available in various forms. Some are shaped like toothbrushes and can be used for applying spirit-gum remover to hairlace in removing wigs, toupees, beards, and mustaches. Available from Alcone, Namies, and Frends.

Brushes, Eyebrow (See Figure A-7I.) Used for brushing the eyebrows. Available from Joe Blasco, Mehron, Kryolan, and Bob Kelly. Eyebrow brushes combined with tiny eyebrow combs (Figure A-7J) are also available.

Brushes, Eyeliner High-quality, sable eyeliner brushes are available from Joe Blasco and from Kryolan. The handle of the Blasco brush is shorter and rounded at the end—a worthwhile safety factor when working around the eyes.

Brushes, Eyeshadow (see Figure A-7K.) Small, soft brushes used to apply pressed eyeshadow. They are also useful for applying dry rouge in small areas, such as wrinkles.

Brushes, Lip (See Figure A-7E.) Narrow, flat brushes used for applying lip rouge. Mehron and Kryolan have excellent short-handled sable ones. Joe Blasco has a retractable lip brush in a metal case.

Brushes, Mascara Small, stiff-bristled brushes for applying mascara.

Brushes, Powder and Rouge (See Figure A-7M and L.) The quality of powder and rouge brushes can be judged to a very large extent by the softness of the bristles.

Brushes, Shading (See Figure A-7A, B, N, and O.) Several flat—preferably sable—brushes of various widths and in long and short handle lengths are practically indispensable in doing character makeups. The bristles should be fine, tapered, and very springy. Wedge-cut bristles are especially useful for modeling nasolabial folds, for highlighting and shadowing around the eyes, and for modeling forehead wrinkles. Sable and synthetic brushes can also be obtained from art supply stores and from all major cosmetic distributors. The often inconveniently long handles can be cut down if you wish.

Brushes, Utility (See Figure A-7G.) Can be used to apply sealer, spirit gum, or collodion. They are available from most cosmetic manufacturers and their distributors or at artists' supply stores.

Burlap An open weave material dipped into plaster and used to reinforce molds.

Cab-O-Sil A fumed silica powder used as a thixotropic agent or thickener. Add to Pros-Aide to make "bondo" or to PAX to make "PAX butter." It will thicken just about any liquid. It can also be used as a matting agent for most adhesives and as a "dulling powder" over various makeup applications. Avoid inhaling this product (use a dust or particle mask). Available from Alcone, Burman Industries.

Cake Makeup A greaseless, water-soluble foundation that is applied dry or with a dampened sponge. There are two types—dry and moist. Kryolan makes a moist type called Aquacolor. (See *Aquacolor Wet Makeup*.) Blending highlights and shadows is somewhat easier with moist cake makeup than with dry. The moist type is also better for stippling. Dry cake makeup is available as Mehron's StarBlend, Max Factor Pan Cake (only the theatrical line has been discontinued), Ben Nye's Color Cake Foundations, and Bob Kelly's Cake Foundations.

Camouflage Creme See *Dermaceal, Dermacolor,* and *Tattoo Covers*.

Carcinogenic A term used to define a product that is known to cause cancer.

Casting Fiber Made of long fibered hemp, this material is used for reinforcing plaster molds.

Castor Oil A highly emollient carrier oil that serves to bind together ingredients of cosmetic formulations such as rubber-mask greasepaint (RMGP). On its own it is ideal for coating latex appliances so creme makeups can be used for coloration (not as effective as using RMGP). Sold as Castor Sealer by Ben Nye and Castor Seal by Graftobian. Available at your local pharmacy.

F I G U R E A - 8 Cake makeup and cream stick by Bob Kelly.

Castorsil A mixture of Cab-O-Sil and castor oil. The resultant gel is mixed with an oil-based liner color to make a non-runny, subtly tinted glaze used to color Old Age Stipple, prosthetic appliances, and three-dimensional latex and gelatin makeups. Glazes are more natural looking than opaque colors and can be built up gradually.

Chamois Can be used to press down the net in attaching hairlace wigs, beards, and mustaches with spirit gum. Can also be used in applying crepe hair. Available at most art supply, paint, or hardware stores.

Character Powders A variety of pigmented powders used on the face, body, and costume to resemble dirt (Texas Dirt by Bob Kelly; Mehron's Texas Dirt in Plain, Silver, Gold, Trail Dust, and Charred Ash; Ben Nye's Plains Dust and Ash Powder [also called Fuller's Earth]; Joe Blasco's Movie Dust; and Paramount's Dry Dirt Powder), powder burns and grease effects (Ben Nye's Charcoal Powder; Paramount's Black Powder) and character face colors (Bob Kelley's Frankenstein Grey and Clown White; Paramount's Death Green; Ben Nye's Super White, and Kryolan's TL 1 White). Powders also come suspended in solutions for spraying, painting, or sponging on skin and costumes. These are available from Joe Blasco as Sta-Charcoal, Sta-Dirt (in several colors) and Simulated Crude Oil; from Transformations Makeup FX Lab as Trans-Mud in light, medium, dark, and red clay, and Trans-Grease in black and green.

Cleansing Tissues Indispensable for removing makeup. They can also be used for creating three-dimensional skin texture (see Chapter 13).

Clown White An opaque white makeup used primarily for clowns. Available from Ben Nye, Mehron, Kryolan, Graftobian, and Bob Kelly.

Cold-Foam Systems A two-part foam system that you mix according to manufacturers' specifications. They require a release agent, a two-part mold, and a triple beam gram scale. These foam systems are hazardous to the user and to the environment and are being replaced by safer water-blown foam systems. Available as Kryolan Cold Foam System and Burman's Polysoft.

Collodion A clear, viscous solution of cellulose nitrates in alcohol and ether. There are two types of collodion—flexible and non-flexible. The flexible is used for building up three-dimensional shapes with cotton and other fillers. The non-flexible or rigid type shrinks as it dries and is used directly on the skin for making scars or pock marks (see Chapter 13). It dries quickly and can be diluted with acetone or rejuvenated with Hexane. It is available from Kryolan, Mehron, and Bob Kelly. Collodion can be peeled off the skin or removed with acetone.

Collodacolor, a pigmented collodion, is available from Michael Davy Film & TV Makeup in transparent and opaque red, transparent yellow, transparent blue/violet, matte clear, and black.

Combs A wide-toothed comb is used for combing out crepe hair and wigs. A kit should also contain a comb to be used for hair with temporary coloring in it, one to be used with clean hair, and a rat-tail comb. Eyebrow combs and brushes combined (Figure A-7J) are available from Kryolan.

Concealer An opaque, highly pigmented creme foundation used to camouflage or conceal unwanted skin discolorations, birth marks, and tattoos. Available from Joe Blasco as Dermaceal and Tattoo Cover, Ben Nye as Coverette Cover-up and Tattoo Cover, Mehron as Tattoo Cover, Kryolan as Dermacolor, REEL Creations as Cover-up Spray, and the department store cosmetic Dermablend. See *Dermaceal* and *Dermacolor*.

Condom Non-lubricated and non-ribbed condoms are used for various bladder effects when special effects makeup applications are required. They are often attached near the surface of foam latex appliances and filled with air or other materials for various effects.

Cornstarch Formerly used for graying the hair. One of the hair whiteners (see *Hair Whiteners*) should be used instead. For quick-change makeups or when the gray must be removed during the play, it may be necessary to use white face powder, which, though not satisfactory, is preferable to cornstarch.

Cotton Swabs Cotton-tipped sticks (such as Q-Tips), used for removing small areas of makeup when correcting mistakes or making minor adjustments and sometimes for blending or for applying dry rouge to small areas. They can also be used in applying latex to open molds and for removing excess latex from them.

Crayons A creme makeup in crayon form. It can be applied directly with the crayon or transferred from the crayon to the face with the fingers, a brush, or a sponge, as with regular creme makeup. Available from Mehron as a Grease Makeup Crayon and from Ben Nye as MagicColor Creme Crayons.

Creme Makeup A velvety, non-greasy makeup foundation applied with the fingers or (for highlights and shadows) with a brush. There are those who prefer to use a foam sponge for applying it as a foundation. The new, lighter varieties contain high-tech silicones in their formulas for a longer lasting natural effect. These products do not penetrate the skin or clog pores and can be removed with facial cleanser and water or makeup remover. (For applying creme makeup, see Chapter 9.)

FIGURE A-9
Creme foundation.
A. Graftobian
B. Joe Blasco

Crepe Hair Used for making beards and mustaches and occasionally eyebrows. There are two types—crepe wool and human crepe hair. Crepe wool comes in tightly woven braids and is usually purchased by the yard. It is available from most of the makeup companies and their distributors in such colors as blond, auburn, light brown, medium brown, dark brown, light gray, and medium gray. Human crepe hair is available from Kryolan and its distributors.

Dep A thick, hair-setting liquid. Available from beauty supply houses.

Depilatory A preparation for removing unwanted hair and to avoid the negative effects of shaving (particularly for men.) Products such as Clean and Easy, Magic Shave, and The Club Man are available from beauty supply stores.

Dermaceal A highly pigmented, waterproof makeup by Joe Blasco for covering skin discolorations, scars, birthmarks, burns, etc. It is available in five colors but can be made up to order in any color in the Joe Blasco line. It can be worn on the street as well as on the stage. It should be applied with one's finger rather than with a brush.

Dermacolor A very effective camouflage creme by Kryolan. It is designed primarily for street wear for both men and women to cover skin discolorations, such as birthmarks or uneven pigmentation. It can also be used for the stage to cover temporary or permanent skin discolorations difficult to cover with most stage makeup. It can be used as a foundation color over the entire face or applied only to the discolored areas, then covered with stage makeup for the overall foundation. It has been used successfully by actors who are allergic to other kinds of makeup, and it has the additional advantage of being waterproof. It can also be used as a foundation color to successfully change a skin tone from light to dark or dark to light. If you are uncertain about what shade you should have, there are two very handy mini-palettes, each containing 16 of the available colors. There are two regular sized color palettes with 12 colors each in 2 different compositions for a total of 24 colors. If no one color is exactly right, you can experiment with mixing the colors in the palette and order the ones you require. They can also be thinned with alcohol or cosmetic fluid GP-20 to create translucent skin colorations for truly natural effects. (See Figure A-10.)

Dermatex A Joe Blasco foundation makeup for use on prosthetic appliances. Available in 40 colors. It does not need to be powdered, and it will not rub off on costumes.

Derma Wax A soft wax for building up areas of the face. It is easier to apply and to remove than nose putty but is less adhesive. It can also be mixed with nose putty as explained in Chapter 13. It is available from the various makeup companies and their distributors. Ben Nye's Nose and Scar Wax and Mehron's Putty/Wax are mixtures of derma wax and putty. (See *Putty-Wax*.) Kryolan has a special wax for street wear (called Dermacolor Skin Plastic) for concealing scars. The wax is then covered with Dermacolor makeup. Mehron has a sturdy wax compound mixed with fibers called Extra Flesh for creating warts, cuts, and scars.

Drawing Mats (See Figure 15-10.) Used in wig making for drawing and blending hair.

Epoxy Parfilm A spray release for easy removal of gelatin from stone molds. Available from Burman Industries and Factor II.

Equipoise A pre-base lotion for dry skin available from Joe Blasco. Also called Blasco Pre-base.

Eyebrow Pencils Wooden pencils with soft grease lead used for darkening the eyebrows. (See *Makeup Pencils*.)

Eyebrow-Pencil Sharpeners Because ordinary pencil sharpeners are not really satisfactory for eyebrow pencils, special eyebrow-pencil sharpeners should be used. Particularly well-designed ones are available from Kryolan. Other eyebrow-pencil sharpeners can be obtained at most cosmetic counters. For giving pencils a flat cut, a single-edged razor blade or a sharp mat knife can be used. Tip: place the pencil in the refrigerator or freezer for a few minutes before sharpening to obtain a more useful point.

Eyebrow Plastic (Figure A-11) A firm wax from Bob Kelly or plastic from Kryolan in stick form for blocking out eyebrows. For further information and additional illustrations, see *Eyebrow Plastic* in the index. Available from Kryolan distributors, Bob Kelly, Alcone, and Namies.

Eyeliner Brush A narrow round brush suitable for lining the eyes. Very good sable eyeliner brushes are available from the various makeup companies and their distributors.

Eyeliners Water-soluble cake eyeliners, liquid liners, pencils, and dry powder are available in a variety of colors. Brown, charcoal, navy, and black are most often

FIGURE A-10 Dermacolor Palette and Camouflage System from Kryolan.

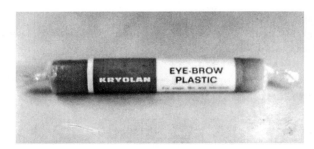

FIGURE A-11 Kryolan's Eye-Brow Plastic.

recommended. Never apply liners to the inside rim of the eye. This technique will increase the risk of injury and infection. Available from all cosmetic manufacturers. Try Nina Ricci.

Eyeshadow Available in creme and brush-on pressed powders. Available from all cosmetic manufacturers. Apply with a beveled shadow brush, sponge-tipped applicator, or your fingers.

Extrinsic Coloration Any coloration system or product added on or applied to a given surface.

Face Powder Used over creme or grease makeup to set the foundation, it will, in most cases, produce a waterproof finish. It comes in a variety of tints and shades. Translucent and no-color face powders cause less distortion in makeup colors than the regular powders and are available from the various makeup companies and their distributors. Most translucent powders, unfortunately, have some darkening effect when used over white or very light colors. Mehron's Colorset, Joe

Blasco's No-color, Ben Nye's Neutral Set Translucent, and RCMA's No-Color, however, have relatively little effect and are, therefore, recommended for any makeup in which there are light highlights.

For a light coverage over foundations, tinted loose powders are available from Kryolan, Ben Nye, Joe Blasco, Stein, Cinema Secrets, LeClerc, and Viseart. When a slightly heavier coverage (to produce a true matte finish) is needed, pressed powders such as Ben Nye's Poudre Compact, Joe Blasco's Hi-Tone Intensifier, LeClerc Pressed Powders, Visiora PC, and Viseart Poudre Compacte, can be used.

If you want to add a satiny sheen to your makeup, try Kryolan's Satin Powder, Ben Nye's Lumiere Luxe Powder, Joe Blasco's Punch-up Powders, and LeFemme Sparkle Dust. Available from the manufacturer and from Namies, Frends, and Alcone.

False Eyelashes Used for straight or corrective eye makeup. They come in individual (single and cluster), half, full, and bottom lashes. They should usually be trimmed before using. Sometimes each lash can be cut in half to make a pair (see Chapter 10). Lashes with a feathered look are available and tend to look more natural. False eyelashes can be obtained from Kryolan, Paramount, or any cosmetic counter. They are applied with special eyelash adhesive or with Duo Adhesive.

Flesh Putty A silicone putty that stays flexible yet holds texture and shape. It comes in seven translucent colors to give a realistic skin-like appearance. Sculpt or press into molds for build-ups, cuts, gashes, and bullet holes. Blends easily and tints with any powder colorant for a perfect skin match. Adheres to skin with or without adhesive and is waterproof and safe. Use with Putty Melt, a silicone solvent, to achieve a perfect blend into

FIGURE A-12 Ben Nye's loose face powder "Visage Poudre" and pressed powder *"Poudre Compacte."*

FIGURE A-13 Art Anthony's Flesh Putty, Matte Patte, Putty Melt.

the skin. Available from Art Anthony Creations and Namies. See *Nose Putty*.

Flocking Fine nylon or rayon fibers in a variety of colors used to give a "capillary" look in the manufacturing of gelatin appliances. Can also be mixed with K-Y Jelly and applied on the surface to produce similar results. See *K-Y Jelly*. Available from Burman Industries, Cinemafx, Namies Beauty Supply, and DonJer Products, Inc.

Fluorescent Makeup This makeup will glow in the dark as long as it is exposed to ultra-violet light.

Foam Latex There are several different companies that produce foam latex kits, each including their own instructions. Burman Foam, GM Foam, McLaughlin Foam, Paramount Foam, and MD (Michael Davy) Foam are some of the most recognized names. Foam latex kits are available from Alcone, Michael Davy, Burman Industries, Cinemafx, and *The Monster Makers*. (See Appendix B for suppliers and Chapter 14 for essential information).

Foam Latex Injection Gun Used to inject large quantities of foam latex or other casting material into a closed mold to produce flexible skin and body parts. Skins are often attached over mechanical skeletal structures when animated creatures are required. An open pour is when the foam latex or other casting material is placed into an open mold and then the mold is closed around it.

Foundation Colors Colors used to provide an appropriate skin color or texture (natural or matte) for the character and to serve as a foundation for *contour* and *accent colors*. Foundation colors are available in creme makeup, cake makeup, liquid, and greasepaint in a wide range of flesh colors. Foundation colors are also known as base colors.

Gafquat 734 A resin found in commercial hair spray used to control the hair. Often used to flatten the hair under bald caps. Mix with mustache wax and 70% alcohol to make H-10 (See H-10.)

Gauze, Surgical Can be dipped in plaster and used over negative moulage molds. Available in drugstores and surgical supply houses.

Gelatin Can be used for certain types of quick three-dimensional work (see Chapter 13). Also used for manufacturing gelatin appliances. An industrial quality called 300 Bloom gelatin is recommended. Available from Burman Industries, Cinemafx, and Alcone. Other gelatin-based special effects materials include Kelly's Kel-Gel, Mehron's 3-D Gel, Ben Nye's Effects Gel, Kryolan's Gelatin Kits, and Gelefects available at Burman Industries, Namies, and Alcone. Ready-made gelatin appliances (scars, cuts, bullet holes, etc.) are available from The Makeup Designory and W.M. Creations.

Glatzan L. A Kryolan product used for making bald caps. See *Plastic Film, Liquid*.

Glitter Available in a variety of colors, including gold and silver and in three forms–powder, tiny bits, and stars. The glitter can be easily attached by coating the skin with Glitter Gel, then transferring the glitter to the gel-coated area with a soft brush. Available from Ben Nye as Sparklers, Kryolan as Glitter and Glitter Stars (Moons, Dots and Hearts), Graftobian as Face Painting Glitter, Mehron as Glitter Dust.

Glitter Gel A transparent gel for attaching glitter directly to the skin or over makeup. It can be applied with the fingers and removed with water. Most manufacturers incorporate the glitter into the gel for ease of application.

Glycerin Can be brushed or sponged onto the body to resemble sweat or tears and to make it shine. It is often sold as Tears and Perspiration or Sweat and Tears. It can be used as a base for metallic powders. The powders can be either patted on over the glycerin or mixed with it before it is applied. Mehron has a *Mixing Liquid* that can

FIGURE A-14 3-D GEL (Gelatin Effects) from Mehron.

be used with metallic powders as well as with other dry pigments. Glycerin is also used as a "plasticizer" for gelatin (Chapter 14). Glycerin is available at drugstores and from most makeup manufacturers and distributors.

GP-20 A makeup base for many commercial liquid makeups. It is used as a makeup extender and works to make colors more translucent. This product can be mixed with any dry makeup or tinted powders to produce a custom "liquid" makeup. A small amount on a sponge will remove excess powder and eliminate lines under the eyes caused by makeup gathering in the creases.

Greasepaint A term derived from the use of petrolatum in the makeup is the traditional foundation paint used to give the skin basic coloring. It is made in a variety of colors and in both a soft and a hard consistency. Mehron's soft, lanolin-enriched foundation paint comes in the same type of container as their cake makeup. Kryolan's soft greasepaint comes in convenient plastic cases in three sizes. Kryolan also has greasepaint sticks in two sizes. (See also *Shading Colors* and *Creme Makeup*.)

Greasepaint (including rubber-mask greasepaint) deteriorates with age. If any makeup smells rancid, throw it out.

H-10 A material used to flatten the hair at the hairline to eliminate the "bump" under a bald cap and to control the hair around the ears and nape of neck. It is made by mixing one part Gaf Quat 734 into one part mustache wax in a double boiler. After these products are mixed completely remove from the heat (extinguish the flame) and slowly add one part 70% alcohol (all measurements are by volume). Note: the flame must be extinguished before adding the flammable alcohol. H-10 is applied with a toothbrush or dental spatula. This product will hold hair in most any position.

Hackle An instrument combining the functions of a comb and a brush, constructed of metal spikes in a wooden block, used for combing or untangling skeins of hair. Available from wig making suppliers.

Hair, Human Used for fine wigs, toupees, falls, and other hairpieces, and for ventilated beards and mustaches. Waved hair comes in a loose corkscrew curl that forms a natural wave in the wig. Unlike crepe hair, real hair should not normally be straightened before use. It is usually available in lengths from 10 to 24 inches, in a variety of colors, and is sold by the pound (or the ounce). The price per pound varies with the length and the color. Available from DeMeo Brothers, California Merchandise Company, and Giovanni & Son. Human crepe hair is available from Kryolan.

Hair, Synthetic See discussion in Chapter 15. Synthetic hair with a high sheen is suitable only for certain stylized wigs and beards. Synthetic hair of a better quality can be used as a substitute for human hair or blended with human hair. Available from Kryolan and California Merchandise Company in a number of shades, which can easily be mixed. Synthetic hair is sold by the ounce and is considerably cheaper than human hair.

Hair, Yak Sometimes used for wigs but more often for beards and mustaches. It is also less expensive than human hair. See Figure A-15.

Hair Coloring Temporary color sprays are available from Kryolan and Stein and at drugstores and cosmetic counters. Kryolan has a number of opaque shades that can be used for covering dark hair with light colors. REEL Hair Color Palettes are available for the makeup artist and hairstylists who need many colors at their disposal without the inconvenience of open bottles and confined spaces. The palette is used for quick, long-lasting hair touch-ups (sideburns, mustaches, eyebrows, highlights, and shadows) and for scalp shadow to conceal balding areas. See Chapter 16 for more information.

Hair Dryer Can be used to speed the drying time of latex and other rather slow-drying liquids and, of course, for drying hair. Make sure the one you use does not contain asbestos. Available at drugstores, appliance shops, department stores, etc. (Do not use a heat gun for drying hair or wigs.)

Hairlace See *Wig Lace.*

Hair Spray A spray used for keeping the hair in place. (See also *Hair Coloring.*) Colorless hair sprays are available in drugstores, at cosmetic counters, and from Kryolan. Colored, Glitter, and Fluorescent hair sprays are available from Kryolan and Stein.

FIGURE A-15 Yak hair wig and beard by makeup artist Joe Rossi.

FIGURE A-16 Brändel Temporary hair color sprays from Kryolan.

Hair Whiteners Adding white makeup or hair color to dark hair often produces a slightly bluish cast. This can be avoided by mixing a small amount of yellow into the white product. Most of the temporary *Hair Whiteners,* on the market have been formulated to avoid this problem. Ben Nye has excellent liquid whiteners in Silver Grey and Snow White that produce a very natural effect. Bob Kelly has creme formulas in Grey-white and Yellow-white and a liquid Silver-grey. Kryolan has a liquid called Temple White, and Mehron has two liquids called Hair White and Hair Silver. All are available from the makeup companies and their distributors.

Highlight Colors Contour colors used for highlighting in corrective and character makeups. The values in standardized numbers usually range from 1 to 3½ for light and medium highlights, the hues from FS to OF, and the values from a to d.

Ice Powder Simulates frost and ice when sprayed with water. Available from Namies.

Intrinsic coloration Dry or liquid colorant added to a product before it is used, therefore becoming an essential part of that product. For example, mix Bob Kelly's cosmetic grade pigments into latex to match skin tones.

Key A key is attached or built into plaster, stone, or silicone multi-part closed molds to insure proper alignment and stability between parts. A key can be a small circular indentation, a wedge-shaped block, or a narrow slanted rail along the outer edge of the mold. See Figure A-17.

Krylon Crystal Clear A brand-name clear acrylic spray used to coat clay sculptures to protect the clay surface during the mold making process. There are other brands available. Before you choose another brand make sure the drying time is less than fifteen minutes. Available at art supply and hardware stores. (Note: Do

not confuse the Krylon Paint brand name with the Kryolan Cosmetic Corporation.)

K-Y Lubricating Jelly Can be used in blending nose putty and derma wax. Can also be used as a protective film over a grease or creme makeup, then removed for a quick change (see Chapter 19). Mix red flocking with K-Y and apply over the foundation to create the effect of broken blood vessels. Available in drugstores in large and small tubes.

Latex, Liquid Used for building up flexible prosthetic pieces (see Chapter 14), attaching crepe hair (Chapter 15), or creating wrinkles and texture for age (Chapter 13). Latex is normally off-white but can be colored by the addition of small amounts of concentrated vegetable dye, food coloring, cosmetic grade pigments, or pigment dispersions (highly recommended) to arrive at whatever flesh tone is required. White latex dries clear; colored latex normally dries darker. If your bottle of latex has a brush in the cap, always return the cap to the bottle as quickly as possible so as not to expose the brush to the air any longer than necessary. Once latex dries on the brush, the brush is ruined. Protect your own brush by first coating the bristles with liquid soap. Citrus cleansers may also help to clean resistant latex from the brush. Rinse with distilled water rather than tap water to avoid curdling. Liquid latex is available from the

FIGURE A-17 **A matrix mold with keys.** *A Matrix Mold has two parts: the inner silicone matrix and outer plaster jacket. Notice the long narrow rails or keys placed in the center of the silicone matrix and the wedge-shaped keys placed along the edges of the plaster jacket. The rails and keys keep the mold parts securely in place during the casting process. This example was executed by makeup effects artist Robert Phillips.*

various makeup companies. Kryolan, Ben Nye, Paramount, Stein, Bob Kelly, and Graftobian have latex available in clear and/or flesh-colored in a variety of sizes. Graftobian also has latex available in six colors (see Figure A-18.) Joe Blasco's clear, deammoniated latex is called *Datex.* For coloring latex Bob Kelly offers thirteen cosmetic grade pigments; GM Foam and A-R Products offer six shades of pigment dispersions.

Because some latexes cause a burning sensation when applied to the skin, always test the product on the inner wrist before applying it to the face. The ones mentioned here are intended for use on the skin and do not normally create a burning sensation when applied. However, as sensitivity to a particular latex can vary with individuals, any latex you plan to use should be tried on your skin well in advance of the time you intend to use it.

Latex Caps (See Figures 14-12 and A-20.) For creating a bald-head effect. (See also *Plastic Caps.*) Available from Kryolan distributors, Cinema Secrets (Woochie), and Alcone. The Woochie rubber caps are thinner than the Kryolan caps and are designed to be used only once. When removed with sufficient care, however, they can usually be reused. Use appliance adhesives or medical adhesives for applying rubber caps.

Latex Pieces Ready-made latex pieces (noses, chins, pouches, Oriental eyelids, wrinkled foreheads, scars, warts, burns, etc.) are available from Kryolan, Graftobian (clown noses), Cinema Secrets (largest selection), and Paramount-Alcone. With some pieces, getting a perfect fit may not be possible. Ready-made chins and noses, for example, are usually designed to fit "average" features. Even so, they may not always fit such features perfectly since there are many possible variations in the shape of features of approximately the same size. Other pieces, such as eye pouches, are more easily adaptable.

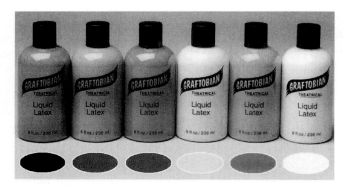

FIGURE A-19 Pigmented liquid latex from Graftobian.

Lip Rouge or Lip Color Creme makeup for coloring the lips. It is usually applied with a lip brush or lip pencil.

Lipsticks These can be used in the individual makeup kit but for sanitary reasons have no place in group kits. Use a makeup spatula to first transfer a small amount of lip color onto a palette. Then use a brush to transfer the color to the lip. This technique will safeguard against improper hygiene habits.

Liquid Makeup Any makeup in liquid form. It is usually referred to as *Body Makeup* except when it is intended only for the face. See *Body Makeup.*

Lumiere A soft, shimmery, luminescent makeup from Ben Nye in creme (Lumiere Wheel and Pencils), dry (Lumiere Grande Colour), and powder (Lumiere Luxe Powder) formulas.

FIGURE A-18 Stein's Liquid Latex

FIGURE A-20 Latex cap placed on an actor's head.

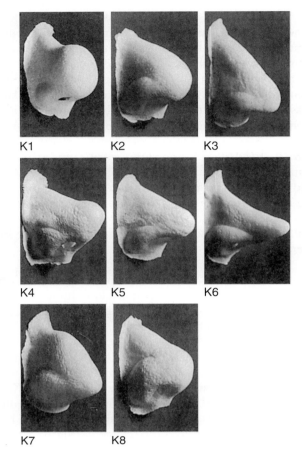

FIGURE A-21 Latex noses. *Available from Kryolan.*

FIGURE A-22 Ben Nye's Lumiere Creme Wheel.

Luminous Paints For a makeup which must glow in the dark, either fluorescent or phosphorescent paints and pigments can be used. The fluorescent ones must be excited by an ultraviolet light; the phosphorescent ones require no ultraviolet light but are less brilliant. A number of shades of both kinds of paints and pigments are available from Kryolan distributors as Luminous UV and UV Dayglo colors, from Paramount as Luminous Makeup, and from Stein's as Phosphorescent and Fluorescent Makeup.

Makeup, Non-Allergenic This term is used to describe a cosmetic product that will not produce allergic reactions on most people. Makeup which is advertised as being non-allergenic may be successful with some individuals and not with others. Non-allergenic or hypoallergenic is usually applied to most oil-free, fragrance-free or to cosmetics with a specific type of preservative. Allergenicity is not a matter of the product but rather the sensitivity of the individual. Products with plant extracts and essential oils pose a greater risk of allergic reactions. Kryolan's Dermacolor (see *Dermacolor*), a high-quality camouflage makeup, has also been used very successfully by individuals with allergy problems when non-allergenic makeups have failed.

Makeup Cape Used for protecting the clothing. Alcone has a translucent white plastic cape, and Kryolan has a plastic bib for covering just the shoulders and the chest.

Makeup Kits (See Figures 8-1, A-23.) Student kits, boxed themed kits, and film and video kits are available from Ben Nye, Joe Blasco, Bob Kelly, Kryolan, Mehron, Graftobian, and Zauder's in creme, creme stick, cake makeup, and moist cake makeup formulas. They usually contain foundations, liner colors, cheek colors, lip colors, shadow and highlights, eyebrow and eyeliner pencils, nose and scar wax (nose putty), hair color, translucent powder, spirit gum and remover, makeup remover, brushes and brush cleaner, powder brush, powder puff, latex sponges, stipple sponge, stage blood, eyebrow/lash brush, and swab applicators.

Makeup Palettes and Stackables These plastic or metal containers provide a convenient way to carry

FIGURE A-23 Ben Nye's Color Cake Foundation Kit.

foundations, lip color, cheek color, eyeshadows, character makeup, rubber-mask greasepaint, concealers, and tattoo covers in a range of colors in one container. (See Figure A-10.) They are available from most makeup manufacturers. You can also buy empty palette boxes from Japonesque and Grumbacher (obtained from artists' supply stores) and fill them with colors of your own choice, as suggested in Chapter 8.

Makeup Pencils Wooden pencils with soft grease lead. When used for darkening the eyebrows, they are usually called *eyebrow pencils*. They are available in a variety of colors in addition to the usual brown and black. Pencils to be used for shading can be sharpened flat with a razor blade, rather like an artist's shading pencil. (See Figure 12-11 and the discussion in Chapter 12 in the section on eye pouches.) They are also used as eyeliner and come in lip color formulas.

Before using any red pencil in a makeup, test it on the skin to see if it leaves a red stain when removed. If it does, try another shade, or use another type of red makeup.

Makeup Removers Available in cream or liquid formulas from a variety of makeup companies and their distributors. Various brands of cleansing cream, cold cream, and baby oil can be obtained in drugstores. All makeup removers and skin care products should be carefully chosen to meet the needs of individual skin types. Consultation with a skin care specialist is recommended.

Mascara Used primarily for coloring the eyelashes, sometimes the eyebrows, and occasionally the hair. It is made in clear, brown, black, white, and various colors, such as blue, green, blond, and henna. It comes in creme and liquid and in regular, thickening, lengthening, and

FIGURE A-24 Makeup removers. A. "E"nriched Cold Cream. B. Makeup Remover Cream. C. Makeup Remover Lotion. *Available from Mehron.*

waterproof formulas. Having a combination of black or brown with white can be very convenient, since the white is useful for aging. It is applied with a spiral applicator brush often attached to a wand for personal use. The disposable type is convenient for maintaining proper hygiene, professional makeup artists, and for group kits. Mascara is available from the makeup companies and their distributors and from any cosmetic counter.

Matte Adhesive A non-shiny spirit gum, available from Kryolan, Joe Blasco, Mehron, W.M. Creations, and Ben Nye. Matte spirit gum can be created by mixing a small amount of T-100 into regular spirit gum.

Menaji First cosmetic line developed specifically for men.

Menthol Blower/Crystals Menthol crystals are placed into a small container that blows fumes toward the performer producing real tears. Available from Frends, Namies, and Kryolan.

Metallic Makeup Metallic makeup in both creme and water-based formulas come in gold, silver, silver-blue, silver-green, silver-lilac, bronze, and copper. Kryolan's non-metallic metallic makeups include Metallic Aquacolor and Metallic Foundations. Kryolan also has a non-metallic liquid makeup, called *Liquid Brightness,* in gold, silver, and copper. It can be applied with a brush, a sponge, or the fingers, directly on the skin or over other makeup. It can also be mixed with other liquid makeup before it is applied. Either technique will give variations on the basic colors (red-gold, green-gold, silver-blue, etc.). Any unevenness can be smoothed out after the makeup is dry by stroking lightly with tissues or cotton.

Joe Blasco has a very effective Metallic Liquid Body Makeup, available in light gold, dark gold, copper, purple, green, brown, red, and blue.

Although gold and silver powders can be used on the hair for graying or adding brilliance, they are difficult to remove and ruinous to any grease or creme makeup upon which they happen to fall. Silver and gold sprays are preferable. The powders can be mixed with Mehron's *Mixing Liquid* and applied to the body for special effects. The powders are usually available in silver (aluminum), gold, copper, red, blue, and green. Mehron has gold and silver.

Non-metallic products that provide a lustrous sheen include Ben Nye's creme formula *Fireworks* in Gold Dust, Silver Satin, Diamond Ice, Ruby Lustre, Copper and Bronze, and dry pressed colors called *Lumiere Grande Colour* in eight vivid shades. Kryolan has an effective water-soluble, non-metallic gold and silver makeup called *Aquacolor Interferenz,* which can be applied with the fingers or with a damp sponge or a brush. Normal application gives a solid metallic effect, but a light application over other makeup gives a slight metallic sheen. Kyrolan also has an iridescent makeup called *Interferenz* (available in a mini-palette of 16 shades, as well as individually).

Flakes or sequins are also available. These can be used for certain scintillating, sparking effects in stylized makeups. Kryolan has glitter in various colors and forms, including Aurora Borealis, gold, red, prismatic in loose, creme, gel and spray. Ben Nye has *MagicColor Glitter Paints and Sparklers,* Mehron has *Glitter Dust* and *Glitterwear* (a paint-on gel), and Graftobian has *Face Painting Glitter.*

No metallic paint should remain on the entire body longer than necessary and should not be used at all unless the actor is in good health. It is considered safe for very short periods, but if it is left too long on the entire body or a large portion of its area, the effects could be extremely dangerous. As a precaution, at least a few square inches of skin—even if the actor is completely nude—should be free of the makeup to allow that much of the skin to "breathe." Should the actor wearing the metallic makeup show any sign of faintness—no matter what you think the cause may be—the makeup should be removed immediately!

Methylcellulose This product when mixed with warm water produces "slime." The thickness and stringiness can be adjusted to suit the necessary effect. It can be tinted with water-based colorants.

Mineral Oil A clear, odorless oil derived from petroleum that is not known to cause allergic reactions. It is used as an emollient cleanser and emulsifier of trapped dirt in pores. It can also be sprayed on the face to simulate perspiration.

Mirror A double-faced mirror (one side magnifying) is very useful in the makeup kit. Whenever possible, of course, makeup should be done before a large, well-lighted mirror, but the small mirror is essential in getting back and profile views. Portable lighted makeup mirrors are very useful—especially those that allow for adjusting the color of the light and have triple mirrors—two adjustable side panels and a center panel with a plain mirror on one side and a magnifying mirror on the other. Professional quality portable makeup mirrors with daylight corrected fluorescent bulbs are available from Cases for Visual Artists, Inc. and Kryolan.

Mixing Liquid A clear liquid for mixing with metallic powders and dry makeup pigments. Available from Mehron and its distributors. Also see *GP-20.*

Modeling Clay There are two types of clay. One is an oil-base modeling clay used to model heads when studying facial structure and when sculpting features for prosthetic appliances. This type does not dry out and is available in a sulphur-based clay (Plastilina) and a non-sulphur based clay (Chavant NSP). It is important to choose the proper clay when making molds from the clay sculpture. Some materials such as tin-based and platinum-based silicones will not cure against sulphur clays. The other type is a water-based clay used for quickly building walls and casings around sculpting. This type will dry out when exposed to air. Available at art supply stores, Alcone, Burman Industries, Cinemafx, and Davis Dental.

Modeling Tools Artists' modeling tools are used in clay modeling and sometimes in modeling nose putty or derma wax. Available from art supply stores and dental supply houses in various styles.

Moisturizer Exposure to harsh detergents, certain makeup products, and climatic conditions can render the skin fragile and dry. The design of modern moisturizers depends on the careful selection of various hygroscopic (a term used to describe an ingredient that readily absorbs and retains moisture) ingredients such as emollients and humectants with properties that maintain the natural moisturizing factor (NMF) found in the skin's corneum layer.

Mortician's Wax Also called Naturo Plasto is similar to derma wax and can be used in the same manner. Available from Alcone, Namies, and Frends.

Moulage An inexpensive impression material that will cast any object including props, masks, and faces. It can

FIGURE A-25 Moisturizers. A. Kiehl's Ultra Facial Moisturizer SPF #13. B. TaUT Hand and Body Moisture Lotion by Leonard Engelman.

be reused over and over and is useful for beginners who are still practicing. Moulage must be heated in a double boiler. This turns the otherwise rubbery product into a smooth, thick, pourable substance. In this state the moulage can be very hot! Care must be taken to avoid burning the skin when facial impressions are being made. For this reason, moulage is no longer recommended for facial impressions. See *Alginate*. Available from Alcone and Kryolan.

Movie Mud   A Joe Blasco makeup for simulating mud or dirt. Also called Sta-dirt.

Mustaches   Excellent ready-made mustaches, ventilated on net (see Figure A-25), are available from Alcone and Kryolan distributors. Instructions for making beards and mustaches are given in Chapter 15.

Mustache Wax/Eyebrow Plastic   Available from Kryolan and from Bob Kelly.

Netting   Used as a foundation for wigs, toupees, beards, and mustaches. Available in silk, nylon, plastic, and cotton. The more expensive nettings (or hairlace) should be used for good wigs, toupees, and beards. Cotton netting can be used for practice work. All nettings and laces are available from Alcone, Kryolan distributors, and a variety of manufacturers listed in Appendix B.

Neutralizer   A translucent creme-based product used to diminish the effects of facial discoloration by employing the science of color theory, specifically that of complimentary colors. Complimentary colors, when mixed together, produce a neutral tone, a shade of brown. By applying the complimentary color over a given skin discoloration (i.e., orange over a blue beard shadow) the skin discoloration will, in theory, be neutralized and disappear. It can be applied over or under the foundation.

Nose Putty   Used for building up the nose and other bony parts of the face. Available from Kryolan distributors in two degrees of stiffness, the softer of which is called Plastici. Ben Nye's Nose and Scar Wax is a blend of putty and wax as is Mehron's Putty/Wax. Also see *Flesh Putty*.

Old Age Stipple   Liquid latex mixture stippled onto stretched skin with a latex, synthetic, or red-rubber sponge which has been torn and plucked smooth. When dried and powdered, old age stipple forms a stiff, yet flexible layer over the skin which buckles when the stretched skin is released. With gelatin as one of its ingredients, it is necessary to immerse old age stipple in hot water for a few minutes to bring it back to a liquid state before application. Old age stipple can be made in three grades: light for around the eyes; medium for the face; and heavy for the back of the hands.

Basic recipe: 90 grams (100 ml.) foam latex base
10 grams (5 teaspoons) talc U.S.P.
6 grams (2 teaspoons) loose pigmented powder or pulverized pancake makeup
2 grams (½ teaspoon) Knox unflavored gelatin
32.5 ml (3 tablespoons) boiling distilled water

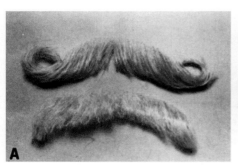

FIGURE A-26   Ready-made mustaches and sidewhiskers. By Kryolan. A. Mustaches. B. Mustache with sidewhiskers.

Light:
1. Combine and stir together talc, powder or pancake, and gelatin in an 8-oz. plastic, glass, or styrofoam cup.
2. Add the boiling distilled water (tap water will change the ph of the latex and cause it to curdle) one tablespoon at a time (mixing after each) until the mixture is smooth.
3. Strain latex through tulle or wig lace to remove any lumps.
4. Slowly add dissolved powders to the latex. Stir rapidly to avoid lumps.
5. Pour the mixture into 2-oz. or 3-oz. glass or plastic jars and label them "Stipple-Light" with the date.

Medium
1. Combine the light recipe (the light recipe yields 140 grams) with either 60 grams of Winsor & Newton Acrylic Gel Medium or 50 grams of Acrylic Gel Medium thickened with 3 tablespoons of Cab-O-Sil.
2. Stir small amounts of the light stipple into the gel until they are combined thoroughly.
3. Pour into jars and label.

Heavy
1. Combine one part (by volume) Medium Grade Stipple with one part (by volume) Sculpture House Pliatex Casting Filler clay.
2. Pour into jars and label.

Note: When stronger adhesion is needed, combine 45 grams of Pros-Aide with 45 grams of foam latex base. See Chapter 14 for removal suggestions. This product must be stored in the refrigerator.

Also available from Ben Nye, Kryolan, Transformations, and RCMA. A stronger, heavier aging formula is available from W.M. Creations.

Old Age Stipple Moistener A mixture of castor oil and 99% isopropyl alcohol applied with a foam latex sponge or the finger tips to dried and powdered old age stipple. This will turn the stipple translucent which allows the skin's natural coloration to show through. It also prepares the surface to accept any type of foundation or liner color (except PAX, which needs no surface preparation over latex or rubber-mask grease paint, which already has castor oil as a vehicle. Excess moistener can be tissued off before makeup application. Also sold as Castor Sealer by Ben Nye.

Pan-Cake Max Factor's trade name for cake makeup.

Pan-Stik Max Factor's trade name for creme stick.

PAX Medium A mixture of approximately equal parts of Pros-Aide and acrylic matte medium. PAX medium will dry crystal clear and can be mixed with water-based or water-soluble coloring agents (food color, pancake makeup, acrylic paint, etc.) to make translucent glazes for character coloration on skin and prosthetics. Note: adding titanium white to a PAX medium glaze will minimize the translucency and lessen the effect.

PAX Paint Paint used on prosthetic pieces and prosthetic applications made by mixing Liquitex acrylic paint with Pros-Aide adhesive in equal proportions. (See Chapter 14.) Available ready-made from Foam Paint Products, from Namies, and other suppliers as "FX Paints" by John Logan and from Thom Suprenaut at (619) 247-1996. They come color-matched to standard popular William Tuttle and RCMA foundation shades. This product is not recommended for direct application on the skin. When removing PAX appliances, soak the adhesive first with the appropriate remover or 70% isopropyl alcohol on a flat brush. Carefully peel the appliance away from the skin. Remove residue with a puff soaked in isopropyl myristate which is milder to the skin than Detachol. Clean the skin with Noxema and finish with a 100% aloe vera gel treatment. See Figure A-27.

Perspiration Glycerin can be used to achieve the effect of perspiration by patting—not rubbing—it on the skin with the fingertips. Glycerin can be purchased at any pharmacy and from most makeup suppliers. See *Glycerin*.

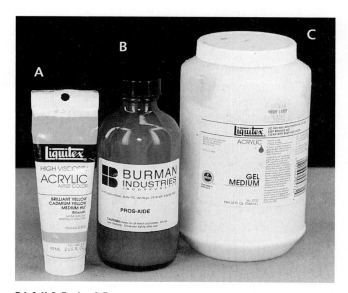

FIGURE A-27 PAX paint and PAX medium components. A. Non-toxic Liquitex Acrylic Artist Color B. Pros-Aide Adhesive C. Non-toxic Liquitex Gel Medium

Phosphorescent Makeup Makeup that glows in the dark after being exposed to light. The glow will soon diminish but will glow again after each exposure.

Plaster Bandage Rolls of gauze impregnated with plaster for use in making molds with alginate and silicone. Gypsona and Johnson & Johnson brands can be obtained from art stores, medical supply houses, Alcone, Burman Industries, and Cinemafx.

Plaster of Paris Used in making both positive casts and negative slush molds for rubber prosthesis (see Chapter 14). Can be obtained from paint stores, art supply stores, craft stores, pottery and ceramics suppliers, and some special effects makeup suppliers.

Plastic and Rubber Caps Used for a bald-head effect. Available from Michael Davy, Alcone (Paramount), Kryolan distributors, Bob Kelly, and Cinema Secrets (Woochie distributor). (See also *Plastic Film, Liquid and Plastic Head Forms.*) If the makeup you are using does not adhere to the cap, use Kryolan's Fixer Spray or Glatzan L (matte finish) to coat the cap before applying the makeup. If a cap has lost its flexibility, warm it with a hair dryer. Use medical or prosthetic adhesives for securing rubber caps and Pros-Aide adhesive for plastic caps.

Plastic Film, Liquid Kryolan has a liquid plastic called Glatzan L, which can be used to make bald caps and can also be painted on glass to make a plastic film in any shape or size. The film can be used for making eyebrow covers (see Chapter 12) as well as scars and sagging eyelids (see Chapter 13). It should be used in a well-ventilated room. Glatzan L matte can be used over Glatzan L to provide a matte finish. A Glatzan hardener is also available for making a stiffer plastic film. The Glatzan *liquid must not be used on the skin.* Glatzan that has become too thick can be thinned with acetone. Other cap materials include Paramount Cap Material and RCMA's Plastic Cap Material.

Kryolan's Old Skin Plast is a clear liquid that can be applied to the skin to wrinkle it. The liquid is brushed on over stretched skin (lightly coated with skin cream or creme makeup). It dries in a matter of seconds and can then be powdered. When the skin is released, wrinkles form. For deeper wrinkles, repeat the process. For still deeper wrinkles, apply torn pieces of cleansing tissue (white or colored) to the first layer of Old Skin Plast, then brush on another layer over the tissue. The liquid plastic is available in a matte finish, which makes powdering unnecessary. It can also be used as a sealer over derma wax, Eyebrow Plastic, etc. It can be removed with Kryolan's OSP Remover or with Kryolan's Mild Spirit Gum Remover. Mehron's Fixative A (see *Sealer*) can be used in the same way as Old Skin Plast.

Plastic/Porcelain Head Forms For use in making plastic caps. Available from Alcone, Kryolan distributors, and Makeup Designory.

Plastici A soft nose putty made by Kryolan. (See *Nose Putty.*)

Powder Puffs Velour powder puffs are available from Ben Nye, Mehron, Bob Kelly, Shiseido, and any cosmetic counter. Large (5-inch diameter) velour puffs are available from Joe Blasco.

Pressed Eyeshadow Dry cake eyeshadow. (See *Eyeshadow.*)

Prosthetic Adhesive or Medical Adhesive A special adhesive for use with prosthetic appliances. Available from Alcone, Mehron, Bob Kelly, Ben Nye, Namies, and others.

Putty-Wax A soft putty made by melting nose putty and derma wax together (see Chapter 13). Mehron's Modeling Putty-Wax and Ben Nye's Nose and Scar Wax are ready-made mixtures of derma wax and nose putty.

Rouge, Creme For coloring cheeks, lips, and other areas of the face. Also used for stippling. Available from the various makeup companies.

Rouge, Dry A pressed cake (or sometimes powdered) rouge that can be applied with a puff or a soft brush, or with a damp sponge, over an otherwise completed makeup. Brush-on rouge a somewhat powdery cake, sometimes called a "blusher," is applied dry with a soft brush. It is available in softer, more subtle colors than most dry rouges.

Rubber-Mask Greasepaint A special castor-oil base greasepaint for use on slip latex, foam latex, and gelatin appliances. Mineral oil-based products tend to absorb into the latex and turn slightly grey in color. Available from Mehron, Bob Kelly, RCMA, Cinema Secrets, Joe Blasco (TPM-Traditional Prosthetic Makeup), and Kryolan. Ben Nye's Castor Sealer, Graftobian's Castor Seal, and Kryolan's Castor Sealor applied to latex products allows regular creme makeups to be used.

Satin Powder Kryolan's nonmetallic powder which gives a satiny sheen to the makeup. It comes in fourteen shades—pearl, gold, copper, flesh, red, rose, blue, petrol, green, lilac, red-brown, peach, black, and silver. Available from Kryolan distributors.

Scar Plastic Available from RCMA as Scar Material and Blister or Scar Making Material. See *Tuplast* and *Gelatin.*

Scars and Wounds Molded latex scars and wounds can be made quite easily by obtaining a Vacu-form mold of scars and wounds (available from Kryolan), making a negative plaster cast in the Vacu-form mold, then making latex positives from the negative plaster cast.

Scissors Necessary for trimming crepe hair and frequently useful for other purposes, such as trimming latex pieces. Barbers' shears are best for hair work.

Sealer A liquid plastic skin adhesive containing polyvinyl butyral, castor oil, and isopropyl alcohol. It is used to provide a protective coating for various makeup constructions. It is an important item in any makeup kit. It is available from Mehron and their distributors in a convenient bottle with brush called Fixative A. It is also available in spray bottles from Ben Nye, Kryolan, and Joe Blasco. Blasco's is available in two types–regular and matte. W.M. Creations, Inc. has two types of sealers, A and B. Type A is a lighter strength formula for sealing the outer surface of gelatin appliances while type B, a slightly heavier formula, is for sealing the inner surface of gelatin appliances. See *Barrier Products*.

Sensitex A pressure-sensitive appliance adhesive. Available from Joe Blasco.

Separating Agents (mold release) Used in casting between the positive and the negative molds to make it possible to separate them easily. Vaseline, Frekote Mold Release, McLube, Carnuba Wax, Polyvinyl Alcohol (PVA), Polysoft Mold Release, Green Soap, Epoxy Parfilm, Molder's Edge ME-301 NS Spray Petroleum, Pure Lube Mold Soap, and PAM, are just a few examples.

Shading Colors The term is used in two ways–specifically to refer to contour colors used for shadowing and,

in a more general sense, to include all contour and accent colors. Shading colors (in both the general and the specific meaning) are available from all of the makeup companies.

Silicone See Chapter 14.

Silicone Oil (also DC 200 Fluid) A mold release agent that is also useful when applied over a finished makeup application when a shine effect is needed. The product will not disturb the makeup.

Soap Used for blocking out the hair, especially the eyebrows. Glycerin soaps or good quality, mild bath soaps can be used.

Sorbitol Corn syrup derivative used in formula gelatin mixtures for gelatin appliances. Available from Burman Industries, Cinemafx, and Alcone.

Spirit Gum (See Figure A-29.) An amber colored, alcohol/resin liquid adhesive used to attach crepe hair, wig lace, and other three-dimensional makeup to the skin. There is a difference in the adhesive strength and in drying time among the various brands. Regular spirit gum is shiny when dry. For use with hairlace, a matte gum (dull surface when dry) is preferable. If the brush that comes in the bottle is too small, a larger brush can be used instead. In applying crepe hair, you should wipe the brush from time to time with an old cloth to remove the hair that sticks to it. And it's a good idea to tape the bottle to your makeup table to avoid the possibility of knocking it over. Or you may prefer to use the spirit-gum bottle holders described below. Spirit gum is available from the various makeup companies and their distributors. Kryolan's unusually adhesive spirit gum comes in regular, matte, quick-drying, and

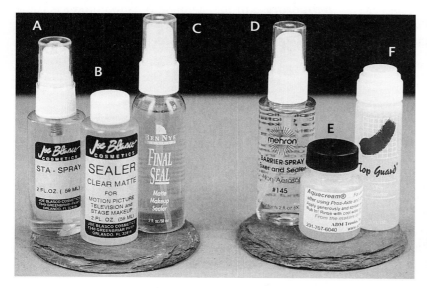

FIGURE A-28 Makeup sealers and skin barriers. A. Sta-Spray by Joe Blasco B. Clear Matte Sealer by Joe Blasco C. Final Seal by Ben Nye D. Barrier Spray (Fixer and Sealer) by Mehron E. Aquacream by ADM Tronics, Inc. F. Top Guard by Premiere Products, Inc.

FIGURE A-29 Mastix spirit gum and spirit gum remover from Kryolan.

water-soluble. Their bottle and brush are the best available. In ordering Kryolan spirit gum, be sure to specify the plastic bottle with brush unless you prefer one of the larger, more economical sizes, in which case you can order any number of the small, empty plastic bottles with brushes and fill them yourself. Kryolan also has a thinner spirit gum for those who prefer it. It comes in a square glass bottle with a smaller brush. Ben Nye's Matte Adhesive Spirit Gum comes in a plastic bottle and is available in both 1-ounce and ½-ounce sizes. Adding a small amount of T-100 to regular spirit gum will produce a matte finish. Joe Blasco and W.M. Creations have superior matte spirit gums.

Spirit-Gum Remover (See *Adhesive Removers*.) Available from the various makeup companies. Kryolan has an Extra-Mild Spirit-Gum Remover (MME) that is particularly recommended for sensitive skins. Spirit gum can also be removed with alcohol or acetone.

Spirit-Gum Bottle Holders Lightweight rigid urethane holders for spirit gum and adhesive bottles to prevent spilling and messy accidents. Useful whenever there is an open bottle of spirit gum or adhesive on the dressing table, especially during quick changes. Available from W.M. Creations, Inc.

Sponges Natural-silk sponges are used primarily for applying cake or liquid makeup. Red-rubber sponges are used for creating skin-texture effects with stippling and for applying rubber-mask grease. Foam sponges are sometimes used for applying creme makeup or for stippling with latex. Black stipple sponges are, of course, used for stippling. Natural-silk sponges are available from Mehron. Black stipple sponges, red-rubber sponges, wedge-cut latex, and polyurethane foam sponges are available from most cosmetic manufacturers and from nearly any place makeup is sold.

Stacolors A 99% alcohol-based pigmented plastic, non-smearing makeup used on gelatin appliances, to cover up and create tattoos, and to cover up bruises and blemishes. Comes in 23 colors including 10 flesh tones. Available from W.M. Creations, Inc.

Stick Makeup Various kinds of makeup are made in stick form—lipsticks, blemish-cover sticks, creme sticks, crayons, beard-stubble adhesive, eyebrow cover, hair white, etc. But the term is used, more often than not, to apply specifically to greasepaint foundation and shading colors in stick form, though it can logically refer to creme sticks as well.

Stone, Dental Comes in powder form to be mixed with water and is used for making casts in the same way as plaster. The resulting cast is harder than plaster and must be used when the cast is to be subjected to considerable pressure. Available from dental supply houses, Burman Industries, and Cinemafx.

Stoppelpaste A wax adhesive for attaching hair particles for simulating beard stubble for the unshaven look. Can be washed off with soap and water. Available from Kryolan. Clear morticians wax can also be used.

Stumps Paper stumps are small, pointed, pencil-like rolls of paper sometimes used for shadowing and highlighting. Brushes should be used instead, but stumps are useful for blending when drawing with charcoal and chalk. They can be obtained from any artists' supply store. Chamois stumps are more expensive but last much longer.

Styptic Stops bleeding from minor cuts. Available in pencil, powder, and liquid from Namies, Frends, and most drugstores.

Tattoo Covers See *Concealer* and *Dermacolor*.

Temporary Tattoos Temporary tattoo products come in the form of paints and transfer sheets. Transfer sheets from Temptu Body Art and Reel Creations contain pre-

FIGURE A-30 Tattoo Cover Ring from Mehron.

FIGURE A-31 Paint-on Temporary Tattoos by TEMPTU.

designed tattoo art that can be transferred to the skin using 70% isopropyl alcohol. Body Inks by the same companies can be painted directly onto the skin when original long-lasting designs are preferred. These products are also useful for any makeup design that requires a waterproof or smudge-proof application (i.e., bruises, black eyes, cuts, even foundations, and hair color). Tattoo designs cut from acetate or plastic sheets can be successfully airbrushed onto the skin using Dinair Airbrush makeup.

Tears Apply glycerin with an eyedropper just below the corner of the eye. Glycerin can be purchased at any pharmacy.

Temple Stick A hair-graying stick made by Kryolan. Available in three colors from Kryolan distributors.

Texas Dirt An effective body makeup that comes in powder form and is applied with a damp sponge. It can be removed with soap and water. It is available from Mehron in Gold, Silver, and Plain, and from Bob Kelly in one color only. Mehron's Plain dries with a dull finish; their Gold is about the same color but has a gold sheen; and their Silver has a silver sheen. (See also *Body Makeup* and *Character Powders*.)

Thixotropy A thixotropic agent, such as Cab-O-Sil, is one that thickens other materials. See *Bondo*.

Thread Common cotton or silk thread or dental floss is useful in removing nose putty. When the thread is passed between the skin and the putty, most of the putty will come off easily.

Tooth Enamel The enamel is applied to dry teeth with a brush that comes in the bottle. The enamel can be removed by wiping the teeth firmly with cleansing tissues. Any specks of color remaining can be removed by brushing the teeth. The nicotine is particularly effective in aging the teeth. The black can be used for blocking out teeth, shortening them, or making them appear broken. Ben Nye has Natural White, Black, Nicotine, Zombie Rot, and Decay. Mehron has Black, Nicotine, and Gold. Kryolan has Black, Nicotine, White, Ivory, and Red.

244 Fluid A silicone brush cleaner designed to dissolve oils and grease. Used also for cleaning plastilina out of molds. It is safe on the skin and has no fumes. Also used as a mold release agent.

T-pins T-shaped pins for securing wigs to wig blocks. They come in various sizes and can be obtained from any wig supply company. Kryolan has a very convenient magnetic container for t-pins.

Toupee Tape A very thin double-sided adhesive film for attaching bald caps, wig lace, and toupees, and for simulating scars. Available as Kryolan's Leukoflex and Special Tape T, Stein's Toupee Tape, Topstick Toupee Tape from Kryolan distributors, Namies, and Alcone.

Tuffy Head A life-size rubber head (face and neck only) that can be used for making beards with a latex base rather than making them directly on the face. If the beard is to be sprayed, it should be done with the beard on the Tuffy head rather than on the face. The Tuffy head is available from Kryolan distributors.

Tuplast A thick, liquid plastic that can be used on the skin to build up three-dimensional scars. It can also be

FIGURE A-32 Bruise Palette by TEMPTU. *Waterproof, smudge-proof Body Ink.*

used in open molds to make three-dimensional molded pieces. (Eye pouches, for example, can be made in much the same way as in using gelatin. Edges can be dissolved with acetone for blending.) Available from Kryolan distributors.

TS-100 A clay-based matting agent usually added to spirit gum and other adhesives to remove the characteristic shine.

Tweezers Handy for removing stray hairs when shaping eyebrows and dressing crepe-hair beards or mustaches or in attaching small latex pieces.

Ultracal 30 A gypsum cement-based powder to be mixed with water and used for making molds when casting foam latex and gelatin appliances. Available from Burman Industries, Cinemafx, and from your local pottery or ceramics supplier. Add Acryl 60 to Ultracal 30 to increase its structural strength and hardness. Also available from Burman Industries.

Ultra Ice This clear face-building gel simulates ice on the face and body. It is a flexible, sculptable gel that visually becomes part of the actors skin transmitting the most subtle expression and movement. Available from Alcone and Namies.

Velvet Stick Stein's trade name for creme stick.

Ventilating Needles Used for knotting hair into net or gauze for wigs or beards (see Chapters 15 and 16). Available from Kryolan, Alcone, or any wigmakers' supply company. They should be ordered by number, the smallest usually being 00 or 0, and are often available in six sizes. The needle holder is ordered separately.

Weaving Frames For weaving hair into wefts. Available from wigmakers' supply houses.

Wig Blocks (See Chapter 16.) Canvas and wood blocks available from Kryolan and other wigmakers' supply houses. Lightweight, durable urethane wig blocks from 21 inches to 24½ inches are also available from Mane-Sta'.

Wig Hangers Kryolan has a lightweight, easily stored wig hanger made of cloth-covered wire. It is available in two styles—N for hanging from a hook and K for hanging over a rod. Available from Kryolan distributors.

Wig lace A net foundation used in making wigs, toupees, beards, and mustaches (see Chapters 15 and 16). Available from Mane-Sta is a non-fraying lace impervious to 99% alcohol and acetone. It comes in two grades: film quality (20 denier) and prosthetic grade. Also available from Kryolan in five grades. Numbers 01 and 0 are their finest flesh-colored nylon lace, excellent for street wear or for films but finer than necessary for the stage. Number 1 is only slightly less fine. Number 2 is a more durable lace, practical for stage wear. Number 3 is strong and slightly stiff nylon netting, which can be used by students for practice in ventilating as a substitute for the rather fragile hairlace. Available from Kryolan distributors. Alcone also carries wig-making supplies including wig lace. Also see *Wig and Hair Resources* in Appendix B.

Sources of Makeup Materials

Makeup Suppliers

ADM TRONICS UNLIMITED, INC., 224-S Pegasus Avenue,
Northvale, NJ 07647
Ph: 201/767-6040
Fax: 201/784-0620
Email: *sales@admtronics.com*
www.admtronics.com

Pros-Aide I and II adhesive and remover.

ALCONE COMPANY, INC., 549 49th Avenue,
Long Island City, NY 11101
Ph: 718/361-8373
Fax: 718/729-8296

Mail-order source of makeup of all brands; professional makeup artist supplies; hair supplies; special effects; books and videos. Call for their comprehensive and educational catalogue.

ALCONE N. Y. C., 235 West 19th Street,
New York, NY 10011
Ph/Fax: 212/633-0551

Complete line of makeup and professional makeup artist supplies.

A-R PRODUCTS, 11807 7/8 Slauson Avenue,
Santa Fe Springs, CA 90670
Ph: 562/907-7707
Fax: 562/907-7708
www.arproductsinc@earthlink.net

Latex pigment dispersions.

ART ANTHONY, STATE OF THE ART CREATIONS
14743 Sierra Highway
Canyon Country, CA 91351
Los Angeles, CA
Ph: 800/896-0515
Email: *ArtsEfx@aol.com*

Source for silicone putty, two-part silicone, silicone adhesive. Distributed by Namies.

BEN NYE MAKEUP, 5953 Bowcroft Street,
Los Angeles, CA 90016
Ph: 310/839-1984
Fax: 310/839-2640
www.bennye.com

Complete line of dealer makeup for stage, screen, and television. Call or fax for catalogue and for the nearest distributor.

BOB KELLY COSMETICS, INC., 151 West 46th Street,
New York, NY 10036
Ph: 212/819-0030
Fax: 212/869-0396

Complete line of makeup for stage, screen, and television. Also makes wigs, beards, and mustaches. Call or fax for brochure and for the nearest distributor.

BURMAN INDUSTRIES, 14141 Covello Street, Suite 10-C,
Van Nuys, CA 91405
Ph: 818/782-9833
Fax: 818/782-2863
www.burmanfoam.com

Complete line of products for prosthetic makeup effects. Mold-making supplies; sculpting supplies;

Foam latex; silicone; gelatin; blood; tools; books and videos. Also a great source for technical support. Mail-order. Call for catalogue.

CINEMAFX, 7347 Ethel Avenue,
North Hollywood, CA 91605
Ph: 818/765-4994
Fax: 818/765-5847

Mail-order source of makeup effects supplies. Urethanes; dental stone; Ultracal-30; dental acrylics, sculpting products. The makeup effects branch of Davis Dental. Call for catalogue.

CINEMA SECRETS, INC., 4400 Riverside Drive,
Burbank, CA 91505
Ph: 818/846-0579
Fax: 818/846-0431

Complete line of house brand and other makeup lines and supplies. Known internationally for their brush cleaner. Primary source for Woochie rubber products and Halloween and horror masks. Call for catalogue.

DINAIR AIRBRUSH MAKEUP SYSTEMS, INC.,
5315 Laurel Canyon Blvd.
N. Hollywood, CA 91607
Ph: 818/780-4777
Fax: 818/780-4748
www.dinair.com

Complete line of Dinair Airbrush cosmetics and supplies. Workshops and videos also available. Call for catalogue and information.

DONJER PRODUCTS, INC., Ilene Court, Bldg. 8,
Belle Mead, NJ 08502
Ph: 908/359-7726 or
800/336-6537
Fax: 908/359-0275

Source for flocking, flocking supplies, and custom flocking.

FACTOR II, P. O. Box 1339,
Lakeside, AZ 85929
Ph: 520/537-8387
Fax: 520/537-8066
Email: *imagination@factor2.com*

Source for tin and platinum cure silicones, mold-making supplies, intrinsic and extrinsic coloration systems, adhesives and removers used in making silicone prostheses. Call for catalogue.

FRENDS BEAUTY SUPPLY, 5270 Laurel Canyon Blvd.,
North Hollywood, CA 91607
Ph: 888/7-frends or
818/769-3834 or

213/877-4828
Fax: 818/769-8124
www.frendsbeautysupply.com

Complete line of cosmetics, makeup artist supplies, hair and skin care, for the theater and film industries. Also carry mustaches and beards and will rent wigs. Call, fax, or buy on-line.

F/X SOLUTION, 820 Thompson Avenue, Unit #14,
Glendale, CA 91201
Ph: 818/242-74FX
Fax: 818/242-7430
Email: *fxsolution@earthlink.net*

Urethanes, silicones, sculpting products, mold making supplies, blood. Call for catalogue.

GERDA SPILLMANN SWISS COSMETICS
640 Glass Lane
Modesto, CA 95356
Ph: 800/282-FACE (3223)
Fax: 209/529-1844
Email: *gerdaspillmann@msn.com*

Complete dealer line of cosmetics and skin care for stage, film, and television. Call for catalogue.

GM FOAM, 14956 Delano Street,
Van Nuys, CA 91411
Ph: 818/908-1087
Fax: 818/908-1262

Foam latex kits in quart, gallon, and five gallon size.

GRAFTOBIAN, 510 Tasman Street,
Madison, WI 53714
Ph: 608/222-7849
Fax: 608/222-7893

Complete line of dealer makeup product for the professional and amateur makeup artist. Call for catalogue.

IMAGE EXCLUSIVE, 8020 Melrose Avenue,
West Hollywood, CA 90046
Ph: 213/651-4678 or
888/734-3444
Fax: 213/651-1710

Complete line of cosmetics and professional makeup artist supplies.

JAPONESQUE PROFESSIONAL MAKEUP SUPPLIES, INC.
P. O. Box 644, Sausalito, CA 94966
Ph: 415/454-6662 or
800/955-6662
Fax: 415/454-8230

Complete line of makeup containers, organizers, palettes, brushes, brush cases, and makeup cases. Call for catalogue.

JOE BLASCO COSMETICS, 1670 Hillhurst Avenue,
Hollywood, CA 90027
Ph: 323/671-1091 or
800/553-1580
Fax: 323/671-1098

Complete line of dealer makeup for stage, screen, and television. Call or fax for catalogue and for the nearest distributor.

KRYOLAN CORPORATION, 132 Ninth Street,
San Francisco, CA 94103
Ph: 415/863-9684
Fax: 415/863-9059

Complete line of dealer makeup for stage, screen, and television. Call or fax for catalogue and for the nearest distributor.

THE MAKEUP CENTER LTD., 150 West 55th Street
(6-7th Avenue),
New York, NY 10019
Ph: 212/977-9494
Fax: 212/977-9497

Complete line of dealer brand of theatrical makeup. Also distributors of Mehron and Stein cosmetics.

THE MAKEUP SHOP, 131 West 21st Street,
New York, NY 10011
Ph: 212/807-0447
Fax: 212/727-0975

Distributors of Mehron, Ben Nye, and Kryolan cosmetics. Professional makeup course offered by Toby Britton.

MEHRON, INC., 100 Red Schoolhouse Road,
Chestnut Ridge, NY 10977
Ph: 914/426-1700
Email: *info@mehron.com*
www.mehron.com

Complete line of dealer makeup for stage, screen, and television. Call or fax for catalogue and for the nearest distributor.

MICHAEL DAVY, Film & T. V. Make Up,
P. O. Box 570309,
Orlando, FL 32857-0309
Ph: 888/225-7026
www.bitstorm.net/mdftv

Film and television makeup including: Airbrush cosmetics; Collodacolor; foam latex; plastic bald caps; foaming sponge gelatin. Call for catalogue.

THE MONSTER MAKERS, 7305 Detroit Avenue,
Cleveland, OH 44102
Ph: 216/651-7739
Fax: 216/631-4329

Email: *arnold@monstermakers.com*
www.monstermakers.com

Complete line of makeup for stage, film, and television.

Distributor of Tom McLaughlin Theatrical Latex Foam Products.

NAMIE'S BEAUTY CENTER, 12640 Riverside Drive,
Valley Village, CA 91607
Ph: 818/655-9933
www.naimies.com

Complete line of professional cosmetics and makeup artist supplies. Call for catalogue.

PREMIER PRODUCTS, INC., P.O. Box 12422,
La Crescenta, CA 91224
Ph: 800/346-4774
Fax: 818/897-7458
Email: *premprod@aol.com*

Telesis and Beta Bond silicone adhesives, solvents, and skin preparations. Call for catalogue.

REEL CREATIONS, INC., 7831 Alabama Ave., #21,
Canoga Park, CA 91304
Ph: 818/346-7335
Fax: 818/346-9664

Manufacturer of Reel Body Art Inks for temporary tattoos, tattoo cover, bruises. Also, Reel blood products. Call for catalogue.

RESEARCH COUNCIL OF MAKE-UP ARTISTS
(RCMA),
P.O. Box 850,
Somis, CA 93066
805/386-4744

Complete dealer line of professional makeup for stage, film, and television. Produced by and for professional makeup artists. Call for brochures. Distributed by Namies and Frends.

RINO CARBONI STUDIO, 00154 Roma.
Via C. Citerni 31/33
Ph: 06 5746433

Complete dealer line of professional makeup for stage, film, and television.

Call for information.

STAGE DOOR STUDIO SUPPLIES, 3500 Aloma
Ave. #F17,
Winter Park, FL 32792
Ph: 407/679-9621
Fax: 407/679-5609

Complete line of products for the special effects makeup artist. Call for catalogue.

M. STEIN COSMETICS (Division of Zauder Bros., Inc.)
10 Henry Street,
Freeport, NY 11520
Ph: 516/379-2600
Fax: 516/223-3397

Complete line of Zauder brand and Stein theatrical makeup. Call for catalogue.

TEMPTU BODY ART, 26 West 17th Street,
New York, NY 10011
Ph: 212/675-4000
Fax: 212/675-4075
www.temptu.com

Producers of Temptu temporary tattoo and body art paint for film, theater, television, and advertising. Call for catalogue.

W.M. CREATIONS, INC., 5755 Tujunga Avenue,
North Hollywood, CA 91601
Ph: 818/763-6692
Fax: 818/763-6693
www.nu-products.com

Brush and adhesive holders, Old Age Stipple, Stacolors, brushes, plastic sealers A and B, Xtra hold spirit gum. Also, slip rubber and foam latex appliances.

ZAUDER BROS., INC., 10 Henry Street,
Freeport, NY 11520
Ph: 516/379-2600
Fax: 516/223-3397

Distributor of Zauder and Stein brands of theatrical makeup. Call for catalogue.

Wig and Hair Resources

ALCONE COMPANY, INC. (See previous address)

CMC (CALIFORNIA MERCHANDISE COMPANY), 2133 South Harbor Boulevard,
Anaheim, CA 92802
Ph: 800/262-9447
Fax: 714/971-1876

Synthetic, human and yak hair wigs; falls chignons, wefting.

DE MEO BROTHERS, INC., 129 West 29th Street,
New York, NY 10001-5105
Ph: 212/268-1400

High quality lace and netting; human hair; wig making supplies; ventilating needles.

GIOVANNI & SON, 14318 Victory Blvd.,
Van Nuys, CA 91401
Ph: 818/908-0183

Human and yak hair; wig making supplies; drawing cards; ventilating needles.

GOLDEN SUPREME, INC., 13033 Park Street,
Santa Fe Springs, CA 90670
Ph: 562/903-1063 Order: 1/800/332-9246
Fax: 562/903-1064

Complete line of makeup artist styling tools: stoves, irons, and carrying cases.

HAIRESS CORPORATION, 880 Industrial Blvd.,
Crown Point, IN 46307
Ph: 800/332-4247

Wholesale beauty supplies; styro and canvas wig blocks; styling tools; wig dryers; bulk wig caps.

MANE-STA', 5755 Tujunga Avenue,
North Hollywood, CA 91601
Ph: 818/763-6692
Fax: 818/763-6693

Supplier of non-fraying lace impervious to 99% alcohol and acetone in 2 grades: film (20 denier) and prosthetic (excellent for foam and gelatin appliances). Urethane wig blocks, full and half face beard forms.

Schools

THE ADVANCED PROFESSIONAL MAKEUP COURSE
Dick Smith
27 Wilford Ave.
Branford, CT 06405

AIRBRUSH MAKEUP INSTITUTE, 5315 Laurel Canyon Blvd.,
No. Hollywood, CA 91607
Ph: 818/508-8800 or 800/785-4770
Fax: 818/780-4748

CINEMA MAKEUP SCHOOL, 3780 Wilshire Blvd., Suite 300,
Los Angeles, CA 90010
Ph: 213/368-1234
Fax: 213/739-0819
Email: *info@cinemamake-upsch.com*
www.cinemamake-upsch.com

EAST COAST SCHOOL FOR MAKEUP, 1 Rutgers
    Court, Suite B-4,
Belleville, NJ 07109
Michael R. Thomas
Ph: 973/759-4977
Fax: 973/844-9044

JOE BLASCO MAKEUP CENTER EAST,
    7340 Greenbriar Parkway,
Orlando, Fl 32819
Ph: 407/363-1234 or
800/252-7261

LOS ANGELES SCHOOL OF MAKEUP, INC.,
    10139 ½ Riverside Drive,
Toluca Lake, CA 91602
Ph: 818/752-4276
Fax: 818/752-6962
www.makeupschool.com

See THE MAKEUP SHOP, address listed above
    Professional makeup course by Toby Britton

NORTH CAROLINA SCHOOL for the ARTS,
    School of Drama
NCSA, P.O. Box 12189
Winston-Salem, NC 27117-2189
Dept.: 336/770-3238
FAX: 336/770-3369

STUDIO MAKEUP ACADEMY, Sunset Gower
    Studios,
1438 N. Gower Street,
#14 Studio 308,
Hollywood, CA 90028
Ph: 323/465-4002
www.studiomakeupacademy.com

TRANSFORMATIONS MAKEUP FX LAB and
    SCHOOL, 2016 Princess Place Drive,
Wilmington, NC 28405
Ph: 910/343-0070
Fax: 910/343-0038
www.transformationsfx.com
    Check web site for latest products and course
    dates.

UNIVERSITY OF CINCINNATI, College
    Conservatory of Music
Theatre Division
P.O. Box 210096
Cincinnati, OH 45221-0096
Dept.: 513/556-5803
www.UC.edu/www/ccm

UNIVERSITY OF ILLINOIS, Urbana–Champaign
    Department of Theatre
4-122 Krannert Center
500 S. Goodwin Ave.
Dept.: 217/333-2371
FAX: 217/244-1861
www.theatre.uiuc.edu/theatre/

WESTMORE ACADEMY OF COSMETIC ARTS,
    916 W. Burbank Blvd., #R,
Burbank, CA 91506
Ph: 818/562-6808
Fax: 818/562-6617
www.westmoreacademy.com

Books and Videos

See ALCONE COMPANY, INC. Order catalogue
    for a complete listing.

MAKEUP ARIST MAGAZINE, P. O. Box 4316,
    Sunland, CA 91041-4316
Ph: 818/504-6770
Fax: 818/504-6257
See Makeup Artist Magazine Book & Video Store
    @ *www.makeupmag.com*
same fax number open 24 hours a day

See ALL MAKEUP RETAIL STORES

Sources Outside the United States

COMPLECTIONS INTL. MAKE-UP SCHOOL
    AND STORE, 85 St. Nicholas Street,
Toronto, ON, M4Y 1W8 CANADA
Ph: 416/968-6739
www.complectionsmake-up.com

FISCHBACH + MILLER, Postfach 11 63,
    Poststraée 1
D-88461 Laupheim, Germany
Ph: 0049-(0)7392-9773-0
Fax: 0049-(0)7392-9773-50
    Complete line of makeup and supplies including
    wigs and beards. Distributors of Kryolan makeup
    products.

CHARLES H. FOX LTD., 22 Tavistock Street,
London, WC 2 / England
Ph: 0171 / 240-3111
Fax: 0171 / 379-3410
Distributor of Kryolan makeup products.

KRYOLAN GmbH, Papierstr. 10,
D-13409 Berlin, Germany
Ph: +49/30/499-892-0
Fax: +49/30/491-4994
Distributor of Kryolan makeup products.

CONTACT KRYOLAN CORP. for a list of
distributors outside the U.S.

CONTACT MEHRON, INC. for a list of distributors
outside the U.S.

CONTACT BEN NYE COMPANY, INC. for a list of
distributors outside the U.S.

Contents of a Professional Makeup Kit

The following is an excerpt from the makeup course taught by Michael R. Thomas, Director of the East Coast School for Makeup (see Appendix B). The suggestions and recommended list of materials are to be used as a point of departure.

Where I have indicated *Recommended:*, get each item after the word. For example, under the heading "Adhesives," *all three* adhesives are recommended, so get all three. Sometimes, only one item is listed after *Recommended:*, in which case, get only that item. (I will list the names of other manufacturers in case you would rather purchase from a manufacturer other than one I have recommended.)

Some items are a matter of personal preference and are made by so many manufacturers, that I have not made any specific recommendations. However, please keep in mind that you are going to makeup many people, each with their own particular needs, and you'll need to cover all the bases as far as color and type of makeup are concerned. You're going to find that the requirements of each job will vary, sometimes wildly, and you want to be prepared.

Please note that in my experience, I have found that most people who wish to become professional makeup artists are usually lacking in three things:

- **Brushes.** You must have a wide variety of brushes, both round and flat, that range in size from $\frac{1}{16}$-inch wide (or around) to 1-inch wide (or around). You must have a variety of types of brushes (blush brushes, adhesive brushes, lip color brushes, etc.). It is far better to have too many brushes than too few.
- **Foundations.** There are lots of different skin tones and types, and you must have a wide selection of both creme and liquid foundations.

- **Liner Colors.** I don't mean lipliners or eyeliners. I mean the rainbow of creme (usually) accent colors used to contour the features, to create realistic and fantasy effects, and to break up the unnatural smoothness of a base of foundation to make it look more like skin.

Absorbent Cotton
Acetone (Please note: *Pure Acetone* not to be confused with nail polish remover)
Adhesives:
    Recommended: RCMA Matte Adhesive #16, Duo Surgical Adhesive, Pros-Aide. (Please note: Dow 355 has been determined to be harmful to the environment and is no longer being manufactured, so it will not be discussed as part of the East Coast School Crash Course.)
Alcohol (70% & 99%)
Baby Wipes
Blood:
    Recommended: Paramount Stage Blood, Kryolan Fixblood (Fixblut), Paramount Congealed Blood
Blush:
    Creme—Iman, Bob Kelly Creme Rouge, Bob Kelly Mirage Rouge Blusher-Creme, Mehron Blushtone, Ben Nye Creme Rouge, RCMA Cheekcolor & Genacolor, William Tuttle Blusher
    Dry—Iman, Bob Kelly Dry Rouge, Ben Nye Dry Rouge, Ben Nye Professional Cheek Blushers, Kryolan's 10-Shade Dry Rouge Palette, MAC Blushers, Paramount Dry Rouge, RCMA EC #2 Dry Blushes
Brush Cleaner—Acehol (a product made and named by Mr. Thomas using equal amounts of acetone

and 99% alcohol), commercial brush cleaner (these must clean and disinfect thoroughly while leaving no residue on the brush), shampoo, and conditioner

Brushes (Please note: The type of bristle in each brush must ultimately be determined by how it feels against the skin. Do not purchase brushes according to their price! Many synthetic bristles are kinder to the skin than natural bristles. Go to a large art store which carries a variety of popular brands, such as Grumbacher, Winsor-Newton, etc., and remember—it is much better to have too many brushes than too few.)

Acetone Brush (for melting the edge of a bald cap)—get one 5/16" or 3/8" round

Blush Brush—get at least two

Dye Brush (toothbrush type)—get one or two

Detail Brush—get two 1/16" or 1/8" rounds

Eyebrow Brush

Eyeliner Brush

Eye Shadow Brushes (rounded tip and flat)—get at least four; two of each

Hairbrush (rat-tail)

Lipstick & Lipliner Brushes—get at least two reusable types and a dozen disposable types

Mascara Brushes (disposable)—get a dozen

Powder Brush

Highlighting and Shading Brushes—get at least two 3/16" or ¼" flat or bright, and at least two ½" flat or bright

Spirit Gum Brush (the small ones that come attached to the bottle cap are too small and flimsy to be of much use)—get one 5/16" or 3/8" round

Castor Oil

Chamois

Cleansers (cold cream, liquid)

Clown White (cake, grease, liquid)

Collodion (flexible, used as a sealer and non-flexible used as scar material)

Combs

Cotton Swabs

Cortisone Cream 1%

Crepe Hair (real & wool):
    White, blond, light brown, medium brown, red, dark brown, black

Dental Spatulas (flat & wax)

Dermacolor:
    Recommended: D-5, D-10, D-17, D-30, D-32, D-34, D-40, D-56, D-305, D-1W (get 2)

Derma Wax (soft & firm)

Detachol (a liquid solvent made especially for removing Pros-Aide, but which can be used for removing spirit gum, PAX, RMGP, etc. A must have!)

Emery Boards

Eyebrow Pencils (assorted):
    Blond, medium brown, brownish black, black, auburn, grey

Eye Drops

Eyelash Curler

Eyelashes (false, assorted strip, and individuals)

Eyeliners (assorted cake, pencils, and liquid)

Eye Shadows:
    Dry—Ben Nye Pressed Eye Shadows, Ben Nye Pearl Sheen, RCMA 12-Color Dry Eye Shadow Palette, RCMA Eyecolor #1 Water-Applied, RCMA Eyecolor #2 Dry-Applied, Paramount Eyeshadow.
    Creme—William Tuttle Eye Shadows

Foundations:
    Cake—Max Factor Pancake, Bob Kelly Cake Makeup, Kryolan Aquacolor, Mehron #110 Star Blend Cake Makeup, Ben Nye Color Cake Foundation.
    Creme—Joe Blasco Cre me Bases, Max Factor Panstick, Iman Cream to Powder Foundation, Bob Kelly Cre me Sticks and Mirage Creme Foundation, Kryolan Supracolor Creme Foundation, MAC Studio Series, Mehron Celebre and #400 Creme Blend Makeup, Ben Nye Theatrical Creme Foundation, RCMA Color Process Foundation, William Tuttle Creme Foundation, Visiora MV Modeleur Creme Visage.
    Liquid—Clinique, Iman, MAC Face & Body Foundation, Mehron #111 Liquid Makeup, Visiora VN Fluide Visage Liquid Face Makeup, Visiora CN Fluide Corps Liquid Body Makeup.

Rubber Mask Greasepaint—Bob Kelly RMGP, Mehron RMGP. *Recommended:* Kryolan RMGP 12 or 24 Shade Palette

Gloves (disposable examination gloves, latex or plastic)

Glycerin

Hair Clips (large and small)

Hair Coloring (assorted liquid, powder, spray, stick)

Hair Dryer (small hand held)

Hair Gel

Hairpins (large and small)

Hairspray

Hair Trimmer (buzzer)

K-Y Jelly

Lining Colors:
    Recommended: Kelly's Soft Liners in black, bronze, blender tone, chestnut brown, gray-violet, leaf green, maroon, medium rose, mikado, ocean blue, spice, sunburn, white.

Lip Balm

Lipliner Pencils:
    Bob Kelly Lip Lining Pencils, MAC Lipliner
       Pencils, Ben Nye Lip Pencil, Ben Nye
       Professional Pencils
Lipsticks:
    Bob Kelly Lipstick, Ben Nye Lipsticks, RCMA
       Lipstick, Kryolan Lip Rouge Color, Mehron
       Glostone, Mehron Lip Rouge.
Makeup Cape
Makeup Palettes (commercial or homemade)
Mascara (black, brown, clear)
Mirror
Moustache Wax
Nose Putty
Pencil Sharpeners (lip pencils, eyebrow pencils, and
    eyeliner pencils)
Personal Hygiene Items:
    Breath drops, tooth paste and brush, deodorant,
       soap, etc.
Perspiration/ Tears (50/50 glycerine and water)
Polaroid Camera
Portable Makeup Box(es), Bag(s)
Powders (assorted loose and pressed):
RCMA No-Color, pigmented (any brand), translucent
    (any brand)

Powder Puffs
Razors (disposable and single edge)
Safety Pins
Scissors:
    Barber shears, cuticle, safety, thinning shears
Sea Breeze Antiseptic
Sealers (water based, plastic)
Shaving Cream (travel-size can)
Soap
Spirit Gum Remover
Sponges:
    Black plastic stipple, foam rubber, natural silk (sea
      sponge), red rubber
Stopplepaste (by Kryolan. A soft wax in a bullet-type
    applicator for adhering chopped hair to the skin
    for a stubble effect.)
Tissues
Tooth Enamel (black, stain, white)
Top Stick (toupee tape)
Tuplast (scar material)
Tweezers
Water (aerosol spray and squeeze bottles)

Health and Safety

by Monona Rossol

from her book on safety in Theatre, Film and TV
by Allworth Press

appendix **D**

Throughout history men and women have sacrificed health for cosmetic effects. Women in the court of Queen Elizabeth I persisted in wearing white lead paint (ceruse) on their faces even though they knew it ruined their skin and made their hair fall out. In the eighteenth century, one well-known actress died from using lead-laden makeup.

Lead and Mercury

Today, acutely toxic chemicals like lead and mercury still are found in foreign cosmetics—even some sold in the U.S. For example, kohl, a mascara made of lead sulfide and antimony sulfide, has been used for centuries to make up children's eyes in the Middle East, India, Pakistan, and some parts of Africa. One U.S. health department found high levels of kohl in the blood of eight children. Two of the children's mothers purchased the kohl in this country.[1]

For another example, several Mexican-made mercury-containing beauty creams are also used in this country. One is known to have caused elevated mercury levels in 104 people. Because mercury can penetrate the skin so easily, elevated mercury levels also were found in some persons who never used the cream but were close household contacts of cream users![2]

[1]Am. Journal of Public Health, Vol. 86, No. 4., April 1996, p. 587–588

[2]*Physicians' Bulletin,* San Diego Dept. Of Health Services, May 1996, Press Release # 31–96, CA Dept. Of Health Services, Sacramento, *The Mortality & Morbidity Weekly Report* (CDC) 45 (19), May 17, 1996, pp. 400–3, and *Ibid.,* 45(29), July 26, 1996, pp. 633–5.

Mercury is still allowed in cosmetics by the Food and Drug Administration (FDA) in the eye-area products in very low concentrations (0.0065 percent) in order to prevent serious eye infections in users. Mercury preservatives in these very small amounts may cause allergies in a few people, but they are not enough to cause toxicity.

These incidents are reported here to emphasize the importance of using only FDA ingredient-labeled makeup.

Hazards to Wearers

Despite FDA regulations, some individuals will have reactions or allergies to makeup. Both ordinary consumers and performers are at risk. There are numerous documented incidents of makeup affecting individual actors adversely. One well known example is Buddy Ebson's serious reaction to a shiny aluminum makeup which cost him the role of the Tin Man in the movie *Wizard of Oz.*

Hazards to Makeup Artists

A number of studies show that beauticians and cosmetologists suffer a higher incidence than average of lung problems like asthma and chronic bronchitis, more skin rashes, and more frequent kidney and liver damage. Some studies also show that they have a higher incidence of cancer and reproductive problems like toxemia in pregnancy and miscarriages.

No similar studies have been made of diseases in theatrical makeup artists, but it is clear that they are exposed to some of the same chemical products. It is important, then, to understand the nature of these substances.

How We Are Exposed

In order to harm you, makeup and beauty products must enter your body. They must do this by one of three routes of entry: skin contact, inhalation, or ingestion.

Skin Contact
Some makeup chemicals can cause skin problems such as irritation, infection, and allergic reactions. Some makeup chemicals, hair dyes, and solvents also can penetrate the skin and enter the blood stream.

Inhalation
Inhaling powders, aerosol sprays, and airbrush mists is another way makeup and cosmetic chemicals can enter your body. Studies have shown that inhalation of aerosol hair sprays can damage or destroy the tiny hair-like cilia which sweep foreign particles from the lungs. When the lungs' defenses are weakened in this way, inhaled substances can cause even more damage.

The smaller the particles of dust or mist, the deeper they can penetrate the lungs. In the deepest part of the lungs, the air sacs (alveoli), are the most vulnerable. Face powder particles and air brush mists are examples of small particles that can be deposited deep in the lungs. Studies show that tiny particles of inert minerals, such as those used in cosmetics (e.g., talc and kaolin) can remain in the alveoli indefinitely.

Ingestion
Ingesting lipsticks, wetting brushes with the mouth, and eating, smoking, or drinking while applying makeup can put cosmetic ingredients directly into your digestive tract. Cosmetics are also ingested when the cilia in the upper portion of the lungs raise mucous and dust particles up the back of the throat where they are swallowed.

Skin Diseases

Acne
The most common reaction to cosmetics is an infectious reaction of the skin. Especially common is a condition known as "acne cosmetica," or cosmetic acne. (Cosmetic acne should not be confused with "acne vulgaris," which is associated with the onset of puberty.) Cosmetic acne usually is a mild condition. Small pimples appear and disappear intermittently and affect women from their twenties through their fifties.

Other types of acne and skin infections can result if cosmetics support bacterial growth or irritate the skin.

Allergies
Many people develop allergies to chemicals in cosmetics. It is estimated that one person in ten is allergic to fragrances in cosmetics. Some of the preservatives and humectants (e.g., propylene glycol) also cause allergic responses in a few people.

Chrome and nickel compounds have been known to cause severe allergies and skin ulcers in industrial workers exposed to them. Chrome compounds can be found in some eye cosmetics, especially in blue and green hues. And while nickel should not be used in cosmetics, nickel allergy has been documented in hairdressers.

In fact, the percentage of the general population in the U.S. that are allergic to nickel has risen in the last few years from 10 to over 14 percent. Experts think that intimate contact with nickel in metal alloys used in earrings and body piercing jewelry is the reason.[3]

The greatest potential for serious allergic reactions to theatrical cosmetics is in our use of natural rubber latex and foam products such as eyelash adhesives, special effects makeup, and face molding compounds.

Allergies to natural rubber are well-known through the experience of doctors and other medical workers who wear latex gloves daily. Somewhere between 10 and 17 percent of medical professionals have developed the allergy. Symptoms may include: skin rash and inflammation, hives, respiratory irritation, asthma, and systemic anaphylactic shock. Between 1988 and 1992, the FDA received reports of 1000 systemic shock reactions to latex. As of June 1996, 28 latex-related deaths had been reported to the FDA.

While there are no systematic studies of special effects latex makeup allergies, this author can testify that her eyes have swelled completely shut on application of rubber latex eyelash adhesive. Many other people have had reported similar experiences. Fortunately, there are synthetic substitutes for almost all natural rubber makeup products and gloves.

Irritation
Chemicals which are caustic, acid, or strong oxidizers can harm the skin by attacking its surface. Examples include sodium and potassium hydroxides which can be found in cuticle softeners and hair relaxers and removers. An example of a strong oxidizer is peroxide which is used to lighten facial hair. Organic solvents such as alcohol and acetone also can irritate the skin or dry it out by removing natural oils.

---

[3] *The New York Times,* "When Body Piercing Causes Body Rash," Denise Grady, Tuesday, October 20, 1998, p. F8

Cancer Sunlight is the major cause of skin cancer, and both natural and tanning-salon light can cause cancer. Some chemicals have been shown to cause it, too. One example is old fashioned carbon black, which was common in mascara until it was banned for use in cosmetics by the U.S. Food and Drug Administration (FDA).

Many cancer-causing and highly toxic pigments are approved for use in artists' paints and materials. Some may even be labeled "non-toxic" because, used as directed, there should be no significant exposure. Using these products directly on the skin, however, is not a directed use and is not advised!

Eye Diseases

The skin around the eyes is more sensitive and more easily penetrated than facial skin. All types of skin diseases (infection, irritation, allergies, and cancer) which affect facial skin also can affect the skin around the eyes. The membrane covering the eye and lining the eyelids (the conjunctiva) can be affected by cosmetic chemicals, producing inflammation (conjunctivitis).

Scratching the eyeball during application of eye makeup is the most common eye injury related to cosmetics. Once an eye abrasion has occurred, the possibility of infection increases. The most important thing to remember about these infections is that they proceed with extreme rapidity and immediate treatment for all painful scratches is recommended. Although most scratches from mascara brushes do not result in infections, those that do can cause ulcers on the cornea, clouding of the cornea, and, in rare cases, blindness.

Infections Transmitted

Makeups can provide a hospitable environment for many microorganisms. The preservatives in makeup are added to increase shelf life and they cannot prevent an infectious organism from one person being transmitted to another.

Examples of just a few of the microorganisms that could survive on makeup include: cold viruses; bacteria such as staphylococcus, streptococcus, and impetigo; fungal infections; and highly infectious viruses such as hepatitis A and herpes simplex. Hepatitis A in particular can remain active for months even on dry surfaces. The AIDS virus probably cannot be transmitted by makeup. But makeup and all personal items such as razors, nail care tools, and similar personal grooming items which might draw blood or contact acne or open sores should not be shared.

Label Reading Tips

Consumer Makeup Labels on consumer makeup are required to carry a complete list of ingredients. An exception is occasionally granted by the FDA to certain manufacturers who claim that certain of their ingredients are trade secrets. These products can be identified when the phrase "and other ingredients" is included on the label. Trade secret ingredients should not be used by people with skin allergies since it may not be possible to find out what is in the makeup.

Professional Makeup Manufacturers of professional makeup are exempt from complete ingredient labeling requirements. Many, however, list their ingredients anyway. These are the products that should be preferred both for the ability to identify ingredients which may be causing symptoms and to choose products best suited for the intended theatrical effect.

"Not Tested on Animals" The FDA requires testing of all cosmetic ingredients. Products that claim not to be tested are only claiming that the product as a whole has not been tested. But to market legally in the U.S., they must have purchased their ingredients from sources that provide tested and certified cosmetic grade chemicals.

Natural Ingredients There is absolutely no reason to trust a "natural" ingredient more than a synthetic one. Somehow we have forgotten the millions of years and the millions of deaths it took people to distinguish between the mushrooms and the toadstools; the henna and the hemlock. We need to be reminded that the deadly allergies to rubber are cause only by *natural* rubber because proteins from the sap of the rubber tree are present. And if we trust natural minerals mined from the earth, we need to be reminded that asbestos is a natural mineral.

Both synthetic and natural ingredients can be hazardous. Be suspicious of any product label that induces you to prejudge the product's safety by its natural origins. Instead, you want the ingredients to be certified, tested, cosmetic grade ingredients that are disclosed by name on the label.

Use As Directed The FDA has different safety standards for makeup ingredients intended for use around the eyes, for lipsticks, and for face makeup. For example, lipstick ingredients must by tested for ingestion hazards. The eye makeups must be tested for ingestion hazards. The eye makeups must protect against infection and be suitable for the especially thin and sensitive skin around the eyes. Makeups, therefore, are considered safe only when used as directed.

Cosmetic Ingredients

Most makeup ingredients fall into a few basic categories: minerals such as talc and kaolin, vegetable powders such as corn starch, oils and waxes, pigments and dyes, and preservatives.

Minerals
Face powders, makeups, and rouges are likely to contain minerals such as talc, kaolin (and other clays), chalk, zinc oxide, titanium dioxide, mica, and bismuth oxychloride. These minerals are harmless to the skin or even when ingested. They also do not cause allergies. They are only hazardous if they are inhaled from dusty products or from airbrushed makeups.

Industrial experience confirms that mineral dusts can irritate the eyes and respiratory system. Talc, kaolin, and mica also can cause long-term lung damage. In addition, talcs in the past often contained significant amounts of asbestos. Anyone who collects antique containers of baby and face powders should never use them.

No law prevents manufacturers from using asbestos-contaminated talcs. Instead, a voluntary industry standard is honored. Nevertheless, a study of commercial cosmetic talcs found traces of asbestos in 6 of 15 samples.[4] But the amounts of asbestos should not be significant if people use the products without creating clouds of dust.

Bismuth oxychloride added for a metallic or pearl luster has produced photosensitivity (skin reactions provoked by sunlight) in some people. Mica can also be used for luster.

Vegetable Powders
To avoid the hazards of mineral powders, some manufacturers have switched to organic substances such as corn starch or rice flour. Like all powders, these are also capable of irritating the respiratory system. They are also more likely to cause allergies especially in people who have food allergies.

Oils, Fats, and Waxes
Cream makeups, rouges, mascaras, and lipsticks are suspended in a base made of either oils and fats alone or oils and fats emulsified with water. There are dozens of cosmetic oils, fats, and waxes. In general, natural oils such as lanolin and cocoa butter are more likely to provoke allergies. Al-

[4]Blount, A. M., "Amphibole Content of Cosmetic and Pharmaceutical Talcs," *Environmental Health Perspectives*, Vol. 94, pp. 225–230, 1991.

most no one is allergic to oils derived from petroleum such as baby oil and Vaseline.

Some of the oily cream products also contain detergents which enable the makeup to penetrate the skin for longer "hold" but which may also result in irritation.

Dyes and Pigments
The FDA assigns names to dyes and pigments. These names indicate whether they are approved for food, drugs, and cosmetics (for example, FD&C Yellow #5) or only for drugs and cosmetics (for example, D&C Red #7). Most cosmetic pigments and dyes have had long-term testing. The FDA approves of these only for uses that will not expose consumers to amounts above a threshold for causing harm.

Lipsticks contain the most dyes and they are associated with a special form of dermatitis called "cheilitis." It is a drying or cracking of the lips, and usually is caused by eosin dyes which stain the lips. Commonly used eosin dyes are D&C Red #21 and 27, lipsticks. Lanolin and perfumes also may cause cheilitis.

Preservatives
Preservatives such as thimerosal (a mercury preservative), methylparaben, and other biocides are found in small amounts in makeup, but are needed to extend shelf-life and keep microorganisms from multiplying in the cosmetics. Most of these are quite toxic, but are in amounts small enough that most people will not be harmed.

Special Effect Makeups

Putty, wax, beeswax, and morticians' wax all can be used to build up a part of the face for theatrical purposes. Collodion can be used to fake age or scars. Natural rubber latex can be made to function in many of these ways, and it also acts as a glue or adhesive, as does spirit gum.

Spirit is an old term applied to alcohol solvents (usually ethyl alcohol). Gum can mean any exudate of a number of plants or trees. Spirit gums today usually are a mixture of natural and synthetic resins in ethyl alcohol. Ideally, the resins should all be identified so users can know if they are likely to have an allergy to one or more of them.

Many people are allergic to these products. One well-known makeup artist told of a case of spirit-gum allergy severe enough to require hospital treatment. Another makeup expert avoided an actor's allergy to spirit gum by placing surgical adhesive tape on his face before applying the spirit gum. Collodion allergies also are well known. People who are allergic to one of these products usually can find another that will do.

Spirit gum can be replaced with synthetic resin surgical adhesives in some cases. Removing spirit gum and adhesives by pulling them off the skin can be harmful, as can removing them with acetone or alcohol, which can dry or crack the skin. Some spirit gum removers are mixtures of solvents that even include toxic chlorinated solvents and skin-absorbing methanol. Take care using these products by peeling spirit gum off gently and using as little solvent as possible. Once removed, use oil, emollients, or moisturizers on the skin to counter drying effects.

Nail Products

Nail polishes, when used properly, are probably reasonably safe because the amounts of solvents which can be inhaled when they dry are very small. Polish removers, on the other hand, consist primarily of a acetone, a solvent which can be a fire hazard and cause narcosis when significant amounts are inhaled (see chapter on Solvents). Although serious poisonings are rare, inhalation of acetone and other polish remover solvents can cause headache, fatigue, and bronchial irritation.

Of greatest concern are the new liquid nail products which harden to create long false nails. Some of these contain plastic acrylate monomers (see the chapter on Plastics), formaldehyde, and other highly sensitizing and toxic chemicals. Take special care to apply these in very well ventilated areas and to avoid exposure to skin and broken skin (cuts, abrasions, etc.). Should symptoms occur, discontinue use immediately.

Use of these products is also associated with nail fungus infections. These infections are extremely hard to treat and sometimes result in permanent disfigurement of the nails.

When Skin Trouble Strikes

When skin problems arise, consult a dermatologist who can tell you which type of dermatitis you have and how to treat it. In general, if your problem is diagnosed as irritant dermatitis or cosmetic acne, you should identify the offending cosmetic and not use it again until healing is complete. If the doctor decides you are allergic to a particular product or ingredient, there are several steps you can take:

1. Try "hypoallergenic" makeup. The term "hypoallergenic" has no legal meaning. However, reputable manufacturers honestly try to eliminate those ingredients known to produce allergies in many people.
2. Try unscented makeups or products with a wholly different scent. One person in ten has an allergy to fragrances and you may be one of them.
3. Try a makeup with a different preservative. Preservatives are known to cause allergic dermatitis in some people. Three preservatives recognized as es-

pecially hyper-allergenic are Quaternium 15, imidazol idinyl urea, and parabens (both methyl and propyl parabens). Look for them on the label.
4. Try comparing labels of products to which you respond, looking for an ingredient they have in common and avoid it.

General Rules for Makeup Users

1. Use only cosmetic products on your skin. Never use paints, dyes, or other non-cosmetic substances.
2. Purchase only ingredient-labeled cosmetics. Many good professional theatrical brands of makeup are now ingredient labeled.
3. Use makeups only as directed. Use face makeup only on the face, eye makeups on the eyes, and so on.
4. Eliminate products which contain ingredients known to cause allergies in many people such as natural rubber, or products with toxic ingredients such as solvents.
5. Wash your hands before and after applying makeup.
6. Never lend your makeup to anyone, and never borrow or accept used makeup from anyone.
7. Do not use aerosol sprays or airbrush products unless there is good local ventilation in the dressing room or makeup room to remove the overspray.
8. Replace old cosmetics regularly. Do not buy cosmetics which look old or shopworn.
9. Avoid creating clouds of face powder or talcum which can be inhaled. Discard old face and bath powders.
10. Moisten brushes or pencils with clean tap water, not with saliva.
11. Seek medical advice and treatment for eye injuries, dermatitis, acne, and other skin and eye conditions.
12. Avoid smoking, eating, or drinking when applying makeup. Do not smoke or stay in dressing rooms where others smoke.
13. When removing spirit gum, latex, etc., avoid prolonged skin contact with solvents like acetone; replace lost skin oils and moisture.

Additional Precautions for Makeup Artists

1. VENTILATION. Makeup artists are going to spend long hours in the makeup room and need to insist that the ventilation be sufficient for the products used. Most makeup rooms only have inlets in

the ceiling for a recirculating ventilation system. Such rooms clearly are not ventilated sufficiently for spray and airbrush products.

Ideally, makeup rooms should have an exhaust fan or local hood system if sprays are going to be used. This author has seen makeup tables with slot ventilation built in. In another case, a wig room had local exhaust vents at wigform height to catch the hair spray. These kinds of systems are rare now, but should become a standard in the industry.

2. SAFE AND SANITARY. Makeup artists should wash their hands before they start on each client. They should also be observant about the skin condition of their clients and use gloves if open sores, acne, or signs of skin disease are present. Gloves must be changed between clients.

3. GROUP MAKEUP PRECAUTIONS. Makeup artists need to insure that their clients' makeup is not shared. Cream sticks and lipsticks can be sliced into pieces and put into small containers and labeled with each client's name. Sponges and applicators should be disposable. Powders can be supplied to each in the smallest possible containers. Eyeliners and mascara should not be shared. The water used to moisten pencils or brushes should be changed for each client. Paper cups can be used to make cleaning water containers unnecessary.

4. TRAINING. Makeup artists need training about bloodborne pathogens similar to the training required for home-care nurses aids. They need to know how these diseases are transmitted, how to put on and remove gloves to avoid recontaminating themselves, how to dispose of contaminated applicators or sponges, and similar skills.

Makeup artists also need hazard communication training about the chemicals in makeup, spray products, disinfectants, and similar toxic products used.

Monona Rossol is the President of Arts, Crafts, and Theater Safety and is the Safety Director for United Scenic Artists, local 829, International Alliance of Theatrical and Stage Employees (IATSE).

Readers with questions about safety may contact Monona Rossol at:

181 Thompson St., #23
New York, NY 10012–2586 or at ACTSNYC@cs.com

Fashions in Makeup

One of the determining factors in any realistic makeup for the stage is the historical period to which the character belongs. This applies not only to the hairstyle but, in many cases, to the facial makeup as well. The kohl-lined eyes of the ancient Egyptians, the whitened faces of eighteenth-century ladies, the fashionably pale lips of the early 1960s—all must be taken into consideration in creating makeups for those periods.

The brief notes in this chapter are intended to give an overall view of the subject and to serve as a reference in doing period plays. Although hair styles are mentioned from time to time along with the makeup, more extensive information can be found in the more than 40 plates of hairstyle drawings in Appendix F.

Ancient Peoples

Among the Egyptians, both men and women used makeup. The eyelids were frequently colored with green malachite and the eyes heavily lined and the eyebrows darkened with black kohl (powdered antimony sulfide). Carmine was used on the lips; for coloring the cheeks, red clay was mixed with saffron. Veins, especially on the bosom, were sometimes accented with blue. White lead was occasionally used for whitening the skin. Both men and women shaved their heads and wore wigs. The hair was usually dark brown, though at the height of Egyptian civilization it was sometimes dyed red, blue, or even green. Beards were often false and tied on with a ribbon or a strap; no attempt was made to make them look natural. Sometimes they were even made of gold or other metal.

The Assyrians and the Persians also dyed their hair and their beards, the Assyrians preferring black, the Persians, henna color. The eyes were lined with kohl,

though not so heavily as those of the Egyptians. The brows, however, were often made very heavy and close together. Both natural hair and wigs were worn, and the hair was curled with tongs. On special occasions it was sometimes decorated with gold dust and intertwined with gold threads.

Upper-class Greek women sometimes painted their cheeks and lips rose or earthy red, whitened their faces, darkened their eyebrows, shadowed their eyelids, and, upon occasion, dyed their hair or wore wigs. Red hair was popular, and blue, it is reported, was not unknown. Fashionable Roman women and some men whitened their faces, rouged their cheeks and lips, darkened their eyebrows, and sometimes dyed their hair blond or red. During the period of the extremely elaborate and rapidly changing hair styles for women, wigs were frequently worn. Men sometimes wore wigs or painted on hair to cover their baldness. Both sexes wore beauty patches made of leather.

The Middle Ages

Upper-class Medieval women liked a pale complexion and in the late Middle Ages frequently used white lead to achieve it. Cheek and lip rouge were often used. In the thirteenth century, rouge was in general use among women; often rose or pink was worn by the upper classes and a cheaper brownish red by the lower. Fifteenth-century French women sometimes painted their cheeks and their lips with a crimson rouge. Throughout the Middle Ages, rouge seems usually to have been applied in a round spot with some attempt at blending. Various colors of eyeshadow were used to some extent in the Middle Ages, and the upper lid was sometimes lined with black. Eyebrows were natural until the late

Middle Ages and early Renaissance, when women of fashion (and in England, at least, even lower-class women) plucked their brows to a fine, arched line (Figure E-1). Sometimes, it seems, the eyebrows were shaved off completely. The hairline was also plucked so that little or no hair would show below the headdresses. The plucking was even done in public.

Both black and blond hair were fashionable, but red was not and would not be until Elizabeth I made it so.

The Sixteenth Century

The Renaissance brought a marked increase in the use of cosmetics but not, unfortunately, much improvement in the knowledge of how to make them safe for the skin. Frequently, irritating and poisonous artists' pigments were used to paint the face as if it were a living canvas. The skin was whitened and the cheeks and lips rouged. In *Love's Labours Lost* Byron says:

Your mistresses dare never come in rain. For fear their colours should be washed away.

FIGURE E-1 Sixteenth-century lady. *Makeup based on a contemporary portrait. Front hair soaped out and brows blocked out with spirit gum and derma wax. Latex nose. Makeup by student Carol Doscher.*

Spanish wool and Spanish papers (wool or small leaves of paper containing powdered pigment) were popular for rouge (and sometimes for the white as well) and continued to be used for several centuries.

By the end of the sixteenth century the artificially high forehead for women was no longer in fashion. Women had stopped plucking their eyebrows to a thin line, and some of them had begun to spot their faces with black patches.

Although some men painted their faces, this was not looked upon with favor by either sex. Nonetheless, Henri III is said to have gone about the streets of Paris "made up like an old coquette," his face plastered with white and red, his hair covered with perfumed violet powder.

Wigs were sometimes worn (both Elizabeth I and Mary Queen of Scots had large numbers of them); false hair was used; and beards, as well as hair and wigs, were sometimes dyed. Elizabeth favored red hair and thus made it a popular color. White or tinted powder was sometimes used on the hair. Venetian women in particular sat for days in the sun bleaching their hair and, according to contemporary reports, occasionally suffered severe reactions from overexposure to the sun. Blond wigs were sometimes worn instead.

Elizabeth's teeth, like so many people's of the time were yellow, spotted, and rotting away.

The Seventeenth Century

Cosmetics were more widely used in the seventeenth century. Spanish papers in red and white were still in use. Samuel Pepys in his diary referred to his cousin, Mrs. Pierce, as being "still very pretty, but paints red on her face, which makes me hate her." On the other hand, the Earl of Chesterfield wrote to his well-painted Miss Livingston: "Your complexion is none of those faint whites that represents a Venus in the green sickness, but such as Apollo favours and visits most."

It is important to remember in doing Restoration plays that country girls still relied on their natural coloring but that ladies who wore makeup made no attempt to conceal the fact. Faces were usually whitened with powder or washes. Dark complexions were considered common.

Rouge worn by the upper classes was usually rose colored, whereas that used by lower-class women was an ochre red, often applied excessively.

Eyebrows were occasionally darkened, and a creme eyeshadow in blue, brown, or gray was sometimes worn by upper-class women. It was usually concentrated on the upper lid near the eye but might occasionally, in a burst of enthusiasm, be allowed to creep up toward the eyebrow.

Rouge, pink or flesh powder, and sometimes a touch of lip rouge were worn by men of fashion in the last decade of the century. Patches were worn by some fashionable men—whether or not they wore makeup—and in profusion by fashionable ladies. Some, according to Beaumont and Fletcher, were "cut like stars, some in half moons, some in lozenges." There were other shapes as well. Their placement was not without significance—a patch close to the eye was called *la passionée,* one beside the mouth, *la baiseuse,* on the cheek, *la gallante,* and so on. Ladies were seldom content with one patch. According to John Bulwer, writing in 1650 in his *Anthropometamorphosis,* "Our ladies have lately entertained a vaine custom of spotting their faces out of an affectation of a mole, to set off their beauty, such as Venus had; and it is well if one black patch will serve to make their faces remarkable, for some fill their visages full of them, varied into all manner of shapes and figures." Bulwer includes an illustration of a "visage full of them." Eight years later, in *Wit Restored,* there appeared a few lines on the subject:

> Their faces are besmear'd and pierc'd
> With several sorts of patches.
> As if some cats their skins had flead
> With scarres, half moons, and notches.

The patches were usually made of black taffeta or Spanish leather (usually red) or sometimes of gummed paper. It was also suggested in *Wit Restored* that patches might be of some practical use in covering blemishes. It is reported, in fact, that the Duchess of Newcastle

FIGURE E-2 **Lady with patches** *English Woodcut, c.1680.*

wore "many black patches because of pimples around her mouth." Plumpers, made of balls of wax, were sometimes carried in the mouth by aging ladies to fill out their sunken cheeks.

The fashion of wigs for men was begun by Louis XIII; black wigs were popularized by Charles II. At the end of the century, light powder (mostly gray, beige, and tan, but not white) was used on the hair. Hairstyles even developed political significance for a time—whereas the Cavaliers wore their hair long, the Puritans cut theirs short and were called Roundheads. Beards and mustaches were carefully groomed with special combs and brushes and kept in shape with perfumed wax.

Teeth were still poorly cared for, and they often looked it.

The Eighteenth Century

Face painting and patching continued to flourish in the eighteenth century. In Wycherly's *Love in a Wood,* published in 1735, Dapperwit, who is trying to arouse Miss Lucy, says to Ranger, "Pish, give her but leave to gape, rub her Eyes, and put on her Day-Pinner, the long Patch under the left Eye, awaken the Roses on her Cheeks with some Spanish Wool. . . .Doors fly off the Hinges, and she into my Arms."

As for patches, a prominent marquise is reported to have appeared at a party wearing sixteen of them, one in the shape of a tree on which were perched two love birds. Sometimes the patches had political significance—Whigs patching on the right side and Tories on the left. Ladies who had not made up their minds patched on both sides.

Face painting became more garish in the second half of the eighteenth century. The ladies "enamelled" their faces with white lead and applied bright rouge heavily and with little subtlety. Horace Walpole, in writing of the coronation of George III, mentions that "lord Bolingbroke put on rouge upon his wife and the duchess of Bedford in the Painted Chamber; the Duchess of Queensbury told me of the latter, that she looked like an orange-peach, half red, half yellow."

In *The Life of Lady Sarah Lennox* we read that a contemporary of Lady Caroline Mackenzie remarked that she wore "such quantities of white that she was terrible" and that the Duchess of Grafton "having left red and white quite off is one of the coarsest brown women I ever saw." A guest at a party in 1764 was described as wearing on her face "rather too much yellow mixed with the red; she . . . would look very agreeable if she added blanc to the rouge instead of gamboge."

The white paints, according to *The Art of Beauty* (written anonymously and published in 1825),

affect the eyes which swell and inflame and are rendered painful and watery. They change the texture of the skin, on which they produce pimples and cause rheums; attack the teeth, make them ache, destroy the enamel, and loosen them. . . .To the inconveniences we have just enumerated, we add this, of turning the skin black when it is exposed to the contact of sulphureous or phosphoric exhalations. Accordingly, those females who make use of them ought carefully to avoid going too near substances in a state of putrefaction, the vapours of sulphur . . . and the exhalation of bruised garlic.

The warnings about the white lead paints were hardly exaggerated. Walpole wrote in 1766 that the youthful and attractive Lady Fortrose was "at the point of death, killed like Lady Coventry and others, by white lead, of which nothing could break her." At least they did not lose their lives through ignorance of the dangerous nature of their paints.

Despite the seemingly excessive makeup used by English ladies, they still lagged behind the French. Walpole reported that French princesses wore "their red of a deeper dye than other women, though all use it extravagantly." Lady Sarah Lennox found the Princesse de Condé to be the only lady in Parisian society who did not "wear rouge, for all the rest daub themselves so horribly that it's shocking."

Casanova was of the opinion that the rouge, though excessive, had its attractions and that the charm of the ladies' painted faces lay in the carelessness with which the rouge was applied, without the slightest attempt at naturalness.

The rouge was sometimes applied in a triangular pattern, sometimes more rounded. About 1786 hairdresser William Barker described French fashions in makeup:

From a little below the eye there is sometimes drawn a red streak to the lower temple and another streak in a semicircular form to the other line. If the eyebrows are not naturally dark, they make them so. . . . Sometimes the French ladies . . . put on rouge of the highest color in the form of a perfect circle, without shading it off at all.

But Mr. Barker added that Marie-Antoinette had introduced a more natural application of rouge. A red pomade was used on the lips as well. One recipe for lip pomade suggested that the lady might add some gold leaf if she wished.

But it was not only the women who used cosmetics. In 1754 a correspondent wrote to *Connoisseur:*

I am ashamed to tell you that we are indebted to Spanish Wool for many of our masculine ruddy complexions. A pretty fellow lacquers his pale face with as many varnishes as a fine lady. . . . I fear it will be found, upon examination, that most of our pretty fellows who lay on carmine are painting a rotten post.

Wigs were almost universally worn by men, much less frequently by women. Powdered hair was in fashion until near the end of the century. White powder was introduced in 1703; but tinted powder—gray, pink, blue, lavender, blond, brown—continued to be worn. Facial hair was never fashionable and rarely worn except, in some instances, by soldiers. Military hairstyles were strictly regulated.

The wigs and high headdresses and powdered hair passed, however, and with them the garish makeup. At the end of the century a more-or-less natural makeup was in vogue.

The Nineteenth Century

In the early years of the nineteenth century, fashionable cheeks were rouged. A portrait by Sir Thomas Lawrence, painted about 1803, shows the rose-colored rouge applied in a round pattern. The lips were also rose. But excessive rouging was not always looked upon with favor. The Countess of Granville wrote disapprovingly to her sister of ladies whose makeup she considered ill-bred: "Mrs. Ervington, dressed and rouged like an altar-piece but still beautiful . . . Miss Rodney, a very pretty girl, but with rather too much rouge and naivete . . . Lady Elizabeth Stuart by dint of rouge and an auburn wig looks only not pretty but nothing worse." A Mrs. Bagot she described as being "rouged to the eyes."

The *Art of Beauty,* published in 1825, noted that it was "not the present fashion to make so much use of red as was done some years ago; at least, it is applied with more art and taste. With very few exceptions, ladies have absolutely renounced that glaring, fiery red with which our antiquated dames formerly masked their faces."

In Victorian England there was a reaction against any form of paint on the face, though creams and lotions and a little powder were acceptable. Makeup was used nonetheless, but so subtly (by "nice" women, that is) that it was often undetectable. A woman who would not dare buy rouge in a public shop was often not above rubbing her cheeks with a bit of red silk dipped in wine or trying some other homemade artifice.

As the Victorian influence became more pervasive, the use of cosmetics became more furtive, particularly in the United States. Despite the example of George Washington, who was perfumed and powdered along with other men of his class, sentiment against any use of cosmetics by men was becoming exceedingly strong—so much so, in fact, that the revelation that Martin Van Buren used such cosmetic aids as Corinthian Oil of Cream, Double Extract of Queen Victoria, and Concentrated Persian Essence helped to end his political career. But in other countries, essential items for the gentleman's toilet included hair oil, dye for the hair and beard, perfumed chalk for sallow complexions, and a little rouge, which was to be used with great care so as to avoid detection. The use of cosmetics was revived to some extent in the 1860s, and it was reported that rouge was "extensively employed by ladies to brighten the complexion" and to give "the seeming bloom of health to the pallid or sallow cheek." Eyebrows were dark, full, moderately thick, and attractively curved. The Empress Eugénie is believed to have introduced the use of mascara, and Charles Meyer, a German teenager trained in wigmaking, introduced Leichner's theatrical makeup—the first greasepaint to be made in America.

By the end of the century the shops were well supplied with fascinating and irresistible cosmetics. Not only did women not resist them, but they were known brazenly to repair their makeup in public. In 1895 the editor of the *London Journal of Fashion* wrote:

> Rouge, discreetly put on, of course, forms a part of every toilet as worn by fashionable women, and some among these are beginning to use their toilet-powders somewhat too heavily. Even those who do not use rouge aim at producing a startling effect of contrast by making the lips vividly red and the face very pale, with copiously laid on powder or enamel—which when badly put on is of very bad effect, and, in point of fact, greatly ages a woman. Still, the entirely unaided face is becoming more and more rare, almost everybody uses other makeup effects, if not rouge, and an almost scarlet lip-salve.

It should be particularly noted, in planning your own makeup for a Victorian woman, that well-bred young girls never used makeup, though they did pinch their cheeks occasionally. Married women might resort to a delicate rouge, very subtly applied so as to look like natural color, but they did not rouge their lips. They might, however, employ various methods of bringing the blood to the surface, such as biting; and they might soften the lips with cream. Lipstick was used mainly by actresses on stage and by courtesans. Victorian eyebrows were natural (Figure E-3).

Early in the century, wigs for women were fashionable. Black and blond were both popular colors. By the 1820s black was favored. *The Art of Beauty* included a recipe for "Grecian Water for Darkening the Hair," which, the reader was warned, was not only dangerous to the skin, but might eventually turn the hair purple. In the second half of the century the preference was for brown or black hair, and dyes were freely used by both men and women—the men for their beards as well as their hair.

In 1878 Mrs. Haweis wrote that red hair was all the rage; and in 1895 the *Journal of Fashion* announced that "the coming season will be one of complexions out of boxes . . . and the new colour for the hair a yellow so deep as to verge on red. It is not pretty, it is not be-

FIGURE E-3 Late nineteenth-century lady. *Natural look. (After a drawing by Friedrich von Kaulbach.)*

coming, and it is somewhat fast-looking because manifestly unreal."

The Twentieth Century

At the turn of the century, many women were using henna to turn their hair fashionably auburn. The purpose of makeup was still to enhance the natural beauty rather than to look frankly painted. Some women, including Queen Alexandra, tended to defeat their purpose by applying their makeup quite heavily, though the colors used were delicate. The English and the Americans lagged behind the French in the frank and open application of paint. In the second decade, the use of eyeshadow, eyebrow pencil, mascara, and lipstick became widespread.

In the early twenties, beauty experts in England and America were still advising natural-looking makeup, but it was a losing battle. In the mid-twenties, geranium or raspberry lips and a pale complexion were fashionable, and eyebrows were being plucked into a thin, hard line. In 1927 it was reported, with marked disapproval, that some women actually used eyeshadow. They were also lining their eyes with black and painting their lips cerise. By the end of the decade, heavily painted, bee-stung lips, plucked eyebrows, and short hair were the mark of the emancipated woman.

It was in the late twenties that sun-tanned faces became popular, and dark powders were made available for those who did not tan well or had no time to lie in the sun. Orange rouge and lipstick were in fashion, and the lips were overpainted with an exaggerated cupid's bow. Beauty experts recommended that eyeshadow be applied close to the lashes, then blended out to elongate the eye. Brown was recommended for day use, blue for night. Rouge and lipstick also came in day and evening colors–light for day, dark for evening.

Early in the thirties, orange lipstick went out and raspberry came in. Even schoolgirls used makeup. Their older sisters bleached their hair platinum, and their mothers or even their grandmothers rinsed away their gray. Hollywood set the styles. For the first time in history women made their mouths larger–Joan Crawford style. The bee-stung lips were gone. Fingernails and toenails were painted various shades of red, gold, silver, green, blue, violet, and even, for a time, black. Polish had been used for some years previously, but it was either colorless or natural pink.

In the forties and fifties, extremes of artificial makeup subsided somewhat, though lips were still heavily painted. Rouge became less and less used and eventually was omitted entirely by fashionable women. Makeup bases in both water-soluble cake and cream form were available in a variety of shades, ranging from a pale pink to a deep tan, and were usually applied too heavily. Eye makeup was still more or less natural. Eyebrows were no longer plucked to a thin line, colored eyeshadow was used mostly for evening wear, and mascara and false eyelashes were intended to look natural.

In the early half of the sixties, however, the natural look was out. Makeup became as extreme as the hairstyles, with a shift of emphasis from the mouth to the eyes. Lips were not only pale (either unpainted or made up with a pale lipstick), they were, for awhile, even painted white. This fashion, like most others, began in Paris. Eye makeup became heavier and heavier, with colored eyeshadow generously applied for daytime wear and the eyes heavily lined with black in a modified Egyptian style. False eyelashes became thick and full, and sometimes several pairs were worn at once. It was a time for restless dissatisfaction and experimentation. White and various pale, often metallic, tints of eyeshadow were tried. Eyebrows were even whitened to try to focus attention on the eye itself, and extremely pale makeup bases were worn. The objective seemed to be great dark eyes staring out of a colorless blob. Hair was tinted, rinsed, dyed, teased, ironed, and wound on enormous rollers, which, during the daytime, were sometimes worn in public. Sometimes the hair was just left to hang (possibly a beatnik influence), framing a pale face with great black furry-lashed eyes.

The 1970s began with a flurry of artificiality–red eyelashes, green hair, colored polkadots around the eyes, doll-like makeup on the cheeks, heavy black eyelashes painted on the skin, eyebrows blocked out with makeup. No innovation seemed too bizarre. But reaction set in, and a greater naturalness in makeup took over. In 1972, however, severely plucked eyebrows were once again in fashion–sometimes no more than the thin line of the twenties. But rouge was natural, and

lip color varied with the season. By 1974 the variations included stronger colors–both very bright and very dark–than had been worn for a number of years. In 1975 the tawny look was fashionable, with cheek coloring tending to be muted and lips either muted or bright and clear. Eyes were shadowed with such colors as Evergreen, Parsley, Walnut, Plum, or Heather and highlighted with tints like pink, lavender, or pale yellow. Eyebrows were light or medium.

In the latter part of 1976 there was a shift among some makeup artists toward pink and rose and plum. Among some women who continued to wear the brown tones, coral lips were popular, but others preferred the deeper, tawnier shades. Lips were outlined with makeup pencils, filled in with brushes, then covered with colored gloss. Eyeshadow colors were often tinged with silver, copper, or gold.

Makeup in 1977 was darker and stronger, with rich, dark reds ranging from brownish to plum. Eyes were shadowed with earth tones–browns, grays, muted greens–and lip coloring might be brownish, deep and rich, or bright and clear. Makeup for evening frequently glimmered with gold or silver.

The emphasis in 1978 was definitely away from the browns and corals and more toward burgundy, magenta, fuchsia, and bluish pinks. The fashionable look was less natural and more sophisticated, with bolder, brighter makeup–deeper eyeshadow colors, bright rouge instead of soft brushers, with even more gloss on the lips. Eye lining was less smudged but still softened with no hard lines. For evening, lighter foundations were worn with smoky, shadowed eyes, bright rouge, and bright, glossy lips.

Continuing the trend, makeup in 1979 was supposed to look like makeup, and a woman with Sunset Rose cheeks, Spirited Rhubarb lips, and Honest Amber eyelids (highlighted with Pearlfrost Pink) might merely be on her way to the supermarket.

The new decade began quietly, on the one hand, with natural-looking eyebrows, soft, opalescent colors, and no hard lines around the eyes. But on the other hand, there were startlingly pale-faced punk rockers with charcoal-smudged eye sockets and bleached blond or dyed black hair shellacked into fierce points and sprayed in streaks or spots with brilliant purple, green, or orange. For summer the tawny look was in fashion–grey-brown or olive green on the eyes and a brownish red on the mouth. This look continued into the fall, when colors were sometimes muted, sometimes exploding into a dazzling array of magentas, mauves, and fuchsias vying with coppery reds and oranges and eyes accented with blue, violet, or green mascara. The eyebrows, however, were still natural-looking.

In 1982 makeup tended to match the natural skin color, with no hard lines and, for awhile, no strong, contrasting colors. In the fall, however, colors deepened, with tones of red, purple, and bronze. Cheek and lip coloring was subtle, but eye coloring was not. Two or three colors, including metallics, might be used on the eyes, along with heavy, slightly smudgy black lines surrounding them. Eyebrows were pale.

Emphasis on the eyes continued into 1983, with charcoal and black still surrounding the eye, but with less color. Eyebrows ranged from pale to very dark. Lip and cheek coloring remained generally subtle, often pale. In mid-year, however, the "assymetrical look" was in vogue. Various colors were applied casually to the eyelids, but not the same colors on both eyelids—nor, in fact, was the same foundation color used on both sides of the face. The effect was, predictably, bizarre. In more conservative makeup, emphasis on the eyes continued for awhile but by the winter had become more natural-looking.

The natural look continued into 1984, with softer, paler tones intended to enhance one's appearance rather than to attract attention. When strong color was used, it was likely to be on a single feature-usually the eyes or the lips.

In the spring of 1985 eyebrows were usually unplucked but darkened a bit if they were light, the eyes accented with deep colors (black, gray, purple, blue, bronze), often with more than one color. Lips might be pink, purplish, bright red, or red-orange. Foundation colors were usually natural-looking, tending toward the warm tones, and the general intent seemed to be to look healthy rather than bizarre. However, the purples, which were fairly popular, tended to defeat this.

In 1986 popular colors, according to *Vogue,* were orange, metallic, and lavender, used separately or in various combinations—a bronze foundation, for example, with lavender on the eyelids, cheeks, and lips, or a pale foundation with bronze on the eyelids, cheeks, and lips. All-bronze makeups were also worn, with variations of brown and bronzy red around the eyes, as well as on the cheeks and lips. In the autumn, colors were warmer and more intense, and there was a greater variety of colors and fewer rules about their application. Metallic eyeshadows were available in gold, silver, and copper; and blushers, in bronzed pink, soft apricot, or coral. The objective for the final makeup was, it was said, to create a "natural" look.

In 1987 glittery, bronzy colors were out, and the new matte makeup featured a variety of tints as well as texture. Although the rose tints were popular, especially among the more conservative, yellow lips, pink eyeshadow, and brightly colored mascara could be seen on the more adventurous. Eyebrows were not only darkened but were sometimes brushed upward to make them fuller and slightly shaggy, with dark eyeshadows surrounding the eye. With this strong emphasis on eye makeup, cheek and lip makeup was fairly natural. But for the young and less conservative, the hair was sometimes boldly streaked with bright colors. And by the end of 1987 women were once again using compacts and powdering their faces in public.

Fashions in Hair

The following pages illustrate men's and women's fashions in hair from ancient times to the present day.

A Sumerian

B Egyptian

C Egyptian

D Egyptian

E Sumerian

F Egyptian

G Hittite

H Egyptian

I Egyptian

J Egyptian

K Egyptian

L Egyptian

M Assyrian

N Assyrian

O Assyrian

P Etruscan

Q Etruscan

R Etruscan

S Etruscan

T Persian

FIGURE F-1 Ancient peoples, men.

APPENDIX F : Fashions in Hair

A
Greek

B
Greek

C
Greek

D
Greek

E
Greek

F
Greek

G
Greek

H
Greek

I
Roman

J
Roman

K
Roman

L
Roman

M
Roman

N
Roman

O
Roman

P
Roman

Q
Roman

R
Roman

S
Egyptian

T
Roman

U
Roman

V
Roman

W
Roman

X
Roman

FIGURE F-2 Ancient peoples, men.

A Egyptian

B Sumerian

C Semitic Akkadian

D Egyptian

E Egyptian

F Egyptian

G Egyptian

H Egyptian

I Egyptian

J Egyptian

K Etruscan

L Greek

M Greek

N Greek

O Greek

P Greek

Q Greek

R Greek

S Etruscan

FIGURE F-3 Ancient peoples, women.

A
Greek

B
Egyptian

C
Greek

D
Roman

E
Roman

F
Roman

G
Roman

H
Roman

I
Roman

J
Roman

K
Roman

L
Roman

M
Roman

N
Roman

O
Roman

P
Roman

Q
Roman

R
Roman

S
Roman

T
Roman

FIGURE F-4 Ancient peoples, women.

A
6th century

B
Byzantine

C
c.547

D
c.750

E
c.879

F
10th century

G
c.1130

H
c.1150

I
13th century

J
c.1150

K
c.1160

L
c.1235

M
c.1245

N
13th century

O
13th century

P
14th century

Q
14th century

R
14th century

S
14th century

T
c.1376

U
c.1390

V
1390

W
c.1409

FIGURE F-5 Medieval men.

A c.400

B Byzantine

C Byzantine

D 1083

E 1180

F c.12th century

G

H 13th century

I 13th century

J 12th or 13th century

K c.1340

L 14th century

M 14th century

N c.1310

O 14th century

P After 1320

Q 1364

R 14th century

S c.1360

FIGURE F-6 Medieval women.

A
Early, French

B
1412

C
Early, English

D
1416

E
Early, French

F
German

G
c.1440

H
1448

I
1445

J
Mid-century

K
Mid-century

L
1480

M
1476

N
1491

O
1488

P
Late, Italian

Q
Late, Italian

R
1486

S
Late, Italian

T
c.1490

U
Late, Italian

V
c.1495

W
Late, Italian

FIGURE F-7 Fifteenth-century men.

A c.1400

B 1st half

C Mid-century

D 1st half

E c.1440

F 1447

G c.1470

H Last quarter

I 1488

J Last quarter

K Last quarter

L Last quarter

M Last quarter

N Last quarter

O Last quarter

P 1495

Q Last quarter

R 1492

S Last quarter

T c.1500

FIGURE F-8 Fifteenth-century women.

A Early years

B 1510

C 2nd. quarter

D 1520

E 1520

F GERMAN

G 1529

H 1530

I 1530

J 1535

K 1540's

L 2nd. quarter

M Mid - century

N

O 3rd. quarter

P 3rd. quarter

Q 3rd. quarter

R c. 1575

S Last quarter

T Mid - century

U 1594

V 1596

W 1599

FIGURE F-9 Sixteenth-century men.

A c. 1512

B c. 1515

C c.1515

D Before 1520

E 1520

F 1st. quarter

G c. 1550

H c. 1550

I c. 1550

J c. 1550

K c. 1560

L c. 1560

M First half

N c. 1575

O Last quarter

P 1560's

Q Last quarter

R Last quarter

S Last quarter

T c. 1595

U c. 1597

FIGURE F-10 Sixteenth-century women.

A
Before
1616

B
1614

C
1614

D
1628

E
Early
1600's

F
c. 1630

G
c. 1630

H
c. 1630

I
c. 1630

J
c. 1630

K
c. 1630

L
c. 1640

M
1632

N
1635

O
c. 1635

P
1645

Q
1645

R
1649

S
c. 1650

T
c. 1650

U
c. 1680

V
1688

FIGURE F-11 Seventeenth-century men.

A c.1610

B 1610

C 1615

D c.1630

E c.1630

F c.1635

G 1640

H c.1640

I c.1640

J 1643

K c.1650

L

M c.1650

N c.1650

O 1660

P 1665

Q 1680

R 1670s

S 1680s

T 1690s

FIGURE F-12 Seventeenth-century women.

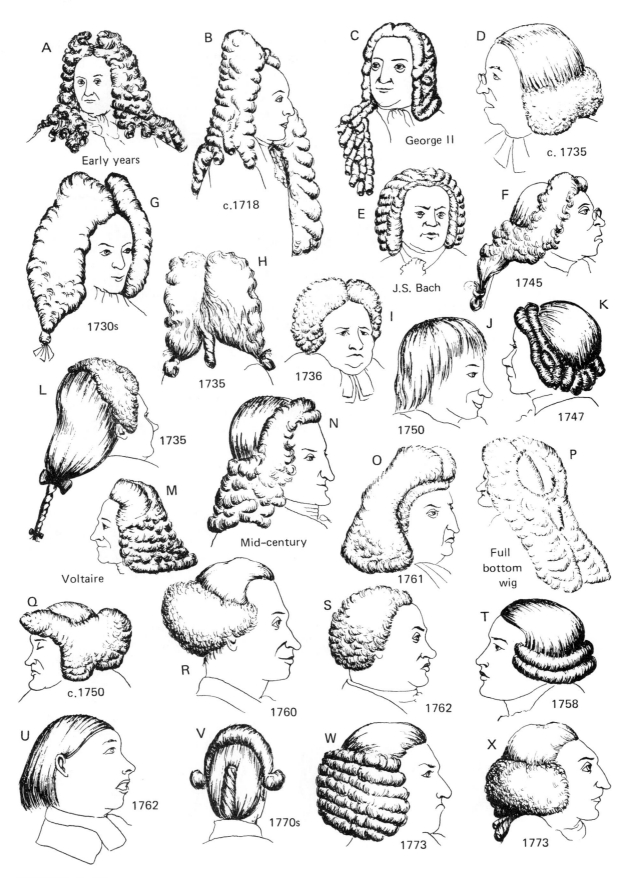

A Early years

B c.1718

C George II

D c. 1735

G 1730s

E J.S. Bach

F 1745

H 1735

I 1736

J 1750

K 1747

L 1735

M Voltaire

N Mid-century

O 1761

P Full bottom wig

Q c.1750

R 1760

S 1762

T 1758

U 1762

V 1770s

W 1773

X 1773

FIGURE F-13 Eighteenth-century men.

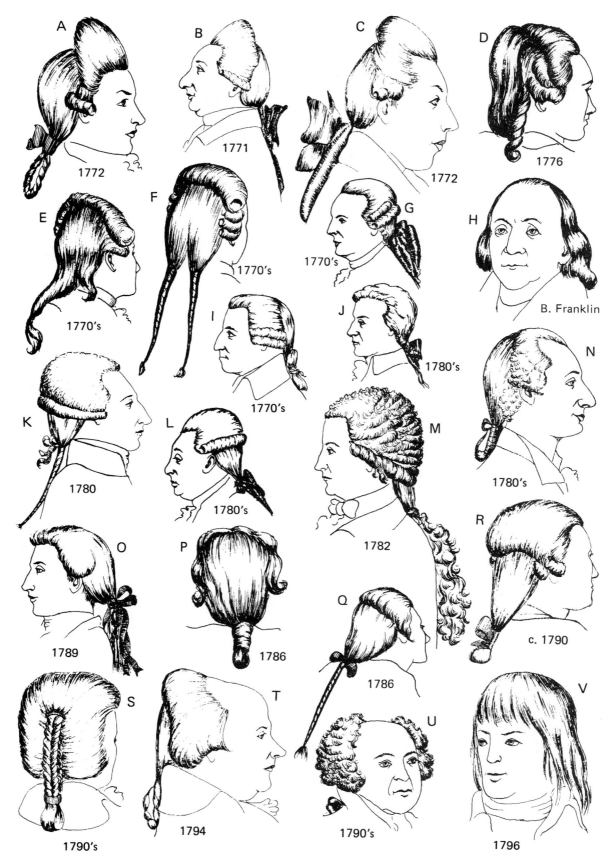

FIGURE F-14 Eighteenth-century men.

A c. 1700

B c. 1702

C 1732

D c. 1730

E c. 1735

F c. 1750

G 1750's

H 1760's

I 1764

J c. 1770

K c. 1770

L 1774

M 1773

N 1774

O c. 1776

P c. 1776

Q 1776

R 1778

FIGURE F-15 Eighteenth-century women.

A 1778

B 1780

C 1780

D 1780

E 1782

F 1781

G 1788

H 1798

I 1794

J 1796

K 1790's

L c. 1788

M 1797

N 1798

FIGURE F-16 Eighteenth-century women.

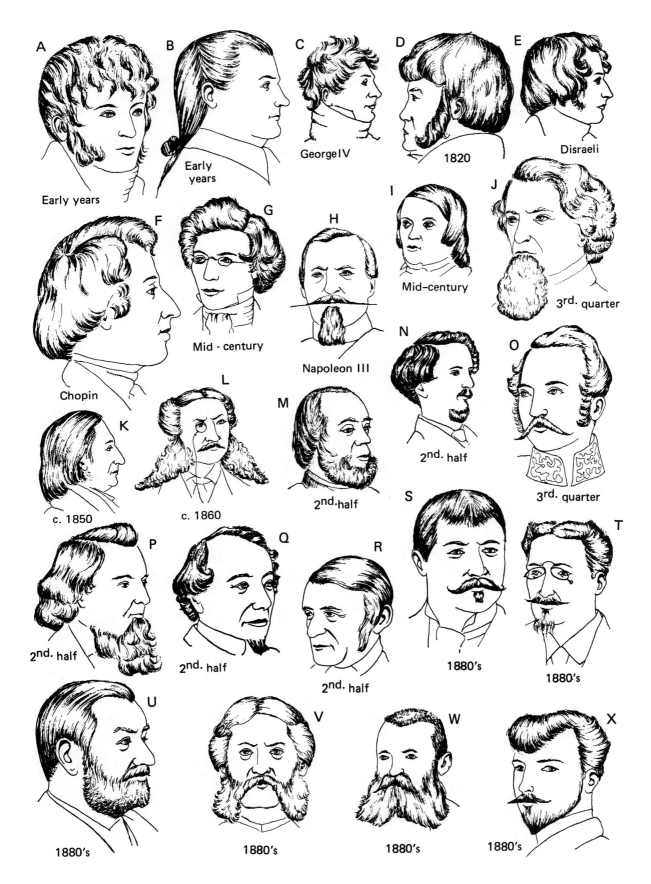

A
Early years

B
Early years

C
George IV

D
1820

E
Disraeli

F
Chopin

G
Mid - century

H
Napoleon III

I
Mid–century

J
3rd. quarter

K
c. 1850

L
c. 1860

M
2nd. half

N
2nd. half

O
3rd. quarter

P
2nd. half

Q
2nd. half

R
2nd. half

S
1880's

T
1880's

U
1880's

V
1880's

W
1880's

X
1880's

FIGURE F-17 Nineteenth-century men.

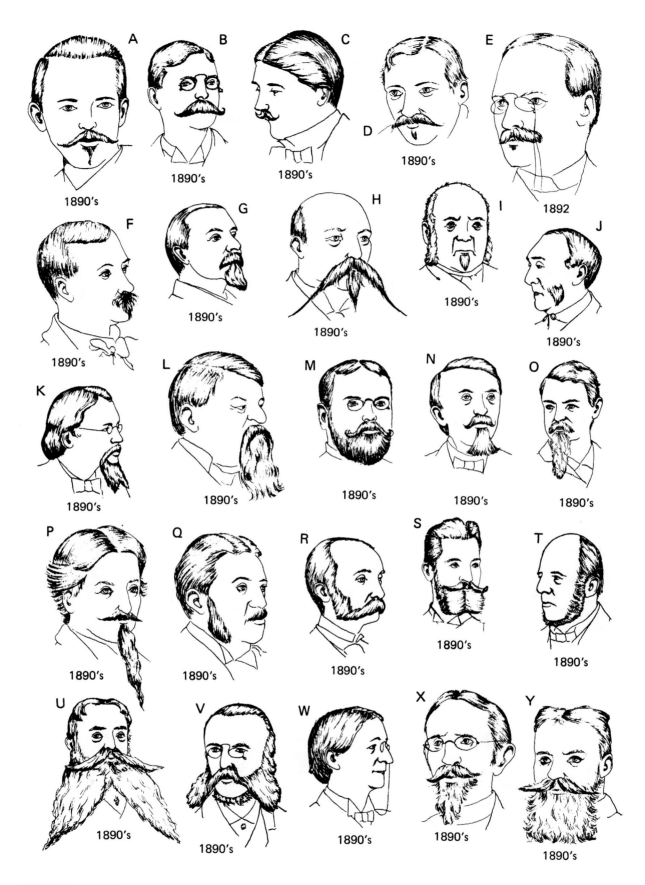

A
1890's

B
1890's

C
1890's

D
1890's

E
1892

F
1890's

G
1890's

H
1890's

I
1890's

J
1890's

K
1890's

L
1890's

M
1890's

N
1890's

O
1890's

P
1890's

Q
1890's

R
1890's

S
1890's

T
1890's

U
1890's

V
1890's

W
1890's

X
1890's

Y
1890's

FIGURE F-18 Nineteenth-century men.

A 1803

B 1808

C 1813

D c. 1820

E 1827

F 1831

G 1841

H 1848

I 1855

J 1860

K 1862

L 1865

M 1869

N 1869

O 1874

P 1877

Q 1879

R 1880

S 1885

T 1888

U 1894

V 1894

W 1894

X 1899

FIGURE F-19 Nineteenth-century women.

A
1905

B
Early years

C
Early years

D
Early years

E
Early years

F
Early years

G
c.1922

H
1926

I
1929

J
1930's

K
1937

L
1940

M
1953

N
1956

O
1958

P
1959

Q
1961

R
1961

S
1961

T
1962

U
1962

V
1963

W
1965

X
1966

Y
1966

FIGURE F-20 Twentieth-century men.

A

B
1910

C
1914

D
1917

E
1919

H
1923

F
1919

K
1934

G
1924

J
1925

I
1925

1904

L
1940

M
1940

N
1941

O
1945

P
1948

Q
1954

R
1959

S
1961

T
1961

U
1964

V
1964

W
1965

X
1966

FIGURE F-21 Twentieth-century women.

A
1966

B
1966

C
1968

D
1968

E
1968

F
1970

G
1971

H
1969

I
1968

J
1970

K
1972

L
1972

M
1972

N
1972

O
1972

P
1973

Q
1973

R
1973

S
1973

T
1973

U
1973

V
1973

W
1973

X
1973

FIGURE F-22 Twentieth-century men.

A 1967
B 1967
C 1968
D 1969
E 1969
F 1969
G 1969
H 1970
I 1970
J 1970
K 1970
L 1970
M 1970
N 1970
O 1971
P 1971
Q 1972
R 1972
S 1973
T 1973
U 1973
V 1973
W 1973
X 1973
Y 1973

FIGURE F-23 Twentieth-century women.

A
1973

B
1974

C
1974

D
1974

E
1975

F
1975

G
1975

H
1975

I
1975

J
1975

K
1975

L
1976

M
1976

N
1976

O
1976

P
1976

Q
1976

FIGURE F-24 Twentieth-century men.

A 1974
B 1974
C 1974
D 1974
E 1975

F 1975
G 1975
H 1975
I 1975

J 1975
K 1976
L 1976
M 1976
N 1976

O 1976
P 1976
Q 1976
R 1976

S 1976
T 1976
U 1976
V 1977
W 1977

FIGURE F-25 Twentieth-century women.

A
1976

B
1976

C
1976

D
1976

E
1976

F
1976

G
1977

H
1977

1978

J
1978

K
1978

L
1978

M
1978

N
1980

O
1980

P
1979

Q
1979

R
1980

S
1980

FIGURE F-26 Twentieth-century men.

A 1977

B 1977

C 1977

D 1977

E 1977

F 1977

G 1977

H 1977

I 1977

J 1977

K 1977

L 1977

M 1978

N 1978

O 1978

P 1978

Q 1978

R 1978

S 1978

T 1978

U 1978

V 1978

W 1979

X 1979

FIGURE F-27 Twentieth-century women.

A 1981
B 1981
C 1981
D 1981
E 1981
F 1982
G 1982
H 1982
I 1982
J 1982
K 1983
L 1983
M 1983
N 1983
O 1983
P 1984
Q 1984
R 1984
S 1984
T 1984

FIGURE F-28 Twentieth-century men.

A 1981
B 1981
C 1981
D 1981
E 1981
F 1982
G 1982
H 1982
I 1982
J 1982
K 1982
L 1983
M 1983
N 1983
O 1983
P 1983
Q 1983
R 1983
S 1984
T 1984
U 1984
V 1984
W 1984
X 1984
Y 1984

FIGURE F-29 Twentieth-century women.

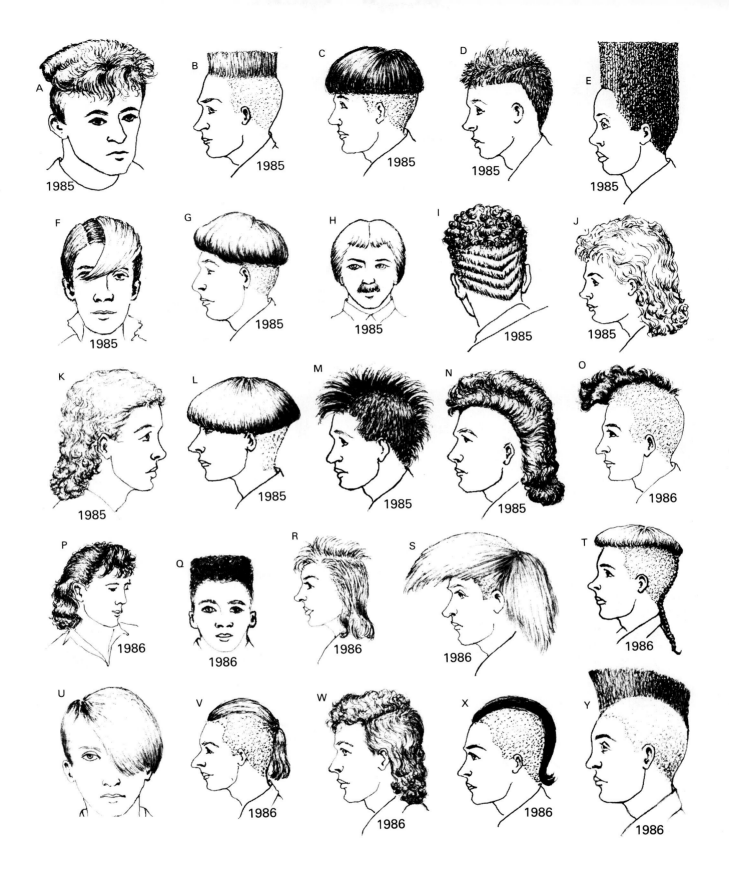

FIGURE F-30 Twentieth-century men.

FIGURE F-31 Twentieth-century women.

A 1985

B 1985

C 1985

D 1985

E 1985

F 1985

G 1986

H 1986

I 1986

J 1986

K 1986

L 1986

M 1986

N 1986

O 1986

P 1986

Q 1986

R 1986

S 1986

FIGURE F-32 Twentieth-century women.

A 1986
B 1986
C 1986
D 1986
E 1986
F 1986
G 1986
H 1986
I 1987
J 1987
K 1987
L 1987
M 1987
N 1987
O 1987
P 1987
Q 1987
R 1987
S 1987
T 1987
U 1987
V 1987
W 1987
X 1987

FIGURE F-33 Twentieth-century women.

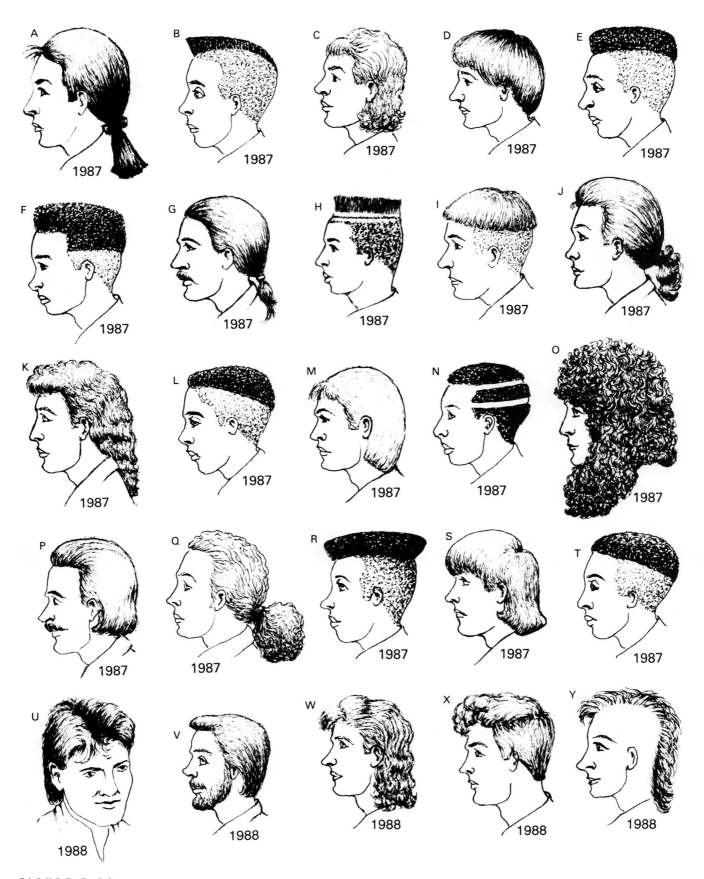

FIGURE F-34 Twentieth-century men.

FIGURE F-35 Twentieth-century women.

1987   A

1987   B

1987   C

1987   D

1987   E

1987   F

1987   G

1987   H

1987   I

1987   J

1987   K

1987   L

1987   M

1987   N

1987   O

1987   P

1987   Q

1987   R

1987   S

1987   T

FIGURE F-36 Twentieth-century women.

A

1988

B 1988

C 1988

D 1988

E 1988

F 1988

G 1988

H 1988

I 1988

J 1988

K 1988

L 1988

M 1988

N 1988

O 1988

P 1988

Q 1988

R 1988

S 1988

T 1988

U 1988

V 1988

W 1988

X 1988

FIGURE F-37 Twentieth-century women.

A 1988
B 1988
C 1988
D 1988
E 1988
F 1988
G 1988
H 1988
I 1988
J 1988
K 1988
L 1988
M 1988
N 1988
O 1988
P 1988
Q 1988
R 1988
S 1988
T 1988
U 1988
V 1988
W 1988
X 1988
Y 1988

FIGURE F-38   Twentieth-century women.

A 1989

B 1989

C 1989

D 1989

E 1989

F 1989

G 1989

H 1989

I 1989

J 1989

K 1989

L 1989

M 1989

N 1989

O 1989

P 1989

Q 1989

R 1989

S 1989

T 1989

U 1989

V 1989

W 1989

X 1989

FIGURE F-39 Twentieth-century women.

A 1989 B 1989 C 1989 D 1989

E 1989 F 1989 G 1989 H 1989 I 1989

J 1989 K 1989 L 1989 M 1989 N 1989

O 1989 P 1989 Q 1989 R 1989 S 1989 T 1989

U 1989 V 1989 W 1989 X 1989

FIGURE F-40 Twentieth-century women.

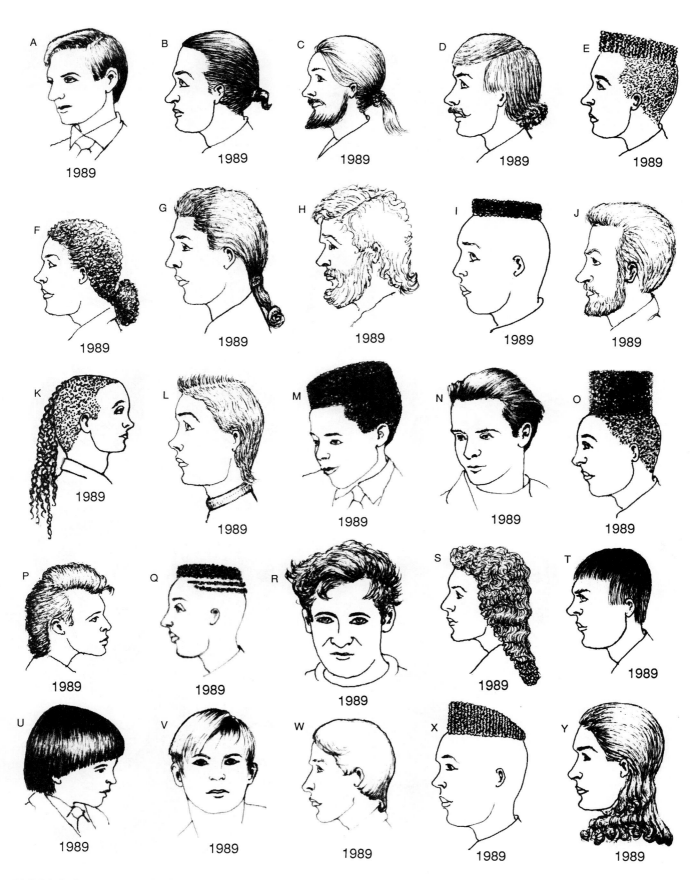

A 1989

B 1989

C 1989

D 1989

E 1989

F 1989

G 1989

H 1989

I 1989

J 1989

K 1989

L 1989

M 1989

N 1989

O 1989

P 1989

Q 1989

R 1989

S 1989

T 1989

U 1989

V 1989

W 1989

X 1989

Y 1989

FIGURE F-41 Twentieth-century men.

A
1990s

B
1990s

C
1990s

D
1990s

E
1990s

F
1990s

G
1990s

H
1990s

I
1990s

J
1990s

K
1990s

L
1990s

M
1990s

N
1990s

O
1990s

P
1990s

Q
1990s

R
1990s

S
1990s

T
1990s

U
1990s

V
1990s

W
1990s

X
1990s

Y
1990s

FIGURE F-42 Twentieth-century men.

A
1990s

B
1990s

C
1990s

D
1990s

E
1990s

F
1990s

G
1990s

H
1990s

I
1990s

J
1990s

K
1990s

L
1990s

M
1990s

N
1990s

O
1990s

P
1990s

Q
1990s

R
1990s

S
1990s

T
1990s

U
1990s

V
1990s

W
1990s

X
1990s

Y
1990s

FIGURE F-43 Twentieth-century women.

A	B	C	D	E
1990s	1990s	1990s	1990s	1990s
F	G	H	I	J
1990s	1990s	1990s	1990s	1990s
K	L	M		N
1990s	1990s	1990s		1990s
O	P	Q	R	S
1990s	1990s	1990s	1990s	1990s
T	U	V	W	X
1990s	1990s	1990s	1990s	1990s

FIGURE F-44 Twentieth-century men and women.

appendix **G**

FIGURE G-1 Vanessa Williams. Print makeup and styling by Kate Best. Photography by Michael Zeppatello.

Concealer:	Laura Mercier #4 (higher value than #6)
Foundation:	Laura Mercier #6
Powder:	LeClerc Banana on center of face
	LeClerc Bronze around the outer areas
	Il Maquillage Banana in a half moon under each eye
Eyeshadow:	Ben Nye Fireworks Creme Fantasy Wheel in Gold, Copper, Diamond Ice
Eyeliner:	MAC Black Creme
Blush:	MAC Cheek (warm orange/gold tone)
Contour:	pinky-brown tone on the cheeks, temple, sides of nose
Brows:	Maybelline Blonde Pencil
Lip pencil:	MAC Spice
Lipstick:	MAC Twig
Mascara:	Maybelline Great Lash

FIGURE G-2 Actress Vanessa Williams in the Broadway musical "Kiss of the Spiderwoman."

Concealer:	RCMA Chinese I and II (light yellow tone) under eyes and on T-section.
Foundation:	Laura Mercier SC 4 (center of the face) & SC 6 (around the edges)
Creme Blush:	William Tuttle Blusher, a pinky-peach tone on apple of cheeks, forehead and temple
Powder:	LeClerc Banana at center of face
	LeClerc Bronze along the rest of face and outer edges. Blend well.
Eyeshadow:	MAC Black creme liner in crease (blend edges with orange toned blush)
	White pencil along lower rim
Eyeliner:	MAC Black creme liner
Blush:	MAC Cheek (warm orange/gold tone)
Contour:	Pinkish/brown tone to add warmth into the edges of the face and to shape and shade nose
Brows:	MAC Black cream liner with a light application near the center.
Lip pencil:	MAC Spice liner, MAC Brun fill-in
Lipstick:	MAC Viva Glam to cover

(makeup and photograph courtesy of Kate Best)

FIGURE G-3 Actress Chita Rivera in the Broadway musical "Chicago."

Concealer:	MAC C-2 (light yellow tone) under the eyes and on the T-section
Foundation:	MAC C-3 (slightly yellow)
Powder:	N-2 adds a bit of pink to the foundation. One shade lighter than foundation.
Eyeshadow:	MAC Vanilla all over (lashline to brows) MAC Chill as highlight, MAC Stencil (pale apricot) on lid and crease MAC Ocre in crease, blend up and out with MAC Rule (bright orange) adds the effect of bright skin color
Eyeliner:	MAC Black creme liner, blend and soften the edges with Rule White pencil along lower rim
Blush:	MAC Cheek (pinkish/peach), blend into the surrounding skin tone with MAC Rule (golden/orange) add a bit of MAC Melba (irridescent)
Contour:	MAC Buff (pinkish/peachy and slightly brown) below cheek
Brows:	Taupe pencil with a lighter application near the center.
Lip pencil:	MAC Spice (scarlet)
Lipstick:	MAC Russian Red

(makeup and photograph courtesy of Kate Best)

FIGURE G-4 A and B. Susan Emerson as Norma Desmond. **Notice the careful color placement, contouring and blending of makeup around the eyes.** *Makeup design by Kate Best.*

FIGURE G-5 Makeup Lesson by Kate Best on actress Julia Sweeney for *Julia Sweeney's God Said "Ha!"* at the Lyceum Theatre. *New York makeup artist Kate Best has been successful in a variety of performance mediums, including Broadway, film, and fashion photography. While her personal choice in makeup includes many products from the MAC line of cosmetics, she is quick to point out that it is simply a product line with which she is most familiar. In many instances on this page and on previous pages she has included a color description of the product along with its name (MAC Buff, for example, is a slightly brown, pinkish-peach tone used as a contour below the cheek bone.) This artist stresses the importance for making appropriate color choices from the product line or lines that best suit your performance needs. The lessons learned from observing these images should focus on color choice, on color placement, and on developing precise application techniques. Many of the makeups have been designed for the bright lights of the Broadway stage and can be modified for other venues by varying the intensity of the effect.*

Step 1   Concealer: Apply concealer under the eye area, along the T-section of the face and over any discolorations. Use Kryolan's Dermacolor #D1.5 and #D2.

Step 2   Foundation: Apply L'Oreal Hydra Perfecte *Nude Beige* foundation with a sponge over the entire face. Blend well towards the neck and hairline.

Step 3   Powder: Set foundation with LeClerc loose powder—*Camille,* with a sponge or puff.

Step 4   Eyeshadow: Apply Il Maquillage pressed eyeshadow—*Banana,* over the entire eye lid up to the brows and at the inner edge of the eye.

Step 5   Highlight the brow bone and the inner edge of the lower lid with *Vanilla* shadow by MAC. For extra highlight on brow bone and in a half moon shape on the upper lid close to the lashes use *Chill* shadow by MAC (use MAC brush #29.)

Step 6   Apply MAC's *Omega* shadow as a contour in the crease of the eye. Begin at the outer edge brushing it three quarters of the way across the lid leaving the inner edge of the eye open. Using a blending brush, blend "up and out" with *Coffee* by Il Maquillage to soften.

Step 7   Apply *Coffee* lightly to the lower lid at the lash line and blend with *Omega* for balance.

Step 8   Eyeliner: Apply *Ebony Pencil* to the back of the hand. Pick up a small amount with an eyeliner brush and with the tip of the brush apply short, controlled even strokes as close to the lashes as possible. Blend with a small blending brush (clean this brush constantly!)

Step 9   Repeat #8 along the lower lid beginning at the center and blending toward the outside corner.

Step 10   Blush: To contour, apply *Coffee* on the temples and below cheekbone with a blush brush. Add *Peach* dry blush by Shu Uemura on the apple of the cheeks, the temples, the tip of the nose and along the jawline.

Step 11   Lips: The lips are lined with Maybelline's *Light Brown* lip pencil and filled in with *Retro* by MAC. Set with powder.

Step 12   Brows: Carefully line the brows with Maybelline's *Blonde* pencil. Starting at the center, draw a light line at the lower edge of the brow up to the arch. Finish the tail of the brow on the top line. Straighten the top line of the brow with the Blonde pencil. Fill in most of the brow with what ever remains on the *Omega* brush. Note: Leave the inner edge of the brow SOFT! Do not add color to this area. (Shu Uemura #60B can also be used for eyebrows.)

* Use Maybelline black mascara

(Makeup and photograph courtesy of Kate Best)

FIGURE G-6 Eye makeup by Kate Best.

A Makeup artist Kate Best.
B. Ensemble from the musical, Aida.
C. Heather Headley as Aida.
D. Ensemble from Aida.
E. Careful blending of eyeshadow into the crease with a Crease Brush. Susan Emerson demonstrating a Kate Best technique.

FIGURE G-7 Actress Kristin Chiles as Zee in natural makeup in the University of Texas at Austin's production of Blind Horses. *(See Figure 18-5 for a list of makeup products and a step-by-step instructions).*

FIGURE G-8 Olga Campos, broadcaster, NBC affiliate KVUE 24 News, Austin, Texas. *(See Figure 18-4 for a list of makeup products and a step-by-step instructions). (photograph courtesy of Olga Campos)*

FIGURE G-9 Mercedes Ellington, professional dancer and Artistic Director of Sophisticated Ellington Symphony and Swing. Artists own makeup for her performance in "Sophisticated Ellington." *(photograph courtesy of Mercedes Ellington) (See Chapter 19 for a list of makeup products.)*

FIGURE G-10 Opera makeup. Soprano Suzanne Ramo as Zerlina in Austin Lyric Opera's 1999 production of Don Giovanni. *Makeup by Leslee Newcomb.*

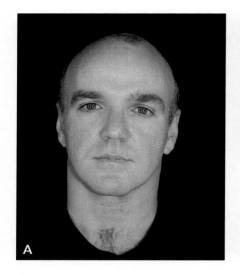

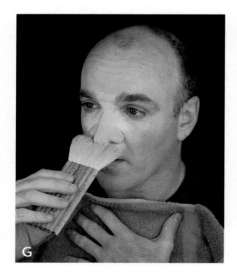

FIGURE G-11 Character Makeup. Actor, James Black as **Ebenezer Scrooge** in the Alley Theatre's Charles Dicken's Christmas Carol, A Ghost Story of Christmas.

A. Actor James Black.
B and C. Applying two coats of Ben Nye Prosthetic Adhesive to his nose and the prosthetic. Let dry completely.
D. Press latex nose into place.
E. James blends the edge with spirit gum, but the spirit gum must be powdered and stippled with Pros-Aide as it will turn gummy when in contact with RMGP.
F. Appling Mehron's Mask Cover—Light Flesh (slightly onto the skin) with a patting motion.
G. Powdering with Ben Nye's Neutral Set.

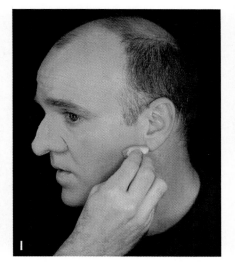

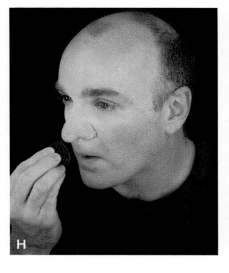

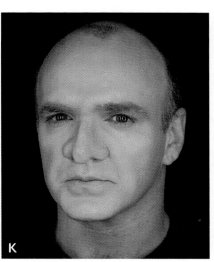

H. Stippling prosthetic with Ben Nye's Capillary Stipple FX-13 to add "life" to the nose.

I. Applying Ben Nye's P-5 (Old Age) foundation to the nose and face with an angle-cut sponge. With a high collared costume there is no need to age the neck.

J. Adding highlights with Nye's P-1 to the brow bone, cheeks, nose and chin. Useing CE-1 (Fairest) above the mouth. Blend.

K. A look at the makeup to this point.

L and M. Adding contouring and wrinkles with a ¼" flat brush using RCMA's KM-3 and KN-8 (darker) character shadows.

N. Working the brush against the edge of the container to maintain a sharp, flat edge.

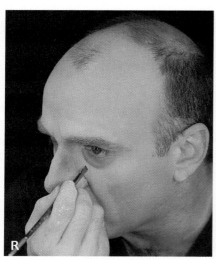

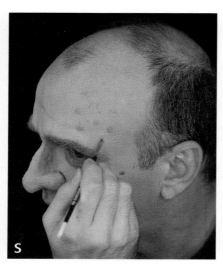

O and P. Painting in nasolabial folds and cheek contour using both light and dark shadow colors. He also introduces a small amount of FX-13 for added color.

Q. Powder.

R. Detailing the deepest edges of bags and wrinkles.

S. Adding age spots with Nye's FX-15 Liver Spot. Also add Capillary Stipple with a black stipple sponge to the nose and front of cheeks.

T. Lining lower eye lid with red pencil.

U. Adding hair whitener (James uses Kiwi Scuff Magic) to the eyebrow with a tooth brush.

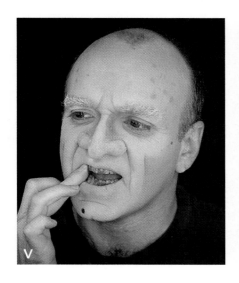

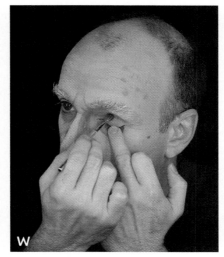

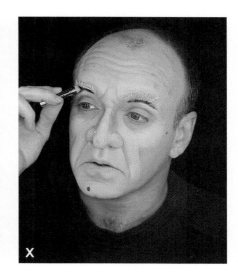

V. Applying a paste formulas tooth color called Tooth Decay.

W. Deepening the eye crease with RCMA's KN-8.

X. Under lining the eyebrow with a black pencil for added definition.

Y. Attaching the wig lace with Matte spirit gum.

Z. Close-up of the finished makeup. A small microphone is attached to his glasses.

AA. James Black as Scrooge. *(Costumes designed by Esther Marquis.)*

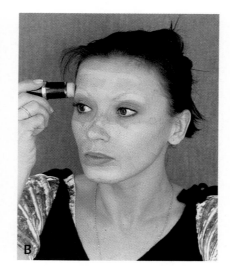

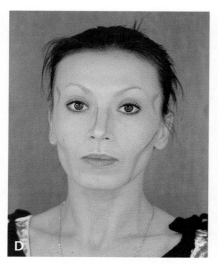

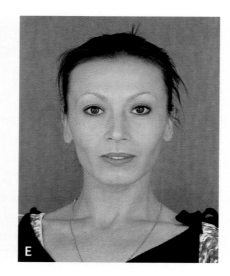

FIGURE G-12 **Makeup for Classical Ballet. Inga Loujerenko, principal dancer, Ballet Austin.**

A. Dampened bar soap used to "soap-out" the ends of eyebrows.
B. Creme foundation applied to the face. Max Factor creme stick, med.-109. Foundation should be slightly darker and pinker than natural skin-tone.
C. Blend foundation with a foam sponge.
D. Apply contour at the temple, nose and under cheek bones.
E. Blended contour and powder. Cover Girl Translucent Ivory/Beige. Powder should be one shade lighter than foundation.
F. Apply dry blush (in the palette of the costume) to the cheek bone, tip of nose, under chin and on the lower half of ear.
G. Apply false lashes along the lash line with Duo lash adhesive. If lashes have been used before apply immediately, if they are new let the Duo set for 30 sec., then apply. Note: the outer end of the lash sits slightly above the lashline.

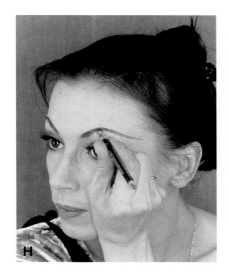

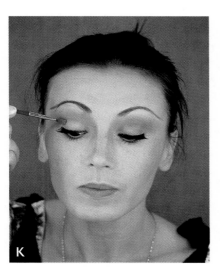

H. Shape eyebrow with a long sweeping arch. Final half inch should be parallel to the floor. Max Factor Expresso pencil with sponge end for blending.

I. Using a dark brown shadow, extend the crease out and up toward the end of the brow. Blend.

J. Extend the shadow along the sides of the nose the bridge.

K. Highlight the upper lid with pale pink eyeshadow.

L. Place white highlight under the brow and blend down and out.

M. Apply dark brown L'Oreal liquid eyeliner along upper lash line. Line should be very thin at the inner edge, slightly thicker at the outer edge. Do not extend past the end of the lash.

N. Using the Expresso pencil draw in a triangle at the end of the lashline as shown.

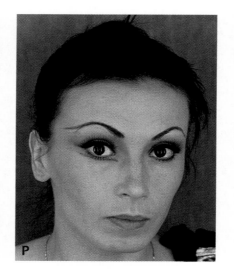

O, P and Q. Using the same pencil draw in a new lower lashline as shown tapering down slightly at the inner corner. Soften edge with sponge end.

R. Apply dark blue pencil or eyeshadow at lower lashline as shown. This line should be thinner at the inner edge and slightly wider at the outer end. Contain this color directly under the eye, do not extend at either end. Blend.

S. Deepen the crease with the brow pencil as shown. Blend up and out.

T and U. Apply a small red dot below the tear duct as shown and blend.

V. Apply eyeshadow (to match costume) above crease and blend up and out. Add a pale pink between the shadow and the white under brow to soften all edges.

W. Line lips with lip pencil to match lip color. Extend the lower lip line down into the foundation at the center only to acheive a slightly fuller lower lip.

X. Fill in lips with lip color. (Lip and cheek color should be similar.)

Y. Apply white at the center of lower lip and blend to add dimension.

Z. Powder all except the eyes. Intensify the cheek color.

AA. Apply black mascara to upper and lower lashes.

BB. Finished makeup. Ballerina, Inga Loujerenko.

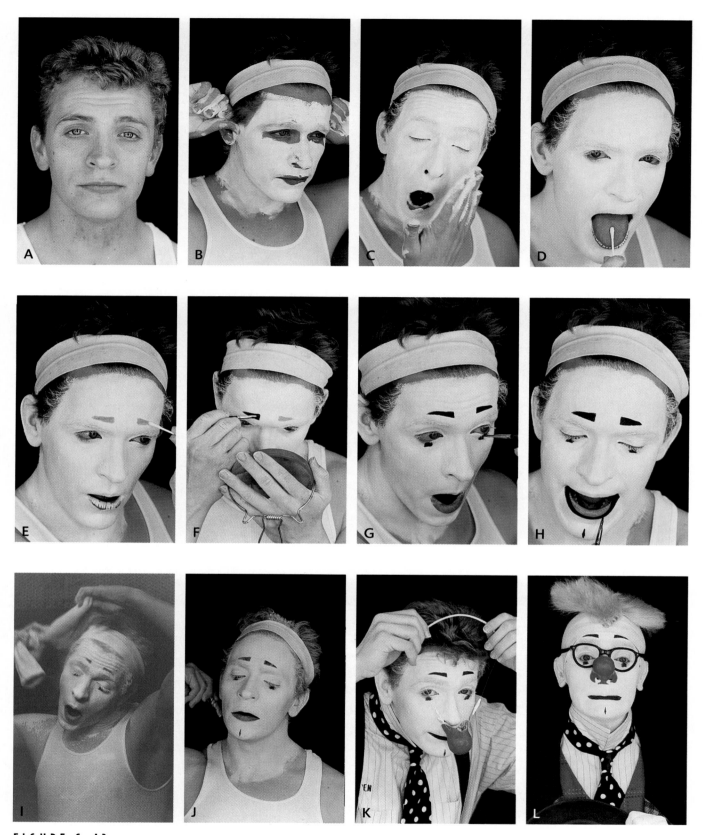

FIGURE G-13 Male Clown

FIGURE G-14 Circus Clowns (top—bottom) Karl Baumann, John Gilkey and Faon Shane-Bélanger.

FIGURE G-13 Male Clown

A. Former Ringling Clown, Ben Schave.
B. Warms Mehron's Clown White between his hands before applying it to his face, neck and ears.
C. Patting the makeup produces a smooth, even finish.
D. Moistening a Q-tip.
E. The moistened Q-tip is used to "cut-out" the design details in the clown white foundation. He cuts out the brows, below the eye, bottom lip and cleft in chin.

F, G and H. Fill in the "cut-out" areas with Mehron's black foundation greaspaint.
I. Powder with a white sock filled with baby powder. Avoid inhaling the powder.
J. Remove powder with a large powder brush.
K. Ben uses a string to hold-on his nose.
L. Ben Schave dressed in his "Agent Suit", knit bald cap and wig.

FIGURE G-14 Circus Clowns (top—bottom) Karl Baumann, John Gilkey and Faon Shane-Bélanger.

This following list of products were used to complete the following makeup designs. Makeup provided by Ben Nye Company, Inc.

A. Karl Baumann. Makeup by Rick Geyer.

Base:	CE-7 Light Tan Matte Foundation
Highlight:	CH-0 Ultralite Highlight, P-1 White Creme Foundation
Contour:	CF-22 Character Shadow MagiCake, ES-395 Terra Cotta Eye Shadow
Cheeks:	DR-9 Dark Tech Dry Rouge
Eye Shadow:	ES-319 Honey (mid-tone), ES-302 Vanilla (highlight) ES-34 Taupe (contour)
Eyeliner:	CF-3 Black MagiCake Aqua Paint
Mascara:	LM-1 Black
Brows:	CF-3 Black MagiCake Aqua Paint
Lip Pencil:	LP-24 Plum (liner)
Lip Stick:	LS-9 Plum
Hair:	ML-01 White Liquid Paint
Powder:	Fair Translucent

B. John Gilkey. Makeup by John Gilkey.

Base:	N-3 Buff Matte Foundation
Highlight:	P-1 White Creme Foundation, P-1 White Creme Foundation
Contour:	P-7 Bronzetone Creme Foundation, DR-71 Desert Coral Dry Rouge
Powder:	Fair Translucent

Cheeks:	DR-7 Coral Dry Rouge
Eye Shadow:	ES-40 Spice (mid-tone) ES-56 Espresso, ES-82 Royal Purple (contour)
Eyeliner:	MC-1 Black Magicake Pencil (eyeliner)
Mascara:	LM-1 Black
Brows:	CF-3 Black MagiCake Aqua Paint
Lip Pencil:	LP-28 Maroon (liner)
Lip Stick:	LS-21 Autumn Red (top lip only) P-1 White Creme (bottom lip)
Hair:	ML-29 Magenta Liquid Paint SD-1 Opal Ice Sparkler (glitter)

C. Faon Shane-Bélanger. Makeup by Rick Geyer.

Base:	CN-0 Ultra Matte Foundation
Highlight:	CH-0 Ultralote Highlight, ES-30 White Eye Shadow
Powder:	CP-1 Ultra Poudre Compacté
Contour:	CP-7 Sienne Poudre Compacté, DR-71 Victorian Rose Dry Rouge
Cheeks:	DR -71 Victorian rose Dry Rouge, DR-12 Pink Blush
Eye Shadow:	ES-82 Royal Purple, ES-80 Deep Violet DR-11 Passion Purple at temples FW-5 Diamond Ice Fireworks on brow bone
Eye Liner:	EL-1 Black Cake
Mascara:	LM-1 Black
Brows:	ES-52 Mocha Eye Shadow
Lip Pencil:	LP-35 Spice (liner)
Lip Stick:	LS-11 Desert Rose, LS-29 Guava Ice

FIGURE G-15

A. Professional dancer, Lyn Elam, without makeup. Coloration: Toffee / Caramel / Cafe Olé.
B. Using an eyebrow razor to shape her eyebrows.
C. After applying MAC Concealor N-9 under the eyes and Fashion Faire Tender Glo creme foundation. (This dancer also uses MAC Studio Fix-NW 40 as a foundation during performances. It is less creamy and "stays-on" better than the Fashion Faire.) Powder with Joe Blasco's "Dark" Ultra-Fine Setting Powder. She applies three colors to the eye lid: MAC Cranberry on the inner corner; MAC Arena 026 on the remainder; and MAC Rap in the crease. Outer crease is then deepened with MAC Espresso. Also apply Arena 026 below the brow line.

D. Lining the lower lashline from the top with L'Oreal pencil eyeliner in black. Also apply pencil eyeliner to the upper lashline, but do not extend lashline at this point.
E. Apply mascara (Lancome Intencils-black) before attaching false eyelashes with black Duo eyelash adhesive. (It will appear dark grey, but will dry black.) Note: the outside end of the false lash should be positioned slightly above the natural lashline as shown.
F. Complete the lashline with a tapered traigular-shape extension, filling in the space between the natural lashline and the false lash. Use a water-proof liquid eyeliner. Then line the entire lashline. Note the coloration of the lid.

G. Create a false lower lashline with liquid liner as shown. Fill the space below the lower lash line with L'Oreal pencil-Kohl Gray. Add additional highlight to the outer eye area between the extended lashlines.

H. Applying Revlon's powdered blush or cheek color—Toast with a blush brush. Also apply cheek color along the jaw line.

I. Applying Wet & Wild creme lip liner pencil in Red (a true red.) Apply lipstick to match (a true red.) Finished makeup for a performance with the dance company, Sophisticated Ellington Symphony and Swing.

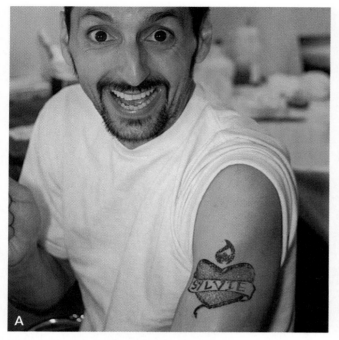

FIGURE G-16 **Temporary Tattoo.**
A. Actor Thom Rivera with his "Sylvie" tattoo made with a rubber stamp and fabric paint. *See Figure 9-9.*
B. Thom Rivera as Alejandro in the Oregon Shakespeare Festival's 1999 production of El Paso Blue by Octavio Solis. *Photograph by David Cooper.*

FIGURE G-17 **Costume rendering with makeup and hair design for the Alley Theatre's production of In the Jungle of Cities. Costume, hair and makeup design by Esther Marquis.**

FIGURE G-18 **Body Paint. Gold body paint using Mehron's Mixing Liquid and Gold Metallic Powders.** *Makeup for this commercial print advertisement by Joe Rossi.*

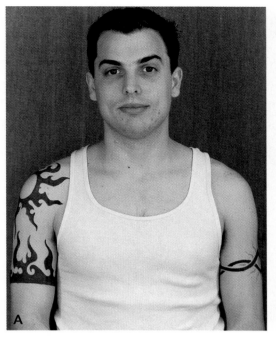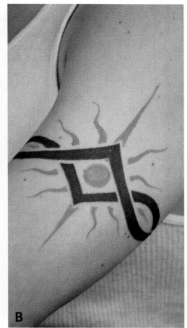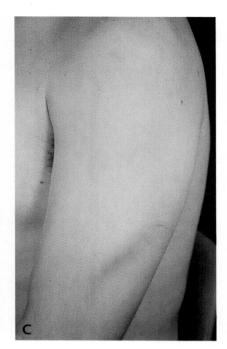

FIGURE G-19 Tattoo Cover

A. Actor Gilford Adams with tattoos.
B. Close up of tattoo.
C. Tattoo cover process: apply Joe Blasco Red and Blue Neutralizers; lightly powder with no-color powder; apply Mehron Tattoo Cover TC-1 and TC-3; lightly powder with Ben Nye Buff Visage Poudre; apply Ben Nye creme foundation P-121 Lite Japonese and stipple (use fingers) with P-12 Japonese; powder with Ben Nye Neutral Set Translucent Face Powder.

FIGURE G-20 Birthmark cover

A. Model Cole Noble.
B. Apply Ben Nye Red Neutralizer over discolorations using a foam sponge. Mehron ProColoRing Concealer in Soft Sandalwood and Honey Glaze are being stippled with a brush over the Port Wine Stain; lightly powder with Ben Nye Visage Poudre Buff. Apply Joe Blasco's Warm Beige creme foundation. Contour with Ben Nye Cinnamon. Powder with Ben Nye BV-71 Beige Suede. Add a bit a color with Blasco's warm Cocoa dry blush.
C. Finished makeup application.

FIGURE G-21 Black eye Makeup by actress Vilma Silva as China in the Oregon Shakespeare Festival's 1999 production of El Paso Blue.

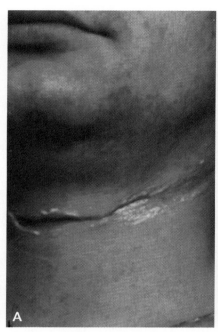

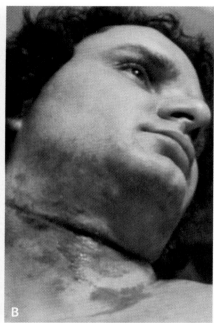

FIGURE G-22 Throat Cut. Latex brushed on and allowed to dry, then pinched together (A) to form a crease. Blood is then added and wiped off (B). *Makeup by Bert Roth, S.M.A.*

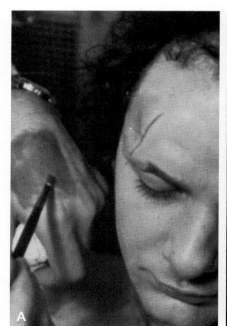

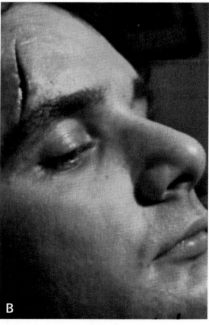

FIGURE G-23 Making a Deep Cut. Forehead area built up with derma wax, then cut with a palette knife. *Grays, purples and reds (A) are mixed to create a bruise. Creme rouge is then painted into the cut (B).*

FIGURE G-24 Scar and Bruise. Collodion scar, artificial blood running from the mouth, and cheek painted to appear bruised and swollen. *Makeup by Bert Roth, S.M.A.*

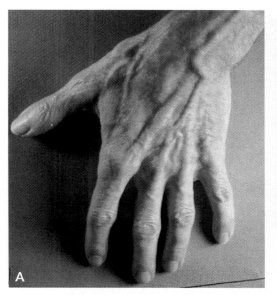

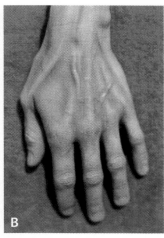

FIGURE G-25
A. Hand (Real).
B. Aged hand. *Makeup by student Gigi Coker.*
C. Hand being aged with makeup. *(Student Joe Allen Brown.)*
D. Aged hand. Highlighted, shadowed, and stippled for texture and color. *Makeup by student Milton Blankenship.*

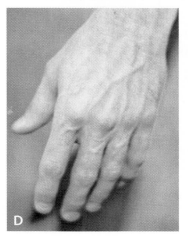

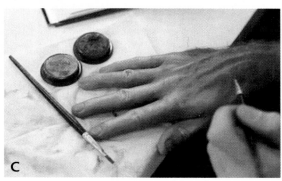

FIGURE G-26 Leopard. *All painting and modeling done with cake makeup. Makeup by student Dianne Harris.*

FIGURE G-27 Stylized rabbit makeup. *By student Barbara Murray.*

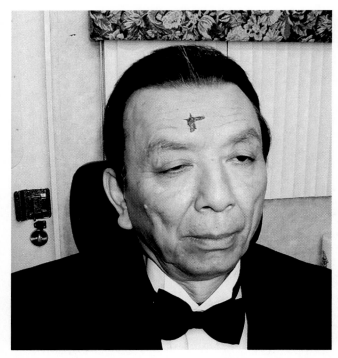

FIGURE G-28 Gelatin bullet hole for actor James Hong in the film "The Art of War." *Applied with Pros-Aide, airbrushed with RCMA rubber mask grease paint thinned with 99% alcohol. Colored with blood paste and liquid blood. Appliance was applied, then digitally removed until the actual shot was fired. Makeup by Adrien Morot and wig by Mark Boley for Steve Johnson's XFX, Inc.*

FIGURE G-29 Synthetic wig for Beau Bridges as P. T. Barnum for A&E. *This ¾ wig is attached to a hard bald cap with side pieces and frontal border added on the actor. Made of white, grey, platinum, golden blonde and light brown hair ventilated on classic cotton cinema lace. Wig by Richard G. Hansen of Les Ateliers in Montreal.*

FIGURE G-30 Gelatin prosthetic age makeup for Sissy Spacek in the film "Blast From the Past." *Makeup by special makeup effects artist Matthew Mungle.*

FIGURE G-31 Prosthetic makeup on actor Colm Feore as the "old man/wizard" in the film "Stephen King's Storm of the Century." Silicone gel-filled appliance. *(Makeup by Adrien Morot for Steve Johnson's XFX, Inc. Wigs by Mark Boley for Steve Johnson's XFX, Inc.)*

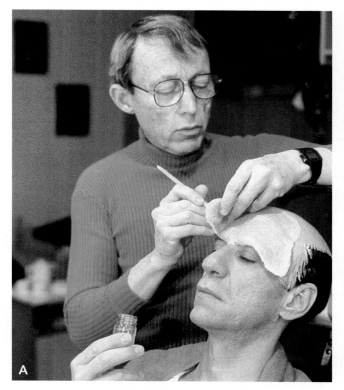

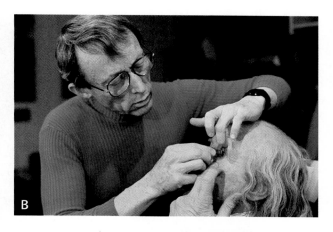

FIGURE G-32 **Foam Latex Prosthetic Makeup**

A. Dick Smith applying H-10 (Gafquat 734+ mustache wax + alcohol) to F. Murray Abraham to smooth and control the hair before applying the plastic bald pate (bald caps cover the entire head.) The bald pate was made from a Union Carbide plasticizer called VYNS. The plastic bald pate and forehead appliance were then glued on with Dow 355 Adhesive (this product has been discontinued, substitute Pros-Aide, Telesis Adhesives or others, see Appendix A—Adhesives.)

B. Contact lenses, with the *arcus senilus* hand painted around the edge of the iris designed to add an ageing effect to the eye, are inserted.

C. Applying beard Stubble. Stubble is made from short (½" or smaller) lengths of crimped (kinky) Yak hair. Attach hairs by hand into a slightly tacky Secure Adhesive (Factor II) applied over the PAX paint. Give the adhesive a matte finish by slowly mixing in the matting agent Cab-O-Sil.

D. F. Murray Abraham as Solieri for the film, Amadeus. *Makeup created by Dick Smith.*

FIGURE G-33 Non-realistic Makeup using Ben Nye's Lumiére Grande Colour and MagiColor Liquid Face Paints. Two lizards from the play Seascape by Edward Albee produced at Actor's Theatre of Louisville.

A. First cover the entire face with a mixture of Lumiére Chartreuse LU-8 and Ice LU-1. Apply Turquoise LU-12 around the eyes of one lizard and Sun Yellow LU-6 around the eyes of the other. Apply a light misting of Final Seal to the makeup. Use the black ML-03 MagiColor face paint to define the irregular-shaped scale pattern, nostrils and mouth area. Fill in mouth and nostrils with MagiColor Rust ML-21.

B. Finished makeup on actors Twyla Hafermann and V. Craig Heidenreich. *Makeup design by Amy Solomon.*

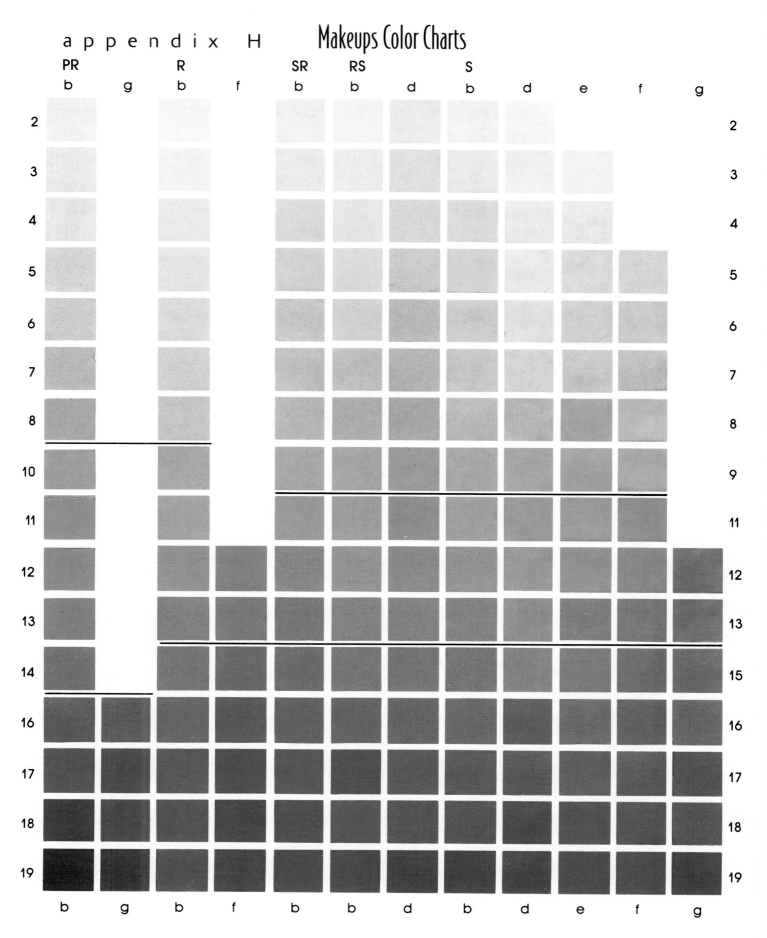

FS

b   c   d   e   f   g

SF

b   c   d   e   f   g

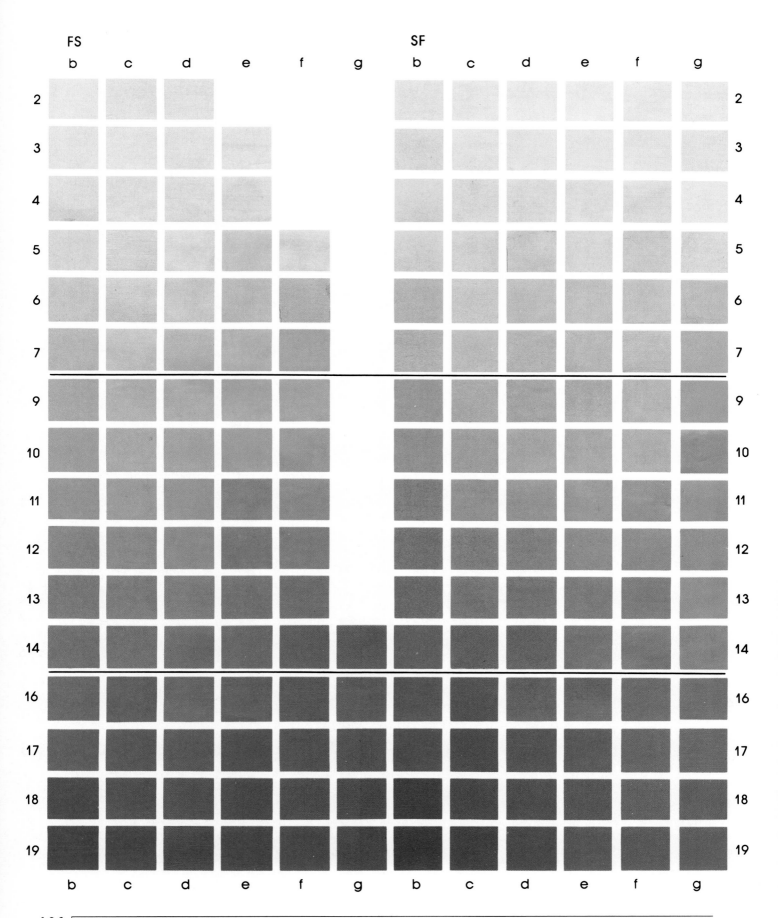

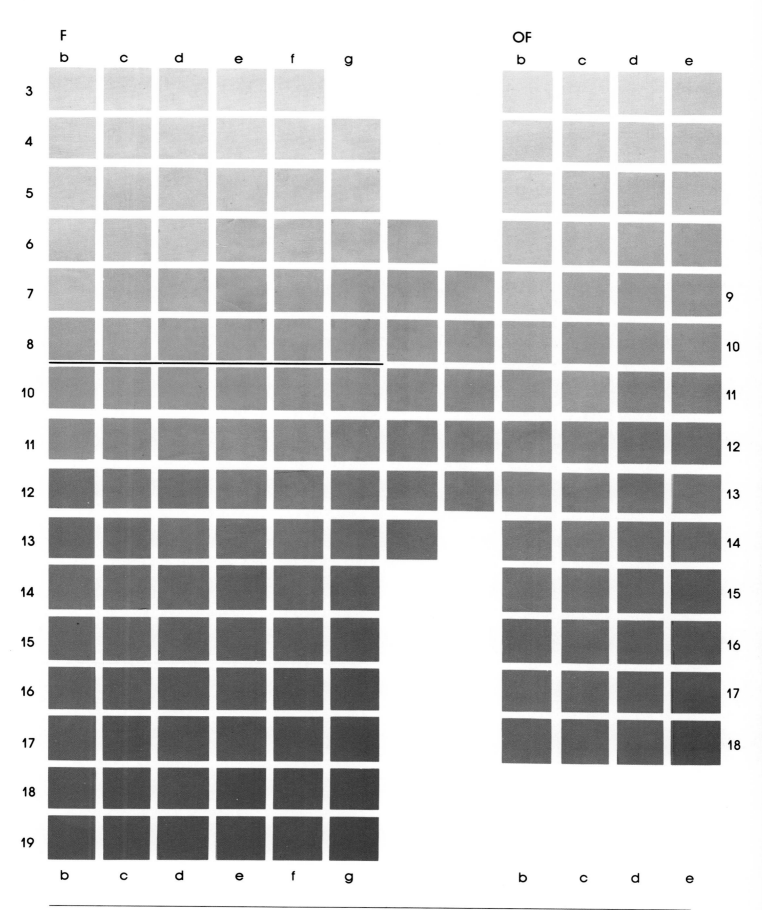

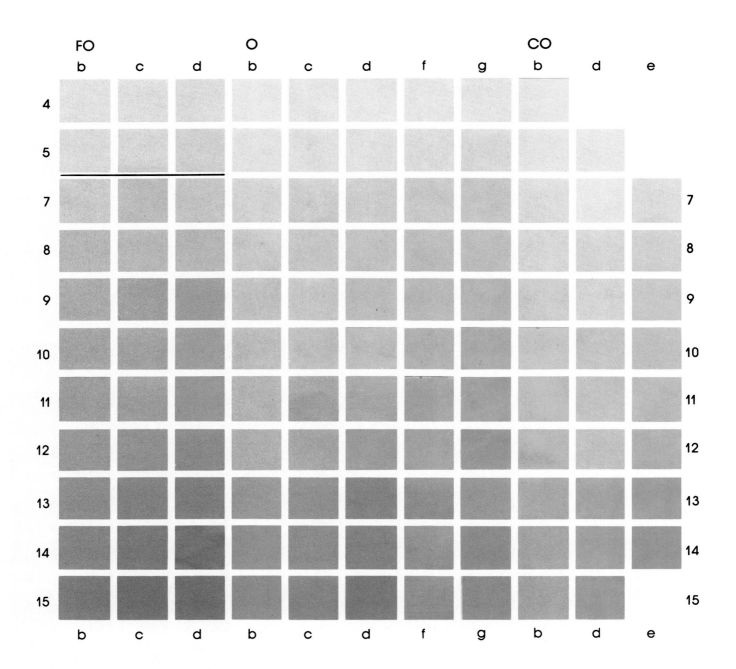

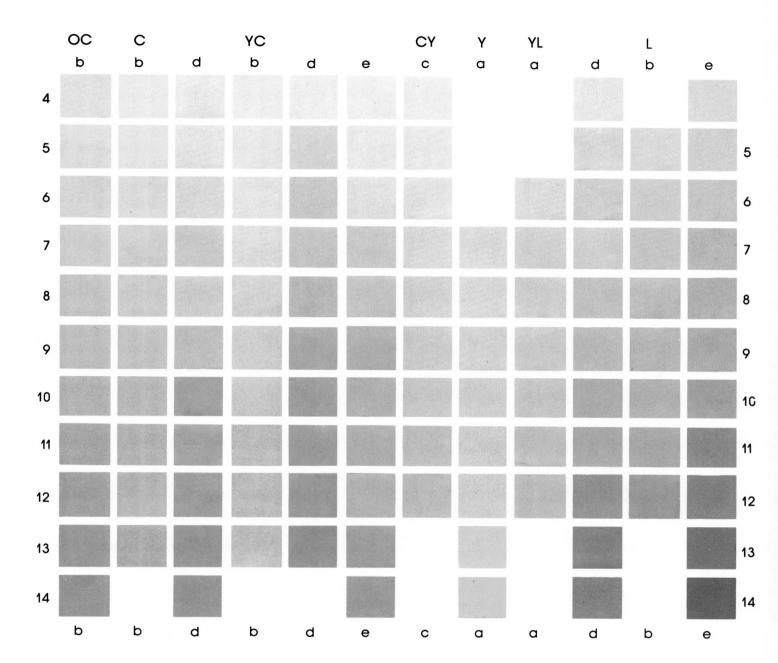

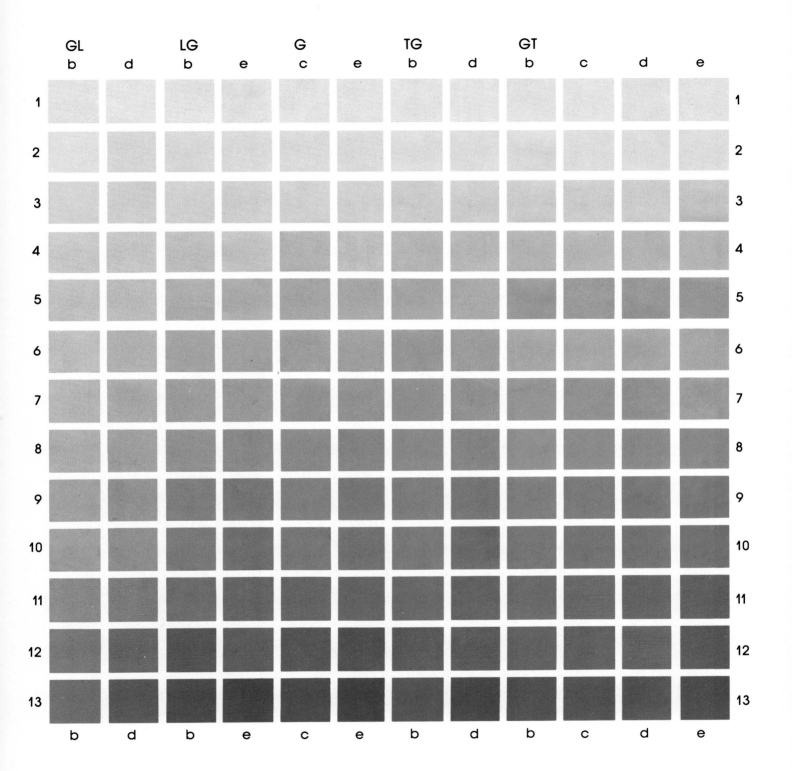

	GL		LG		G		TG		GT			
	b	d	b	e	c	e	b	d	b	c	d	e
1												
2												
3												
4												
5												
6												
7												
8												
9												
10												
11												
12												
13												
	b	d	b	e	c	e	b	d	b	c	d	e

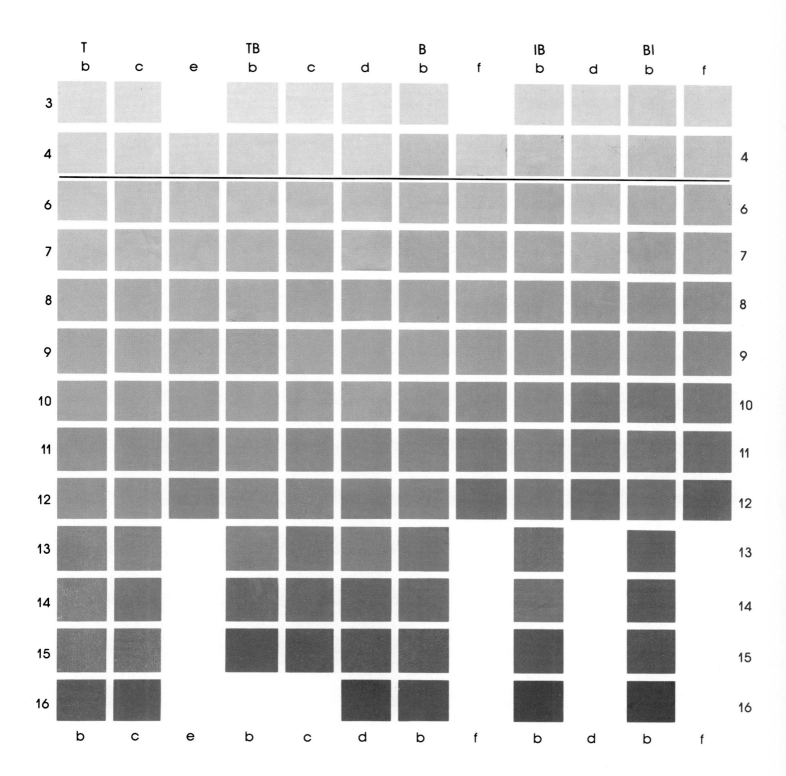

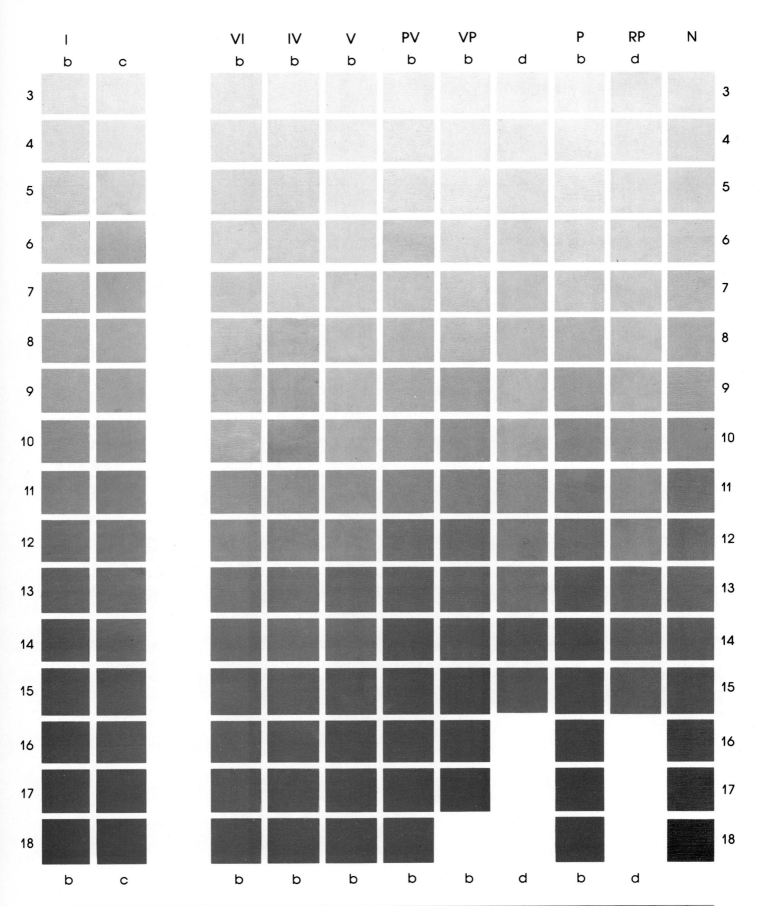

Makeup-color Tables

On the following pages makeup colors are listed by both the numbers under which they are sold by the various makeup companies and by a set of standardized numbers which coordinate the colors of the various makeup companies into a single system of color identification defined by their hue, value, and intensity (see Chapter 4). For example, Ben Nye's Creme Foundation # P-6, named Natural Tan, has a standardized number FS-11-d. This standardized number is a numerical representation of the approximate color of P-6. The color can be found in the Makeup Color Chart in Appendix H. First, find the color grouping or Hue, *FS* (Flame-Scarlet), indicated by capital letters at the top of the page. Then, trace down the left side of the page, to the number *11*. This is the numerical indication of the color value range (in this case, a medium value). Move horizontally across the page to the right to find the color chip in the column indicated by the lower case letter *d*. This is the color representation of Ben Nye's Creme Foundation #P-6, Natural Tan. This process can be repeated for all makeup colors.

The companies represented in the following table include: Ben Nye Comany, Inc., Joe Blasco Cosmetics, Bob Kelly Cosmetics, Inc., Mehron, Inc., M. Stein Cosmetics, Kryolan Corporation, and Dinair Airbrush Cosmetics.

In the Table the abbreviations used are:

R Red
S Scarlet
F Flame
O Orange
C Chrome
Y Yellow
L Lime
G Green
T Turquoise
B Blue
I Indigo
V Violet
P Purple

Color Numbers of the Various Makeup Companies and Their Equivalent Standardized Numbers

Ben Nye Creme Foundations

Series	Number	Corson Chart	Color
P-	1		White
P-	022	SF-4-d	
P-	024	FS-5-b	
P-	2	off chart	
P-	3	S-8-d	
P-	4	FO-8-b	
P-	41	OF-7-b	
P-	5	F-10-f	
P-	6	FS-11-d	
P-	7	F-14-d	
P-	8	S-19-f	
P-	9		Black
P-	10	SF-14-d	
P-	101	RS-11-b	
P-	11	F-14-g	
P-	111	F-13-f	
P-	12	F-11-e	
P-	121	FO-11-d	
P-	13	off chart	
P-	14	YL-13-d	
P-	15	off chart	
P-	16	I-3-b	
L-	0	SF-6-d	
L-	1	OF-10-d	
L-	2	SF-11-f	
L-	3	SF-12-e	
L-	5	SF-13-f	
T-	1	F-15-e	
T-	2	SF-18-f	
M-	1	F-14-e	
M-	2	SF-18-d	
M-	3	SF-19-d	
M-	5	F-19-e/f	
Y-	1	SF-16-f	
Y-	3	SF-17-f	
Y-	5	SF-19-g	
TW-	20	OF-8-c	
TW-	21	OF-9-c	
TW-	22	OF-10-c	
TW-	23	OF-11-d	
TW-	24	OF-13-d	
TW-	25	OF-14-d	
TW-	26	OF-16-d	
TW-	27	OF-17-e	
TW-	28	OF-18-d	
TW-	29	OF-18-e	

Series	Number	Corson Chart	Color
BE-	5	SF-13-g	
NO-	1	off chart	
NO-	3	OF-9-d	
NO-	5	OF-8-e	
NO-	7	OF-9-e	
NO-	9	OF-10-e	
IS-	1	OF-6-c	
IS-	10	SF-9-f	
IS-	18	F-12-f	
IS-	21	F-11-f	
IS-	23	FS-11-f	
IS-	25	SF-11-g	
IS-	31	FO-12-d	
IS-	33	SF-10-g	
IS-	35	SF-14-g	
IS-	41	off chart	
SA-	1	SF-14-f	
SA-	2	SF-16-g	
SA-	3	F-14-f	
SA-	5	F-15-f	
SA-	7	OF-15-e	
SA-	9	F-16-g	
SA-	11	F-17-g	
SH-	0	OF-6-b	
SH-	1	O-9-b	
SH-	2	FO-10-d	
SH-	3	O-12-d	
SH-	4	O-13-d	
CN-	0	F-5-d	
CN-	010	F-6-d	
CN-	001	F-7-d	
CN-	002	OF-8-d	
CN-	003	F-8-e	
CN-	004	F-8-f	
EB-	1	SF-5-e	
EB-	3	SF-6-f	
EB-	5	SF-6-g	
EB-	6	F-10-e	
N-	1	SF-5-d	
N-	2	FS-7-c	
N-	3	FS-7-e/f	
FT-	1	FS-11-e	
FT-	2	FS-14-e	
FT-	6	off chart	
FT-	8	off chart	
FT-	9	off chart	
FT-	11	SF-18-g	
FT-	13	SF-19-g	

Ben Nye Matte Foundations

Series	Number	Corson Chart	Color
CE-	1	O-5-b	
CE-	2	O-8-b/c	
CE-	3	off chart	
CE-	5	FS-6/7-f	
CE-	7	FS-10-f	
CE-	9	FS-12-f	
BE-	1	F-8-d	
BE-	3	SF-7-g	

Ben Nye Cake Foundations

Series	Number	Corson Chart	Color
PC-1	1		White
PC-	02	FO-5-b	
PC-	021	OF-8-b	
PC-	022	off chart	
PC-	2	S-6-d	
PC-	30	OF-8/9-b	
PC-	305	OF-9-b	
PC-	31	FO-9/10-b	

PC-	32	FO-10/11-c
PC-	33	off chart
PC-	34	F-11-d
PC-	36	OF-13/14-d
PC-	4	SF-9-e
PC-	40	off chart
PC-	41	FO-10-d
PC-	42	F-11-e
PC-	43	F-13-f
PC-	46	off chart
PC-	47	SF-9-b
PC-	48	SF-9-b/c
PC-	5	off chart
PC-	51	SF-10-c
PC-	6	off chart
PC-	7	SF-12-d
PC-	8	off chart
PC-	81	off chart
PC-	82	I-3-b
PC-	83	YL-13-d
PC-	87	FS-12-d/e
PC-	89	FS-14-e
PC-	9	off chart
PC-	11	FS-12/13-d
PC-	111	SF-13-e
PC-	114	SF-14-e
PC-	115	SF-17-d
PC-	12	SF-16-b/c
PC-	13	F-14/15-f
PC-	135	F-18-d
PC-	14	SF-16/17-e
PC-	16	SF-17/18-e
PC-	17	F-17-d
PC-	19	F-17/18-e
PC-	20	F-18/19-e
PC-	21	F-18-g
PC-	23	Black

Ben Nye Creme Liners

Series	Number	Corson Chart	Color
CR-	0	RS-8/9-d	
CR-	1	off chart	
CR-	2	RS-12-b	
CR-	3	S-15-d	
CR-	35	S-13-e	
CR-	38	S-15-e	
CR-	4	off chart	
CR-	5	RS-15-d	
CR-	7	off chart	
CR-	8	R-15-b	
CL-	1	White	
CL-	2	off chart	Shades of Green
CL-	211	off chart	Shades of Green
CL-	3	off chart	Shades of Green
CL-	31	off chart	Shades of Green
CL-	32	off chart	Shades of Green
CL-	33	off chart	Shades of Green
CL-	4	off chart	Pink
CL-	5	off chart	Yellow
CL-	6	C-13-b	
CL-	61	C-13-d	
CL-	7	FO-14/15-b	
CL-	8	VP-11-b/d	

CL-	9	F-16-d	
CL-	10	SF-19-c/d	
CL-	11	FS-19-d	
CL-	12	RS-19-b/d	
CL-	13	off chart	Red
CL-	131	R-16/17-b	
CL-	14	R-17/18-b	
CL-	15	PR-17/18-b	
CL-	16	VP-13/14-b	
CL-	17	off chart	Misty Violet
CL-	18	P-16/17-b	
CL-	19	VI-17-b	
CL-	191	off chart	Bright Blue
CL-	20	GT-11/12-e	
CL-	21	GT-13-e	
CL-	22	off chart	Purple Blue
CL-	23	off chart	Purple grey
CL-	25	off chart	Shade of grey
CL-	26	off chart	Shade of grey
CL-	27	off chart	Deep Brown
CL-	28	off chart	Misty black
CL-	29	Black	
CS-	1	F-12/13-e/f	
CS-	2	FS-14-g	
CS-	3	FS-18/19-e	
CS-	4	FS-19-d	
CS-	5	RS-19-d	
CH-	0	off chart	
CH-	01	off chart	
CH-	1	off chart	
CH-	2	off chart	
CH-	4	SF-10/11-d	
CH-	5	off chart	
CH-	6	FS-14-d/e	

Ben Nye Eye Shadows

Series	Number	Corson Chart	Color
ES-	2	off chart	Misty Violet
ES-	30	White	
ES-	302	off chart	Vanilla
ES-	304	off chart	Heather
ES-	31	off chart	Toast
ES-	312	off chart	Banana
ES-	314	off chart	Shell
ES-	317	off chart	Taos
ES-	319	SF-7-d	
ES-	32	off chart	Santa Fe
ES-	34	off chart	Taupe
ES-	38	SF-9/10-c/d	
ES-	39	SF-10-b	
ES-	395	F-9-b	
ES-	40	SF-11-e	
ES-	44	off chart	Goldenrod
ES-	50	F-13-g	
ES-	52	FS-14-f	
ES-	54	off chart	Dark Brown
ES-	56	off chart	Espresso
ES-	59	S-18-e	
ES-	60	off chart	Bark
ES-	62	off chart	Mossberry
ES-	70	off chart	Teal
ES-	72	S-16/17-d	
ES-	75	off chart	Black Plum

ES-	76	off chart	Burgandy
ES-	80	off chart	Deep Violet
ES-	82	V-14-b	
ES-	90	off chart	Navy Blue
ES-	95	N-9/10	
ES-	97	N-12/13	
ES-	99	Black	

Ben Nye Dry Cheek Rouge

Series	Number	Corson Chart	Color
DR-	1	off chart	Flame Red
DR-	2	off chart	Coral Red
DR-	3	off chart	Raspberry
DR-	4	off chart	Fuchsia
DR-	5	R-17-b	
DR-	6	off chart	Misty Pink
DR-	61	off chart	Victorian Rose
DR-	7	SR-11-b	
DR-	71	off chart	Desert Coral
DR-	9	off chart	Dark Tech
DR-	10	RS-17-b	
DR-	11	P-14-b	
DR-	12	RS-9-b	
DR-	13	S-11-b	
DR-	14	S-12-d	
DR-	15	S-13-d	
DR-	16	off chart	Cool Pink
DR-	17	S-18-b	

Ben Nye Lipsticks

Series	Number	Corson Chart	Color
LS-	1	FS-6-b	
LS-	2	off chart	Hot Pink
LS-	3	SR-12-b	
LS-	31	off chart	Hot Coral
LS-	4	off chart	Dusty Rose
LS-	5	R-15/16-b	
LS-	6	PR-13/14-b	
LS-	7	off chart	Natural
LS-	8	off chart	Cranberry
LS-	9	SR-18-b	
LS-	10	off chart	Bordeaux
LS-	11	PR-12/13-b	
LS-	12	PR-16/17-b	
LS-	13	off chart	Magenta
LS-	14	off chart	True Red
LS-	15	off chart	Siren Red
LS-	16	off chart	Ruby Red
LS-	17	Black	
LS-	18	LG-13-e	
LS-	19	off chart	Mocha Rose
LS-	20	off chart	Cappuccino
LS-	21	SR-15/16-b	
LS-	22	off chart	Black Cherry
LS-	23	off chart	Boysenberry
LS-	24	off chart	Ultra Nude
LS-	25	off chart	Blush
LS-	26	off chart	Primrose
LS-	27	off chart	French Mocha
LS-	28	S-13-f/g	
LS-	29	off chart	Guava Ice
LS-	30	E-8-b/c	

LS-	32	off chart	Rose Glaze
LS-	33	off chart	Marilyn Red
LS-	34	off chart	Russian Red

Ben Nye MagiCake Aqua Paints (Face and Body Paints)

CF-	1	White	
CF-	3	Black	
CF-	4	off chart	Shade of Red
CF-	5	off chart	Shade of Red
CF-	52	PR-17-b	
CF-	6	I-11-b/c	
CF-	62	off chart	Bright Blue
CF-	65	I-14/15-b	
CF-	7	I-18-b	
CF-	8	GT-12-d	
CF-	9	off chart	Yellow
CF-	10	CO-13/14-b	
CF-	108	off chart	Lime Green
CF-	110	off chart	Shade of Green
CF-	11	off chart	Shade of Green
CF-	112	off chart	Shade of Green
CF-	12	off chart	Shade of Green
CF-	129	off chart	Shade of Purple
CF-	13	off chart	Shade of Purple
CF-	14	off chart	Magenta
CF-	15	off chart	Shade of Red
CF-	16	off chart	Pink
CF-	17	FO-14/15-b	
CF-	19	SF-17/18-d	
CF-	195	SF-18-e/f	
CF-	20	FS-17-f	
CF-	21	F-19-e	
CF-	22	S-18/19-d	
CF-	23	off chart	Grey
CF-	24	off chart	Misty Violet
CF-	25	off chart	Off white
CF-	26	off chart	Dark Brown

Ben Nye Magicolor Liquid Face Paints

ML-	01	White	
ML-	03	Black	
ML-	05	off chart	Red
ML-	07	off chart	Blue
ML-	09	off chart	Yellow
ML-	11	off chart	Shade of Green
ML-	13	C-9/10-b	
ML-	15	off chart	Shade of Purple
ML-	17	off chart	Pink
ML-	19	FO-14/15-b	
ML-	21	SF-17/18-d	
ML-	23	off chart	Dark Brown
ML-	25	N-14/15	
ML-	27	GT-12-d	
ML-	29	off chart	Magenta
ML-	30	off chart	Fire Red
ML-	31	off chart	Bright Blue
ML-	32	off chart	Kelly Green
ML-	33	off chart	Lime Green
ML-	34	PR-16/17-b	
ML-	35	off chart	Shade of Purple
ML-	36	CO-13/14-b	

Joe Blasco Olive Bases:

TV White: F-1-f
Fair Olive: FO-2-c
Special Olive Beige:
    OF-3-c
Alabaster: OF-5-d
Olive: OF-5-c
Medium Olive: F/OF-5-d
Deep Olive: OF/FO-8-c/d
Suntone: FO-10-c
Olive Tan 1:
    OF/FO-91/2-c/d
Olive Tan 2: OF-10-d
Olive Tan3:OF-111/2-c/d
Hawaiian Tan:
    OF-101/2-c/d
Olive Beige 2: FO-4-c
Olive Beige 4: FO-8-c
Light Oriental: FO-8-c/d
Dark Oriental: FO-9-c/d
CTV 7W: OF-9-c/d

Joe Blasco Ruddy Bases:

Fair: F-3-c
Fair Pink: SR-4-a
Cream: F-41/2-b
Ruddy Ultra Fair 1: F-2-c
Ruddy Ultra Fair 2:
    OF-41/2-c
Ruddy Ultra Fair 3: OF-6-c
Peachtone 1: F-41/2-b/c
Peachtone 2: F-51/2-b/c
Peachtone 3: F-7-b/c
Peachtone 4: F-9-b/c
Blushtone 1: SF-6-d
Blushtone 2: SF-7-d
Blushtone 3: F-8-d
Blushtone 4: F-9-c/d
Ruddy Beige 2: OF-8-c
Ruddy Beige 4: OF-10-c/d

Joe Blasco Stage Bases:

Stage Base #1: SR-3-a/b
Stage Base #2: SR-6-a/b
Stage Base #3: RS-8-b
Stage Base #4: S-16-b
Stage Base #5: SF-12-a\b
Stage Base #6: FS-5-e
Stage Base #7: P-3-b
Stage Base #8: F-2-b
Stage Base #9: OF-7-b
Stage Base #10: F-181/2-b
DW#1: OF-5-b
DW#2: OF/FO-91/2-b
DW#3: SF-9-d
DW#4: F-11-c/d
EF 1: OF-11-a/b
EF 2: OF-12-a/b
EF 3: F-9-a/b
EF 4: F-10-a/b
EF 5: OF-10-b

EF 6: F/OF-11-b/c
EF 7: OF-12-b
EF 8: F-12-b
EF 9: F-10-b
EF 10: F/OF-11-b
EF 11: OF-11-b
EF-12: OF/FO-11-a/b
EF 13: OF/FO-13-b
EF 14: OF-15-a/b
EF 15: OF-16-a/b

Joe Blasco Ruddy Tan Bases:

Bronzetone: OF-9-c
Dark Bronzetone:
    F/OF-10-c/d
Tantone: OF-11-c
Coppertone: OF-10-b/c
Palm Springs Tan:
    OF-FO-91/2-c
Summertan: F/SF-8-d
California Tan: F-11-d
Malibu Tan: OF-11-c/d
Rugged Tan 1: SF-11-d
Rugged Tan 2: SF-10-e

Joe Blasco Natural Beige Bases:

Natural Beige 2:
    OF/FO-7-c/d
Natural Beige 4: FO-10-d
Teentone: OF-7-c/d
SR: OF-8-c/d
Dark SR: OF/FO-10-c

Joe Blasco Dark Skin Bases:

Ruddy Dark Skin Base 1:
    OF-91/2-c
Ruddy Dark Skin Base 2:
    OF-101/2-c
Ruddy Dark Skin Base 3:
    OF-111/2-c
Ruddy Dark Skin Base 4:
    OF-121/2-c
Ruddy Dark Skin Base 5:
    OF-131/2-c/d
Ruddy Dark Skin Base 6:
    F/SF-16-d
Ruddy Dark Skin Base 7:
    F/SF-17-e
Ruddy Dark Skin Base 8:
    F/SF-19-f

Joe Blasco Auxiliary Bases:

Hal Linden: OF-9-d
White Base: White
Clown White: White
Black Base: Black

Joe Blasco Shading Colors:

Shading 1: SF-9-f
Shading 2: SF-10-f
Shading 3: OF-13-d
Shading 4: F/OF-14-c/d
Character Cold: OF-11-d
Character Warm:
    OF-14-c/d
Character Gray: FS-13-g
Natural Shading 1: SF-7-e/f
Natural Shading 2: SF-8-e
Natural Shading 3: F-12-d
Natural Shading 4: OF-
    131/2-c
Dark Skin Shading 1:
    OF/FO-11-c
Dark Skin Shading 2:
    OF/FO-15-c/d
Dark Skin Shading 3:
    F-18-d
Dark Skin Shading 4:
    SF-20-d

Joe Blasco Highlighting Colors:

Pink Highlight 1: FS-1-a
Pink Highlight 2: FS-4-c
Orange Highlight 1:
    F-31/2-c
Orange Highlight 2: F-5-c
Dark Skin Highlight 1:
    OF/FO-11-b/c
Dark Skin Highlight 2:
    FO-13-b

Joe Blasco Cheek Colors:

AD 1: FS-7-c
AD 2: SF-8-b
CTV: SF-9-c
Men's Cheekcolor:
    F-12-c/d
Natural Cheekcolor
    Regular: FS-10-c/d
Coral Rose: RS-10-b
Pastel Rose: FS-8-b/c
Rose Orange: F/SF-10-b
Coral Orange: SF-19-b
Light Burnt Orange:
    SF-121/2-b
Dark Burnt Orange:
    SF-13-b
Brick: F-11-b

Joe Blasco Dry Cheek Colors:

Rose: PR-7-a
Mauve: R-10-b
Coral: SR-10-a
Peach: FS-10-b

Joe Blasco Death Colors:

Death Straw: CY-6-b
Death Blue-Gray: I-6-f
Death Green: L-6-f
Death Purple: SR-14-e
Death Gray: FS-3-g

Joe Blasco Creative Colors:

Blood Color: R-16-a
Red: SR/RS-12-a
Orange: FO-11-a
Gold-Yellow: C-8-b
Yellow-Gold: C-11-b
Yellow: LY-5-a
Gold-Olive: C/OC-10-b
Light Yellow-Green: L-9-d
Medium Yellow-Green:
    L-13-c
Dark Yellow-Green:
    G1S-13-c
Green: LG-13-c
Icy Green: TG-4-d
Turquoise: T-8-c
Gray: N-8
Green-Gray 1: C-8-i
Green-Gray 2: C-9-i
Green-Gray 3: OC-14-g
Green-Gray 4: OC-16-g
Icy Blue: I-7-a
Sky Blue: 1—8-a
Blue: I/VI-12-a
Blue-Gray: I/VI-10-d
Blue-Violet: P/VP-13-d
Gray-Violet: V-13-e
Pink-Purple: RP-8-a/b
Lavender-Purple: RP-10-b
Purple: P-13-c
Maroon: PR-18-c
Gray-Rose: RP-12-e
Light Brown: FO-14-d
Medium Brown: OF-15-d
Dark Brown: F-17-e
Charcoal: N-18

Joe Blasco TPM (Traditional Prosthetic Makeup):

1: FO-1-a
2: OF-5-c/d
3: FO-7-c
4: OF-7-c
5: OF/FO-91/2-c
6: OF/FO-10-c/d
7: O-10-d
8: OF-6-d
9: OF-5-b
10: OF/FO-7-b
11: F-6-b
13: OF-9-c
14: OF-8-c

15: FS-9-b
16: FS/SF-13-a/b
17: F-9-d/e
18: P-3-b
19: OF/FO-10-b
20: OF-10-b/c
21: OF-11-b/c
23: FO-11-b
24: OF/FO-10-b
25: OF/FO-12-b
26: OF/FO-15-c/d
27: White
28: Black
29: F-15-f
30: FO-13-d
31: OF-11-c
32: OF-12-a
33: YC-7-a
34: N-8
35: Y-8-e
36: S-12-a
37: Y-9-a
38: LG-13-c
39: I/VI-12-a
40: OF-16-d

Joe Blasco Dermaceal:

1: FO-3-c
2: OF-7-c/d
3: FO-10-c
4: OF-10-c/d
5: OF-7-c
6: F-7-c
7: OF-8-b
8: OF-11-c
9: OF/FO-12-c
10: OF-12-d

Bob Kelly Creme Stick:

S-1: White
S-2: SR-2-b
S-3: S-5-d
S-4: S-4-b
S-5: S-9-d
S-6: S-7-c
S-7: FS-13-e
S-8: FS-8-e/f
S-9: C-8-b
S-10: S/FS-10-e
S-11: F-161/2-e
S-12: F-16-e
S-14: FS-11-d/e
S-15: S-12-c
S-16: F-17-c
S-17: SF-12-e
S-18: FS-17-e
S-19: O-18-d
S-20: O-18-e
S-21: FS-1-c
S-22: FS-12-d
S-23: FS-12-f
BK-1: S/FS-10-e/f

BK-2: S/FS-12-f
BK-3: F-71/2-e
BK-4: F-81/2-d
BK-5: SF-11-f
BK-6: FS-11-e/f
BK-7: S/FS-12-e/f
32-E: PR-13-h
CVA-Red: RS-13-c
Frankenstein Grey: N-1
SC-50: FS-10-f
SC-54: F-19-f
Fairest: F-4-b
Medium Fair: OF-5-b
Lady Fair: F-41/2-c
Olive: SF-3-b/c
Medium Olive: F-6-d/e
Deep Olive: SF-7-f/g
light Brunette: F-51/2-c
Medium Brunette: F-6-c
Dark Brunette: F-7-d
Tantone: F-6-d
Natural Tan: SF-6-c
Golden Tan: SF-10-c/d
Coppertone: RS-6-d/e
Bronzetone: FS-10-d/e
Blue: TB-9-b
Green: G-9-b
Purple: V-11-a
Red: RS-14-a
Yellow: Y-12-a

**Bob Kelly Cake
Makeup:**

*Since cake-makeup shades are
supposed to match creme-stick
shades, they are not listed
separately.*

**Bob Kelly Moist Cake
Makeup (Rain Barrel):**

Ivory: FS-1-c
Flesh Tone: SF-31/2-c
Natural: F-4-e
Rose: FS-6-b
Tan: FS-9-d
Olive Rose: SF-3-c
Latin: FS-10-d/e
Sunburn: FS-19-b
Sportsman: RS-71/2-d/e
Egyptian: FS-10-d
Bronze: F-13-d
American Indian:
    S/FS-11-e/f
Arabian: FS-12-e
Old Age: FS-8-e/f
Grey: N-13

**Bob Kelly Creme
Shading Colors
(Liner/Eye Shadow):**

SL-1: 1–7-a/b
SL-2: I/VI-12-a

SL-3: VI-16-a
SL-4: PV-10-b
SL-5: G1S-11-d
SL-6: T-17-c
SL-7: O-15-e
SL-8: O-16-c
SL-9: Black
SL-10: N-6
SL-11: N-12
SL-12: White
SL-14: C-5-b
SL-15: OC-8-b
SL-16: PR-12-g
SL-17: P/RP-15-d
SL-18: R-16-b
SL-19: CO-5-b
SL-20: GT-7-c
SL-21: P-15-a
HL-1: OF-1-c
HL-2: OF-31/2-b
KS-1: SF-10-g
KS-2: N-8

Bob Kelly Creme Rouge:

SR-1: SR-6-a/b
SR-2: PR-6-a
SR-3: R-10-a
SR-4: PR-9-a/b
SR-5: PR-10-a/b
SR-6: S-8-d
SR-7: SF-9-b/c
SR-8: S-9-a
SR-9: R-8-a
SR-10: SR-8-a
SR-Bronze: RS-10-d

Bob Kelly Dry Rouge:

Female: PR-5-a
Male: R/PR-7-b
DRC-1: R-9-a
SRC-4: PR-8-a/b
Bronze: SR-7-b

**Bob Kelly Brush-On
Rouge:**

Amber: SF-6-b
Tawny: SF-8-e/f
Cocoa: F-8-c/d

Bob Kelly Lipstick:

LP-1: R-13-a
LP-2: RS-12-b
LP-3: R-12-a/b
LP-4: SR-12-a
LP-5: SR/RS-8-b
LP-6: S-8-b
LP-7: FS-9-b/c
LP-8: S-11-a
LP-9: RS-12-a
Cinnamon: SR-10-d
Coffee: S-9-d/e
Orange: S-12-a

Zebra: R-12-c

**Bob Kelly Rubber-Mask
Grease Paint:**

RMG #1: OF-41/2-b
RMG #2: SF-7-f/g
RMG #3: FS-10-e
RMG #4: FS-16-e
RMG #5: S/FS-12-g

**Bob Kelly Cake
Eyeshadow:**

SESC-1: I-9-a
SESC-2: BI-4-d (Silver)
SESC-3: IB-7-d (Silver)
SESC-4: GT-6-a
SESC-5: White
SESC-6: G1S-6-d (Gold)
SESC-7: FO-20-i
SESC-8: G1S-8-c

**Bob Kelly Blemish-
Cover Stick (Blot-Out):**

Light: SF-3-a/b
Medium: F-6-b
Dark: F/SF-6-d
Bob Kelly Mirage:
Pink: R-1-a
Pink Strawberry: R-10-a
Bronze: R-10-a/b
Warm Red: FS-10-b
Grape: FS/SF-13-a/b
Blender Tone: F/SF-8-d
Terra Cotta: F/SF-10-d
Darkest Tone: F/SF-16-a
Ivory: F-2-e
Rose Glow: F-3-c
Dark Average: F-11-d
Lady Fair: OF-5-c
Light Dark: OF-9-c/d
Bronze Glow: OF-9-d/e
Medium Dark: OF-17-c/d
Dark Skin #4:
    OF/FO-111/2-e
Clear Blue: I-8-a
Cool Grey: RP-12-g

**Mehron Base Colors:
Celebre, Stick, Cake**

OS2: O-d-8
OS4: O-f-10
OS6: O-f-13
OS8: O-f-14
OS10: O-g-15
22A: SF-d-4
24A: SF-c-6
26A: SF-f-9
28A: SF-f-10
30A: SF-f-13
TV2: F-f-4
TV4: F-h-7
TV6: F-h-10

TV8: F-g-14
TV10: F-g-18
1B: RS-b-1
2B: SF-c-4
3B: SF-e-7
5B: SF-d-6
6.5B: F-g-13
8B: F-f-17
11B: FS-g-17
12B: R-f-17
18B: N-13
19B: I-c-2
TT: F-f-11
FT: F-f-12
4C: S-f-19
7C: RS-d-19
10C: PR-b-19
LE: F-g-17
ME: FS-g-19
Contour I/37: R-f-19

Mehron Additional Colors: Stick, Cake

22: F-e-6
24: F-e-12
26: F-e-16
28: F-d-18
30: FS-c-19
9.5B: F-g-8
10B: SF-c-16
14B: FO-b/c-4
16B: OC-b-8
R/B Red: R-b-16
Lt. Grey: I-b-6
Purple: P-b-14
Orange: O-b-15
Red: R-b-17
Blue: I-b-15
Green: LG-b-13

Mehron Latex Mask Cover

CS2: O-D-8
CS4: O-f-10
CS6: O-f-13
CS8: O-f-14
CS10: O-g-15
TV4: F-h-7
TV6: F-h-10
TV8: F-g-14
TV10: F-g-18
16B: OC-b-8
10C: PR-b-19
Red: R-b-17
Blue: I-b-15
18B: N-13
25A: SF-f-7
28A: SF-f-10
30A: SF-f-13
10B: SF-c-16
Green: LG-b-13
Yellow: Y-a-13

Mehron Creme Rouge (cr):

9: R-b-8
10: PR-b-8
11: PR-b-10
13: PR-b-16
14: RP-d-13
15: F-b-16
19: S-e-16
20: FS-b-16/17

Mehron Dry Rouge (dr):

Rosewood (RW): PR-b-8
Tropicoral (TC): R-b-8
Nutberry (NB): S-b-19
Just Peachy (JP): F-b-15
WineBerry (WB): R-b-10
Bronzer (BR): F-f-15
Bold Red (BR): PR-g-12
Contour (C): S-f-12
Mojave (MJ): S-f-11
Pale Peach (PP): FS-d-11
Arizona (A): R-f-11
Mocha (MC): RP-d-13

Mehron Lip Rouge:

Light (L): PR-b-14
Medium (M): PR-b-17
Dark (D): PR-c-18
Brick (B): R-b-19
Cherry (CH): PR-b-16
Maroon (MN): PR-b-19
Plum (P): PR-e-14
Special #5 (SP5): SR-b-18
Ebony Red (E): PR-g-17
Crimson (CR): PR-a-18

Pressed Eye Shadow (es)

Natural Wheat (NW): SF-d-5
Cashew (CW): FO-d-8
Adobe (A): SR-b-5
Espresso (EO): R-f-18
Fawn (F): F-g-13
Cocoa (CO): FS-g-17
Merlot (M): VP-b-15
Toffee (T): R-f-12
Cinnamon (CN): S-g-17
Eggplant (E): P-b-16

Cream Shadows (cs)

1: I-b-15
2: I-d-8
3: I-b-2
4: TB-d-8
5: T-c-16
6: RP-d-14
7: N-11
8: SF-c-19
8.5: RS-d-19
9: FS-g-17

RC10: S-g-17
RC11: S-e-18
RC12: S-g-19
17: SF-c-2
18: OF-c-4
Y: Y-a-13
LP: RP-d-7
SB: I-b-4
C: N-6
N: CO-b-7

Stein Greasepaint:

11/2: S/RS-11/2-a/b
2: S-4-a
21/2: SF-3-alb
3: FS-5-A
31/2: F-7-a/b
4: FS-1-b
5: OC-3-b
51/2: OF-5-a/b
6: OF-81/2-a/b
7: F-8-b/c
7F: S/FS-9-b/c
8: SF-9-a/b
9: S-13-d
10: S/FS-11-d
11: O-20-h
12: C-8-b
13: S-5-g
14: F/SF-10-c
16: F-20-f
21: SF-3-a
22: FO-2-b
23: O-4-d
24: OF-6-c/d

Stein Creme Makeup (Velvet Stick):

Natural Blush: FS-5-c/d
Natural A: FS-2-b
Natural B: S/FS-6-d/e
Cream Blush: SF-3-b
Cream A: F-3-b
Cream B: SF-3-c
Tan Blush: FS-5-d/e
Tan Blush #2: F-6-d
Tan Blush #3: F-8-c/d
Tan A: SF-7-e
Tan B: SF-10-e
2: SF-9-c
7: FS-10-c
9: SR-17-b
32: OF-18-d
33: Black
34: N-4
35: SF-13-c/d
36: SF-14-d
37: S/FS-14-c/d
38: FS-11-e
39: SF-12-d/e
391/2: O-10-c
40: O-12-f

411/2: OC-7-b
41: S/FS-15-b/c
41A: S-16-d/e
42: FS-13-b
43: White
44: SF-31/2-b
45: FS-9-c
46: G1S-14-g
47: I/VI-11-a
48: RS-13-a
49: IV/VI-8-b
50: R-12-f
51: O-19-c
52: FO-18-d

Stein Cake Makeup:

Since cake-makeup shades are supposed to match creme-makeup shades, they are not listed separately.

Stein Soft Shading (Lining) Colors:

1: F-18-b
2: FO-16-b
3: N-8
4: N-13
5: N-15
6: OF-16-e
7: OF-20-c
8: I-11-a
9: I/VI-10-a
10: VI-15-a
11: BI-8-b
12: R-16-b
13: PR-18-b
14: SR-13-a
15: White
16: Y-11-a
17: Black
18: RS-13-a
19: G1S-121/2-d
20: TB-15-b
21: RP-16-a
22: S-19-b
23: VP-111/2-b

Stein Creme Eyeshadow:

1: FO-16-c
2: VI-10-a
3: T-10-e
4: VP-111/2-b
5: RP-16-a
6: GT-6-a
8: N-13
11: I/BI-8-g
16: G1S-121/2-d
17: G1S-13-f
18: N-7
19: I-19-a/b
20: VI-15-a

Stein Eyeshadow Stick:

1: S-2-g
2: SF-13-f
3: I-11-b
5: IB-6-d
6: BT-8-c
7: SF-19-d
8: PV-7-b
11: GT-9-b/c

Stein Creme Rouge:

1: RS-13-a
3: R/PR-13-a
4: SR-14-a
5: PR-12-a
6: SR-12-a
7: PR-13-a
8: SR/RS-11-a/b
9: SF-16-a/b

Stein Lipstick:

Since lipstick shades are supposed to match creme-rouge shades, they are not listed separately.

Stein Dry Rouge:

3: RS-10-a
12: FS-12-b
14: PR-10-a
16: PR-13-a
18: RP/PR-11-a
20: RP/PR-11-d

Factor Greasepaint:

1: SR-2-b
1A: S-4-b
11/2: R-4-b
2: SR-21/2-c
2A: SF-4-c
21/2: S-5-c
3: S-10-c/d
4: OC-1-afb
4A: F/SF-2-c
41/2: FS-2-b
5: CO-6-b
5A: SF-41/2-c
51/2: F/SF-7-d
6: FS-10-h
6A: F/SF-8-d
7: F/SF-5-c
8: F-9-c
8A: F-16-d/e
9: SF-91/2-b
10: S-11-c
11: O/CO-18-g
14: VP-1-d
16: OC-18-f
17: CO-18-h
18: SR-11-b

Factor Pan-Cake:

Pan-Cakes and Pan-Stiks with the same numbers are approximately the same color.

Natural No. 1: F-3-b
Olive: F-4-d
Deep Olive: F-5-d
Tan No. 1: F/OF-6-e
Tan No. 2: F-9-d
Café Honey: OF-10-f
Cocoa Tan: OF-12-h
Chinese: CO-8-d
Dark Egyptian: O-15-h
Indian: SF-10-e/f
Negro No. 1: O-16-h
Negro No. 2: FO-15-g
Eddie Leonard: FS-19-g

The following shades have been discontinued but are included for the convenience of those who have them and wish to replace them with similar colors in other brands:

21: FS-2-b
22: FS-3-b
23: FS-4-b
24: F-5-c
25: F-6-c
26: F-7-c
27: F-8-d
28: F-9-d
29: F-10-d
30: F-11-d
31: F-12-d

Factor Pan-Stik:

1N: FS-3-a
3N: SF-3-a
5N: OF-5-b
6N: OF-6-b
7N: OF-7-b
8N: F-8-d
10N: F-10-b
2A: SF-7-c
4A: SF-2-a
7A: S/FS-11-c
Olive: F-4-d
Deep Olive: F-5-b
Natural Tan: SF-7-e
Golden Tan: SF-10-f
Light Egyptian: SF-14-f/g

Kryolan Makeup Colors:

The same Kryolan color numbers are used for all of their paints.

01: SF-11/2-b
01s: FO-2-b

02: SF-3-a
03: SR-3-a
04: O/CO-6-c
04a: OC-4-b
05: FO-41/2-b
06: FO-6-c/d
07: O/CO-7-b
08: F-18-b
09: OF-12-e
010: FO-8-c
012: SR/RS-10-c
014: OF-10-e
015: O-4-b
016: OF-6-b
017: F-8-c/d
021: OF/FO-7-c
022: OC-12-b
022a: CO-10-c
024: OC/CO-16-c
030: OF-8-a
031: SR-8-a
032: F-10-a
033: F-51/2-b
034: F-5-d
035: FS-10-d/e
039: FS/SF-12-g
040: O-12-g
041: OC-15-e
043: O/CO-18-f
045: O/CO-15-d
046: RS-17-d
047: FS-19-e
050: S-18-e
072: R-3-f
073: N-2
074: N-31/2
075: S-12-d
078: SR-11-a
079: RS-12-a
080: RS-15-a
081: SR-14-a
082:R/PR-16-alb
083: R/PR-14-b
086: PR-18-a
087: IV/VI-31/2-a/b
088: N-16
089: N-5
090: TB-8-b
091: I-10-b
092: G1S-3-a
093: TB-14-c
094: T-14-b
095: T/GT-16-a
096: GT-14-a/b
097: T-2-a
098: PV-15-b
101: 0–19-f
102: 0–20-g
103: FS-19-f/g
160: S-6-e
173: VI-4-h
193: TB-11-d/e

303: OC-6-a
304: LY-15-d
305: CY-10-b
308: YC-14-b/c
406: F-1-a
416: S-14-a
421: CO-17-c
425: F-11-g
431: S-11-e
436: YC-4-a
438: F-7-e
449: S-5-a
452: CY-12-d
453: SF-17-f
454: G1S-13-g
459: YC-15-h
462: CO-18-g
466: O/CO-10-b/c
468: FO-13-d
470: F-17-c
477: Y-11-d
481: IV-1-a/b
482: V-3-a/b
483: VI-6-a/b
501: N-14
502: L-14-d
503: YC-14-f
504: Y-13-d
507: OC-13-c
508: FO-8-a
509: Y-12-a
510: I-13-a
511: LG-5-a/b
512: LG-12-b
513: F-21/2-f
517: N-13
521: YC-2-b
522: YC-4-d
523: YL-1-a
534: YL-11-a
545: PV-16-a
549: B-9-b
576: FS-2-a
579: O-16-d
587: BI-6-a
606: Y-14-e
607: Y-13-c
Fl: CO-21/2-b
F2: F-41/2-c
F3: F-6-d
F4: F-51/2-d
F5: FS-4-e
F7: FS-2-e
F8: OF-6-e
F9: F-10-i
F10: F/OF-8-f
F11: O-6-f/g
F12: O-8-g
F15: O-10-f
F16: F-7-d/e
F17: F-7-d
F18: O/CO-4-d

Kryolan "B" Series:

00: LY-1-c
2: S-21/2-b
21/2: SF-4-a
3: SF-7-d
31/2: S-6-b
4: FS-11-d
41/2: S-11-g
5: CO-4-b
6: FS-5-c/d
7: FO-17-d
8: SF-13-e
8a: C-9-b
8b:CY-111/2-d
9: FS-11-c
10: YC-13-c
11: O-20-h
12: Black
13: F-14-d
16: CY-17-f
28a: O-16-h
30: S-17-d
32a: N-10
32b: N-4
32c: N-15
101: S-3-c
104:SF-41/2-a/b
106: O/CO-8-a
107: CO-13-b
108: OF-8-b
109: O-8-c
111: FO-9-b
113: SF-18-c
115: OF-11-d
118: OF-11-b/c
B: RS-61/2-a/b
C: O-11-b
EC1: SF-91/2-e
EC2: PR-10-g
EC3: F-15-f
EC4: F/SF-101/2-g
EC5: S-9-h
EC6: SF-8-h
EC7: SF-10-h
EC8: FS-9-f
F2: F-5-b
F3: F/OF-51/2-c/d
F4: F-5-c
F6: FS-9-e
F10: S/FS-4-c
F11: S-4-d
F12: FS-8-e
F13: FS-8-d/e
F14: FS-13-e
F31: SF-11-e
FA: FS-41/2-c
FB: SF-5-b
FC: OF-6-c
FD: OF-6-d
FE: SF-9-c/d

FF: F-61/2-c/d
FF1: FS-4-j
FF2: SF-3-b
FF3: SF-3-b/c
FF4: SF-6-f
FF5: F-61/2-c
FF7: TG-1-c
FF13: F-6-c
FF14: SF-8-e
FF21: FS-3-c
FL: OF-7-d
FN: OF-9-c
FP: OF-5-b
FS4: F-3-d
FS8: F-6-a/b
FS9: F/OF-5-b
G1: F-12-f
G2: FO-8-b/c
G3: FO-5-b
G4: FO-9-c
G5: FS-12-f
G7: Y-4-d
G9: Y-2-b
G10: Y-1-a
G14: SR-2-b
G15: S-3-c/d
G16: OC-2-b
G24: O-8-b
G41: FS-31/2-c
G56: I/VI-4-a
G81: BT-6-e
G82: GI-4-a
G83: BI-4-d
G92: Y-6-a
G103: YL-8-e
G104: S-3-e
G108: P-6-b
K: CO-5-b
K1: S/FS-3-e
O: FO-3-b
P1: OF-21/2-b
P2: F-51/2-c
P3: SF-41/2-b
P4: OF-7-c
P5: OF-7-e
R3: RS-8-a
R5: SR-9-a
R6: R-10-a
R9: S-7-a
Naturell: SR-2-a
Mandarine: OF-13-a
Jugendrot: RS-14-a
Zinnober: FS-12-a
Carmin 1: RS-13-a
Carmin 2: SR/RS-12-a
Carmin 3: PR-14-b
Carmin 4: PR-17-a
Hellrot: S-14-b
Altrot: PR-17-b
Schattierrot: RS-12-b
Schattierbraun: FO-15-b/c

Blau 1: BI-6-c
Blau 3: I-10-a
Blau 5: I/VI-11-a
Lila: VP-12-c
Grun 1: L-9-c
Grün 9: G1S-5-b
Grün 11: YL-2-b
Grün 20: GT-11-b
Grün 21: GT-11-a
Grün 30: T/GT-11-a
Grün 31: T-13-b

DINAIR AIRBRUSH MAKEUP 800-785-4770

Glamour Shades Group: Matte finish, *alcohol free!*

Stage Makeup

Gradient Range-
Cross Reference

Dinair #	Dark Coverage	Light Coverage	Dinair Color Name
100-02	SF-C5	SF-C2	Alabaster
100-04	F-D7	OF-B3	Olive Beige 2
100-06	FS-E11	F-B3	Light Golden Beige
100-08	OF-E9	OF-B4	Natural Beige 2
100-10	OF-C6	OF-B2	Dark Golden Beige
100-12	OF-D10	OF-B4	Golden Tan 2
100-14	F-E13	F-B3	Bronze 2
100-15	OF-D11	OF-B4	Dark Olive
100-16	OF-C11	FO-B7	Golden Olive
100-18	FS-F14	FS-F3	Egyptian Bronze
100-30	FS-D17	FS-D2	Fawn Brown
100-32	N-13	BI-B3	Gray Frost
100-34	I-C6	I-B3	Silver Blue
100-35	RP-D10	P-B3	Orchid Plum
100-36	SF-C10	SF-C2	Peach Beige
100-37	RS-B8	RS-D2	Dark Peach Pink
100-40	S-B8	S-B2	Peach Pink
100-42	S-E12	S-B2	Bronze Rose
100-44	PR-B13	PR-B2	Mauve
100-45	RS-D7	RS-D2	Light Mauve
100-46	PR-14	RS-B2	Cinnabar

Alcohol Free to be used as Glamour colors or adjusters.

100-20			White Glamour
100-22	N-18	N-7	Black (Charcoal) Glamour
100-24	CO-B5	CO-D5	Light Yellow
100-25	YL-A11	YC-B4	Bright Yellow
100-26	GT-C3	GT-B1	Light Green
100-27	BL-B12	BL-B4	Bright Green

DINAIR AIRBRUSH MAKEUP 800-785-4770
Fantasy Colors Group: Matte finish, low alcohol

Stage Makeup
Gradient Range-
Cross Reference

Dinair #	Dark Coverage	Light Coverage	Dinair Color Name
200-10	N-18	N-3	Black
200-12			White
200-14	F-B16	R-B2	Red
200-16	YL-A11	YC-B4	Yellow
200-18	I-B12	I-B3	Blue
200-20	TG-D10	GT-C1	Green Oliv
200-21	TG-B8	TG-B1	Bright Green
200-22	TB-B10	TB-B4	Turquoise
200-24	OF-B17	SF-E2	Orange
200-26	PR-B10	PR-B2	Pink
200-27	RP-D7	RP-D3	Light Purple
200-28	VI-B11	VI-B3	Purple

DINAIR AIRBRUSH MAKEUP 800-785-4770
Fluorescent Colors Group: Matte finish, low alcohol

Stage Makeup
Gradient Range-
Cross Reference

Dinair #	Dark Coverage	Light Coverage	Dinair Color Name
200-71			Yellow
200-74	CO-B14	FO-B5	Orange
200-77			Red
200-81			Pink
200-83	P-B10	P-B3	Magenta
200-84	GL-B10	GL-B2	Green
200-86	B-B11	B-B4	Blue

DINAIR AIRBRUSH MAKEUP 800-785-4770

Opalescent Colors Group: Matte finish, low alcohol

Stage Makeup
Gradient Range-
Cross Reference

Dinair #	Dark Coverage	Light Coverage	Dinair Color Name
200-31	N-9	BL-B3	Silver
200-32	N-7	BL-F3	Light Silver
200-33	CO-B5	CO-D5	Gold
200-37			Opal White
200-39	N-14	N-3	Onyx Black
200-45	PR-B10	SR-B2	Ruby Red
200-49	TG-D10	GT-D1	Emerald Green
200-55	BL-Bl5	BL-B4	Sapphire Blue
200-61	TB-B9	TB-B4	Sparkling Turquoise
200-67	O-B11	O-B4	Topaz

Conclusion

MAKEUP is a fascinating art—at least, I find it so. You will agree or disagree with me, depending largely upon your recent experiences with it. At the moment I am interested only in those who have been favorably impressed and who intend to continue making up themselves and others for the stage.

I hesitate to fill these last pages with advice, for they will probably prove to be of value only as an exercise in writing. But there is one warning which I feel compelled to issue to all those who have stayed with me this long. Would that it be more widely heeded by makeup artists of today! It is simply this: You have not now learned to do makeup. You have only begun to learn—you will never finish. Don't stop experimenting and practicing now, but continue always.

Makeup is not by any means a static art. It is far different today from what it was ten years ago. Ten years hence you may expect it to have gone through many more changes. Unless you progress as rapidly as the art itself, you will soon be in the position in which far too many makeup "artists" now find themselves—they are doing makeups for theater of 1890 and putting them in modern, realistic settings. The result, of course, is ludicrous.

Do not be afraid, then, to discard materials or techniques suggested by books and teachers of today in favor of something better which may appear tomorrow. By all means, don't fail to experiment with every new material or idea which is even so much as rumored. Then, perhaps, you will be able not only to keep up with your art but—what is still better—to keep ahead of it.

From the first edition of *Stage Makeup* by Richard Corson, published in 1942 by F. S. Crofts & Co.

Index